Telecommunications in Europe

COMMUNICATION AND SOCIETY
edited by George Gerbner and Marsha Siefert

Telecommunications in Europe

Eli Noam

New York   Oxford
OXFORD UNIVERSITY PRESS
1992

Oxford University Press

Oxford   New York   Toronto
Delhi   Bombay   Calcutta   Madras   Karachi
Kuala Lumpur   Singapore   Hong Kong   Tokyo
Nairobi   Dar es Salaam   Cape Town
Melbourne   Auckland

and associated companies in
Berlin   Ibadan

Copyright © 1992 by Eli Noam

Published by Oxford University Press, Inc.,
200 Madison Avenue, New York, New York 10016

Oxford is a registered trademark of Oxford University Press

Library of Congress Cataloging-in-Publication Data
Noam, Eli
Telecommunications in Europe / Eli Noam.
p. cm.—(Communication and society)
Includes bibliographical references and index.
ISBN 0-19-507052-6
1. Telecommunication—Europe. 2. Telecommunication policy—Europe.
I. Title. II. Series: Communication and society (New York, N.Y.)
HE8084.N63 1992 384'.094—dc20 90-22969

9 8 7 6 5 4 3 2 1

Printed in the United States of America
on acid-free paper

72652

Preface

This book, together with its companion volume, *Television in Europe,* covers many subjects and many countries. It is therefore necessary, at the outset, to state what it is and what it is not.

The book is an analysis of the rise and beginning fall of the telecommunications monopolies in Europe. These Post, Telegraph, and Telephone administrations (PTTs) are vast and powerful; in many countries they are the largest employer, investor, and buyer. They often run vast financial savings and payment systems, and even provide services such as bus transportation in some countries. Their physical presence is ubiquitous, and their services reach daily into almost every home and office. But despite the importance and scale of these institutions, social scientists have paid little attention to them.[1]

One reason for such lack of interest is that the subject of telecommunications seems forbiddingly technological. Actually, most of the issues in telecommunications are quite accessible once they are stripped of needless jargon. Another reason is that for a long time most experts had grown up within the traditional system and mutually reinforced each others' views. Only recently did expertise begin to diversify, and more detached judgments became possible.

To understand the future one must know the past. Hence, this book deals in some detail with the historical and political context. This is done especially in Part I which describes the dynamics of changes and the forces that transform the traditional PTT system.

Part II is given to discussions of individual countries. All Western European countries are analyzed, hence this section serves as somewhat of a handbook on Western European countries' telecommunications systems, and provides a bird's-eye view of the continent. At present, telecommunications knowledge is highly segmented along territorial lines. It has proved to be an enormous undertaking to treat so many countries and write a book that tries to transcend national systems and go beyond theorizing. Some priorities had to be set, and several of the larger countries received a more detailed treatment. Eastern Europe, whose societies have only recently rejoined the European mainstream and the dynamics of its telecommunications evolution, is treated only briefly.

In the discussion of some countries, I have selected particular issues for emphasis. For example, procurement of equipment by a PTT is given greater attention in the chapter on Germany; industrial policy is emphasized in the chapter on France; and the United Kingdom chapter looks at a PTT reorganization and its aftermath. Thus, the country chapters, taken together, also provide a mosaic of policy issues across Europe.

Part III discusses several special topics in European telecommunications, such as industrial policy, the struggle with American interests, internationalization of conflict, and vertical integration into new fields. Value-added services, integrated networks, transborder data flows, and international services are further examples of new policy issues. The last part of the book analyzes the future of networks, the instability of the international system, and the modularization of networks. It concludes with an outlook on the future policy agenda and the emerging new open network environment, which is very different from the traditional one.

The book is not a comparative study in the sense of contrasting different countries' approaches to a problem and evaluating the best of them. This is done only occasionally, both among European countries and with respect to the United States. More interesting than the comparative approach—''which PTT procurement system is best?''—is the institutional one—''how and why did Germany's procurement system evolve? How and why is it changing?''

Although the treatment of an entire subcontinent with some specificity is worthwhile, it is also difficult. In each country there are numerous experts who know more about the subject matter for their own country than any single author could. Hence, it is easy to be critical of the broader analysis by reference to superior knowledge of the details in a subplot. I have tried to deal with the specifics by investing much time in visits; in reading academic, trade press, governmental, and consulting literature; and in engaging in voluminous correspondence. Drafts of the chapters were sent in each country to a dozen or more individuals and institutions, sometimes in several rounds, and most of the comments and corrections were incorporated. Often the replies and corrections from the same country were contradictory, mirroring the policy debates in those countries themselves. Even after the corrections, I am sure that national experts will be able to identify some inaccuracies. Some may be based on sources, of which many are unavoidably secondary rather than primary; others will be due to updates to information presented in the book. Some perspective is necessary. Although a change in the particulars may be of critical significance to those directly involved, the broader picture is rarely affected by it.

In numerous contacts with PTT officials, I have become used to defensive reactions to any suggestion that the traditional arrangement was not solely aimed at optimally serving the public's need for a telecommunications infrastructure. One form of response was dismissal of alternative views as having an ''American perspective'' (i.e., not being grounded in the traditions of another country). It is, of course, true that all institutions are historically grown. Indeed, that is the very premise of this book. But PTT officials, who are typically electrical engineers turned civil servants, are rarely familiar with the genesis and evolution of their own systems. Their perspective tends to be ahistorical. Indeed, a second type of response, at tension with the first, has been that the discussions in this book are relevant to the past but are ''dated'' in that things have recently changed, perhaps due to a reorganization, a new technology, or a new directive yet. This is as if one negated the relevance of childhood and youth to an evaluation of an adult. Episodes along the way do not become irrelevant to the understanding of an ongoing institution simply because the rules have recently been changed. A third and related type of response has been the flight into detail. It is this expert-oriented view of the world, favoring the trees over the forest, that has kept discussions of telecommunications policy out of the public realm.

Another form of defensiveness is to consider an evaluation that contains a critique of the monopoly system as adversary and possibly inspired by business designs. I have no such ties or commercial engagements. Nor do I ignore the significant historical contribution made by PTTs to the evolution of their countries' communication infrastructure. PTTs were very important in the first phases of network evolution; but as this book argues, telecommunications are moving into a third stage, that of the pluralistic network. Its origin lies in the success, not the failure, of the traditional system. The unravelling of that system by various centrifugal forces cannot be contained, and we are merely at the beginning of that process. Such a conclusion may be unwelcome, but it is not adversary.

This is not a book about U.S. telecommunications. To be critical of a practice in a European country does not necessarily mean to approve of its U.S. counterpart. But it is of course true that the perspective of this book has benefitted from participation in American telecommunications policy and research. I should clarify that much of it has been written or conceived before I took a leave as a professor at Columbia University and as director of its Center for Telecommunications and Information Studies (now the Columbia Institute for Tele-Information: C.I.T.I.), and before I was appointed to the New York State Public Service Commission. Nothing in this book reflects the views of that regulatory body (whose international involvement is, at any rate, negligible). The PSC and its staff of 650 regulate intrastate telecommunications for 10 million lines in the state, as well as electricity, gas, and water. It is in frequent disagreement and litigation with the Federal Communications Commission in Washington.

Thus, the views of this book do not defend the views of official Washington. The New York State PSC, for example, instituted low-income telephone service, based on a blueprint by the author, that provides basic telephone service for about 1.5 million poor households for $1 per month, with similarly low installation charges. This makes telephone service virtually free for poor people. I mention this because one of the self-images of traditionalists in telecommunications policy is that only they are socially concerned. A large body of literature sees change in telecommunications as a challenge by large business interests, many of them multinational firms, to existing socially motivated and home-grown arrangements. The reality, however, is much more complex. Domestic monopolies are less rooted in social benevolence than its defenders claim. The imperatives of an information-based economy and a rapidly developing technology do not leave unscathed the institutional structure under which the informational nervous system of society functions, and it makes little sense to slay the messenger of that news. Changes came to the surface first in America, and subsequently reached Europe and Japan. It would be surprising if this process were not to continue for decades and if at its end the various national systems were not very different from those of today.

At the conclusion of this project, thanks are owed to a large number of people; only a few can be recognized in these pages, and none should be held responsible.

The project was made possible by financial assistance from the German Marshall Fund of the United States and later from the Gannett Foundation. Peter Weitz and Gerald Sass deserve the credit for supporting the work and keeping it alive as its scope grew.

At Columbia, a lively collection of student assistants, editors, cite and quote checkers, and typists participated in the project, later helping to update the information. They were supervised first by Christopher Dorman and then by Richard Kramer, who contributed in many valuable ways. Assisting them were Hüseyin Bayazit, Andrew Blau, Theresa Bolmarcich, Laura Bulatao, Dawn Chang, Paul Chew, Andrew Day, Peggy Danneman, Sherry Emery, Christine Enemark, Valere Gagnon, Rhonda Harrison, Christopher King, John Kollar, Jessica Lee, Junno Lee, Catherine Lim, Alfred Lucas, Michael McManus, Kurt Miller, Altagracia Miranda, Erica Simmons, Wendy Stryker, My-Phuong Tran, and Mark Young. Barbara Martz was enormously helpful with press and articles from many sources. Roberta Tasley and Douglas Conn, as managers of the Columbia Center, provided the necessary organizational structure. Áine NíShúilleabháin supervised the last and strenuous phase of the project. Rachel Toor, Herbert J. Addison, and Steve Bedney of the Oxford University Press guided the project to conclusion.

Among academics, private experts and public officials, both at home and elsewhere, I am grateful to Per Klitgaard Andersen, Elena Androunas, Francisco Pinto Balsemâo, Johannes Bauer, Marino Benedetti, Hans Bergendorff, Catherine Bertho, Martin Bullinger, G. Buyck, Tom Byrnes, Farrell Corcoran, Andrea Costa, James Cowie, William Drake, Martin Elton, Beth Eres, Ugo de Fusco, Paul W.J. de Graaf, Bruce Greenwald, Karl Erik Gustafson, Jaakko Hannuksela, Mario Hirsch, Johann Hjalmarsson, Wolfgang Hoffmann-Riem, Janos Horvat, Elfriede Hufnagl, C. Jacobaeus, Herman Cohen Jehoram, Tuen de Johngh, Tanya Kiang, Leon Kirsch, Christian Kobelt, Ismo Kosonen, Geovanni Lanza, Michael Latzer, S. C. Littlechild, Giovanni Maggio, Pennetti Mannisto, Horst Edgar Martin, Fergus McGovern, Heikki Myllo, Gosta Neovius, Godefroy Dang Ngyuen, Sam Nilsson, Mogens Kuhns Pedersen, Francois Pichault, G. Russell Pipe, Gerard Pogorel, Remy LeChampion, Sheizaf Rafaeli, Anthony Rutkowski, Shaul Hai, Joachim Scherer, Donald Smullin, Charles Stabell, Matthias Steinmann, Jan Thurmer, Sylviane Toporkoff, Rudolf Trachsel, Sergio Treves, Jeremy Tunstall, Thierry Vedel, Timo Viljakainen, Lennart Weibull, Christian von Weizsäcker, Eberhard Witte, and Glenn Woroch. To those whose names have been inadvertently omitted, my apologies.

Most of all, I owe this book to my wife Nadine Strossen, champion of free speech and human rights in America and abroad; to my mother, who provides the bridge across the Atlantic; and to the memory of my father.

New York   E.N.
November 1991

Contents

Telecommunications in the Mediterranean Countries and Eastern Europe

III   BATTLEFRONTS IN TELECOMMUNICATIONS POLICY

IV   THE FUTURE OF TELECOMMUNICATIONS

I

TRADITION AND CHANGE

1

Public Telecommunications: A Concept in Transition

The Monopoly System

A number of far-reaching changes in telecommunications policy originated in the United States. Because many were passed under a conservative political regime, they were usually viewed in Europe as the product of American business interests, wrapped in a Chicago free market economic ideology. But more recently, Japan and several European countries have begun to adopt similar policies, or at least to discuss changes that previously seemed unthinkable. This indicates that the changes in telecommunications go deeper than the nature of the respective governments in power and that they reflect a more fundamental transition.

For a century, telephony throughout Europe had been a ubiquitous, centralized, hierarchical network operated by a monopolist. The operating entity was usually a state administration for post, telephone, and telegraph (PTT), though in some instances, the post was separated from telecommunications. The entire arrangement was therefore known as the PTT System. In the United States, AT&T fulfilled much the same function in telephony. Western Union, the telegraph monopolist, and the Post Office Department (later the U.S. Postal Service) added the T and the P. The physical and organizational structure of PTTs was hierarchical. Major policies were set by technical experts, largely outside public scrutiny. To be sure, the arrangement served the important goal of interconnecting society and operated as a mechanism of redistribution. It was not merely a technical system, but a social, political, and economic institution based on the sharing of resources and the transfer of benefits toward favored groups, often the economically weak and almost always the middle class and farmers.

The origin of the centralized network system for communications preceded electronics by centuries and was embedded in the emergence of postal monopolies. In 1505, the Hapsburg emperor Maximilian granted exclusive mail-carrying rights to what one would call today a multinational company, the Taxis family of Italy. Although this concession proved to be an unexpectedly rich source of revenue to the Hapsburgs, who shared in the profits, it also required vigilant protection from the incursion of mail systems, of which there was a multitude (Dallmeyer, 1977). Neighboring Prussia went one step further,

3

and in 1614 established a state-run postal monopoly (Stephan, 1859). Thus, the PTT system was born as a creation by the absolutist state for the absolutist state. Later, this system was rationalized as based, depending on one's point of view, on economies of scale, national sovereignty, cross-subsidies, or public infrastructure needs; but the early creators of the postal monopoly system were quite forthright in their mission to generate profits for the state and its sovereign. The postal system became a major source of revenue, at a time when European rulers had insatiable needs for cash. As the goose that would lay the golden eggs, the system was ardently protected through the centuries against encroachment by private competitors and by other states.

When the telegraph emerged in the nineteenth century, it was rapidly integrated into the monopoly. Later, much was made of the military importance of state control over telegraphy. Although this consideration may have been significant for the major powers, it was less relevant for the many other countries that also banned private telegraphs. Even for the larger states, the strategic importance of the new medium did not really require operations by the state itself any more than it did for overseas mail—an important service in the era of imperialism—where private delivery under contract was regularly used.

When the telephone made its appearance in 1876, it too was soon integrated into the state monopoly once its financial viability became clear. Here official histories claim that the purpose was to bring telephony to rural areas neglected by commercial interests. This is true in some cases, but in other instances (for example, Norway), the historical record is quite different, and does not lead to find an aim of spreading telecommunications service across the country. At the same time, telecommunications were integrated into an international system of collaboration, with the official goal of technical coordination, but also, from the beginning, with a cartel agenda on prices and service conditions.

For almost a century, a tightly controlled system of telecommunications was in place in most developed countries. Its structure was supported by a broad coalition that provided political support in return for a share in the monopoly rents. This rent-seeking coalition can be termed the "postal-industrial complex." It encompasses the government PTT as the network operator and the private equipment industry as its supplier, together with residential and rural users, trade unions, the political left, and the newspaper publishing industry, whose postal and telegraph rates were heavily subsidized. The traditional system worked in particular to the benefit of the equipment industry, which was provided large markets by huge PTT procurements, especially after World War II. These markets were also almost always protected from foreign competition by buy-domestic policies. Within most industrialized countries, equipment manufacturers often collaborated in formal or informal cartels that set prices and allocated shares of the large PTT contracts. The structure of telecommunications in the United States, although private, was not all that different, because it was a near-monopoly, with a full integration of network operation and equipment manufacturing. Its corporate ideology was shaped by AT&T's patron saint, Theodore Vail, himself a former postal man as the head of the U.S. Railway Mail Service.

The system was profitable and reassuring for insiders, and its inefficiencies were hidden by the general downward trend in the cost of electronic technology (which was due, on balance, more to computer and component firms than to traditional telecommunications firms.) The PTTs also set standards for equipment in a way that would often discourage or delay outsiders, and they often collaborated with favored domestic firms in equipment development and in export promotions.

In Switzerland, for example, the PTT in 1984 set standards for cordless telephones by issuing a fifty-five page specifications manual and requiring no less than forty duplex channels and automatic scanning. Because of these rules, which were allegedly passed to protect the users, only one company, a Swiss one, could meet the standards quickly (and not surprisingly, since it had played a major role in developing the rules). Moreover, the manufacturer's estimated price to the PTT for a set was almost $800, and monthly rentals came to about $15 (Wolf, 1983). At the same time, one could buy a simpler but perfectly adequate cordless telephone in the United States for less than $75. Swiss users resorted to buying cheaper but illegal foreign equipment in the many stores where they were marked "for export only."

Although the traditional monopoly system—though not always its execution—operated to the economic advantage of equipment firms, its principle long enjoyed broad public approval from the constituent groups of the postal-industrial coalition. The monopoly followed concepts of public service: universal, accessible, affordable, and redistributive. As a public service, telephony was outside the mechanism of the market, even in otherwise free-economy countries. Any change in that status was bound to be controversial; an expansion of the realm of the market into the realm of rights and politics has always been a painful transition.

Thus, a partial relocation of telecommunications from the public domain into the economic one was objectionable to many. Indeed, the single most powerful argument in defense of the traditional centralized system is a value preference for the principle of state ownership in infrastructure as distinguished from the "scientific" arguments that a monopoly is necessary for engineering and economic reasons.

PTTs were not entirely frozen in their institutional development. After many decades of stability, some of them were transformed in the late 1980s into "PTOs", public telecommunications organizations. The new designation connotes a separation from postal services, and change from a governmental administration into a state-owned semi-independent organization. Furthermore, some new types of activities such as value-added services and mobile telephony were permitted to be offered by private firms. But these changes do not prove that a major reorientation had taken place, and that the problem of state monopoly had been resolved in most countries.

The exaggeration of the extent of actual change can lead to bureaucratic doublespeak. For example, the Danish government, in creating the PTO teleDenmark, declared, "As a consequence of decisions made at the EC level, there will be competition within all spheres of telecommunications in the next few years, apart from telex, ordinary telephones, radio-based mobile services, satellite services, the infrastructure and the use of telecommunications network for broadcasting. . . .'' (Ministry of Communications, 1990). In other words, ''everything'' will be competitive, except for the remaining 95%. In almost every country there still exists a tight monopoly over transmission infrastructure, switched services, and voice service—the vast majority of telecommunications activities. The liberalized exceptions are minor in comparison, and, in the case of value-added services, consist of sophisticated computer-based activities in which the PTTs had only a limited participation. Similarly, the separation from postal service and the creation of a more independent status represents no reduction in economic power. To the contrary, postal services had become a financial drag on telecommunications. Independence permitted a branching into new activities, including the vertical expansion into manufacturing, and the horizontal expansion internationally. Regulation was left to tiny government departments that were hard-put to control some of their countries' largest and most complex organizations.

This is not to say that no change has taken place. The traditional PTT system was stable for a century. But in the 1980s pressures emerged, just as they did in the television sector, that could no longer be contained. This was accompanied by harsh political disputes. By the end of the decade, change was in the air everywhere. The postal and telephone monopolies were being reorganized in most countries; some competitive suppliers were emerging; intraorganizational private networks were increasingly taking traffic from the public network; and the European Commission in Brussels was hectoring the national governments to loosen restrictions. The actual extent of the change should not be exaggerated, given the inertia of the past; but once the process is set in motion, further transformation is inevitable. This process will continue, and will lead to a telecommunications infrastructure that is very different from today's.

These are the themes this book discusses, both in general and in country-specific terms.

2

The Establishment of the PTT System

Early Postal Systems

The key institutions of European telecommunications are the PTTs—the government administrations of posts, telephone, and telegraph. These formidable organizations did not emerge overnight, but are the result of centuries of struggle. Most Europeans are not aware of the historical background that led to the formation of a monopoly system and to its institutions that are part of their environment.

Pressures for liberalization of the monopoly system are not a recent phenomenon. The history of postal monopoly from the Middle Ages onward has been one of the efforts to establish and defend monopolies against the competition of private services and rival governments. These drawn-out rivalries put into question the assertion that postal service—and later telecommunications, which were usually merged into the postal system—is a "natural monopoly" whose economic and technical characteristics secure it from competitors. It was only in the late nineteenth and early twentieth centuries that governments had finally successfully suppressed attempts at rival service and consolidated postal powers in an enforceable fashion. To understand how the monopoly institutions emerged, it is necessary to take a look at their history.

Postal services go far back. In antiquity, the Medes and the Persians had systems for conveying messages that used human shouts transmitted from hill to hill, as well as routes of runners. Xenophon observed that the Persian kings had established rider routes with stations at which horses were changed. The Romans set similar routes. In the thirteenth century, Marco Polo described regularly spaced "poeste" on China's main roads, where imperial messengers would change horses. He reports that there were 10,000 posts in the Mongol Empire with 300,000 horses. "The thing is on a scale so wonderful and costly that it is hard to bring oneself to describe it" (Collins, 1960). Messages moved at 25 miles a day, but urgent dispatches could be speeded up to an incredible 400 miles a day. The Spaniards observed similar Inca runner systems in Peru in the sixteenth century.

In medieval Europe, the origins of commercial postal service were messenger services run by such disparate institutions as city-leagues, guilds, religious orders, and commercial operators. In many instances, traveling merchants and journeymen (particularly butchers, for some reason) carried messages. Over time, regular routes developed, centered around inns at which messengers would rest. It became customary for patrons to leave messages for delivery and transportation at these "posts," and for messengers to exchange horses, thereby considerably speeding up transportation. Two basic forms of organized postal service emerged. The first was private service, subject to governmental authority. Its prime example was the Thurn-and-Taxis postal system. The second was a state-operated postal service, such as the ones in Prussia and in England that became the direct ancestors of the modern European PTTs. These two types of systems and their struggle with each other will now be described.

Private Postal Service: The Taxis System

The Tassis family had already provided courier services in Italy for several generations, when in the fifteenth century the Hapsburgs required better communications for their far-flung European possessions. King Maximilian I turned in 1489 to Janetto Tassis, appointing him as exclusive postmaster. In 1501, Phillip the Fair of the Spanish branch of the Hapsburgs similarly appointed Janetto's brother Francesco Tassis, now Germanized as Franz von Taxis, to rule as the captain and master of the post in the Netherlands. Five years later, Taxis also received a concession to run postal courses between Spain and the emperor in Austria, at his own initiative and risk (Dallmeyer, 1977).

From the beginning, the Taxis were obligated to transport state letters at no charge as a benefit to the Hapsburgs, and to contribute to the imperial coffers. This was the origin of the system of cross-subsidies that still survives today; from the outset the Taxis family consciously used it as an argument for its legal monopoly. Their system also received operational privileges, including the use of the postal horn (which established priority on the highway), freedom from local road and bridge tolls, royal protection for its messengers, and the right to requisition local help.

The Taxis monopoly franchise proved unexpectedly profitable. One commentator observed in 1748:

> Everybody considered such [postal] institutions as misguided, and nobody could imagine that the letters and items of merchants and other people would generate so much postal revenue that horses, wagons, coachmen, and postal servants would be supported. But as soon as the German merchants became aware that they could obtain the [information] on the rate of exchange, the tariffs and the prices of all goods, for little money, without therefore having to travel to Antwerp, Brussels, etc., the new post of Taxis drew such an incredible number of letters together, that the von Taxis had such a rich surplus of money from the postal service, as a medium-size German principality could barely generate [von Beust, 1748].

Now the government authorities' appetite was whetted. The previously ignored postal service was recognized as a rich source of revenue, and this led to bitter disputes about the rights of regional principalities and of the free cities to operate their own systems. It was readily understood that the coexistence of rival services would lower profitability. The Taxis were supported by the German emperor, who advanced the legal theory, profitable to both, that the right to grant a postal franchise was an imperial prerogative. But this was frequently challenged or ignored, and the Taxis had to work ceaselessly at suppressing other private messenger services and governmental postal services of smaller principalities and cities.

In particular, during the period of the Dutch rebellion against Spain, the Taxis system of a loose family confederation operating under various government concessions unraveled, and competing local messenger guilds emerged. Since competition posed a threat to the imperial revenues, Emperor Rudolf II initiated in 1579 what has since become second nature to European governments: He prohibited private competition and appointed a blue-ribbon commission to study postal reforms. The commission included two members of the Fugger family—bankers to the emperors and large-scale merchants (in today's terms, user and creditor representatives). The commission, unsurprisingly, restored control to the Taxis. In 1595, Leonhard von Taxis was appointed imperial postmaster general. He and Emperor Rudolf II sent notices around to suppress the "lesser, butcher and messenger posts."

But competitors and rival authorities kept disputing the monopoly privileges granted to the by now Count von Taxis. Duke Frederick of Württemberg annotated the emperor's missive, in his own hand: "Because there is no obligation, one must not obey, as we will not do, but ask Your Majesty to place your posts elsewhere, as it has been in past days, so it shall remain" (von Beust, 1748). The states also accused the Taxis monopoly of unreliable service and of excessive charges. Yet subsequent Hapsburg monarchs renewed the Taxis rights. Charles V even extended them, after his coronation in 1630, for his entire realm, over which the sun did not set. The Thirty Years War complicated the Taxis fortunes by introducing commercial, religious, and diplomatic intrigues of major proportions. Emperor Ferdinand III, whose war finances depended upon Taxis contributors, was induced again to proclaim the prohibition of rival messenger service where the Taxis operated, even though this antagonized many cities and principalities that still operated their own systems.

The eighteenth century was the zenith of the private Taxis system. The Emperor's financial needs continued, of course, and the head of what had been a humble family of messengers was now promoted to hereditary imperial prince, head of the House of Thurn and Taxis. But this concealed the decline of the system: The powers of the emperors were waning, and with them the foundation of Taxis power. The Thirty Years War had created a more decentralized governmental structure in Central Europe, and the territorial rulers no longer recognized the imperial postal monopoly claim. Whatever the constitutional legalities, the territorial rulers controlled roads over which postal service had to pass. Furthermore, the emperor's arguments for a monopoly system were much weakened when he established state-owned posts in his own Austrian domains.

These disputes over postal monopolies lasted for centuries. The major states unilaterally established their own posts on whatever routes they found profitable. In today's language, they engaged in "cream skimming," though it was done by governments against a private operation. Eventually, Taxis operated mostly in the smaller or less desirable territories.

The Development of the Classic PTT: The Prussian Post

The Prussian Post established the institutional model of a state postal administration for much of Europe and the rest of the world. Its early history is one of a centuries-long struggle against the private Taxis system. And although most of this rivalry is long forgotten, traces of antagonism are no doubt left within its institutional subconscious.

The direct ancestor of today's giant German Bundespost Telekom system started out as tiny semigovernmental service in Brandenburg (Prussia's predecessor) with twenty-four messengers. Initially, the system operated only for governmental use. Soon, however, some private service was provided on the initiative of the postmasters who directly shared in the profits. In 1649, the Prussian government formally took over the system and expanded routes, relay stations, postmasters, and agreements with foreign governments.

Government monopoly did not necessarily mean state provision of postal services. Local postmasters were not paid a salary, but could levy charges on letters. Private concessionaries that were compensated by the local postmasters provided much of the actual transportation of the mail. They were required to keep to the established schedules; fines were levied for tardiness.

Soon rivalries flared up with the messenger services of free cities who were prohibited to pass through Prussian territory. Danzig messengers armed themselves; pitched battles broke out and led to temporary warfare that also involved other states. The Taxis were able to buy rights of transit through Prussia, but were prohibited from picking up or distributing any letters on Prussian territory. The state's monopoly was extended to transporting coach passengers, an arrangement directly leading to today's railroad monopolies.

Where state monopolies were not enforced, a wide diversity existed. In 1695, postal customers in the Free City of Hamburg could choose among local postal offices affiliated with Sweden, Denmark, Prussia, Brunswick, Thurn and Taxis, Holstein, Mecklenburg, Saxony-Gotha, and Nuremberg, plus various private messenger and delivery services. In 1712, the General Prussian Postal Order was issued, reiterating the governmental monopoly. On occasion, private operators were licensed, but only on routes or for time periods that were noncompeting. They were usually not permitted to change horses and were otherwise restricted. However, the suppression of private service providers was not easy. As Heinrich Stephan, later the Prussian Postmaster General, writes:

> The civil and military administrations were instructed to carefully seek the maintenance of the state postal rights. If the efforts in that respect were not always as successful as desired, one should not overlook that the total elimination of the previously very extensive private-messenger institutions is a difficult task, whose

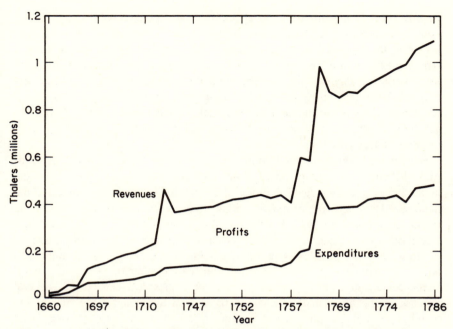

Figure 2.1. Revenues, Expenditures, and Profits of the Prussian Postal Service. (*Source:* Stephan, 1859, pp. 130, 297–299.)

successful solution could have been reached only gradually. (Stephan, 1859, p. 51).

The postal system became highly profitable. In 1662, Prussian postal profits were 7000 Thalers on 10,000 Thalers expenses. Twenty years later, profits had quadrupled to 29,058 on 22,902 expenses, a substantial margin. And in 1688, they were 39,213 on 40,758 of expenses (Stephan, 1859, p. 59). See Figure 2.1. The profits of local postmasters were similarly considerable. Neumann, the postmaster of Königsberg, enjoyed an annual income of about 2000 Thalers. To put these figures in perspective, in 1623 a meal of about four courses in a Berlin inn "suitable for persons of nobility" cost about 1/4 of a Thaler; day labor cost 1/24 of a Thaler, plus meals. Messengers were compensated at 1/12 of a Thaler per day, plus about 1/5 of a Thaler for an average day's mileage.

In subsequent years, the profits of the Prussian postal service continued to increase. These profit figures are still understated, because they do not include the sale of postmasterships.

What were the profits used for? In 1699, the first year for which a breakdown is available, profits were a remarkable 85,000 Thalers on 68,000 expenses. Of the net gain, 45,000 Thalers went to the monarch individually, 6000 to his wife, 6000 to the crown prince, and 4000 into construction of the elector's Berlin residence. Three thousand Thalers were used to support the sciences (Stephan, 1859, p. 130). Thus, almost two thirds of the considerable profits of the post directly benefitted the royal family, and 4 percent went into what we would call today research and development.

During the forty-six years of Frederick the Great's rule, the postal service generated 20 million Thalers, much of it going directly to the king, who depended considerably on this revenue. In addition, appointment to a postmastership was accompanied by payment to the royal coffers. The king paid an extraordinary amount of attention to the details of the postal service. Given the rich flow of revenues, protection against postal competition became an important part of foreign policy.

Seeking still higher returns to defray the cost of the Seven Years War, Frederick the Great decided to raise postal rates considerably and to expand the state monopoly to packages. A group of French fiscal specialists organized the changes. Users and foreign postal administrations initially refused to pay the higher rates, but to no avail. For the postal civil servant Heinrich Stephan (later a celebrated postmaster general), writing in a later age in which postal administrators were still guilelessly proud of making profits for the state rather than skillful in understating them, this was proof of the strength of the monopoly: In the seventeenth century when private companies still existed, "a general increase in the letter mail rate would have been a signal for the ruin of the postal institution, and for the reemergence of a whole number of private postal institutions" (Stephan, 1859, p. 294). But this was no longer true in the eighteenth century. The power of the absolutist state made it possible to increase rates that a century before would have been unsustainable because of competition.

Internally, however, the increase of postal rates was controversial. Frederick's ministers, in a report to their sovereign about the decline of Prussian commerce, ventured respectfully that the postal rate increase was a contributing factor. This 1766 report is a remarkable document in its aversion to mercantilistic restrictions and its support for a free-market philosophy, in the same vein as Adam Smith's *Wealth of Nations,* published a decade later. The report is a direct ancestor of today's pleas by various ministries of economics or industry in favor of less restrictive postal policies. And it was similarly controversial. Within twenty-four hours, the king strictly prohibited his ministers from engaging in any discussion along these lines. But it turned out that the king's ministers, accused by him of ignorance, malice, and corruption, had a better understanding of economics than their sovereign, since the total revenue of the postal service declined for some time. Even the absolutist monarch was unable to abolish demand elasticity. Moreover, several foreign postal services avoided Prussia as a transit route. Thus, whatever competition that did exist for routes exerted itself. In time, revenues recovered. But to Heinrich Stephan, the architect of the telecommunications monopoly system a century later, one of the lessons of the initial setback must have been that rate coordination between neighboring countries was necessary to protect monopoly power, just as domestic exclusivity was its precondition.

In the 1720s, several European states contemplated the establishment of a cooperative postal arrangement that would permit a route from Amsterdam all the way to Danzig and Petersburg, entirely bypassing Prussia and establishing a major alternative to its postal service. Prussia stood to lose 75,000 Thalers a year in revenue. It took all its diplomatic, secret service, and commercial efforts to stifle the establishment of the rival system, but the competitive pressure also led to considerably improved postal service on the threatened route. Most important, it entered into an alliance with its long-time rival Taxis, which was similarly threatened by the proposed new system. In 1723, the former competitors reached a treaty against the common enemy; they agreed upon a code of conduct, and divided routes among themselves. Though they hardly needed the reminder, they also promised to be vigilant in their suppression of independent postal carriers. The relations between the Prussian and the Taxis systems became even closer, when Alexander von Taxis, elevated to prince in 1754 because of his enormous wealth and financial support of the emperor, also sought to buy a seat in the imperial electoral college, which included the handful of the highest nobles of the realm. Frederick the Great supported him in return for postal concessions. But the agreement proved short-lived, because of the Seven Years War that engulfed Europe. Taxis eagerly displaced Prussian posts when Frederick's war fortunes were low, and when Prussia turned the tide of war, it too expelled the Taxis postmasters and substituted its own.

During the Napoleonic Wars, the Prussian Post and the Taxis system were again in conflict over their rights. When the Holy Roman Empire came to an end in 1806, the position of the Taxis post, based upon the grant by the emperor, had lost its foundation. In a conflict with strong secular powers, it was pushed aside, regardless of its performance as a carrier.

After the Vienna Congress in 1815, the increased flow of traffic led to a large number of bilateral agreements modeled after the Prussian-Taxis arrangements, which regulated the relationships of postal services. In the following decades, coordinating bodies developed both for post and for the newly developed telegraphy. A regional postal union was created in 1850 and was soon expanded to telegraphs. It provided the model for later European and later global collaboration of state telegraphs and telephones.

In 1866, the Thurn und Taxis Reichspost, which still existed in fifteen small states, had shrunk to 15 percent of the size of the Prussian Post. In that year, Prussia went to war with Austria over hegemony in Central Europe, and occupied Frankfurt, the Taxis's headquarters. Thus ended the 350-year-old Taxis system. The family, left with a huge fortune but no postal routes, was henceforth relegated to an active role in the society pages.

Von Stephan, Germany's postmaster general and later state secretary and minister, played a remarkable role in the development of European postal and telecommunications institutions. Born in 1831, as the son of a tailor, he began working as a postal scribe and rose rapidly (Grosse, 1931). A man of unusual breadth, he wrote monographs on the history of transportation and postal service, contributed such innovations as the postcard, and restructured German and international postal service. Stephan became postmaster general and integrated the German postal systems; later he was instrumental in the international agreements that led in 1874 to the establishment of the International Postal Union.

In 1876, the newly established German state decided to expand its backward telegraph system. Von Stephan, a postal man, was appointed to head the telegraph office. Within a short time, he had merged the two services, despite opposition from the more technical telegraph personnel. Von Stephan also rapidly introduced the telephone. Its purpose, however, was distinctly different from that of its American counterpart, where the telephone became established in private homes and businesses. The Reichspost viewed the telephone as an extension of state telegraphy, to be used in rural post offices, where trained telegraph operators were economically infeasible.

In the German state of Württemberg, which maintained its independent postal system even after the German unification, the American Bell Telephone Company sought a government concession to provide telephone service in the capital city of Stuttgart. Impatient after bureaucratic delays, the Bell representative started wiring without a license until he was stopped by the police. The postal authorities soon took over. This was Germany's only brush with private telephone service for more than a century, until the 1990s. In 1892, the comprehensive telephone authority of the state was cemented into law.

An account of the further history of German telecommunications is provided in Chapter 7 on Germany.

The Establishment of the PTT Monopoly in Britain

In the United Kingdom the monopoly for postal and telecommunications services was also far from "natural," but rather the outcome of fierce economic and political battles for control. This struggle for a British postal monopoly and its extension to telecommunications will be discussed in greater detail than the similar developments that took place in other European countries.

British postal service began with informal messengers for the royal household. In 1481, Edward IV created a more organized route system for governmental use with stations 20 miles apart. It was not a monopoly, however. Private letters had to be carried by a variety of messengers until 1512, when Sir Brian Tube, the first recorded English postmaster general, opened the Royal Post to nonofficial letters. The system stagnated during the reign of Queen Elizabeth (1533–1605). In 1590, John Lord Stanhope was made hereditary master of the posts. Stanhope obtained a national monopoly and subcontracted specific postal routes to local postmasters, often for substantial sums. These postmasters, frequently innkeepers, also held the local monopoly over the hiring out of horses to travelers. For some services, particularly international ones, the official postal service had to compete with the rival Foreigner's Post and the Merchant Adventurers' Post (Hemmeon, 1912).

In 1591, a royal proclamation affirmed the government's claim to monopoly over postal services to foreign countries. But in 1619, a rival operator by the name of de Quester, attracted by the potential profits, obtained from the King the monopoly rights for "foreign parts," leading to protracted litigation and intrigue. Eventually, de Quester transferred his interests to Thomas Withering, who revolutionized English postal history in 1635 by transforming a tottering system whose profits accrued to licensed private operators into a rich source of revenue for the state (Clear, 1940, pp. 21–32). Withering, supported by Charles I's royal proclamation, brought remarkable operational planning to his postal reorganization, which endured for more than two centuries. Withering spearheaded a postal reform that regularized and speeded up service considerably, to up to 120 miles in twenty-four hours. In the process of reform, however, Withering made enemies: Within two years he was dismissed and replaced by the two powerful secretaries of state, Lords Coke and Windebank (unlike Withering members of the High Nobility) and by a wealthy creditor to the king. Petitions by the London merchants to retain Withering's control were to no avail.

Under Cromwell's Commonwealth, the farming out of postal routes was resumed. The postmaster-generalship itself cost an annual £10,000. After the Restoration, Lord Stanhope resurfaced with claims, but the monopoly patent was eventually given to the Duke of York, in a grant estimated by Parliament as worth £21,500 per year. Another £5000 of postal income was assigned by the king to his mistresses and favorites. Slowly, postal service improved with political stability. But the Royal Post still operated primarily on a handful of great roads emanating from London. "Cross-and-bye" posts linking provincial towns were rare, and neither urban nor rural service was provided. These could be offered by private "common carriers." Disputes between the official and private posts led to physical casualties and forced the government service to cut its rates substantially.

In 1680, a London entrepreneur, William Dockwa, set up a remarkable private urban mail system, the London Penny Post, which created at once a level of service unsurpassed ever since: hourly collection at 179 postal points, four daily deliveries for residences, and six to eight for business centers. The charge per letter and parcel was a uniform 1 penny for up to 1 pound. Postage was payable in advance and was credited by stamping the letters, a novelty. Dockwa's venture required a risky initial investment of £10,000; but when it proved highly profitable, the Duke of York muscled in with the help of the courts. Dockwa was pushed aside, and compensated with a minor pension, while a multitude of courtiers with no connection to the postal system drew large revenues. The Duchess of Cleveland, for example, was given £4700 a year. In contrast, the universities of Edinburgh and Glasgow received a meager subsidy of £210 each from the postal revenue. The lease of postal offices generated crown income of £65,000 in 1685. In 1650, when a London municipal postal service was proposed whose profits would benefit the poor, Parliament suppressed it.

More fortunate than Dockwa was another private businessman, Ralph Allen, who obtained permission in 1721 to serve the cross-and-bye posts linking provincial towns in return for £6000. After two years of heavy losses, the service

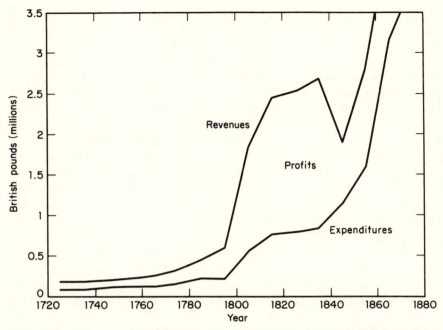

Figure 2.2. Revenues, Expenditures, and Profits of the Post Office in Great Britain. (*Source:* Hemmeon, 1912, pp. 245, 247, 252.)

turned very profitable. (Allen died with an estate reportedly worth £500,000.) After 1765, major road improvements were undertaken, which led to the establishment of stage coach service by private operators who soon undercut the official postmasters by also carrying mail. The Royal Post set up its own rival "mail coaches" in 1784.

Postal service was highly profitable, as Figure 2.2 illustrates. Until the mid-nineteeth century, for each pound of expense there were more than one or even two pounds in pure profits. Nevertheless, the appetite of the exchequer for more revenues was unlimited; the urban Penny Post became the Two-Penny Post in 1801, and soon thereafter the Three-Penny Post. Interurban and international rates were similarly increased. Part of the reason for the rate increases was the need to finance the Napoleonic Wars. Another significant reason was the need to cover the increasingly costly exemptions from postage—the franking privilege—of members of Parliament, which at times degenerated into extensive rackets operated by members for their constituents and supporters. The revenue drain was estimated at £140,000 for the year of 1763 alone. Another major revenue loss was the virtually free mailing of newspapers.

Throughout the seventeenth and eighteenth centuries, royal proclamations reaffirmed the government's monopoly over the lucrative postal service. Their very repetition suggests a steady challenge of the exclusivity of mail service, particularly when it was expensive and unreliable. Many of the private common carriers conveyed some letters over the official routes, and government regulations were enacted literally to slow them down. Later, the 1855 *Annual Report of the British Postmaster General* argued forthrightly: "The object of the Crown in establishing this letter post was probably quite as much the formation of a profitable monopoly as the accommodation of the public" (Stephan, 1859). The system became intolerable for a country in the midst of the industrial revolution. In its late stages, the monopoly was widely evaded. Private parcels crammed with letters were sent by coach to the major cities for redistribution and delivery. Stagecoach guards traveled with pockets full of letters which they posted in their city of destination (Edwards, 1879, p. 87). In one location, calculations showed that only one letter in fifty went through the official post office. One witness freely admitted violating the postal monopoly about 20,000 times and being caught only once. The postmaster of Manchester testified that probably half of all letters between Liverpool and Manchester were transported illegally. Another witness estimated that more than five-sixths of all letters between London and Manchester bypassed the postal service.

Thus, postal reform was not only proposed to aid commerce, but also to reduce the role of private services.

In 1840, the postal service underwent major change. Sir Rowland Hill, a noted reformer of taxation and education, though no postal expert, issued a private report in 1837 advocating that postal service be a tool for promoting economic activity rather than an instrument of revenue generation (Hill and Hill, 1880; Smyth, 1907). The key to reform was a significant reduction of the postal rate for a regular letter to a distance-insensitive penny, creating the famous "penny post." Another feature was the use of postage stamps for prepayment of charges. These measures radically reduced the cost of handling a letter. Before the postal reform, the tariffs for a regular letter were, for example, 4 pennies for distances up to 15 miles or 9 pennies for a destination between 18 and 120 miles away. Hill expected traffic volume to increase and eventually offset the revenue lost due to rate reduction. In the first year after reform, traffic volume more than doubled, and the number of routes increased. Postal revenues dropped, however, from £12.4 to £11.4 million. It took ten years for the old revenue level to be regained, and almost twenty years to reach the former profit level. When the post office showed a £7 million deficit, the Whig government, which had instituted the "supply-side" reform as a measure of its initiative to liberalize trade, was compelled to resign from office. The reform, nevertheless, greatly improved postal service in Britain. It also secured the previously discredited state monopoly system by making it uneconomical and illegal to compete against the low penny rate.

The Struggle for a Telegraph Monopoly in Britain

The telegraph was introduced into the United Kingdom almost at the same time as the postal monopoly was made secure. Edward Cooke and Charles Wheatstone filed for a patent in 1837, four months before Samuel Morse registered his own system in the United States. In contrast to Morse's system of dots and dashes—an early variant of digital transmission—the British telegraph relied on an analog system in which a needle pointed to letters of the alphabet. The Cooke-Wheatstone system was easier to operate, but much more expensive in its capital equipment. It originally required five wires, eventually reduced to two, as opposed to Morse's one-wire system. Despite the technical differences, Cooke and Wheatstone successfully prevented Morse from obtaining a British patent.

Construction of the telegraph commenced in Britain earlier than in the United States. The first operations, undertaken by the privately owned Electric Telegraph Company, proved profitable. Subsequently, the Magnetic Telegraph Company entered the market in a competitive fashion and maximum rates fell from 10 shillings to 4 shillings; but because of the high elasticity of demand, total industry profits increased (Brock, 1981). Eventually, the two companies entered coordinating agreements.

The telegraph network expanded rapidly: Between 1851 and 1855, the Electric and International Telegraph Co. and the British and Irish Magnetic Co. alone tripled their mileage and multiplied their business volume by 700 percent. In 1861, a rival firm, the United Kingdom Telegraph Company (UKTC), entered the market with a low-rate service. The new company was vociferously opposed by the earlier entrants, but under the competitive regime rates dropped to less than 1 shilling for those routes that were served by UKTC. In 1865, the new company was integrated into a new cartel and rates were fixed at 1 shilling for under 100 miles and 2 shillings for distances above 200 miles.

Soon, however, the private cartel character of the telegraph was challenged, particularly by the newspaper publishers, for whom telegraph rates had become a large expense. Because they expected lower rates and better service under public ownership, newspaper owners began calling for nationalization. They were supported by the British Post Office, which argued that the telegraph was related to the mail-carrying function, on which it had a monopoly. Proponents of nationalization claimed that duplication would be eliminated, that smaller towns would receive service, and that telegraph employees would be better paid. Parliament, persuading itself that it could reduce telegraph rates and at the same time compensate the cartel for future monopoly profits, in 1868 authorized a takeover of telegraphs by the Post Office. Consistent with the goal of self-financing, it did not appropriate funds for compensation. The telegraph companies received a settlement of twenty times the 1868 profits, or about £10 million, which was four times as high as had been originally estimated. This created a public furor, as well as difficulties in repayment, and deeply influenced attitudes toward telephone policy in the coming decades.

The press came out well ahead, with new rates at one tenth of the regular charge during off-peak, and one seventh of the regular charge during regular times. Its traffic volume was prodigious. By 1895, the press transmitted two fifths of the total number of words sent over the telegraph, generating an estimated revenue loss of £1 million. The number of telegraph offices was greatly expanded and salaries increased. Overall, the financial position of the telegraph was shaky, and by undercutting its revenue the introduction of the telephone threatened to make the government policy toward the telegraph look even worse than it already did.

In 1850, a submarine telegraph cable was laid from England to France, but it failed after a short time. A transatlantic cable project was started by the Atlantic Telegraph company but was soon abandoned. In 1858, another transatlantic cable between the United States and Britain resulted in exchanges of messages between Queen Victoria and U.S. President Buchanan, but the cable broke down almost immediately and could not be revived. Eventually, another cable provided more durable service.

The Struggle for Telephone Monopoly in Britain

The establishment of a British telephone monopoly was also anything but natural. When the telephone arrived in Britain, its spread was slow compared to the United States and several continental European countries. This was not due to a lack of public attention to the new technology; indeed, from the beginning the telephone created a sensation. Alexander Graham Bell gave demonstrations to audiences that overflowed into the streets, and he was received by Queen Victoria for a private showing. Government users, however, were conservative in adopting the new medium. The chief constable of Exeter, for example, did not seek to have an office telephone installed until 1901 (Perry, 1977, pp. 69–96). The advent of the telephone was not enthusiastically received by the Post Office, which had only recently taken over the telegraph. Its chief civil servant questioned the practicality of the new instrument. In 1878, the postmaster general, Lord John Manners, declared that there were no plans for the Post Office to use telephones as a supporting part of telegraphy.

Since the telephone was regarded a luxury, its development received no priority. And indeed, the telephone was expensive. Limited local service cost three times as much as employing a maid or messenger boy. It could pay for a household's annual expenses for coal, firewood, and electricity. When in 1902 the London County Council protested against high telephone rates, *The Times* editorialized, "When all is said and done the telephone is not an affair of the millions. It is a convenience for the well-to-do and a trade appliance for persons who can very well afford to pay for it" (Perry, 1977, p. 75).

The growth of the telephone industry was further affected by patent disputes. Both Bell and Edison had received British telephone patents and were soon involved in litigation (Meyer, 1907). Both companies offered the patent rights to the Post Office, but negotiations failed. The parties then jointly formed the United Telephone Company in 1880. In the meantime, the government tried to include authority over the telephone in a pending telegraph bill. This proved unsuccessful in Parliament, but a court of law soon held that the original 1869 Telegraph Act encompassed telephones.

The postmaster general then offered to license the United Telephone Company if it waived its right to appeal the court decision; a royalty payment of 10 percent was required. The Post Office concession did not include the power to erect poles or use public rights-of-way. For this it was necessary to obtain the local authority's or private property holder's permission. The concession was not exclusive, and additional licenses could be granted to other companies as well as to the Post Office itself. Furthermore, the provision of long distance telephone communications was severely restricted in order to protect the government's investment in the telegraph system. For the same reasons, public pay telephones were precluded in most instances. When a local company in Manchester wanted to provide public pay telephones at 2 cents per conversation, it was required to charge 24 cents, the equivalent of the charge for a twenty-word local telegram.

Similar protectionist restrictions were put on messenger services' use of the telephone. In 1891, messenger companies were forced to be licensed under the following conditions: that they not use the telephone, that they pay a minimum license fee per year, that they affix a 2-cent stamp on every letter delivered by messenger, and that no messenger take more than six letters at a time from one center. Moreover, messenger companies were prohibited from using a messenger call box with telephone attachment, an American invention that could summon a messenger.

United Telephone applied for and received a license for London. For other areas, it set up regional firms that it provided with patent rights in return for equity. These subsidiaries then applied for Post Office operating licenses.

In 1882, when a competitor to the United Telephone Company applied for a license, the application was granted by postmaster general Henry Fawcett, one of the leading economists of the time. Fawcett favored competition and free trade between private firms and between the private firms and the government. He opposed nationalization and abolished restrictions such as size limitations of exchange areas; he also permitted the company to engage in some long distance transmission.

In 1884, the Post Office began to install telephone exchanges itself, despite the opposition of the Treasury, which did not want the government to engage in competition against private firms. The Post Office also eliminated the prohibition of private interurban trunk lines, and interconnected several local exchanges. With a growing national network, the United Telephone Company began a consolidation, eventually absorbing twelve subsidiaries into the National Telephone Company (NTC).

By 1892, telephones were installed in about 400 cities by the NTC. The company suffered, however, from problems in acquiring way-leaves (rights-of-way). Finally, in 1892, partly in response to pressure from the newspaper publishers, the government improved the company's rights-of-way situation by a quid pro quo that sought to protect the ailing long-distance telegraph service, which could barely cover costs after Parliament had reduced its charges by half. In return for the NTC's right to acquire rights-of-way, the Post Office sought full control of long-distance telephone service. Under pressure and dependent on the government (the telephone company's long-distance lines were strung along government railroad tracks), the company sold its trunk lines to the Post Office in 1896.

However, the agreement required the company to obtain the consent of the local authority for each right-of-way. This turned out to be an insoluble problem and made the agreement virtually useless. The slow expansion of the national trunk system created another bottleneck. The Post Office and the Treasury were apprehensive about incurring financial obligations. Trunks were laid only if local authorities guaranteed adequate revenues for the construction and maintenance of the new line. The company was forced in many instances to issue that guarantee.

Local authorities demanded approval rights for telephone service partly to obtain financial payments. Many cities refused to give rights-of-way, because some wished to operate a municipal telephone service themselves. Circuitous routings became necessary, and there was no access to certain areas. For example, in 1885 the NTC was unable to reach the Middle and Inner Temple areas in London in which most barristers had their offices. The arrangement also delayed the introduction of so-called metallic circuits which were of substantially higher quality than single-wire circuits, and of underground cables.

The situation was further complicated by the emergence of the Duke of Marlborough as a promoter of a rival venture, the New Telephone Company. Founded in 1884, it had obtained a Post Office license but was not actually operating. In 1891, the Duke began to campaign for his company with several letters to the *Times,* in which he offered to provide London subscribers with metallic-circuit telephone service for a flat rate of 12 guineas for an unlimited number of calls, a rate much lower than the existing one. In 1892, stock for the New Telephone Company was offered to the public at a fairly high price. The National Telephone Company bought one-third to keep leverage over the potential rival. But when the time came to make the promises real, the Duke published yet another letter in the *Times,* this time repudiating the possibility of low-cost, high-quality telephone service. Referring to himself as having "bleated a good deal" about the lower-priced telephone (Meyer, 1907, p. 102), he vaguely referred to future efficiencies that would establish the conditions he had described in promoting his venture. The remainder of the New Telephone Company's shares were subsequently acquired by the National Telephone Company for $2.2 million although actual property value was estimated at $1 million or less.

Beyond the blue-sky aspects of these securities transactions, some of their long-run effects were to unreasonably raise expectations. Public opinion, once made to believe in cheap flat rate service, saw higher rates as an expression of private monopoly power. The tide began to shift toward the advocates of nationalization.

The House of Commons appointed a select committee in 1895 to report on the feasibility of municipal telephone service. The government's own attitude ran at first from lukewarm to negative. The postmaster general, Arnold Morley, declared in a parliamentary debate in 1895 that telephony was not a specific municipal responsibility, as were gas and water. He went on to predict: "gas and water were necessaries for every inhabitant of the country; telephones were not and never would be." [1] He further explained patiently to Parliament that "in a town like London, Glasgow, or Belfast, an effective telephone service would be practically impossible if the large majority of houses were furnished with telephones, so great would be the confusion caused by the increased number of exchanges." But in 1898, another select committee concluded that the municipalities should provide effective competition to the NTC. The government accepted this recommendation, and authorized municipal telephone services as well as Post Office exchanges in the 1899 Telegraph Act. The Act also precluded the NTC from entering areas in which it had not already been operating.

This policy proved an utter failure. Of the 1300 local authorities that were eligible to engage in telephony, only six actually installed telephone exchanges, one of which was sold almost immediately to the NTC. In London the Post Office made little headway with customers against the NTC.

Its competitive strategy in ruins, the government pursued outright takeover. In 1901, the company capitulated and agreed that upon the expiration of its license in 1911, its London facilities would be purchased by the postmaster general at the cost of reconstruction (i.e., much below market cost, minus depreciation). The purchase price was fixed by the Railway and Canal Commission and arbitrators on the basis of replacement cost without allowance for goodwill or future profit. This principle of government acquisition was subsequently extended in 1905 to the entire country, also to become effective in 1911. For the few areas for which licenses had been granted to extend beyond 1911, the postmaster general agreed to buy the unexpired license from the company. The entire system was nationalized for a mere $12.5 million. Even so, this purchase price proved highly controversial in Parliament. The Post Office also acquired the meager band of municipal systems. In the end, only the Hull telephone system was left independent, and has remained so until today.

Thus, after a long struggle, the unified state monopoly system of post, telegraph, and telephone, all under one roof, was complete and would stay so for almost three quarters of a century.

The PTT System at Its Maturity

Developments similar to those described for German and British telecommunications took place in most other European countries; details can be found in the respective country chapters.

In time, the Post, Telephone, and Telegraph administrations that were established throughout Europe achieved enormous power, partly because telecommunications became ever more important and partly because the PTTs cemented their monopolies through an extensive system of economic and political alliances with key constituencies in society, in a system that can be termed the "postal–industrial complex."

Today PTTs are among the largest employers in their countries. In Germany, for example, the combined Bundespost had the single largest work force in the nation, some half a million employees, even before unification. A similar number are on its retirement rolls. Add to that 1 million of their families and relatives, and one has a substantial voting bloc. Employees in these systems are usually reasonably well-paid and secure in their positions, typically as civil servants. To some extent, the lower-skilled but more numerous postal employees benefit at the expense of their telecommunications colleagues, but they also provide political backing. In several countries, such as Sweden or Spain, postal and telecommunications operations have always been separate. More recently, several countries have divided the functions of telecommunications operations from the regulatory functions and have often given a greater independence to the former than under a state administration; they often use the term *PTO* (Public Telecommunications Organization, or Operator) instead of *PTT*. But they are still state controlled virtual monopolies. These changes will be discussed further in Chapter 5.

Closely linked with PTT employees are the workers in the large equipment supply and electrical industries, who are well aware of the threats to their jobs due to the migration of electronics industry production to the Far East. The trade union movement in general is rooted by history and membership in the manufacturing sector of the economy. The interests of employees of telecommunications users are less represented, partly because white collar service industry unions, although they exist, have played a lesser role in the trade union movement.

Unions have traditionally strong interests in supporting the principle of PTT monopoly. First, as employees of huge enterprises, they are fearful for the potentially lower employment levels and wage rates of a competitive regime. The example of the United States, where deregulation of the airlines and the divestiture of AT&T led to a reduction in employment and to attempts at rollbacks in wage settlements, is certainly a deterrent. Second, as members of the socialist wing of the body politic, unions often held a political preference for a nationalization of key industries. There was a strong general feeling across the political spectrum that a critical part of the infrastructure, particularly one with such future importance to the information economy, cannot be entrusted to business owners and managers dedicated to the profit motive and to the protection of their positions of power in society.

Beyond those factors is the notion that the PTT is an important planning tool in the development of information technologies, and as such must be under government control. Additional arguments are that a PTT monopoly is an aid in social redistribution because it provides subsidized telecommunications services to the poor and to inhabitants of outlying areas.

Apart from their own positions of direct influence, much of the PTTs' power arises from allowing other groups of society to share in the benefits of their monopoly. One such group is equipment manufacturers, typically very large private companies (Siemens in Germany, CGE and Thomson in France, GEC and Plessey in the United Kingdom, BTMC in Belgium, Italtel in Italy, Philips in the Netherlands, NEC and Fujitsu in Japan, and Ericsson in Sweden). In most European countries the market share of the largest four manufacturers in total telecommunications equipment is above 90 precent. Such companies are among the most potent European firms; for a long time they set the tone for the private sector's telecommunications policy preferences within general industry associations. In the equipment markets, PTTs fill the role of a monopsonist, or primary buyer. The maximum of joint profit for both monopsonist (who is a monopolist supplier of the final product) and a group of oligopolists usually lies in some form of cooperative behavior. The PTTs are instrumental in coordinating the industry, an arrangement that can be advantageous to suppliers, who as a result need not compete vigorously against one another.

A variety of barriers were set to protect this cooperation, including a reluctance to procure foreign equipment, a coordinated development of new technology, and PTT-organized equipment standards. One consequence of this protective system was that European prices were said to be 60–100 percent higher for switching equipment and 40 percent higher for transmission equipment than prices in North America (OECD, 1983), or even 200 percent higher (see table on page 330).

The office equipment manufacturers, new computer companies, and data processors—the grouping that may be termed the "second electronic industry"—were partly outside the postal–industrial complex. In combination with the service industry, these firms were a potential counterweight. But in time the PTTs drew them into their orbit, especially by assuming a key role in domestic industrial policy. This role made the PTT an important financial backer, valued customer, domestic protector, and international promoter in high-technology markets. It could channel development contracts to domestic industries and undertake tests of such technology. It could also coordinate R&D among manufacturers and provide nontariff protection and export advantages. The PTTs thus assumed some of the costs of the early part of the learning curve, and in effect subsidized the development of products that were then offered in the world market, in a way similar to the role of defense spending in the U.S.

The scope of telecommunications grew to enormous proportions. In the European Community alone, in 1986 there were 173 million telephone customer lines served by telecommunications organizations employing 922,000 people (excluding the more labor intensive postal services), annually generating 64.8 billion ECU (about $77 billion), and investing 22.5 billion ECU (about $27 billion). Average penetration of main lines per 100 population in 1990 was 37.75, ranging from 17.8 in Portugal to 56.0 in Denmark.

The broad coalition of government bureaucracy, private equipment suppliers, labor unions, intellectuals, good-government advocates, the political left, the press, the poor, and the rural areas is formidable. The other side includes service industry users who are denied certain communications services, and the "unborn technological generations." Organizations of large users within European countries, although they exist and are joined in umbrella organizations, are relatively weak.

For all its strength, the traditional system became subject to a host of forces of change. The dynamics of this transformation constitute the subject of the next chapter.

3

Network Tipping: The Rise and Fall of the Public Network Monopoly

According to John Kenneth Galbraith, the "great advantage of being in the same world as the United States is that it reveals to other countries the pleasures and horrors that will afflict them only a few years hence."[1] Although such a generalization must be taken with caution, it suggests that some recent American change in telecommunications may be part of a broad and general trend and may be relevant to circumstances as they evolve elsewhere. More recently, several other industrialized countries have begun to adopt similar policies. Japan, for example, has seriously contemplated splitting its near monopolist NTT into local-exchange and long-distance companies and giving them a greater distance from equipment suppliers. Britain, Germany, and the Netherlands have lowered entry barriers. Other countries are considering similar changes. Much of Latin America is engaged in the privatization of telecommunications. These developments raise the question of whether change may have explanations more fundamental than the nature of the respective governments in power. Of course, there are unique aspects to any country, and they will keep national telecommunications systems to some extent distinct. But the variations should not obscure central themes that repeat themselves elsewhere.

There has been little attempt at a broader interpretation of the formation and transformation of networks that can explain the dynamics of change, and this is the subject of this chapter.[2]

The discussion is more theoretically oriented, and includes some equations that readers can skim without loss of the general argument. We begin with a look at the general concept of networks.

The Concept of Network

Networks are an important concept in society and economy. They abound as *physical* facilities, such as those of electric utilities, communications, and transportation. They also exist as *relational* systems, such as those of "old boys," political supporters, and intelligence agents.

The term *network* is old; in the Bible's King James translation, it is used by the Supreme Regulator: "And the Lord spake unto Moses, saying . . . You shall also make it a grating, a network of brass . . ." (*Exodus* XXVII, 4). In the original Hebrew, the word is *reshet* (net), similarly used today for telecommunications and other networks.

The term is used by most academic disciplines, and with a variety of meanings. Chemists apply it to arrangements of molecules (Zacharisen, 1932, pp. 38–42); biologists, to cell structures (Knox, 1830, p. 214); mathematicians, to topology (Klingman and Mulvey, 1981); electrical engineers, to distribution systems (for high voltage), or for circuit configurations of components (for weak voltage) (Karni, 1986, pp. 1–4).

Operations researchers use a network terminology to solve shortest-path problems, maximum-flow models, and optimal routing (Elmaghraby, 1970, pp. 1–3). Computer scientists apply the term for computer interconnections in hardware and to implementation algorithms in software.

In the social sciences, political scientists use the concept of networks in discussing hierarchies, interactions, gatekeepers, and policy communities (Richardson et al., 1985, pp. 6–8). For sociologists and social anthropologists, networks are a major way to see the world; a basic point is that the nature of linkage affects behavior (Barnes, 1954; Bott, 1971; Boissevain, 1979). Sociologists speak of network *dyads*—interpersonal linkage between two persons in which each is indebted to the other, similar in some ways to the exchange relation of economics.

Among the social science disciplines, economists have probably paid less attention to networks. There is no body of analysis for the network concept. Somewhat related is work on market structure by some industrial organization theorists (Baumol et al., 1982). Closer are public choice theories of group formation, discussed in the following section. Other writings on networks are by Noam (1988), Heal (1989), and Economides (1989).

Corresponding to different disciplines' use of the network concept, economists also approach concrete applications differently. Thus, when it comes to telecommunications networks and network policy, several ways of thinking can be distinguished. They are the golden calves worshipped by different professional denominations.

For technologists a primary organizing concept is *economies of scale* and their first cousin, *standardization*. Economists, on the other hand, worship at the altar of *competition*, mostly to the trinity of structure, conduct, and performance. The increasing disenchantment with this view is represented more in academia than in the regulatory environment.

Lawyers in this field often judge policy issues in terms of conflict of interest, which translates here to potential for *cross-subsidies*. This perspective is particularly developed in the United States (hence, the AT&T divestiture).

Finally, many other social scientists as well as most politicians and journalists organize reality in telecommunications policy around the concept of *income distribution* (i.e., around the question of who pays and who receives and of what factors of political power lead to such distribution).

All these concepts are legitimate but have been carried by their proponents beyond their explanatory power. Used single-mindedly, they have degenerated from tools of analysis to rallying slogans in policy disputes.

Perhaps the greatest common failing of these traditional organizing ways of looking at telecommunications principles is that they concentrate on "supply-side" analysis. That is, they look at the subject from the angle of production and producers: AT&T versus MCI; Intelsat versus Cable & Wireless; value-added networks versus basic carriers, and so on.

It is not surprising that this approach would be taken. After all, policymakers deal primarily with carriers, technologists deal with networks, and economists deal with competitors. Moreover, journalists love a horse-race angle to their coverage. But this supply-oriented perspective obscures the other side of the coin—what could be called a *demand*-side telecommunications analysis. At its most basic, one should not think of telecommunications primarily as a service produced by carriers, but as an *interaction* of groups and subgroups in society, facilitated by service suppliers called carriers. The supply structure, if left to its own devices, is a reflection of the underlying interaction of communication users with each other, whether in one all-encompassing "user coalition" or in several user groupings. A ubiquitous public network that interconnects every-body with anybody, under a single organizational roof, is technically and finan-cially merely one arrangement out of several.

Thus, one should not view the liberalization of telecommunications as a pol-icy of primarily permitting the *entry* of suppliers. Just as important, though less obvious, it is the easing of *exit,* by some partners, from a previously existing "sharing coalition" of users that has become confining.

Integration and centrifugalism are two basic types of forces—call them com-munalism versus particularism, order versus diversity—common to many social processes. Telecommunications are only one instance for the widespread ascen-dancy, in recent years, of centrifugalism in previously shared arrangements. Wherever one looks, people break up all kinds of social networks of interaction and form new ones.

Examples abound. They include public education, mass transit, dispute res-olution, pension systems, health provision, electrical power and gas distribu-tion, stock exchanges, and so on. It is beyond the scope of this chapter to discuss the factors underlying these transformations. But if we focus on tele-communications, we can look at its key institutional relation, the shared net-work, and analyze why its unity breaks down.

Theories for the Emergence of Multiple Networks

A number of explanations have been offered—explicitly or implicitly—for the demise of monopoly in telecommunications. There are four major types of the-ories.

Technological Explanations

The technological perspective comes in two variants:

1. "More powerful technology leads to new transmission options, thereby to competition, and thus to the breakdown of monopoly."
2. "The merging of telecommunications and computing technologies breaks down traditional barriers separating different industries and undermines monopoly power."

These views are typically held by technologists and are influential in an engineering-oriented industry such as telecommunications. But they are not sufficient as explanations; otherwise one would observe a diversity of physical networks also emerging in, say, France, Australia, or Mexico. After all, the same transmission and switching technologies are available anywhere on the globe.[3] Yet their impact on network structure has varied and provides no evidence for technological determinism. Technological change provides a precondition for change, but it is not a sufficient one.

Political Explanations

There are three related *political* explanations, all using the perspective of countervailing powers:

3. "In the information age, a telecommunications monopoly becomes too powerful and its scope needs to be limited."
4. "Government regulation proves incapable of controlling a monopoly and is therefore replaced by policies encouraging a competitive industry structure."
5. "Large business users successfully fight the monopolistic restrictions."

The problem with these views is that the introduction of a multiplicity of carriers is only one policy option out of several. An alternative response to political power or regulatory inefficiency might well be a stricter or more effective regulation, as would be nationalization or a size reduction along geographical and/or functional lines while maintaining monopoly. Thus, it is not clear why competition is the necessary remedy to monopoly power.

Nonsustainability Explanations

Another view is that a monopoly, even if efficient across its multiple products, cannot protect itself from entry into some lines of business:

6. "The diversification of telecommunications makes it difficult for any one provider to serve all submarkets without competitive entry."

This view is essentially that of an economic nonsustainability theory advanced by Baumol et al. (1982), applied to telecommunications (Woroch, 1990). It can explain the emergence of entrants for new products of a multiproduct firm, but it does not adequately cover competition in traditional core markets of a telecommunications monopolist, unless one accepts very restrictive assumptions (Shepherd, 1983).

Market Structure Explanations

There are two variants to the market structure approach, one passive and the other active:

7. "Monopoly's inefficiency eventually leads to the emergence of competition."
8. "Competition is a policy chosen to enhance efficiency and technological development."

These views are held by many economists. Theory 7 is similar to the views of Milton Friedman on the impermanence of privileged economic arrangements. Theory 8 expects governments not simply to wait for competitors' entry but to institute proactive and pro-competitive policies (e.g., the United Kingdom and Japan, where competition was introduced from above). These two views share the premise of inefficiency of monopoly. In other words, a multicarrier market structure is believed to be emerging because of some failure of the traditional system. Yet this assumption is at odds with the reality of network performance in those countries where structural changes in networks are most rapid. If inefficiency were the causal force for rival entry, Egypt or Mexico (to use two almost random examples) should have introduced competition long before the United States and Japan, whose networks were among the most advanced and ubiquitous networks in the world even *before* embarking on their liberalizing policies.

It has always exasperated the proponents of the traditional network system to be told that their problem was inefficiency. This clashed with their observations of economies of scale, benefits of long-term technological planning, and effectiveness of end-to-end responsibility. Thus, explanations premised on the inadequacies of the monopoly system are not persuasive.

A New Approach: The Tipping of Network Coalitions

None of these eight theories for the emergence of multiple networks provides an adequate explanation, although they all contain truth and in the aggregate hold explanatory power.

In contrast, a ninth and alternative view is proposed, that of the dynamics of group formation. The thesis is not based on the *failure* of the existing system, but rather on its success. Changes in technology, politics and cost are merely enabling a more fundamental shift of coalitions.

9. "The breakdown of monopoly is due to the very *success* of the traditional system in advancing telephone service and in making it universal and essential. As the system expands, political dynamics take place that lead to redistribution and overexpansion. This provides increasing incentives to exit from a sharing coalition, and to an eventual 'tipping' of the network from a stable single network coalition (the public network) to a system of separate subcoalitions."

This view of success undermining its own foundations is, from the monopoly's perspective, deeply pessimistic, because it implies that the harder their efforts and the greater their success, the closer is the end to their special status. As in a Greek tragedy, their preventive actions only assure their doom.

A Model of Networks[4]

It may be useful to ask why there is usually only one public telephone network in a country. It is not for the interconnectedness of all participants, since this justification would lead one to have only one large bank for all financial transactions. Interaction does not usually require institutional integration. This was Adam Smith's major insight. To distinguish telecommunications from this observation by labeling it *infrastructure* requires us to define that term in a way that is not vacuous or circuitous, an almost impossible task.

Another explanation is "natural monopoly." Although such a monopoly may exist for a local exchange area, the examples of the United States, Canada, Denmark, and Finland prove that a widespread horizontal integration of local exchange areas is not required. Even if it were, one must ask, why these economies end miraculously at the national frontier. Has there ever been a national monopolist that asked a larger neighbor to take over its system in order to reap the benefit of economies of scale? Moreover, it has not been established that an integration of local and long-distance service is based on economies of scale. These services are institutionally separated in several countries.

Perhaps the best way to look at a network is as a *cost-sharing arrangement* between several users. Fixed costs are high, marginal costs low, and a new participant, C, helps incumbents A and B to lower their cost. In this respect a network is similar to a "public good," such as a swimming pool or national defense. But although there is basically only one national defense system, there are many types of arrangements for swimming pools. A user may want to share the pool with a few dozen families, but not with thousands. A pure public good admits everyone, a pure private good admits only one. But there is a wide spectrum between the pure private good and the pure public good (Buchanan, 1965). A telecommunications network is one intermediate example. It is not a private good yet it does not meet the two main conditions for a public good: nonrival consumptions and nonexcludability. In fact, nonexcludability has to be established as a legal requirement—the universal service obligation. What has been happening in recent years to telecommunications, and what goes by the more dramatic labels of divestiture and deregulation, is largely a shift in the degree of its intermediate position, a shift toward the direction of private good.

We shall now develop, in a stepwise fashion, a model for network evolution and diversification to explain the breakdown of the network monopoly.

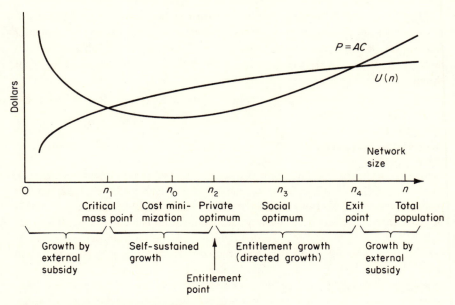

Figure 3.1.   Stages in Network Expansion.

The Basic Model[5]

Let the total cost of a TC network be given by a cost function that depends on the number of subscribers.[6]

$$TC(n) = C(n); C'(n) \geq O)$$ (1)

Let an individual's utility be given by a function $u(P, n)$, where P is the price for network usage and n is the number of network members.[7] We assume that the more members there are on the network, the better it will be for an individual subscriber, other things remaining equal (including network performance and price),[8] that is, we assume that network externalities exist. This means that $(\delta u/\delta n > 0)$, though at a declining rate $(\delta^2 u/\delta n^2 < 0)$.

We assume that the network membership is priced at average cost (i.e., that users share costs equally). Then price P is also a function of n: $P = P(n)$. (This assumption will be dropped later.[9])

These relations can be shown schematically in Figure 3.1, where $u(n)$, the benefit of participation in a network, is steadily increasing with network size, though at a declining rate. The price of participating in the network

$$P = AC = C(n)/n$$

is declining, at least at first.

Critical Mass

Subscribers will find it attractive to join a good-sized network, because total costs are shared by many, making average costs low, while the number of subscribers n adds to utility. This can be seen in Figure 3.1, where the utility of joining a network rises at first. Conversely, where the network is small, the average cost is high, and externalities are small. In that range, below a "critical mass" point n_1, a network will not be feasible, unless it is supported by external sources. We define critical mass as the smallest number of users such that a user is as well off as a nonuser $u(n) = P(n)$.[10]

To reach n_1 requires a subsidy of sorts, either by government or by the network operator's willingness to accept losses in the early growth phases of operations. The strategic problem is to identify in advance a situation in which such a break-even point n_1 will be reached within the range $n < N$, where N = total population. Such a point may not exist, and subsidies would have to be permanent to keep the network from imploding. We shall return to the critical mass issue later in the section entitled "Subsidies for Reaching Critical Mass."

Private Optimum

Through the cost-sharing phases of network growth, the earlier network users can lower their cost by adding members. However, at some point average cost AC increases in the range beyond the point n_0 where AC $= f'(n)$.

Beyond n_0, expansion becomes unattractive for the members of the network for cost reasons because (for example) they are in more remote locations with lesser population density, and thus are more costly to serve. But some further expansion would be accepted by the network members, since newcomers beyond the low-cost point would still add to utility. This will be up to the point n_2 where the total derivative with respect to the number of users is equal to zero.

$$\frac{du}{dn} = -\frac{\delta u}{\delta c}\frac{\delta AC}{\delta n}\frac{1}{p} + \frac{\delta u}{\delta n} = 0 \tag{2}$$

which holds where the marginal utility of an added subscriber is

$$\frac{\delta u}{\delta n} = \frac{\delta u}{\delta c}\frac{1}{p}\frac{\delta AC}{\delta n} \tag{3}$$

The optimal point lies in the range of increasing AC. Graphically, n_2 would lie where the two derivatives are of equal size, $u'(P) = u'(n)$. Left to themselves, the existing subscribers of the network would not accept members beyond n_2, the private optimum. From size 0 to size n_2, the network is in its *cost-sharing* stage.

Social Optimum

From a societal point of view, however, the optimal network size in an equal-price system may diverge from the private optimum.

Assume social welfare given by the sums of utilities.

$$W = n[u(P(n)) + u(n)] = n[C(n)/n + u(n)] \tag{4}$$

so that its derivative

$$\frac{dW}{dn} = C'(n) + nu'(n) + u(n) = 0 \tag{5}$$

$$u'(n) = \frac{1}{n}[C'(n) - u(n] \tag{6}$$

Since $u(n) > C(n)/n$ below the point of intersection n_4, social optimum n_3 is greater than private optimum n_2. (It should be noted that the same size will be chosen by an unconstrained monopolist that sets the price at $P = u(n_3)$ to exhaust consumer surplus.)

What is the implication? Left to itself, the network will cease growth beyond n_2, at least as long as costs are equally shared. Existing network subscribers would not want to admit newcomers beyond n_2. Latecomers beyond that point add cost, because they raise AC and add fewer externality benefits. [In reality, of course, networks are "public" and not able to reject members (B. Greenwald, 1990, communication).] The socially optimal size n_3 will not be reached by itself, but requires some external direction (e.g., governmentally mandated expansion and/or a differentiated pricing scheme) or some internal politics of expansion, which will be described later.

Entitlement Point and Universal Service Obligation

To understand the politics of government-directed network expansion, let us assume that political decisions are made by a mechanism in which majorities rule. When private optimum size $n_2 < N/2$, there are more people outside than inside the network, and there are positive net benefits (i.e., $u(n_2) - AC(n_2) > 0$). A majority consisting of $N - n_2$ network outsiders would therefore outvote the n_2 network insiders and require the opening of the network to additional members. This would be the case up to the point where network size reaches $N/2$, at which point the network insiders would have grown to a majority and would resist further growth. Beyond $N/2$, then (or where $n_2 \geq N/2$ and a majority against expansion exists from the beginning), a politically directed growth will occur if the coalition of network insiders can be split by aligning the remaining outsiders $N/2$ with some of the insiders who are offered a more favorable share of cost (i.e., by price discrimination). It can be shown that this coalition formation will lead to an overexpansion of the network. The dynamics of such price discrimination and its impact are discussed in greater detail later in this chapter, in sections entitled "Political Price Setting and Redistribution," "Monopoly and Expansion," and "Network Tipping."

Politically directed growth beyond private optimum n_2 can be termed an "entitlement growth," because it is based on political arguments of *rights* to participate in the network where average net benefits are positive (encouraging attempts of entry) while marginal net average benefits are negative, leading to attempts at exclusion. In economic terms, the argument is made to expand the network at least to where $C'(n) = P = u(n)$, leaving fixed costs to be distributed unequally, for example, by a Ramsey pricing rule. When the marginal net benefits are positive, there is no need to resort to the language of entitlements, since growth is self-sustaining and sought by network insiders. It is only beyond that point that entitlements, rights, and universal service rights (i.e., obligations by the network) become an issue. We can thus define n_2 as the "entitlement point."

This way of analyzing entitlements serves to clarify the often asked question; "For which services will universal service be extended?" The analytical answer is to those services that

1. have grown beyond minimum critical mass, and
2. have reached, through self-sustained growth, a private optimum, beyond which further growth is not internally generated because *marginal* average net benefits are zero, but where
3. average net benefits are positive (and therefore encourage demand for entry), and
4. the number of those excluded is sufficiently large to lead to an opening by means of internal and external redistributive politics.

Exit from the Network

If $n_2 < N$, with N being the total population, some people would be left out of the network. But as discussed in the previous section, a government would require for the network to be open to other users. Yet there may well be a point where the network is expanded to an extent that, given its increasing marginal cost, a user is better off by not participating. We define n_4 as the "exit point" (i.e., the largest n such that the indifference exists between dropping off the network and sharing in the cost of supporting the expanded network).

$$u(n) = u(P) \tag{7}$$

This exit point may lie beyond the total population, $n_4 > N$. But this seems unlikely under an average-pricing scheme, because the last subscribers may impose a heavy burden on the rest of subscribers, and the subsequent departure of some subscribers would lead to further reduction in the utility of the remaining members and may induce a secondary exodus. Thus, assuming $n_4 < N$, a government's aim to establish a truly universal service, without resorting to a subsidy mechanism or price discrimination, is likely to be infeasible. In other words, a universal service policy is likely to depend on a redistributive policy.

In the range of size n_2 to n_4, the network is in its second phase, the *redistributive* stage.

Political Price Setting and Redistribution

We have so far assumed that universal service is something imposed externally by government. In this section, however, it will be shown that the *internal* dynamics of network members will take the network toward universal service and toward its own disintegration.

As has been shown, a network will cease to grow on its own after private optimum n_2. But this conclusion was based on a pricing scheme of equal-cost shares. Yet there is no reason for such equal-cost shares to persist if they are allocated through a decision mechanism that permits the majority of network users to impose higher-cost shares on the minority. (This assumes that no arbitrage is possible.) Unequal prices and a departure from cost could be rationalized benignly as merely "value-of-service" pricing (i.e., higher prices for the users who value the telephone greatly).

Suppose for purposes of the model that decisions are made through voting by all network members.[11] Let us assume at this stage that all users are of equal size (or that voting takes place according to the number of lines a subscriber uses, which in terms of the model is the same thing) and that early network users have lower demand elasticity for network use. The determinative vote is provided by the median voter located at $n/2$. A majority would not wish to have its benefits diluted by a number of beneficiaries larger than necessary. This is the principle of the "minimal winning coalition." Its size would be $n/2 + 1$.

A majority will establish itself such that it will benefit maximally from the minority. The minority that can be maximally burdened are the users with less elastic demand for telephone service, which are the early subscribers. But there is a limit to the burden, given by utility curve $u(n)$. If price gets pushed above $u(n)$, subscribers will drop off. Hence, the majority ($n_2/2 + 1$) will burden the minority ($n_2/2 - 1$) with a price up to positive utility, and they will bear the rest of the cost. The minority's price P_1 will be such that

$$P_1 = u(n_2) \tag{8}$$

The majority's price will then be[12]

$$P_2 = n - \frac{n_2}{2} = 2AC - P_1 = 2AC - u(n_2) \tag{9}$$

This, then, is the redistributory outcome, assuming no discrimination within majority and minority.

Monopoly and Expansion

Such redistribution, however, is not a stable equilibrium. Before network size n_2 was reached (once the critical mass threshold was crossed) by voluntary association. Additional members were not admitted, because they lowered utility for the incumbents. But with internal redistribution, several things happen. There are now incentives for the minority network members to exit the network and form a new one in which they would not bear the redistributory burden. This is economically feasible if the minority is larger than critical mass, $n_2/2 > n_1$. Even when this is not the case, the minority can band together with those beyond network size n_2 who desire telephone service but were previously excluded.

This exit would deprive the majority of the source of its subsidy and is therefore held undesirable. The only way for the majority to prevent this "cream skimming" or "cherry picking" is to prohibit the establishment of another network, both by those wanting to leave the original network and by those not admitted to it in the first place because they are beyond n_2. Thus, a monopoly system and the prevention of arbitrage become essential to the stability of such a network system.

At the same time, the model predicts that the network will expand beyond n_2. For the majority, there is added utility from added network members, while most of its cost is borne by the minority, who are also willing to bear a greater burden as the network expands due to its greater utility. The majority will therefore seek expansion beyond n_2. The cost to the majority is only that the subsidy by the minority must be shared with more network participants. Therefore, the majority would admit new members up to the point n_5 where marginal utility to its members is equal to the marginal price increase due to the diluted subsidy.

But this is not the end of the story. With expansion to n_5, the majority is now $n_5/2$ rather than $n_2/2$ (i.e., larger than before), and it can tax a larger minority ($n_5/2$) than before. Hence, the expansion process would take place again, leading to a point $n'_5 > n_5$. This process would continue until an equilibrium is reached.

n^*_5 is the point up to which the network will grow under the internal dynamics described earlier. The greater the marginal utility from added network members, and the smaller the marginal costs, and the greater the fixed costs are, the larger n^*_5 will be.[13]

Network Tipping[14]

As this process of expansion takes place, the minority is growing too. The likelihood that its size will increase beyond the point of critical mass n_1 is increased, and the utility of its members, given the burden of subsidy, may well be below that of membership in a smaller but nonsubsidizing alternative network. We have so far assumed that there is only one network and that a user's choice is whether to join or not. Suppose there are no legal barriers to the formation of a new network. In that case, a user's choice menu is to stay, to drop off altogether, or to join a new network association. Assume that the new network has the same cost characteristics as the traditional network. (In fact, it may well have a lower cost function for each given size if there has been accumulated monopolistic inefficiency in the existing network and rent-seeking behavior by various associated groups.) Then minority coalition members would find themselves better off in a new network B, and they would consider such a network, abandoning the old one. The only problem is that of transition discontinuity. A new network, in its early phases, would be a money-losing proposition up to its critical mass point n'_1.[15]

The point where exit becomes possible, given the redistributory burden that keeps utility just balanced with price, is the point n beyond where

$$u(n/2) > AC(n/2) \qquad (10)$$

which is at the critical mass point. Hence, the minority will strive to exit the redistributory network once its size is more than twice the size of critical mass.[16]

The majority may attempt to alleviate these pressures to exit by reducing the redistributory burden and thus keeping the minority from dropping out. But that means the network size n_7 would not be optimal to the majority anymore, and members would have to be forced out. And this, in turn, would reduce its majority, so that it would have to drop the subsidizing burden from at least some minority members as the $n/2$ point separating the majority from the minority shifts to the left.

This means either higher burdens on the shrinking minority— frustrating the purpose of bribing it into staying—or still less benefits for the majority if it wants to keep the network from fragmenting. Such a disequilibrium process will continue up to the point where network size $n = 2\,n_1$ (i.e., where the minority may be too small to create a self-supporting new network). One might call this the effect of *potential* exit by the minority, and it results in a lessened redistribution of newcomers to the network in order to keep the first entrants inside.

It might be argued that in a new network, internal redistribution based on coalitions might exist. But this is not likely. Once the possibility of exit is established, each burdened subgroup can simply join another network. Thus, internal redistribution will happen only if a network is unique, and thus if a burdened user will not readily switch into another network.

Unequal User Size

We have assumed so far that network voters are of equal size. In reality, however, some users are much larger in terms of lines n than others. The minority's position would be further weakened if voting were governed by a principle of "one subscriber, one vote" rather than the "one line, one vote" previously assumed.

Suppose users are ordered according to size on Figure 3.1; in other words, the largest users are those that joined the network first. This is not unrealistic, since users with great needs for telecommunications are likely to have been the first to acquire a telephone, and early subscribers had the longest time to expand usage. Let us further represent the distribution of lines n for a user v by

$$n = Av^{-a} \qquad (11)$$

where $A > 0$, $a \geq 1$.

The median voter (or median account) is $v/2$ and its preferences govern. But the network size provided by the users arrayed to the left of such median user is larger than those to the right.

In Figure 3.1, n_m, the median account, is to the right of $n/2$. In other words, the median voter whose preferences govern is at a network size greater than the median point of the network size. The more the distribution of lines is skewed (the larger the coefficients A and a) the further to the right is n_m. And the more skewed the distribution, the more likely it is that the voting minority will reach by itself a size beyond the critical mass point.

Interconnection

The process of unraveling of the existing network would commence even earlier if a new network has the right to interconnect into the previous one, because in that case it would enjoy the externality benefits of a larger reach $n_A + n_B$, while not being subject to redistributory burden. This is why interconnectivity is a critical issue for the establishment of alternative networks, as the historical U.S. examples demonstrate, from the *Kingsbury Commitment* in 1913 to *MCI Execunet* in 1976 and today's *ONA* and *collocation* proceedings.

Since the benefits of network reach remain, a subscriber's exit decision is cost-driven, and takes place if $C(n_B)/n_B < c(n)/n$. With redistribution under the primary network, but not in the new network B, the test would be, for a subscriber i, if $c(n_B)/n_B < P_i(n)$.

Would there exist, for any subnetwork, internal redistribution based on coalitions? Once the possibility of exit is established, each burdened subgroup could join another network. Thus, internal redistribution will happen only if a network is unique to its users.

Network interconnection means that the network still centers around a society-wide concept of interconnected users. But it consists now of *multiple* subnetworks that are linked to each other. Each of these subnetworks has its own cost-sharing arrangements, with some mutual interconnection charges. Interconnection facilitates the emergence of new networks and lowers entry barriers. But given entry, it may reduce competition by establishing cooperative linkages instead of end-to-end rivalry (Mueller, 1988). Interconnection is a useful concept, because it responds to the frequent claim that a single network is necessary for universal reach. This assertion is clearly incorrect. Interaction does not usually require institutional integrations. Otherwise, we would have only one large bank for all financial transactions, as mentioned. But as the next section will show, it may also lead to market failure in the establishment of the original network.

Subsidies for Reaching Critical Mass

We have mentioned that waiting for demand to materialize prior to the introduction of a network or network service may not be the optimal private or public network policy. Demand is a function of price and benefits, both of which are in turn functions of the size of the network. Hence, early development of a network may require internal or external support to reach critical mass.

This suggests the need, in some circumstances, to subsidize the early stages of the network—up to the critical mass point n_1—when the user externalities are still low but cost shares are high. These subsidies could come either from the network provider or its membership as a start-up investment, or from an external source (e.g., a government) as an investment in "infrastructure," a concept centered around externalities. The question is how the internal support is affected by the emergence of a system of multiple networks.

The private start-up investment in a new form of network is predicated on an expectation of eventual break-even and subsequent positive net benefits to members. But if one can expect the establishment of additional networks, which would keep network size close to n_1, there would be only small (or no) net benefits realized by the initial entrants to offset their earlier investment. This would be further aggravated by interconnection rights, because a new network could make immediate use of the positive network externalities of the membership of the existing network that were achieved by the latter's investment. Hence, it is less likely that the initial risk would be undertaken if a loss were borne entirely by the initial network participants while the benefits would be shared with other entrants who would be able to interconnect and thus immediately gain the externality benefits of the existing network users, but without contributing to their cost sharing. The implication is that in an environment of multiple networks that can interconnect, less start-up investment would be undertaken. It pays to be second. A situation of market failure exists.

How could one offset this tendency if it is deemed undesirable? Patents are one solution. If a contemplated new network arrangement is technologically innovative, it might obtain a patent protection for some period. Where a service is innovative but not patentable, one might create a "regulatory patent" for a limited period of protection, or the initial approval (where necessary) might be accelerated. Similarly, interconnection rights might be deferred for a period, or joint introductions might be planned that eliminate the first entrant penalty. But these measures would also reduce the usefulness of alternative networks and hence could lead to the dynamics of political expansion, redistribution, and break-up described earlier. Another approach is to require access charges that cover the externality benefits for interconnection. But this requires market power, since otherwise no price above cost could be sustained. And if that market power exists, it could be exercised in a restrictive fashion.

It is quite possible that none of these measures would be as effective in generating the investment support as a monopoly network that can reap all future benefits. This would mean that the private and social benefits of networks in the range between n_1 and n_4 would not be realized. In such a situation, there may be a role for direct outside support, such as by a government subsidy. At first, this may seem paradoxical. One would expect a competitive system of multiple networks to be *less* in need of government involvement than a monopoly. But there is some economic logic to this. Just as the subsidies to individual network users that were previously *internally* generated by other network users would have to be raised *externally* (through the normal mechanism of taxation and allocation) if at least some users are still to be supported, so might subsidies to the start-up of a network as a whole have to be provided externally, also through taxation and allocation, where network externalities as well as start-up costs are high enough to make the establishment of a network desirable.

Social Welfare and Multiple Networks

If network associations can control their memberships, stratification is inevitable. They will seek those members who will provide them with the greatest externality benefits—those with many actual or potential contacts. Furthermore, they will want to admit low-cost, high volume, low risk customers as club members. Thus, different affinity-group networks and different average costs will emerge.

But what about social welfare in such a differentiated system? The traditional fear is that the loss of some cost sharing and externalities brought by a second network would reduce social welfare. But the news is not necessarily bad. Where mutual interconnection is assured, one can keep the externalities benefits (and even increase them) while moving down the cost curve toward a lower AC. Furthermore, the cost curves themselves are likely to come down with the ensuing competition.

The welfare implications of the formation of collective consumption and production arrangements are analyzed by theorists of clubs (Schelling, 1969; Tullock, 1971; Rothenberg, 1976; Tiebout, 1956; McGuire, 1972).

Optimal group size will vary according to the dimension to be optimized: It depends on the ratio of marginal utilities for different dimensions, set equal to the ratio of transformation in production, and is in turn related to size (Buchanan, 1965, pp. 4–5). But this does not imply that one should keep networks nonubiquitous and unequal. Financial transfers can be used. However, it is generally not Pareto-efficient to attempt income transfer by integrating diverse groups and imposing varying cost. It is more efficient to allow subgroups to form their own associations and then to redistribute by imposing charges on some groups and distribute to others. The set of possible utility distributions among separate groups dominates (weakly) the set of such distributions among integrated groups (McGuire, 1972, p. 124). User group separation with direct transfer is more efficient than the indirect method of enforced togetherness with different cost shares. In other words, differentiated networks plus taxation or another system of revenue shifting such as access and interconnection charges can be more efficient than monopoly and internal redistribution.

Conclusion

The theoretically based analysis of the model means that a network coalition, left to itself under majority-rule principles, expands beyond a size that would hold together. Such an arrangement is therefore inherently unstable. It can stay together only as long as arbitrage is prevented, as long as the minority cannot exercise political power in other ways, and as long as it has no choice but to stay within the burdensome network arrangement.

But beyond that point, the over expansion policy creates incentives to form alternative networks. And the more successful network policy is in terms of achieving universal service and "affordable rates," the greater the pressures for fracture of the network.

This chapter has shown that networks become unstable with expansion beyond their optimal size to participants, and because a democratic decision-making mechanism establishes expansion through a redistributive mechanism. Stability can be maintained only through coercion, which becomes increasingly difficult to maintain.

The analysis also shows that a subsidy is necessary in the early stages of a network to reach critical mass and that such a subsidy is less likely once the monopoly network is supplemented by other networks with the right to interconnect. In such a situation, market failure may well exist that would reduce start-up investment in innovation. This suggests that in a competitive network environment where interconnection exists, alternative subsidy mechanisms must be established if new types of networks are to reach critical mass.

Thus, the very success of network expansion bears the seed of its own demise. This is what might be called the "tragedy of the common network" [in the Greek drama sense of unavoidable doom, and borrowing from the title of Hardin's classic article "The Tragedy of the Commons" (1968) on the depletion of environmental resources]. In the words of Alfred North Whitehead: "The essence of dramatic tragedy is not unhappiness. It resides in the solemnity of the remorseless working of things." In the case of telecommunications the tragedy is that the breakdown of the common network is caused not by the failure of the system but by its very success—the spread of service across society and the transformation of a convenience into a necessity.

4

Forces of Centrifugalism

The model of Chapter 3 identified an evolution of network development with three stages:

1. *The cost-sharing network.* Expansion of the network is based on the logic of spreading fixed costs across a large number of participants, beyond a take-off point ("critical mass"), and of increasing the value of network connectivity.
2. *The redistributory network.* At this stage, the network grows beyond the size that is optimal to its original members, through a politically directed expansion caused by the formation of internal coalitions that lead to transfers from some users to others.
3. *The pluralistic network.* Beyond a certain point, the cohesion of the unitary network breaks apart because the dynamics of expansion and redistribution lead to a divergence in the interests of its participants that can no longer be reconciled within one network. The results are exit, formation of new networks, and the emergence of a federation of subnetworks. The network has progressed to its "tipping point," where its cohesion breaks up and a multinetwork system emerges.

These trends have a logical progression. At first the network expands because it makes economic and technical sense. Later it expands because it makes political sense. But as the network provider succeeds in providing full service to every household, it also undermines the foundation of its exclusivity.

Most countries in the world are still in the phases of the cost-sharing or redistributory networks. In Europe, first stage countries are Portugal, Turkey, Greece, and the nations of Eastern Europe. All others have reached substantial universal penetration of telecommunications for a number of years, and it is here that the transformation of the network system has begun progressing toward its third stage, which the United States entered first, followed by Japan. Since there is a strong correlation of economic growth and telephone penetration (roughly an additional telephone per $50,000 GNP), countries with high economic growth are likely to progress rapidly through the first two stages. Eventually, through economic growth and the instabilities transmitted from the more advanced nations, many other countries will move into a pluralistic network environment and will be faced with the policy issues inherent in such a system.

We have seen how the centralized and hierarchical system of the traditional network, despite its public popularity, has been subject to forces of centrifugalism that have undermined its stability. The present chapter looks at the contributing factors that make this breakup more likely. Technology is one such factor, though one should not exaggerate its contributions. It is not microwave and satellite transmission that has made long-distance telephone competition possible. Several other factors have contributed to the disintegration of the centralized monopoly.

The Service Economy and Increases in User Size

The driving force for the restructuring of telecommunications has been the phenomenal growth in user demand for telecommunications, a force that in turn is based on the shift toward a service-based economy. The largest users of telecommunications are major providers of services; they include corporate headquarters, banks, insurance firms, airlines, health delivery organizations, engineering and consulting firms, law offices, and media organizations. The growth of these service industries in highly developed countries has been due in part to diminished competitiveness in traditional mass production, where newly industrialized countries have excelled. It was also partly due to their large pool of educated people skilled in handling information. These advantages were reinforced by productivity increases in information transactions through computers and advanced office equipment. Information-based services, including headquarters activities, therefore emerged as a major comparative advantage of developed countries. Manufacturing and retailing, at the same time, became far-flung and decentralized.

Within the service sector, the number of people performing functions related to information and its creation, processing, and manipulation has grown particularly large. According to one study (Beniger, 1986), 37 percent of the work force in 1980 was engaged in information jobs, 22 percent in industrial jobs, 2 percent in agriculture, and 29 percent in other services. Another study asserts that 54 percent of the American work force and 63 percent of all working time are now devoted to information work (Strassman, 1985, p. 56). An earlier study found a similar trend (Porat, 1978).

As electronic information transmission (i.e., telecommunications) became increasingly important to the new services sector, it turned into a major expense item. For instance, for Citicorp, America's largest bank holding firm, telecommunications are the third largest cost item, after salaries and real estate. Consequently, the purchase of communications capability at advantageous prices is much more important than in the past. Price, control, security, and reliability have become variables requiring organized attention. This, in turn, led to the emergence of the new breed of private telecommunications managers whose function is to reduce costs for their firms, establishing for the first time sophisticated telecommunications expertise outside the postal–industrial coalition. These managers aggressively seek low-cost transmission and customized equipment systems in the form of private networks of power and scope far beyond those of the past (Schiller, 1982). These private networks, which start out as systems of dedicated lines leased from the monopoly network carriers, can become large and far-flung. Some require hundreds of skilled technicians and managers to operate and administer, and they are carving out slices from the public network. It does not take a large number of private networks to have an impact. In the United States, for example, the largest 3 percent of users typically account for 50 percent of all telephone revenues. These activities are spearheaded by private firms but are not exclusive to them: Nonprofit institutions (e.g., hospitals and universities) and public organizations (e.g., state and local governments) are actively pursuing similar cost-reduction strategies. The U.S. government, for example, awarded in 1989 a $25 billion contract for a "private" network to serve its civilian activities (FTS-2000).[1]

The Saturation of Basic Service

The model of Chapter 3 argued that the expansion of a single network can eventually lead to its fragmentation. What has been the path of such expansion? For a long time the primary policy goal of most industrialized countries was to establish a network that would reach every household; this also benefited the supplying industry. Even in highly developed countries, the achievement of substantial network penetration is a very recent phenomenon. In West Germany, penetration in 1960 was 12 percent. In 1980, it was 75 percent (Schulte, 1982); and in 1990 it was getting close to 100 percent (Pfeiffer and Wieland, 1990). In France, it was 6 percent in 1967 (Guerard and Lafarge, 1979), 54 percent in 1983 (AT&T, 1983), and 97 percent in 1990 (Steckel and Fossier, 1990). Similar trends existed in almost all European countries. Hence, the imposition of the costs of the last subscribers is a fairly new development, and responses to it are only now beginning to work themselves out. In the United States, universal service was substantially achieved some twenty-five years earlier.

An Activist Role by the Equipment Industry

Once universal penetration was reached, the industry had to reorient itself, because its activity level would otherwise have dropped dramatically.

Having been successful in spreading telephony, the supplying industry too became a victim of its own success. It was left with several strategies:

1. *Upgrade.* After achieving universal penetration, the equipment industry advocated an upgrade of the network. This means an accelerated supply push rather than demand pull. It also means moving into videotex, integrated services digital networks (ISDN), integrated broadband networks, and cable television as ways to provide the industry with procurement contracts.

2. *Export.* Increased attention to international activities can substitute for the shrinking basic domestic market. However, many of the more interesting markets in industrial and industrializing countries are protected by their governments, which use the network as a way to promote a domestic electronic industry. The results are trade frictions around the world and eventually partial opening of national markets in order to achieve reciprocity. This reduces the traditional territorial compartmentalization of the industry and loosens the close relation between equipment industry and network monopoly. One of the positive consequences of this is that prices fall even beyond the gains of technology.

3. *Target users as equipment buyers.* Perhaps most important in the long run, manufacturers turned to large users as a market for equipment. Whereas in 1975 virtually 100 percent of United States capital investments in telecommunications equipment were made by the carriers, that figure had dropped to 67 percent by 1986. About $15 billion was invested by non-carriers, mostly large users (Crandall, 1988). Such equipment includes PBXs, multiplexers, concentrators, network management equipment, satellite and microwave facilities, etc.

Users increasingly assumed control over the network segments closest to them—first, over equipment on their premises; second, over the wiring segments in office and residential buildings. It was the natural next step that they began to share in a full array of telecommunications services within their building through "shared-tenant services," which shifted some of the switching from the public exchange to a common PBX and moved transmission from the public network to a private one. Next, users moved to switching and to local area networks (LANs) for high-volume links serving the data flows within an organization.

The implication is that the equipment industry, in the past a protector of the traditional monopoly, has increasingly become part of the process of creating alternative networks.

Reductions in Equipment Costs and Increases in Productivity

Another factor leading to new networks is that the underlying economics of transport and switching have shifted the cost curve for telecommunications considerably downward. A unit of communications has become much cheaper to transmit and switch. The cost of a network drops as electronic and photonic equipment becomes cheaper, more powerful, and less expensive to operate. In the United States, the price for switches paid by one telephone company, for example, came down in price per line from $230 in 1983 to $144 in 1988.[2] Manpower requirements declined considerably,[3] and productivity increased.

Similarly, the price per meter of fiber fell from $7 in 1977 to 23 cents in 1988, and its transmission capacity increased enormously. LEDs dropped from $2000 a few years before to less than $30 in 1990. According to some predictions, in three to five years fiber will be cheaper to install than copper (Elton, 1991; Egan, 1990).

In terms of the model, as the cost curve drops, the critical mass point n_1 shifts to the left to a smaller minimal size, and it becomes easier to start an alternative network. The growth of large users also means that it takes fewer of them to reach any given network size n. This reduces transaction costs of organizing and coordinating a new network club and makes it possible for a smaller number of users to enjoy the economies of scale.

Diseconomies of Scale and Scope

Economic and technological development lead to increased specialization and to a divergence rather than convergence of options. In telecommunications, the rapid technological development has spawned a large number of applications. For examples see the chapter on value-added services. It has become difficult for the traditional network to keep up with all these options and customized needs. Thus, the growth of technological and operational alternatives undercuts the economies of scale and scope once offered by the centralized network. This will be discussed in detail in the chapter on ISDN.

The Emergence of the "Second" Electronic Industry

Throughout the 1960s and 1970s, many traditional telecommunications firms gradually lost their technological preeminence. Insulated from competition and secure in their profits, they had not been highly successful technologically relative to their resources. Most missed out on the development of computers or tried unsuccessfully to enter that industry. Their lack of success came despite major national efforts and subsidies for the development of computer and semiconductor components. (This will be discussed in the chapter on industrial policy.)

Over time, an independent computer and component industry evolved in most developed countries, forming a "second" electronics sector. These firms, which were based on direct relations with users without the mediation of the PTTs, provided an element of a new coalition that began challenging the traditional postal–industrial complex. They were allied with the large service industry users in a "services–information industry coalition." In the United States, this grouping includes, for example, American Express, IBM, Time-Warner, TWA, Silicon Valley firms, and Citicorp. Defending the traditional system was primarily AT&T, but this was not enough to stem the tide. Hence, the victory of the services–information coalition over the traditional forces was inevitable in the United States. (For a discussion of the AT&T divestiture, see Cole, 1990.)

In Britain, the new coalition was slower to gather than in the United States, and the defense of the traditional industrial sector was more tenacious and ideological. But the balance of power swung in the 1970s.

The British electronics industry was not successful internationally, particularly when one subtracts Britain's former colonies as a market. On the other hand, British service industries such as banking, insurance, trading, publishing, and media were doing well. London, along with New York and Tokyo, was the major center for international services, and it was the preferred European headquarters of non-European firms. Although the Thatcher government argued for the deregulation of telecommunications largely on the grounds that it would make British high technology more competitive, the most important effect of its policy was to help make London the center for European business transactions. This is a role with which Britain, given its traditions, was comfortable. A similar story can be told for the Netherlands.

In Japan, where the "first" telecommunications industry transformed itself better than anywhere else into the "second" electronics industry, the changes were smoothest, since the private industry did not stand to lose while the service sector was gaining strength. Reform was accomplished as a continuation of industrial policy. The national monopoly carrier, NTT (Nippon Telephone and Telegraph), was privatized, and competition was introduced under the prodding of the Ministry of International Trade and Industry (MITI) without the bitter public conflicts of the United States or Western Europe (Ito, forthcoming; Nambu, forthcoming; Nagai, forthcoming; Komatsuzaki, 1986).

In several continental European countries, such as France, the service sector is relatively weak in comparison to manufacturing. French banks, most of which were nationalized, do not play the same role in international business as London banks. On the other hand, the industrial sector has been close to the heart of the French left. The weakness of the service sector can be explained in part by the traditional socialist emphasis on the production of goods, with its proletarian connotations, in contrast with the more middle-class rooted white-collar service activities such as finance and international trade. It also reflects the traditional electoral base of socialist parties. The emphasis on high-technology manufacturing also fits neatly into France's traditional concern with national autonomy, which appeals to the political right.

Increasing Cost of Incremental Subscribers

Over the years, low-cost subscribers have been added to the network earlier than high-cost subscribers. As the network reaches universality, connecting the last members increases cost. In the Bell system, the average capital investment cost per new telephone grew steadily (in 1982–1983 dollars) (*Telecom Factbook,* 1986):

1945:	$1928
1955:	$2050
1965:	$2580
1975:	$3960
1985:	$4624[4]

Upward Drift of Cost Curve of the Old Network

Costs and efficiencies of networks are a question not simply of engineering but also of market structure. The existing network, operating as an exclusive arrangement, tends to drift upward in terms of cost for a given technology vintage. This can be exacerbated by regulatory arrangements that lead to wrong incentives, such as to overcapitalization (the Averch-Johnson effect). Some indicators for this are the cost reductions achieved by U.S. companies when competitive pressures started to make themselves felt.

For example, AT&T's equipment installation and maintenance cost, at the time of divestiture, was estimated at $61 per hour as opposed to $33 for IBM and $28 for MCI.

The implications are that a new network, unencumbered by the accumulated high-cost attributes of the old one, could operate on a lower cost curve even in the absence of technical progress.

Pluralism in Network Usage

Another related factor contributing to the increase in specialized telecommunications networks is the growing number of groups in society that interlink via telecommunications. As the communications needs of groups have become specialized, private user clusters have emerged. Early examples are travel agents and airlines, automobile parts suppliers, and financial institutions, all of which have established group networks that combine some economies of scale with customization. Thus, pluralism of association has led to group communications, which we can locate conceptually somewhere between private and public network activities.

Again, these trends are discernible in all Western industrial countries. They go back to the changing nature of the production process itself. Michael Piore and Charles Sabel (1984) coined the term *industrial divide* for points where the path of technological development itself is at issue. In such periods the very nature of technology is determined by the social and institutional realities which shape economic institutions far into the future. Accordingly, we may be at a second industrial divide, the first being the emergence of mass industrial production. Today we are witnessing difficulties stemming from the transformation of the economy from an industrial base to a service base, and to smaller-scale production units. Adam Smith illustrated the importance of economies of scale in production in his famous example of the needle factory. Size made it possible to deploy specialized tasks and skills and to gain productivity increases. An advanced economy based on mass production was the synonym for capitalist-era production for both Smith and Marx, and an even more advanced economy, or so it seemed, would be based on still *more* mass production. This policy became the "corporatist" interpretation of political economy, justifying policies that care for and protect those economic entities that are already large and powerful, and allying the public interest with that of its largest economic organizations. The PTT system is a classic example of this approach.

But the mass production view of economic advancement needs revision. Significant activity takes place in small and medium-sized firms, and it is difficult to reconcile their role with the mass production theory.

One way to do so is to take note of the clustering of small firms. The ability to provide specialized services through clusters of firms creates economies of scale too. One need not think of the economic process as having to take place under a single roof or ownership structure. The entrepreneurial function is to bring together factors of production, not necessarily to own them. Thus, in terms of neoclassical economic theory, whether the services are performed by employees or outside contractors, by owned or leased capital is immaterial, though Marxist economists will not agree.

Hence, the logic of continuing specialization may lead to clustering of firms. Instead of large-scale vertical integration, a functional specialization may lead to a disintegration of the traditional functions of a firm. Within those specialties, supplier firms may have horizontal economies of scale even though their size may be moderate because of their high specialization. In the aggregate, these firms form a production and service complex that can be large, but it is not under one corporate control. The easy availability of telecommunications and information technology plays a key role in this development, because it makes decentralization possible. Telecommunications networks provide the glue that keeps such a production system together. At the same time, this trend leads to specialized network functionalities and equipment options, which in turn accelerate the evolution of telecommunications into a pluralist system.

Provider Specialization

As the information flow requirements of large users become larger, they also become increasingly specialized. Equipment offered by numerous vendors permits many configurations to accommodate the requirements and procedures of organizations. It is no longer as necessary to forgo benefits of specialization in order to benefit from cost sharing.

By their very nature, the traditional networks provide standardized and nationwide solutions, carefully planned and methodically executed. In the old days, sharing a standardized solution was more acceptable to network members, because the consequential loss of choice was limited and outweighed by the benefits of the economies of scale gained. As the significance of telecommunications grew, the costs of nonoptimal standardized solutions began to outweigh the benefits of economies of scale, providing the incentive for nonpublic solutions. Furthermore, some users aggressively employed a differentiation of telecommunications services as a business strategy to provide an advantage in their customers' eyes, and affirmatively sought a customized rather than a general communications solution. Although these considerations are most important for large firms, the differentiation of communications needs for small business and residential users has been moving rapidly as well.

The desirability of opting out of the traditional sharing arrangement depends, among other things, on traffic *densities*. Where these are high, private networks of different types emerge, depending on the degree of traffic *specialization*. For high-density general-purpose use, private networks emerge, but for low-density general purpose use the shared public network may last longest. For intermediate density, "virtual private networks" provide an intermediate option. For specialized services, the network types to emerge, depending on traffic densities, are strategic private networks, closed-use group networks, and value-added networks. These classifications[5] can be charted as follows:

Network Specialization

Traffic Density	General	Specialized
Dense	Private networks	Strategic private networks
Intermediate	Virtual private networks	Closed-use group networks
Low-density	Public networks	Value-added networks

As traffic densities and usage specialization grow, the core of the traditional public network (the lower left corner) shrinks.

Telephony has gone far beyond simple switched voice connections. Many "value-added services" have been developed and introduced, including voice mail, videotex and audiotex, and electronic message interchanges. Conceptually, most advanced telecommunications services can be analyzed as four layers superimposed on each other: basic transmission, data packet transmission, generic services, and applications packages. Although in many instances several of these layers can be integrated within the same carrier, they need not be. Thus, when a bank customer uses an automatic teller machine, several functionally different service providers may be involved on the same layer, and several other firms may provide communications on different geographical segments. The underlying banking transaction, in turn, may trigger interbank electronic transfer networks of similar complexity. Such structure calls for specialized service providers and packagers. This will be described in greater detail in the chapter on value-added services.

Technology of Alternative Transmission Paths

With multiple transmission technologies, total control has become increasingly difficult for one organization. In large countries, PTT exclusivity in long-distance communications is already sustained more by politics than by economic or technological advantages. For local distribution—the segment exhibiting the greatest characteristics of "natural" monopoly—several different transmission systems have emerged, including coaxial cable television networks, stationary cellular radio, microwave multipoint distribution, metropolitan areas, fiber-nets, and infrared transmission (Noam, 1986). For the PTT to control all the transmission paths means to assert control in new areas, some of which may be already occupied by other actors, such as cable network operators or satellite organizations. Alternative transmission routes have become economically feasible, opening new channels of communications and upsetting traditional patterns, much as advances in navigation and ship building resulted in Columbus and Vasco Da Gama upsetting traditional shipping routes.

Distance Insensitivity of Transmission Cost

The attractiveness of global transactions has increased as cost has become less sensitive to distance (Pool, 1990). For satellite transmission, in particular, the marginal cost with respect to distance is virtually nil. Fiber-optic links have also lowered distance-sensitive costs. As a result, communication flows can be routed indirectly to circumvent regulatory barriers and restrictive prices. This will be discussed in Chapter 32.

If a country's PTT exercises restrictive policies, its firms will be disadvantaged internationally, and foreign firms may choose not to domicile themselves in the country. Similarly, companies in countries with those restricted policies may pressure for change when they learn about options available elsewhere.

The challenge to the monopoly is that once it is breached by one country, the change may become irreparable. If the United Kingdom, with its liberalization policy, or one of the smaller European countries finds it profitable to change its policies and become a communications "haven," it becomes difficult to contain the dynamics. There are strong incentives for arbitrage if a carrier tries to charge above cost. This will be discussed in Chapter 40.

Merging of Technologies

Other challenges to the centralized network arise when traditional telecommunications networks and equipment increasingly become contiguous and overlap with previously separate sectors, such as computers, office equipment, and broadcasting. One response for PTTs has been to enter new fields, such as cable television, master television antennas, electronic publishing, computer utilities, electronic mail, modems, answering machines, and so on. Such moves lead to conflict with interests that were not previously part of the postal–industrial sector, leading to unsecured boundary regions and to confrontations with other powerful government entities.

Governmental Industrial Policy

Governmental industrial policies and regional economic collaborations also have implications for telecommunications monopolies. In most developed countries, governments have established support programs in electronics. While the PTTs usually have been an important practical and regulatory part of this effort (Nora and Minc, 1980), such industrial policy has created a support structure for their future rivals. For example, several European countries finance satellite development programs in order to enhance their electronic and aerospace industries through civilian programs. The development of such satellites establishes the imperative for their actual operation and their financial viability, which in turn opens the door to potential future use by new types of carriers. In other countries, such as Britain, cable television is supported as part of technological development, with the goal of establishing optical switched-star cable systems. These networks could be used in the future for more general telecommunications purposes. Elsewhere, various local governments are advancing so-called teleports as part of regional developments, thereby providing the facilities for bypassing the public network.

Regional Collaboration

Regional and supranational economic collaborations like the European Community have challenged protective domestic arrangements between industry and government. The European Commission has overturned a whole range of domestic and collaborative policies defended by PTTs. This is discussed in the chapter on international organizations.

A Breakdown in Intra-PTT Cohesion and Labor Support

The traditional organizational integration between the postal and telecommunications components of the PTTs has become subject to strain. Increasingly, telecommunications employees have backgrounds and salary expectations similar to those of workers in the high-technology sector, yet they are constrained individually by civil service standards and collectively by the burden of the postal service's deficits. At the same time, PTT managers have begun to recognize that a change in organizational status can give them substantial flexibility and independence. Therefore, they have become willing to transform telecommunications operations from government administrations into government-held corporations. Thus, the growing significance and attractiveness of the electronics sector led PTT employees and managers to begin defining their interests as different from the collective PTT and to seek a more advantageous non-civil service status in a semi-independent private-law organization separate from the governmental regulatory organization, especially if they could maintain most of their civil service benefits at the same time. As its constituent parts began to redefine their interests, the PTT's traditional coalition weakened.

This chapter has described the centrifugal forces which have led, after a long period of stability, to changes in Europe. The policy options will be the subject of the next chapter.

5

Defense of the Telecommunications Monopoly

As telecommunications moved in new directions, the PTTs were increasingly faced with the task of justifying the existence of a rigid monopoly in essentially market-oriented economies, delivering a service that could be provided by the private sector. This is not, after all, a situation where the public subsidizes unprofitable but socially desirable enterprises such as railroads. The arguments in favor of the traditional system will be discussed in what follows. It is important to stress at the outset that the issue is not the *existence* of publicly supplied telecommunications services, but rather their *exclusivity*.

The Need for Social Subsidies

It is often believed that a monopoly is necessary to ensure socially meritorious goals such as service for the poor. The fulfillment of this obligation necessitates subsidization, which must come out of revenues from more profitable telecommunications services. Liberalization would attract competitors to precisely those areas and customers that are most profitable, and such "cream-skimming" would reduce PTT profits and cut into the cross-subsidies of their socially desirable services. But it is elementary in the analysis of public finance issues to separate conceptually the mechanism of taxation from that of distribution. There are various ways of providing subsidies to support universal services. Alternative mechanisms for the allocation of government subsidies are readily used for the distribution of most other goods and services. Such subsidies can be distributed through welfare or social service programs, cash payments, entitlement stamps, tax incentives, or producer subsidies. Therefore, it is not necessary that telecommunication services be supplied by a monopoly to ensure their adequacy. Nor is supply by a governmental entity required. Even if there is a role for government in assuring the maintenance of universal service, for example, as a "supplier of last resort," this does not prove the need for total monopolization. Railroads, for example are frequently government owned, yet they compete with private truckers, barges, airlines, and, often, supplementary private railroads. Nor is there any reason for the source of a subsidy to be the telecommunications system itself. It can be provided from general revenues and raised through general and progressive taxation.

The usual response to these points is that they are politically unrealistic. Advocates of the monopoly argue that the political system would not permit massive cross-subsidies if they were transparent to the government and the legislature of a country. This is probably true in Europe, as it is in the United States. But the argument is at heart antidemocratic. If European governments and legislatures, faced with a transparent choice, choose to cut back some subsidies in favor of other social goals, they merely exercise their role of setting priorities for public expenditures. (In the author's view, some such subsidies can be justified; he drafted New York State's lifeline program, entitling 1.5 million poor households to telephone service at $1 per month. See, additionally, the arguments for a critical mass subsidy to initiate a service, provided in Chapter 3.)

The cross-subsidy rationale is normally used in support of basic services for disadvantaged categories of users or areas. But similar arguments have also been advanced to support new and advanced services such as data transmission and value-added services, with the claim that new technological services generally lose money initially, and their introduction therefore necessitates some form of critical mass subsidy. But this argument can easily become circular. A government monopoly is defended on the grounds that it is necessary to encourage the introduction of new services that would not otherwise be supplied by private firms. But the private firms cannot enter because they are not allowed to undercut the monopoly that is deemed necessary to support the new services.

Many people sincerely believe that universal service depends on a public monopoly. This, however, is not correct. First, for most of the monopoly period there was nothing close to universal service in existence, and investments were targeted highly unequally. In France, for example, telephone service was offered far more extensively in the Paris region than in the provinces (see Figure 9.1, p. 141). At the turn of the century, Berlin and New York City had similar telephone densities (one telephone per twenty-nine persons in New York, and one for forty-three in Berlin). But in the rural state of Iowa, telephone density was twice as high as in New York State (one telephone per nineteen people), with 170 different telephone companies and cooperatives providing service, whereas rural districts in Germany had one phone per 500 people, less than one-tenth of the Berlin density (Brock, 1981). In 1960, the percentage of German farmers with telephones was an extraordinarily low 9 percent (Schulte, 1982). In 1980, it had gone up to 80 percent. In France, it was 9 percent in 1968, 73 percent in 1980, and 93 percent in 1985 (T. Vedel, 1988, communication). In the United States, according to the Rural Electrification Administration, 96 percent of all farms had telephones in 1988. In typical farm states such as Iowa and Kansas, telephone densities were higher, with 95.1 and 95.2 per 100 households, than the national average of 92.4 (Federal–State Joint Board, 1988), even after a more liberalized telecommunications regime.[1]

Natural Monopoly

A serious argument for PTT exclusivity is that communications services are a "natural monopoly," that is, that single-firm production is cheaper, at every level of output, than multifirm production. This is true when average (and marginal) costs are continuously declining with output. In that case, there are efficiency advantages to the largest network the market will bear. But if the underlying characteristics are truly naturally monopolistic, there should be little or no danger of competitive entry, since new entrants, unless they could support losses for a sufficiently long growth period, would inevitably fail. What then is the purpose of prohibition of entry if economic barriers would be enough?

The counterargument is that, although theoretically no entry would be profitable, in reality the rate structure is based on social goals, which leads to tariffs above cost for some services in order to provide for the subsidization of others. These high-profit services would then become the object of "cream-skimming" in a liberalized environment, even though it would be economically inefficient to provide them outside the monopoly. This reasoning links the cross-subsidy argument with the natural monopoly argument.

The most sophisticated analysis along these lines was advanced in the United States as part of new industrial organization theory linked to William Baumol and others such as Elizabeth Bailey, Gerald Faulhaber, John Panzar, and Robert Willig. These writers demonstrated that in a multiproduct setting (i.e., where a firm supplies an array of related items), such a firm may have overall economies of scale, but under certain conditions its position may become "unsustainable" because particular product lines are vulnerable to competition, even in the absence of cross-subsidies (Baumol et al., 1982). Such loss of the monopoly would result in a loss of economies of scale and scope, that is, of size and of joint production. This implies that even in a system free of cross-subsidies, a natural monopoly could be subject to competitive entry. The argument is effective in the abstract, but it is based on certain theoretical and empirical assumptions that have been criticized (Shepherd, 1983).

There are other problems with the economies-of-scale argument. The first is the question of whether they actually exist beyond some point, a question that is a theoretical and empirical morass. Most older U.S. and Canadian econometric studies of economies of scale, in the days of the AT&T monopoly, seem to show that they are of a modest size (Meyer et al., 1980). A review of several studies finds that, excluding one AT&T study, the range of scale elasticities for the Bell system was between 0.98 and 1.24 (Mantell, 1974). Another study (Nadiri and Schankerman, 1981) finds a much larger value of around 1.8, though it was declining over time. An AT&T submission in the antitrust law suit (AT&T, 1976) shows a great range (0.74–2.08). Much lower results were found for Bell Canada (0.85–1.11) (Dobell et al., 1972; Fuss and Waverman, 1977). The FCC concluded, based on most of these studies, that the existence of economies of scale was not definite.

Furthermore, even if the existence of economies of scale is accepted, they

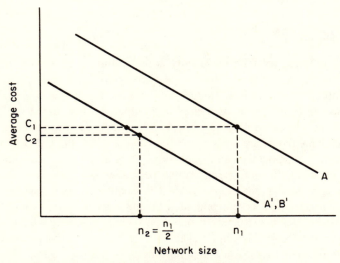

Figure 5.1.   Economies of Scale and Shift of Cost Curve.

must also be shown to offset the inefficiencies of monopoly and regulation. For example, regulation of rate of return has been shown to create an incentive for overcapitalization (the Averch–Johnson effect). There is also the matter of simple, accumulated high-cost operations. The operating costs of MCI per revenue-minute were estimated as 24.8 cents, only three-fourths of the costs of the much larger AT&T, which were estimated as 31.8 cents per revenue-minute at the end of its near-monopoly phase (Chrust, 1985, p. 10).

These numbers indicate that economies of scale cannot be observed in the abstract but must be considered with reference to the competitive pressures on efficiency under which they are realized. The shape of average cost curves may be downward-sloping, but the actual location of the cost curves is not independent of different institutional arrangements and their dynamics. In other words, one must distinguish between movement along a cost curve and a shift of the cost curve itself. The latter, induced by competition, may be greater than the lost economies of scale.

In Figure 5.1, for example, the average cost in the monopoly network is declining, suggesting benefits of economies of scale.

At size n_1, the cost is C_1. However, suppose that competition is permitted. A second network enters, and its rivalry leads to a lowered cost function at each level of production, for either network, depicted as A', B'. Let us assume that both networks split the market equally, that is, that the network size of each is $n_1/2$. At that size, the cost of each is C_2, which is *lower* than the cost in the monopoly network.

This does not even take into account the increased demand due to lowered prices and increased marketing efforts of the competitors, which should move average cost further downward on the competitive-cost curve. In other words, the existence of economies of scale does not dispose of the question of lower cost.

Furthermore, if the realization of economies of scale were the governing issue for telecommunications policy, why would they coincide with the size of a country? Should not logic suggest supranational carriers who can realize still greater economies? Why not a Nordic or a Benelux PTT? Why not serve Denmark through the German Bundespost, just as Germany supplies many of Denmark's automobiles? These arrangements do not exist for a variety of reasons, in particular because of the loss of sovereignty. But that simply means that economies of scale, even where they exist, are only one factor among several and are regularly disregarded for a variety of political or control reasons.

Technical Integrity

Yet another argument in favor of monopoly is that it is needed to assure the technical integrity of the network. Liberalized entry into network services and equipment could permit users to utilize equipment that might damage the network and thus impose negative externalities on others.

In the equipment field, the need to protect the integrity of the network is not a persuasive argument. It was used by AT&T for many years to prevent even the attachment of nonelectrical equipment, such as plastic noise guards on telephone sets. These restrictions were struck down in 1956 in the *Hush-A-Phone* decision. Similarly, the German Bundespost at one time prohibited emergency telephone number stickers supplied by private parties from being put on telephones. Harm to the network can be prevented by establishing safety standards, just as for other products.

Compatibility

A close cousin to the technical integrity argument is the claim that a monopoly is necessary to ensure that all participants can actually communicate with each other. If several carriers supply services and equipment, technical incompatibility could fragment the network, leading in time to the need to have multiple telephone instruments on one's desk. This argument is flimsy at best. Standards setting takes place in numerous industries without the need for monopoly production. In telecommunications, much of it already takes place through various international bodies. There are also economic incentives to compatibility. But where these are not adequate, legal requirements and technical standards of interconnection and access can assure that there will not be fragmentation into incompatible networks.

Comprehensive Planning

Telecommunications, it is argued, requires a complex and long-term planning process, for which a market mechanism is not well suited. This claim tends to view competing carriers as tiny operations rather than as large corporations whose very essence is their ability to engage in long-range planning. Furthermore, it assumes that the traditional dominant carriers would cease to engage in planning and that an overarching plan could not be fashioned by a government in the absence of a full monopoly. It is true that planning becomes more complex as the number of participants increases. On the other hand, there is likely to be a more dynamic planning and execution process in a nonmonopolistic setting. This issue is discussed in Chapter 39 on the open network system, where the necessity of a move toward a modularized network system is argued.

Communications as a Responsibility of the Government Infrastructure

Another argument in favor of PTT monopoly is that control over communications, because it is an essential infrastructure service, is the responsibility of the government. This view holds it to be undesirable to leave the sector under private control, since control over a country's electronic highways would afford unacceptable private power. Telecommunications is considered a quintessential public service, as is transportation over roads, canals, and railroads. This argument does not usually distinguish between a government *assuring* such services and a government *providing* them. For example, the state should assure that no part of the population will starve. But this does not mean that the government itself must grow the food, and still less that it must control all food stores or supermarkets.

Still, the view that private power over communications is to be avoided is a legitimate one. And although it might be said that competition would prevent one firm from becoming predominant and that competitive rates would make manipulation of communications difficult, these are essentially market-oriented arguments, and they are based on value judgments. For those who support public ownership of the means of production and a reduced role for the private sector, they will not be persuasive. Clearly, if government ownership per se is a preferred value, arguments made for the pursuit of efficiency or for the use of alternative means of achieving redistributory goals are inadequate. Advocates of state control over communications see liberalization as an increase in the political power of business, as a subordinating of communications to the profit motive, and as a potential threat to national sovereignty. One can disagree with these views or with the reality of the threats, but not with the legitimacy of holding them.

6
Policy Directions

Policy Options

Given the forces of change, what are the policy directions? It is necessary to distinguish between several very different reform concepts that are frequently intermingled under the vague heading of "deregulation."

Corporatization

Under corporatization, the status of telecommunications operation is transformed from a state administration (i.e., part of the civil service) into a publicly owned corporation. Such a course is usually advocated to encourage efficiency and flexibility. The monopoly status is not touched by corporatization as such, though once the close link to the government is severed, a process is set in motion that makes further changes more likely. Sometimes the corporatized entity is described as a "private" firm, in the sense that it may be organized under private law provisions (which determine its status in, for example, contract and labor law), but that description confuses legal detail with the reality of control, which is still governmental. Corporatization is usually accompanied by the creation of a regulatory mechanism of government, typically as part of the PTT ministry.

Privatization

A privatization policy may follow corporatization as the government sells part or all of the shares in the telecommunications entity to private investors. Privatization, too, need not affect the monopoly status. In the United States, AT&T was private and a near monopoly for a very long period.

Ownership per se does not determine economic performance. For example, the nationalized French banks have performed quite well. More relevant is the extent of state political interference. Such interference can take place in nominally private organizations such as Italy's SIP. In contrast, a government organization such as France Télécom has established significant independence regardless of its legal status.

Liberalization

Liberalization involves a more pronounced change in market structure. By opening equipment supply and services to entry, liberalization changes the nature of markets and the power of the established suppliers. Privatization is more dramatic, but liberalization is by far the more important policy. Advocates of telecommunications reform tend to combine and sometimes confuse these two policies.

Devolution

A prime example of devolution is the divestiture of AT&T in America. It is not necessary for either liberalization or privatization, although it addresses the problems of competitive barriers and market power. A devolution can also be part of liberalization, where some segments of the market are opened up, and others are not. If different regulatory treatment of carriers active in both open and restricted markets is sought, a policy of devolution may make sense. Devolution is also possible without liberalization. In Denmark and Italy, for example, the public network had been segmented but monopolistic.

Deregulation

Despite the frequent usage of the term deregulation, it is an imprecise concept and is usually used as a synonym for liberalization, that is, for a lowering of entry barriers or other restrictions. But it is also used to mean a reduction in red tape and government involvement. This second meaning can easily be at odds with the first: Partial liberalization as a process tends to complicate things much more than an outright prohibition and can lead to a more extensive set of rules to address the new problems. To analogize: It is much simpler to ban all trucks from using a highway than to permit some of them to use the road. In the latter case, one must establish rules on weight, speed, time of day, and so on, and enforce them.

Deregulation is often a euphemism for laissez-faire, a term discredited by nineteenth-century robber barons. In America, deregulation has a more benign sound, since aversion to the heavy hand of government regulation has been a theme on which a wide range of the political spectrum can agree as a general proposition, though rarely in a concrete case. In America, the accelerated penetration of electronic technology into the telecommunications sector coincided and interacted with an intellectual and political move toward more laissez-faire. In Europe, the new technology was similarly available, but the ideological receptivity to new institutional arrangements was different. For most Europeans the trend of economic history had been toward increased forms of public control. The political left took the scientific inevitability of this trend as dogma; the conservative right, though parts of it were fighting against public control, was in doubt of its own long-term prospects in stemming the trend.

The American historical experience, for a long time, followed the expected path from relatively unbridled laissez-faire capitalism to a regulatory system that kept steadily but unspectacularly expanding in the decades following the Great Depression and World War II. The unusual aspect of recent developments in U.S., U.K., and Japanese regulatory policy is their reversal of this historical trend.

Within the spectrum of European policy response, one extreme is the United Kingdom, whose government, under former Prime Minister Margaret Thatcher, supported a free-market economy. The British government brought about separation of the telecommunications monopoly British Telecom from the postal services, and reorganized it as a privately owned corporation subject to some competition.

While Britain was consciously attempting to raise its high-technology standards through market forces, with the government attempting to create an entrepreneurial environment, French policies increased the governmental role. The Socialist government set development of a high-technology electronics industry as a national priority and nationalized much of the French electronics and telecommunications equipment industry to gain a lever for the achievement of this goal. This policy, only partly reversed by conservative government, had the support of a large part of the public and intelligentsia. The effect is that the French actually created, for a time, a state-owned analog of the old AT&T system: a vertically integrated complex of equipment manufacturing coupled with a telecommunications transmission monopoly and an R&D laboratory. At the same time that the Bell telecommunications monopoly in the United States was being segmented into several component parts, the French did the opposite and integrated, for the first time, the major elements of telecommunications under one ownership (though the French state is admittedly a very large umbrella whose spokes may be at odds with one another). Equipment manufacture was partly privatized again and the telephone administration was made more independent in 1990. But the state and its affiliated institutions are strongly in charge.

The telecommunications policy of the Federal Republic of Germany lies somewhere between the liberalization of the United Kingdom and the nationalization of France. For a long time, the Deutsche Bundespost was loath to relinquish its monopoly power over domestic and international telecommunications, and it has labored to protect the status quo. Only reluctantly, under the prodding of other parts of the government and following the Dutch example, were institutional reforms moved forward in 1988. The telephone administration was separated from postal matters and corporatized as a state organization, with greater operational separation from the PTT Ministry, which now functioned as the regulatory agency. Similar courses were taken by the Netherlands, Denmark, and several other countries.

These four positions—corporatization, privatization, liberalization, and devolution—constituted the primary policy menu of European countries in the 1980s. Yet for all their differences, European strategies also had an important common element: assigning the national telecommunications carrier a role as a locomotive for national high-technology development. This is discussed in the following section.

Political Telematique: The New Role of the PTTs

For a long time, the mission of the postal–industrial complex in developed countries centered around the achievement of a high degree of penetration. "Universal service" was the organizational goal, and it happily brought together the interests of the manufacturers, users, and politicians. With the goal of universal service largely achieved through effective collaboration of PTTs and industry, a new organizational ideology needed to be articulated, both to instill a sense of purpose internally and to legitimize the continuation of the institutional regime externally. The new views were influentially expressed in the 1978 French Nora–Minc report. This government report concerned itself at length with the threat to national sovereignty posed by the government's lack of control over electronics, that industry of the future whose paragon, IBM, was viewed as threatening French sovereignty:

> As a controller of networks, the company would take on a dimension extending beyond the strictly industrial sphere; it would participate, whether it wanted to or not, in the government of the planet. In effect, it has everything it needs to become one of the great world regulatory systems [Nora and Minc, 1980, p. 72].

How was the government to deal with IBM, "one of the great actors on the world stage"? The growing interaction between computer technology and telecommunications made control possible. Although governmental influence over the computer industry was limited, the latter's overlap with telecommunications—over which the state traditionally had control—provided the state with a lever of power.

> [National governments need to] strengthen their bargaining position with a solid mastery of their communications media. . . . However, the difficulty lies even more in the fact that no country can play that role alone. . . . But the internationalization of the stakes means that today no economic Gallicanism is sufficient to keep Rome out of Armonk. Independence would be vain and as easy to outflank as a useless Maginot Line if it were not supported by an international alliance having the same objectives [Nora and Minc, 1980, pp. 72–73].

Nora and Minc coined the term *telematique* for the sector that is also variously referred to as IT, C & C, informatics, or compunications. Their analysis, which may be termed *political telematique*, became extraordinarily influential as PTTs embraced its notions, which assigned to them a central role in high-technology policy and in the preservation of the national interest against American (and later Japanese) economic and technical interests. The equipment industry was also supportive since the Nora–Minc report created a presumption in favor of government subsidies and protectionism as a matter of preserving national sovereignty.

Political telematique's view of liberalization is negative. In 1984, the influential French daily newspaper *Le Monde* carried the Nora–Minc theme forward in a series of lengthy articles assessing U.S. deregulation (le Boucher and Quatrepoint, 1984). It viewed the United States as engaged in two wars: militarily against the Soviet Union and industrially against Japan, with the advanced technologies of computers and communications vital factors in both battles.

To win this international war, the United States deregulated and broke up AT&T. At first glance this may be surprising. "Why smash this power [AT&T] in the middle of a war against Japan?" (*Le Monde*, 1984). The answer is, "Deregulation of communication in the U.S. has as its main goal to give American industry a good 'kick in the pants,' in order to get it to start a conquest of the rest of the world."

Given the energizing effects of divestiture and deregulation, one would expect the United States to prefer to be the sole custodian and beneficiary of such a system. Nevertheless, *Le Monde* saw the United States as proselytizing the rest of the world. Opening the American equipment market to foreign imports is part of a U.S. export offensive. International liberalization gives the United States several advantages. It reduces the communications costs of multinational (i.e., American) users and it pries open the European equipment market. Once "liberated," European telecommunications would be captured by American firms. "Would not abandonment of state control over communications cause them to fall under the control of IBM?" Having posed the issue in such a way, the analysis leads to advocacy of political solutions, such as international agreements and domestic restrictions. Liberalizing change is described as profoundly threatening to French and European economic and sovereignty interests, and therefore requires energetic containment by government.

The past several chapters of this book have laid out a more theoretical or general framework for the evaluation of telecommunications. The next sections will analyze, in much greater detail, the past, present, and future of the various national systems.

II

THE TELECOMMUNICATIONS SYSTEMS OF EUROPEAN COUNTRIES

7

Germany

History of the Reichspost

For a discussion of the early history of German postal services, telecommunications, and institutions, the reader is referred to Chapter 2, in which the emergence of the country's PTT system is discussed.

The history of German telecommunications can be said to have begun in 1832, when Prussia introduced an optical telegraph system that connected Berlin with Koblenz on the Rhine. The system was designed for official dispatches only, and a petition by the Berlin Chamber of Commerce to transmit stock market information was emphatically rejected (Allentier, 1973). Later, civilians were permitted to use the telegraph during slack periods, as an effort to supplement state revenues.

After the invention of the electrical telegraph, Werner Siemens' newly established firm was instrumental in promoting a Prussian governmental line from Berlin to Frankfurt in 1848, where the first German parliament was then meeting.

In governmental debates on the establishment of Prussian telegraph service, strict state control and monitoring over civilian messages was held necessary to protect the postal service, to supervise politically oriented telegraph messages, and to limit "unfair stock market maneuvers."

Most German principalities introduced their own state telegraph service. In 1850, the German Telegraph Union was created for technical and operational coordination. In 1876, the newly established German state decided to expand the backward telegraph system. The government appointed Heinrich Stephan, director general of the postal system, to also head the telegraph office. Within a short time, Stephan merged the two services, despite some opposition from the telegraph personnel.

The invention of the telephone included German participation. An early version was conceived by Philipp Reis (1834–1874), a teacher who demonstrated the principles of voice transmission in 1861. His device, however, never worked in practice.

In 1877, news of Bell's invention of the telephone reached Berlin. After reading about it in *Scientific American*, Stephan immediately wrote to Boston to obtain sample equipment and then personally experimented with it. In a handwritten memorandum to Bismarck, he predicted a great future for the telephone. But the purpose of German telephony was distinctly different. Stephan viewed the telephone as an extension of state telegraphy, to be used in rural post offices where trained telegraph operators were not economically feasible. It took Emil Rathenau, a noted Berlin industrialist with a particular interest in applications of electricity, to establish the concept of public telephony on users' premises.

Because Bell's telephone was introduced in Germany three months after the German patent law was passed on July 1, 1877, Bell's invention fell between the cracks and received no patent. Thus, the manufacture of Bell equipment was free in Germany, and Werner Siemens began producing and improving it (Siemens, 1949, p. 199). Through their companies, Siemens and Rathenau henceforth became the main protagonists in German telecommunications equipment manufacturing. Together with Stephan, they created German telecommunications, from the beginning a close alliance of governmental and business interests.

Stephan called upon Rathenau to organize the Berlin business community for the first telephone exchange in Germany. Rathenau, one of the more interesting figures in German economic and political history, agreed to work on the introduction of telephone service in Berlin (Goetzler, 1976, p. 6). After considerable difficulty, the Berlin exchange opened in January 1881, connecting eight subscribers. Official German accounts of the introduction of telephone service traditionally describe the Berlin exchange as the country's first. Actually, the first system was established in Mulhouse in what was then German Alsatia, and by private rather than postal initiative. However, not wishing to be upstaged by its reluctant province, the Berlin authorities denied the Mulhouse system an official permit to operate until after the Berlin state system was opened.

Local exchange areas were consolidated into territorial districts, and after 1884 these were interconnected by long-distance trunks. Telephone service expanded, and Germany had 10,000 local post offices with telephone service by 1890. Besides these state-run telephones, however, there was little penetration. But the spread of electronic outposts into the countryside was immensely welcome, and the Reichspost, and Stephan at its helm, became enormously popular.

In 1882, the Reichspost established conditions of private interconnection with the public network. Ten years later there were more than 2000 private lines connecting with the public system, and almost 3000 purely private telephone systems within private properties such as factories. In 1892, the comprehensive telephone authority of the state was established by law.

The next decades witnessed steady improvements of technology, services, and penetration of the telephone. In 1886, the first international public telephone communications were established between a town in Alsace and Basel, Switzerland. A trial for an American-made automatic exchange was inaugurated in 1900, and German equipment came on line in 1908. In 1909, wireless telegraphy was introduced.

After the initial push into rural post offices, the development of telephony in

Germany was much more centered in the cities than in the United States. In 1902, overall telephone density in the United States was one telephone for each thirty-four persons, as compared to a much lower density of one telephone per 128 people in Germany. But for the cities, the ratio was more similar. The number of people per telephone in New York was thirty-nine, in Chicago, thirty; and in Boston, nineteen. In Berlin the density at the same time was forty-three persons per telephone. It was fifty-two in Hamburg, seventy-seven in Frankfurt, and thirty in Stuttgart. But in rural areas the matter was quite different. In New York State, telephone density was one telephone per thirty-one inhabitants; in Illinois, twenty-four, and in Iowa, a largely agricultural state, one per nineteen. In Germany, on the other hand, one eastern Prussian district had one telephone for 634 inhabitants, and in many others the density was less than one per 500 (Holcombe, 1911, p. 432).

During the years of the Weimar Republic, technology, subscribership, and services all steadily expanded. In 1923, subscriber trunk dialing was introduced in Bavaria. Intercontinental telephone service to the United States was inaugurated in 1928.

Rampant postwar inflation made the Reichspost dependent on government subsidies, until the 1924 Imperial Postal Finances Act (*Reichspostfinanzgesetz*) established financial autonomy and control by an administrative council rather than parliament.

When the National Socialists assumed power in 1933, Adolf Hitler appointed W. Ohnesorge as state secretary (later upgraded to minister) in charge of the Reichspost.[1]

History of the Equipment Industry

The histories of German public telecommunications and of the private Siemens firm are closely intertwined. From its humble beginnings, Siemens rose to become a giant in international telecommunications, thoroughly dominating most aspects of telecommunications equipment in Germany and one of the world's largest electrical and electronics groups (Dodsworth, 1987). Siemens is the largest electronics and second largest industrial firm in Germany. The company's equipment is manufactured in more than two dozen countries, and its employees worldwide number about 376,000, with 10 percent in research and development (Äppel, 1990). Siemens has a strong presence in components manufacture and information systems and is an integrated supplier of information technology. Outside of telecommunications, its products include power-generating equipment, nuclear power technology, and medical apparatus. Siemens makes over 200,000 products through some 300 divisions (Fuhrman, 1990, p. 98).

Siemens has been involved in telecommunications since its inception in 1847. Entering the telegraph business, it initially bet on the Wheatstone pointer telegraph (Siemens, 1949, p. I-29). But when an address by the king of Prussia, transmitted to the 1848 Frankfurt parliament by the Morse telegraph in a quarter of an hour, took the Wheatstone system seven hours, postal authorities shifted their preferences. Siemens adopted the new equipment but found himself almost immediately embroiled in a public debate about the effectiveness of his buried telegraph lines. After he published a pamphlet that criticized the state authorities' construction method, the firm lost all governmental contracts and almost went out of business. Fortunately, other governments, particularly Russia's, had their own needs for telegraph equipment and the firm was thus kept alive.

Siemens and his brothers set up operations in several major European countries (Scott, 1958). Werner was the "Berlin Siemens," and the driving force of the main firm, Siemens & Halske. (The related firm, Siemens & Schuckert, manufactured locomotives and heavy electrical equipment). A gifted engineer and a courageous entrepreneur, he was also a political liberal of sorts who did not hesitate to have himself elected to the Prussian Parliament as an opposition deputy, despite the fact that the government was the major customer of the fledgling company. His brother, Carl Wilhelm, who lived in London and eventually became Sir William Siemens, was the main figure in the separate British firm Siemens Brothers. Heinrich, known as the St. Petersburg Siemens, looked after the family's substantial Russian business. A close relative, Georg Siemens, was the founder and head of the Deutsche Bank, which rapidly became the most important financial institution in Germany and which still remains the *Hausbank* of the firm.

With his relatively liberal views, Werner Siemens was similar to two other major figures in the German electric industry, Emil Rathenau, the founder of AEG, and later Robert Bosch, founder of the Bosch Company (Heuss, 1946). AEG-Telefunken became the second most important German telecommunications company. After its decline in the 1970s, its position was assumed by the increasingly diversified Bosch, a very successful firm that began in automotive component supply and consumer durables and increasingly moved into telecommunications. The electronics industry was progressive and internationalist in comparison with the heavy industry that set the image of German business.

The relationship between Rathenau and Siemens was characterized by both competition and cartel behavior. Rathenau founded the German Edison Company in 1883. According to an agreement, Siemens stayed out of electric distribution, which was reserved to Rathenau's firm, which in turn bought all of its equipment, except for light bulbs, from Siemens. Rathenau introduced electric lighting into Germany by creating a complex supporting structure. His firm was transformed into AEG (Allgemeine Electricitaets Gesellschaft, or General Electric Company), with the Siemens firm as one of its major investors. When alternating current was developed as a rival to the untransformable direct current, both Siemens and Rathenau fought its introduction vehemently, just as Edison did in the United States against Westinghouse, and just as unsuccessfully.

At Stephan's request, Siemens started to produce unpatented telephone equipment. When Michael Pupin, a Columbia University professor, developed the so-called Pupin coil, which greatly improved the amplification of signals,

Siemens acquired the German patent rights for a large sum and defended the patent against challengers, which included the Reichspost. He told the inventor, "As far as I know, this is the highest price that has ever been paid for a mathematical formula; it goes far beyond the hundred oxen of the Pythagoras. The Post Office knows very well why it led us in such a dance last year, for it is now its turn to pay" (Siemens, vol. I, 1957, p. 181). Previously only one among several competing firms for local systems, Siemens now acquired technical leadership in long-distance telecommunications equipment through the Pupin license.

Siemens still had no dominance in switching, however. When the Reichspost experimented with the introduction of the Strowger automatic telephone exchange, a clear advance over the hand-operated exchanges, Siemens waved the flag to discourage the purchase of American equipment. Serious about automatic switching, the Reichspost set up a consortium of companies to develop such equipment. The consortium included Siemens despite its lack of experience in the area, but it eventually became the driving force and acquired the German rights for the Strowger patent, and improved it. This was the beginning of Siemens dominance in German switching equipment. As a family member, Georg Siemens, wrote, "Siemens and Halske had created for themselves, with their [exchange] systems, a technical monopoly" (Siemens, vol. II, 1949, p. 53). To deal with this situation, the Reichspost united other exchange equipment companies in joint ventures.

Competition, cartelization, and the breaking of cartel agreements continued to characterize relations among Germany's main electric equipment producers. The "Big Three" of power generation agreed that they would explore and inform each other of each request for a bid over a specified value. They also agreed that they would bid predetermined prices that varied only slightly from each other, and that they would permit the contracting firms to give price discounts only if the order threatened to be lost to an outsider. This agreement operated under the code name V.C., for *Vertrauliche Correspondenz*, or confidential correspondence. Similar relations existed in the production of incandescent lamps. According to Georg Siemens, "Due to senseless price slashing, it had come to the point where lamps which twenty years earlier cost twenty Marks, cost the same amount in Pfennig, and this could not go on. Thus in 1904, the 'Sales Organization United Incandescent Lamps' was established in Berlin, a syndicate in which Siemens & Halske and AEG held a quota of 21 percent of total production" (Siemens, vol. II, 1949, p. 240). To tighten cartel cooperation, a joint firm for incandescent lamps (Osram) was established in 1919, into which Siemens, AEG, and Auer brought their production facilities and patents. Another selling cartel syndicate was founded in 1911 for insulated wires. As Georg Siemens describes it, the wire cartel "claimed in its favor that it kept its members to a strict adherence to the standards of the Association of German Electro-technical Engineers, and provided them in return with a fairly undisturbed independently wealthy existence" (Siemens, vol. II, 1949, p. 24).

Perhaps the longest-lived and most successful cartel in the German electrical sector was the cable cartel, which dates back to 1876 and a large cable order by the Reichspost to Siemens & Halske and Felten & Guilleaume. That cartel set supply quotas for members in 1914 and established an enforcement office that instructed each firm what price it could quote for an order. Any violation led to a large contractual penalty. If a firm exceeded its quota, it was instructed to quote high prices to avoid winning further contracts. The system operated very successfully under strict cartel management which had access to relevant financial records of the firm.

At AEG, meanwhile, Emil Rathenau was succeeded as president by his son Walter. In addition to being a company executive, Walter was a novelist, essayist, designer of the value-added tax (which fifty years later was adopted in Europe), and head of Germany's wartime economic planning. After World War I, the younger Rathenau gave a speech that discussed critically the reasons for Germany's defeat. Even though he had been an essential figure in the economic mobilization during the war, his speech led to vituperations against him that were frequently anti-Semitic. According to Georg Siemens, "Particularly in the circles of heavy industry, a virtual boycott against AEG was commenced, and a number of large and important orders, which it would have received otherwise, went to various competitors, primarily the Siemens-Schuckert firm" (Siemens, vol. II, 1949, p. 283). AEG's central administration, aghast at its president, forced him to resign. He then entered the political arena and served as minister of foreign affairs until he was assassinated in 1922 by right-wing students.

In the early development of the radio, Siemens and AEG were competitors. Later, Emperor Wilhelm II, who was obsessively interested in naval matters and therefore in the development of radio for navy and merchant marine, expressed his displeasure that two German groups were competing against each other and weakening themselves in relation to the Marconi company. The military authorities preferred a uniform solution. This led to a great deal of political pressure on Siemens, and in 1903 to the formation of a joint company with AEG. The joint company became the renowned Telefunken company, eventually part of AEG. The pioneer of German broadcasting, Hans Bredow, was a director of Telefunken before he moved to the Reichspost, which he then established as the undisputed ruler of the airwaves.

Telefunken held rights to an extraordinarily important amplification tube under the Lieben patent. Without it no other company could produce an effective radio set. For a while, Siemens, AEG, and Telefunken all sold the identical product with different exteriors, under the protective umbrella of Reichspost licensing.

In telephone equipment, Siemens produced a 2500–subscriber central battery telephone exchange in 1909, the first PBX in 1912, automatic trunk dialing equipment in 1923, and long-distance public telephones in 1929. In 1930, the development of a full-wire transmission technique made possible a nationwide telephone service, and in 1933 the company established the first telex network in the world.

During the Nazi period, the firm's leader, Carl Friedrich von Siemens, kept some distance from the regime, but the company benefitted from the rearmament that took place. The war caused major destruction to Siemens plants, and a large portion of its facilities in Berlin was dismantled by the victorious Russians. Both Siemens & Halske and Siemens & Schuckert were restructured, and most of the headquarters was moved to Munich. The firm soon resumed its place as the foremost name in the German electronics sector.

The Present German Telecommunications Industry

In addition to Siemens and AEG, the important German equipment suppliers are Standard Elektrik Lorenz (SEL), an ITT and later Alcatel subsidiary; AEG-Telefunken's subsidiary Telefonbau und Normalzeit, renamed Telenorma and acquired by Bosch; Deutsche Telephone und Kabel Werke (DeTeWe), a Siemens subsidiary that is also a part owner of Telenorma; ANT, with a heavy Bosch participation; and Tekade, a Philips subsidiary.

The German telecommunications industry is particularly dependent on exports, which represent nearly 30 percent of sales. This is larger in percentage terms than any other large industrial nation, except for Holland and Sweden. According to the electronic industry's trade association, Germany in 1983 was the largest exporter of communications products in the world (ZVEI, 1983, p. 58). Nonetheless, the government determined in that year that German information technology was lagging in the world market (Neumann, 1986). Similarly, in its 1983 annual report, the Bundesbank, Germany's central bank, found Germany's export of high-technology goods to be inadequate.[2]

In the 1960s Siemens tried to participate in the new world of computers, but with mixed success. It produced computers under RCA's licenses but was left in the lurch when RCA left the computer market. It then joined the Dutch Philips and the French CII in Unidata, a joint venture, which, however, also soon faltered. Next, it joined forces with the Japanese Fujitsu for IBM-compatible machines, and in 1974 it acquired the firm Computer GmbH, an unsuccessful joint venture of AEG-Telefunken with Nixdorf (Malerba, 1985, p. 177).[3]

During the 1970s, Siemens seriously miscalculated in its development of a semielectronic space division switch, which became obsolete before completion. It then intensively developed the successful digital EWSD switch. EWSD has operated in South Africa since 1980 and in Germany since 1982. The EWSD system is used for very large exchanges as well as for the German mobile radio network and is the cornerstone of German ISDN efforts. In digital development, Germany lagged somewhat behind the French, who began experimenting with digital switches in 1966.

Siemens has also established a presence in integrated broadband fiber network development and was in charge of two "BIGFON" broadband network pilot projects. It is also a leader in electronic mail (teletext) systems.

In 1985, German government procurement was about 9 percent of total sales for Siemens. The percentage was much higher in telecommunications, where the Bundespost accounted for almost one-third of Siemens's 1986 sales of about $4 billion.

For its American marketing, Siemens established a corporation in Boca Raton, Florida, to adapt its digital switch to American specifications, including software that permitted centrex service. The undertaking was difficult and expensive: Siemens spent $200 million to adapt its products and had to pay Bellcore, the local Bell companies technical arm, $10 million for equipment testing (Dodsworth, 1987). To help its entry into the American market, Siemens considered a collaboration with the large and vertically integrated American telecommunications company GTE. The arrangement would have permitted the two companies to share development costs. The negotiations were on and off for almost two years. But during this period, Siemens successfully courted several American regional Bell companies and no longer needed GTE. In the end, a 1986 agreement created a company into which GTE brought its American transmission equipment manufacturing as well as its manufacturing subsidiaries in Belgium, Italy, and Taiwan, thus providing Siemens with an entry into these markets. Siemens controlled 80 percent of the new company and paid GTE $400–$500 million. The American switching business of the two companies was left outside the venture, however. This transaction was not much noted at the time, because of the commotion over ITT's almost simultaneous sale of control over its international equipment operations to the French firm CGE. Together, these two transactions resulted in the large-scale withdrawal of the two major American firms most active in the European telecommunications equipment market.

In 1989, Siemens purchased the PBX manufacturer Rolm from IBM, thus ending the U.S. computer giant's frustrating attempt to establish a telecommunications presence that had led to losses of $100 million in 1987 and 1988.

In 1990, Siemens restructured itself drastically, creating fifteen operating groups and two divisions from the original seven. It continued acquisitions with the American Bendix Electronics, the French computer firm IN2, and especially the German computer company Nixdorf. It also participated in a hostile takeover—an unusual event in Europe—with GEC of the U.K.'s Plessey, discussed in the following chapter on U.K. telecommunications. But the collaboration with GEC was not an easy one. The merger led to its assuming control in North America of GPT Stromberg-Carlson, a supplier of switches to independent telephone companies. It gained a major contract from Bell South, and was on its way as the third supplier of the U.S. market.

AEG-Telefunken has been less prosperous than Siemens. The firm was active in technical development, but since the mid-1970s was engaged in a constant battle for survival. Losses were severe in home electronics and office equipment, and it managed to lose money even in construction projects in Saudi Arabia and Iraq. The firm would have gone bankrupt in 1983 without major government involvement. Daimler-Benz, Germany's major industrial firm, subsequently acquired a majority share.

Standard Elektrik Lorenz (SEL), now an Alcatel subsidiary, was acquired by ITT in 1925 from AT&T's Western Electric. It is one of Alcatel's largest West European units, with an annual volume of operations of about $2.2 billion. Switching and transmission products accounted for 48 percent of sales in 1989.

The company had 21,000 employees in 1989 and was successful in worldwide home electronics business, in particular through its television sets and digital television system DigiVision.

SEL played a major role in the development of ITT's System 12 digital switch. With the Bundespost's order for System 12 in 1982, SEL obtained potentially 30–40 percent of the German digital exchange market.

Bosch, long a leader in automotive parts and household durables, is controlled by a private charitable foundation. Like SEL, it is located in the Stuttgart area. It acquired Telenorma and its 18,000 employees from AEG, and added more than 40 percent of ANT (a company with 6500 employees and a leader in digital broadband switching, communications satellites, fiber optics, and cellular telephones). Bosch also owns the mobile radio company Blaupunkt, which is also active in automobile video display systems, television and stereo, and Btx terminals. Bosch increased its investments in Telenorma, JS Telecommunications, in France; Hasler, in Switzerland; and Telettra, in Italy and created a mobile communications division. Taken together, the Bosch group is a contender for the number two position in German telecommunications equipment.

Nixdorf Computer was perhaps the greatest challenge to the established order of Germany's electronic industry. The company was founded by Heinz Nixdorf in a factory basement in 1952 with an investment of $6000, and it has remained innovative and untraditional. By identifying market niches in the computer field, it left behind large companies such as Siemens, Triumph-Adler (formerly of AEG), and Kienzle. For example, Nixdorf had a large share of the German market in computerized banking equipment and automated teller machines. In 1983, Nixdorf introduced Germany's first digital PBX, and by 1989, telecommunications accounted for over 10 percent of its revenues.

Nixdorf was also one of Europe's largest software developers. Four thousand of its 20,000 employees are directly involved in the development of software and provided about half of total revenues. Unlike other European computer companies, Nixdorf also moved aggressively into the American market.

In 1978, Volkswagen made a bid to acquire a controlling share of Nixdorf but was rebuffed. Eventually, however, Nixdorf's undercapitalization and technical ambitions caught up with the company. After its 1989 losses of close to DM 1 billion, it was forced to sell a 51 percent stake to Siemens. Siemens then merged its own computer operations into Siemens-Nixdorf Informations Systems, which became Europe's largest computer company.

Telecommunications Since 1970

Expansion of Service

The "democratization" phase of German telecommunications achieved universal service in a remarkably short time. Between 1970 and 1986, telephone density increased from 14.3 to 43.8 lines per 100 population (DBP, 1987).

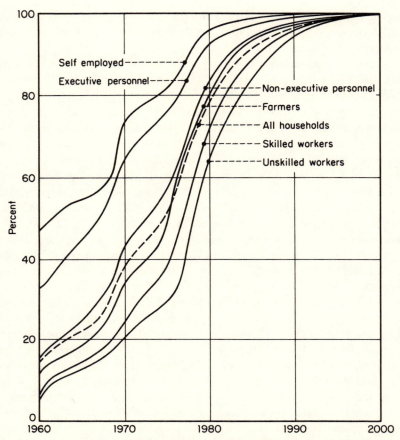

Figure 7.1. Telephone Main Lines per 100 Households by Occupational Group in Germany. (*Source:* Schulte, 1982.)

The 1970s, in particular, was a time of telephone expansion, engineered by the Social Democratic government, which was in power for the first time in forty years. In 1970, there had been about 9 million main stations, but by 1980 there were more than 22 million. The use of telecommunications services per subscriber household rose along with the greater penetration. The average household increased its expenditure on telecommunications from 0.3 percent of its total consumption in 1960 to 1.9 percent in 1980.

As can be seen in Figure 7.1, telephone penetration varied by economic and social class (Schulte, 1982). Workers (skilled and unskilled) had the lowest penetration rate: in 1980, 58 percent of unskilled workers and about 70 percent of skilled workers had telephones. These figures are not particularly high. In contrast, the rural population is well supplied, with a penetration rate for farmers of about 80 percent in 1980. As recently as 1970, less than 20 percent of unskilled workers had a telephone. Skilled workers were only slightly better off, and farmers had a penetration rate of only about 30 percent at that time. In other words, their penetration had almost tripled in a decade.[4] In 1960, penetration had been less than 10 percent for these social groups! But for white-collar employees too penetration was 84 percent in 1980, in contrast to 42 percent in 1970 and about 15 percent in 1960. Thus, for the vast majority of German households, the telephone is a fairly recent acquisition. In Germany, a sense of appreciation still exists toward the supplier of the service, the Bundespost, for making it possible to join the telecommunications network.

With the task of universal service largely completed, the next phase in telecommunications, starting in the early 1980s, was to refocus priorities to increasingly sophisticated telecommunications services, and this meant toward the needs of large users, whatever the official philosophy proclaimed.

New Services

The usage and density of telex service in Germany are high. Germany's telex network is the world's largest, three times denser than that of the United States, and had thirty-nine telex accesses per 10,000 inhabitants in 1988. In 1988, there were about 155,000 telex subscribers, down from the 1986 figure (ITU, 1990). Most likely, this number will continue to decline because of the emergence of fax and electronic mail, known as teletext. (Teletext should not be confused with the broadcast text service of the same name).

Teletext was introduced by the Bundespost after seven years of development in 1981, following the recommendations of the blue-ribbon Commission on Communication Techonology (KtK) panel. Growth was disappointing.

ISDN and videotex in Germany are discussed in other chapters of this book. A few details will suffice here. In 1986, Germany conducted two ISDN trials in Stuttgart and Mannheim. In addition, the Bundespost tested, after 1983, fiber-optic broadband networks under the name of BIGFON, providing to users two digital telephone lines, data and text services, two to four centrally switched TV channels, twenty-four stereo audio channels, and a videophone video capability.[5]

Regular ISDN service was introduced in 1989 at a Hanover trade fair. The DBP signed up its first ISDN applications customer, a retail drugstore chain in August 1989, but subsequent user demand was low (Schwarz-Schilling, 1990, p. 58). The DBP therefore created a "U2000" network strategy, shifting emphasis from ISDN transmission to an intelligent network. ISDN plans were expanded to include the distribution of 50,000 microcomputer boards to stimulate demand (Gilhooly and Schenker, 1989).

The Deutsche Bundespost as an Institution

By any calculation, the Bundespost is a gigantic enterprise. The German Monopoly Commission observed that the DBP's 1980 budget of DM 55.4 billion was significantly above that of Nordrhein-Westfalen, the largest German federal state, which encompasses nearly one-third of the West German population. Its revenues were also much higher than those of any German manufacturing firm. This comparison is even more impressive, since most of the Bundespost's activities are domestically achieved.

Similarly significant are profits. The Monopoly Commission report found a real profit of approximately DM 5 billion in 1980. It noted that, according to the calculation of the Association of Postal Users, another DM 0.75 billion ought to be considered profit, which would result in a profit margin of 15.8 percent. Total telecommunications profits are even larger if one disaggregates them from postal services, which have been substantially in the red for many years.

Telecommunications accounted for 70 percent of total DBP's revenue, with postal services 26 percent and banking and financial services 4 percent.

By its own estimate, the Bundespost's share in Germany's GNP more than doubled between 1960 and 1982, from 1.4 percent to 3.4 percent. In 1982, the Bundespost provided secure jobs for more than 500,000 employees (about 216,000 in telecommunications). Not counting the effect of technology development on exports, its procurement orders and investments provided jobs for an additional 200,000 people (DBP, 1982a). Together with the hundreds of thousands of retirees, relatives, and neighbors, this means a very large voting constituency. In 1988, the combined DBP had DM 52.5 billion in revenues and DM 16.9 billion in investments. The Postal service reported losses of DM 2.26 billion (Blau, 1989; Möschel, 1988; ITU, 1990).

Article 87 of the Basic Law (constitution) of the Federal Republic of Germany postulates governmental control of telecommunications. The Postal Administration Law of 1954 established the Bundespost as the organization serving the communication needs of Germany (Elias et al., 1980). The Telecommunications Facilities Law of 1928 gave the Bundespost what it interpreted as the sole right to erect and operate telecommunications facilities. The exceptions were private facilities not crossing property lines (and, under certain conditions, connections between separate properties of the same owner) and certain government authorities (such as the state railway Bundesbahn and the armed force Bundeswehr) which are allowed to run their own internal communications operations. The Minister of Postal Affairs could, in principle, grant waivers to other providers, though this had not been done for many years.

Overall responsibility for the Bundespost lies with the Federal Minister of Post and Telecommunications, who is a cabinet member and typically an influential party figure.

The DBP operated a substantial telecommunications technical center (FTZ) in Darmstadt, a central approval office for telecommunications in Saarbruecken (FZZ), two engineering colleges, a scientific institute, and more than 18,000 post offices throughout the country. Until 1982, the Bundespost also provided a far-flung postal bus service that carried 281 million persons during its last year of operation. For a long time, it was the largest bus operation in Europe (Stuebing, 1982). The Bundespost had no monopoly over its bus routes but could establish them virtually everywhere, while private competitors could run lines where the Post buses already operated only by demonstrating that additional service was necessary.

The Bundespost also operates a huge postal financial system. In Germany, the typical method of paying bills is not through a bank check but through a postal pay order. Several billions of such financial transactions take place each year. The Postal Savings Bank is a major thrift institution. In 1986, it had 20.9 million accounts in a country of 61 million and held an average aggregate credit balance of DM 35 billion (DBP, 1987). The postal reform of 1989 made financial operations a semi-independent public corporation.

The bulk of Bundespost profits were raised by telephone services. Telegraph services were subsidized at between 2 percent and 5 percent of cost, and postal services covered only 86.2 percent of their very large costs in 1986 (DBP, 1987). By far the largest relative subsidy is extended to newspaper delivery, which covered only 47.8 percent of its cost. Newspaper publishers thus benefit substantially from the telecommunications sector subsidy of the postal service. In 1982, 8111 newspapers were approved for the low-cost newspaper rate.

In addition to the internal subsidies mentioned, there were explicit levies on the Bundespost. In 1982, over DM 4 billion were transferred to the government. In percentage of total expenditures, the levy amounted to 7.1 percent in 1950, 6.0 percent in 1970, and 9.6 percent in 1982. In comparison, depreciation charges were only 50 percent more, and expenditure on outside capital was substantially lower (DBP, 1982b). In 1986, the levy was DM 4.8 billion, or 11 percent of profits (DBP, 1987). While the levy was a drain for the Bundespost, it also created a special interest of the government in its profitability. In consequence, the Finance Ministry was a champion of institutional status quo in discussions of DBP reform.

In addition to its role in high-tech development, one of the roles of the DBP is its ability to function as a counter-cyclical investment vehicle. In 1982, with German industry in general recession and its investment level decreased, BDP investment was at a record level of 12.7 billion DM, and it was by far the largest investor in Germany.[6] Furthermore, the DBP's procurement targeted "preferred suppliers" which are often located in economically weak regions or employing disabled individuals (Henneman, 1984, pp. 70–77).

Procurement Practices

General

Procurement practices of the DBP have been a particular bone of contention, both internationally and domestically. The German Monopoly Commission found equipment prices to be generally higher domestically than in North America, and the equipment was of a costly design.

In 1960, only 25 percent of total procurement was subjected to at least a limited bidding process. This increased over the next twenty years to 40 percent. A set-aside process was used in competitive procurement: Bids for part of the quantity were solicited first, with the resultant price the upper limit for the remaining quantity. The problem is that the supplying companies could tacitly agree on a price leader and then set a high "market price" for the second stage in which they would participate. In 1976, the Cartel Office imposed fines totaling DM 1 million against twelve telephone equipment manufacturers and twenty of their managers, after finding that in 1974 and 1976 they had rigged bids for DBP terminal equipment.

The DBP's renowned research and development arm, the Fernmeldetechnisches Zentralamt (FTZ), played a key role in the process through its power over the selection, licensing, and development of equipment. Almost 60 percent of the DBP's procurement contracts were awarded by the FTZ. Traditionally, it collaborated with a chosen supplier to develop products, with the other manufacturers acting in effect as subcontractors to the primary firm.

In 1963, the German Federal Accounting Office issued a report criticizing the Bundespost's procurement practices. A two-volume DBP response asserted that it saw "no reason and no possibility for a fundamental change" (Scherer, 1985, p. 79). The theme of liberalization was then sounded by academics (Mestmäcker, 1980). Similarly, the German Monopoly Commission, in a major report, found in 1981 that the DBP's practices contributed to the rigidity of the supply market structure by its reliance on uniform equipment technology, and a de facto concentration of procurement (Monopolkommission, 1981). The principle of uniform technology (*Einheitstechnik*) was a key element in the Bundespost's procurement practice. All suppliers had to conform to an agreed-upon technology for a product; the four main development firms (*Entwicklungsfirmen*) shared patents that were obtained in the course of the product development. The Bundespost defended this policy, citing its advantages for technical planning, in particular in the postwar reconstruction, where it reduced duplicative R&D. For digital switching, the Bundespost modified its principles, but it had in any event no realistic alternative. It also opened procurement of public packet switching systems to international bidding, and Northern Telecom, despite its views about domestic market restrictions quoted earlier, obtained the order.

Procurement of Central Exchanges: A History

The closed nature of the procurement system, at least in the past, is observable in the central exchange market. Here the Bundespost accounts for practically all domestic purchases. Traditional suppliers included Siemens, with 40 percent of the market; SEL (ITT, later Alcatel), with 30 percent; DeTeWe, with 14 percent; and Telenorma, with 10 percent. These figures understate the importance of Siemens, which also owns a substantial share in DeTeWe. Furthermore, Siemens had developed the switching system, was the system leader, and had assured itself a dominant position through agreements with other suppliers (Monopolkommission, 1981).

The basic procurement system for switching equipment was created in the 1920s, when the Reichspost introduced its "postal dial system," developed by Siemens with a smaller partner. The Reichspost, not wanting to depend on a single supplier, pressured Siemens to license its technology to the predecessor of today's SEL (Mix & Genest), as well as DeTeWe, Lorenz, Berliner, and other manufacturers, in return for an assured procurement quota. Starting in 1924, together with its small partner, Siemens received a set quota of 60 percent of the procurement for the next five years. The agreement was renewed in 1927. In 1933, with the National Socialists in power, the nine major telecommunications equipment manufacturers, some of them now under new Aryan ownership, entered into the so-called Telecommunications Domestic Contract with each other. This contract governed all telecommunications transactions with state agencies and private users. They carved up the market among themselves, with the Siemens group receiving 54 percent; the Standard group (which consisted of Mix & Genest, C. Lorenz, and Berliner), 36 percent; and DeTeWe, 10 percent of the Reichspost procurement volume. The contract was to run for ten years. The Reichspost was notified of the agreement and stayed within its provisions.

For the six firms that survived World War II, the quotas were maintained, now justified by the need to stabilize the market where overcapacity existed and to permit national planning. After 1951, the Bundespost notified the central exchange manufacturers, by then three in number, to plan their production capacity each for a specific volume. In the following years, the watchdog Federal Accounting Office began to show concern about the arrangement. The Bundespost insisted that even though the participants acknowledged the nature of its coordination, it was only an internal administrative matter and did not include an agreement between the Bundespost and firms or between the firms themselves. After 1954, the exclusive circle was expanded to include the firm T&N (later renamed Telenorma), following that firm's legal pressures.

In 1955, the Bundespost decided to substitute its System 55 with the new EMD switch developed by Siemens. Because it did not wish to depart from its practice of using only one type of equipment, rival equipment by SEL was not adopted. However, the DBP required Siemens to grant licenses to the other three switch manufacturers. The decision to move to the new switch was undertaken without involvement of the Bundespost's Supervisory Council. As part of these transactions, in 1955 a highly confidential agreement was signed by the Bundespost and the four industry manufacturers. The preamble of this "Heads of Agreement" document stated that the Bundespost wished in the future to include T&N in switching equipment contracts. The firms then agreed to a quota of 46 percent for Siemens, 31.3 percent for SEL, 15.2 percent for DeTeWe, and 7.5 percent for T&N. For trunk switches, a quota of 55 percent for Siemens, 32 percent for SEL, 10 percent for DeTeWe, and 3 percent for T&N was agreed upon (Scherer, 1985, p. 441). The firms also agreed not to contest each others' market shares.

In subsequent years the Bundespost, with considerable legal agility, denied the existence of quotas, but it largely adhered to the figures of the Heads of Agreement. These market shares, combined with the Bundespost's detailed three- to five-year projections of its total equipment needs, made reasonably accurate production planning by the firms possible. In practice, orders for equipment came up from the regional telecommunications directorates, together with preferences for equipment suppliers. These orders were then aggregated, and, if necessary, centrally modified to reach the target quotas. In other words, the preferences of the Bundespost's own regional directorates could be disregarded in order to meet the industry's agreement. Although the practices were criticized by the Federal Accounting Office, the Bundespost—defying reality, economics, and common sense—insisted that the quotas were only representing real market shares and that its procurement practices did not establish any economic power relationship or market concentration.

In the mid-1970s, as residential telephone service neared saturation and the economy suffered from recession, telephone expansion dropped considerably. In 1971 the waiting list for telephones had been 600,000, but by 1974 it had shrunk to 17,000. Equipment volume contracted, and workers were laid off. Alternative export markets were not easily available. The reliance on the safe and traditional electromechanical switching technology, by then twenty years old, left the manufacturers without a product that was competitive in the world market.

In 1975, the Bundespost started to introduce price competition by permitting limited changes in the procurement quota, according to prices offered. As a result its bargaining position strengthened. The system provided for a quota increase of 2 percent above that of the previous year for the lowest bidder. If the Bundespost considered the lowest bid to be still too high, it could withdraw the entire offer. If other firms lowered their prices to that of the lowest bidder, they would share the remainder of the market among themselves, absorbing the 2 percent reduction of market share.

One problem in the adoption of the procurement method was that the smallest and the most recent of the suppliers, T&N, behaved like a maverick, insisting on a larger share than before. This forced the Bundespost to ask for the blessing of the Federal Cartel Office for the scheme, which it received. T&N, however, did not give in, and argued that violations of German and European anticompetitive laws were taking place and demanded a quota of 15 percent. This led again to intense negotiations with the four firms, the Bundespost, the Cartel Office, and the Ministry of Economics. The firms and the Cartel Office reached an agreement, but the Postal Ministry, in an uncharacteristic procompetitive stance, decided to challenge it. Eventually, a compromise was reached that protected T&N's market share from an undue retaliatory drop. In 1977, the Bundespost cemented T&N's cooperation by giving it the largest increase in its share, from 7.5 percent to 8 percent.

The development of first-generation electronic switching proved to be a dismal chapter in the joint R&D efforts of Bundespost and private industry. In a major miscalculation, a fully digital development was considered and then dropped in favor of a semielectronic space division system. The project foundered, because technical progress occurring during its development continuously led to changes in the project goals, and because the firms had problems coordinating the development among themselves. The system was intended to be introduced in 1977 or 1978, but these target dates were pushed back to 1981 or 1982. It became clear that the TDM digital technology was considerably superior to the one on which the Bundespost and the manufacturers had bet. In 1979, Bundespost Minister Kurt Gescheidle pulled the plug on the development program. He declared that technical development hit the Bundespost and its suppliers like a "natural catastrophe" but that the Bundespost had learned from its mistakes, and as a result, it would now closely follow technical developments in the international telecommunications markets. The large losses in the project were borne chiefly by the equipment industry.

After the dropping of the ill-fated analog system, the Bundespost initiated a crash program in digital switching. It approached the major manufacturers to submit new development models, though only up to three models would be tested by the Bundespost, and of those, at most two would be chosen, with cutover dates in 1984–1985. This led initially to three proposals, by SEL (ITT), by Siemens and its affiliate, and by DeTeWe, T&N, and Tekede. The latter group, possessing no digital exchanges of their own, did not meet the May 1982 deadline to continue the project, and thus only two models were presented to the Bundespost. A competitive selection was not instituted, and both the EWSD system of Siemens, and ITT's System 12 were accepted in 1983.

Customer Premises Equipment

Similar cartel arrangements existed for PBXs. Since the first private branch exchange (PBX) was introduced in Germany in 1900, the penetration of PBXs was substantial. There are more than a million PBXs in Germany, connecting about 10 million extension stations. About 60 percent of total traffic volume originated from or reached a PBX (ZVEI, 1983). The DBP's market share was about 40 percent of units, but less in DM volume.

Until 1934, the market for PBXs was relatively free. All private suppliers could enter and install equipment on private premises, though the Reichspost was also a supplier. Competition led to technological development, but it also led to severe price wars. In particular, the Reichspost was being undercut by private competitors in a variety of ways. Until 1934, only compatibility standards were set for PBXs. In 1934, however, the PBX manufacturers considered the price competition to be "ruinous" and set out to stabilize it. This was accomplished through the establishment of uniform technical requirements and performance standards.

The private suppliers agreed to conform to uniform conditions of supply as well as to the prices of Reichspost-supplied PBXs. Any new supplier had to be admitted to the production of PBXs. In other words, the Reichspost achieved the elimination of competition that would undercut its own position while providing an umbrella for a price-fixing agreement among private suppliers.

The 1934 PBX rules also explicitly aimed to slow down technological development. They sought to "cut back the overdeveloped (*überspitzte*) technology to the actual needs and to the associated reasonable extent, and to assure that in further development only pertinent considerations would be determinative" (Wittiber, 1934, p. 184, footnote 48).

In the 1980s a government report described the historical growth of this regulatory system since the 1930s and found that "The result was a cartel situation which divided the market among the suppliers. This did not come about through prices, but through . . . standards regulation" (Mestmäcker, 1980, p. 185). The DBP bought, leased, and resold customer terminal equipment. Traditionally, it was the sole supplier of simple terminal equipment. It also provided, though not exclusively, PBXs, modems, and other more sophisticated equipment, including telefax equipment. It had exclusive rights for servicing telex equipment but did not supply it.

Problems with this arrangement arose due to the Bundespost's triple function in the telecommunications field: It regulated, operated, and competed. It was the primary telecommunications regulatory authority of the country, with the powers of government. At the same time, it was also the predominant network operator: In equipment supply, it competed with private firms. The tension between these several functions led to the appointment of a Kommission Deutsche Bundespost in 1969–1970, which drafted a new charter, including the organizational separation of political leadership and supervision, on the one hand, and the actual operation, on the other hand. This bill was not passed by the Bundestag (Elias et al., 1980).

The industry's attitude toward the Bundespost as a supplier was complex. The DBP is, after all, its major customer and often a friendly supporter of the industry's technical development and exports. But as a supply competitor, it enjoyed advantages they resented: The Bundespost's equipment licensing authority provides it with information about its own competitors' products; it had no risk of bankruptcy; it did not have to set its pricing according to costs; and it was able to subsidize its products internally for market penetration and deterrence of competitors (Monopolkommission, 1981).

The legal framework supported any DBP pricing policy. When equipment was offered at a loss, it could be justified as a fulfillment of a public obligation; when it was profitable, it was said to be part of the Bundespost's function to balance its budget or to raise revenue for the federal budget.

In the customer terminal equipment market, there are eighteen firms, of which the usual four (Siemens, SEL, T&N, DeTeWe) are the "development firms," while the others are "follower firms." According to the Monopoly Commission, these four have protected their technology through hundreds of patents. The commission maintained that the "overlap [of patents] is obviously tolerated with mutual good will. Apparently the comprehensiveness of patent licenses is not utilized offensively to restrict competitors, but rather serves defensively to secure individual production programs. The development firms show a common interest in a peaceful coexistence in technological competition" (Monopolkommission, 1981, para. 131).

The remaining eight suppliers of terminal equipment had a substantial 60 percent of the terminal set market. Those companies are fairly obscure and depend on the Bundespost's good graces. They have no domestic distribution system and have no need for one, since the Bundespost is their predominant German customer.

The industry's ardent defense of the Bundespost suggests the symbiotic relationship between the network monopoly and the equipment suppliers. The trade association's (ZVEI) position on the role of the Bundespost has been: "The German telecommunications industry is convinced that the functional integrity of the public telecommunications network, the nationwide availability of services under the same conditions, the compatibility of communications networks with all terminal devices, and the resulting freedom for all users to communicate can be guaranteed only by a network monopoly" (ZVEI, 1983, p. 43). The industry also defended the Bundespost's role as a distribution system for small producers. "Participation of the Deutsche Bundespost in the terminal equipment market is extremely advantageous for small and medium-sized communication companies, which cannot meet the costs of a nationwide sales and services network of their own, and therefore supply their product directly to the Deutsche Bundespost. This allows them to achieve a notable share of the market" (ZVEI, 1983, p. 45). This was in conflict with other industries, where medium-sized producers were able to market their products, whether through their own sales organization or through agents and intermediate wholesalers, rather than having to depend on a state organization.

A complex bidding system was employed for terminal equipment that provided for greater competitiveness than for switching equipment. In the mid-1970s the Bundespost charged suppliers with a breach of the price and quantity agreement. They were fined, and the DBP tightened its procurement rules. Immediately, the new system proved unworkable. The Siemens bid was by far the lowest, and only SEL agreed to match it. The other ten firms refused and made their high prices a David vs. Goliath issue for the survival of small and medium sized companies. With business organization, unions, and politicians being involved, the Bundespost retreated and announced its willingness to accept not the highest, but rather the third highest price as its guide. This was accepted by eight of the ten companies, but the small firms were still unhappy about the loss of the previously cozy arrangement. With the Federal Cartel Office joining in to support the existence of a diversity of firms, the Bundespost retreated still further.

The Bundespost strongly opposed the liberalization of terminal equipment on legal grounds, based on a Telecommunications Order that declared terminal equipment to be part of the public network. The order was confirmed by the Federal Constitutional Court in 1978. The DBP also argued on technical grounds that the separation of network and terminal equipment was impractical, since terminal equipment fulfills a network protection function. To a certain extent this is true, though other means of protection can be easily established. The logical consequence of the Bundespost's view was that much of the office equipment, as it becomes "smart" and connected to the network, could be claimed to be subject to the Bundespost's regulatory jurisdiction and potential control.

Conflicts about the Bundespost's role in equipment supply go far back. In later years, controversy arose over telefax service initiated by the Bundespost in the 1970s. The Bundespost wanted to ensure that it would play a major, if not exclusive, role in the expected success of telefax equipment. The matter came before the Administrative Council of the Bundespost, which was conscious of the potential controversy with office equipment manufacturers. The union representatives on the board were unanimously opposed to a provision of telefax equipment by private suppliers only and considered exclusive provision by the Bundespost a viable alternative.

Within a short time, a rare public debate concerning the liberalization of equipment began. In particular, the Federal Ministry of Economics championed a liberalization, and in 1977, it opposed Bundespost participation in advanced terminal equipment. It argued that such participation was not necessary, that it was potentially discriminatory against its competitors which were also its suppliers, and that it encouraged internal subsidies that distorted competition. The Bundespost countered that operational experience with equipment was essential for a network provider to be able to improve services. The Economics Ministry pointed out, however, that the Bundespost could easily acquire equipment for its own use and in that way gather operational experience. The Conference of the State Economics Ministers took up this matter in 1978 and came out on the side of the Federal Ministry of Economics. When that ministry conducted a public "telefax-hearing" in August 1978, Siemens, the largest manufacturer, favored a role of the Bundespost as equipment supplier.

The Ministry of Economics softened its position and demanded that (1) there be a ceiling on market share of the DBP for telefax equipment at 15 percent and (2) the DBP not be able to refuse its customers use of competing suppliers' equipment. Eventually, the minister for posts and telecommunications agreed but did not make a commitment to a specific percentage of market share, except that it would not be a "market-dominating" position. In German cartel law this terminology implies a share of less than 20 percent.

Equipment cases were a constant source of friction. Because much of the terminal equipment was Bundespost owned, a slower rate of technological change in the network and in terminal equipment was suspected, since the Bundespost had to consider whether innovations would make its own equipment base obsolete. Under such an argument, network performance and design become the prisoner of the existing terminal equipment base. But it is also true that change in network performance could make much of the terminal equipment base obsolete, and that is an argument for an integrated provision of network and terminal services.

In a study commissioned by the Monopoly Commission, three economists—Carl Christian von Weizsäcker, Jürgen Müller, and Günter Knieps—argued that the Bundespost's participation in terminal equipment was not a serious problem, because it already held a monopoly in telecommunications services, which are closely complementary to equipment. Since the Bundespost did not produce terminal equipment itself, it had an interest in seeing terminal equipment as inexpensive and as widely distributed as possible, creating a positive contribution to its network monopoly. The terminal equipment was characterized by a supplier oligopoly, which led to prices that were above cost. Therefore, the participation of the Bundespost could lower prices; its large economies of scope and scale allowed it to underprice the other market participants. Thus, the DBP should actually be required to participate in the terminal market (Knieps et al., 1981).

The Monopoly Commission decided that the question of whether economies of scope would be more beneficial than the Bundespost's exclusion from the market was largely an empirical one, and best resolved by making competition a "discovery procedure" (Snow, 1983). In the telefax market, competitors noted that the Bundespost's rental fee was only half as high as that of private firms, allegedly because of cross-subsidization. To avoid this problem in the future, the Monopoly Commission discussed, though it did not recommend, the isolation of parts of the Bundespost's activities in separate independent subsidiaries (DBP, 1985).

In arguing against equipment liberalization, the Bundespost claimed that the "result of the liberalization of the terminal equipment market in the United States—with the exception of the telephone handset for the simple telephone main station—is a situation that has existed in the Federal Republic for a long time" (DBP, 1981, p. 97a). This statement shows a lack of familiarity with the terminal market in the United States that existed by 1980. The 1956 *Hush-a-Phone* and the 1968 *Carterfone* decisions had made equipment connections possible. Although AT&T attempted to impose restrictions by requiring expensive buffer protection devices, the FCC overrode AT&T's rear-guard resistance and adopted instead a system that simply defined minimum safety standards that manufacturers had to meet.[7] Under this system there is no testing or approval. Competitors have twenty days to contest a filing, and responses are due within ten days. A ruling on such disputes, which is rare, takes generally less than two months.

Competition in equipment supply for customer terminals had markedly positive effects in Germany. Until the mid-1970s there was no particular reason for the Bundespost, given its monopoly position, to seek customers and to engage in marketing for terminal equipment. As an official in the Ministry for Post and Telecommunications noted, the demand for telephones far exceeded the supply. In addition, "Since the telephone, by itself, was already a status symbol, subscribers did not have particular demands concerning form, color, or performance" (Wolf, 1982).

In the 1970s, however, economic recession, market saturation, and the emergence of a gray market in terminal equipment brought a reduction in demand for terminal equipment, leading, as the Bundespost noted, to "serious consequences for the German Bundespost and its suppliers. . . . New ways had to be pursued to move quickly from this low point. The German Bundespost tried for the first time to reach the customer and more than in the past to respect his desires and to fulfill them more exactly" (Wolf, 1982, p. 26). This led to market research, an advertising campaign, and changes in the design, color, performance, and price of telephone equipment. The surcharge for telephones of a color other than gray was eliminated. As another Bundespost official acknowledged, "Through the increasing supply of unlicensed equipment, often with considerable defects, a certain pressure had already developed in the market. The Deutsche Bundespost recognized this trend" (Schulte, 1982, p. 328).[8]

The Bundespost fiercely protected its equipment monopoly. At one time, its advertising subsidiary informed potential customers of other advertising agencies that the Bundespost's permission was necessary to affix a sticker containing an emergency number and an advertising message to the telephone set. The competitors sued. The lower courts found that this behavior was an attempt to extend the postal monopoly into the competitive realm.

This case corresponds to the American *Hush-A-Phone* decision, in which the Bell System had similarly tried to prevent a trivial nonelectrical attachment to its equipment but was rebuffed in court. In Germany, however, a 1980 court decision accepted the prohibition of stickers on telephone equipment owned by the Bundespost. ''The prohibition of attaching stickers serves therefore the security and maintenance of an undisturbed telecommunications operation . . .'' (DBP, 1981, para. 76).

Despite (or because of) such defensive measures, pressures on the Bundespost grew. In 1981, the state economics ministers created a working committee, Deutsche Bundespost and Telecommunications Monopoly, and charged it with proposing a modification of telecommunications equipment law. The proposals asked for a DBP exclusion from equipment provision, except when technical, economic, and reasons of national economy, or other interests of society required it. In 1982, partly because of diffuse criticism against its dual role of supplier in competition with private firms and as the approval authority, the DBP established a new central office for telecommunications licensing (ZZF) with a semi-independent status and a location in Saarbrücken, at some distance from the Bundespost establishment in Bonn and Darmstadt.

The DBP was slow to approve modems and similar devices. Until 1986 only the DBP could sell modems. Its modem monopoly was broken after a 1985 EC Commission intervention. Even after 1986, the DBP continued to drag its feet on accepting the technical specifications approval of different modem suppliers. It wanted data communication to use its public data networks. Similarly, up to 1989, the DBP would not allow standard fax boards on the telecommunications network since it did not want the fax machines permanently connected (Pfeiffer and Wieland, 1990, p. 84).

In 1982, the European Commission joined the chorus, issuing a complaint against the DBP regarding modem and baseband equipment, citing it in violation of Articles 85 and 86 of the Treaty of Rome. European legal provisions—specifically, Articles 37, 85, 86, and 90—have some applications to the behavior of postal authorities. Article 37 requires member states of the European Community to treat their trading and distribution monopolies so as to eliminate potential discrimination among countries. This article has exceptions for reasons of governmental function, security, and consumer protection. Article 90 applies competitive requirements to companies imbued with the public interest. This area and the application of antimonopoly rules require much more judicial clarification. (For an analysis, see Scherer, 1985, and Mestmäcker, 1980). The DBP subsequently modified its practices. In 1986, it also agreed that modems could be sold by manufacturers directly to users rather than relying on the bulky SEL or Siemens modems it had provided. These restrictions, coupled with the Bundespost's own marketing, were important, since only 59,000 modems were in use in the entire country at the time, in comparison with 300,000 in the United Kingdom and 115,000 in France (Bruce, 1986). The decision had to be made by the German Cabinet, so strong was the resistance of the Bundespost. The DBP, however, was left with the powers of setting standards and approving all modems, an arrangement that could cause considerable delay. (The firm Deutsche Fernsprecher Gesellschaft, for example, waited more than a year before receiving approval for a modem). Furthermore, modems connected to the Btx videotex service remained under Bundespost monopoly.

In 1985, the European Commission also forced the Bundespost to give up its monopoly over cordless telephones. A Siemens cordless phone sold for $665, whereas similar Japanese models cost $79 in the United States (Schares, 1989, p. 137).

The American government, prodded by its industry, was critical of German procurement practices. Negotiations over liberalization of the German telecommunications market reached some agreement about a reduced domestic orientation by the Bundespost, as well as tenders that permitted a streamlining of the approval process, greater ease for leased lines, and liberalized specifications for PBXs.

As part of the 1989 reforms, Germany's equipment market, including first sets, was officially liberalized on July 1, 1990. The Telecommunications Installation Act (Fernmeldeanlagengesetz) specifies a "no harm to the network" standard for type approvals.

Reform Debates

For a long time there was no public discussion of the Bundespost's role, in marked contrast to the intense discussion in Germany over cable television and media policy in general.

More than interest group politics is at work in Germany. The ideology of a mixed economic system goes back a long time and has intellectual roots in an important school of thought, *Gemeinwirtschaftslehre* (Public Economics), which argues for government involvement in economic activities (Thiemeyer, 1983; Snow, 1983). The *Gemeinwirtschaftslehre* goes back to Adolph Wagner, who, in "Wagner's law," postulated the necessary growth of the public sector (Wagner, 1887).[9]

Reform discussions of German postal affairs are not new; organized attempts to study the system and recommend reforms go back at least to 1579, when Emperor Rudolf II appointed a blue-ribbon panel (including representatives of large postal users and financial institutions) to report on the Thurn and Taxis postal monopoly. Four hundred years later similar questions were still being studied. In 1969 a commission was set up to investigate the organization and role of the Bundespost. The panel proposed the separation of political supervision from management of the Bundespost and recommended that a presiding body of five, without the traditional civil service status, manage the PTT in the manner of a private company, though with social obligations as well as financial goals. But when the government attempted even such a modest reorganization, it was blocked, partly because there was no agreement on the extent of participation of the postal unions in the proposed governing boards. Later, pressure by the postal unions prevented a reemergence of the proposal.

The general reformist spirit of the early 1970s, when the Social Democrats held the federal chancellorship, led to the appointment of a Commission on Communications Technology (KtK), at the initiative of the Social Democratic government official Prof. Horst Ehmke, who happened to be simultaneously minister of postal affairs and minister for science and technology. [It is interesting to observe that in Germany, academic researchers have been more actively involved in issues of telecommunications policy than they were elsewhere in Europe (Hoffmann-Riem, 1984).] The KtK was set up in 1974 to formulate proposals for the development of a "socially desirable and economically feasible telecommunications system for the Federal Republic of Germany." The commission was chaired by Eberhard Witte, an economist at the University of Munich (Commission for the Development of the Telecommunications System, 1976). In the area of telephony, the report touched institutional concerns only lightly; liberalization of equipment supply or the opening of communications services to carriers other than the Bundespost were rejected. But the KtK also examined media policy issues in cable television. As a result, the federal states, traditionally in charge of broadcasting, initially refused to cooperate with the committee, and political maneuvering was required to effect a compromise.

The KtK report established general guidelines that were adopted by the government cabinet in 1976 and became the foundation for the subsequent establishment of pilot cable projects to test the technical, economic, and social feasibility of the new cable medium. Perhaps most importantly, they led to the creation of politically acceptable institutional models. The report also encouraged the development of a data network and recommended the establishment of a planning body for telecommunications outside the postal authority. The latter, however, was never implemented.

In 1977, the German Constitutional Court dealt a negative ruling to proponents of reform by holding that the Bundespost's exclusive rights for the construction and operation of telecommunications facilities covered the entire telecommunications sector, including transmission, switching facilities, and terminal equipment, and that it encompassed all new forms of information transmission in network and user segments.

Nevertheless, in the early 1980s, the German Monopoly Commission, an advisory commission to the government, launched an investigation of the Bundespost and issued a report on the Bundespost's role in telecommunications (Monopoly Commission, 1981). This report was unusual because it was the first time that the commission investigated the market power of a public enterprise. It traced in detail the problems of telecommunications monopoly, and forcefully advocated liberalization in some areas. Even where it recommended maintenance of the existing policy, it did so typically as the lesser of the evils, and rarely without a fairly negative analysis of the existing system.

The leading spirit behind the report was Professor Ernst-Joachim Mestmäcker, who served at the time as the commission's chairman. He thought it a "mercantilistic view of the state" to believe that the public interest is adequately served by a monopoly enterprise simply because it is the state that operates it (Mestmäcker, 1980, p. 196).

The Monopoly Commission concluded that economies of scale were not particularly important for the connection of network and terminal equipment but that the DBP's involvement with the terminal equipment market had negative effects for market structure and competition. The commission also determined that the argument of natural monopoly had to be doubted, based on the American experience, particularly in long-distance communications. However, it was better, at least for a while, not to go ahead with a development of parallel network infrastructure, given the necessary large investment. But the commission held that specialized, privately supplied value added services should be permitted on Bundespost facilities. Direct network competition could be permitted with the development of technology, in case of a potential deterioration of DBP services, and a reduction of internal subsidies to some of the DBP's services. Given its own scathing criticism of the existing arrangement, the commission's policy conclusions were somewhat modest and probably represented an adjustment to the political realities.

Also in 1981, the German Bundestag, in a major effort to formulate public policy in this field, created an Inquiry Commission on New Information and Communications Technologies. The commission had as its mandate the exploration of all international aspects of the new technologies. The major political parties appointed their communications experts to the commission. For example, the Christian Democrat representative was Christian Schwarz-Schilling, who soon thereafter became minister for post and telecommunications. The parties also appointed seven nonparliamentary experts from the outside, including Wolfgang Hoffmann-Riem, a law professor and head of the media research center Hans-Bredow Institut in Hamburg.

The commission was active in its two years of existence. But the heavy party politicization of media issues which is prevalent in Germany as in much of Europe, prevented constructive proceedings. Another set of conflicts existed between the commission and the federal states. During the commission's tenure, the government changed hands, and elections were held sooner than expected. No final report could be agreed upon by the deeply divided commission. A lengthy preliminary report was supported by parts of the commission and eventually printed as a publication of the German parliament. The report reflects what must have been frustrating proceedings. Dissenting opinions, even on purported factual matters, appear frequently, as do references to the lack of agreement on many of the questions. Even on the simple statement that technologies not only provide "opportunities" but also "could lead to dangers," the commission could find no agreement. The commission discussed the liberalization of the postal monopoly's innovative communications services—specifically, the Monopoly Commission recommendation that the network should be opened up by admitting more specialized networks and giving general permission to lease resale lines in order to increase competition. It listed several arguments for such service competition, such as encouraging an improved utilization of resources in telecommunications. This more efficient resource utilization would not negatively affect the economies of scale of the telecommunications network, since the DBP would remain the sole network carrier. Allowing private suppliers to explore and develop new telecommunications services not yet offered by the DBP, including information and communications services, was seen as improving the potential for innovation. And the Bundespost would still be needed in the initial phases of development to subsidize new services.

The commission approvingly cited the German Constitutional Court's decision that private parties can be prevented from offering only lucrative services, whereas the Bundespost, because of its legal obligation, must also supply less lucrative services. The commission therefore concluded that the "Post is entitled to exclude such 'cherry-picking' by private competitors" (Inquiry Commission, 1984, p. 180).

The commission was also negative about competition in basic networks. "Permitting competition would easily lead to an economically inefficient duplication of investment" (Inquiry Commission, 1984, p. 174). The report conceded that it was empirically unclear whether telecommunication is indeed a natural monopoly and admitted that there had been no investigations of that question for the Federal Republic. However, empirical studies of economies of scale for the United States, Canada, and Great Britain were cited that suggested that the telecommunications sector as a whole was a natural monopoly, although the economies of scale had decreased over time. (This literature, some of which was commissioned in support of embattled service monopolists, is more ambiguous than the commission's reading.)

The commission's stance on the Bundespost's role in equipment markets was evasive. After a description of the complexity of the equipment licensing process, the report concluded that: "Whether there are real [distorting] effects cannot be determined" (Inquiry Commission, 1984, p. 185). The report stresses that the network needs to be protected technologically, and users of equipment need to be protected from malfunctioning or incompatible equipment they have acquired.

Faced with criticism, the Bundespost began to act more flexibly and to bend its principles quietly, as long as its monopoly was left intact. It began to permit some resale of capacity in data lines. Resale of voice transmission was still out of bounds, though the DBP seemed to have tolerated it in some instances. Resale was formally limited to 50 percent of the lines' capacity, although this limit was impossible to enforce. But criticism persisted. The free-market position, as explained by a member of the subsequent blue-ribbon reform commission, was essentially that "Reputable expert opinions commissioned by the Bundespost itself lead to the conclusion that the state-run enterprise also earns a rather mediocre grade in an international comparison. . . . It pointed out that the Federal Republic lagged far behind in the number of public telephones, with 162,000 compared with the 1.7 million in the US and 828,000 in Japan, and that it had for a long time no itemized billing, cordless phones, call-waiting, call-forwarding, etc.'' (Möschel, 1988, p. 3).

In 1984, the government published another report to serve as a conceptual document for the advancement of information technology. The report, *Regierungsbericht Informationstechnik 1984*, stressed the importance of governmental initiative in order to keep German information technology competitive (Lange, 1984).

In the 1980s, even the Social Democratic Party, which had faithfully supported the Bundespost monopoly, began to criticize its rate of upgrading of the network. Its General Secretary, Peter Glotz, himself a media expert, criticized the Bundespost's low level of investment in digital switching (Glotz, 1983), and urged a rapid development of the Bundespost networks. As Glotz asserted, if no modern public networks would be offered, private networks would emerge on leased lines, which would provide the same efficiency benefits, but would be less sensitive to social politics and other requirements such as data protection.

The Reform of German Telecommunications

Partly in response to pressure for liberalization from the United States and the European Community, a commission was established in 1985 to make recommendations for the reform of telecommunications policy. The panel, chaired by Eberhard Witte of Munich University, who had also headed the KtK, was composed of twelve members who represented the four major parties and a spectrum of economic interests. From the beginning, the commission was subject to criticism. To some it was a threat to the established order; to others it was a legitimization of minimalist reform steps which largely served the Bundespost's interests. It took almost one year to set up the panel, and another two and one-half years until it produced its report in September 1987.

Internally, the commission was split in various ways. The free market or liberal wing consisted of the Free Democratic Party representatives, a law professor, the banks' representative, and the president of the Federal Associate of German Industry. In the past, the telecommunications industry interests had generally defined the position of the German industry association. The orientation of the association's president was thus significant, because it indicated that users and other electronic firms' interests had gained in importance and influence.

The traditionalist wing consisted of the trade unionist, the Social Democratic delegate, and in key questions, the representative of the Bavarian Christian Democrats. That conservative party favored the status quo, because it wished to satisfy its large rural population, and perhaps because Munich was the headquarters of Siemens, which also did not wish to see an upheaval in well-established relations.

The commission was split six to six over the key question of whether to permit competition in physical networks. Chairman Witte, who had two votes, elected not to break the tie, which was likely to have been in favor of network competition, for pragmatic reasons: Even if a majority had recommended such competition, the minority would have included the representatives of three of the four major parties, representing more than 80 percent of the parliamentary deputies. Political realities had to be taken into account if the recommendations were to be adopted. The economically liberal opponents believed that the recommendations had to reflect what was best, not just what was most realistic politically. The approach ultimately taken by the commission majority on this issue was to initiate a process and then to expect its dynamics to lead in future development. Thus, it recommended a number of modest pro-competitive steps that would, in time, its majority hoped, obtain a momentum of their own and lead to a more significant change in German telecommunications.

It is important to note that the commission found that the existing telecommunications monopoly was not enshrined in, or protected by, the German Basic Law. Structurally, it recommended a separation of telecommunications from postal services, and a separation of "sovereign tasks," or regulation, from the entrepreneurial tasks of organization. It recommended that regulatory tasks be vested in the ministry and others reside with operational organization Deutsche Telekom, which would have greater operational and legal independence. Deutsche Telekom would also have greater flexibility in compensation, payment methods, and deployment of labor. Deutsche Telekom would retain its monopoly on the basic network and on voice telephony. But data, text, and other non-voice communications would be open to competition from the private sector, using the Telekom network. It would also lose its monopoly on the basic telephone set, and the terminal equipment market would be fully liberalized. The commission also proposed that tariffs be set by the Ministry of Communications and be more in line with costs, thus eliminating tariff distortions. Greater freedom would be granted in the interconnection of leased lines with switched service. In a departure from existing controversial practice for leased lines, Telekom would develop a tariff structure not based on volume-sensitive charges. Satellite-delivered slow-speed data would be opened to transmission by others, another first.

The commission also recommended that the government reevaluate market conditions every three years, with the option of permitting the establishment of competing networks if the market was not developing satisfactorily (Witte, 1987). The commission thus provided, at least rudimentally, for a previously missing mechanism of policy change.

Most of the recommendations were accepted by PTT Minister Schwartz-Schilling and by the government in a somewhat more restrictive bill. It rejected a conditional DBP monopoly but allowed the following: value-added services, a second cellular network, usage-sensitive leased-line tariffs, liberalized terminal equipment, liberalized type approval, slow-speed satellite service for data, and limited resale. It imposed special obligations on private carriers (Möschel, 1988, p. 17). But the new telecommunications organization was not to be fully freed under its own board of directors, and its name was slightly but pointedly changed to DBP Telekom—indicating its ties to the Bundepost. It must contribute 10 percent of income to the Federal budget. (The total that the DBP paid to the government through its annual contribution in 1988 amounted to 5.25 billion DM, approximately 10 percent of its annual income). After the reforms, the three different sectors of the DBP are subject to taxes, as if they were private enterprises. Furthermore, an "infrastructure council" with mixed state-federal membership was established to respond to the desire of several states to have input into telecommunications policy and to address their fear of neglect by a profit-oriented Telekom.

After bitter debates and opposition by the trade unions, the Law on Restructuring the Bundespost passed on July 1, 1989.

The objective of the 1989 reform was to eliminate the structural conflict between the regulatory and the production activities of the DBP and to encourage participation and competition from the private sector for new services and hardware. To accomplish this, a separation of responsibilities was mandated. Managerial responsibilities over the PTT were taken away from the Ministry of Posts and Telecommunications, so that the ministry could in the future concentrate on regulatory issues without any conflict of interest. The ministry, which would retain cabinet representation, would now set and implement standards, establish access rules, allocate spectrum, license entrants, and so on.

The 1989 Reform (the *Poststrukturgesetz*) created three distinct public corporations, for telecommunications, for postal service, and for the PTT's traditional financial services. Each of these corporations would have its own board of directors, its own published balance statements, and its own organizational structure. Further, these new entities would have the legal responsibilities of private corporations to their customers and suppliers, rather than their previous protection of being part of the German state.

The chairpersons of each of these distinct entities meet in a single Deutsche Bundespost directorate, which is responsible for consolidating the individual balance sheets of the different PTT entities, coordinating service between the different groups, and handling joint labor compensation issues. Each of these entities, however, was still required to make a profit on its own.

The staff members of the new operating entities are still civil servants, and as such retain their traditional protections from dismissal. It remains difficult to reward employees for merit.

The telecommunications entity, DBP Telekom, retained exclusive right to all voice transmission. Since this service amounts to 90 percent of all the telecommunications business in Germany, it is still in control of the most important and profitable sector. Further, in part because of monopoly conditions, it can charge above cost for these services. The rationale for allowing DBP Telekom such profit was that it would be able to invest this money into infrastructural changes, including fiber optics and to cross-subsidize service to more remote regions in the country.

No alternative physical network can be set up except under very special circumstances (internal use of public administration or transportation concerns, or between singly owned parcels of land no more than 25 kilometers away from any of the other parcels of land). Many users complained that the new law still allowed DBP Telekom to move slowly in servicing their needs. In response, Schwartz-Schilling drafted stronger legislation in 1990 aimed at reducing DBP Telekom's ability to block competitors with limited access and high tariffs.

Competition for nonvoice transmission began shortly thereafter. Germany already had 185,000 cellular subscribers in 1989, connected to DBP's then monopoly service. But in May 1989 the government solicited bids for the construction of a second (D2) cellular network, based on the European GSM standard. Several American firms—NYNEX (with BT and Daimler-Benz), Bell South (with Siemens, Olivetti, and Shearson-Lehman-Hutton), and Pacific Telesis (with Mannesmann and Deutsche Genossenschaftbank)—sought licenses. Mannesmann, a large steel and engineering conglomerate, led the winning consortium, but its service was delayed by a year of negotiations with DBP Telekom over interconnection and carriage tariffs. A third and digital, in principle, mobile telephone network was decided upon in 1991.

In 1991, the ministry granted 22 companies licenses for private satellite networks that did not interconnect with the public network. Services above 15 kbps required special approval. Most systems are, at least in part, over the 15 kbps threshold. Licenses were also awarded for paging and radio data.

Although it is important to note the DBP's new services, a perspective must be kept. Most of the DBP's telecommunication revenues derived from traditional telephone service. Of the DM 38.4 billion of telecommunications revenue, traditional telephone service made up DM 34.2 billion, or 90 percent. Data services (including videotex) and telegraph were DM 2.67 billion (7 percent), and radio and other telecommunications sources were DM 1.5 billion. Of the data service figure, 40 percent was earned by leased lines (Pfeiffer and Wieland, 1990, p. 11), until rates were drastically rebalanced.

East Germany—German Democratic Republic

Despite the vast differences in political systems, East Germany's telecommunications operations were organized in some ways similarly to those of West Germany prior to the latter's 1989 reform. Telecommunications were provided by a monopoly PTT "Deutsche Post" (DP), which had a standard two-part structure of Directorates and regional offices. The PTT was subject to the Ministry of Posts and Telecommunications, or "MPF," which controlled central strategic and regulatory offices and exercised management, coordination and planning functions over the full range of communications technologies.

In the period immediately prior to unification, the Ministry dominated a vertically integrated structure of state owned companies that provided telecommunications services, manufactured telecommunications equipment, and installed cable, switching and terminal equipment. This structure included two classes of entities. The PTT directly owned the VEB Fernmeldebau, which provided installation services. (A VEB or "volkseigner Betrieb" was a state-owned company of the type that predominated in the German Democratic Republic's centralized economy.) The MPF also controlled the "Kombinat Nachrichtenelektronik," a state cartel that organized and directed all fourteen of the VEBs that manufactured telecommunications equipment. In addition, the Minister headed a government commission that coordinated the various state-owned networks and directed their interconnection with the public network, and the MPF controlled a public frequency commission that oversaw the allocation of radio spectrum space.

In addition to its telecommunications services, the DP provided extensive postal services, such as distribution, billing and marketing for all newspapers and magazines. It also was responsible for radio and television receivers and transmission stations, as well as all studio production equipment. The PTT's control over public communication was so extensive that if individuals needed a microphone for any public purpose, they had to rent it from the PTT (Neumann, 1990).

Before 1989, the telecommunications equipment industry had been under the control of a manufacturing industry ministry. Under that arrangement, the PTT was forced to report its investment requirements to a central planning bureaucracy that allocated resources based on its own political priorities instead of on the needs of the telecommunications sector. Telecommunications services were considered a nonproductive part of the economy and were thus assigned a low priority. Conversely, equipment export was a high priority, and approximately 75% of all telecommunications goods were sent abroad, especially to other East European countries. In 1989, the telecommunications industry was put under the control of the MPF in a controversial effort to improve economic performance and turn its productive capacity to domestic uses (Neumann, 1990).

The 1985 Law on Posts and Telecommunications gave the state the exclusive right to provide postal and telecommunications services. While some leased line networks were operated by businesses that had obtained waivers to do so from the MPF, the only nonpublic telecommunications systems were those operated by the army and the police. All terminal equipment was provided by the PTT, except for a small number of PBXs that received a special waiver. There was no private telecommunications equipment market.

Although the GDR had one of the most advanced telephone systems in the Eastern Bloc, the infrastructure was inadequate and outdated. There were only very basic services. In 1965, there were 1.6 million telephones, with a waiting list of 84,000 people. The waiting list for phones grew to 660,000 in 1983 (A. Rutkowski, 1990, communication; Kelly, 1990, Figure 2). By 1990, there were 1.8 million main exchange lines, twice as many as 1969, serving 4 million telephones. Nevertheless, only one out of seven households had a phone, and party lines were common. Moreover, the few residential phones available were unevenly distributed. In East Berlin, 50 per cent of homes had service, while in other cities, such as Dresden, only one out of nine homes had service. By 1990, the official waiting list was approximately 1.2 million people (almost as many people as had telephones), and was growing twice as fast as installed main lines. At the previously planned rate of construction, the backlog would have taken at least ten to fourteen years to fill (U.S. Department of State, 1990, p. 51); some estimates suggest as much as a twenty year delay. Moreover, as in many Eastern European countries, the list probably did not include discouraged potential users.

Telegrams were a significant form of public communication. In 1965, 8 million domestic and 3 million international telegrams were sent from 6000 telex connections. In 1989, those figures were 11 million and 3 million telegrams, respectively, and 18,000 telex connections.

The East German network structure prior to unification was composed of 1,500 local networks, 2,700 local switching centers, and 182 switching centers at the trunk level. While almost all of the main exchange lines were connected to automatic exchanges, just 20 per cent could be switched automatically for international calls. Almost a quarter of the local and trunk switches were ancient, installed between 1922 and 1934, while 42.6 per cent were installed in 1950. Another 28.1 per cent were installed between 1963 and 1965. Part of the switching system was so old that it had already been fully depreciated more than twice. At the local and trunk levels, the switches were analog and electro-mechanical; 25 per cent of all East German switches were crossbar. Most of the transmission system was analog, although since the mid-seventies PCM-systems were used. Fiber optic cable amounted to less than 1 percent of the transmission network.

The network could barely support facsimile and data transmission, and there was neither a circuit-switched nor packet-switched data network. The first modem use was reported in 1969 when eight modems were put on line. By 1983 there were 500. There was an operator-assisted data network that connected 1,500 subscribers, and another 3000 subscribers leased lines for data transmission. (The PTT had planned to build a packet-switched network since the mid-eighties and had signed an agreement with Siemens to do so, but CoCom restrictions on the packet-switching technology prevented the project.) As a result, only a few hundred fax machines and modems were in use before unification, while over 10,000 prospective subscribers were on the waiting list for data connections. Mobile and value added services were unavailable. There were 18,000 telex connections, transmitting text at 50 bps over thirty to forty year-old technology, and 3,000 data circuits with a capacity of 2.5 kbps (Gärt-ner and Habenicht, 1990, p. 13). The only well-developed part of the telecommunications network was that operated by the GDR's secret police for surveillance and domestic control (Hafner, 1990).

The German political unification in 1990 created an urgent need to upgrade East Germany's antiquated infrastructure. In December, 1989, a Joint Government Commission was created by the East and West German governments to manage the process of unification for all aspects of telecommunications. The government of Prime Minister Hans Modrow, still a Communist party official, decided to shift the PTT toward financial independence from the government and make it a public enterprise. By early 1990, the MPF concluded that it would move toward the West German organizational structure in an effort to secure necessary support. In March 1990, a non-Communist East German government was elected. Soon thereafter, it replaced the old PTT structure with three public enterprises along the same lines as West Germany.

Simultaneous with the negotiations on economic and currency union, the East and West German Ministers of Posts and Telecommunications negotiated a Joint Declaration that outlined the plan for integration. Targets were for the East German network to be on par with West Germany's by 1997. DBP Telekom planned to install 7.3 million new subscriber lines, 10 million miles of fiber-optic and copper cable, 68,000 public phones, 360,000 facsimile connections, and 50,000 packet-switched connections by that time, and add 2000 digital central office switches. The newly united PTT planned to add 100,000 East German subscribers in 1990, 300,000 in 1991 and over a million annually thereafter. In contrast, the growth rate before unification had been approximately 60,000 subscribers per year. In addition, DBP Telekom, which needed to rely on satellite and cellular services to accommodate the extra load as the landlines were being installed, planned to add 300,000 mobile phone connections. The quick availability of cellular service relieved some of the pressure on the standard network, which experienced a 500 percent increase in traffic within eight weeks following unification (Hafner, 1990; Gärtner and Habenicht, 1990).

Before unification, consideration was very briefly given to the possibility of privatizing the PTT. While such a move could be done fairly straightforwardly through legislation (as opposed to the situation in West Germany, where privatizing the DBP would probably require a constitutional amendment), this option was not pursued. The interest in unifying the East and West German systems took precedence. Instead, the Eastern DP was merged into the Western entity. Almost all employees were retained (the exceptions were primarily the numerous secret police workers within the PTT whose major function was to wiretap calls and open letters).

Another option was to operate the East German network as a separate regional company interconnected with the Western DBP Telekom. Such an arrangement would have made the transfer of investment funds and expertise from the West to the East more difficult, though creative alternatives could have been devised. But the tradition of national monopoly was too strong for such an option to be seriously considered.

The merger of East Germany's telephone system into DBP Telekom was not a smooth one. Soon, East Germany's 130,000 postal and telecommunications employees went on strike for a more rapid equalization of pay levels. DBP Telekom, meanwhile, was asked by the government to contribute an additional 1.3 billion annually to the federal budget for four years, to help pay for the general cost of unification. This was beyond the substantial amounts that were needed to upgrade East Germany's telecommunications. It was also difficult to move West German technical employees to the East, where their skills in digital communications were needed. Another problem was how to integrate the two dozen East German private networks, a legacy of the GDR's separate ministerial and state industries' systems, into the national system. One of them was acquired by the West German chemical industry for its own use. Service upgrade in the East was slow, leading to some calls in the East for the entry of alternative service providers. In an effort to speed up development, the government initiated turnkey projects in which SEL, Bosch, DeTeWe, Deutsche Aerospace AG (Daimler-Benz), and Siemens would construct full-scale local networks in various cities. These substantial burdens gave ammunition to those traditionalists in the Bundepost and the Ministry who had never been happy about liberalization, and who could argue for slowing down its pace. Indeed, had German unification burst upon the scene only one year earlier than it did, it is probable that the entire Bundespost reform would have been put on hold. The Monopoly Commission in Bonn, on the other hand, looking at the same set of problems, advocated the relaxation of monopoly to accelerate the development in the East. Thus, the old controversies continued.

In 1991, DBP Telekom invested about $4 billion in eastern Germany, and anticipated the need for an additional $100 billion before the year 2000. These huge financial demands took place at the same time that revenue-eroding liberalization was being introduced by the telecommunications ministry for terminal equipment, value-added and mobile services, interconnection of private leased-line networks, satellite data, and even resale and switching. The company was also criticized for having some of Europe's highest rates for leased lines.

DBP Telekom, run by Helmut Ricke, a manager hired from outside the organization, responded with a massive rebalancing of tariffs, systematically reducing leased-line and long-distance rates, and raising rates for local service. It moved into value-added services, forming a joint venture with IBM. Still, the company was limited by law from certain activities, for example, directly offering service in the newly opened countries of Eastern and Central Europe. In consequence, the government in 1992 gave serious consideration to changing DBP Telekom's status, and privatizing up to 49 percent of its shares through an international offering. Such plans, unthinkable only a few years earlier, demonstrate how far the dynamics of change have taken hold in transforming Heinrich von Stefan's monolithic state instutition.

8

The United Kingdom

The Reorganization of British Telecommunications

The early history of British telecommunications, up to their nationalization in 1911, is provided in Chapter 2.

In the years following nationalization, the telephone system developed only very slowly. In 1912, the first public automatic exchange was opened; in 1916 amplification for long distance service was introduced; the Strowger switching system was adopted in 1922 and remained the mainstay well into the 1980s (Foreman-Peck, 1985, pp. 215–28). Demands for network investment were made in 1920 by a Parliamentary Select Committee, the Telephone Development Association (formed in 1924), and the Liberal party. But the General Post Office, the Treasury, and the Union of Postal Workers (though not the technical unions) resisted change until a 1932 Act of Parliament demanded reorganization. An opposition group, the "Memorialists," was formed to press for telecommunication reform. It had the support of 320 MPs. A commission was set up (the Bridgeman Inquiry) that recommended moderate change. But the Post Office maintained its inefficient structure; even in the face of a substandard system, the postmaster general declared that he could not see how additional capital could be more usefully spent.

A structural reorganization of telecommunications was accomplished only in 1969. It transformed the General Post Office from a governmental department subject to Treasury and parliamentary interventions to a more autonomous public corporation. But it also reaffirmed the Post Office monopoly over telecommunications. While Post Office autonomy was the primary objective of the 1969 Act, it remained an elusive goal because of the frequent interventions of the Conservative government that came to power shortly thereafter. Government cutbacks in capital investment as well as limitations on telecommunications tariffs forced the Post Office to operate under increasing financial strains, and to implement unpopular rate increases in 1975 (Morgan, 1987).

During that time, the Post Office's level of service also attracted strong criticism. In response, the government in 1977 commissioned another panel to propose reforms (Littlechild, 1983b). These recommendations—the Carter Report—were relatively modest: to separate the Post Office into its postal and telecommunications parts, with both still operating as monopolies. The Post Office brushed off the proposals, feeling unthreatened. But times had changed.

The traditional equipment industry–labor–rural coalition could not prevail anymore against Prime Minister Margaret Thatcher and her inner circle's determination to change the system after their electoral victory in 1979 (Locksley, 1983).

Under Thatcher, who dominated British politics through the 1980s until her fall in 1990, the right wing of the Conservative party, rather than the more moderate followers of former Prime Minister Heath, set economic policy. Their economic perspective was one of classic economic liberalism. They were alarmed by the decline of the British electronics industry; for example, Britain's share in telecommunications equipment trade had fallen from 25 percent in 1960 to 5 percent in 1980. In pursuit of economic growth, the government sought a major redirection of British industry from traditional and stagnating industries to those with a strong knowledge base—electronics, information, biotechnology—all closer to the white-collar interests of Tory followers than to the traditional smokestack firms with their unionized workforce.

There were three distinct elements to the Conservative government's telecommunications policy: (1) a separation of telecommunications from the Post Office; (2) a liberalization of terminal equipment, service competition, and enhanced services; and (3) the privatization of the public network provider.

In 1980, Sir Keith Joseph, a member of Thatcher's inner circle, announced to Parliament the government's intention to end the monopoly on telecommunications. The government soon presented a far-reaching bill that became the British Telecommunications Act 1981. The Act separated telecommunications from the Post Office and established a new state-owned corporation, British Telecom (BT), to operate telecommunications. The Act also ended the near monopoly over terminal equipment. Before 1981, the Post Office supplied, leased, and maintained nearly all telephone equipment, with the exception of PBXs of more than 100 lines. The 1981 Act maintained the supply monopoly for the first telephone set only, although that set could now be privately serviced. Terminal equipment still required technical approval from the Department of Industry, which delegated standard setting authority to the British Standards Institution (BSI). The Secretary of State for Industry appointed the British Electrotechnical Approvals Board (BEAB), which set up a laboratory, the British Approvals Board for Telecommunications (BABT), to undertake testing to determine whether consumer apparatus met BSI standards.

The 1981 Act also permitted either the Secretary of State for Industry in consultation with BT, or BT itself, to grant licenses for competitive networks. Almost immediately, and with active government prodding, a consortium including the telecommunications company Cable and Wireless (C&W), Barclay's Merchant Bank, and British Petroleum (BP) founded Mercury Communications as the first alternative carrier for long-distance network services. In time, Mercury became fully owned by C&W.

Other changes rapidly followed the Telecommunications Act 1981. The government decided to sell a majority of BT's shares, and BT itself was internally restructured as a business rather than as a civil service administration. In a White Paper announcing its intention to privatize BT, the government argued that private management would increase efficiency and permit easier access to capital markets. Run as a public corporation since 1969, BT was subject to restrictive rules on borrowing, and had to self-finance approximately 90 percent of its investments, an extremely high rate (Department of Industry, 1982). By 1982, after two years of energetic prodding, BT's per capita investment was still only two-thirds that of France's and just over half that of West Germany, and revenue per employee was $4200, compared with $4900 in France, $6200 in West Germany and $7900 in the United States (*Journal of Commerce*, 1983).

A second telecommunications bill was introduced in 1982 to implement the privatization goals of the White Paper. Although the bill was not immediately passed because of the general election, it was reintroduced after the Conservatives formed the new government.

As part of the privatization terms, the government forgave or assumed £2.9 billion of BT's long-term debts and shouldered pension obligations of £1.25 billion. Together, £4.15 billion of liabilities were taken off BT's books, a huge amount in relation to the £4 billion for which 51 percent of the entire enterprise was sold.

One of the major obstacles to privatizing BT was its sheer size. The sale of BT for about £4 billion accounted for 30 percent more than the total amount raised for *all* U.K. companies in 1983, itself a ten-year high. It was therefore feared that the floating of BT shares would disrupt the capital markets. This led briefly to the suggestion of an AT&T-style divestiture whereby BT would be sold in parts, either by function—local, long-distance, international, and business services—or along geographic lines, or both. Prime Minister Thatcher allegedly favored this idea for a brief time. In the end, 51 percent of an undivided BT was offered to the public. To assure the success of the issue, the government chose a fairly low share price. Opponents argued that the Tory strategy was to make it expensive and unpopular for the next government to renationalize BT. The Labour opposition called for a renationalization, to be financed by an exchange of shares for nonvoting bonds; their initial price would be the stock issuing price and would thus not reflect appreciation of shares.

And an appreciation there was. On the first day of its public offering, the price of BT's shares almost doubled. But the success of the public offering also had its cost in terms of subsequent policy flexibility, because it created a large constituency opposed to deregulatory actions which might reduce BT's profitability.

Prior to privatization, British Telecom had almost a quarter of a million employees, most of whom belonged to one of BT's several labor unions. The largest of these was the National Communications Union (NCU)—formerly the Post Office Engineering Union (POEU); others include the Union of Communications Workers, the Society of Telecom Executives, and several smaller unions.

BT's unions strongly opposed privatization and competition. Their opposition was based on fears that labor would bear the brunt of the 25 percent cost savings that BT's chairman, Sir George Jefferson, publicly projected for the first three-year period. The unions also felt that opening the market to competing networks was a step toward eroding BT's monopoly position and profits, in which they indirectly shared. They also stressed the negative impact on residential service and R&D and feared a change in their civil servant status. Consequently, the unions fought the licensing of a competing carrier and staged work protests against the new company. Union fears proved not unfounded. In its first year as a private company, BT reduced its staff by 17,000 employees, mostly by attrition. However, although the number of BT's employees declined, its total labor costs increased (Oftel, 1985a).

BT's unions argued that the government should reestablish the monopoly over the trunk network and the first telephone set, integrate Mercury into BT at market value, and, most importantly, maintain control of 75 percent of the company's shares. They also advocated filling 50 percent of BT's board with employee representatives, with other directors coming from consumer organizations, other industries, major users, and the government.

Oftel: The New Regulatory Framework

It would be simplistic to believe that the privatization of BT alone would make it more efficient and responsive to its customers. A public monopoly is subject to political supervision, and therefore potentially more accountable than an unrestricted private monopoly. Hence, in the absence of a competitive environment, a regulatory mechanism is essential to complement privatization. Accordingly, the government established a regulatory body to perform that function, and named it the Office of Telecommunications (Oftel).

The government also remained BT's largest shareholder, though it announced in 1991 further privatization of its shares. Though the Thatcher government promised not to assert its right as a shareholder in commercial decisions or even to vote at shareholder meetings, this promise does not bind future governments. Furthermore, the government can affect BT's actions through the Department of Trade and Industry and the Monopoly and Mergers Commission.

BT is also obligated under its license to provide universal telephone service, a public emergency system, and public coin telephones where they previously existed. It also must permit terminal equipment to be connected to its network, provided that such equipment conforms to technical standards.

Oftel is headed by a director general of telecommunications (DGT), who is appointed by the secretary of state for industry for a five-year term of office. It resembles the Federal Communications Commission in the United States but lacks the FCC's formal independent status and its power over broadcast communications. In 1988, Oftel's staff numbered 116 in comparison with the FCC's 1900, to which one should also add the American state public utility commissions' considerable personnel (The New York and California commissions, which are the largest, have more than 600 persons, though they are responsible for regulating other utilities as well. The FCC also regulates broadcasting.)

Unlike the commissions in the United States or Canada, Oftel has no direct authority to set rates and can only make recommendations. However, almost from the beginning Oftel has expanded the scope of its investigation into rate issues under its mandate to assure the provision of "good services to consumers" and to insure that BT does not abuse its monopoly power.

Oftel supervises existing licensees and makes recommendations on applications for new licenses. Licensees include British Telecom; Hull Telephone Company, the only independent local telephone company; Mercury, the new long-distance carrier; Cable & Wireless, its parent, with many international involvements; value-added networks; Vodaphone and Cellnet, the cellular service companies; and other telecommunication service providers.

Despite Oftel's activity, the Department of Trade and Industry has retained significant authority over telecommunications, including spectrum allocations, cable television, technical licensed satellites, and resale of BT capacity (S. Littlechild, communication, 1989). Customer and manufacturer concerns are also channeled to Oftel through Advisory Committees on Telecommunications in England, Scotland, and Wales (Manning, 1988).

Consumer and advocacy organizations have criticized Oftel's powers to protect consumers as inadequate, claiming that Oftel can only require BT or other communications carriers to respond to grievances. Actually, Oftel can also sue in court or alter and amend the operating license; and although Oftel's power to protect consumers directly may be limited, they are far larger than those of the earlier consumer protection body, POUNC, which had a primarily consultative role. But Oftel's procedure is not open to the public when it comes to information. British Telecom, for example, was not required to make public the information on revenues, profits, costs, and quality performance that was provided to Oftel for a determination of its price formula.

Bryan Carsberg, a professor of accounting at the London School of Economics, was appointed as the first director general of Oftel in 1984.[1] Carsberg established a more active supervision over the telecommunications industry than many expected, helping, for example, to prevent a venture between BT and IBM on value-added networks, forcing an interconnection policy on BT that was favorable to Mercury, and requiring BT to change its accounting system to make it more possible to detect cross-subsidization. However, Oftel drew criticism when it involved itself in BT's procurement practices. Carsberg recommended that BT's purchase of digital exchanges from a second source ("System *Y*") be limited to 20 percent, for at least three years. This looked like a protectionist measure that favored the "System *X*" of the British firms GEC and Plessey. In public, BT rejected Carsberg's "recommendation" for a voluntary purchase quota, though as a practical political matter it went along with the allocation.

One important initial decision involved the basic choice of regulatory technique (Littlechild, 1983a). An interministerial working group recommended linking the BT license to a maximum rate of return on capital and a specific rate of return for the local, long-distance, and international services, with a share of excess profits returned to consumers. As long as the rates of return were not exceeded, specific prices would not be subject to control. The U.S.

experience with rate-of-return regulation had demonstrated the problems of this method, including the difficulty of calculating the rate base and allowable expenses; incentives for overcapitalization (gold-plating), known as the Averch–Johnson effect; disincentives against risky investment, since they are not rewarded by a higher rate-of-return; inadequate incentives for efficient and lean operations in general; and absence of price control within broad rate of return categories. The chief economic advisor to the prime minister, Professor A. A. Walters, advocated an alternative incentive mechanism to keep prices low and raise output, under which regulators would project a five year revenue growth rate. Overfulfillment of this target would lead to a lower company tax rate, while underfulfillment would lead to a higher rate, and therefore to a penalty. Although Walter's method included no price control and made the government a de facto partner in monopoly prices, it reduced the incentive for monopolistic restrictions of output. It remains questionable, however, whether the administrative problems of this method would be less complex than those of rate-of-return regulations. Profits need to be calculated, which is always a slippery matter. Still more difficult to define is output, particularly in an industry where the number of services and their quality dimensions are large, complex, and changing.

Professor Stephen Littlechild of Birmingham University suggested as a third option substituting partial control over prices for control over profits. For those services in which BT was dominant, tariffs would be increased only by the rate of inflation, minus a specified percentage. Hence, a real reduction in telephone rates would be built into the system, based on the expectation of advancing technology and productivity. The Littlechild approach can be a useful transitional technique, since it is simpler to handle and implement than the other proposals. However, it is unlikely that the pricing of monopoly telecommunications services could continue for an extended period of time to be based on long-past prices. Any evaluation of the price formula was likely to involve reference to profitability (and eventually did). Another problem is the need to regulate service quality, since BT might seek to cut costs and raise profits through service quality deterioration. Furthermore, what should be the correct productivity offset? If it is too low, BT reaps a windfall; if it is too much, it will suffer financially. Littlechild prudently did not wish to resolve all of these questions, but proposed a five year transitional period for his method, after which the entire system would be reconsidered.

In 1983, the government, having weighed the various possibilities, accepted the recommendation. It decided eventually on a formula for overall changes, a "tariff basket" based on the retail price index (RPI) inflation rate, minus 3 percent annually for the productivity offset. Furthermore, BT assured that rates for consumers would not rise by more than 2 percent above inflation. Subsequently, the pricing formula was incorporated into BT's license.[2]

Oftel modified the price formula in 1989, raising the productivity offset from 3 percent to 4.5 percent. In discussing the proper RPI discount, Oftel tacitly admitted that price cap regulation was predicated upon rate of return calculations. BT's rate of return was consistently above the RPI from 1983 to 1989:

Year	Rate (%)
1983	19.3
1984	17.5
1985	19.2
1986	20.2
1987	21.4
1988	21.3
1989	21.6

Oftel also redefined the basket to include residential, business, domestic long-distance, and directory assistance services, and forced BT to introduce a reduced tariff for infrequent users. BT was able to retain its RPI + 2 limit on installation connection and rental charges. Critics of BT argued that rates had simply been lowered where competition from Mercury existed and raised for other customers. Local calls had risen 35 percent from 1984 to 1986 and peak rate trunk calls fell 32 percent in the same period (Gist, 1990, p. 47; Dixon, 1990b). In 1990, BT raised line rental charges 11 percent and introduced customized tariffs.

The Changing Network Environment

Cable and Wireless

With British liberalization, Cable & Wireless (C&W) became one of the most interesting telecommunications carriers in the world. Until the 1980s, it was a sleepy postcolonial governmental enterprise. But thereafter it became the first truly global telephone company, linking the world's major trading centers.

C&W, which was nationalized in 1947, used to operate Britain's international telegraph service as well as telecommunications services in many of Britain's overseas possessions. After decolonialization, the company continued to operate domestic public telecommunication services in more than two dozen countries, and the international communications of 37 countries. Many of C&W's overseas operations were joint ventures with local governments or local private interests.

In 1981, the Conservative government privatized more than half of the company; in 1985, the remainder of C&W was sold in the second largest stock sale in British history after the BT sale earlier that year.

Privatization made it possible for C&W to expand rapidly and aggressively. As a government company it needed Treasury approval to spend more than £10 million, but as a private firm it could freely invest in new projects. C&W's profits increased rapidly from £90 million on sales of £500 million in 1981, to £360 million on revenues of £1.3 billion in 1985 and £500 million in revenues of £2.2 billion in 1990.

The centerpiece of C&W's operations and profits is in Hong Kong, where it operates the franchise for international telephony and holds a controlling interest in the Hong Kong Telephone Company, of which it sold a 20 percent share in 1989. The firm also has an agreement with the People's Republic of China to upgrade the Chinese telecommunications network in the nearby provinces, in Beijing, and in the Yangtze Delta, and has a 49 percent interest in the Shenda telephone company in a Chinese special economic zone next to Hong Kong. C&W also owns 75 percent of telephone operations in Macao and operates international and domestic service in Bahrain, the commercial center of the Persian Gulf region, through a firm in which it has a 40 percent interest. In 1990, C&W had operations in forty-eight nations, including most Caribbean countries.

In the United States, C&W operates through TDX Systems and has become the fourth largest long-distance company. Another C&W activity is its joint venture PTAT for a private submarine fiber-optic cable between the United Kingdom and the United States. C&W also participates in the trans-Pacific cable venture IDC, and increased its share to 17 percent. It is also represented in domestic Japanese service through Fair-way. These pieces fit together as part of a strategy to link the four major financial centers in the world—London, New York, Tokyo, and Hong Kong—with Bahrain and Singapore as additional link-up possibilities. Aside from the PTAT and North Pacific cables, C&W also backed the Asiasat project and co-won a mobile license in Germany (Cable & Wireless, 1990, p. 8). C&W also entered in 1991 telecommunications in Sweden through the first competing public network service. Tele2 AB was owned 40 percent by Cable & Wireless and 60 percent by Kinnevik, and used fiber lines belonging to the Swedish railroad. C&W also established facilities management centers in continental Europe.

Mercury

In the U.K., C&W is the sole owner of Mercury, the alternative to BT in long-distance service. Originally, C&W's partners in Mercury were British Petroleum and Barclay's Merchant Bank. Although Mercury was modeled on the U.S. company MCI, there are great differences between the two. Whereas MCI was a small, maverick firm that entered the market by prevailing in court over the opposition of both AT&T and the federal authorities, Mercury was born with three silver spoons in its mouth and the government as its godparent. Mercury emerged through a classic insider deal rather than on the basis of competitive bidding. Furthermore, because the Conservative government staked the credibility of its telecommunications on Mercury's effectiveness, it protected the company by giving it an exclusive license to compete with BT until 1990. There are, however, similarities to MCI. Both initially stated that their intention was only to provide limited service offerings, in particular leased lines, aimed at users underserved by the monopoly. However, their ambitions grew rapidly, and they sought to gain many additional customers by interconnecting into the public network and by providing switched public domestic and international long-distance service.

Mercury's intentions raised the stakes for BT considerably. To both BT and

AT&T it seemed unfair that they should be required to let competitors use their carefully nurtured local distribution network. The notion of common carriage, however, is based on the premise that service must be provided to anyone who pays the posted price. Although British Telecom was understandably not enthusiastic about its new competition, Mercury's presence provided the basis for further liberalization of BT's operations, which was a positive prospect for the large company.

After Mercury's initial license was granted in 1982, it quickly established a microwave network service within London, and connected this network by digital microwave with Birmingham and Manchester. It also began construction of a national fiber-optic trunk system centered in Birmingham. In London it made substantial use of subway tunnels and acquired rights to lay cable through the underground cable network of the London Hydraulic Power Company.

Mercury, as a subsidiary of C&W with its substantial international presence, also established itself abroad. In 1983, it received permission to provide international service. In 1984, transatlantic service to the United States was introduced. In 1987, Mercury also penetrated the continental European market when it arranged to exchange public telecommunications traffic with Italy. This was troublesome for BT, which derived about 20 percent of its profits from international service.

To meet its switching equipment needs, Mercury went outside the traditional British manufacturers GEC and Plessey to Northern Telecom in Canada. In 1986, Mercury entered an agreement with the largest domestic computer company, ICL (through their parents C&W and STC), for a joint venture in specialized data communications and value-added services.

Although Mercury's regular license, granted in 1984, is similar to British Telecom's, it has several important differences: (1) Mercury does not have to fulfill BT's universal service obligations; (2) it does not operate a full national system and is under no obligation to do so; (3) it cannot provide maritime services other than for offshore installations; and (4) it is not price regulated.

Mercury started its public switched operations in Britain on May 15, 1986, with long-distance rates that were about 15 to 20 percent lower than BT's, despite the latter's anticipatory tariff reductions. Mercury's goal was to reach a 5 percent market share by 1990 (about £8 billion) and a much larger share of large user business.

By 1987, 37 percent of major telecommunications users in Britain were using Mercury for some of their service. Of eighteen financial institutions in the City, seventeen became Mercury customers. The share of large users in BT revenues is about 30 percent. It was not merely a matter of price: large users were seeking to be less dependent on one supplier, an important factor in a country as prone to strikes as Britain. But when it came to small and medium-sized users Mercury was lagging.

BT's primary leverage over Mercury is through interconnection into its local distribution network, and the regulatory determination of that interconnection relation is therefore critical. The question of how much BT can charge Mercury involves murky conceptual and accounting issues. Additionally, technical aspects such as the numbering system, the points of interconnection, the quality of service, the number of digits to be dialed, and so on, have to be considered. BT has some reasons to be less than fully cooperative, and Mercury has an incentive to cry wolf and seek an advantageous interconnection arrangement. Without a period of protection, Mercury argues, it could not compete with BT, and its failure would undermine the entire base of government pro-competition policy. It would be embarrassing (at least for the Conservatives) to see Mercury fail. One government minister commented:

> If we opened up to free competition, there is a danger that British Telecom would be able to wipe the floor with all the tiny competitors. We think the method of introducing a little competition begins with the Mercury rival network. It is our duty to look after Mercury, to nurse it. (Jason, 1985, p. 4)

Hence, Mercury has a certain leverage over British policy makers that is disproportionate to its economic power. With a Labour government in power, the reverse is possible and Mercury could be choked to death by "technical" regulatory decisions rather than by decisions debated and passed by Parliament.

The problem of interconnection, and the respective licenses of BT and Mercury, came before Oftel. In 1985, Bryan Carsberg decided on a framework for the interconnection of Mercury and BT, a ruling that was considered a major success for Mercury. The ruling stipulated that BT had to provide Mercury with local interconnections at both ends of a telephone connection, set the compensation that Mercury must pay BT, and established a time schedule of payment for one-half of the cost of providing the additional capacity. BT must also provide full international interconnections for Mercury.

The issue of fair interconnection is complicated. In the United States it has led to two decades of dispute and was a major issue leading to the AT&T divestiture. The Justice Department, and with it Judge Harold Greene, concluded that one could not expect a local monopoly to provide genuinely nondiscriminating access to its long-distance competitors. The divestiture established the principle of complete and equal access and allowed users to choose a "primary long-distance carrier." But the question of the cost for such access to the local network, whether by AT&T or by its competitors, precipitated fierce battles between long-distance carriers and local exchange companies, and among long-distance carriers themselves.

The issues are hardly trivial. The total of access charge payments that long-distance companies must pay to the local exchange companies can comprise more than half of their entire revenues; they are also a major source of revenue for local exchange companies (Noam, 1986). In the United States, according to some calculations, the actual cost of access to the local company was approximately $0.03 per minute, but charges to the long-distance carrier were between $0.07 and $0.08 per minute. This substantial gap exists because, in most views, long-distance calling has subsidized local telephony. In a competitive environment, a substantial markup for access above cost creates an incentive for long-distance carriers to "bypass" the local public switched network entirely and reach users directly. Especially for large users it begins to make economic sense to lease local circuits from the local telephone carrier to the long-distance carrier, which are not governed by the access line charges, or to create communication links entirely outside of the local telephone network.

At the heart of this complex matter is the question of the allocation of the joint costs, largely of a fixed nature, that are incurred to make the provision of *both* local and long-distance services possible. Conceptually and practically, the allocation between the two types of services is difficult, and in some views, arbitrary. After much dispute, the FCC decided to resolve this problem by imposing a flat-rate "user charge" to be borne by end users. In theory, this charge would be partially offset by lower long-distance charges, as carriers would pass on their savings from reduced access charges to end users. The economic logic was that since flat-rate user charges were not usage sensitive, users could not avoid them by decreasing the number of telephone calls they made through the local public switched network. Hence, it would reduce the incentive for "uneconomic" (i.e., purely regulation-induced) bypass.

A related question is whether a differentiated access charge should be set for different long-distance carriers for access to the local exchange network. (AT&T had to pay more than its competitors.) Once customers could use all carriers under equal terms, unequal access charges for different carriers appeared to be unequitable. However, because the alternative long-distance carriers did not have the economies of scale of AT&T, equal access rates could have, in effect, made them uncompetitive. Therefore, the alternative carriers asked for at least a temporary handicapping of AT&T in their favor.

Mercury reached profitability in 1989. However, its total income was 1.6 percent of BT's and its shares of international traffic (4.3 percent), inland phone calls (0.7 percent), and leased lines (7.6 percent) were miniscule. Mercury invested a total of £825 million from 1981 to 1989, less than one-third of BT's investment for the year 1990 (Arlandis and Gille, 1989).

Mercury's status was reviewed in the 1990 'duopoly review,' leading to further opening of telecommunications and to potential competition for Mercury. This review is discussed at the end of this chapter.

Value-Added Networks and Resale

After the government announced in 1980 that it intended to reduce BT's monopoly, Professor Michael Beesley of the London Business School, a transportation expert, was commissioned by the government to study the economic implications of permitting third parties to offer services over BT's network. The main focus of Beesley's inquiry was the feasibility of value-added network services (VANs) and their benefit to the customers, as well as any resultant effects on BT's pricing and profitability. Beesley expanded the analysis to include the pure resale of network capacity as well.

Beesley received many complaints that BT's monopoly had delayed new services and new technologies, such as digital technology, packet switching services, and memory telephones. The various restrictions, including the prohibition of resale and sharing, were criticized. They inhibited usages such as direct debit arrangements between customers and banks, computer access for storing and forwarding messages, and the extension of radio paging services to include storage and forwarding of messages. All these services were impossible because they required the sharing of leased circuits. BT permitted a number of value-added services as long as they did not require private switching or compete with BT's actual or planned services. Other proposed services, however, were turned down. In Beesley's views, these restrictions were only the tip of the iceberg because innovative services do not flourish in the abstract; they await opening of the rules under which business can take place (Beesley, 1981).

BT estimated that unconstrained reselling of capacity would result in a net loss of revenue from domestic calls of £30 million for 1984–1985. With more generous assumptions for potential "cream skimming," it calculated a net revenue loss of £110 million. If these figures are taken as the lower and upper ranges, they represent between 0.4 percent and 1.5 percent of BT's gross revenues and between 3.2 percent and 12 percent of its profit. A 12 percent reduction of profit is hardly a small loss. Beesley, however, did not share this apprehension, for he believed those estimates to be very "vulnerable." Even using BT's estimate, Beesley found that revenue loss would amount at the maximum to only £6.4 per residential customer, a loss that would be offset by about an 11 percent increase in the residential rate. This would, however, be accompanied by gains to consumers in reduced long-distance rates and by potential innovations in services. Beesley concluded that resale should be permitted without use restriction because it would encourage ingenuity in meeting customers' demands with favorable effects on productivity and exports.

Beesley also expanded the analysis to international service. BT was highly sensitive on this issue, considering the great profit contribution of international traffic. One study estimated that a hypothetical London to New York private satellite link would cost £5300 per year, in contrast with the BT tariff for such a connection of about £50,000. For approximately the same distance, a leased line coast-to-coast in the United States costs £4500 per year, again less than one-tenth of BT's price. The pricing of international calls seemed to be close to its revenue maximizing high. According to Beesley, for a three-minute U.S.-to-U.K. call the mean expected elasticity was -0.936. For a U.K.-to-U.S. calls, it was -1.094. These figures are close to the maximizing 1.0, which indicates revenue vulnerability to a price reduction induced by competition or resale.

Beesley recommended easing all restrictions on the offering of all services on the BT network, including resale. He further recommended that constraints on BT's pricing be reduced or eliminated so that rates could move toward costs. BT, in turn, should be free to enter nonvoice markets as a competitor, provided safeguards were in place to prevent unfair competition. Domestically, leased rates ought not to discriminate on the basis of total usage. Internationally, however, differentiated rates could be instituted. And this liberalization, Beesley argued, should be seen in the context of a possible rival entry into transmission and switching, which he advocated.

BT opposed the recommendations of the Beesley Report, pointing again to revenue losses. BT's chairman, Sir George Jefferson, conceded that "change in the way telecommunications services are provided in Britain is inevitable; BT is not seeking to preserve the status quo . . .'' (British Telecom, 1981). But he also warned that ''precipitate implementation of the Beesley recommendations [would] cause irreversible damage . . . Further detailed studies are necessary.''

In addition, BT waved a warning flag in the direction of equipment manufacturers: ''British Telecom is concerned about the possible impact on its suppliers . . . If it is faced with the competition from separate networks, it may be unable, as a result of the activities of its competitors to make long term decisions that support the British national telecommunications industry'' (British Telecom, 1981).

In July 1981, the government partly accepted the recommendations and announced that it would permit private suppliers of VANs to receive licenses but that it would not presently permit the resale of leased line capacity, since this could undermine universal service. The government did provide, however, for the possibile resale in the future.

In 1984, the government changed course by deciding that resale of services would be permitted after July 1989. In the meantime, it liberalized the leasing of shared capacity on privately owned networks and the third-party use of private circuits, thus coming close to resale.

In 1989, the DTI approved an Oftel report that allowed simple resale of capacity leased from BT, Mercury, or Hull. The United Kingdom was the first European nation to allow leased line resale. DTI began issuing licenses to private network operators and lifted restrictions on the number of connections to other private networks. British Rail, Istel, and Racal quickly established virtual network services, private pay phones, and other services on their leased lines. In response, BT raised leased-line tariffs by 11 percent.

Even the Post Office returned to offering telecommunications services. It started National Network (Natnet) to resell 30 percent of the capacity on its own private network. The Post Office network carries 12 million calls yearly from 25,000 users and 4500 terminals to 200 locations throughout the United Kingdom (*The Economist,* 1990a; Purton, 1990).

Beesley had indicated the difficulties in distinguishing simple resale from value-added services. In the United States, where the FCC's First, Second, and Third Computer Inquiries grappled with a related problem, experience demonstrated the fluidity of the separation. The British approach to VAN licensing has been to try to proceed pragmatically, without getting into philosophical or semantic disputes. VANs are required to offer more than just transmission. The question of whether packet switching could be considered a value-added service was particularly controversial. Against the opposition of BT, the government recognized packet switching as a value-added service, thus allowing licensed competitors to provide this service.

The primary British regulatory structure is based on the separation of the two categories of service: ''basic conveyance'' and all other services, which are defined as ''value-added.'' The definition of basic conveyance service is ''the conveyance of a message by means of a telecommunications system to a single destination . . . in the same form that it was received without any additional services having been provided . . ." (Department of Trade and Industry, 1985, p. 16). Drawing on the experience of other countries, especially the United States, the government wisely regarded its definitions as only temporary.

More specific rules for VANs were set in 1982 (Department of Trade and Industry, 1985). By February 1987, 841 VANs were licensed, operated by 221 different companies (Department of Trade and Industry, 1987). Of these, the most popular were store and retrieve systems (112), mailboxes (90), protocol conversion between incompatible computers and terminals (90), customers' databases (66), deferred transmission (63), user management packages (58), viewdata videotex services (62), wordprocessor/facsimile interfacing (46), multiaddressing routing (56), and speed and code conversion between incompatible terminals (49). Other VANs include automatic ticket reservations, conference calls, long-term archiving, secure delivery services, telesoftware, and text editing.

VANs with a volume of more than £250,000 per year were subject to rules that prevent the establishment of a dominant market position. These limitations were aimed at BT and IBM. Under its license, BT must provide services nationwide, unlike some of its VAN competitors. BT is also subject to rules that prevent a cross-subsidy of its VANs out of its other services.

In 1986, the VAN rules were further modified to encompass managed data networks, which had thrown the separation between basic service and VANs into disarray, thus illustrating the complications of partial liberalization and partial approval requirements. The legislation was again changed in 1987 when the VANs license was replaced by the Class License for Value Added and Data Services (VADS). Under the new classification, those wishing to run under license from Oftel, other than major service providers, need no longer register with Oftel.

In 1984, BT and IBM teamed up and announced their intention to establish a joint VAN venture for data network management services, and applied for a value-added license under the name JOVE. This set off a strong domestic protest in Britain, and about 100 computer and communications companies registered their opposition. They were concerned with the reliance on IBM's SNA architecture, which they feared would threaten British industry and government development toward an open systems interconnection (OSI). The two partners argued that their venture allowed for an OSI protocol standard, but by then the opposition had grown to a clamor. There was also much concern expressed about the feasibility of competition if two dominant firms in closely related markets were permitted to link together. With Britain actively introducing competition into its telecommunications and computer fields, the government felt that such a move would have been counterproductive. Not only would it make competitive entry more complicated, but it would remove the potential rivalry between IBM and BT.

Other critics of the JOVE venture feared that it would permit IBM to achieve some measure of control over BT. They pointed out that IBM-UK had six employees in 1951 and 16,000 by 1984 (Bird and Huxley, 1984). Given the determined opposition, the British government, through the Department of Trade and Industry, rejected the application in October 1984 but left the door open for either company to offer such services on its own.

In response to JOVE, several other VAN operators consolidated. The United Kingdom's two leading competitors, ICL and General Electric Information Services, merged their VAN operations into International Network Services Limited (INS) in 1987. In 1989, one of the United Kingdom's largest VAN operators, Istel, was acquired by AT&T.

Hull Telephone Department

The Hull Telephone Department (HTD), the only independent local telephone company in Britain, received its original license in 1902 to operate in an area already served by the private National Telephone Company. Four years later, Hull Telephone was the only municipal company that resisted acquisition by the Post Office. The offer was rejected by the Hull chairman's tie-breaking vote. In 1914, Hull Telephone purchased the National Telephone Company plant from the Post Office and has renewed its original license every twenty to thirty years since then. With the privatization of British Telecom and the creation of Oftel in 1984, a new regulatory system was established, and Hull received another twenty-five-year license. Hull as a city, and with it HTD operation, is controlled by the Labour party. In the first eighty years of its existence, HTD had only four general managers, all of them exhibiting unusual political longevity.

Hull Telephone is officially known as the City of Kingston-upon-Hull Telephone Department. It serves a population of 375,000 with a total of 128,000 lines and fourteen telephone exchanges. The company has semielectronic exchanges and digital System X switches. Its main exchange is located adjacent to the British Telecom exchange to which it is connected through a hole in the wall.

In contrast to the United States, local service in Hull is not subsidized from long-distance revenues that originate in its territory. Originally, Hull Telephone paid 10 percent of its revenues to the Post Office and retained 5 percent of the trunk and international revenues that it initiated. After 1979, both types of charges were eliminated and Hull instead paid the government a license fee of £150,000 per year. After liberalization and BT privatization, Hull still pays a license fee and has negotiated with British Telecom for a different division of revenue involving both companies. Hull customers have split usage of long distance service fairly evenly between BT and Mercury, offering a potential model for the rest of Britain.

HTD telephone service has been cheaper than that of BT; Hull provided an unlimited local call at 5 pence in 1985, whereas BT provided for that price local service ranging between thirty seconds and two minutes, depending on the time of day. Hull's fee for residential line rental per year was £50, and £84 for businesses, compared to £65 and £102 for BT (*The Economist*, 1985). Hull's local service is profitable, in contrast to BT's. But it is cheaper to provide local service in a city of Hull's size than in rural areas.

Cellular Telephony

With Oftel especially concerned about competition in new service, mobile radio received special attention. Professor Bryan Carsberg was interested in protecting new services offerings against BT dominance and concluded that "BT should not be a network operator, either directly or indirectly, or have more than a minority share in providers of service for new p.m.r. [public mobile radio] networks." A public telecommunications operator running a public mobile radio system would have "unmatchable advantages over competing systems" (Oftel, 1985b, p. 2).

After applications were solicited, licenses were granted to two providers, Cellnet and Vodaphone, with the obligation to cover almost the entire country by 1989. Cellnet is a consortium of BT and Securicor, a security services company that had also been active in telemetry services; Vodaphone is a joint venture of Racal, Millicom, and Hambros. The competitive structure that had been set up gave advantages to early starters, and the two companies rushed headlong into the service. Cellular telephone service became operational in 1985, drawing a very strong demand.

Cellnet and Vodaphone, however, cannot sell directly to users, they must go through service providers who resell to the public in return for a commission of approximately 15 percent. The terms for dealing with these service providers must be published and must be equal for all, with the exception that the terms can be volume-related. For service providers, the commission is approximately 15 percent. In practice, the principals of the two cellular telephone operations set up their own independent retail service providers to deal with the public: BT established BT Mobile Phone, and Racal set up Racal Vodac. Importantly, however, these companies cannot receive advantages over other service providers. Service providers are allowed to market both networks; and resellers, in turn, can employ independent agents for transactions (Fuller and Mitchell, 1986). In 1987, there were about fifty reselling organizations, including established firms such as Marconi and Motorola. Also involved in the sale or resale of equipment and installation was a legion of local agents, ranging from garages and telephone stores to office equipment suppliers. This structure permitted the emergence of vigorous competition, although mostly for equipment packages rather than for "air time" tariffs. Because the retailers share in the profits from cellular phone calls, they often sell equipment at low cost to increase the subscriber base. In 1990, mobile phones were available for as little as $300. There were 650,000 subscribers.

In the competition between the two network operators, Cellnet started with the significant advantage of BT's resources, an established telephone network, and existing mobile telecommunications operations with an established customer base. With the privatization of BT, it also had the good will of millions of British shareholders. Racal's Vodaphone, on the other hand, was an unknown entity. Its advertising slogan was "Racal—the largest company you've never heard of" (Raggett, 1986).

The relation between two companies moved from hostility to cooperation, partly because there was enough business for both companies' services in the initial phase. BT provides interconnection service for Vodaphone, thus creating a delicate relationship. In the technical field, the companies must cooperate to achieve the required full cellular interconnection that would permit "roaming" between the two systems. By 1990 there were nearly 800,000 cellular users, the second highest number in Europe behind Sweden, split evenly between Cellnet and Vodaphone. Each had invested some £200–300 million in their networks and each was gaining 15,000 new subscribers monthly. Even with success in gaining subscribers, there was substantial user criticism with the performance of Racal (22 percent dissatisfaction in a survey) and Cellnet (32 percent dissatisfaction.

In 1989, the United Kingdom moved to the forefront of mobile communications by licensing two entirely new forms of operation, Telepoint and PCN. Telepoint or CT-2 (cordless telephone second generation) consists of hand-held units that can be used within 200 meters of a base station.

Telepoint service operators install low-cost base stations ($180–$500, depending on estimate). In 1988, the DTI awarded four Telepoint licenses to Ferranti, Phonepoint (BT, France Télécom, STC, NYNEX, and the German DBP), Callpoint (Mercury, Motorola, and Shaye), and BYPS Comms (Barclays, Philips, and Shell).

CT-2 employs a frequency division multiple access system, as opposed to the EC's Digital European Cordless Telecommunications (DECT) standard, which uses time division multiplexing and which was especially promoted by Ericsson. The DTI asked for the European Telecommunications Standards Institute (ETSI) to determine the appropriate standard, GSM or DECT, for the U.K. system after operators were unable to reach an agreement (Green, 1990b).

Personal Communications Networks (PCN), is another form of mobile communications. It employs very small mobile transceivers (though at low power, with less reach and less mobility than cellular).

DTI received eight applications for PCN service and granted licenses to three consortia in 1989: Mercury PCN (C&W, Motorola, and Telefónica), BAe (British Aerospace, Millicom, PacTel, and Sony), and Unitel (STC, Thorn EMI, US West, and the DBP). BT's Cellnet and Racal's Vodaphone did not receive licenses but will be allowed to configure their systems for PCNs. Each consortium aimed to invest $1–$2.5 billion for service available by 1992 (Sims, 1989; Oftel, 1990a, p. 1).

Optimistic projections of 12–30 million Telepoint and PCN users by the year 2000 were quickly scaled back. For Telepoint, only 3500 transmitters were installed in 1990, compared with 86,000 public call boxes and 358,000 private pay phones (Lynch and Hayes, 1990). By 1991, Telepoint had proved to add

little value to existing cellular service, and all but one of the operators had
gone out of business. PCN did not fare much better. PCN figures were adjusted
downwards and yearly losses were foreseen until the turn of the century.

Cable Television as a Telecommunications Carrier

Cable television policy in the United Kingdom is dealt with in the companion
volume on European television. However, the effects of cable television and
broadband transmission on the telephone system and its providers will be briefly
discussed here.

Traditional telephone and cable television transmission cross paths in two
ways. First, broadband cable systems have the potential to be used for the
distribution of traditional and new telephone services. Mercury had unspecified
plans to use local cable networks to link customers to its long-distance system.
To the extent that arrangements such as these are possible, competitive local
distribution may emerge (Noam, 1982).

To provide more than fixed line service, cable distribution requires some
switching ability, such as a star network architecture, as opposed to the tree-
and-branch systems in cable television. In its 1983 specification for cable licenses, the British government required that a certain number of cable franchises
were to be in the star configuration. This proved to be a decision that undermined the prospective viability of many proposed cable systems. The second
way in which cable television and the traditional telephone services overlap is
through BT's own role in the installation and operation of cable systems. Such
involvement in cable television is in marked contrast to the United States (Noam,
1985).

In defining the role of BT (and to a lesser extent of Mercury) in cable television transmission, the government was faced with a dilemma. On the one
hand, if BT and Mercury were to be granted an active role in laying cable and
in local operation even on a common-carrier basis, BT's power would be increased even further, and thus the entry of new telecommunications carriers
and services would be less likely. On the other hand, the availability of the
two companies as actual or potential operators would put pressure on all other
companies for efficient performance and could also lead to cabling of marginal
areas. The government adopted a compromise position. It permitted the entry
of BT and Mercury, either independently or in consortia with other companies
as potential licensees. Because of the centralized licensing mechanism, it was
quite unlikely that British Telecom would receive a predominant number of the
licenses, at least under a Conservative government, even if it could point to
some superior economies.

At the same time, the government sought to protect BT and Mercury's traditional lines of business from competition by cable operators, because this
would tend to have a negative effect on the national public system and weaken
Mercury's position as the "official" competitor to BT. Cable operators are
permitted to offer a variety of interactive services, but voice and much of data
communications remained exclusively the domain of BT, Mercury, and Hull.

Similarly, data communications in major business centers are the exclusive province of the three carriers, although a cable operator could offer them in conjunction with BT and Mercury. In 1987, Oftel granted temporary licenses to two cable television companies to offer telephone service in cooperation with Mercury Communications. The role of cable carriers became an even more interesting question after many cable franchises were granted in 1989 and 1990 to American phone companies such as NYNEX, US West, and PacTel, which proposed to offer basic telephone service and interconnect cable networks without using BT or Mercury networks. At the same time, Mercury and BT were pressing for the right to offer cable TV service. The government's 1991 White Paper increased cable companies' flexibility in telecommunications. It also kept BT out of their turf until at least 1997.

Britain Breaches the European Cartel

Britain's liberalization policy put the United Kingdom into conflict with its partners in the European Economic Community and the European Conference on Post and Telecommunications (CEPT), the organization of European PTTs. This conflict was exemplified in the "British Telecom Case" before the European Court, a case that illustrates the British dilemma of reconciling its European role while pursuing a telecommunications policy somewhat different from its partners.

Britain had about 100 private message forwarding agencies, which receive or transmit telex messages from customers who themselves do not have a telex subscription (Dumey, 1983). At first operating only within the United Kingdom, several agencies then expanded their message relaying service into continental Europe, North America, and Asia. This was profitable because British Telecom's international telex rates were quite low, particularly to North America, creating an incentive for continental European users to route their telex traffic via London when sending their telex messages across the Atlantic. Initially, firms went directly through their British subsidiary's office if they had one. For users without related U.K. branches, the telex forwarding agencies started to fulfill the same function. In some instances, the agencies offered superior service, including a money-back guarantee if the message was not transmitted within a certain time.

The PTTs, facing the loss of revenue and an emerging competitive price regime, fought back by mustering the rules of CEPT and the CCITT that "harmonize" the PTTs behavior. CCITT telegram recommendations required PTTs to block telegram and telex messages that were sent to forwarding agencies for transmission in order to "evade" full charges of the complete route. In 1975, the British Post Office, still operating under the traditional policy guidelines, clamped down on the forwarding agencies and required messages to be charged a rate by the forwarding agencies equal to the tariff that would have been paid for a direct telex route bypassing the United Kingdom. But it was impossible to enforce this provision. The telex bureaus had no incentive to check on rates between third countries. In early 1978, the provision was dropped. It was, however, replaced by other and stricter rules prohibiting telex agencies from providing international services for their customers altogether when messages were in data form (from computer to computer) and were received through the telephone lines and then converted to telex, facsimile, or other visual form.

One of the telex agencies lodged a formal complaint with the Commission of the European Communities in June 1979. Proceedings took place in 1980, while the British government reorganized its telecommunications system and set up British Telecom. BT at first maintained the previous prohibitions. The case before the European Commission therefore proceeded, and the decision was announced in December 1982 (*Official Journal, L360*, 1982, p. 36). In its decision, the commission found BT's rules to be a violation of Article 86 of the Treaty of Rome. Ironically, however, BT had withdrawn these restrictions two months earlier, in light of Britain's changed attitude toward service competition; the issue was thus moot as far as the British situation was concerned.

In its decision, the commission found that the Post Office, and later BT, had abused their position as a statutory monopoly. The 1976 restrictions would have required telex agencies to discriminate in their rates for equivalent transactions according to the country of the customer or the country of destination. The 1978 restriction was similarly discriminatory, because it prohibited telex traffic both to and from countries, including EEC members. It also found that the prohibition of use of a combined telephone line and telex link for computer data transmission imposed restrictions on the development of a new market and new technologies, as well as on the efficient use of existing facilities, thus restricting interstate European trade.

The British government, when it was still opposing the telex bureaus, used Article 90(2) of the Treaty of Rome in its defense, contending that this section exempted public enterprises from the EEC competition rules. That section, however, contains a broad principle that applies competitive rules of the treaty to public monopolies where important services of "general economic interest" are at stake. Hence, where the PTT's obligation is to cooperate with other PTTs, the commission found that the "development of trade must not be affected to such an extent that it is contrary to the interest of the community," even if this resulted in the inability of the PTT to fulfill its duties. Thus, the limitation of Article 90(2) did not apply.

Though the court ruled against BT's provisions of 1976 and 1978, it imposed no fine, taking a number of factors into account: BT had acted originally under the pressure of other European PTTs; it had not profited by these rules in the sense of additional revenues; and it had suspended and not enforced the prohibition during the commission proceedings (Dumey, 1983).

Thus, the commission announced that the restraints upon telecommunications services, even when undertaken within a concerted European policy, were in violation of the European antitrust provisions. This could have been the end of the story, but the commission's principle was too important to be left unchallenged. The British government, by now firmly embarked on a course of liberalization and possibly coveting the role of London as a communications hub, was in no mood to appeal the decision, but other European countries were. The Italian government therefore took up the defense of BT's lost virtue and challenged the commission's decision before the European Court of Justice (case 41–83) in an appeal that had implications far beyond telecommunications. It was the first time that a Common Market member state had appealed a decision of the commission in an individual competition case. Moreover, it was the first time that a member state appealed a decision that concerned a company over which it did not have direct jurisdiction.

The Italian government made several arguments. It claimed that BT's actions were part of the exercise of legislative power, rather than entrepreneurial activity, it claimed that these activities were regulatory and public law activities essential to BT to accomplish the task of providing telecommunications services domestically and internationally. Furthermore, Italy argued that BT, as a member of the ITU, was required to implement international regulations adopted by the ITU (such as the 1947 Atlantic City Convention) such that international agreements must be honored even if the effects were contrary to the EEC treaty rules. Furthermore, according to Article 222, the treaty "does not prejudice the system of property ownership within the Member States." Italy argued that the legality of BT's action in its capacity as monopoly could not be brought into question without questioning the legality of the monopoly itself. Instead, the claim continued, the British government needed to protect itself from unfair competition by cream-skimming enterprises that jeopardized the economic integrity of the telecommunications systems.

The commission had declared the regulations against telex message forwarding to be anticompetitive and in violation of Article 86 of the Treaty of Rome. In response, Italy argued that the Community's competition rules did not apply to monopoly telecommunications services authorities and that regulatory activities of public companies should not be considered as an activity of an "undertaking" within the meaning of Article 86.

The European High Court of Justice announced its decision in March 1985, two years after the case was appealed to it and ten years after BT's regulations of 1975 and 1976 (Court of Justice of the European Communities, 1985). The court firmly rejected all of Italy's claims, thus putting an end to the legal attempt to block third-party traffic in telex. In all likelihood, similar arbitrage services by a European country functioning as a communications hub will thus be upheld against PTT cartel prohibitions.

The Equipment Sector

The British telecommunications service monopoly was traditionally closely linked with the country's equipment industry. In consequence, the industry took a decidedly unenthusiastic view of the liberalization and privatization of its main customer, British Telecom.

A tradition of oligopoly pervaded the early history of British equipment manufacturing. Before 1920, cable procurements by the Post Office were allocated among themselves by the members of a cartel, the Telephone Cable Manufacturers Association (TCMA) (Foreman-Peck, 1985, p. 224). In the 1920s, cartel agreements were reached with the Post Office to limit the number of orders submitted to companies outside of the association's members. Later, during the Depression, the Post Office pressured TCMA members to reduce prices and cost by concentrated production. The TCMA, in return, asked for a ten year supply agreement and a promise not to go outside of the cartel, which was agreed upon.

Similar market-stabilizing arrangements were made for switching equipment. After World War I, the GPO decided to concentrate on the Strowger system produced by the Automatic Electric Company. Four companies—AEC, STC, Siemens (Britain), and GEC—entered into an agreement to share orders during the years 1923–1928. In 1928, the four companies committed themselves to a "bulk supply" agreement for another five years, at prices already agreed upon. A committee of the manufacturers themselves determined the various manufacturing quotas. Similar bulk supply agreements (BSAs) existed for other types of equipment. When they were abandoned, the effects on procurement prices were often dramatic. For example, when the BSA for batteries was abandoned for competitive contracts in 1956, prices fell by almost 50 percent. Similarly, when the BSA for telephone cords was abolished in 1953, prices decreased by more than 50 percent within five years. The BSAs also had the effect of reducing incentive for research and development, since the market shares were already fixed.

In the 1960s, the Post Office Engineering Union (POEU) issued a report entitled *The Telephone Ring,* which described the cartel of British equipment manufacturers (the "ring") and the decline of telephone exports from Britain. The report pointed out that telephone dials made by ring companies cost almost twice as much as the same dial made by a continental European company.

More recently, the protective impact of the BT supply monopoly, which has kept prices high, has also been obvious in the PBX market. Prior to liberalization of PBXs with less than 100 lines, the cost of a PBX line in London was £650, compared to £200 in Dublin for similar equipment (Stapley, 1981). Monopoly also affected diversity. When BT chose not to compete in the market for PBXs above 100 lines, a wide array of products became available.

BT's newly independent equipment practices were viewed with apprehension by the manufacturing firms. The Telephone Equipment Manufacturers Association (TEMA) accused BT of a variety of unfair trade practices (*Connections,* 1985). When BT announced its intention to purchase the Canadian PBX maker Mitel, TEMA vociferously opposed this vertical integration into manufacturing and argued to the Monopolies and Mergers Commission, with some justification, that it would strengthen BT's power in terminal equipment and threaten British PBX manufacturers. Against the advice of Oftel, the commission nevertheless recommended an approval of the merger, albeit with some tough conditions attached: structural separation, absence of cross subsidies, and no BT purchases from Mitel for the public network or for supply to end users at least until 1990. But even these conditions were softened by the government when it approved the merger, though with a ceiling on procurement from Mitel. BT promised not to acquire more Mitel equipment for the public network than it had bought in 1985 in terms of value. Since PBX prices have fallen, however, this amount has actually permitted a quantitative increase. In 1989, the DTI allowed BT to increase its procurement of PBXs from Mitel. Mitel's financial performance kept deteriorating, and British Telecom eventually tried to sell it, although it found no buyers after two years of efforts.

In response to complaints from manufacturers that equipment liberalization was being slowed by lengthy approval procedures, Oftel convened the Birtwistle Committee, which in 1987 suggested eliminating any mandatory test. BT opposed these changes. Even after CPE equipment and handsets were liberalized, BT controlled 70 percent of the U.K. market for equipment.

The General Electric Company (GEC) is the largest electrical and electronics company in the United Kingdom (Locksley, 1982). Traditionally, it has had strong ties with the government through its telecommunications, electric generation, and defense procurement, and it is British Telecom's major supplier. GEC is involved in the development of the System X digital switch, and it markets private PBXs, partly using the technology of Northern Telecom and NEC. The company also designs and manufactures semiconductor components and electronic office equipment. GEC also sought entry into cable television franchise operations.

Plessey is the second major telecommunications equipment manufacturer. It was the lead developer of the System X digital switching system. The company is also active in the defense aerospace industries and in microelectronic components. Other Plessey products include satellite ground terminals, radio relay systems, telex, packet switching systems, and coin-operated telephones. It acquired the American switching manufacturer Stromberg-Carlson, subsequently controlled by Siemens, and is a part owner of Scientific-Atlanta, a major American producer of satellite and cable television equipment.

In 1985, Plessey's profits declined dramatically. At the same time, the company had to carry the losses of Stromberg-Carlson. It sought a major American military communications procurement order, jointly with Rockwell International, and even persuaded Prime Minister Thatcher to raise the matter personally with President Reagan. What Mrs. Thatcher reportedly had not been told was that the Plessey/Rockwell bid was almost twice as high as the bid submitted by the U.S. firm GTE with the French Thomson-CSF. Plessey consequently lost the bid.

Plessey's major headache was the digital exchange System X, jointly developed with GEC. System X development had cost £800 million and was far behind schedule.

In 1985, GEC offered about $1.7 billion in a takeover bid for its rival Plessey. Plessey resisted and counterproposed its taking over GEC's System X operations. Both companies argued that all they wanted was to end duplication of telecommunications equipment development. Overall, GEC was in a much better position, with a large cash surplus and a strong management team headed by Lord Weinstock. GEC was four times larger then Plessey, with an annual revenue of £8.9 billion and 165,000 employees, compared to Plessey's £2.1 billion annual revenue and 37,000 employees.

GEC's bid for Plessey divided the government. Both GEC and the Department of Trade and Industry argued that it would require a large company to compete in world markets. But the Monopolies and Mergers Commission and the Ministry of Defense—a major customer—objected. The commission concluded that although the merger would result in cost savings for System X production, it would reduce competition for PBX transmission equipment and traffic control systems. Moreover, the commission found that the System X rationalization could be achieved without a full-scale merger between the firms, but with a merger of only the System X part of their business. Based on a more sober assessment of the export potential, it found excess capacity in System X production and did not believe that the loss of competition between these two System X manufacturers would outweigh the cost savings of rationalization. Thus, it virtually recommended a joining of System X interests, but opposed approval of the overall merger (Monopolies and Mergers Commission et al., 1986). Plessey and GEC's telecommunications interests subsequently merged in 1987 to become GPT. Both companies maintained equal ownership in the joint venture.

In early 1989, GEC itself became the target of merger talks, with various interested parties involved in purchase discussions, including Plessey, STC, Siemens, and others. Later that year, GEC combined with Siemens in a successful hostile takeover of Plessey, despite protests from its largest customer, BT. Hostile takeovers in Europe are extremely rare. Political concerns were also raised over Plessey's defense contracts and radar systems falling under Siemens' control. Siemens was expected to gradually phase out GPT's System X technology, and the partnership was not an easy one.

The other major telecommunications equipment supplier is the Standard Telephone Company (STC), for many years a subsidiary of ITT (Young, 1983). STC was originally the British manufacturing outpost of AT&T. In 1925, it was sold to ITT, at that time a fledgling outfit of two Virgin Islands brothers with great ambitions. AT&T was under pressure in the United States for having international operations that, it was claimed, were subsidized by U.S. telephone subscribers. A deal was struck for $30 million, the same price for which the United States had purchased the Virgin Islands only eight years earlier. The name of the British subsidiary company was changed to Standard Telephone and Cable, Ltd. STC became a mainstay of British telecommunications manufacturing. One of its specialties is submarine cables, where the company holds a large share of the world market. It designs, manufactures, and installs these cables and has moved into use of fiber-optic technology. The company also has a major presence in maritime radio.

In the 1970s and 1980s, successive parts of STC were offered by ITT to the public, and by 1982 ITT's stake was only 35 percent and STC had become, at least briefly, a British-controlled company. ITT withdrew partly because it needed the money for operations and acquisitions and partly because STC had always been seen as an American Trojan horse, a liability in a politicized business such as telecommunications equipment. The company minimized the public visbility of its ITT connection.

With Plessey and GEC, STC was a partner in the original development consortium for the digital-exchange System X. But it was later dropped, partly because of its American ties and the conflicts with the ITT System 12. In recompense, it received a large contract for the less advanced TXE4 switches.

In 1984, STC acquired the major British computer manufacturer ICL for about $550 million after quietly buying up about 10 percent of the shares and then bidding for the company. The British government feared that significant British computer technology would leak into the United States through ITT. Thus, a separation of technology sharing was arranged. STC's acquisition of ICL was also sensitive since ICL represented the British government's major efforts of promoting a British computer industry. Only three years earlier, the British government provided ICL with a £200 million loan guarantee to rescue it. It also favored this company in British governmental procurement contracts. Part of ICL's problem was to move from being a classical technology-driven firm to a demand-oriented firm concentrating on specialized systems.

To finance the ICL acquisition, STC issued securities which dropped disastrously from 190 pence in the spring of 1985 to 86 pence a few weeks later. Amid the unfavorable publicity from the London financial community, STC's chairman and chief executive resigned. Northern Telecom acquired first 27 percent of STC, and the rest of the firm in 1990. It then sold 80 percent of ICL for £743 million to Japan's Fujitsu.

Thorn-EMI is another main electronics manufacturer. In the equipment market, in partnership with the Swedish manufacturer L. M. Ericsson, it offered Ericsson's AXE switch. That switch, modified as "System Y," became the second source for BT, next to the System X. BT chose Thorn-Ericsson to ensure itself a consistent supply of switches and to exert competitive pressure on its System X suppliers, GEC and Plessey. Thorn-Ericsson emerged from a pool of eight international candidates to fill this role.

Telecommunications Services

The introduction of Marconi's wireless telegraphy around the turn of the century greatly worried those who held shares in British submarine cables. The Post Office, which after 1889 operated submarine cables between Britain and its European neighbors, also felt negative effects. In an effort to forestall the development of radio, the Wireless Telegraphy Act of 1904 was passed, prohibiting installation and operation of wireless telegraphy stations without license by the postmaster general. Although proponents of the Act claimed they were acknowledging the importance of wireless to national security, it is clear that the government feared the emergence of a new monopoly, which it would then have to purchase. An application in 1905 by the private General International Telegraph and Telephone company for a commercial license for wireless service within Britain was refused because it was in direct competition with the government telegraph monopoly. The government eventually signed agreements with the Marconi interests for wireless transmission to North America and Italy. In 1920, long-distance ship-to-shore radio telegraph service was introduced; in 1927, long-wave radio telephone service to the United States was begun; and in 1932, ultra-shortwave radio telephone links were put into domestic service.

Following World War II, Britain greatly increased its international telecommunications links. In 1956, the first transatlantic telephone cable connected Britain with Canada. Six years later, the first satellite ground station was opened to connect with Telstar. Domestic direct-dial long-distance service was introduced in 1958, and in 1963, international direct-dial service was introduced. In 1976, the first TXE4, a large electronic telephone exchange, began operating. Two years later, Europe's first fiber optic cable link was installed as an integral part of the public network. International traffic accounts for 1.3 percent of U.K. revenues and nearly doubled from 1983 to 1988. The most frequently called nation is the United States which receives 23.3 percent of calls, far ahead of Germany (10.9 percent) and France (9.5 percent) (Staple, 1990, p. 30).

Given its island location, it is not surprising that Britain is a major user of submarine cable. In 1986, there were twenty-five cables operating between Britain and the Continent. The first submarine fiber-optic cable began service in 1985 between the United Kingdom and Belgium, and operating at 280 Mbps. Seven submarine cables connect Britain with the Irish Republic, the Channel Isles and other offshore islands. Britain also has two cables to Canada, two cables to the United States, and shares five other cables to the United States.

From the beginning, Britain was a primary site for satellite communications. A satellite earth station was constructed in Goonhilly, selected for its far western location—important for the earlier low-altitude satellite. The Goonhilly station aerials are vast, up to 30 meters in diameter. A second station, Madley, is even larger. For both locations, Marconi was the prime contractor.[3]

The main data service on the public switched network is Datex, which has medium speed. Packet switching was introduced in 1981. Private circuits for high-bit rate digital services exist under the names of Kilostream, Megastream, and Satstream. With Finland, BT was the first in Europe to implement videotex, which is described in greater detail in Chapter 36. But in 1990, only 95,000 terminals were hooked up to BT's Prestel system, and 55 percent of those connections were by business users (Woollacott, 1990b, p. 41). BT was first with videoconferencing and was an early entrant into third-party-provided mass message service. Public facsimile service is offered via Bureaufax in cooperation with the Post Office.

Among European countries, Britain has the lowest cost for the lease of a private circuit from Europe to the United States. A 1985 study found the line cost to be twice as high in West Germany as in the United Kingdom, £48,000 versus £24,000 (Garnham, 1985). By 1990 the gap had narrowed somewhat, with the cost of a voice-grade circuit over 50 percent higher to Germany than to the United Kingdom.

BT began ISDN service on a trial basis in 1985. The service, Integrated Digital Access, had limited applications but was aimed at determining user requirements for eventual ISDN service. BT upgraded its IDA service in 1990 with ISDN 2, a CCITT-compatible service offering 2B + D channels. BT's ISDN 2 tariffs, like those in France and Germany, are priced the same as regular calls but include a one-time connection charge and yearly rental fees.

As in all developed countries, telegraph service is in decline. In 1983 alone, international telegraph service decreased by 23 percent, and telegram service lost £20 million. A large computer-based international telex exchange opened in 1982. London became Europe's telex hub because its rates to North America were substantially lower than those on the Continent. Telex bureaus emerged to handle the retransmission of telex traffic from Europe to North America. The continental PTTs opposed this process, leading to the important *British Telecom* decision of the European Court of Justice. In 1988, the United Kingdom had the most telex terminals (111,500) and lowest rates of any European country (ITU, 1990).

"Chatlines" became popular after 1986, but they also caused consumer protection problems. In response to consumer criticism, Oftel imposed restrictions in 1988 that effectively terminated such services. Complaints stemmed from both the high cost and the nature of these services. Without itemized billing, consumers could not keep track of the number or type of such calls; employees could amass large bills for their employers, as could children for their parents. To curb such abuses, the corporate consumer was forced to incur the expense of devices that block calls to specific exchanges. These devices, however, were not available to residential consumers. In addition, message *content* also proved to be a source of controversy. Many consumers felt that Oftel should take action against message services whose content could be characterized as soft pornography. At the same time, however, Oftel also received complaints that some advertisements for message services suggested pornographic content without delivering it.

Addressing these complaints, Professor Carsberg of Oftel encouraged the establishment of the Independent Committee for the Supervision of Telephone Information Services (ICSTIS) in 1986 to monitor message content. In addition, in July 1988, Carsberg advocated controls on Chatline services that would provide access to these lines only to consumers who actively requested them (Oftel, 1988). In 1989, Oftel instituted Codes of Practice for Chatlines, which restricted access to minors and taxed service providers to establish a fund for subscribers who faced large bills because of unauthorized use.

Telecommunications Service Improvements

After privatization and reorganization, BT embarked on a long-term modernization program estimated at over £20 billion. But it found the sailing rough. System X switches were delayed and flawed in several London installations. Oftel generally received so many complaints that it considered instituting dam-

Table 8.1 Performance Comparison of New York Telephone Co. and
British Telecom

	New York Telephone	British Telecom
Operator response	Average, 4 seconds	87% within 15 seconds
Long distance blocking	<1%	3.6%
Service orders filled	92% within 5 business days	62.2% within 8 business days
Complaints to Company per Line	0.04	0.22
Complaints cleared	75–80% within 24 hours	74% within 5 hours; 90.2% within 2 days

Source: BT, and communication to the author by NYT, 1988.

age liability against BT. A BT line averaged a technical problem every two years, ten times the rate of the Bell companies in the United States. Even BT conceded the fault rate to be two to three times higher than that in the United States (Hudson, 1987).

Overall penetration in 1988 was forty-two main lines per 100 households. As a private firm subject to some competition, BT's sensitivity to its customers increased. Business customers, in particular, benefitted from service improvements and rate reductions. The waiting time required to install private circuits in the City of London, used to be several months, was rapidly shortened. Performance profit centers were created within the company. Management employment contracts began to include performance and profitability clauses and were limited in duration in order to break a civil-service, lock-step salary environment. A sales force with major-account managers was created in 1980 to help the company protect and increase its business.

The U.K.'s liberal telecommunications policy and relatively lower international telephone rates helped attract large users. The Ford Motor Company, for example, set up the communications center for its European operations in the United Kingdom. Nevertheless, there was much dissatisfaction with BT's service. In an effort to rebut the criticism directed at it for service quality, in 1987 BT announced a quality strategy that included expenditures of over $400 million to improve both international and domestic service. In response to the complaints, Oftel resumed its publication of survey figures on service quality. Oftel's 1990 *Annual Report* noted and increase in complaints, from 23,800 in 1988 to 31,650 in 1989, despite increases in percentage of faults repaired in one day from 65 percent to 86 percent (Oftel, 1990a, p. 8).

Table 8.1 shows the comparison in quality of service between British Telecom and New York Telephone. The quality performance of New York Telephone does not rank high among the more than thirty telephone companies in New York State. However, Table 8.1 shows that its service quality is above BT's.

According to Sir Brian Carsberg, head of Oftel, "The largest area of complaints is billing. People say they could not have run up the amount that appears on their bill . . . In the United States where they have itemized billing, this is a relatively small area of complaint'' (*Connections,* 1985). BT began to offer itemized billing when it introduced the System X digital switches, but set an extra charge for this service.

The service quality of public coin telephones was poor. In 1983, BT provided more than 350,000 pay phones, many of them rented on private premises. BT was not enthusiastic about this service. According to its accounting, it lost more than £77 million on it in 1982–1983, about 20 percent of its total profits. The requirements of BT's license led it to upgrade service. The company embarked on making the instruments more vandal-proof, a goal that is particularly important, since in some areas vandalism accounted for 75 percent of the cost of pay phone maintenance.

Nevertheless, the state of public telephones was for a long time the single worst aspect of British telephone service. In response to a 1985 survey by the *Daily Mail* that showed almost 60 percent of public telephones out of order at any given time, Oftel commissioned its own study, which found a still extraordinary rate of 50 percent. Over two years of effort aimed at improving this statistic produced progress. At the end of 1987, Oftel found 23 percent of public phones out of order, a number that declined to less than 10 percent by mid-1988 (Oftel, 1988). Another area of complaint about BT concerned its rates. Local telephone charges in 1988 were among the highest in Europe, although business and residential service baskets were slightly below OECD averages. In 1990, BT raised residential rates 9 percent after Oftel refused steeper increases. Business rates remained unchanged, but line rental charges for home users increased 12 percent. In 1989, Oftel began an investigation into excessive international rates.

BT followed an increasingly international strategy and expanded its global presence by buying in 1989 a 22 percent stake in the second-largest U.S. cellular service provider, McCaw, for $1.5 billion, thereby gaining access to 30 percent of the U.S. mobile market. It also bought an 80 percent stake in the paging firm Metrocast in 1988, and it acquired McDonnell Douglas's data communications operations, Tymnet, for $355 million in 1989. In 1986, it acquired Dialcom from ITT. Through Tymnet, BT also purchased Edinet, Ontyme, and a 25 percent stake in Japan's Network Information Service Co. BT also bid for a German D2 cellular license. Soon, BT's international investments led to criticism of its modernization programs in the United Kingdom as inadequate. Furthermore, the fate of its global investments was mixed. Metrocast had to be closed; McCaw's debts escalated to over $5 billion, and Mitel was heavily in the red. BT shifted away from owning equipment and further foreign carriers, and into the servicing of major users and their global networks. It pursued various international alliances and established Syncordia, an Atlanta-based managed data service.

Despite some liberalization of entry, BT still vastly predominates almost all British telecommunications. Although in the past it played no role in manufacturing, its acquisitions after privatization indicate a trend toward vertical integration.

Mercury's status was reviewed in the 1990 'duopoly review.' After Oftel submitted a report in 1990, the review was opened to public comment. Over 200 groups responded. In 1991 the Department of Trade and Industry, which oversees Oftel, presented its findings in *Competition and Choice: Telecommunications Policy for the 1990s*, a title reminiscent of the government's parallel efforts in television liberalization through the broadcasting White Paper (Home Office, 1988). The duopoly review decision signalled a move from managed competition to a more open system, but with a more level playing field.

Equal access provisions were envisioned only in two stages, and not before the 1992/3 review of BT tariffs, since BT (and some user groups) had argued that the costs (£300 million) and technical problems of developing switching capability for multiple operators were extensive. The decision also changed British Telecom's tariff structure; it included international services in the tariff basket after a one-time 10 percent reduction, and it tightened the price cap to RPI-6.25 percent from RPI-4.5 percent. While cable, satellite, and cellular firms received greater flexibility (and interconnectivity) to offer telecommunications services, there was no symmetry. BT was prohibited from offering cable television service until at least 1997.

The reaction to the White Paper was mixed. Some welcomed its further liberalization and viewed it as a challenge to BT's market power. Others thought it too lenient on BT, perhaps in order to protect the value of government shares prior to full privatization. They also saw Mercury as the loser since it faced new competition in its core business of serving large users. BT also received the right to grant special tariff packages to large users. On the other hand, the consortia which were expected to offer telecommunications services (such as British Rail, British Waterways, Racal, British Aerospace, and the Post Office) were hampered by the unresolved interconnection issues. And few cable operators actually had networks in place that might have offered local services.

Thus, British telecommunications policies have created an entity similar to the predivestiture AT&T in the United States—a private, dominant, and regulated carrier with a limited competition in the long distance field. Such a system had been considered problematic in the United States (even without BT's domestic quality problems), and led to further liberalization and divestiture. Analogously it was unlikely that the transformation of British telecommunications had reached a stable equilibrium.

9

France

Early History of French Telecommunications

Throughout the 1980s, no West European government controlled telecommunications more comprehensively than France; French state organizations were the principal operators, developers, customers, export promoters, and, for a time, primary equipment producers. This statist role has a long history. Organized French communications date back to the thirteenth century, when the University of Paris operated a messenger service. In 1464, Louis XI established a government courier service system for official use, and by 1622, there were also regular postal routes for the public. In 1725, the government declared the entire transportation system, including postal service, to be the exclusive domain of the state. Since most private operators leased postal routes from the state, postal routes became a significant source of state revenues. In 1790, the transportation of persons and parcels, but not of letters, was partially liberalized. In 1794 (the third year of the Republic), interested parties were allowed to provide postal services, except for the delivery of letters and small packages. However, after losing postal service revenues to the emerging competition, the government soon imposed a 10 percent tax on the receipt of private posts and raised letter rates considerably, in some instances by more than 500 percent.

Always in need of revenue, Napoleon reestablished the governmental monopoly in 1804 by a decree that lowered postal rates somewhat but kept them considerably above the original rates. Napoleon also centralized the postal administration and established a system of postal inspectors in every department. This governmental monopoly was zealously enforced, with 750 violations prosecuted in 1805 alone.

The high rates, which the Bourbons maintained after the Restoration, provided considerable profits for the state. In 1847, profits were FFr 17.8 million on expenses of FFr 35.5 million. According to Heinrich Stephan, later Germany's postmaster general, the French profits were the highest of all European postal administrations (Stephan, 1859, p. 630).

In the eighteenth century, French, German, and British inventors tried to create reliable high-speed communications. Claude Chappe, a one-time seminarian and later a physicist, developed a novel optical telegraph system; in 1792, his brother, Ignace, a member of various revolutionary bodies, successfully introduced a proposal to initiate a route from Paris to Lille. Chappe called his invention the *tachygraphe* ("rapid writer"), but this fortunately was changed into the term *telegraphe* for "distance writer," and this Graeco–Latin designation has stuck.

The Paris–Lille telegraph route was completed in 1794. Signals were conveyed by various positions of mechanical arms on windmill-like stations located on hilltops at intervals of 6–12 miles. In 1803, the route reached Brussels and a few years later, Amsterdam. In 1798, another Chappe brother established a line to the German and Swiss borders. Lines were extended to Milan in 1805, and Venice in 1810. The Napoleonic Wars made rapid communications important. After the Bourbon Restoration, the systems continued to expand within France. By 1845, the system encompassed 535 optical telegraph stations linking Paris with twenty-nine cities. The Chappe optical telegraph system and variant systems were also used in England, Scandinavia, Prussia, and Austria.

A message from Paris to Lille, a distance of 225 kilometers, was relayed by twenty-two stations and required, in theory, only several minutes for transmission. But the Chappe system was complicated and required a skilled operator, usually trained and supervised by military officers. The British optical system was simpler but slower. Signals on the Chappe telegraph could be transmitted at a rate of one signal every sixteen seconds. Because of this time-consuming procedure, elaborate codes were developed for standard phrases and expressions. Codes also served to protect the secrecy of the official messages. Transmission at night or in bad weather was not possible and the system was plagued with problems. It was exceptional for a telegraph line to transmit even six telegrams of about twenty words a day. The entirety of this network could handle a maximum of 7000 dispatches annually. It was therefore not surprising that military, diplomatic, and administrative messages of the state claimed absolute priority and that the system was operated by a board of the Ministry of the Interior. Initially, no private messages at all were transmitted on the system. In 1833, Alexander Ferrier created a private company to respond to private demand. Although his effort failed, it demonstrated the interest in developing a private telegraph.

In 1837, such private efforts were outlawed by a law that declared the telegraph a government monopoly within the expanding postal monopoly. Private communications networks were discouraged primarily to inhibit the exploitation of financial information by speculators. A French legislator argued: "Governments have always kept to themselves the exclusive use of things which, if fallen into bad hands, could threaten public and private safety: poisons and explosive are given out only under the state authority, and certainly the telegraph, in bad hands, could become the most dangerous weapon. Just imagine what could have happened if the passing success of the Lyon silk workers insurrection had been known in all corners of the nation at once" (Brock, 1981). The law provided substantial fines for unauthorized transmission. Succeeding governments of varying political persuasions have never significantly deviated from this principle. The French government monopoly over telecommunications was thus established by law even before the introduction of electric telegraphy. When the latter arrived, the French government was far from enthusiastic. An explicit ban on private electric telegraph lines was quickly declared when the advent of the railroad led to an attempt to create a private telegraph line between Versailles and Saint Germain. Although private entry was thus made impossible, the government was reluctant to enter electrical telegraphy itself because it feared undermining its own elaborate optical telegraphic system. The advent of the electric telegraph threatened state power, as one minister complained: "No, the electric telegram is not a sound invention. It will be always at the mercy of the slightest disruption, wild youth, drunkards, bums, etc. . . . All that is unnecessary with the electric telegraph are those destructive elements within only a few meters to a wire over which supervision is impossible. . . . The visual telegram, on the contrary, has its tower, its high walls, its gate well guarded from inside by strong armed men" (Allentier, 1973, p. 100).

Eventually, however, the French government constructed an electrical telegraphic system which was operated and controlled by a unit of the Interior Ministry until 1878, primarily for governmental and only secondarily for public use. In 1853 the optical telegraph was discontinued, its low capacity and relatively high cost of operation being factors in its rapid demise.

In 1852, in an important departure, Louis Napoleon Bonaparte (Napoleon III) allowed private users to access the telegraph system. Control was gradually relaxed, though state control was still used against opposition newspapers and coded messages (Bertho et al., 1984), to name two examples.

When it came to international submarine telegraph cables, England had, until 1880, virtual control, and French colonies often had to use English lines to communicate with Paris. Given her rivalry with Britain, France found such dependence intolerable. Meanwhile, several attempts by French companies to enter the submarine cable market ended in failure or in buyouts by American or English companies. The Ministry of Posts and Telegraph began to invest in several cable companies. After 1879, the government operated its own cables to Algeria and Africa. The Compagnie Française au Câble Télégraphique (CFCT) was formed in 1889 and operated privately until its nationalization in 1945.

The Establishment of Telephony

The telephone debuted in France at the Paris World Fair of 1878 (Holcombe, 1911). In contrast to Germany, where it was the state that seized upon the new invention with enthusiasm, in France the private sector played a significant role in the establishment of the new medium. The Third Republic was pushing for economic liberalism in areas of public services, usually through concessions to private companies which would shoulder the burden of investment and risk. The telephone was included in this framework, and in 1879 the government announced its decision to award private concessions. But all construction had to be supervised by state engineers.

Concessions were not exclusive and lasted only five years; a 10 percent royalty payment was required, and the government could purchase all the telephone equipment it needed from the concessionaires at an agreed upon or arbitrated price. At the same time, there was no rate regulation. The concessionaires thus had both the incentives and the ability to try to recoup their investment as quickly as possible. In 1879, licenses were issued to the firms of Edison, Gower, and Blake-Bell. Before construction began, however, these franchises were merged into the Société Générale de Téléphone (SGT). This process of consolidation was based on cartel advantages as well as the Paris municipality's wish to avoid multiple and unsightly wire networks.

The first Paris exchange opened in 1881. Development however, was slow. Service was limited in quality and expensive. The two viable policy options were either to increase the government's role or to allow telephone companies to expand and develop. The government instead chose to increase restrictions on private operations, without strengthening its own role as an operator by committing resources.

In 1882, the government determined that the SGT was inclined to provide services only to the dozen or so large French cities. The National Assembly was persuaded to support governmental telephone construction in various medium-sized cities. But the annual budget allocation for this endeavor was a paltry FFr 250,000.

In 1884, the French government renewed the existing private licenses over strong opposition, but without a clear-cut policy of its own. Soon it became desirable to link the local exchanges by long-distance connections. The telegraph authority, sensing a threat, began construction, starting in 1885 between Paris and Rouen, and in 1887 between Paris and Brussels.

In subsequent years, French policy continually changed. In 1887, Grannet, the minister in charge of telegraphy, introduced legislation to strengthen private telephony to alleviate the backward condition of French telephony. His successor, however, opposed the plan. With some justification, the public believed the French telephone system had become a complete morass in less than ten years. By 1889, the Grannet plan was rejected, largely on the argument that private telephony would jeopardize the financial soundness of the state telegraph system (Holcombe, 1911).

Backed by a coalition of dissatisfied business users, small towns, and leftist republicans, the government soon decided to take over the entire network. Opponents argued against too much state power and against support for what was considered a luxury. But the French National Assembly approved nationalization in 1889, at the end of the second five-year concession period, fired by the national enthusiasm of the revolution's centennial. The companies' installers were given the option of setting up installation businesses of their own, originating a system of private installation firms still in use today, and whose origin is thus not a liberalization but a nationalization.[1]

Nationalization and Its Aftermath

Since the SGT refused to surrender its property willingly, it was literally taken over by force, with compensation paid after the fact. At the time, there were only 8500 subscribers, of which only 2000 were outside Paris (Nouvion, 1984). After extensive court action, the company received about FFr 11 million, twice the amount the telegraph authority had been willing to pay, but less than the company had demanded.

Having taken control of the telephone and telegraph, and having placed it under the Office of the Under secretary of State for the Postal and Telegraph Service, the government now had to figure out what to do with it. Because the telephone held no priority in general economic development, the government was not prepared to make the significant investment necessary to finance construction. It had, over two generations, built up an extraordinarily high general debt burden and was reluctant to increase it.

Instead, it devised a system in which potential subscribers and municipalities were forced to extend interest-free loans that would eventually be repaid from the profits derived from their own receipts. Futhermore, subscribers were required to purchase telephone sets themselves to save the state's money. This was the origin of France's subscriber equipment policy, which was presented in the 1980s as an example of liberalism.

This system of financing was also expanded to long-distance transmission. Local systems resembled cooperatives in that they united the first group of subscribers, who paid for the construction of the network. As in other cooperative ventures, the admission of newcomers and the potential integration of systems into the national network presented problems.

Financing proved problematic when it came to the replacement of obsolete equipment or making improvements. By 1900, this situation was referred to as a "telephone crisis." The system was congested, unreliable, and expensive. There were still only 30,000 telephones in the entire country! By comparison, in 1909, there were 27,000 telephone lines alone in the 100 largest hotels of New York City (Attali and Stourdze, 1977, p. 106).

A number of improvements were achieved under A. Millerand, a Socialist who became minister of the PTT. Millerand established a new system of financing telephone expansion out of public revenue rather than subscriber charges, but he was unsuccessful in obtaining appropriations from the legislature. Even the French business community shortsightedly opposed additional budget allocations. The Chamber of Commerce argued that construction had to be financed not by government budget but by greater internal economies of PTT operations. Millerand was dropped from the cabinet.

In the early years of the century, service remained abysmal. There was only one line between Paris and Marseilles, and during one twelve-month period (1905–1906), it had 204 interruptions with an average duration of 14.5 hours. Between Paris and Lyon there were five lines, with 550 interruptions of an average duration of ten and a half hours (Holcombe, 1911, p. 302). Local exchanges were enormously congested. In 1905, operators in Paris took almost two minutes on average to make a local connection.

By 1906, the government acknowledged the problem and a special law passed to transfer the Post and Telegraph Department from the Ministry of Commerce and Industry to the Ministry of Public Works. It also authorized a budget of 19 million francs but required that the funds be spent within the same fiscal year, leading to insufficient planning and excessive costs. Millerand, back in the government, instituted a labor relations reform for PTT workers, featuring eight-hour days, security of tenure, overtime payment, and full payment during illness.

The destructiveness of World War I further deteriorated the telephone network. Industry was not up to the task of rebuilding it. French equipment makers were merely manufacturers of general electrical machinery, small companies, or subsidiaries of foreign firms. In 1920, when the Paris network was to be upgraded, several foreign firms—Western Electric, Siemens, Ericsson, and ITT—sought the business. ITT bought two French manufacturing firms, created a large research laboratory in Paris, and studied the needs of the French network in depth. As a result of its commitment, it was awarded the major French orders for automatic central offices. But this foreign dominance created resentment in the 1930s and after World War II, leading to a French industrial buildup against ITT's position.

The first automatic exchange opened experimentally in 1913 in Nice using the Strowger system. The PTT also ordered semiautomatic systems from the French company Le Matériel Téléphonique (LMT) then owned by AT&T and using Western Electric's rotary technology. The first such exchange opened in Angers in 1915 (Nouvion, 1984, p. 80). However, the spread of the automatic exchange was slowed by World War I and the economic problems in its aftermath. Crossbar exchanges were not introduced in Paris until 1964. Six years later, the electronic time division switch, the E10, was introduced, leapfrogging a generation of technology.

During the period of economic conservatism of the 1920s, the magnitude of the investments required for the telephone network sparked a debate over its denationalization. Two proposals emerged from the debate: ITT, eager to put down roots in the French market, offered to take over and operate the entire national network as it did in Spain; the second proposal was from the Société Industrielle du Téléphone (SIT), a predecessor of the telecommunications operations of CGE.

In 1921, a law was advanced to study denationalization. Louis Deschamps, who advocated privatization of various government monopolies, including the telephone, served briefly as PTT minister. Because of the project's difficulty and opposition from PTT employee associations, his successors did not pursue his course. From 1923 onward, the PTT was instead directed to operate like an administration with industrial and commercial purposes, under a separate budget (subject to parliamentary approval) and required to cover its costs.

In 1920, the PTT awarded the concession for international radio-electric links from France to the private company Compagnie Sans Fils (CSF), which created Radio France for this purpose. The concession to CSF caused a vigorous debate. Because the international radio-electric link posed promising opportunities, the labor unions and the political opposition were against privatizing this sector.

PTT relations with Radio France were generally poor because radio links of the PTT and Radio France (SRF) were at times in competition. A FFr 60 million station opened in 1923, allowing France to build a wireless network that included PTT links to Africa and Indochina, communications links to central and northern Europe, and Radio France transmission to most of the world.

Meanwhile, the PTT slowly upgraded the domestic telephone network, with the first long distance cables in France using Pupin coils put into service in 1924. Still, the average wait for an interurban connection was five hours. To address this problem, the government adopted a separate budget for the PTT as an annex to the general budget, giving it access to special loans. In addition, it approved another modernization plan for the telephone network. Between 1924 and 1934, the number of subscribers increased annually by an average of 45,000, almost double the previous rate, though growth was still excruciatingly slow.

The automation of the Paris network started in 1925 and led to major industrial struggles over procurement contracts. The competing firms included the French Compagnie des Téléphones Thomson–Houston, and the Société Industrielle du Téléphone (SIT), both of which proposed a Strowger system. LMT, now acquired by ITT, proposed a rotary system, and the Ericsson subsidiary proposed its own method. The French Compagnie Générale de Télégraphie et de Téléphonie was also in contention, but its system depended on a Siemens patent, and the French government did not want Parisian telephones to rely on German technology.

At the time, ITT had experienced several setbacks in Europe: Germany and England chose the Strowger system, and although Spain opted for exclusive use of ITT's rotary system in 1924, the Spanish could have changed their minds if the French had not also chosen that system. With so much at stake, ITT hedged its bets and bought the Thomson–Houston telephone division in 1925 (later to become CGCT), giving it a stronger position for the French procurement. This was accomplished just as Thomson–Houston patented its new R6 switching system.

The PTT awarded the project to LMT (the ITT subsidiary) in 1926. The firm's promise to build a large manufacturing facility and to release its processes to other companies designated by the PTT weighed heavily in the decision. These companies were the Société Grammont, which withdrew in 1931 because of financial problems, and Ericsson.

The ITT contract, however, did not eliminate demand for the R6 system. Rural exchange contracts went to Thomson–Houston, ITT's other subsidiary, which was considered "more French" than LMT. The PTT also extended a license for the R6 to SIT. This period marked the low point for French switching firms and the high point for ITT. Through its two subsidiaries it dominated this key sector. A few years later, in 1932, the large French electrical firm Compagnie Générale d'Électricité (CGE) took control of SIT and sought unsuccessfully to forge links with the American firm Automatic Electric of Chicago. This marked the beginning of the CGE's long march against ITT. With substantial help from the French government, it eventually took control of ITT's worldwide telecommunications equipment operations in 1986, more than half a century later.

Between 1924 and 1934, the number of lines increased an average of 7.6 percent annually. Because of budgetary restrictions, this rate fell to 2.6 percent between 1935 and 1939. The number of lines served by automatic systems rose from 3.6 percent in 1926 to 45.6 percent in 1938. The corresponding 1938 figure for Germany was 84.9 percent, and for the United Kingdom, 54 percent. While telephone penetration in France rose, it was still very low: 3.7 per 100 inhabitants in 1938, compared to 4.6 in the UK, 15 in Germany (Nouvion, 1983, p. 84), and 15.1 in the United States (U.S. Department of Commerce, 1939). Even that figure for France overstates the actual situation, because of the imbalance in favor of Paris. Only a handful of the French departments had a telephone density above five telephones per 100 inhabitants. In many, the density was less than two.

World War II destroyed parts of the French telephone network, though some of the long distance telephone network had been expanded by the German occupiers for military use (Bertho et al., 1984). From 1941 to 1944, the Vichy government consolidated various research centers into one organization, the CNET, as part of a modernization effort. After Liberation, telecommunications fell behind the rest of Europe in rebuilding because of inadequate investment funds. The network became a drag on France's otherwise rapidly developing economy. This is not to say that there was no innovation; there was progress in switching, transmission, and telex. France was the first European country to use coaxial cable for long distance trunks (Paris to Toulouse, in 1947). France was also first to use such a cable for a totally automatic service, starting in 1952. Yet demand for telephone lines vastly outstripped supply. Telex advanced partly through the exertions of the firm Sagem and the liberal equipment policy for telex and PBXs. Complaints became endemic.

In 1969, the PTT admitted that the average long-distance call had to be placed three times before it found a clear circuit, an efficiency rate of less than 40 percent. According to a Western Electric report, only one call out of four during business hours was completed on the first attempt. The report also claimed that in 1969 "it was not unusual for a telephone subscriber to wait anywhere from 30 minutes to more than an hour and a half for a dial tone and more than two days to get a call through" (Western Electric, 1978, p.1). Under pressure to improve this performance, the government budgeted FFr 45 billion for telecommunications development in its Sixth Plan (1971–1975). This amount was ten times greater than that provided in the Fourth Plan, but it was still far from adequate.

Telephone distribution was also quite unevenly spread across the country. Figure 9.1, from a Direction General de Télécommunications (DGT) staff study,

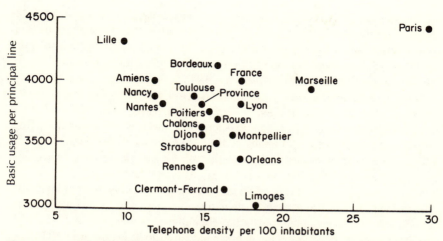

Figure 9.1. Telephone Diversity and Usage in France: Paris versus the Regions.
(*Source:* Guérard et al., 1979.)

shows the vast difference in telephone density between Paris and other cities and regions of the country (Guérard et al., 1979).

On the horizontal axis, the telephone density is mapped. Vertically, telephone usage per main line is traced for the year 1977. As can be seen, the telephone density for Paris was almost twice that of major areas of activity in the provinces, which were, in turn, much higher than in the countryside.

The Great Leap Forward

By the mid 1970s, French telephone performance had deteriorated to the point that it became one of the campaign issues in the 1974 presidential election that brought to power Valéry Giscard d'Estaing, a right-of-center finance minister with a technocratic image and an interest in telephone issues. Giscard d'Estaing, as an Assembly deputy, had introduced legislation in 1967 to establish the telephone administration (DGT) as an independent entity. In 1974, the bitter joke was that half of the country was waiting to get a telephone installed, and the other half was waiting for a dial tone. Only 5 million lines served a population of 52.6 million, whereas the United Kingdom, with roughly the same population, had twice the number of telephone connections. In 1974, telephone densities were extraordinarily low. For blue-collar workers they were only 10 percent; for junior executives and clerks, 22 percent; and for the agricultural professions, 19 percent (*Logica,* 1979).

In 1975, the French government set a national priority of modernizing and expanding the domestic network, while at the same time using telecommunications as a base to develop a high-technology industry strong enough to compete in the world market. President Giscard d'Estaing launched a five year plan aimed at giving the entire population access to telephone service, with emphasis on bringing the particularly low quality of telephone service in the provinces in line with the standards enjoyed in Paris. The number of subscribers quadrupled in eight years to over 20 million in 1983, aided by the VIth and VIIth Plans, which allocated FFr 405 billion and FFr 120 billion, respectively, for telecommunications (*Scientific American, 1983*).

Telecommunications were set as the first priority in the VIIth five-year plan for the French economy. Its goals were to reach parity in density with West Germany and the United Kingdom and to reduce the wait for a telephone from 16.4 months in 1974 to 0.5 months in 1982. In equipment, accelerated conversion to electronic switching was planned, both for increasing the effectiveness of the French system and as a basis for export (Connaughton, 1982).

With money and attention, French telecommunications were remarkably transformed. For the first time in their history, they were a national priority supported by the state and by now a largely indigenous industry. In 1976 alone, 2 million lines were added. This number increased to 2.7 million in 1979, and almost 3 million in 1980. In 1981, the number of new installations began to plateau and decline. This was an impressive performance, but less unusual in the European context than is often believed. Other European countries were also rapidly increasing their investment in telecommunications infrastructure at a similar pace. French telecommunications investments, as a percentage of the total national investment, were 3.36 percent in 1981. In Germany, without telecommunications being proclaimed a national economic priority, it was 3.20 percent at the same time. Italy spent 3.26 percent, and the United Kingdom spent 3.5 percent (Benedetti, 1983).

France Télécom

Until 1989, the Ministry of Post, Telegraph and Telephone (PTT, later PTE, when it also included the space portfolio) controlled French telecommunications, operating through the Direction Générale de Télécommunications (DGT), renamed France Télécom (FT) in 1988. Postal service was provided by another PTE General Directorate, the DGP (later La Poste). The DGT, established as an autonomous directorate in 1946, employed about 166,000 people (about 7.2 per 1000 lines) and was composed of twenty-two regional directorates, which were in turn divided into operational subregions. Some of its operations were carried out through a subsidiary or a separate entity, and others through a mixed investment firm controlled by the state but constituted according to private company law. In 1985, these subsidiaries were placed under the control of the state holding company Compagnie Generale de Communication (COGECOM). Two dozen of these subsidiaries operated in foreign countries or ran satellite ground stations and submarine cables. In 1989, COGECOM had revenues of more than $1.8 billion. Other subsidiaries operated in France, including Entreprise Générale des Télécommunications (EGT), for advanced terminal equipment, and France Câbles et Radio for new services to large users. Télésystèmes provides computer services and software. Transpac is the packet-switched data network.

Before the reforms of 1990, the annual telecommunications budget was part of the overall state budget and therefore had to be passed by the National Assembly; long-term program authorization and advance credit approval, however, reduced the uncertainty of the process. In the 1960s, telecommunications investment had to be self-financing, which proved inadequate, particularly when rates were restricted and the number of lines was low. These limitations were eased, and the self-financing ratio was reduced to about 40 percent. Telecommunications obtained financing through the public Caisse Nationale des Télécommunications (CNT). It also obtained some financing from private finance companies which purchased telecommunications equipment specified by the DGT (later France Télécom) and then leased it to the latter for ten to fifteen year periods; the equipment then reverts to the DGT upon payment of a 3 percent residual value fee (Voge, 1986).

After 1982, the DGT was subject to large financial transfers to the general government budget and was required to contribute to the French electronics industry. French telephone users thus directly subsidized the electronics industry, in addition to contributing indirectly through procurement and R&D support. In 1985, the DGT contributed $2.3 billion out of $12.2 billion in revenue to nontelephone operations of the government, including the Post Office Directorate, which received $0.5 billion, and the general budget, which received $0.3 billion (Morley, 1986).

The Organic Law of 1959 provides for domestic tariffs to be set by cabinet decree. Long distance traffic was heavily profitable whereas basic subscription and local service was being subsidized. According to one study by DGT economists, 1983 revenues were FFr 8.7 billion for basic subscription, FFr 6.9 billion for local message units revenues, and FFr 20.5 billion for long-distance service (Curien and Brunetiere, 1984). The ratios of revenues to costs were, respectively, 0.4, 0.79 and 2.3. For a long time, local telephone traffic was not time-measured, long-distance calls were highly differentiated by distance, and off-peak pricing was rudimentary (Pautrat, 1984). After 1984, the network has distinguished between four levels of price, depending on the time of day (red, white, black, and light blue tariffs).

The DGT and later France Télécom did not manufacture equipment, but supported and guided most of the telecommunications R&D in France through the Centre National d'Études des Télécommunications (CNET). The CNET was derived from PTT labs that had existed before World War II. CNET was created to increase independence from foreign firms and provided an authority to regulate the competition between PTT suppliers.

In 1957, a Department of Research on Electronic Machines was created within CNET. Its purpose was to apply developments in electronics to telephone switching. The first prototype of electronic switching appeared in the early 1960s and led directly to Alcatel's dominance, since that firm was closely allied with CNET. In 1989, CNET had 1500 researchers and a budget of $350 million (Steckel and Fossier, 1990, p. 38; Arlandis and Gille, 1989, p. 37).

Services

Partly because of its fairly recent major expansion, the French telephone system achieves high technical standards. Development was particularly successful in both digital switching and transmission. In 1989, 71 percent of all lines were electronically switched, with the rest using crossbar switches; rotary type switches had been totally phased out.[2] In 1989, nearly 4 million electronic lines were put into service. By 1989, 58 percent of switches were digital, 12 percent analog, and 30 percent crossbar. Total network digitalization was set for 1996 (Steckel and Fossier, 1990, p. 22).

France was a leader in public packet-switched networks. Available since 1978, Transpac is the world's largest packet-switched network. Subscribers were especially attracted by the distance-independent tariffing. Private companies are involved in the network, which the GCE subsidiary SESA designed. Transpac was originally operated through a mixed public–private economic organization. To spread risk, maintain commitment, and increase input, Transpac users were also shareholders. Later only 3 percent remained in private hands. In 1985, Transpac was placed under the control of the state holding company COGE-COM.

Transpac had 5.5 million users (including the 5 million subscribers of the French Minitel service) and 86,000 direct access points in 1991, carrying 2 billion characters per month. It also introduced a range of new services, including Atlas 400, a X.400 electronic data interchange, and a mass market electronic mail system, Minicom. Transpac also moved internationally by acquiring a 15 percent stake in the U.S. VAN Infonet, together with several European PTTs. It entered ventures with the German DBP Telekom and the Swiss and Danish PTTs. In 1991, Transpac began to offer service in the United Kingdom, as part of an international expansion program. Other data services are Transfix, Transcom (a medium-speed public switched service), and Transdyn (a satellite service). These services were bundled and upgraded as Transmic.

France Télécom moved toward ISDN, known in French as RNIS (Réseau Numérique a l'Intégration de Services). In 1987, the DGT introduced its ISDN service Numeris in Brittany. By 1989, 18 million telephone subscribers had potential access to Numeris and several dozen companies were developing applications in partnership with France Télécom.

Limited resale of leased line capacity was allowed for data services in 1987, but tariffs were set to prevent arbitrage. Sources were divided into Category I (under 3.5 Mbps) and Category II networks. All networks required a license. By 1990, some 120 applications were filed but only one authorization was granted for a Category II network. Restrictions on VANs were further lifted in a 1989 regulatory ruling, which allowed automatic authorizations of Category I (Roussel, 1989d, p. 13). VAN providers were still limited to a single connection to the public network, ruling out network bypass, and they must support OSI protocols for data transmission (Steckel and Fossier, 1990, p. 10).

French policy toward VANs has been somewhat reluctant. When the European Community proposed in 1989 to liberalize data service provision, France protested, suggesting that network operators be given authority to issue licenses and levy access charges on private VANs operators. France also led the opposition to the E.C. Commission's Open Network Provision.

On the other hand, France is a leader in public videotex. Its Teletel system is accessed by 5 million Minitel terminals installed and distributed free of charge by France Télécom. This is discussed in detail in chapter 36 on European videotex.

In contrast to data transmission, where France is strong, mobile communications had a slow start. In 1982, cellular radio was introduced in Paris. In 1985, the system still had only ten repeaters. Matra, in collaboration with France Télécom, manufactures the systems.

In 1987, a second mobile communications license was awarded to a consortium that included the water utility Compagnie Generale des Eaux (also active in cable TV); Racal, of Britain; and Bell South, one of the seven regional telephone holding companies in the United States. This consortium, the Société Française du Radiotéléphone (SFR), installed a network in direct competition with the France Télécom system, using equipment by Nokia and Alcatel (Chamoux, 1988, p. 6).

In 1990, cellular penetration was still low, at 0.27 percent of the population, compared with 1.25 percent in the United Kingdom and 3.68 percent in Sweden. France Télécom's Radiocom 2000 had over 90 percent of the 170,000 subscribers. The DRG threatened to intervene in 1990 if France Télécom could not agree with SFR on interconnection arrangements to the GSM mobile standard.

France Télécom also introduced a telepoint cordless service (Pointel) based on the U.K. CT2 system (Dawkins, 1990a). In paging services, a closely related duopoly exists. Télécom Systèmes Mobiles Alphapage service grew to 200,000 in 1989. TDF-1 Radio Service, in which control was acquired by France Télécom, had only 18,000 subscribers in 1989, partly because of the high cost ($700) of its paging devices (*Telecom France*, 1990, p. 5). Both services are offered through COGECOM, France Télécom's holding company.

Network improvements were aided by steady increases in productivity. Turnover per employee rose steadily by over 10 percent from 1984 to 1987 before leveling off in 1988. France Télécom's productivity was consistently higher than that of British Telecom (Arlandis and Gille, 1989, p.8).

The Restructuring of the Telecommunications Industry

As part of a high-technology renaissance, the VIIth Plan of 1975 set the development of France as an international leader and exporter of telecommunications equipment as a main goal of French telecommunications policy. Since the government wanted to retain domestic control over these key industries and the major subsidies they received, government policy aimed to minimize foreign competition in the electronics industry in France. Thus, the government financially backed the involuntary acquisition by Thomson-CSF of ITT's share in LMT and 40 percent of Ericsson's French subsidiary, SFT. This restructuring in 1976 raised the domestic equipment market share of French firms from 43 to 71 percent; and for public exchange switches alone, from 39 to 80 percent (Connaughton, 1982, p. 14.)

When François Mitterrand was elected president and a Socialist government came to power in 1981, telecommunications seemed to be a perfect industry for its goals. It was a sector that already had a strong tradition of state control, long-range planning, and close cooperation between government and industry. Thus, the new government, like its predecessor, seized upon telecommunications as a vital sector. But there was an important difference of emphasis: the more technocratic Giscard d'Estaing era was the golden period of telecommunications engineers. They were accorded status, investment funds, and relative operational freedom to expand the network. Under Mitterrand, telecommunications were not a goal in and of themselves, but one tool for a more general modernization of society and the economy. As a result, telecommunications policy became more political and less technocratic; engineering bureaucrats yielded the center stage to empire builders straddling the public and private sectors. The focus of governmental policy moved from the network to its supplying industries.

The General Commissariat of Planning assembled a study group to investigate the economic effects of DGT's investment on employment, internal trade, and economic growth. Using a multisectoral econometrics model, the commission attempted to gauge the effect of an increase in telecommunications investments each year between 1983 and 1988 (Bienaim and Picaud, 1984). The DGT passed the test of investment effectiveness. Politically, it reasserted its autonomy and achieved predominance in its planning, development, and financing functions in the *filière électronique*, the technological–economic–political complex of electronics.

Initially, the Directorate for Electronic Industries and Data Processing (DIELI), a board of the Ministry of Industry Planning, supervised government planning in the electronics industry. It was in charge of setting guidelines for the development of the French electronics industry, but the relation of those plans to telecommunications was not clear. In time, the DGT asserted increasing influence.

The Socialists had come to power on the campaign slogan of "nationalization, decentralization, planification, and democratization." Of these goals, they accomplished the first and pursued the third in telecommunications. The second and fourth goals inspired the creation of local radio, television, and cable television. On the other hand, the reorganization of the telecommunications sector served to further concentrate the industry rather than to accomplish the declared fourth goal of decentralization.

Despite the substantial governmental efforts to expand the role of the French electronics industry, it claimed only 5 percent of the world market in 1981–1982. Without the domestic market, French firms had only 1.4 percent of the world electronics market, including France's former colonies. France had only 0.3 percent of the U.S. electronics market (*Scientific American,* 1983)

Furthermore, government plans had generated little success for French consumer electronics, office equipment, and computers. In 1982, Bull amassed losses of FFr 1.35 billion, while IBM France posted identical profits.

To improve this situation, the incoming Socialist government's five year plan of 1982 provided as one of its four main objectives the development of French expertise in electronics. At that time, telecommunications had a turnover of about FFr 26 billion (i.e. sales revenue), and comprised more than one quarter of France's *filière électronique,* the chain of technical, social, and economic activities associated with the electronics industry. The investment target for the five year-period (governmental, private, and academic) was FFr 140 billion (approximately $21 billion) for the five-year period. This was approximately $4 billion annually, a sum comparable in magnitude to IBM's $2 million R&D expenditure at the time (Darmon, 1985, p. 79).

For a long time, France maintained a policy of promoting ''national champion'' firms and projects of high prestige and visibility such as the Concorde, the first light water nuclear power plant, the largest solar energy furnace, and a high-speed train. *Le Monde* dubbed these projects the ''new cathedrals'' (Crane, 1979). A major theoretician behind the Mitterrand government plans and policies was Jacques Attali, counselor to the president, who described his French economic model as ''based on a mathematical model influenced by linguistics and psychoanalysis.''

The Socialist government implemented its policy in three major steps. The first was the nationalization of the electronics sector. The second was a restructuring that, in effect, assigned specialized functions to the various nationalized companies: CII–Honeywell–Bull (CII–HB) was designated for computers; Alcatel for telecommunications and office automation; Thomson and Matra for semiconductors; and Thomson for consumer electronics. The third step was a five-year, $20 billion government development plan for electronics, which was only partly implemented.

Industrial planning designated the electronics area as the hoped-for ''locomotive'' for French industry. Economic models of the demand for goods and services corresponding to the growth of telecommunications services supported this industrial plan. Studies concluded that telecommunications represented one of the best investment choices for the stimulation of production (Bonan et al., 1985). Nationalization and government control were justified by the charge that French private business had not been stoking the locomotive hot enough. According to Jean-Pierre Chevènement, then the minister of research and industry, ''If capitalism had worked the way it was supposed to, things might be different today—but capitalism did not work'' (Locksley, 1983, p. 134). Similarly, for Pierre Dreyfus, the French minister of industry and one-time head of the Renault automobile company, ''private enterprise in France does not take risks; it is chilly, timid, shy, against taking risks even when they are necessary for new products and long-term needs'' (Delamaide, 1982, p. 167).

Still, France had fared relatively well in the global recession of 1981, and it is not obvious why the government—already the dominant force in the electronics industry through the DGT, military procurement, and R&D financing—had to target this sector for nationalization.

Americans speak of *nationalized* industries, but the French call them *national* industries. France has a well-established tradition of national industries, including firms such as the tobacco monopoly, Seita; the advertising agency and communications firm, Havas; the automobile firm, Renault; and all the major banks, in addition to the more conventional state activities in heavy industry, utilities, and transportation. The state's role in industrial policy dates back at least to Colbert, under whom state enterprises such as the Gobelins tapestry and Sevres porcelain works were established in 1681. Three centuries later, in 1982, Prime Minister Pierre Mauroy celebrated this tradition by proclaiming "nationalization is a form of the French genius" (Delamaide, 1982, p. 167).

The industry is enormously dependent on government procurement. In 1988, France Télécom provided a market of $2.5 billion, or 45 percent of production, for the French telecommunications industry, whose exports accounted for 15 percent ($800 million), with the French private sector and the military together adding another 40 percent (Steckel and Fossier, 1990, p. 6). The industry is also highly concentrated. Of the forty companies comprising the sector, the largest five accounted for 90 percent of total production. Three of these five were nationalized: CGE (including CIT–Alcatel), Thomson (Thomson–CSF and LMT), and CGCT. Additionally, the computer manufacturer CIT–Honeywell–Bull, and the defense and electronics firm Matra—both increasingly moving into telecommunications—were nationalized. Altogether, the French state became an owner of three quarters of the telecommunications equipment business. Several smaller groups remained in private hands, such as G3S, which included CSEE and SAT (Société Anonyme de Télécommunications Radio-électrique et Téléphonique) affiliated with the Dutch company Philips and active in microwave, radio, and data communications and switching. The company Jeumont-Schneider produced electronic PBXs.

The nationalization of the electronics industry was part of a larger pattern. By 1982, 30 percent of the country's entire industry was state owned, and the government had holdings in more than a thousand firms. These firms controlled 95 percent of bank assets and about half of all French business activities (Monsen, 1984). But by the end of 1983 the franc had been devalued three times, and nationalized companies had lost an estimated $4.5 billion. Whereas initially they retained considerable flexibility under Industry Minister Dreyfus, who as head of Renault had learned the benefits of decentralization, they were subsequently burdened by much more interference under his successor, the more left-leaning Jean-Pierre Chevènement. This led to a rebellion of company presidents, who appealed directly to Mitterrand. Laurent Fabius, the pragmatic budget minister, was reassigned to the ministry of industry. After becoming prime minister of France in 1984 at the age of thirty-seven, Fabius renewed a flexible, decentralized policy and reestablished the priority of high-technology fields over aging industrial sectors such as steel.

The initial nationalization costs about $6 billion. But the losses that had to be carried mounted from $226 million in 1980 to $4.6 billion in 1982, and $4.2 billion in 1983. Thus, the *annual* subsidy of losses was more than two-thirds higher than the initial costs to the government of taking over the companies. Under the pressure of these losses, the government began to emphasize financial accountability. Meanwhile, it reduced capital infusions, issued non-voting shares on the Paris stock exchange, and even encouraged venture capital markets. At the same time, the opposition, both Gaullists and Giscardists, formulated sweeping economic platforms in which they advocated reduced governmental ownership and regulation, greater tax incentives, lower taxes, and some forms of deregulation. Former President Giscard d'Estaing defined the goal as seeking a "liberal economy—something that has never existed in France before" (including under his presidency).

The direct government aid package for the electronics industry expanded from $1 billion in 1983 to $1.2 billion in 1984, a level maintained in 1985. This did not include substantial support through DGT procurement and R&D. In both 1984 and 1985, Bull received $100 million. Thomson received $100 million in 1984 and $130 million in 1985. It also shared R&D costs with the state. At CGCT, the government's equity participation grew from $300 million in 1984 to $450 million in 1985.

Eventually, ending state companies' deficits became a priority and French companies rapidly cut jobs. Alcatel–Thomson eliminated 1700 jobs, LMT 1300, and Thomson 4000. Personnel in the telecommunications industry steadily diminished. There were 94,000 people employed in 1977 and 77,000 in 1983, a 25 percent decline (Darmon, 1985, p. 88). This was not altogether surprising. After the years of vast expansion of the telephone network, the industry experienced surplus capacity and inevitable decline once the backlog was eliminated. In 1985, export orders also fell below the levels of the previous two years. Some reprivatization was considered. Edith Cresson, the new minister for trade and industry, and prime minister after 1991, began to argue that nationalization targeted parent companies and not necessarily their subsidiaries, which could have substantial private elements.

Losses continued in the 1990s. In 1991, the government had to promise more than $1 billion of support to the state companies Groupe Bull and Thomson. Bull's 1990 deficit was $1.2 billion, and the government promised $700 million to alleviate the computer company's problem. Thomson, in similar dire straits, received $350 million. France Télécom had to contribute toward those amounts.

All in all, the Socialist experience was sobering. It dampened the government's high-technology ambitions and challenged traditional socialist ideology. This was important, given France's considerable influence in the world of ideas, particularly in the developing world. The question was whether the retrenchment of the French Socialist government was only a temporary measure, dictated by the reality of then-existing conditions, or whether it could in fact be viewed as a historic reorientation of the idea of state control. Conservative thinkers began to receive a respectability that they had not enjoyed—with the possible exception of Raymond Aron—since World War II. A number of best-sellers by writers Jean-François Revel, Guy Sorman, and François de Clossets popularized the idea that French society had become too state-controlled, too full of privilege and constraints, and that as a result it could not grow and innovate. They advocated certain forms of deregulation and denationalization. On a more philosophical level, André Glucksmann, a leader of the "new philosophers" and a former Maoist, analyzed the problems of traditional socialist ideology in modern industrial society and what he referred to as the "emptiness" of the Mitterrand goal of modernization. These views began to set the stage for the temporary return to power in 1986 of conservative government, which rescinded some of the nationalizations, a path not contested by the Socialists when they regained a majority in 1988. But first, we will discuss the industry itself.

The French Telecommunications Industry

Following nationalization, the Socialist government restructured the telecommunications industry with the goal of streamlining and rationalizing it, in the hope of reducing its heavy losses and increasing exports. An important question is whether the state's interventions deterred the industry or encouraged it. There can be no simple answer here to this issue central to business–government relations in general. But one can observe that the government's interventionist attitude, complemented by the strong polarization of French politics, leads to strong policy swings and creates uncertainty and risk for managers. Consequently, they invest time and effort in building supportive coalitions. Where governmental support is the ultimate variable for success or failure, securing it will be a priority. Conversely, governments and parties in a polarized political environment need the support of powerful economic entities. This symbiotic process leads in time to politicized managers and managerial politicians. It is an environment conducive to empire builders, but not necessarily to product innovators. Its effect may be offset by the protection and funding that arise from government actions, though such help can also be extended through a hands-off policy rather than by microinvolvement in management. In the case of French digital switching, much of the technology was state-developed; the market was a state market; the risk was the government's, and export deals were subsidized in various ways as part of foreign commercial policy. The role of the managers, thus, became one of dealing with and manipulating such actions. The two main players in this game were CGE and Thomson.

Compagnie Générale d'Électricité (CGE) is the largest French industrial company outside of the automobile and oil sector. Founded in 1898, it had 1989 sales of about FFr 143.9 billion, and FFr 4.9 billion in net income. The CGE group includes over 100 subsidiaries in electronics, electric generation, transmission, publishing, transportation, engineering, and construction. The group's organizational structure is decentralized to the extent that some of its subsidiaries have stocks that are independently traded on the Bourse. It has a major presence in two key governmental infrastructure projects in France: nuclear power generation and telecommunications equipment. In 1982, CGE was nationalized, and in 1987 it was reprivatized. To deal with the problem of raising capital as a nationalized firm without a priority in the government budget, CGE issued "participatôry certificates" to private investors. The nationalized CGE was one of only three such French companies that were profitable (the other two were Saint Gobain and Matra). In the first year of its nationalization, the group spent $2.4 billion on R&D, half of which went into telecommunications and informatics (Vasseur, 1984).

Foreign firms had long dominated the French market. In 1939, as discussed earlier, Thomson–Houston, controlled by ITT, had 31 percent; LMT, also an ITT firm, had 41 percent and SFT Ericsson had 23 percent. French firms supplied the remainder: Société Industrielle des Téléphones (SIT) (3 percent) and L'Association des Ouvriers en Instruments de Précision (AOIP) (2 percent) (Bertho and Nouvion, 1986, p. 60). In stark contrast, by 1985 a single state firm, the merged company Alcatel-Thomson, had 84 percent of the market and exerted a major influence on the remaining 14 percent of then state-controlled CGCT, which survived largely for political reasons.

Key dates for the foreign and French victories, respectively, are 1925 and 1976. In 1925, in what became known as the battle of the Carnot exchange, multiple firms competed for the Paris area automatic exchange equipment order. Paris was one the last European capitals to automate its telephones. Several systems had been introduced earlier elsewhere in France. In 1913, Thomson–Houston installed an American Strowger unit in Nice under license; in 1915, AT&T's LMT cut over a rotary system in Angers; in 1924, SFT-Ericsson similarly installed its own Strowger system in Dieppe: Britain's GEC and Germany's Siemens offered other Strowgers. French suppliers were Thomson–Houston, Grammont, and SIT, and SIT had no technology licensing agreement with a foreign developer. Within a short time, the fledgling ITT acquired LMT from AT&T's Western Electric, and it acquired a minority interest in Thomson–Houston. The PTT chose the ITT rotary technology and its price offer, provided that equipment was produced in France by LMT, licensed to SFT Ericsson and to Grammont, and backed up by an ITT lab located in Paris. Defeated, Thomson–Houston sold its telecommunications divisions to ITT in 1925, where they became the foundation for what was named in 1939 CGCT, ITT's other French subsidiary. ITT subsequently also won the contract for medium-sized and rural exchanges. Its successful R6 was actually an earlier Thomson–Houston development. With the advent of the Great Depression, Grammont also exited from the switching business; CGE briefly participated with SFT and SIT, but by 1932 French firms played a minimal role in the field (Aurelle, 1986). ITT dominated directly, and whatever Ericsson produced was under ITT license. More important to the government than switching was long-distance transmission, which had strategic importance in light of the potential for war with Germany. Hence, the government encouraged the strengthening of the firm SAT, which in time became part of today's CGE.

After World War II, cross-bar switches were introduced on an experimental basis. In 1955, the ITT Pentaconta was chosen, to be manufactured by LMT and CGCT. Ericsson's CP 400 was selected for medium-sized exchanges and licensed to AOIP and CIT (which had evolved from SIT in 1946). This license was the seed for the global CGE–Alcatel empire, since CGE soon acquired CIT, after being unsuccessful with its own electromechanical switch. CGE also took a substantial minority interest in SFT–Ericsson. The French firms were aided by the PTT's encouragement of re-creation of the Socotel, a cartel for switching firms dating back to the end of the Vichy era, when several French firms allied themselves for mutual protection against postwar competition from foreign firms. The market was stable until the mid-1970s, when the electronic switching generation was decided upon. CGE, through its telecommunications arm, CIT–Alcatel, offered a D-10 system. Joining with Ericsson in the firm Citerel, it also promoted the Ericsson AXE. ITT's system was the E11. Other competing firms were Thomson CSF (offering Northern Telecom's Sp-1); SAT (with Siemens EWS); and TRT (a Philips subsidiary). Thomson's reentry into switching was remarkable insofar as it had just concluded a market division agreement with CGE in 1969, under which it concentrated on components, low-tension technology, consumer electronics and professional materials. CGE, according to the agreement, would specialize in high-tension, telecommunications, and electric power equipment. But the government persuaded Thomson to participate in telecommunications. The government, intent on a greater and more diverse French presence, also forced Ericsson and ITT in 1976 to transfer to Thomson their French firms, SFT and LMT. Meanwhile, CGE was still looking for a foothold, but it had the critical advantage of a close alliance with the PTT's technology laboratory, CNET. This relationship was forged in the late 1950s by CGE's Ambroise Roux. Later, CNET developed the concept of time division multiple switching (TDM), and CGE created the applications in close collaboration with CNET engineers. Thomson, on the other hand, developed its MT20 without such governmental ties (Bertho, 1987) and chose the space division multiplex technology. Of course, the DGT chose TDM as its preferred technology, as advised by CNET. Just then the government established expansion of the network as a top investment priority, thereby creating a huge order boom.

By 1976, Thomson's long-running commitment to manufacturing switches had become equivocal; the DGT strongly encouraged it to set aside its agreements with CGE and reenter the telephone industry. Research on digital switching was undertaken, culminating in 1982, when Thomson's MT system became operational.

ITT, in the early 1980s, was the only meaningful foreign presence left; it still supplied PBXs and central office equipment through CGCT. But not for long. In 1982, the Socialist government nationalized CGCT. In that period CGE and Thomson–CSF also took over AOIP, a workers' cooperative for central office equipment and PBXs, which had been unable to make the transition to electronic switches and maintain its 10 percent share of the market. The Socialists did not want AOIP to die. It also preferred the DGT to have several equipment manufacturers to choose from. The government had already intervened in 1979, requiring Thomson and CIT–Alcatel to hire part of AOIP's personnel, to use its factories, and to manufacture a switch developed by the AOIP, the URA 2G. CIT–Alcatel already had an equivalent product, and it could dodge the order, but Thomson had to comply. Some of the difficulties Thomson experienced in the early 1980s can be traced to its forced adaptation to the URA 2G (Darmon, 1985, p. 171).

CGE's telecommunications, on the other hand, prospered. The emergence of digital exchanges coincided with the great expansion of the French network. Together, they made CGE the European leader in TDM switching. In 1977, the DGT opted for the CIT–Alcatel E-10 as the centerpiece of its large-scale expansion. To reduce CIT–Alcatel's bargaining strength, the DGT also designated the Thomson MT system as its second source. CGE's Alcatel produces TDM switching systems, submarine cable systems, PBXs, and PCM equipment. Its subsidiary, Alcatel Electronique, is involved in peripheral equipment. Another subsidiary, SESA, is a leader in packet switching networks (Quatrepoint, 1984). CGE was also active in transmission lines and cable television through its subsidiary Câbles de Lyon. It also became dominant domestically in nuclear reactor construction.

The second major player in the telecommunications equipment field, already repeatedly mentioned, was Thomson–CSF a part of the Thomson Group agglomeration of more than 100 companies and subsidiaries. Under a variety of labels, it held over 30 percent of the European Community's color television market. In 1987, it also acquired RCA's consumer electronics division in exchange for some of its own subsidiaries (particularly those involved with medical equipment), and became the world's second largest TV manufacturer. Thomson owned the major German television set manufacturers—AEG, Telefunken, Nordmende, and Saba—accounting for about one-quarter of the German market.

The Socialist government nationalized Thomson in 1981. To facilitate its nationalization plan, it pledged $900 million in financial support to Thomson for telecommunications development. Alain Gomez, a graduate of ENA and the Harvard Business School and a former leftist, was appointed to replace the previous group of managers, whose career backgrounds had been predominantly in the military and who were known for a slow moving management style. Of the top eleven managers under Thomson's former regime, only two had come from civilian industry. Five top executives, including the president, hailed from the navy. The company focused on military business and was less profitable in consumer markets. When it became a state-owned enterprise, it was directed to focus on consumer markets. The government hoped to avoid repetition of Thomson's failure to exploit the potential of video disc players. In 1972, the company had been at the forefront in developing the video disc player, but rather than applying the technology commercially, it sold it as a tool for teaching the maintenance of military equipment, without promoting its applications in consumer electronics. Eventually, Thomson left video disc production and licensed its technology to a Japanese firm, which produced the machines at half the French cost (Pierrand, 1984). (Of course, it was in good company, since Philips and RCA were similarly unsuccessful.) Thomson is also the largest French producer of electronic components. In 1987, Thomson merged its semiconductor activities with those of the Italian firm SGS, then a member of the STET group.

As part of its nationalization activities, the French government bought out in 1982 ITT's remaining French telecommunications companies, mainly CGCT. ITT valued its French companies at \$375 million but got much less in compensation. The government argued that CGCT was unprofitable, but this was a self-fulfilling prophecy. ITT lost money in France because its equipment, which sold well around the world, was rejected by the DGT in favor of French switches. As a result, the government could point to the company's relative lack of commercial success and argue for a low compensation for its expropriation.

The government assured CGCT's allocated share of about 16 percent of the DGT procurement. This was augmented by government contributions of FFr 188 million to CGCT's capital. Still the company asked for FFr 1 billion in various forms.

But things kept changing. In 1983, Gomez reached a transfer agreement with George Pebereau, director-general of the CGE, handing over all of Thomson's civil telecommunications activities in exchange for CGE's departure from military procurement until at least 1990.[3] Thomson was heavily in the red, having not only devoted itself to developing the MT system, but spread itself using over different switching systems (Darmon, 1985, p. 95). The reorganization was by no means forced on the companies by the government. Gomez and Pebereau persuaded Laurent Fabius that France's telecommunications needed consolidation and "rationalization" in order to be internationally competitive.

The restructuring was unprecedented in its size or scope in Europe. Its main aspect was that CGE and Thomson swapped major assets. After the exchange, a new telecommunications group was created that combined the telecommunications businesses of Thomson and CGE, controlled by the CGE subsidiary CIT–Alcatel. Thomson, for its part, received CGE's electronics component business, military division, and consumer electronics operations. There were several reasons for the reorganization. It attempted to simplify the existing structure (i.e., to reduce competition[4]) and generate economies of scale. But more important, it attempted to stop the substantial financial losses at Thomson, which had been FFr 2.2 billion in 1982, with no end in sight.

The DGT, however, opposed consolidation because it did not wish to be dependent on a single equipment supplier. In its view, rivalry between competitive suppliers would benefit technological innovation (a perspective it did not usually extend to its own operations) and make the DGT less dependent on one company. For the previous right-of-center government, it had been axiomatic to provide for multiple French suppliers; it had encouraged Thomson–CSF to enter by having it absorb ITT's LMT and Ericsson's interests. To prevent the CGE–Thomson reorganization, the DGT argued that a single domestic supplier could only provide about 65 percent of these needs, whereas two national suppliers could provide about 90 percent. Thus, it concluded that the consolidation had negative implications for the French balance of trade and for French jobs by opening up the domestic market to foreign competitors.

In the end, Fabius accepted the Gomez and Pebereau proposal and consented to financial support: In 1984, FFr 1.7 billion in capital endorsements and FFr 250 million in public credits were extended toward the reorganization, with FFr 500 million earmarked for 1985. Ironically, Thomson got the same amount of government money for leaving the field as it had unsuccessfully requested in order to stay in the telephone business (Darmon, 1985, p. 96).

The agreement led to the creation of Alcatel-Thomson, a manufacturer with sales of FFr 12 million and 40,000 employees. The combination represented 70 percent of French domestic telecommunications production and ranked at that time fifth in world telecommunications production. Alcatel–Thomson controlled 85 percent of public switching, 75 percent of electromagnetic transmission, 6 percent of cable, and 60 percent of private telephone sets.

The Ascendancy of CGE and the Expulsion of American Firms

In the past, the American and French markets for telecommunications equipment had barely overlapped. In the mid-1970s the U.S. Department of Commerce found that imports were only 3–4 percent of total telecommunications equipment sales in France, and of those, the U.S. share was only 1 percent of the total, made up primarily of teleprinters, modems, microwave components, and test equipment. (This, however, did not include ITT's substantial activities in France; its ownership was American but its production and R&D European.) The DGT created or continued cartels with leading manufacturers (U.S. Department of Commerce, 1975, p. 3). Sotolec was formed in 1947 for companies in transmission equipment. Two years later, Socotel was similarly established for the switching equipment industry, continuing an arrangement of the Vichy regime. Members of the Sotolec cartel included the firms LMT, SAT, TRT, CGE, CIT–Alcatel, and Thomson–CSF, and their main purpose was to "prohibit ruinous and savage competition." Though sometimes characterized as paper organizations, these cartels controlled equipment specifications, patents, and development. CNET maintained technological control over suppliers and at the same time provided suppliers with access to design specifications and to each others' patents on a royalty-free basis.

French firms similarly found much of the U.S. market difficult to reach. But with the AT&T divestiture, the close link between the Bell Operating Companies and AT&T, which had assured AT&T dominant access to the world's largest market for telecommunications equipment, was severed, and French producers began eyeing this opening with great hopes. In consequence, CGE's Alcatel subsidiary worked hard at breaking into U.S. markets.

French telecommunications equipment exports to the United States grew from

4.4 percent of the French export market in 1983 to 19.3 percent in 1988. Total French exports in 1988 were Ffr 10.156 billion, more than double the 1983 figure. Exports to Western Europe, on the other hand, declined relatively from 17.3 percent to 13.8 percent. However, Alcatel's success was limited mostly to the small independent telephone companies. Eventually, the firm reduced its U.S. switching activities for lack of a major market success.[5]

During the same period, AT&T found itself unable to crack the French market. This led to an important agreement in 1985 between AT&T–Philips (APT) and Alcatel involving a partial mutual opening of each others' markets. Behind the agreement was the question of what to do with the remaining French public switch manufacturer, CGCT, which the French government had nationalized from ITT in 1982. CGCT was losing large sums of money, but it had one major asset, the traditional allocation of 16 percent of the French public switching market, or approximately 300,000 lines per year, as a second source for the DGT. CGCT was initially given the task of manufacturing the Thomson MT digital switch under a license, but it was in no position to develop and upgrade it for the future. The question then of who would be the second source supplier to the DGT therefore remained unresolved. One would think that the DGT itself would be the one to decide with what other firm it would like to deal. However, CGE, which already held 84 percent of the market, was in fact negotiating with a foreign consortium about whether it should be admitted to the market as CGE's competitor, in return for export benefits to CGE. CGE was, in effect, selling the share of the French market that, for political reasons, it did not supply. Specifically, CGE agreed that APT would receive CGCT's 16 percent market share for its 5–ESS PRX switch, to be manufactured in France by CGCT and adapted to French standards. CGE would receive several types of benefits: AT&T would supply marketing and technical assistance in adapting its E10–5 switch for North American use; it would include it in its product line and pay indemnities if sales did not reach a specified amount. Second, Philips would transfer the microwave equipment manufacturing of its French TRT subsidiary into a joint venture controlled by CGE, while AT&T would undertake to buy at least $200 million of such microwave transmission equipment over four years. In other words, Philips would relinquish control over one of the few activities competitive with CGE in France, and AT&T would help sell the products in the United States. Lastly, CGE would receive $100 million.

CGCT, unenthusiastic about AT&T, preferred to deal with Siemens or Ericsson, but for CGE, AT&T was a more compliant partner. Given the close European collaboration between France and Germany, including the heavy involvement of French companies in German consumer electronics, a company such as Siemens, once it had a toehold in the French market, could not be easily subjected to political protectionism. In contrast, any AT&T involvement in France could receive much greater government scrutiny and future pressure, since public opposition against it could always be easily organized.

The agreement required government approval and was criticized on a variety of grounds. First, French trade unions sought guarantees, fearing that AT&T

involvement in CGCT might lead to a reduced labor force. More generally, they and others were concerned about the entrance of an American high technology company into France, with possibly irreversible results for French industry.

Siemens began to pursue the possibility of substituting for AT&T in the 16 percent CGCT quota. The DGT supported the APT deal, while Siemens argued along political lines for a "European solution," even though Philips, AT&T's partner, was Dutch. Other French ministries did not want to antagonize Germany. The matter soon reached the highest political levels, with discussions between West German Chancellor Helmut Kohl and French Prime Minister Jacques Chirac, warnings from the American ambassador, and hints of retaliation from FCC Chairman Mark Fowler. Because of DGT's preferences, APT seemed to have the inside track. But then the ITT–CGE merger burst on the scene and changed everything.

In July 1986, CGE entered into an extraordinary agreement culminating in its taking control of the telecommunications operations of the American-based conglomerate ITT. ITT's international telecommunications equipment activities had been originally acquired in 1925, when AT&T left the international market. Despite its American headquarters, the company had only a limited equipment presence in the United States, and in the telecommunications business it was a multinational company without a real home base.

But the company, which had become a far-flung conglomerate in the 1960s and 1970s under Harold Geneen's leadership, had subsequently come upon hard times. Led by Rand Araskog, it needed money, and it was unable to sustain the large funds necessary to extend its System 12 digital switch to the U.S. market or to finance development of the next generation of technology.

Meanwhile, CGE's Alcatel had difficulties of its own, especially in export sales; it had almost no public switch sales in the rest of Europe, and most of its international sales were political arrangements with former French colonies or part of foreign aid packages. ITT's international presence combined with CGE's financial resources made them a formidable combination. A deal was arranged.

The complex agreement provided that ITT merge its telecommunications equipment, office automation, and consumer electronics divisions into a holding company. CGE brought in it its own Alcatel equipment subsidiary. ITT held a 37 percent share of the new firm, whereas CGE, together with other European entities, controlled the rest. CGE had 53.6 percent, Société Générale de Belgique, 5.7 percent, and Crédit Lyonnais, 1.7 percent. ITT received $1.3 billion, and the holding company assumed $800 million of ITT's debt. In 1990, ITT sold an additional 7 percent to CGE for $640 million.

The new company was unambiguously called Alcatel, the name of CGE's telecommunications subsidiary. Management and organization was set up in decentralized fashion, with some support staff functions in Brussels, and nominal headquarters in Amsterdam.

One of the new firm's major problems was that it had no less than three different digital switches, each incompatible with the others and each with its own problems. ITT's System 12 has advanced fully distributed processing, and when widely deployed, the intercommunication between its different modules can cause overloads. The MT20 switch was transferred to Alcatel from Thomson in 1983 and found few fans, even in France. Alcatel's own E10 switch itself was losing international market share and needed modernization. Alcatel's main challenge, however, was not technical, but political and managerial: It had to hold together a wide array of subsidiaries functioning under divergent policy environments, management styles, and product lines.

The newly merged firm became the second largest international telecommunications firm after AT&T, amassing $7 billion in assets, almost $10 billion in sales, and 150,000 employees. It supplied a huge 42.5 percent of all European public telephone switches. CGE heralded the agreement as establishing, for the first time, a large-scale European telecommunications firm, but few Europeans got enthusiastic over such a French state-dominated arrangement. CGE claimed that it required the merger to give it sufficient size to operate the economies of scale necessary for success. In other words, it asserted that it took almost half the European market to be economically viable.

This deal finally established the French victory over ITT after more than half a century of struggle. Georges Pebereau had been its strategist. But soon after his triumph, the new conservative government replaced him with Pierre Suard.

The deal put into question CGE's separate arrangement, also negotiated by Pebereau, with AT&T. Now, with CGE inheriting much of ITT's footholds in many other European countries, it was likely that these countries would expect greater reciprocity. In return, the 16 percent market share that had been allocated to AT&T might be more usefully employed to assuage one or several European countries, notably Germany. In other words, it was time for CGE to reassess its contract with AT&T. The tug-of-war grew acrimonious. Within the French government, the DGT preferred APT, while other ministries did not wish to antagonize Germany, which was backing Siemens. The rival companies successively sweetened their bids. In the end,the French government chose the Swedish Ericsson as a neutral compromise, together with the French defense firm Matra, which thus gained a foothold in its country's telecommunications.

Subsequently, Alcatel Chairman Pierre Suard strongly opposed AT&T's involvement in Italy. Suard stated that the goal of European telecommunications policy must be to maintain and improve the leadership of European industry.

In 1989, CGE had 210,300 employees, an increase over the 192,000 in 1982, but this concealed significant staff cuts prior to and following its integration of ITT's international telecommunications operations in 1987. For example, Alcatel cut its new acquisition's work force by 25,000 to 125,000 and closed seven of ITT's eighteen national research labs (Tully, 1989). As CGE became the second largest manufacturer of central switching equipment worldwide, active in over 100 countries, it lent the domestic French industry a major international presence.

Alcatel's opposition to the AT&T/Italtel partnership contributed to its acquisition of Italy's Telettra in 1990. Alcatel thereby bought Telettra's 33 percent market share in tranmission equipment in Italy and a 45 percent share of the same market in Spain. Combined revenues of Alcatel and Telettra were $10.9 billion in 1989 compared with total of $11.1 billion in 1990. But in an effort to reduce anti-competitive vertical integration, the European Commission required Spain's Telefónica telephone monopoly to divest itself first of its 21 percent share in the Spanish Alcatel subsidiary and of its 10 percent share in Telettra, as well as open its purchasing policy. Alcatel merged its satellite operations with Aerospatiale and bought the transmission equipment division of U.S. giant Rockwell.

The French Computer Industry

The early mainstay of the domestic French computer industry was Groupe Bull, which began in 1931, when a French group, partly owned by the Callies family, cousins of the Michelin tire owners, bought the patent for punched card machines from the Norwegian inventor Fredrik Bull. Its first significant product was a tabulator–printer that successfully competed against the French subsidiary of IBM, which had been established in 1920 (McInnes, 1964).

In 1952, Bull introduced its first computer, reputedly more innovative than IBM's most advanced 604 computer, though IBM was just then starting in the computer business. Bull's revenues rose tenfold in the decade from 1952 to 1962; exports grew 30 percent annually, and its labor force increased sixfold to 14,000. Bull became the darling of the Paris Bourse, with its shares reaching a price of 1470 francs by 1960, although its earnings never exceeded 3.80 francs per share.

Trouble soon followed, as IBM's more advanced 650 computer started to recapture market share from the Bull models. Bull fell further behind when IBM introduced its 1401 transistorized computer. While trying to recoup its losses with the high-priced and innovative Gamma 60 computer, Bull's production and development lagged behind schedule. The machines had chronic problems, and Bull sold or leased only fourteen of them. IBM came out with a still more advanced series, the 7070 model (Bransten and Brown, 1964, p. 154). Stymied in its products development, Bull sought help in America, entering a ten-year agreement for the sale of RCA's computers in France under the Bull label. It also obtained access to RCA's patents and production knowhow and soon marketed RCA's Model 301 in France, promoting it as a French product competing with those of the foreign IBM (some of whose products were manufactured in France for export to other European countries). Unfortunately for Bull, RCA soon left the computer business altogether.

Despite the success of its shares, Bull was undercapitalized and met with economic difficulties. Instead of reducing their control to raise equity, the owners took on large debts. When they faced the necessity of raising equity, the stock had begun to drop and it was too late. Between 1959 and 1962, total indebtedness increased fivefold, exceeding capital and reserves. In desperation, Bull restructured, to gain access to the Swiss financial markets, and sold off its share in Olivetti-Bull, a computer venture with Olivetti in Italy.

By 1963, the French government urged the state banks to assume control of Bull. Bull's chairman, Callies, sought links with the American company General Electric, at that time a computer maker with European ambitions, as preferable to control by the French government. Although GE agreed to buy 20 percent of Bull, the two companies had not reckoned with President Charles de Gaulle, who personally ordered the deal stopped, believing it contrary to the French interest in its computer industry to have an American firm share ownership. But after the government failed to line up French support, it was, embarrassingly, forced to permit an even larger participation of GE in Bull (49 percent) than the one it had previously vetoed, and at a lower sale price, amounting to a virtual control of Bull by the American company. The French government insisted, however, on segregating GE's control from Bull's defense contracts, which at that time involved developing France's nuclear capability. The deal was rationalized as part of a strategy of teaming up with another American giant against IBM.

Not surprisingly, General Electric soon experienced major headaches with Bull. Though it was clear that Bull was overstaffed, GE had committed itself to not reducing employment. When it was confronted with reality, a period of labor strife ensued. GE also canceled two ongoing computer developments at Bull. Eventually, GE left the computer business entirely, with Honeywell assuming its share in Bull, to form the Honeywell-Bull company.

French concerns over computer "sovereignty" were not ill founded. The French were shocked by the U.S. State Department's refusal of an export license for large scientific computers to the French atomic energy commission for use in H-bomb research. Realizing its vulnerability, the government formulated its Plan Calcul in 1966 and 1967, among other projects, merging two French-owned computer manufacturers, CAE (owned by CSF and CGE, both important telecommunications manufacturers) and SEA (a subsidiary of the Schneider industrial group) to create the firm CII (Compagnie Internationale pour l'Information). Another element of the Plan Calcul was financial support to establish consortia for the development of electronic technology. Bull, the main computer firm, was excluded from the Plan Calcul because of its American links. A computer czar, with the title of "Delegate Generale," was to oversee the projects and the government procurement, although the position largely became a public relations affair.

Plan Calcul delineated goals for the development of scientific computing, leaving much of commercial office computer market to IBM. This misjudged the explosive growth of business applications of computers, while failing to recognize the innovativeness of the American Control Data Corporation (CDC) in the scientific computing field.

The product strategy behind the Plan Calcul also missed other developments. The emergence of time-shared use of computers, linking terminals to a powerful central computer, led the Plan to predict a future with only a few giant mainframes and consequently to set product development priorities toward developing such machines. The subsequent trend was almost the opposite; mini- and microcomputers proliferated, and IBM was not the dominant firm in that market. On the other hand, one benefit from the Plan Calcul was to provide digital technology skills to Thomson and to CGE, which were later applied to digital telecommunications switches. This link was not foreseen in the Plan Calcul, but it was its major success.

A second Plan Calcul was instituted in 1971, again amidst much publicity: in absolute terms, however, the support levels were small. For the first Plan between 1966 and 1971, government support had been $140 million. For the second five years (1971–1976) support was $263 million.

CII had been nursed along with infusions of government capital. But after a while, a strategic rift developed between CII's two major owners, Thomson–Brandt and CGE, then rivals in the telecommunications field. The French government, Thomson, and CII were in favor of CII's participation together with Philips and Siemens in the European computer venture Unidata, designed as a competitor to IBM. However, CGE wanted a link with the second semi-French computer company, Honeywell–Bull, and refused to put up money for Unidata.

By 1976, neither CII nor Honeywell–Bull were doing well; with some government pressure and financial help, they were merged into CII–Honeywell–Bull, which was 53 percent French and 47 percent owned by Honeywell. The new firm had an extraordinarily complex structure to assure participation by major French electronic firms, by the French government itself (9.5 percent), and by Honeywell. Recognizing the importance of orders, the government promised $800 million of public sector procurement within the next four years, to provide necessary economies of scale. If that target was not met, major contractual damages would have to be paid to the company by the government.

It turned out to be expensive for the French public sector to buy the French computers to replace IBM systems. In particular, the cost of converting software turned out to be much higher than the cost for computers themselves. For the government, this more than doubled the amount it had planned to spend on CII–Honeywell–Bull computers.

With the Mitterrand nationalizations, Honeywell was forced to reduce its involvement in Bull substantially. But because its participation was still deemed to be desirable because of its access to advanced technology and the American market, it retained 19.9 percent of Bull and entered into a ten-year marketing and technology agreement with it. The French government also invested 1.5 billion francs in Bull. In 1986, Honeywell exited from computer manufacturing altogether.

In the 1980s, Groupe Bull's guiding philosophy shifted. It had not been able to manufacture its DPS7 computer, which was on the drawing board since 1979. Bull began to rely on cooperative agreements with other firms, including Honeywell, Convergent, Trilogy, and NEC. Such a strategy brought with it the risk of transforming Bull into a marketer of others' products, while contradicting notions of French autonomy in the computer field that underlie much of the government's financial efforts.

Bull was the twelfth largest computer manufacturer in the world. In the European market for minicomputers, it was second, with 11 percent of the total.

It was weaker in low-end minis and especially mainframes; the latter market was dominated by IBM (57 percent) and Siemens (15 percent), leaving Bull with a 6 percent share. In 1988, Bull received 18 percent of its revenues from U.S. operations (Schenker, 1989a, p. 13). It then sought a greater share of the U.S. market and acquired in 1989 the computer division of Zenith, an American manufacturer in financial difficulties because of its television manufacturing.

Groupe Bull continued to receive some $150 million annually from the French government (Petersen, 1989, p. 80). But its finances were in trouble. At the turn of the decade, Bull suffered heavy losses. In 1990, Bull's incurred a $1.2 billion deficit, necessitating a $700 million government contribution together with France Télécom. Bull also sought minority participation by NEC. The Japanese company already provided it with mainframe technology.

Other Efforts in Industrial Policy

Semiconductors

In 1982, French companies accounted for only 5 percent of their domestic microprocessor and MOS/memory market (though this number rises to 45 percent when foreign companies producing in France are included). To increase the French share has been a major development priority for the government's *filière électronique* industrial policy in the 1980s, an "action program for the electronics sector" aimed at creating at least 1000 jobs. To attain its aims, the government encouraged the creation of two new French-American ventures, Matra-Harris Semiconductors (MHS) and Eurotechnique, by Saint-Gobain and National Semiconductors (Malerba, 1985). Other major French microcomponent manufacturers were Thomson and Schlumberger; The latter acquired the American company Fairchild, a pioneer in integrated circuits that had lost its leadership position partly because of the flight of some top personnel into entrepreneurial start-ups. Schlumberger played an important role for a while, headed by the legendary Jean Riboud, an intimate of President Mitterrand. It was at one time called the best managed enterprise in the world, but Riboud died in 1985 and the company was beset by problems in its declining oil drilling business. Heavy losses on its Fairchild semiconductor operation led Schlumberger to sell it in 1986.

A second "Components Plan" (Plan Composants) was adopted in 1983, seeking to promote specialized components in telecommunications, military applications, and MOS (metal oxide) technology. The plan's economic goals included raising French volume of production to 4.65 billion francs in 1986. The plan's budget was FFr 3.2 billion (FFr 700–800 million annually), mostly benefitting four companies. The government's telecommunications research arm CNET also played an important role in this area.

In 1987, Thomson merged its semiconductor operations with those of SGS, the microchip firm controlled by the Italian government's STET group, to form Europe's second largest microchip firm after Philips.

Communications Satellites

In cooperation with Germany, France developed an experimental satellite system called Symphonie, launched in 1974 and 1975. The next generation of satellites, Telecom-1, was decided upon in 1978 and contracted from Matra with the limited involvement of Alcatel and Thomson CSF. Telecom-1A and -1B are used for domestic civilian and military applications as well as for transmission of telecommunications and television programs to France's overseas possessions.

This domestic French satellite must be distinguished from the European ECS satellite, produced by a European consortium with British Aerospace as prime contractor, administered by the European Space Agency (ESA), and operated by the European satellite organization Eutelsat.

Telecom-1's coverage of most of Europe allows it to provide links beyond the French borders. Two agreements were signed in 1981 with Germany, permitting it to offer domestic national communications in German territories using part of the system's capacity. A second agreement was signed in 1982 with Eutelsat for offering international European links. A 1980 agreement between France and Germany led to the launch of the TDF-1 direct broadcast satellite in 1988. TDF-2 was launched in 1990.

The Restructuring of France Télécom

France Télécom itself continued to widen the scope of its activities. It had 155,000 employees and revenues of $166.6 billion in 1989. It had 27 million access lines, forty-five main lines per 100 persons. It established international partnerships in Germany, Spain, Italy, and Singapore (the latter cable project involved a $600 million fiber optic cable from France through the Middle East to Singapore), and joint projects with Germany's DBP Telekom, a Phonepoint bid with BT, as well as participation in Infonet and a Pacific Cable with other partners (Steckel and Fossier, 1990). After the Chirac conservative government came to power in 1986, Gerard Longuet, a leader of the right-of-center Republicans, became PTT minister. Although the conservative government took an early and active role in privatizing the broadcasting field, it moved more carefully in telephony. It promised to propose legislation that would establish private competition in the telecommunications field by the end of 1987.

Marcel Roulet, a PTT veteran, was appointed as the Chirac government's director of the DGT. He recommended ending the DGT's dual role of network operations and regulation and establishing the DGT as a state enterprise rather than as a government administration. Under this plan, the industrial policy role of the DGT would move to the Ministry of Industry and some of the DGT's competitive subsidiaries would be partly privatized. At the same time, the DGT would be free, under such an arrangement, to participate in joint ventures with private companies and to purchase its equipment more freely.

Longuet was succeeded by his party colleague, François Léotard. He expanded the High Authority of the Audiovisual Sector, an agency created by the Socialists a few years earlier to supervise broadcasting, into a National Commission for Communications and Liberties (CNCL), with some regulatory powers also over telecommunications. In October 1986, the ministry set up the Mission à la Réglementation to handle postal and telecommunications regulation. Jean-Pierre Chamoux headed this task force, developing new policy initiatives along these lines, but many of its proposals were slowed down when the labor unions threatened disruption and presidential elections interfered.

The government did not recommend an opening to competing service providers in transmission. This left the liberalization of value-added networks services (VANS) as a major focus. Since 1987, VANS had been legalized and usually needed only to notify the PTT administration to commence operations. The decree distinguished between closed, user group networks and universal networks open to third parties.

The Chirac government moved more actively in the reprivatization of the electronics industry. CGE was sold, undivided, to the public in May of 1987 for $3.7 billion. Thus, a private near-monopoly in telecommunications equipment succeeded the public one. Next was CGCT, which was sold to Ericsson and Matra in January 1988. The privatizations of Thomson and Bull were delayed after the stock market crash of 1987 and were later abandoned after the presidential elections confirmed Mitterrand in 1988.

Furthermore, it was more difficult to privatize painlessly the two money losing companies. In 1990, Thomson had a deficit necessitating a $350 million contribution by the government. Bull's deficit was $1.2 billion. Alcatel's profit for the same year was $750 million.

Chirac's efforts at privatization had been opposed by Paul Quilés, former oil company engineer and minister of defense, though not particularly well versed in telecommunications issues. A savvy politician, Quilés became PTT minister in the Socialist government that soon returned to power. At the same time, the PTT became the Ministry of PTE—Post, Telecommunications, and Space—reflecting the growing importance of satellite to network communications.

In 1988, the regulatory and operational functions of the DGT were split into the Direction de la Réglementation Générale (DRG), and France Télécom, the new name for the DGT. The DRG (the former Mission à la Reglementation) has authority over type approval, value-added services, and the electromagnetic spectrum (Roussel, 1989b). Its first head was Bruno Lassère, formerly legal counsel to the DGT, while Marcel Roulet was appointed the first director general of France Télécom. The DRG also represents France in international negotiations. Authority over France Télécom's most significant decisions such as network investments, public service obligations, and management remained under the control of the PTE through the Direction des Services Publiques (DSP). The DRG had only authority over competitive services, which was still limited to a handful of VANs and a small second cellular service provider, and its powers to bring competition to the French market were limited.

In 1989, Quilés commissioned an analysis of French policy from civil servant Hubert Prévot. Originally a defender of the DGT monopoly, Quilés stated publicly that growth should not be constricted by "archaic structures." Quilés also had the support of France Télécom's management, which had complained about political control (Dawkins, 1990b). The Prévot report recommended the formal separation of post and telecommunications services, and the removal of France Télécom's equity from the Treasury to create a more autonomous and competitive entity. The autonomy would also change the civil servant status of employees. This resulted in union opposition. Led by the Communist CGT labor federation, one fifth of PTT workers went on to strike in 1990. Despite the national debate they triggered, the proposed reforms passed the National Assembly with surprising ease. In the Senate, however, the proposal's detractors were many. The strongest criticism came from a group of conservative senators led by Gerard Larcher, a strong supporter of former PTT minister Longuet. They issued a scathing report that charged Quilés with being weak-kneed in his proposed reforms. The report claimed that, despite gaining autonomy, France Télécom would still answer to the government in setting tariffs and before making large investments or purchases. The senators found particular fault with the program's hiring provisions, labeling them too rigid to stop the chronic "brain drain" from management ranks.

The Larcher committee also proposed that a larger contingent of lawmakers be chosen for the proposed twenty-one-member France Télécom board and that more autonomy be given to the board than was recommended by Quilés. The Senate conservatives also wanted to create a European Telecommunications Foundation to promote the continent's interests in telecommunications.

After promises of job security for employees, the government's reform proposals passed the National Assembly and Senate in May 1990. The law provided that France Télécom be separate from La Poste and managed by a twenty-one-member board, including representatives of French ministries and users groups. France Télécom's president is nominated to a three-year term by the government. It must negotiate its budget with the government and set rates according to a price-cap scheme, instead of the past 6 percent rate-of-return system. In addition, the COGECOM subsidiaries, including TDF, Transpac, and France Cables et Radio, were all removed from the control of the Finance Ministry.

Paul Quilés was succeeded in 1991 by Jean-Marie Rausch, and in 1992 by Emile Zuccarelli, head of a small leftist party and a mayor in Corsica, but without a telecommunications background. The position of PTE Minister was downgraded to a junior minister reporting to the Minister of Finance, Economy and Budget.

Limited proposals to liberalize terminal equipment and value-added service markets were introduced in 1990, and France Télécom's monopoly over basic telephone, telex and national network services was reaffirmed. V-sat licenses were issued in 1991 to France Télécom, but also to BAeCom, Alpha Lyracom, Reuters, and PolyCom. A second mobile license was awarded to SFR.

Thus, the first steps in what will be a continuing journey toward an industry structure of greater openness had been initiated, though they still represent primarily a strengthening of the traditional operator, liberalizing its ability to function successfully rather than altering the structure of the communications sector.

Telecommunications in Benelux and the Alpine Countries

10

The Netherlands

Historically, the Netherlands has been a center for transportation, insurance, banking, and trade. The port of Rotterdam is the largest in the world and a major hub for the oil business. Much of the extensive European Rhine and Meuse barge traffic reaches Holland through inland shipping. In addition, the country accounts for a quarter of international trucking within the EEC (PTT Telecommunicatie, 1983). Holland is also the headquarters for three of the largest multinational companies in the world—Shell, Philips, and Unilever. In 1980, the sum of the country's imports and exports was 60 percent higher than its entire GNP, a ratio five to six times higher than that of the United States or Japan, and twice as high as those of other European countries (Wieland, 1986).

It is therefore not surprising that the Netherlands targeted its telecommunications system to help establish itself as a major European economic center. In 1985, the government decided to reorganize the PTT by forming a semi-independent telecommunications company separate from the basic network provider. This moderate reform, which went into effect in 1989, marked the second European PTT transformation, following the more far-reaching changes in the United Kingdom.

The Dutch reorganization was particularly significant because it served as a model of corporatization for other European countries. The extensive competitiveness in the United States made its system institutionally too distant to be directly applicable. The British policy, favoring privatization and the establishment of a competitive carrier, was also too radical for the continental countries. The Japanese model suffers from the lack of transparency of Japanese governmental and economic processes. Holland, on the other hand, is a close and respected neighbor, and its policies cannot be easily dismissed as attempts at hegemony. The Dutch PTT reform was therefore watched with particular interest by other European countries.

The Dutch PTT

A national postal service existed in the Netherlands since 1799, when it was created to supplant the private postal services (Kingdom of the Netherlands, 1981). Telephone service was begun in 1881, when the private Nederlandse Bell Telephoon Maatschappij opened in Amsterdam. Other companies followed elsewhere, operating under governmental concessions (Dabbs et al., 1982). Private companies also established long-distance interexchange telephones starting in 1888. However, the government took over the long-distance licenses when they expired in 1897 in order to protect the revenues of state telegraphy; subsequently, the Government Telephone service was formed.

In the meantime, as a consequence of monopolistic charges levied by private local companies on subscribers, most municipalities co-opted local telephone service. In the largest cities—Amsterdam (1896), Rotterdam (1896), and The Hague (1903)—the municipal governments built completely new systems rather than purchase the deteriorated Bell plant (Holcombe, 1911). Starting in 1907, the PTT collected the local networks under its aegis, and by 1927, it operated all but the networks in Amsterdam, Rotterdam, and The Hague. Eventually, the PTT gained full national control over telephone service when the last three municipal systems were forcibly incorporated in 1940 during the German occupation in World War II.

Strictly speaking, the PTT, as defined by the 1904 Telegraphs and Telephones Act, was not a statutory monopoly; in practice, however, it played that role ever since it absorbed the remaining municipal systems. Formerly called the Staatsbedrijf der Posterijen, Telegrafie en Telefonie, the Dutch PTT provided telecommunications as well as postal and financial services. It was the country's largest employer, with 29,000 of its 100,000 employees working in telecommunications.

The PTT was controlled politically by the minister of transport and public works and financially by the minister of finance. Its governance was subject to the PTT Raad (Council), a board that included all major political parties, and to provincial PTT Kamers (PTT chambers), representing the provincial governments, the PTT unions, and users. Since the PTT depended on the government for approval of its budget, it had to conform to governmental economic policy, such as restrictions on price increases. As a result, a government ordinance was required to change charges for rental equipment, for example.

The PTT was affiliated with Nepostel, a technically independent foundation that provides Third World consulting and assistance, and with CASEMA, a central cable television antenna system company, of which it held 51 percent. CASEMA's other major shareholders were the national broadcast transmitting organization NOZEMA (22 percent), which provided radio and TV broadcast transmission services in the Netherlands, and several of the country's semi-independent broadcasting associations, such as AVRO, KRO, VARA, and NCRV. The PTT also constructed and maintained NOZEMA's facilities and shared facilities with the Dr. Neher Laboratories (DNL) and PTT Telematics Laboratories (PTL) for technical research and development.

Services

Telephone line density increased more than sixfold in twenty years, from 1 million in 1960 to 6.4 million in 1980. This growth rate slowed in the 1980s from 13 percent to 4 percent and lower, since most households had been reached. Long waiting lists of potential subscribers had accumulated during the 1970s, peaking in 1977 at 200,000. By 1982, this backlog had been reduced to 1 percent of main stations.

By 1988, telephone density in the Netherlands reached sixty-six sets per 100 population. According to the OECD, the 1990 tariffs in the Netherlands are Europe's lowest for business services, $430.21 yearly, and the third lowest for residential customers ($224.48 yearly), behind Iceland and Sweden. The density of the Dutch network allows the Netherlands to offer low rates (Montgomery, et al., 1990).[1]

Despite the country's small size, PTT Telecom was the world's eighth largest international carrier in 1988.

In 1962, the Netherlands became the second country in the world, after Switzerland, to achieve a fully automated national telephone service. Electronic switching started in 1972, with the Ericsson AKE-13, a stored-program-controlled (SPC) exchange. The Philips PRX-205 local switch followed in 1974. In 1980, Ericsson's AXE exchange was also put into service in order to provide a second supplier. In that year, 30 percent of subscribers were served by SPC switches, the highest such density in the world at the time according to ITT. Since 1984, fully electronic exchanges have gradually replaced electromechanical exchanges as part of a fifteen-year investment program to digitalize the network, using AT&T technology after 1983. PTT Telecom inaugurated a pilot test of international ISDN service in October 1989, linking Rotterdam with Düsseldorf.

The public packet switching service Datanet-1 operated from 1982 on a trial basis, and since 1984 commercially, with transmission rates up to 48 kbps. It provides international access. Telex penetration in the Netherlands is among the highest in Europe, but falling. Since 1984, an electronic mail service was offered over Datanet-1. Multisat provides international broadband data communications via satellites.[2]

Most post offices in the country carry Faxpost, a public facsimile service. Other services include cellular telephone and radio paging through the Benelux system. Videotex, under the name of Viditel, was introduced in 1980. The broadcast text service teletext was started in 1980 by the broadcast associations and NOS, their umbrella state organization. The PTT and several Dutch cable operators formed a joint company in 1989 to develop a videotex service. However, PTT cooperation with cable television was controversial (Tutt, 1990).

Protracted debate occurred on privacy legislation. Following a commission's reports of 1974 and 1976, a bill was introduced in 1981, but it was complex and was withdrawn. The simplified substitute was debated for several years (de Pous, 1988). After twenty years of discussion, a Data Protection Act was adopted in 1988 and came into effect the next year. The Act required self-regulation in the collection of personal data and established the right of individuals to access and correct information files for a minimal fee.

Equipment

In procuring equipment, the PTT has traditionally been close to the Dutch company Philips. Prior to the digitalization of the exchanges, Philips supplied about 70 percent of the PTT's SPC switches, with Ericsson's Dutch subsidiary supplying the rest. In 1985, the PTT awarded a major contract for its 5ESS-PRX digital switching system to the joint APT venture of Philips and AT&T. The government also required the PTT to contract with a third and junior supplier for digital switching, in addition to Ericsson and APT, to satisfy CGE-ITT (Alcatel) with its subsidiary Nederlandsche Standard Electric Maatschappi (NSEM) and its System 12. Subsequently, Alcatel, the second largest telecommunications firm in the world, established its formal headquarters in the Netherlands, partly to soften its image as French dominated and to give it instead a pan-European image. Much of Alcatel's actual management remained in France.

In the recent past, the PTT has had an extraordinary hold over customer equipment. However, there has always been a distinction between the relative severity of the letter of telecommunications regulation and the more flexible reality. For example, large users understood well that the prohibition of sharing leased lines was not an enforcement priority of the PTT. Similarly, although the PTT had a total monopoly on all regular telephone sets until 1989, in practice, much customer equipment was purchased from private vendors (Hins and Hugenholtz, 1986). The PTT also enjoyed a monopoly on the installation and maintenance of PBXs and of the telephone sets attached to them. The PBX remained the property of the PTT and was only leased to the user. In theory at least, the PTT had the right to extend its monopoly into answering machines, telefax, modems, and other data terminals, though it refrained from asserting such broad authority.

Philips

Philips is the largest European electronics manufacturer and by far the largest Dutch high-technology company (Tagliabue, 1987). Founded in 1894 by Anton Frederik Philips and his brother Gerard to make electrical lamps, the company keeps the name Gloewlampenfabrieken (incandescent lamp factory) in its title, even though, beginning with the period after World War I, it has vastly expanded its product line. Gerard, a mechanical engineer and chemist, initiated a scientific tradition in the company that Gilles Holst continued after World War I. The company pioneered the electric dry shaver and was active in X-ray tubes and hot gas engines. Gerard was childless, and the succession of control moved to his brother's children (Philips, 1978).

Philips was hard hit by the Depression and later by the German occupation. In anticipation of the occupation, Philips moved its legal headquarters to Curaçao, a Dutch possession safely located in the Western Hemisphere. Its extensive American and British interests were placed in two separate trusts that were legally separate from the Dutch company. This maneuver guarded these parts of the firm from take-over by the Allies after the German occupation of Holland.

World War II put the company into the difficult situation of complying with German-appointed supervisors while simultaneously trying to avoid attracting Allied bombardment. The German supervisors were not interested in merely running the company. In one instance, Philips was pressured to give up two paintings by Lucas Cranach the Elder and coveted by Field Marshall Hermann Goering, lest its raw material supply be cut off (Philips, 1978).

The Germans ordered Philips to reduce prices for its light bulbs. Frederik Philips' comments on this incident in his corporate history provides a glimpse into the protected Dutch electrical equipment market:

> The former manager of our sales organization for the Netherlands and her colonies had firmly believed in high prices for our lamps and would never budge. The result was that, at the beginning of the occupation, there were in Holland no less than twenty-three lamp factories, large and small, which survived under this heightened price umbrella. Possibly the manufacturers loved us for this, but our lamps were more expensive in Holland than abroad—a fact that the public knew. I decided that we would lower our prices after the war by 50 percent. However, the Germans were ahead of us: they suddenly ordered a substantial cut in retail prices [Philips, 1978].

After liberation, the company expanded substantially into other European countries, the United States, and the Third World. It acquired Pye in Britain and part of a major cable manufacturer in Germany. Philips became a world pioneer in consumer electronics—for example, in compact audio cassettes and in video cassette recorders, where it introduced the world's first consumer VCR (Video 2000) in 1972. In 1986, it adopted the Japanese VHS standards under license for its VCRs, and withdrew its own system. However, by 1990 Philips had only a small share of the European VCR market and a much smaller proportion globally because of vigorous Asian competition. Together with the Japanese firm, Sony, Philips established standards for optical laser compact disc systems, but here, too, it was left behind by Japanese price competition. Similar pressure on its other product lines led Philips to change its strategy from in-house development to one of joint ventures with American, Japanese, and other European firms. In 1984, only 20 percent of Philips' products were manufactured by one of its own companies; many of the others were produced by other companies and sold under the Philips label.

Philips spent over $1 billion a year on research and development, the third largest such budget after IBM and AT&T (Tagliabue, 1984). It was Holland's most important firm in the development of microprocessors and other semiconductors, with its subsidiaries Valvo (Germany), Mullard (Britain), Complelec (France), and Signetics (America) (Malerba, 1985). Philips also took over the German firm Grundig, which, before faltering financially, had been Europe's second-largest consumer electronics company. Together with Siemens, Philips worked on developing advanced memory "megachip" components.

In telecommunications, Philips concentrated on cable transmission, telephone sets, PBX terminals, and smaller switches rather than on large central office switches. Because it had little advanced digital technology, it entered into a joint venture with AT&T in 1982. APT (AT&T-Philips Telecommunications) was carefully structured as a European venture; chartered in the Netherlands, its subsidiaries are entirely European. The venture led Philips to stop developing its own PRXD digital switch and adopt the AT&T 5ESS-PRX switch.

APT competed unsuccessfully in Britain and Italy; it received a Dutch contract, some Saudi Arabian business, and a larger Indonesian award, and combined with Alcatel to modernize the Venezuelan telephone system.

The joint venture was not as successful as originally hoped. Furthermore, Philips was under financial pressure. In 1989, AT&T increased its share from 60 percent to 85 percent in the joint venture. Later that year, Italy's Itatel and AT&T formed a joint venture (the former took a 20 percent stake in the project). In 1990, AT&T purchased Philips' remaining 15 percent share and sold 6 percent to Spain's Telefónica (Wilde, 1990).

In 1990, Philips took a huge $1.4 billion charge against earnings and eliminated 10,000 jobs from its workforce of almost 300,000 worldwide, mostly because of its faltering computer and electronics divisions.

Policy Debate and Reform Legislation

An early attempt at policy discussion took place in the early 1960s, when the so-called Goedhart Committee studied the possibility of PTT autonomy in investments and borrowing. But the committee's 1963 recommendation for greater flexibility was never acted upon (Wieland, 1986).

In 1981, widespread dissatisfaction among users and equipment suppliers led the government to appoint a new commission, chaired by Frans Swarttouw, chairman of the Fokker aircraft manufacturing firm, to investigate the present and future of the PTT and to recommend necessary reforms. In 1982, this commission proposed to grant the PTT more autonomy in order to enter financial markets independently and to set rates and services with greater flexibility. At the same time, it recommended that private competitors be permitted to enter the terminal equipment market, while leaving intact the PTT's monopoly for traditional services. The commission advised that the PTT be transformed into a limited-liability company owned by the government, rather than remain a part of the Ministry of Transport and Public Works. It further urged that the new "enhanced" services—linking computers and communications to potentially include videotex, video conferencing, and electronic mail—should be opened to private service providers using the PTT network. Telecommunications operations would be separate from postal operations, and PTT financial activities would be placed into a separate "postbank."

Shortly after the report's release, the previous center-right government was displaced by a left-of-center coalition. This enabled Philips (the major equipment supplier) and the trade unions to block the recommended changes. In 1985, however, the Christian Democrats and Liberals regained power and declared their support of the Swarttouw recommendations. Another commission was appointed to investigate the possibility of integrating telecommunications with the numerous cable television networks, a move in response to the slow but steady trend toward liberalization that had been going on in Dutch broadcasting since 1969. T. H. Steenbergen, an economic liberal, chaired the new commission, which consisted of two other members, one an industrialist with Social Democratic leanings and the other a professor of engineering whose Danish origin may have encouraged hopes of domestic neutrality. With the assistance of the large American consulting firm McKinsey, and without the cumbersome membership by representatives of every interest group and party, the commission provided a report within the year, in July 1985.

The Steenbergen Commission report proposed a twofold reorganization: first, a functional separation of the PTT's telecommunications activities into three areas. "Public utility services"—to include public networks, basic services, and basic terminal equipment—were distinguished from "competitive services," which included user group networks, value-added networks, and complex terminal equipment. Although both functions would remain under the auspices of the PTT, "competitive services," unlike "public utility services," would lose monopolistic exclusivity. The third function of regulation, equipment approval, and standardization, would be taken away from the PTT altogether and lodged in a newly created department for telecommunications regulation and approval under the jurisdiction of the Ministry of Transport and Public Works (RUPTT).

The minister would regulate the PTT's "public utility" rates and quality, approve equipment and operating licenses for value-added and regular networks, and allocate frequencies. The two limited companies would share a board of directors, top management, and some central administrative functions, although financially they would be independent of each other. In addition, no hidden funds would flow between social and competitive tasks in telecommunications. Competitive services would have to pay the regular value-added tax, and PTT employees would lose their civil service status by 1989. The commission suggested that private value-added services would be a possible way of dealing with competitive and network services without establishing alternative networks, while at the same time solving the resale problem. Licenses for the value-added network services would be sought from the approvals office, and the services would have to be specific enough so that the system would be protected from pure resale.

In addition to this functional separation, the report recommended that the legal status of the PTT itself be transformed into a private holding company (Royal PTT Nederland N.V.), entirely owned by the state, which in turn would own three separate limited companies: for postal services, for basic public telecommunications, and for competitive telecommunications services and products. However, the separation of telecommunications into two segments was not adopted by the government. The basic and competitive tasks were left within PTT Telecom Nederland B.V. after PTT resistance and were separated for the time being only by undefined accounting procedures. The government-stated intention was ultimately to separate the two by legal means. It insisted on continuing to receive from the holding company about the same contribution to its general budget as before.

Both the Swarttouw and the Steenbergen reports proposed to end the PTT monopoly over terminal equipment. But the actual loss to the PTT from liberalization was not great because privately supplied terminal equipment was already de facto widely available. The commission recommended greater competition for PBXs to reduce their price. Partly because of high costs due to the existence of only two suppliers, Philips and Ericsson, the Netherlands had only half as many PBXs as West Germany. According to the commission, only four models of small PBXs (for up to 100 lines) were available in Holland, compared to seven such models available in Germany and twenty-five in the United States. For medium-sized PBXs (100 to 400 lines), only one model was available in Holland, seven in Germany, and sixty in the United States (Wieland, 1986).

The government's official response to the Steenbergen report cautiously acknowledged its conclusions: "Let there be no doubt that this government is in favor of deregulation and privatization/denationalization, but it must be done in a responsible fashion" (Netherlands PTT, 1985, p. 10). The PTT took a critical stance in reaction to the report and presented itself as the last line of defense for order. Hinting at a bias of the commission toward IBM, the PTT claimed, "It is hard to avoid the conclusion that the Committee has chosen in favor of computer suppliers who never cease to distance themselves from telecommunications companies in Europe, mainly PTTs."

But despite several rearguard arguments, the PTT eventually reconciled itself to change and concluded that reform was, in fact, in its own self-interest. The Steenbergen recommendations were, after all, hardly radical. A German Bundespost study of the Dutch situation surmised that the change of heart in the Dutch PTT may have reflected a generational shift in attitude, whereby the younger management in leadership positions preferred a greater managerial independence outside of a government operation. Meanwhile, union members, the majority of whom actively followed the deliberations, concluded that their wages, salaries, and especially pensions would be improved by a switch from a civil service to independent corporate status (Wieland, 1986).

Under the old system, PTT employees were paid as civil servants and were tied to the entire bureaucracy's general pay scale. The many technically qualified personnel needed by the PTT were in great demand by other employers, and the maximum government salary was often not sufficient to draw them into civil service. At the Dr. Neher Laboratories, for example, a large number of all positions remained unfilled for that reason. In many instances, the PTT was able to hire only recent graduates who sought to gain experience before moving on to the private sector.

The PTT's new stance was strengthened by the fact that the Dutch equipment industry that opposed the reform, fearing a loss in market share, was less powerful than those in other countries. Since Philips is a greatly diversified global corporation, it was not as dependent on the PTT's status quo as some manufacturers in other European countries.

The government cabinet approved the Steenbergen proposal in 1985 and established a phase-in period lasting until January 1, 1989. The proposal was approved by the Dutch parliament in 1986 and included further provisions to privatize much of PTT Telecom by selling its shares to the public by the mid-1990s. A new department of telecommunications was created in the Ministry of Transport and Public Works. The ministry oversees operator licenses, equipment type approvals, and public service requirements.

Following the 1989 restructuring, PTT Telecom Nederland had exclusive responsibilities for basic service, transmission, telex and telegraph service and data transport services. Valued-added services and customer premises equipment were liberalized.[3] But these changes still left many large users, VANs, and equipment suppliers dissatisfied. PTT Telecom faced complaints from users over this role as equipment supplier and service provider. It did not allow interconnection with the public network. Value-added services may be provided only on the condition that the public infrastucture is used.

The $800 million equipment market was liberalized in 1989 but exclusive distribution contracts between the PTT and Ericsson and Philips limited competition and raised prices. The PTT still supplied a majority of basic phone sets. However, a significant portion of the PTT's PBX market now belongs to Ericsson and Philips. A Philips PBX costs 25 percent to 33 percent more in the Netherlands than in the United States or West Germany. Responsibility for testing was given to two independent institutes, KEMA and NTK.

A blue-ribbon panel, the Zegveld Commission, was appointed to investigate the newly organized PTT's possible relationships with the municipal, independent, and private cable networks. In 1986, it advised the gradual integration, over a period of twenty years, of the cable network with the PTT-owned infrastructure.

11
Belgium

With the erosion of its traditional economic base of heavy industry, Belgium's economic priority is to become Europe's administrative center. Brussels already serves as the headquarters for both the European Community and NATO. The country also seeks to draw nongovernmental organizations; its capital city is home to the European headquarters of many overseas companies and associations. Telecommunications links should therefore be an especially important factor in the country's economic development. However, Belgium's traditional monopolist Régie des Télégraphes et des Téléphones (RTT), financially constrained in its goal to be at the forefront of service provision and development, has been one of Europe's strongest defenders of traditionalism. In this position it was supported by its major equipment supplier, Alcatel's BTM, and by the labor unions. As a consequence, Belgium has not become a center of European telecommunications, a role that would be otherwise natural. Partly in order to achieve that goal, a 1991 reform reorganized RTT into the semi-independent Belgacom.

Telephony and the RTT

The telephone was first demonstrated in Belgium in 1876. When the government showed no interest in the new invention, a private telephone company was formed in 1879. Other companies soon followed and intense competition developed in several cities. Encouraged by national and local governments, the private firms merged in 1881 into the Compagnie Belge des Téléphones Bell. In 1883, telephone service was made subject to concessions granted in the context of the public telegraph monopoly. Concessions were granted for twenty-five years, at the end of which the physical plant was to be turned over to the government at no cost to the state; the government also had the option of choosing to purchase the plant after ten years. Concessionaires had to compensate the government at the rate of 5 francs per telephone station.

In 1884, the government began construction of interexchange long distance lines. Two years later, it started to provide local exchange service to small and medium-sized cities that were left out by the private concessionaires and it stopped issuing new licenses. When the ten-year option periods began to run out, the government took over the private Bell telephone systems. By 1896, no private telephone exchanges remained.

The first central battery network in Europe was opened in Brussels in 1902, with 4800 subscribers. Much of the telephone plant was destroyed during World War I, and it took until the end of 1920 to reestablish regular service. In 1922, the first automatic central office was inaugurated. The establishment of telephony and its improvement were hampered, however, by the weak financial situation of the government. A submarine cable to England was laid in 1926 and established Belgium as an important transit point for international traffic.

A 1930 parliamentary act removed the telephone monopoly from direct state control and placed it under the authority of the newly created RTT, an independent state agency that has since been the nation's sole provider of telecommunications services. The act provided parliamentary controls, and RTT was subject to the Ministry of PTT. It gave RTT some accounting flexibility, which a pure state service would not have been granted. In an effort to unify the status of the various semipublic organizations, however, parliament changed the law in 1954, making RTT also report to the ministers of the budget, finance, and civil service, all of whom had some authority over aspects of RTT operations. Subsequently, RTT lost even more autonomy. This was the reverse of trends elsewhere, where PTT organization became more independent over time. As a result, prior approval from one or several of the ministers in question was needed before RTT could take action. Decision-making speed was thus considerably reduced just when the opposite was needed in light of technological and business developments. These restrictions were supplemented by additional ones, including controls on equipment procurement implemented in 1976.

During the early 1980s, RTT found itself in dire financial straits and had difficulties meeting its debt burden. In 1985, its total outstanding debt was about Bfr 180 billion ($3 billion), the service of which required nearly 30 percent of the agency's revenues. This situation created particular problems in light of RTT's intention to enter in a significant way into digital switching.

The debt crisis created an impetus for rethinking the role of RTT, a process that divided both the government and the PTT Ministry itself. In 1985, the minister for communications, Herman de Croo, advocated a loosening of the RTT monopoly. In contrast, RTT itself, the labor unions, and his parliamentary state secretary, who was a member of another party, were opposed to such a step, because they viewed these measures as steps toward privatization. Only a limited liberalization of RTT activities took place; in 1985, the RTT was given permission to invest in private telecommunications companies and to establish "joint economy companies." Within RTT, there is a generational transition. Older managers defended the monopoly, based on their notion of its social and engineering function; younger managers tended to be more willing to experiment with new structures.[1]

In 1986, the government established a commission of four university professors headed by F. DeBount to look into the question of RTT autonomy. This commission of "four sages" delivered a very cautious report, staying within the narrow confines of what was deemed to be politically feasible. It advocated a liberalization of terminal equipment, more autonomy to RTT managers, and transformation of RTT into a public limited company, but only within several years.

In the center-right government coalition, the powerful faction of Christian Democrats was reluctant to liberalize. The conservatives' minister for the budget, Verhoffsdt, was most strongly in favor of private initiatives but had little support within the cabinet. The Social Democrats, the main opposition party of the time, saw no need for new structures. The parties were also divided among themselves according to language regions. Social Democrats from Flanders were more flexible on telecommunications issues than some members of the Liberal party from French-speaking Wallonia, since the protective attitude toward employment was much stronger in lagging Wallonia than in Flanders.

A force for change in Belgium has been the European Community's Commission, which resides in Brussels and whose officials thus have daily firsthand experience with RTT service and equipment options. Thus, RTT faced pressure from the EC to end the embarrassing delays of up to eighty days for telephone service for firms establishing offices there (Kellaway, 1990, p. IV). In 1986, for example, the commission issued a directive to RTT to liberalize equipment approval for terminals supplied by other countries.

After over thirty drafts and three years of debate, a reform bill finally passed the Belgian Parliament in 1991. The law created a category of public autonomous enterprises for state-owned firms, and separated RTT into an operator Belgacom and a regulatory body, the Belgian Institute for Telecommunications. The Institute plays only an advisory role to the powerful Minister of Infrastructure of Economic Affairs, who is responsible for telecommunications matters. Belgacom negotiated by 1992 a management contract outlining its budget, service offerings, and investment priorities. A Competition Council was also established to oversee public enterprises (R. Queck, 1991, communication). Belgacom provides basic transmission as a monopoly, and enhanced services in competition. However, authorized VAN licenses may be denied in the public interest, or if the license would cause financial losses for Belgacom. Conditions for the use of leased lines were also established. Belgacom also kept substantial power over equipment, and its employees kept civil-servant status. On the other hand, Bessel Kook, the former chief of the major user network SWIFT was appointed as Belgacom's head.

In 1992, the privatization of Belgacom was proposed, partly in order to balance the national budget.

The Equipment Industry

RTT had a monopoly on some PBXs, which it procured mainly from its main supplier BTM, and on first telephone sets. Liberalization emerged in the markets for more advanced equipment such as facsimile, teletext terminals, and cordless telephones. Policy debates focused on liberalizing all interconnection equipment.

The Belgian telecommunications industry grew at a rate of more than 15 percent during the decade 1975–1985. More than half of its equipment production was exported, and the country was in seventh place worldwide in net telecommunications exports in 1983 (Belgian National Committee, 1983).

Among the manufacturing firms, ATEA predominantly supplies private users, providing equipment such as computer terminals, telephones with magnetic card readers, and PBXs. In the United States, the firm's equipment for credit card checks has a major share of the market. ATEA was owned by the American firm GTE until 1986, when GTE sold control to Siemens. Siemens employs more than 2000 people in Belgian telecommunications and has engineering facilities for telecommunications and data-processing systems, as well as production facilities for telex terminals and for radio, transmission, and switching equipment.

The Dutch electric giant Philips has a Belgium telecommunications subsidiary with about 1000 employees. The subsidiary produces transmission equipment, multiplexers, integrated circuits, fiber-optic systems, PBXs, and radio communications equipment.

ACEC, a large company employing 1500 in telecommunications, produces teleprinters and satellite and fiber transmission systems. ACEC is owned by the Société Générale de Belgique and has links with Ericsson.

By far the most important Belgian equipment firm is Alcatel Bell Telephone, formerly Bell Telephone Manufacturing Company (BTMC or BTM). Despite its name, for many years BTM was an ITT firm, having been sold by AT&T to ITT. It became a pillar of ITT's European operations until the 1987 ITT–CGE deal transferred ITT's manufacturing operations into Alcatel, controlled by France's CGE. Partly because of the importance of Alcatel Bell Telephone in Belgian high technology, there is a special Belgian financial participation in Alcatel via the holdings of the large conglomerate Société Générale de Belgique. In 1985, BTM employed more than 10,000 people, 85 percent of which were in telecommunications. In 1990, Alcatel Bell Telephone employed 7455 people, all of them in telecommunications. The company exports to more than eighty countries, and its digital switches are sold, for example, in Denmark, South Korea, Israel, Taiwan, Switzerland, Mexico, Nepal, China, and Turkey (G. Buyck, 1987, communication).[2]

In 1985, BTM won a contract to supply China with System 12 digital exchanges for several cities, including Shanghai, and entered a joint manufacturing venture with a production capacity of 300,000 lines annually. The United States government objected to a transfer of such technology to China.

Historically, RTT had a relatively cozy relationship with BTM and ATEA in the procurement of switches, and it maintained an informal "three-to-one" order ratio between the two. In view of its location in the heart of European integration, RTT cannot be blatantly protectionist. Nevertheless, RTT's 1987 digital switching contract—dubbed "the sale of the century"—was granted to

BTM (66 percent) and ATEA (33 percent) (Müller, 1988). Technically, both companies are controlled by firms in other EC countries. The procurement process is also complicated by the traditional rivalry between Flanders and Wallonia. During price negotiations, the firms asked for $514 per line, whereas the RTT refused to offer more than $420 per line. The RTT then decided it would place the extra $92 per line into a R&D budget independent of the individual suppliers but benefiting them (*Euro-Telecom News,* 1987). In the United States, digital exchange for 1987 delivery was priced between $180 and $213 per line, according to the U.S. Justice Department (U.S. Department of Justice, 1987).

In 1987, RTT filed a complaint against GB-Inno, a supermarket chain that was selling nonapproved second telephone equipment. GB replied with a counterclaim against RTT's equipment approval methods. European court proceedings revealed that RTT's charges for equipment testing were often inflated. Further inquiries demonstrated that the RTT was more likely to approve Belgian equipment: 45 percent of overseas terminals applications failed compared with 11 percent of Belgian terminals[3] (Tutt, 1989).

In 1989, the government reluctantly agreed to follow EC liberalization policies; but the actual process fell behind other European countries because of the government's fear for the impact on jobs. It similarly opposed the EC's policies on tariff principles and Open Network Provision.

Services

In 1988, telephone set density was 49.8 per 100 population (RTT, 1987). There were 3.7 million telephone main lines in 1990. Rates were sixth lowest for business and eighth lowest for residential service among the twenty-four OECD countries. Residential and business users faced up to a six-month wait for service.

An important first occurred in 1956, when RTT inaugurated, together with France, international direct-dial telephone service, the first such service in Europe. The installation of semielectronic space division stored program-control switches began in the early 1970s. The first fully electronic digital exchange became operational in 1983. In 1989, digital exchanges comprised 20 percent of the total network.

Data transmission began to grow strongly in the early 1980s. The RTT had a monopoly on low-speed modems. It was strict in preventing resale. Shared use was authorized under certain conditions, provided that volume tariffs were applied. RTT was particularly concerned with the leakage into the public switched network of calls carried on international leased lines (Pichault, 1985). Alcatel entered the data services market in 1990 through a joint venture with RTT to operate private networks and VANs.

Telex is also well developed in Belgium, though declining. (ITU, 1990a). Mailbox service and video conferencing were made available experimentally in 1986.

In 1982, a packet-switched network was put into operation under the name of Data Communication Service (DCS-NET), with transmission rates up to 48 kbps. In 1990, RTT agreed to lift restrictions on international leased lines, including mandatory routing through DCS-NET, after a lawsuit by GE Information Services charged RTT with violating the EC competition policy.

In 1984, RTT initiated prototype ISDN trials, using the BTM System 12 and ATEA switches. Belgium became the fourth European country to launch an ISDN service, under the name of Aline.

Mobile telephone service was first provided in 1977, with equipment provision under the monopoly of the RTT and produced by BTM. A cellular system went into operation in 1987 and is integrated within a Benelux system. In 1989, RTT chose Siemens and Philips as the suppliers of a new digital mobile network.

Videotex was launched by the RTT in 1986. Databases are mainly supplied by private parties. One important and delicate task in language-divided Belgium is how to allow connection to the surrounding countries that follow different protocols. Therefore, the system follows the British Prestel standard used in the Netherlands, but it also allows the French Antiope standard, with access to host computers in France. Connection to the German Btx was also provided. In 1990, the RTT began testing the service over cable networks, since over half a million Belgian television sets had teletext decoders suitable for some videotex service.

12

Luxembourg

Luxembourg's tiny size and population seem to provide little incentive for new entrants. The country is active in international financial services, incorporations, television, satellites, and even shipping registration. Telecommunications is an important input for each of them. The PTT, under the supervision of the minister for transport, communications, and information, held the national service monopoly. It followed a policy of providing services compatible with those of neighboring countries. In contrast to Luxembourg's minor role in telecommunications, its position in mass media transmission was far more significant. Here both the television company CLT and the broadcast satellite provider SES were at the forefront of Europe-wide change.

Between 1862 and 1880, the Luxembourg government installed a telegraph network connecting Luxembourg with its neighbors to promote the country's economic expansion. Telephone service was introduced in 1881, initially only for verbal transmission of telegraph messages. In 1883, the administrations for posts and for telegraphs were united to become the Administration for Posts and Telecommunications (APT), and the Ministry of Finances proposed the first telephone legislation. Under the provisions of the law of 1884, which is still in effect, the government was authorized to construct or operate the telephone network for its own use or to concede construction or operation to a private firm. The government decided to undertake the project and built a network in the capital city, which was eventually expanded (Bode, 1985). This network opened in 1885.

To deal with low rural penetration, public phone booths, called auxiliary telephone agencies, were installed, managed by private individuals but financed by the state. Communities without such service could connect a line to the general network for an annual fee and the cost of line construction.

User tariffs were flat-rate (unlimited communications) until 1920, when a volume-based tariff replaced it. But this led volume to fall by 66 percent in the first year of its implementation.

Luxembourg's geographical position fostered the early development of an international network, with connections to Belgium in 1898 and to France, Germany, and Switzerland by 1904. During World War I, Germany controlled the network and suspended civilian communication until the 1918 armistice.

Following the war, Luxembourg made an effort at modernization. In 1922 the first electromechanical automatic switches were installed and transmission quality was improved by converting all lines to double wire circuits.

The German invasion in 1940 severely damaged the communications infrastructure, especially in the north. Reconstruction was completed in 1948, and automation of the domestic service was finished in 1963.

Telex service, introduced in 1951, became fully automated in 1958. That year also marked the first stage of automation for international connections when Luxembourg interconnected with West Germany.

During the 1970s, the APT set out to improve network penetration. The Budgetary Law of 1973 created investment funds specifically for telecommunications. Telephone density increased from 34.4 per 100 population in 1971 to 48.0 in 1990 (ITU, 1990). In 1974 a public airbill network opened. The first digital connections were installed in 1976. Digital switching arrived in 1979, and fiber trunks were installed in 1983. In the same year, the packet-switched network Luxpac was inaugurated. Cellular service began in 1985 with a connection to the Dutch MTX network. Teletex (e-mail) and videotex services have been offered since 1986. By 1990, teletex had forty subscribers, videotex had forty-four information providers and 360 subscribers (L. Kirch, 1990, communication). Advanced data services, however, were slow in being offered. Users had to wait six weeks for international leased lines and six months for 64–kbps data lines (Schenker, 1990). There were also waiting lists of three months for regular service. Digital lines to France, Belgium and Germany were established in 1989.

Luxembourg has no telecommunications equipment manufacturing industry, and procurement is based on international tenders. The APT provides ordinary telephone sets and detached modems.

The APT is liberal-minded when it comes to upper level services and resale but strict on basic infrastructure. The notion of rival transmission for a small country like Luxembourg is not entirely far-fetched. A potential rival transmission system, at least for international service, already existed through the Astra television satellite system of the Société Européenne des Satellites (SES), which could potentially also be used for data and voice. APT opposed any loosening of the infrastructure monopoly. But resale was permitted, and VAN and resale services did not require licenses.

APT was hampered by its lack of independence over its budget and hiring levels, since these were determined as part of the national budget. It therefore sought and obtained in 1990 legislative approval to convert into a public, state-owned corporation, effective in 1992. Regulatory functions were left with the Minister of Communications, and APT was divided into posts and telecommunications branches, with a monopoly over public and infrastructure services. Employee rights were maintained. The state retained the right to 20 percent of income, and ordered APT to invest LuF 2 billion, the equivalent of 2 percent of the national budget, in network digitalization.

13

Switzerland

The Swiss PTT is one of Europe's last "classic" PTTs: It is an exclusive and monopolistic government administration where telecommunications subsidize the postal service with which they are fully integrated. In its equipment interconnection policy and procurement practices, the Swiss PTT is among the more rigid in Europe. At the same time, the quality of its service—in terms of both equipment and manpower—is good, and the density of its coverage is among the highest in the world. Thus, the traditional arrangement has worked reasonably well when the priority was to spread service to every household and when technology and large-user demands were relatively stable.

Switzerland is a traditional center for financial and other international services. However, rural interests are also very strong. In telecommunications policy, they are allied with the labor movement and the advanced but high-cost electronics sector, which in turn has close ties with the banking industry that owns much of it. Nevertheless, it seems inevitable that Switzerland will have to reconcile telecommunications with its traditional economic function as an international cross-roads. The increasingly electronic form of financial transactions and their resultant distance-insensitivity puts Swiss banks into direct competition with such centers as London, New York, Singapore, Tokyo, and Hong Kong. It is therefore likely that the country will move toward a more liberal system that has characterized the rest of its economy, while finding new ways of safeguarding its traditional concerns.

History

Historically, the postal service has been one of the relatively few central governmental functions of the Swiss Confederacy. With the advent of the telegraph in 1851, telegraph service was similarly put under national control of the Telegraph Directorate. The Swiss telegraph network began operation in 1852 and international telegram service was started in the following year (Swiss PTT, 1983). When the telephone was introduced, the Swiss Federal Council passed restrictive licensing regulations, distinguishing between telephone traffic in areas where telegraph service existed and areas where it did not. Where the government telegraph monopoly was affected, a license fee had to be paid that amounted to at least two to three times the costs that had already been spent on telegraph service in the area. Protection of the state monopoly was a major policy goal from the beginning of the development of Swiss telecommunications. An early telephone pioneer, Wilhelm Ehrenberg, challenged these restrictions, but his proposal was rejected. The Telegraph Directorate was slow in providing service itself, however. After a series of discussions, a license was extended to a company led by J. Ryf, a member of parliament, and T. F. Wild, a partner in a major publishing and printing firm. As it later transpired, Wild also represented the International Bell Telephone Company.

In 1880, the private Zurich Telephone Company was granted a license. Service began almost immediately. In the first telephone directory, more than 10 percent of the subscribers were affiliated with Wild's publishing firm (Hofmann, 1980). The status of the new company, however, soon became uncertain. Following a series of disputes, the International Bell Telephone Company withdrew, leaving the Zurich Telephone Company as a purely Swiss enterprise. But this did not help to alleviate the political problems concerning the scope of the Zurich company's license. The term of its franchise was reduced from twenty-five years to five years. Recognizing the profitability of telephone service, the Swiss government then decided to cease granting further private licenses and instead to establish a state-operated service wherever feasible. In December 1880, this decision was ratified by the parliament, which wrote into law the telephone monopoly of the federal government.

The telegraph administration opened its first urban telephone system in Basel in 1881 and then in Berne at the bankers' association initiative. In 1883, the first local networks were interconnected. In 1884, the operating license of the private Zurich Telephone Company expired and was taken over by the governmental system, with compensation paid. Today the Swiss PTT is more gracious than other PTTs in acknowledging the role of early private operations. Its official publication notes that "with hindsight, one must concede that the Zurich Telephone Company performed a valuable service in acting as a driving force and saving the Federal Government from paying dearly for their experience" (Kobelt, 1980). By 1892, nearly all local systems were interconnected. Trunks were initially run on overhead lines along railroad tracks and were later buried.

Because of Switzerland's status as an international financial center, international telephone communications were implemented almost immediately. Experiments were undertaken as early as 1878 with a connection to the Milan telegraph office using telegraph lines. Cross-border telephone service on a regular basis was started in 1886 from Basel to Alsace and then rapidly expanded to other countries. The first transatlantic radio telephone service opened in 1928 via London. During World War II, direct shortwave service to the United States was introduced. In 1956, the PTT offered transatlantic calls over submarine telephone cables, and after 1965, via satellite.

Semiautomatic switching was begun in 1917, using equipment from the Belgian Bell Telephone Manufacturing Company (BTM). BTM, then owned by AT&T, set up the Swiss subsidiary Standard Telephone and Radio (STR) and became a major supplier. As an ITT company, STR introduced the crossbar switch into Switzerland in 1965. Much of the automation of the network was done with Strowger switches in cooperation with Siemens through a Swiss subsidiary that is now named Siemens-Albis. Automatic long-distance service began in 1950 and was completed by 1959. Automated international service was introduced in 1964. Some international telecommunications services were also provided by the government-owned Radio Suisse.

Services

Switzerland has one of the highest telephone densities in the world. In 1988, density was fifty-four telephone lines and eighty-eight telephone units per 100 population. Like Sweden, Switzerland's neutrality during the world wars spared it from the destruction and resource drain that other countries suffered (Ducommun and Keller, 1980).

Expansion in international traffic was especially great. More international calls are made per capita from Switzerland than from any other country, averaging twenty-eight per person yearly. Calls to West Germany, France and Italy account for over 60 percent of that total (ITU, 1989, p. 764; Staple, 1990, p. 35). With Germany, Switzerland has the highest telex service density in the world, with 530 telex connections per 100,000 population in 1988. Switzerland's extensive telex service is partly due to its importance in the financial sector.

Not surprisingly for the world's center of watch making, Switzerland's first special service was the transmission of the time signal: In 1935, a "speaking clock" was introduced. Also provided today are regularly updated weather forecasts, reports on avalanches and on ski and road conditions; sports results and betting information.

Additional services include car radio paging, introduced in 1958, and mobile telephony, available regionally since 1952 and nationwide since 1980 under the name of Natel. Cellular telephony was introduced in 1978, and digitally after 1991. In 1982 the public packet-switched network Telepac became available. Other PTT services include teletex (electronic mail), telefax, as well as a popular call forwarding service, Omnitel. Leased lines are available, under restrictions, and the need for private networks must be demonstrated. According to the PTT, customer requirements should generally be met through the public network. In 1988, the PTT began a Communes Modèles Suisses pour la Communication (CMC) program. This introduced advanced services—such as videoconferencing, remote database, access and distance learning—to twelve municipalities to assess their communications needs. Videotex operations began in 1983 as a field test, and in 1987 as a regular service, with a faster Supertex version offered in 1989. Switzerland has been and remains among Europe's leaders in cashless public telephony, with its prepaid "taxcards" (Purton, 1990).

The PTT has been in charge of radio transmissions for the official Swiss Broadcasting Corporation (SBC) since 1931. It offered, almost from the beginning of radio, transmission service over wire lines in areas of poor reception, an important consideration in a mountainous country such as Switzerland. In 1933, one foreign and three national radio channels were available over wire. By 1956, there were six channels. The number of wire radio subscribers reached its peak in 1969 with 440,000 subscribers. The service continues and is used particularly in such institutions as hospitals, hostels, and hotels. In 1952, wire radio broadcasting moved from the PTT to the SBC in terms of program content. The success of Swiss cable radio, preceding that of cable television by decades, was remarkable, though it did not receive much attention.

A small additional provider of Swiss telecommunications service is Radio-Suisse, a mixed-economy service organization 95 percent owned by the government. Until 1986, Radio-Suisse provided international telex, land-to-ships and land-to-aircraft communications, and such services as voice storage and retrieval, paging, consulting, and databases. It also provided civil air navigation for Switzerland. Radio-Suisse's service with ships at sea had a good reputation, and ships in the Atlantic or the Mediterranean often interconnected via Radio-Suisse into the European public telephone or telex networks, despite Switzerland's being a land-locked country. Throughout the 1980s, however, Radio-Suisse had difficulties, partly because the PTT occupied profitable lines of telecommunication service in international telex and data transmission. It was also in a legally complicated situation insofar as it provided services both in monopolistic and competitive fields. This led to a 1984 report by the Federal Ministry of Justice raising the question of the legality of the nominally private Radio-Suisse providing monopolized governmental services in Switzerland (even though the government owned 95 percent of the company).

Between 1986 and 1988, much of Radio-Suisse's telecommunications facilities were transferred to the PTT. Radio-Suisse was thereafter left with a consulting business and information service activities (i.e., largely competitive services).

Switzerland participated in various European efforts on transborder data flow protection, but a national privacy law was slow to be enacted, because of the problem with Swiss banking and financial secrecy.

The PTT and Reform

The postal, telegraph, and telephone administration was formed in 1922 by combining existing functions. It is the largest Swiss employer, with 61,000 employees in 1989, about one-third of which are in telecommunications (Wührmann, 1989).

The monopoly of the Swiss PTT is based on Article 36 of the Swiss Federal Constitution. The primary legislation is the Federal Telegraph and Telephone Law of 1922, which controls the activities of the PTT itself. The Federal Department of Transport, Communications, and Energy provides political supervision. It is run by a governing board and by three directors-general, one of whom is in charge of the telecommunications department. Labor union representatives occupy three of the board seats. As stated in the PTT's master plan, its service principles are to work for the benefit of the community, to provide service for the entire country under the same conditions and economic principles, to provide unrestricted access, to protect privacy, and to be aware that "not everything technically achievable and economically viable is necessarily beneficial for society as a whole." In interpreting the specific applications of these principles, the PTT has considerable discretion.

Following the takeover of the private Zurich Telephone Company in 1890, the government had promulgated an installation monopoly for the telegraph administration. This was changed in 1921, after pressures from the Association of Swiss Electrical Installation Firms, when the government ceded interior installations to officially licensed private firms. Despite agitation in the 1930s, only equipment supplied and maintained by the PTT could be used for all telephone sets and telex machines. Approved data and fax terminals could be privately supplied. PBXs were supplied by the PTT, and only PTT modems were permitted for data transmission over the switched network.

Because the Swiss telecommunications law dates back to 1922, many new telecommunications services have had to be governed by regulations and decrees. The Swiss political system makes it particularly difficult to modify the telecommunications structure. Any legislation must be approved by the Swiss upper chamber, in which the rural cantons, with their small populations, have a disproportionate influence. They resist any modification that might lead to an increase in telephone rates or postal service in rural areas.[1] During the 1980s, questions began to be raised about the scope of the PTT's monopoly. In 1980, Zurich groups sought a referendum initiative to reduce PTT power, but they did not succeed in getting enough signatures (Knieps, 1985a).

These signs of public dissatisfaction started a legislative reform process in 1981, when the PTT directorate general decided to draft provisions to revise the old Telecommunications Law. In 1983, the council of the PTT approved an early version of such a bill. However, other parts of the government and various interest groups claimed that the draft was overly protective of the PTT and demanded a draft legislation to be designed by a body independent from the PTT. In 1984, the minister of transportation and energy appointed a study commission for a new telecommunications law. The commission, however, was chaired by the secretary general of the ministry itself. Other members represented interest groups, such as PTT officials, the PTT union, the national chamber of commerce, the consumer federation, the small business association, the equipment industry, and large users. Independent members included Professor Carl Christian von Weizsäcker, an economist who had also been active in German telecommunications commissions. In 1985, the commission submitted to the department a preliminary report that was endorsed by the governing PTT boards.

The study group's recommendations and the 1985 draft legislation were cautious. Even in terminal equipment, some areas would be left entirely to the PTT, with governmentally drawn lines based on vague criteria such as "interest of the country" and "security of transmission." Main stations terminal equipment and telex machines would remain under the control of the PTT. Furthermore, approval was left to the PTT and thus subject to its time schedule. The proposal also prohibited resale of transmission capacity (Blankart and Knieps, 1985).

The partial liberalization of terminal equipment was largely a confirmation of reality. PTT exclusivity for simple terminal equipment had been undercut by the illegal attachment of widely available telephone sets, marked "for export only." Article 28 of the draft law provided that terminal equipment can be advertised, sold, leased, or rented only if it is technically approved, that the PTT has the right to control all terminal equipment, and that the owner of a terminal must provide physical access to it. In accordance with Article 3, the cabinet would decide which types of terminal equipment would be exclusively provided by the PTT.

The ministry describes such restrictive equipment rules as a "step-wise liberalization," which is an overstatement unless the government exercises its line-drawing powers in a liberalizing fashion. The government's report alleged that a competitive system would put into question the ability of some customers to reach others, and that it would create disparities within the country. It also stated that a small country such as Switzerland could provide an efficient telecommunications network only under a single organization, and according to unified norms. Despite these assertions, interconnection and compatibility could be legally mandated; even if additional or specialized Swiss networks were not economically feasible, there could still be general or specialized Europe-wide networks, which would have the economies of scale that Switzerland might be unable to provide. It would be pure happenstance if the optimal size of the network coincided with the size of Switzerland.

The PTT also argued that the Swiss telecommunications industry cannot presently compete with foreign imports:

> A spontaneous and unrestricted opening up of Switzerland to the telecommunications markets would pose a serious threat to the Swiss telecommunications industry and consequently affect the social and economic life of our country. At present the Swiss telecommunications industry cannot offer products at competitive prices in comparison with cheap products from the Far East or countries with a large domestic market. As long as foreign markets remain closed to products from the Swiss telecommunications industry, the existence of the latter can only be assured by supplying equipment to the PTT. The PTT monopoly may thus, to some extent, serve as a defensive measure against the protectionist attitude of foreign markets with regards to indigenous products [Bütikofer, 1987, p. 7].

To alleviate the problem of foreign competition, the government's position was that it needed to ensure an adequate domestic supply by granting its industry enough time to adjust to liberalization. The government acknowledged the industry's interest in a PTT monopoly arrangement more honestly did than the government of most other countries. The argument that protectionism abroad has harmed Swiss manufacturing, however, is unpersuasive. It is true that many countries have such protectionist rules on the first terminal set (though these rules are fading in favor of EC norms), but if it were competitive in price, features, and performance, Swiss equipment could be sold more widely across Europe, America, and the developing world.

In 1989, a parliamentary draft of the new law proposed that services be divided into basic and extended categories, with the former, such as transmission and switching, remaining the sole province of the PTT. Extended services "which complement, modify, store, or otherwise manipulate messages" would be opened to private competition. This would include second telephone sets, telefax, modems, PBXs, and teletype terminals. Regulatory and operational functions of the PTT would be separated.

The Equipment Industry

The Swiss telecommunications industry is hampered by the relatively small size of its home market (the PTT procures equipment costing about 1 billion Swiss francs a year). Import orders are about 30 percent of sales, which is relatively low for Swiss industry. The PTT is closely linked to the well-organized domestic equipment industry. According to a survey by the Swiss Industry Association, the share of the PTT in the total of Swiss telecommunications manufacturing was 80 percent in switching equipment, 60 percent in customer terminal equipment, 42 percent in transmission equipment, and 40 percent in cable.

Upon the initiative of the major suppliers and a high PTT official, a "Pro Telephone" trade association was formed in 1927 by representatives of ten firms, renamed later Pro Telecom (Piquet, 1980). Its objective is to promote telephone usage and to organize collaboration with the PTT in many areas. The PTT is represented on two advertising committees, and Pro Telecom's managing director is a member of the PTT's marketing board. Several working groups of Pro Telecom's R&D committee played a role in joint development by three suppliers of a new electronic set telephone, TS85. Similarly, the semiconductor components group promoted the use of Swiss components in electronic PBXs and telephone sets. The manufacturers also cooperate in export drives through Swisscom, Teleconseil, and Telesuisse.

Total telecommunications manufacturing employment in Switzerland numbered approximately 20,000. The largest Swiss telecommunications companies by market share in 1990 were the following: (1) Ascom, which controls 51.6 percent of the market and makes mobile, standard, and cordless phones; PBXs; and banking systems. (2) Siemens-Albis, with 18.5 percent of the market, providing cables, wires, exchanges, modems, and multiplexers. (3) STR (Alcatel), with 19.0 percent of the market. For those three large companies, telecommunications equipment was by far the predominant part of their business (Blankart and Schneider, 1984). Other firms in the telecommunications market include BBC, Alteau, Landis & Gyr, and Gretag (Northern Business Information, 1990).

The narrowness of the market has led to concentration. In 1984, the Swiss firms Hasler, Zellweger, Uster, Autophon, and Gfeller (the last of which is controlled by Autophon) joined to form a cooperative arrangement under the name of Ascom, for development, export, production, and purchases. This led to the merging of the top two firms, Hasler and Autophon, in 1987 as part of the Ascom holding company, which in turn owned 50 percent of Zellweger and has a connection to the German firm Bosch. Ascom, through a holding company, became the dominant Swiss equipment firm, strengthening the position of the purely Swiss companies versus Siemens-Albis and Alcatel's STR. Another cooperative venture is the Tritel telephone production agreement involving Gfeller, Autophon, and Zellweger (Union Bank, 1986).

After 1970, the PTT cooperated with Siemens-Albis, STR, and Hasler to create the Integrated Telecommunications System, or ITS. The primary aim was to develop a digital system to replace about 1000 analog switches. In 1983, 140 million Swiss francs later, the PTT decided instead to opt for a foreign-developed system and was criticized that it had not established an effective project management organization for such a large-scale project and that the scope of the project had been underestimated (ASUT, 1983) .

The PTT decision did not, however, eliminate the three companies as potential suppliers of a digital switch. After the failure of the initial IFS concept, it introduced in 1985 the concept of a new IFS-Swissnet, with foreign-developed switches. Both Siemens-Albis and STR provided their parent companies' electronic switches, EWSD and System 12. Hasler, a Swiss company, offered the AXE 10 switch of its traditional technology source L. M. Ericsson. However, digitalization of switching was slow, with the first full digital exchanges being put into operation in 1987 (Ducommun, 1987). The PTT predicted the connection of 90 percent of subscribers to SWISSNET by 1995 (Trachsel, 1987).

In the supply of customer equipment, the cumbersome system of approval and adoption of PTT-owned equipment led to a substantal gray market. A consumer movement magazine reported that the *annual* rental price for the PTT telephone model TS85 with twenty-number storage was SFr 192, whereas a corresponding foreign model could be purchased illegally in a store for only SFr 125. Cordless telephones were officially introduced only in 1985, although an active market in illegal equipment already existed.

When the official equipment was introduced, the monthly rental charges were SFr 26 (then about $12). In the United States, these rates would pay for purchasing the equipment in less than half a year. This also corresponds to a study that found that the cost of some equipment available for purchase in the United States was equal to its rental fee for three to four months in Switzerland (Blankart and Schneider, 1984).

In 1983, the PTT still believed that the cordless equipment would cost SFr 1500–2000 (about $1000) per station. After much criticism, this was reduced to a still high SFr 1000. At the same time, a letter to the editor of the major newspaper *Neue Zürcher Zeitung* pointed out that they were available in the United States for only $59. After a lengthy development process, the PTT in 1984 and 1985 issued a fifty-five page technical specifications manual that happened to match the system developed by the largest Swiss telecommunications manufacturer. For example, the PTT required that each telephone have forty duplex channels and an automatic frequency search scanner. Furthermore, the timing of procurement for distribution was a few months hence, which was almost impossible for foreign competitors to meet (letter to *Neue Zürcher Zeitung*, January 6, 1984). The PTT's response (*Neue Zürcher Zeitung*, January 20, 1984) was that the cheaper equipment was probably an inferior Far Eastern product and that it permitted others to eavesdrop or to illegally use someone else's main stations.

Switzerland was not under a liberalization pressure from Brussels like most of its neighbors since it was not a member of the EC. But in time, it could not remain apart from the broader trends, with EFTA moving close to the EC. In 1990, even the PTT's telecommunications head admitted that

> Switzerland has too long under-estimated the significance of developments outside its borders. Given the worldwide expansion of markets and the European Community's internal market, our insular solutions could no longer be tolerated, especially for telecommunications. If our country is to profit from the economic liberalization and deregulation of Europe and remain competitive, liberalization is unavoidable (Wührmann, 1990).

Recognizing the significance of telecommunications to the Swiss role in international transactions, the PTT unveiled in 1991 an ambitious $10 billion three-year plan to establish Switzerland as a European telecommunications center.

Telecommunications in Liechtenstein

Although the principality of Liechtenstein is independent, its telephone service is largely handled by the Swiss PTT. Telephone service in Liechtenstein dates back to the turn of the century, when it was operated by the Austrian government telegraph administration and was linked to the Austrian system. With the outbreak of World War I, Liechtenstein telephone service was totally isolated from the rest of the world for a year, until it was connected to Switzerland. Since 1921, the Swiss PTT has operated Liechtenstein telephony as part of Swiss domestic service.

14

Austria

Austria's telecommunication system is a classic postal–industrial complex: a powerful PTT monopoly closely allied with labor unions and with a virtual cartel of private equipment firms known as the "Four Sisters." Because large users are frequently state-owned firms or international organizations, little counter-pressure exists.

History

Telecommunications began in Austria in 1846, when a railroad company constructed a telegraph line from Vienna to a suburb and onward to the city of Brünn (Brno) for its evolving operational needs (Holcombe, 1911). Emperor Ferdinand quickly declared telegraphy a governmental monopoly, the *Telegraphenregal,* assigning the new technology solely for the service of the railroads and the state. His successor, Emperor Franz Joseph, cast the future of the telecommunications monopoly by his 1849 decree, which, among other things, permitted public access to the telegraph system.

Telephony was introduced in 1879 within the Austrian military. Civilian service started in 1881 by the Vienna Privat-Telegraphen-Gesellschaft. Two years later, the London-based Consolidated Telephone Construction and Maintenance Company began service in the outlying cities of the Austrian empire, including Prague, Trieste, Pilsen, and Brno. Once the various private companies had demonstrated the profitability of the new service, the government, despite the emperor's pronounced skepticism, put telephony within its domain in 1887 and introduced a long-distance service connecting Vienna to Brno and then to other cities. In 1888, the private and state networks were interconnected. The forty-seven local networks that were linked in 1892 rapidly swelled to 198 by the turn of the century. Full state monopoly was achieved in 1895, when the last of the private systems was taken over. Communications became part of the Commerce Ministry, were later moved into the Ministry of Transportation, and were reunited with the postal service in 1923.

At the beginning of World War I, Austria was a sprawling empire with one of the most extensive long-distance telephone systems in Europe. The first regular automated local exchange opened in 1910 in Graz. After the war, local exchange service was considerably expanded. In 1938, Austrian telecommunications became part of the German Reichspost. During World War II the trunk lines, exchanges, and equipment were substantially damaged, and afterward, the Soviet Union dismantled some of the remaining equipment in its occupation zone. With funds provided by the Marshall Plan during the reconstruction, the second Austrian republic recovered rapidly to become a leader in the introduction of coaxial cable and microwave transmission (PTV, 1984).

The Structure of the PTV

Operating under the Telecommunications Law of 1949, the Österreichische Post und Telegraphenverwaltung (PTV) has a monopoly on telecommunications services in Austria. The PTV, which employs about 58,000 people, 18,400 of which are in the telecommunications sector (ITU, 1990), is a branch of the Federal Ministry of Public Economy and Transport, with the PTV's director general appointed by the minister (Bauer, 1986). Telecommunications (the "gray post") is organizationally linked with the mail service (the "yellow post"). A central office for telecommunications technology (FZA) oversees specifications and type approval.

The PTV is subject to the parliament for its budget and investments, and for the rates of inland tariffs. Parliament shifted rate-setting responsibility for international tariffs to the ministries of Finance and Public Economy and Transportation. Domestic rate changes, five-year investment plans, and various regulations must be approved in the form of legislation (Eward, 1984). There have been minor modifications and some additions to the law, such as the 1977 law on private telecommunications installations. The legal framework has been criticized as outmoded and inconsistent, although there have been no serious attempts to rewrite it. Most of the parliament's discussion of telecommunications law is centered on tariffs. In Austria, an informal body known as the "Social Partnership," which combines the major economic interest groups, considers and resolves many of the country's significant issues, including those concerning telecommunications. Telecommunications reform was not deemed necessary.

Strictly speaking, the PTV's monopoly applies only to the public network.[1] It can provide other services itself or license others. The 1977 law on private telecommunications installations *(Privatfernmeldeanlagengesetz)* specifies that license applications can be rejected by the PTV if it deems the services technically inadequate, if the needs "can be served with the required reliability and speed by existing services or facilities of the PTV," or if it is "against the business interests of the PTV" (quoted in Bauer and Latzer, 1987, p. 8). In effect, the PTV has a right of first refusal on new services. In one instance, the PTV rejected Philips' interest in providing a videotex service on the grounds of its "right of priority," and proceeded to provide Btx itself. Only the state-owned Radio Austria, close to the PTV, received a license to provide transcontinental telex and data transmission.

Services

In response to criticism throughout the 1960s that the PTV's restricted budget and bureaucratic organization prevented modernization, the government granted it a five-year investment plan. As a result, the organization could expand the reach of the network.

Between 1970 and 1988, telephone density almost tripled from 13.1 to 39.5 per 100 population. At the end of 1989, there were 3.1 million main telephone stations and about 21,500 telex connections in a population of about 7.6 million. Telex density was a very high 0.34 percent of the population, but telex traffic dropped 25 percent from 1988 to 1989 alone. It should be noted that there is a marked difference between the number of main line installations and actual telephone sets (3 million lines to 4.1 million sets in 1988) due to the frequency of party lines. After 1970 there were periods when the waiting list contained more than 200,000 applicants for telephone service and when delays were over two months. But by 1989, the number of applicants on the waiting list had greatly decreased to 35,000 (ITU, 1990).

Tariffs are high. Calls placed from Austria to other European countries tend to cost twice as much as calls traveling in the opposite direction (TDR, 1988, p. 9). Although the PTV claims to be adapting tariffs to real costs, Austria's rates for business ($1408 per year) and residential ($529 per year) users are among Europe's highest (Montgomery et al., 1990).

The Austrian telephone network is technically complicated, because it employs two sets of technologies, one of which uses nonlinear hybrid circuits at the junction of two- and four-wire circuits, and thus suffers from performance problems in data transmission. ITT electromechanical (HK8) and semielectronic (11E) exchanges were installed in the south, west, and northeast of the country. Elsewhere, Siemens ESK-A3, A5 and F semielectronic switches were primarily used.

In 1978, the PTV decided in favor of digitalization. A concept was developed by the consortium organization ÖFEG, which brought together the Republic of Austria (51 percent), represented by the PTV and the Social Partners, and the telecommunications manufacturers Siemens, ITT (now Alcatel), Kapsch, and Schrack, which are collectively known as the Four Sisters. Not surprisingly, the consortium decided to ''carefully adapt'' a foreign system to Austrian specifications under control of the Four Sisters and the PTV, thereby foreclosing the market to others.

Two supplier groups were chosen. The first group was comprised of the two domestic Austrian firms Kapsch and Schrack, and offered a version of the Canadian Northern Telecom DMS-100 switch as the OES-E system. The second group, Siemens and ITT, offered a Siemens EWSD system. There was some competition between the two groups whereby the lower bidder receives an extra 10 percent of orders while the higher bidder adjusts its prices to the lower bid. In 1986, digital operation commenced in Vienna. By 1990, there were more than 500,000 digital subscriber lines linked to seventy switching centers. PTV planned to increase that number to 2.3 million, or about two-thirds of all phones, by 1995 (Sindelka, 1990, p. 50; CWI, 1990, p. 4). Since 1989, the PTV invested in its broadband fiber trunk network ("Ö-Netz") (Purton, 1990, p. 13). ISDN trials began in 1991.

In 1982, two new data services—circuit-switched, Datex-L and packet-switched Datex-P—were introduced. Together with the existing telex network, they form the integrated telex and data network (IFSD). In 1988, Datex-L had about 4000 subscribers and Datex-P had 2500. All Datex services had 10,300 total subscribers in 1989.

Videotex, known in Austria as Btx, was introduced to the public in 1985. Btx telephone rates are the same as those of local calls, even though the transmission distance may be considerably greater. However, indicative of user apathy, there were only 9717 registered subscribers in 1989.[2] The Austrian Btx terminal MUPID failed to gain acceptance after nine years of state support. The market for videotex terminals was subsequently liberalized in 1989 (M. Latzer, 1990, communication).

Cellular mobile telephony (Network C) was introduced in 1984 with Motorola equipment, joined shortly thereafter by Ericsson (with Schrack) and Siemens (with Kapsch). In 1990, the PTV awarded a contract for digital mobile radio to Motorola, in cooperation with Austrian firms.

Private leased lines are available. Resale of lines is not permitted, but because of the difficulty of enforcement it exists informally. Since the introduction of its data networks, the PTV has discouraged, through rate setting, the use of leased private circuits, and even aimed for regulatory measures to convert all private leased circuits into circuits that can be used by public data networks (Bruckner, 1982).

Because the Austrian telecommunications law has not been updated, the legal status of value-added services by alternative providers is a complex matter. The law does not differentiate between equipment and service. Approval by the PTV is required for both the technical specifications of the connected equipment and the corresponding software of value-added network services. The extent of scrutiny varies between the various regions and depends partly on the use of public networks versus leased lines and the applicability of public versus private laws and contractual arrangements (J. Bauer, 1987, communication).

Equipment

Subscribers' equipment is supplied privately or by the PTV. The basic telephone set, however, must be rented or bought from the PTV. The PTV is both supplier and regulator of equipment. After 1987, the PTV followed a more liberal policy for consumer premises equipment. In 1988 a triple socket for connection of privately owned telephone terminal devices was introduced to foster greater liberalization of equipment markets in practical terms (Sindelka, 1988).

Telex terminals can be obtained privately, but this policy is less open than it may appear. In 1987, the PTV alone maintained all telex terminals and it had certified only four telex models. The Four Sisters—Siemens, Alcatel[3], and the domestic firms of Kapsch and Schrack—supply from 90 percent to 95 percent of telecommunications equipment to the PTV (Bauer and Latzer, 1988; CWI, 1990). They employ 20,000 people, with 11,000 in their telecommunications divisions. A comment in a PTV report reveals its attitude to foreign equipment: "Since only a small share of the computer market is held by Austrian equipment manufacturers, no restrictions are imposed on foreign [computer] equipment" (Bruckner, 1982, p. 12).[4]

Telecommunications in Scandinavia and the North Atlantic

15

Sweden

Televerket, Sweden's telecommunications operator, has long pursued an effective technological and social agenda while creating a vertical integration that reached into equipment manufacture. No statutory monopoly exists and the introduction of competition was accomplished smoothly. The market reality is one of Televerket dominance, given its managerial effectiveness and its political support. Aggressive rivalry from a well-connected small rival, Comvik, and a move toward partial privatization of Televerket promise to make Swedish telecommunications one of the more interesting scenes of network evolution.

History

From 1853, Swedish telegraph service was mainly run by the government, but no legal state monopoly on telecommunications existed when the telephone was introduced (Holcombe, 1911). Initially, the government refrained from involvement in telephone service, but by the 1890s its role had changed dramatically.

The first telephone connections were established in Stockholm in 1877. One of the earliest users, H. T. Cedergren, later founded the General Telephone Company (Gustafsson, 1987). In 1880, the International Bell Telephone Company opened local systems in Stockholm, Gothenburg, and Malmö. Almost immediately, several domestic firms were attracted to this market by Bell's high prices. Although Bell would not sell equipment to its competitors, L. M. Ericsson entered the field in 1878 and proved a viable alternative in the absence of telephone patents. The first non-Bell network, established in 1881, charged lower rates than Bell. In 1883, Cedergren started the General Telephone Company, Allmanna Telefonaktiebolag, and within one year served three times as many subscribers as Bell. The two firms engaged in a lively head-on competition in price and service, particularly in Stockholm. In 1887, General Telephone opened the world's largest exchanges (7000 lines). By 1888, Bell succumbed and relinquished control to its Swedish competitor, which merged the two systems.

Still, the demise of Bell did not signal the end of competition, although Sweden's second phase of competition was less dramatic than its first. Small stock companies, mutual associations, cooperative societies, and municipal systems rapidly established themselves in rural areas and began to coexist through long-distance trunk lines. The government Telegraph Company (Telegrafverket) also began to construct long-distance lines, and in some instances acquired or built local networks. In 1881, it started a local network interconnecting government offices. In 1883, a Royal Ordinance required the state's permission for interconnection, and it has survived to the present day.

In 1889, General Telephone applied for rights-of-way to establish trunk lines to connect its three municipal systems. Thus prompted to review its role in long-distance telephony, the government decided to be the main builder of interurban lines. Significantly, long-distance telephone service would only be readily available to subscribers of state local exchanges. In 1891, General Telephone reached an agreement with the state. It was licensed to operate and use other rights-of-way for fifty years and allowed it access to the state's long-distance lines. Outside a 70–kilometer radius from Stockholm, the telegraph authority imposed access fees and technical requirements on private systems that were so burdensome that many sold out to the government. Within three years, the government had taken control of three-fourths of all the local systems.

General Telephone, however, did not give in. The government thereupon expanded its small system in Stockholm, which had previously operated for official administrative use only, into a general public network. In 1905, an act on wireless telegraphy strengthened the state's centralized authority in granting transmission rights (Heimburger, 1931), and by 1907, it renounced its willingness to interconnect. At that time, General Telephone had 37,000 subscribers in Stockholm, and the government had 13,000, but in the competition between the two that ensued, the government, with its resources and long-distance interconnection, held the upper hand.

Within Stockholm the vigorous rivalry led to reduced rates, high technical performance, and experimentation by the government with new types of service and billing (including usage-measured tariffs), making Stockholm's telephone system the most advanced in the world. Whereas the original flat rate of the Bell company had been about $40 in the inner city of Stockholm and $60–70 elsewhere, after a few years of this unique competition, rates fell to about $12 for residential customers and $15 for businesses—the lowest in Sweden (Holcombe, 1911).

The government, with its superior resources and power, ultimately took control of General Telephone in 1918, and integrated it by 1923. General Telephone's management moved to L. M. Ericsson, which became General Telephone Company–L. M. Ericsson. The Swedish telecommunications administration, subsequently named Televerket, thus assumed its role as sole actor in Swedish public telecommunications. The exceptions to its monopoly are several other state administrations that can provide for their own communications—the state railway company, the state power board, and the Swedish defense forces, to name a few. The only real private encroachment to the monopoly since General Telephone has recently emerged. Technically, however, Televerket never held a legal monopoly. To satisfy the distinction, in the following the word *monopoly* should be read as *de facto monopoly*.

Televerket

Telecommunications in Sweden became more vertically integrated than almost anywhere else in the world after the United States broke up much of AT&T's integrated structure. Televerket (often referred to internationally as Swedish Telecom) had a de facto service monopoly over local, long-distance, and international communications; in 1988, however, Comvik AB received permission to begin an international satellite communication network. Televerket has also long held a connection monopoly over much of the customer equipment in voice telephony and telex, though that was stepwisely relaxed. In 1989, terminal markets were fully liberalized for PBXs and high-speed modems (Thorngren, 1990). Televerket still produces much equipment itself. Not even AT&T in its heyday had the same end-to-end control over production, services, and equipment connections; AT&T had no monopoly on international service, was excluded from telegraphy, coexisted with about 2000 other local telephone companies, and had to share its equipment patents with others.

Part of Televerket's reason for success has been that it has been long outside the postal administration. It is a public service corporation and reports to the Ministry of Transport and Communications. But whereas Televerket has over 40,000 employees, of whom about 30,000 serve basic telephony, the entire ministry has seventy employees, of whom only six deal with telecommunications issues (Televerket, 1989, p. 7). In 1989, Sweden's pool of telecommunications policy expertise was severly depleted by the deaths of the finance director of Televerket and several members of the Ministry of Communication in a plane crash.

Since 1975, Televerket has been organized into twenty local areas, each operating with substantial independence. Televerket's board, appointed by the government, represents the political parties, the business and scientific communities, and several of Sweden's labor unions. A director general manages day-to-day operations. In the past, the annual budget was proposed by the government and passed through the budgetary process of the parliament. Profits had to be returned to the Treasury. Since 1980, the budget became independent from the public sector budget, and profits are now returned to the Treasury only at a predetermined rate-of-return on the capital that the government supplies to Televerket. Televerket has also been allowed to borrow on the open market and is thus unencumbered from general state budget difficulties, nor does it need to subsidize other governmental functions, such as the postal service. Since 1984, Televerket's supervision has followed three-year programs, which it submits to the government for parliamentary approval. This plan includes an investment and finance schedule, production goals, and a rate-of-return proposal. Once this plan is approved, Televerket is substantially free to operate within its parameters. In 1989, Televerket proposed the expansion of the existing de facto price cap system (Krzywicki, 1990), and in 1990, it sought to be privatized.

Sweden's telephone penetration is high. Like Switzerland, Sweden was lucky to escape the drain and destruction of two world wars, and it experienced the Great Depression in a relatively mild form only. Between 1930 and 1940, the number of telephones increased by 70 percent (H. Bergendorff, 1987, communication). The country enjoys high standards of public services and significant income equality. In 1988, telephone density was 66.2 main lines per 100 inhabitants (ITU, 1990). (For a discussion of Televerket's data, see Chapter 32.)

Vertical Integration

The Televerket monopoly, for a time, extended beyond services to all customer hand sets; after the 1970s it was liberalized for secondary sets, telex, and low-speed modems. It maintained PBXs and high-speed modems until 1989.[1] Videotex terminals and cellular telephone equipment were never restricted (Brown, 1985).

With respect to equipment provision, Sweden is therefore similar to the more liberal parts of Europe. The difference to most other countries is that Televerket is also involved in equipment manufacturing and R&D in two major ways: first, through its wholly owned manufacturing arm, TELI, which dates back to 1891; second, through its partnership with L. M. Ericsson in the development firm ELLEMTEL.

TELI has 3500 employees and produces much of Televerket's domestic equipment. Ninety percent of TELI production is destined for Televerket. Televerket also buys some equipment from Ericsson, but Ericsson relies primarily on export markets for its revenues. TELI produces digital AXE switches, PBXs (including Northern Telecom-licensed products), hand sets, and a variety of other transmission and data-processing equipment, as well as a limited number of electromechanical switches. It has also been involved in the production of low-cost computers used especially for school instructional purposes.

Ericsson and TELI established ELLEMTEL in 1970 after earlier disappointing experiences for each in the development of electronic SPC switches. They developed independently the prototypes (ATE12 in 1968 and A210 in 1970, respectively). However, both Ericsson's chairman Wallenberg and TELI feared the large costs of such endeavors and decided to pool expertise and costs. As part of this decision, the two partners divided the market for ELLEMTEL products, especially its AXE digital switch, with TELI getting its traditional Swedish (i.e., Televerket) market and Ericsson getting the rest of the world. Losses are shared by Televerket (27 percent) and Ericsson (73 percent) according to expected sales (OECD, 1987). In 1990, Televerket purchased Ericsson's domestic telecommunications sales interests.

Televerket claims that vertical integration into manufacturing enabled it to purchase equipment at favorable prices and pass these savings on to its customers. It also sought to avoid being captive of one national equipment firm. Before liberalization, however, subscriber terminal hand sets were available in competitive markets at one quarter of the Televerket price (Brown, 1985). Liberalization of hand sets, largely ratifying the reality of customers' self-help, legalized competition and forced prices down. Televerket also argued that, through its manufacturing arm, it gains useful information about manufacturing costs, which helps it in its other procurements. An example was its successful effort to convert Northern Telecom equipment to European standards in the late 1970s. Only 10–20 percent of Televerket's telecommunications equipment was imported,[2] although it has no formal "buy Swedish" procurement policy. After TELI ceased headset production in the face of Asian competition, their imports rose to fifty percent.

Televerket's vertical integration is not without critics. In 1980, the Swedish parliament passed a telecommunications law with broad support to specify its role. While emphasizing Televerket's position in modern information technology, the law encouraged a further market orientation and required that Televerket's competitive activities be undertaken in separate subsidaries. Teleinvest, the resulting company, was set up with several affiliates, including Tele-Larm, for security systems; Nerion, a Norwegian electronics manufacturer; Swedtel, an international consulting company; Swedcom, for telecommunications systems development abroad; Telefinans, a finance company for access to the international commercial financial markets; and Telelogicab, a software design subsidiary. The 1980 law limited Televerket's connection monopoly to voice communications equipment, medium- and high-speed modems, and telex equipment, but its provision for Telefinans significantly enhanced Televerket's competitiveness by allowing it to borrow on the open market. In 1987, TELI was integrated into the Teleinvest subsidiary Teleindustrier and given corporate status. Teleindustrier dwarfs all other subsidiaries.

A 1982 law made certification of privately supplied equipment subject to a liberalized procedure. Other equipment required type approval, for which a department of Televerket itself was in charge. In other words, potential entrants had to submit technical drawings and detailed descriptions of their equipment to their major manufacturing and marketing rival for approval. Since 1984, suppliers were allowed to have their equipment tested by any independent laboratory, private or public, and even, in some instances, to be self-certified. But approval was still lodged in the Televerket authority (Gleiss, 1983). A 1985 law scheduled further liberalizations in several steps. A 1988 parliamentary decision mandated open markets for payphones, PBXs, and modems of any speed, partly in response to trade friction with the United States, where Commerce Secretary Malcolm Baldridge had threatened to bar Ericsson from the United States if no reciprocity was established. In 1989, the technical approval functions of Televerket were moved to a separate regulatory entity, the National Telecommunications Council (Statens Telenämnd, or STN) (Thorngren, 1990). Control over monopolistic activity or competitive policy are performed by Sweden's Fair Trading Ombudsman (SPK). By 1990, Televerket's only formal and disappearing regulatory power was related to spectrum management (Whitehouse, 1989, pp. 3–6), which still afforded it a level of power against its competitors in the mobile telephony field.

Televerket has a close relationship with its 48,000 employees through its unions. The three unions (for blue-collar, white-collar and college-trained staff) are involved in all major decisions and must be consulted on matters affecting workers. Most Swedish firms operate similarly. The unions have opposed equipment liberalization, relaxation of monopoly, and the transformation of TELI into a corporation.

Ericsson

Sweden's major telecommunications equipment firm, Telefonaktiebolaget L. M. Ericsson, was founded by Lars Magnus Ericsson in 1876. Its two largest stockholders are the Wallenberg Group and the financial institution Handelsbanken. The firm successfully offered stock (in the form of deposit receipts) on the American market.

L. M. Ericsson began to manufacture telephone equipment in 1878, aided by the absence of patent protection. Its first major customers were the telephone companies to which Bell-affiliated manufacturers would not sell equipment. Later, in 1918, when the state Telegraph Administration forced the General Telephone Company out of network operations, the latter's management joined Ericsson.

Internationally, Ericsson is a medium-sized but very active corporation. Its net sales in 1989 were $6.3 billion and grew to $7.4 billion in 1991. Of these, public telecommunications accounted for 44 percent of sales. Ericsson's success in the export business (80 percent of its sales) is linked, paradoxically, to the absence of a captive home market. Televerket's TELI is its parent's prime supplier, and Ericsson is only a secondary supplier in Sweden. This is not to say that Ericsson is a small firm in the Swedish context. With 70,000 employees worldwide, it is one of the country's ten largest industrial firms. Its success in both industrialized and developing countries has proven that it is not necessary to be large or backed by a large domestic market to be a technologically competitive developer of sophisticated telecommunications equipment.

To reduce its labor costs and improve its international competitiveness, Ericsson built manufacturing plants in dozens of countries; half of its employees work abroad. It is organized in seven business areas, including public telephony, radio communications, information systems (including its acquisition, Datasaab), defense systems and components (Rifa), and a large cable enterprise. Research and development for its AXE digital switches and other equipment are conducted by ELLEMTEL, in joint operation with Televerket's TELI. In 1987, Ericsson sold its office equipment operations to the Norwegian firm Design Funktion.

Ericsson's technical successes include a photonic switch matrix which represents an important step toward building an optical switch in which photonic signals can be routed without having to be converted into electronic signals for switching purposes. The digital AXE switch was installed or ordered in many countries and increased the company's share in the world market for digital switches to 13 percent by 1984. In the United States, the AXE switches were first used outside the Bell System by special common carriers and independents. Customers included MCI, Western Union, ITT, and US Sprint. The opening of the Bell market through the AT&T divestiture increased Ericsson's potential customers dramatically. But in 1979, the U.S. markets comprised still a minor share of Ericsson's business, representing 5 percent of sales, mostly in traditional technology. By boosting its AXE system with a new central processor and increasing its capacity, Ericsson made it a viable choice for American local exchanges. Although its critics complain that it is based on a central rather than on a distributed processor, the AXE system's modular architecture, for which it is noted, has advantages over more customized designs. Ericsson's hopes of penetrating the Bell companies' central office market, however, were slow to materialize.

In the United Kingdom, Ericsson's AXE switch successfully won acceptance in the public switching market, the first such entry by a foreign firm in decades. This was accomplished when British Telecom, in order to be less dependent on the delay-plagued System-X switch developed by Plessey and GEC, sought a second supplier, dubbed System Y. It picked Ericsson's venture with Thorn EMI, greatly disappointing the French, in particular, who argued that the choice of a non-EC firm was a step in the wrong direction.

Ericsson operates in Italy through its subsidiary Fabbrica Apparechiature Telefoniche Materiale Elettrico (FATME) and several smaller operations which together comprise 19 percent of the Italian market, employ about 5000 persons, and have received export orders for AXE exchanges from Cyprus, Swaziland, Ethiopia, Guatemala, and Mozambique, among others.

In Latin America, Ericsson holds a strong position, particularly in Mexico, Brazil, Venezuela, and Colombia. Ericsson is also strong in Australia, the Netherlands, Denmark, and Spain, where its subsidiary Spain Intelsa has almost 50 percent of the digital public exchange market. In 1990, more than 2000 digital exchanges, including cellular exchanges, were in service in some seventy-five countries, with 27 million lines installed or on order. In 1987, it received a $46 million contract from the People's Republic of China for AXE-10 digital switches, and thirty-six were installed by 1990. Similarly successful was Ericsson's mobile cellular telephone technology, which was selected by numerous countries.

By 1992, Ericsson found itself under financial pressures and a potential merger partner.

Services

Formally, Televerket does not have a legal monopoly over network services. De facto, however, it was the only supplier of public or private network services, with the minor exception of networks of a few governmental departments too powerful to overcome.

To make competition fair, the government resolved in 1986 to permit a move toward cost-based pricing by Televerket (Ministry of Transport and Commu-nications, 1987). In 1987, the government took legislative action to rebalance prices by reducing rates for long-distance calls and gradually increasing charges for local calls (OECD, 1989).

The first significant entry in services occurred with the licensing of the com-pany Comvik as a rival cellular telephone service provider. Liberalization of service was introduced in 1989, when third-party traffic and international ser-vice were opened to new producers (B. Thorngren, 1990, communication). Comvik's Skyport service opened leased circuits for competition and resale. Subsequently, Sweden's national railway also aimed to resell capacity on its fiber-optic network.

Behind Comvik is Jan Stenbeck, a major Swedish industrialist engaged in steel, coal, and other businesses. Stenbeck's strategy is to invest in telecom-munications services with an eye toward their deregulation. He owns Kinnevik, a major media company, and its subsidiary Comvik. Comvik was the first to compete with Televerket with mobile telephone service and international satel-lite connections. Stenbeck's TV3 channel, Sweden's first commercial cable channel, was transmitted from London via the Astra satellite, in which he was part owner. He also owned the pay service TV1000 and cable television systems (Finvik), and was a partner in an American DBS venture and in Mil-licom, the holder of interests in cellular licenses in the developing world. Through his diversified communications holdings, and subsequent partnership with Brit-ain's far-flung Cable & Wireless, Stenbeck positioned himself to be the Nordic equivalent of Berlusconi or Murdoch, but with a much stronger telecommuni-cations presence. Forty percent of Comvik's satellite operations were held by Cable & Wireless.

Cellular telephony is a special Swedish success story, primarily through the joint Nordic cellular telephone system (NMT). In 1981, the initial year of its operation, Televerket predicted it would have 50,000 subscribers by 1991. But in 1987, there were already 120,000 subscribers, and by 1990 there were 450,000, or 9 percent of all automobiles (Boan, 1990, p. 3). Other mobile services in-clude Mobitex, which permits mobile transmission of data as well as voice developed especially for intraorganizational use. National and local paging (Mbs and Minicall) are also available.

Comvik holds about 7 percent of the cellular market and has the right to interconnect with its rival's public network. In 1990 Comvik submitted accu-sations of unfair practices by Televerket to the Ministry of Communications and to the Fair Trading Ombudsman. One inquiry concerned the charge that Televerket influenced Ericsson to refuse Comvik's order for mobile equipment in an attempt to squeeze Comvik out of the market for mobile telephony. Also, Comvik applied for spectrum capacity to expand its proposed GSM network across all of Sweden by 1995. Televerket allegedly limited Comvik's original frequency allocation. Televerket also responded with a 300 percent increase in the fee on calls made between its system and Comvik's. On the other hand, Televerket's view was that Comvik's difficulties were partly due to its decision to support only its own equipment standard. Another potential mobile competitor, Nordictel, was formed by Scandinavian Airlines (SAS), Volvo, Custodia, Pharos, and Racal. It was licensed in 1991.

Several public data networks exist. Datel service has long been offered for moderate transmission rates. Datex-L is a circuit-switched network linked with similar Scandinavian networks. Tariff rates per time unit were proportional to the transmission speed, making the cost per bit relatively constant but reducing the incentive to use data lines more intensively. The third public data network is Datapak (formerly Telepak), a packet-switched network that has operated since 1984. Rates were structured to make public data networks more advantageous than private lines, particularly for small users.[3] In 1990, Televerket served 1 million data terminals (Boan, 1990).

The first competing public network started service in 1991. Tele2 AB was owned 40 percent by Cable & Wireless and 60 percent by Kinnevik. It leased fiber lines from the Swedish railroad. Thus, competition in transmission had come to Sweden.

A major digitalization program for the public network was initiated in 1985, following basic decisions of the 1970s. Digital upgrading proceeded rapidly. In 1990 almost 50 percent of exchange lines were digitally switched. However, Televerket was not giving ISDN the same priority as many other European telephone administrations did.

Televerket's broadcast activities include more than 1200 radio and TV transmitters. Televerket was also in charge of national frequency management and runs coastal, maritime, and aviation communications. It also provides cable television and SMATV services, with over 50 percent market share. In 1990, the market for VSATs and TVRO dishes was liberalized, subject to frequency coordination.

Videotex began in Sweden in 1982 under the name Datavision. The involvement of Televerket is substantially smaller than that in many other European countries. It limits itself to providing network services and does not manage information provision. This is done by a private company, Telebild (in which Televerket held 30 percent until it sold it off) and by the postal administration's Postal. Televerket also introduced "071" service in 1989, a type of dial-it service offering news, weather, jokes, sports scores, and other information.

Sweden's strong social welfare tradition has led it to the forefront of the innovative Nordic "telecottages" program, which it began in 1985. Telecottages bring telecommuting, distance learning, telefax, videotex, and some video services to remote rural locations. In 1989, Sweden had seven existing and twenty-one planned telecottages (Qvorturp, 1989).

In 1990, Televerket proposed to have its status changed from a Crown Corporation and to sell a 45 percent stake to private investors. Regulatory powers would be lodged in the National Telecommunications Council. The plan met some opposition from socialists, greens, and communists; its passage would give the company much greater autonomy, but would also lead to increased competitiveness in the market. Evidently, Televerket was confident that it would hold its own, though it also began to forge alliances with other medium-sized PTOs, such as the Dutch PTT.

16

Finland

The Finnish telephone system is one of the most interesting in Europe. Instead of a national monopoly, there are about fifty companies, either subscriber co-operatives, municipal enterprises, or private firms, that provide local telephone service and are directly accountable to subscribers. There is also a national PTT (the P&T), which is the largest operator of local telephone service (covering about one-third of all subscribers and three-quarters of the land area). The P&T also offers domestic and international long-distance service, mobile telephony, and other services.

Thus, the Finnish telecommunications system has forgone the economies of scale and the unity of control that are sanctified elsewhere. Yet its telephone system is among the most advanced in the world, moved along by a healthy rivalry among the various participants, and especially by the responsiveness of local companies to their subscribers/shareholders. The number of equipment options is high. Despite the country's small domestic market, Finland's electronics and telecommunications industries are quite successful both in domestic and export markets.

History

The Finnish state postal system dates back to 1638, when Queen Christina of Sweden issued an edict that led to the establishment of five post offices. This system first operated as part of the Swedish and later as part of the Russian post. In 1812, the system became semiautonomous, and it received a monopoly status in 1874. Savings bank services were added in 1886, which led to a rapid increase in the number of offices. After national independence, a postal administration was set up in 1918 and was combined in 1927 with the Telegraph administration into the P&T (Finland PTT, 1983).

The first telephone sets arrived in Finland as early as 1877. Within five years, a number of local telephone companies began operation, the first started by a Helsinki telegraph mechanic, Daniel Johannes Waden. Since Finland was still a Russian province, it was subject to the Russian telegraph bureaucracy. By forming local cooperatives, the Finns became less dependent on the Russian authorities. After 1917, the new Finnish government inherited the imperial Russian role in telegraphy and some long distance service, but independent local telephony was already in place in the cities.

In 1894, the Interurban Telephone Company of Southern Finland was started. The P&T, which gradually established telephone service in the northern part of the country, acquired this company in 1935. Since then, the P&T has operated long-distance service as a monopoly. Service with Russia began in 1909, extending to Sweden by 1919. Automatic telephone exchange was first introduced in Helsinki in 1922 (AT&T, 1975).

The P&T acquired a private long-distance company, and expanded it until it included all long-distance and international service, plus the new offering of telex. It also provided local service in those areas where local organizations did not exist (Bruce et al., 1986).

The basic laws of Finnish telecommunications were set by the Czarist Telephone Manifest of 1886, the Telegraphy Law of 1919, and the Radio Law of 1927. Efforts were made to update the laws, but for a long time there was no political consensus to accomplish more than minor changes (OECD, 1982, p. 10). Eventually, a new telecommunications law was passed and became effective in 1987. It provided a legislative framework to promote development of the telecommunications industry. The traditional operational division of responsibilities between the telecommunications bodies remained the same, but the Ministry of Transport and Communications assumed the supervisory functions previously under the jurisdiction of the P&T.

The P&T and the Local Companies

Telephone service in Finland is unique in that it is provided by both the government through its P&T and by fifty-one local telephone companies that operate with a state concession. These local companies serve more than 72 percent of the telephones in Finland, with the P&T serving the others. By population, the local telephone companies' service covers 68 percent of households, and the P&T service covers 32 percent. In terms of area, however, the P&T serves 75 percent (i.e., the rural parts of the country). The Ministry of Communications has overall responsibility for telecommunications and also sets the P&T budget.

The local companies provide data transmission, but the P&T provides telegraph and telex services. Transmission of TV and radio broadcasts is undertaken by the Finnish Broadcasting Company YLE and by private local radio broadcasters rather than by the P&T. A data network (circuit-switched Datex) is operated jointly by the P&T and the local telephone companies. Nationwide cellular telephone (the Nordic Mobile Telephone Service) is also provided by the P&T.

Organizationally, the P&T is headed by a director general and a deputy director general for telecommunications, and is divided into departments of general telecommunications and radio. The radio department provides mobile radio and paging services.

The local companies are either private firms or cooperatives owned by their subscribers or municipal companies. In the 1930s, over 800 private telephone companies operated (Williamson, 1986, p. 52). The smallest company supplies approximately 1900 connections; the largest, the Helsinki Telephone Company, supplies almost 650,000. By their charters, the cooperatives' pricing is supposed to be cost-based and not for profit. Subscribers elect management and directors, either at a general meeting or by mail. This process is taken seriously. At the board election of the Helsinki Telephone Company, 50 percent of the 350,000 owners participated in the mail balloting. Subscribers, when joining the system, provide a payment and receive a negotiable share certificate. Nearly three-quarters of subscribers are shareholders. No single shareholder can have more than twenty votes, however, and each shareholder must pay an annual telephone subscription, whether a telephone is used or not, which discourages the holding of multiple shares and of speculation. This system affords about 1 million telephone subscribers a direct role in telecommunications matters (Myllo, 1984). A wide variety of organizational structures exists among the companies, including in several cases outright municipal ownership. Mergers have reduced the numbers of companies to fifty-one. In matters of service quality and tariffs, the independent telephone companies are bound by general conditions of their concessions and are otherwise free to set their own policies. No direct popular involvement exists for the P&T, but it has public advisory committees and is subject to oversight by the government.

The state-owned P&T is Finland's largest employer, with 45,000 employees. Of those, more than 20,000 worked in telecommunications in 1988. It is a profitable organization: in 1988, its surplus was 13 percent of revenues (which was contributed to the state budget) and its return was 20 percent of fixed assets (ITU, 1990). Before 1989, it was headed by Pekka Tarjanne, who became the secretary general of the ITU in Geneva.

In 1988, P&T's profits were about FIM 800 million ($200 million). The 1989 telecommunications act requires the P&T to contribute a fixed amount of profits, about $100 million, to the general budget each year. The P&T contribution is more than that of all other state industries combined. Sixty percent of P&T revenues come from domestic service, with the rest split among mobile equipment leasing and international and telex service (Whitehouse, 1989b).

The relation between P&T and the local companies is characterized by both cooperation and conflict. The local operators are collectively represented by the Association of Telephone companies of Finland. Known also as *toimilupalaitokset,* or "licensed ones," they are a strong voice against the P&T. The P&T has long claimed that to ensure the goal of social equity, a full national monopoly is required; but the local companies have stressed, just as adamantly, their century-old tradition of technical progressivity and political legitimacy through the participation of owners/subscribers. Friction arises over the extent of the P&T monopoly, control of advanced services, and revenue and cost allocations.

Legislation and Change

The Finnish system bears a certain resemblance to that of the United States after the AT&T divestiture, in that it is composed of independent local companies interconnected by a powerful long-distance carrier. However, the Finnish P&T, at least before a 1987 law, both acted as regulatory and franchising authority over the local companies and approved equipment that the local companies supplied in partial competition with it. It also held a monopoly over long-distance and international services. The P&T's dual role of service provider and regulator, as well as its claim of monopoly power over the ambiguous data services, was a source of criticism and growing discord between the P&T and local companies.

The 1987 telecommunications law was an effort to define jurisdictions and thus end the disputes. Regulatory powers moved to the Ministry of Communications. Although the new law allowed the local telephone companies to enter parts of the market for data services, various overlapping service issues remained unresolved. An example for such a dilemma is the long-distance data communications services offered by OY Datatie, owned by a number of local telephone companies. The P&T maintained that Datatie should first have a license, granted by the P&T, to enter this market. Similarly, overlap problems exist for electronic mail and videotex which are now regarded as competitive services.

The independent companies must also pay for carriage on the P&T's long-distance network; these payments help keep the P&T's local telephone rates low. Sixty percent of the independent companies' income goes to the P&T for long-distance charges, whereas 80 percent of all calls are local. Not surprisingly, the independent companies are interested in long-distance competition that would provide them with alternatives. (In the United States, long-distance carriers support, through access payments, the local exchange companies, not vice versa.)

In 1980, the local telephone companies terminated an agreement on data transmission. Two court decisions in 1982 restricted the P&T's ability to limit the activities of private telephone companies.

The local telephone companies feared that the P&T would limit them to basic telecommunications services and even compete with them, while reserving for itself the potentially lucrative advanced commercial services. The P&T, could, for example, operate in the areas of the local companies by using their lines to link the PBXs of large users directly to the distant P&T exchange, in effect "bypassing" the local companies.

To deal with these and other problems an early governmental proposal was presented in 1982, but it found no approval. The fight was on between the P&T and the companies and led to the appointment in 1983 of the so-called Rekola Commission. This panel proposed independent equipment approval, simplified attachment by users (a bow to reality), liberalized resale of services, and introduced the possibility of "special" private networks without common carrier obligations. The commission, seeking to fashion a characteristically Finnish consensus, proposed more control for the P&T over its own activities and financing, and greater institutional distance from the government. But it also recommended ending the situation in which the P&T was both a licensing authority and a competitive equipment provider.

However, the P&T opposed the proposed regulatory entity within the Ministry of Communications. The 1987 law followed most recommendations but provided for type approval authority to be lodged in the ministry. The ministry can, however, delegate this authority to a control body that can employ outside laboratories, including those of the P&T and the local companies. In general, the new law's regulatory structure distinguished between services provided as "official duties" and "commercial activities." Private companies can be licensed by the government for general telecommunications. For separate networks, they must seek a license from the Ministry of Communications, assisted by an expert advisory committee. Carriers being granted a general telecommunications license are subject to a variety of duties and rights. Among the former is a universal service requirement, and the obligation to lease connections, including those for further uses such as value-added services.

The 1987 law gave the Ministry of Communications authority to set P&T rates and to decide the basic guidelines for the tariffs of the private companies or to issue unfavorable equipment approval. The local companies tried to prevent P&T exclusivity for long-distance and international service to be written into law. In 1991 they applied again for permission to offer such services.

In addition to defining the role of the P&T, the 1987 legislation set requirements on its efficiency and productivity. Although the P&T remained a state-owned enterprise, there were plans to enact further legislation separating its corporate and government budgets.

In 1989, the Finnish parliament passed two telecommunications laws (Law 748 and Decree 928) to make the P&T a public company on January 1, 1990. However, the sale of P&T stock was delayed well past that date, as was the split of postal and telecommunications activities.

Services

Telephone density and quality of service are high in Finland. In 1988, density was 49.86 subscribers and 68.5 sets per 100 people (ITU, 1990). This is particularly remarkable in light of the low population density. Although Finland is Western Europe's fourth largest country, its total population is less than 5 million. Also, despite its rural character, Finland maintains rates well below the OECD average for residential and business lines (OECD, 1990).

Local exchange automation dates back to 1922 and was completed in the 1960s. Long-distance automation began in 1958, with Ericsson ARM equipment. Electronic Analog SPC switches were introduced in the 1970s, and digital trunk exchanges were introduced in 1978. The P&T introduced digital switching in the trunk network as well as in the local exchange in 1983.

The decentralized Finnish system permits substantial flexibility. Because of Finland's multiplicity of standards and operators, it is an ideal testing ground for new products and services. The Helsinki Telephone Company set up, among others, a packet-switched network and a special data network, a subsidiary to sell subscriber equipment throughout Finland. It also began construction of a cable network. According to its managing director, "We didn't ask anybody, we just did it" (Williamson, 1986). The "Dataway" network was introduced in 1985 by the Helsinki Telephone Company and Finland's biggest bank, K.O.P., to operate an intercity data network. It aimed to bypass the P&T's trunk lines with fiber-optic transmission.

In 1985, thirty-eight local phone companies formed a long-distance operator, Datatie, to compete with the P&T. Datatie carries voice and data traffic and leased line services but no switching. Its shareholders and customers are major banks and insurance companies. Its leased line prices tend to be 25 percent below the P&T's tariffs. In response, P&T invested in Business Networks' (Yritysverkot) bypass network for high-speed leased lines.

In 1990 local companies began fiber-distributed data interface (FDDI) service through Datatie. Helsinki Telephone offered its own service over a 100-mbps backbone, and P&T planned two FDDI rings for Helsinki, one for government and one for commercial uses.

Since 1981, a circuit-switched data network (Datex) has been in operation, in cooperation with other Scandinavian countries. The P&T and the local companies also provide a packet-switched network, which became fully operative in 1984. This packet-switching system was developed separately by the local companies and the P&T.

In 1992, the rivalry between P&T and the local companies intensified, when they sought permission to enter each other's core markets of long-distance and local services.

ISDN trials began in 1987. An intermediate digital service, Diginet, has been available since 1986, offering one 64-kbps channel. Full service began in Helsinki in 1990 under the cooperation of P&T, Helsinki Telephone, and the manufacturer Nokia, and also used Ericsson and Siemens ISDN exchanges (T. Salo, 1990, communication). In 1989, the independent telephone organizations formed the joint company Teleryhamä, which offers data transmission services.

In 1978, Finnish local telephone companies were the first in Europe to provide public facsimile. In the same year, Finland became the second country in the world to offer videotex. Fiber links were introduced into the standard telephone network after 1979. Electronic mail and teletext services were introduced after 1983.

P&T's cellular service operates at 450 MHz and 900 MHz and is part of the Nordic system NMT. Demand for mobile telephony has far exceeded predictions, with some 100,000 Finns using the NMT 450 system and 25,000 using NMT 900 in 1989. A digital GSM service and telepoint CT-2 are being introduced. There will be two separate networks for GSM: Radio Linja's and the P&T's.

An interesting indigenous technical development is the Wilderness and Island

Telephone Network, developed by the P&T and introduced in 1977 as an emergency service (Karvonen, 1984). These are unmanned telephone booths, located in distant locations, and operating by radio with a special battery that lasts two to four years. The conditions of the telephone and the battery can be monitored from a central facility. The telephones are connected to a base station powered by generators, windmills, or solar cells.

Equipment

For a country with a small population, Finland has a well-developed electronics industry. In principle, the equipment market is open to foreign firms, but most equipment is supplied by domestic companies, such as Nokia or the Finnish subsidiaries of Ericsson, Siemens, and Alcatel. Telephone companies attempt to buy from several sources to maintain competition among suppliers. There are four digital exchange suppliers: Telenokia, with 40 percent of the market; Ericsson, with 34 percent; Siemens, with 25 percent; and Standard Electric Puhelinteollisuus (formerly ITT, subsequently Alcatel), with 1 percent.

Telex terminals are provided solely by the P&T; cellular telephones and paging equipment generally are privately supplied, rather than provided by telephone companies. This is due to the liberalization of interconnection rules. In the past, the telephone companies and the P&T provided most equipment, including telephone sets, modems, and data terminals. Interconnection of subscriber-owned equipment has subsequently become permissible.

Other internationally successful Finnish Telephone equipment manufacturers are VISTACOM (videophones), BENEFON (mobile telephone) and TECNOMEN (paging, automatic voice-messaging, encryption). The largest Finnish equipment manufacturer is Telenokia, part of the electronics division of Nokia, Finland's largest private company. In 1989, it controlled 19 percent of the Finnish telecommunications market (Northern Business Information, 1990). The Nokia group is also involved in forest products, machinery, plastics, and chemicals. A sister organization, Nokia Data Systems, produces PBXs, LANs, and other equipment and terminals. Nokia Cables is an important European cable manufacturer. Still another sister company, Mobira, is Scandinavia's largest producer of mobile telephones.[1]

In 1989, Nokia had approximately 37,000 employees and its turnover was about $5.6 billion (*Nokia Annual Report,* 1989, p. 3). Although in the early 1970s Nokia was not very active in the electronics field, by 1990, electronics and electronic products comprised 90 percent of the group's business, mainly in the consumer area. Telecommunications represented 9 percent of sales, or $570 million.

Nokia is active in exports. Only 32 percent of its sales in 1989 were in Finland, with other Scandinavian countries accounting for another 16 percent (*Nokia,* 1989). It holds 35 percent of the digital transmission market in Sweden, 95 percent in Qatar, and supplies the U.K., France, China, and the United Arab Emirates with its DX-200. In 1990, Nokia had 37 percent of the mobile phone market in Thailand, 35 percent in Hong Kong, and 10 percent in the United Kingdom. In 1990, it formed a joint venture with Moscow Telephone Network to provide the Soviet Union's first mobile telephone network. Its success contradicts the conventional wisdom that it takes a large company and a protected home market to survive internationally, because of economies of scale. Nokia has demonstrated that there are niche markets, and it has found one in small rural exchanges with less than 1000 lines.

17
Norway

History

The Norwegian state telegraph company was established in 1855, four years after the first telegraph line was installed. The telephone was introduced in 1880 by the International Bell Telephone Company. Within a year, Bell established local franchises in Oslo and Drammen. A second private system was launched in the capital to compete with the Bell System, but the two were combined in 1886 into the Christiana Telephone Company when the vigorous competition between them yielded what municipal officials deemed were counterproductive results. The city government thus committed itself to a role in the development of Oslo's communications system and retained a share in the new company (Holcombe, 1911).

Norway soon faced the question of who would provide the long-distance link between the Oslo and Drammen exchanges and what role the government should play in telephony. In 1881, the parliament established state control over telephony and telegraphy and provided for private telephone concessions. A private project for the Oslo–Drammen line collapsed when the state telegraph authorities demanded full compensation for all revenue losses incurred as a result of intercity telephone service. The project was also impeded by the merchants of Drammen, who feared that a readily available means of communicating with the capital would hurt their businesses. Similar to other European states' shortsighted protection of the telegraph, the state telegraph office decided not to provide long-distance service on its own to guard the health of the telegraph. In an attempt to block all intercity telephone service, the telegraph administration forced local exchange systems of adjoining communities to maintain a 2–kilometer buffer area between their respective service areas. However, as demand in rural areas increased and companies responded with expanded service, interconnection was permitted, although still only where no equivalent telegraph connection existed. This restriction was abolished as it became increasingly clear that the telegraph could not substitute for the telephone. In 1885, the first interurban telephone line parallel to a telegraph route was constructed and some telegraph offices were converted to public telephone offices. But where telephone companies interfered with its revenue sources, the telegraph administration still required compensation for the resulting falloff in its business.

Because of the dispersed nature of settlements in Norway, the telephone was well-received. Within a decade of its introduction most villages in the country had their own systems. This extraordinarily rapid expansion of telephone service was neither supervised nor operated by any central state organization. Most of the local telephone systems were built by small joint stock associations, cooperatives, or public ventures. The majority were small efforts with neighbors helping each other and contributing rights-of-way, materials, and labor. The systems initially used different equipment and standards. This lack of technical coordination impeded later attempts to link systems through trunk lines. By 1908, however, local systems began to cooperate to create a homogeneous national network.

In 1892, a royal commission was appointed that recommended that long-distance service be privately provided too. Several of the larger local companies attempted to become involved with the plan. But the telegraph administration began to buy local exchanges when their concessions expired and entered the long-distance service field. By 1906, provision of both local and long-distance service was about half private and half public, with the government serving primarily the larger cities and the private companies serving the rural areas. This is the reverse of situations ordinarily prevailing in countries with mixed public-private systems. Eventually, the state system absorbed all private and cooperative networks. In 1899 the agency that would later become the NTA was established and its authority remained largely unchallenged until the 1980s (Nyheim, 1987).

The Norwegian Telecommunications Authority (NTA)

The Norwegian Telecommunications Administration (NTA or Televerket) is the country's de facto telecommunications monopolist. It operates under the 1899 Monopoly Act, which delegated to the state exclusive control over telecommunications in all forms except broadcasting but which does allow private parties to provide telecommunications services under government license. The NTA is supervised by both the minister of communications and an Advisory Council on Telecommunications. In 1988, it was the country's largest non-defense employer, with a staff of 6400.

The NTA's development proceeded in accordance with a planning document whose focus led to significant increases in telephone penetration and productivity in the 1980s (Foreman-Peck and Manning, 1988). In 1980, the government appointed a commission to recommend long-range telecommunications policy. Its report, issued in 1983, was supportive of a strong state role. By then, however, the government was led by a right-of-center coalition which did not particularly care for the recommendations and instead established the Stette Commission to re-examine the telecommunications organization in light of deregulatory trends.

That panel recommended dividing Televerket into three separate organizations: one for basic monopoly services, another for competitive activities in equipment markets, and a third for technical control functions (Nyheim, 1984).

In 1986, the parliament adopted a resolution to reorganize the NTA beginning in 1988. The parliamentary plan allowed the NTA to keep its basic network monopoly but required that its unregulated businesses be consolidated under a separate subsidiary, Televerkets Konkurranseorganisasjan (TBK). Structural safeguards have been implemented against cross-subsidization of TBK by NTA's monopoly. After the defeat of the social democratic government, the new coalition government began to consider further deregulation. The value-added network services were opened for competition. When the market was opened, there were no competitors. With some reluctance, NTA participation in this market was permitted. Applications for a second cellular service were received from Netcom, owned by Norway's Nova Industrier and Orkla Borregaard and Sweden's Comvik. Aside from telecommunications services such as VANs, TBK markets, sells, installs, and services user equipment and offers cable TV systems.

The reorganization also included the establishment of the Norwegian Telecommunications Regulatory Authority (NTRA), overseen by the Ministry of Communications, which represents Norwegian interests before bodies determining international standards and handles licensing, spectrum allocation, and equipment type-approval.

The privatization of 49 percent of NTA and divestiture of TBK promised by the conservative and Progress parties was averted by a narrow Labor/Left victory in 1989. But competition was assured for mobile telephony.

Services

Penetration of main lines reached 47.7 per 100 persons in 1988 (ITU, 1990). These investments are financed by rates, identical for business and residential customers, which are among the highest in Europe, despite the 1981 elimination of connection charges. (Foreman-Peck and Manning, 1988). In a controversial move, NTA in 1989 decreased the price of international leased lines while increasing domestic leased line prices by 16 percent.

Telex service began operating in 1946. Data transmission, using circuit-switched Datex-L service, is available. A public packet-switched network, Norpak, operating since 1980, offers international connections. In 1990, Norway ordered X.400 and X.500 systems from the British firm ICL. The 1983 government commission recommended the development of ISDN, and in 1986 the NTA started an ISDN research laboratory and a pilot ISDN project. Videotex trials began in 1981 (Nyheim, 1984).

A mobile telephony network began operating in 1966 and was automated and integrated into the Nordic Mobile System in 1981. In 1989, Norway had the highest rate of mobile communications penetration in the world, thirty-two subscribers per 1000 persons. ROGALAND radio, established in 1927 and expanded in 1960, also provides maritime services. A GSM network in Oslo was planned for 1991, with a consortium of Norwegian equipment suppliers, including EB Telecom, Siomonsen, Elektro, and ELAB (Green, 1989).

Equipment

One peculiarity of Norwegian network and equipment has been that since the introduction of automatic dialing in the early 1920s, equipment in the Oslo area has operated with a reversed dial (i.e., the digit 1 gives nine pulses, etc). In contrast, the rest of the country operates on the regular system. Interconnections required dial connectors in the public network and in the leased private networks, and equipment had to be available for both systems. This problem is gradually being solved by the introduction of electronic-tone equipment.

Most telecommunications equipment—including data transmission terminals, paging receivers, and private handsets—is privately available with NTRA type approval. Telex terminals and PBXs were once supplied only through the telecommunications authority, though that did not appear to be lasting. Domestic public switch manufacturers were Standard Telefon of Kabelfabrik (STK) (formerly the Norwegian subsidiary of ITT and subsequently of Alcatel) and the Elektrisk Bureau (EB) Group. EB supplied electromechanical switches. But in 1983, the NTA began to digitalize and adopted STK's System 12 switch. In 1989, STK had monopoly control over Norway's public switching market. By 1991, 40 percent of Norway was digitalized, with STK providing 1.2 million lines.

All this affected EB negatively. Previously owned by L. M. Ericsson, EB was one of Norway's strongest private industry groups. In 1987, EB and Ericsson established EB Ericsson Information Systems to manufacture terminal equipment in which each company has a 50 percent interest. In the same year, Asea of Sweden acquired a majority interest in EB, which it soon merged with its two Norwegian subsidiaries. Asea, in turn, joined the Swiss company Brown Boveri to form the Asea Brown Boveri group. EB became Norway's second largest privately owned industry group and employed 15,000 people, of whom 2800 were in its telecommunications division. However, in 1989, EB traded its public switch, PBX, mobile telephone, and other telecommunications operations to L.M. Ericsson in return for the latter's road and railway signalling interests, and concentrated on satellite and power line communications. Ericsson thus acquired a direct role in Norwegian markets.

There are several manufacturers of PBXs. Northern Telecom acquired an interest in one of the larger ones, G. A. Ring. Other domestic telecommunications manufacturers include Universal Communications, for modems; Tandberg Telecom, for videocodecs; Stentor, for advanced intercoms; SysScan, for optical scanning devices; Simonsen Electro, for mobile telephones; and Scanvest Ring Communications, for telemetry.

18

Denmark

Denmark's telephone system is unusual in Europe insofar as it is a shared arrangement of several state-dominated organizations. An 1897 law established a government monopoly for Danish telephony, but concessions granted since then have transferred actual operations to several telephone companies. This structure was until 1990 remarkably similar to that of the United States after its AT&T divestiture: several regional companies offer local service, and a national carrier (the PTT, subsequently Telecom Denmark) provides national and international long-distance service. A separate body serves regulatory functions. This system contradicted traditional PTT tenets of unified structure, end-to-end technical responsibility, and economies of scale.

But for all of its unusual structure, the Danish telephone system cannot be described as either private or competitive. The local companies were dominated by the government and did not compete head-on. But they were rivals insofar as the public was offered an opportunity, almost nonexistent in Europe, to compare local service and to pressure for improvement in lagging performance. Furthermore, a healthy rivalry used to exist between the regional companies and the national PTT, particularly in the areas of new data and mobile telephone services. In 1986, Denmark even had its own mini-divestiture when the PTT was required to reorganize its small local telephone operations. The telephone organizations, in turn, have to face an influential and aggressive constituency—the housing associations with their television community antenna associations—especially on issues involving broadband services. However, in 1990 the rivalries were reduced by the government's putting the regional companies under the PTT holding company, with the aim of reducing internal competition in order to prepare for the expected European competition.

Structure

The government holds the legal telegraph and telephone monopoly concession in accordance with a 1897 law; it franchised three regional telephone companies—for Copenhagen (KTAS), Jutland (JTAS), and Funen (FKT)—to provide service. A fourth concessionary company (Tele Sonderjylland), under the

Danish Post and Telegraph office (PTT), was added to provide service to the South Jutland region after it was returned to Danish rule in 1920. The individual companies operated trunk lines within the areas of their individual franchises, and the government played no role in local operations for a long time.

Thus, telecommunications services were supplied by two sources, the PTT and four local telephone companies. These local companies were not private. The government held a majority control of the Copenhagen and Jutland telephone companies as well as 100 percent of the South-Jutland telephone company. The Funen Company was a cooperative of local councils, and the government owned the remaining 45 percent. KTAS operates on the islands of Zealand, Lolland-Falster, and Bornholm, and serves 45 percent of the population and 49 percent of all telephones. JTAS has 39 percent and FKT has 8 percent. In 1990, all regional companies were placed under a PTT holding organization, with partial privatization involving investors close to the government (such as pension funds).

The need for long-distance interconnection and approval of rates suggested a government presence. In 1950 an agreement was reached between the state and regional companies (the concordate) in which the state acted as arbitrator for issues of standards, pricing and cost-sharing, and traffic planning (Olsen, 1988). But this agreement proved unstable in the 1980s when new technologies were being introduced. In 1982, the minister of public works, who holds overall responsibility for telecommunications policy, established and appointed a Telecommunications Council comprised of thirteen members, representing the ministries, the PTT, the independent telephone companies, subscribers, industry, and employees.

In 1986, the Telecommunications Council was reduced in significance when the general directorate for Telecommunications was carved out of the PTT. This reorganization came in the wake of the so-called Bernstein Committee report. The regional structure was strengthened by adding a fourth concessionary state enterprise for South Jutland, which was divested from the PTT, though it was still owned by it. The PTT, which in 1978 had still called for a unified system under its control, also lost its operating divisions for data transmission, mobile telephone terminals, telex, telefax, and other customer services to the four concessionary companies. In addition, the PTT was divided into a general directorate for political, administrative, and regulatory functions (including rate setting, spectrum management, equipment certification, and licensing) and two operating divisions for postal service and telecommunications. The latter was named Telecom Denmark, and was in charge of connections between concessionary areas, international long-distance service, the national trunk network, nationwide cellular mobile telephones, and broadcasting. The Telecommunications Council was reduced to an advisory capacity, and regulatory matters were more independently lodged in the ministry and the general directorate (Pedersen, 1987).

The creation of the general directorate was significant in unification and consolidation of regulating authority. The weak arbitrator's approach of the former agency was replaced by a politically strong "caretaker of the public interest". The directorate outlined a timetable of liberalization consistent with EC reforms (Olsen, 1988).

Yet this liberalization was not without opposition. In 1990, the government, moving against the European trend, decided to purchase the Copenhagen and Jutland telephone companies by 1992, arguing that replication of costly services such as ISDN and intelligent networks was inefficient in a small country and that it reduced service quality. Like Italy, it sought to protect monopoly by consolidating it instead of using institutional diversity as an invigorating factor.

In July 1990, the conservative government reached an agreement with the Social Democrats to place the four telephone companies under a new holding firm, teleDenmark, which has 17,000 employees and revenues of $3 billion. The government kept a 51 percent stake and retained control of the tele-Denmark Board, selling the rest to private investors. Much of the private investment, however, is from pension funds with ties to the government. The General Assembly appoints eight out of twelve members of teleDenmark's Board, including the chairman. The employees of teleDenmark, who retain their civil servant status, appoint the other four Board members. Telex, satellite and basic telephone services were reserved to teleDenmark. A second cellular operator (Dansk Mobil telefon, owned by Great Northern, Bell South, and Nordic Tel) was franchised.

Equipment

In 1875, F. C. Tietgen, founder of the Great Northern Telegraph Company (1869), created the first telegraph manufacturing company. Domestic telephone set production began in 1892, followed by a number of foreign subsidiaries. By 1987, the three major companies were GN-Telematic, Alcatel Kirk, and NKT (Nordisk Kabel og Trad) (Pedersen, 1988).

Telecommunications equipment represents a quarter of the country's total output of electronic products. In 1987, the telecommunications industry employed 32,000 people and exported 60 percent of its products (NKT, 1987). The largest export markets are Scandinavian nations and the United Kingdom. Although Danish companies generally have a small share of foreign markets, mobile cellular firms established major shares in several countries.

Microwave transmission was patented in Denmark in 1902 but did not experience major growth until after World War II. In 1947, the Great Northern Company established a terrestrial and maritime radio communications manufacturing subsidiary, Storno, which became the dominant producer of mobile radio equipment after opening a public mobile telephone network in 1963. Storno is no longer Danish owned; it was acquired by General Electric in 1976 and subsequently sold to Motorola in 1985. The other major radio manufacturer, A.P. Radiotelefon, was created in 1953 and acquired by foreign interests in 1978. The only major Danish-owned transmission equipment company left was Dancall (originally Dancom maritime radio manufacturer), which was established in 1980.

All the preceeding companies dominate the Danish equipment industry in certain product lines. NKT manufactures optical fibers. Storno, A.P., and Dancall all produce cellular mobile telephone systems. Alcatel Kirk manufactures PBXs and manufactures telephones and small telephone systems. GN-Communications produces payphones, and GN-Datacom makes data transmission equipment. Yet another company, Regnecentralen (RC), supplies directory systems and the packet-switched network. Danish Telecom International (DTI), owned by the concessionary telephone companies, distributes telephone sets, digital switching systems, PBXs, and the Dikon ISDN switch to international markets (Pedersen, 1988).

In 1979, when optical fibers were first used in the Danish network, Siemens was the supplier. NKT entered the market in 1983 after five years of R&D. In 1987, NKT was joined by AT&T in creating Lycom, an optical fiber production subsidiary.

Alcatel Kirk (SEK) and GN Telematic (both established in 1892) held significant shares of the telephone system market until 1990, when GN Telematic was reorganized. Alcatel Kirk, originally Emil Moller's Telephone Company, adopted its present name after the acquisition of ITT's telecommunications business by France's Alcatel.

GN-Telematic was the only Danish-owned telephone set manufacturer until Bang & Olufsen (B&O) began producing telephones in 1986. Bang & Olufsen was established in 1925 and is the largest Danish-owned audio and video systems producer. The Dikon Systems Division was created in 1979 with the support of JTAS to bring B&O into the telecommunications industry with the production of an advanced subscribers network switch. The Dikon switch had advantages of maintenance and installation, and its success encouraged B&O to expand further into telecommunications (Pedersen, 1988). In 1990 Ericsson acquired 50 percent of Dikon and renamed it Diax Telecommunications.

Regnecentralen Computer (RC) was founded in 1955 and was jointly owned by ICL, the telephone companies, pension funds, and the government. Its greatest success was its 1975 advanced minicomputer (RC 8000), which enabled RC to create a telephone directory system for the local companies. This system is currently used by other countries, including the United States. RC also developed the packet-switched public data network, Paxnet, used by the Danish ROCs since 1983. In 1988, the British firm ICL, subsequently controlled by Fujitsu, bought a 51 percent stake in RC, changed its name to RC International and shifted to UNIX-based systems.

Originally, the PTT and the concessionary companies held an equipment supply monopoly in their respective areas. The four telephone administrations still provide telephone sets, modems, PBXs, and telex, teletex, and data communications equipment. All telephone equipment attached to the network either must be supplied by the telephone administration or must meet the type-approval set by the government Telecommunications Inspectorate.

Reform legislation in 1986 provided for successive liberalization of equipment, first of telephone extensions, then of PBXs, modems, telex terminals, and main telephone sets. In 1989, all but first telephone sets had been liberalized (TDR, 1989). By 1990, the entire terminal equipment market had been liberalized, in line with EC directives to ensure Danish manufacturers' reciprocal access to the export market (M.K. Pedersen, 1990, communication).

Liberalization was slowed by telephone company ownership of the equipment installed in homes and businesses. The electricians association claimed that its Telepunkt stores were unable to compete with the existing de facto equipment monopoly.

Services

Denmark's telephone companies offer a variety of data transmission services. Paxnet is a packet-switched data network. Datex is a public circuit-switched data network. The three local telephone organizations also provide slow-speed Datel service. Until the end of 1986, the PTT provided and maintained all modems, except the lower-speed (300 baud) modems, which were supplied by the local companies. Subsequently, local operators provided all modems above 2400 baud, and the market for lower-speed modems was liberalized. In 1988, all modems were liberalized.

Since 1985, extensive investments in the future of ISDN have been undertaken by both the PTT and the local companies. Field trials were begun in 1989 using Ericsson AXE and Siemens EWSD switches. The local companies also introduced Meganet, a 2-Mbps data transmission service using Dikon switches.

The Nordic Mobile Telephone system (NMT) has offered mobile cellular telephone service since 1982. NMT was provided by the PTT and not by the regional companies. Demand exceeded expectations. The combined subscriber base for the NMT450 and NMT900 systems is almost equivalent to those of France or West Germany.

Next to the United Kingdom, Denmark has the world's second-lowest telex charges (Barnes, 1987). Electronic mail teletext service was introduced in 1984 and operates at a speed of 2400 baud. TeleDenmark also provides a videotex service named Teledata, which operates under the Prestel standard. Prestel development was stopped, however, while the PTT and the regional companies developed a new system based on the CEPT standard. Telex and teletex users have access to the electronic mailbox service, Databoks. In 1988, Denmark liberalized value-added services, subject to registration. Transmission capacity could be resold to data customers on a leased-line basis, although a 5 percent limit was placed on resold traffic (P&T Directorate General, 1988). Anticipating liberalization, KTAS established joint ventures with IBM (danNet) for data processing, teletext, and EDI.

In 1979, the cable manufacturer NKT proposed ambitious plans to connect with local telephone companies to provide an integrated broadband network (IBN). This followed growing concern with the emergence of cable television and direct broadcast satellites. For example, households could have access to their own or community satellite antennas to the exclusion of the established telephone carriers.

In 1983, a Royal Commission on Mass Media proposed that a national broadband network be established that would provide both television and telephone linkages. The independent telephone companies were in favor of a nationwide broadband system because it would free them from prior agreements with the PTT (Qvortrup, 1984). The PTT, however, preferred to separate telephone from broadband services, with a narrowband ISDN network to link telephone connections and a broadband network to interconnect the national cable television and master antenna systems. The latter would use a nationwide PTT microwave system and PTT-operated satellite earth stations. These issues were resolved in the Bernstein Committee's 1988 recommendations, which left broadband services such as data transmission and video service providers to the local companies.

Much of the country was cabled for the Digital Optical CATV Trunk (DO-CAT) system, which allows transmission of eight television and twelve FM channels on each broadband optical fiber.

The PTT and the telephone companies were given a monopoly for the reception of television programs from communications satellites, thus forcing households to partly finance the advanced national cable system. This led to much unhappiness among cable firms and the numerous housing associations that operated master antenna satellite systems. Provocative violations of the law ensued. In consequence, the parliament changed the law in 1987 and permitted a system by which private parties could receive satellite-delivered programs and compete with the traditional telephone carriers, which themselves can transmit these satellite programs to master antenna associations as "hybrid network connection" (hybrid both in terms of analog-digital and fiber-coax combinations). The notion of the unified national broadband network was thus significantly affected, since the new law permitted broadband reception and limited distribution outside of it.

19

Iceland

Iceland is a prime example of a country suffering from the diseconomies of small scale. Its telecommunications are constrained by the country's basic realities: Its rugged terrain is sparsely populated by only a quarter of a million people; its remote geographic location requires advanced international communications; and it lacks an electronics industry. It is difficult even to imagine competitive telecommunications in Iceland. Yet by the same logic of scale, the integration of parts of Icelandic telecommunications with the larger systems of its frequent Nordic partners would be conceivable.

Telephone service began in 1889, when a businessman in Isafjordur, in northwestern Iceland, connected his various offices by telephone lines. In 1890, a private line was opened between Reykjavik and nearby Hafnarfjördhur. Government operations began in 1906 with the trunk connection of Reykjavik to the east coast and the creation of telephone and telegraph exchanges. By 1929, service reached around the country. A large automatic telephone exchange began operating in Reykjavik and Hafnarfjördhur in 1932. In 1935, shortwave radio telephony was opened to England and Denmark. In 1947, service to the United States was implemented.

The Icelandic PTT has a monopoly over telecommunications. It is state owned and reports to the minister of transport. In 1988, telephone density was about 46.6 main lines per 100 persons and there were approximately 117,000 subscribers. Quarterly subscription for residential phone service is 585 Kr (about $16), and a local call costs 1.32 Kr ($0.04) per six minutes in daytime. Long-distance calls up to 100 kilometers cost 1.32 Kr ($0.04) per eighteen seconds. A one-minute call to the United States costs 85 Kr (about $2). These rates were the lowest among *all* OECD countries for both residential and business service (OECD, 1990, p. 30).

Between 1965 and 1975, all the urban exchanges were automated, and full automation of the nation's system was achieved by the end of 1986. In 1981, the PTT decided to replace the older analog switches with digital switches. The first digital exchanges employed Ericsson AXE-10 switches and began operating in 1984 in Reykjavik and Keflavik. Switching equipment by Elektrisk Bureau (EB) of Norway was also used. At the end of 1989, seven AXE central exchanges and twenty-two secondary exchanges served 35 percent of the system's subscribers (Tomasson, 1990). Plans to increase digitalization and deploy fiber-optic cables were slowed by a government austerity program.

Iceland has no telecommunications equipment industry. Siemens, Ericsson, Philips, Telic/Alcatel, and SEK all offer PBXs, most of which are supplied and serviced, but not rented, by the PTT. Also offered are key systems from a wide variety of suppliers, including Japan. All terminal equipment, including modems, is supplied through the PTT. Equipment must not disturb or cause inconvenience for the PTT or its subscribers. Telex for data transmission, telegraph, and telephone circuits can be leased from the PTT.

Mobile telephony was introduced in 1986 with the implementation of the NMT 450 system. In 1987, an AXE exchange was added to the system and the number of mobile subscribers increased to 4400. Such traffic is especially heavy between fishing boats and the shore.

After planning a public data network since 1983, the PTT implemented the Eripax X.25 system ICEPAC for domestic use in 1986. The network is centered in Reykjavik with six remote nodes. ICEPAC was first linked to Copenhagen and London and is now linked to most Western countries. Since 1986, digitalization of the network has been pursued through the AXE exchanges, digital radio systems, and fiber-optic links.

A microwave ring around the country was completed in the early 1980s. Since 1980, the Skyggnir earth station has permitted international direct dialing. By 1987, 500 kilometers of fiber-optic cable had been laid.

20

Ireland

History

The United Telephone Company opened its first exchange (with five subscribers) in 1880.[1] United was taken over in 1882 by the Telephone Company of Ireland, which oversaw a slow growth to 500 lines in Dublin by 1988. The operation was acquired in 1893 by the National Telephone Company, which rapidly developed the network to encompass fifty-six exchanges by 1900. The Post Office, which operated the telegraph and feared revenue losses, began in 1893 slowly to invest in trunk lines and submarine cables. By 1908 the Post owned thirty-three exchanges to National's eighty-five (Litton, 1961).

The threat of Post Office take-over of National Telephone became a reality in 1905; the postmaster general forced a sell-out at the end of National's license period in 1911, paying only £12.4 million where the company had claimed its value was £20.9 million. Military involvement in network construction began in 1909, completely replacing civilians until the outbreak of World War I. By 1918, there were 12,500 lines, half of them around Dublin; three counties were still without exchanges. The network was greatly damaged in the Anglo-Irish and civil wars of the 1920s.

In 1924, the Post Office launched a vigorous program to rebuild and expand the crippled network. By 1930, only western pockets of Mayo and Donegal counties were without exchanges. Dublin received the country's first automatic exchange system in 1927, but economic hardship in the 1930s stalled the network's growth.

In 1937, there were still fewer than 40,000 lines in service (Department of Industry and Commerce of Ireland, 1944). Except for the emergency installation of telephone lines to coastal lookout posts, progress halted altogether during World War II. In 1945 the government earmarked £10 million for a program to reach 100,000 subscribers within fifteen years, which was achieved ahead of schedule. The country's first transatlantic cable was laid in 1956, and Limerick began operating Ireland's first crossbar switch in 1957 (Telecom Eireann, 1987). By 1960, however, Ireland still had only 145,000 telephones in service, fewer than any European nation except Greece, and line density in Dublin was a mere 9.25 percent (Department of Industry and Commerce of Ireland, 1969).

By the late 1960s, connections were accelerated. By 1979, a total of 436,000

232

lines were in operation, but the waiting list was still lengthy (Central Statistics Office, 1979, p. 322).

Telecom Eireann

For Irish telecommunications, the 1980s was an era of catching up. In 1978, the inferior quality of services provided by the government's Department of Posts and Telegraphs forced the newly elected Fianna Fáil government to commission an external and independent group to review Irish telecommunications (Raggett, 1984). Upon completion of its task, the commission issued a report that urged immediate action. The inadequacy of telecommunications was acknowledged. The government established an interim Telecoms Board, and as part of a broad infrastructure program it approved accelerated development.

Soon after, under the P&T minister Albert Reynolds, the government launched a five-year telecommunications spending program of over $1 billion for the early 1980s. The program aimed to modernize and upgrade the network to the quality of other European countries and to increase its availability throughout the country (Ergas and Okavana, 1984). The implementation of this program helped to change the government's previous tendency to consider telecommunications as a money maker for its other services.

The government published legislative proposals based on the review group's report, but enactment of the legislation was impeded by five changes of government in the three years of the interim Telecom Board. The proposals as outlined, however, encountered little political opposition (Keenan, 1985; Raggett, 1984).

Eventually, the Postal and Telecommunications Services Act of 1983 was passed. It created two state-sponsored enterprises, the Bord Telecom Eireann (TE), for telecommunications, and An Post, for the national postal service. Carved from the Department of Post and Telegraphs, a Department of Communications was created to supervise general policy on telecommunications issues (NTIA, 1985). Actual telecommunications operations are provided by Telecom Eireann (TE). Tom Byrnes, an Irish-American who has been the managing director of IBM Ireland, served as Chief Executive of TE. TE was required to operate on a profit basis, with near-monopoly rights of service, and embarked on an ambitious modernization program. In 1987, foreign loans helped fund 50 percent of TE's investment program (Garnett, 1987).

After separating from the PTT, Bord Telecom Eireann was still a state-owned enterprise but operated with greater autonomy, under an exclusive government license. It has an "exclusive privilege," which is somewhat less than a monopoly, up to and including the connection point in the customers' premises. Where TE decides not to provide service, another network operator can be licensed, as in the case of cable service. Such a license can be issued by the PTT minister or by TE itself. Where services are uneconomical, the government can force TE to provide them. In 1985, the cable television committee, established by Communications Minister James Mitchell, recommended the establishment of a national distribution network linking local cable networks through TE.

Compared to other European countries, Ireland has a relatively low telephone density. In 1990, telephone line density was 26 per 100 people, or 64 percent of households. Total number of lines by 1990 was 950,000, of which 34 percent were business and 64 percent were residential. Annual line charges in 1990 were about $201 for residential service and $222 for business.

TE's main problem has been to improve service in Dublin to be comparable to the service existing outside of the capital, a reversal of the usual quality differential (Keenan, 1985). Partly because Dublin was the fastest-growing major city in Europe, telephone installations have lagged far behind. Much of the investment funds, therefore, have been used simply to catch up in the mass provision of basic telephony. TE has also had to grapple with the rate structure, which had been time insensitive for local calls. In addition, it inherited an inflexible, graded employment structure that created problems in the rapidly changing environment.

At first, TE depended on funds from the Ministry of Finance. But as the coalition government of the mid-1980s became increasingly mired in debt, a new strategy was devised that was influenced by the French model. It established a subsidiary, Irish Telecommunications Investments (ITI), which invests funds in the private financial markets and in the telecommunications network. ITI technically owns these assets and charges TE for their use.

Unfilled service orders dropped from 20 percent of total customers in 1980 to 2.9 percent in 1986, and the waiting period fell to six weeks. Operating revenues rose to IR£784 million, a 20 percent increase from 1985 to 1986 (Dillon, 1987). By 1990, the waiting list for main lines had dropped to 6000, less than one percent of total subscribers (ITU, 1990). In real terms, TE's rates were reduced by almost 30 percent between TE's establishment in 1984 and 1990 (F. McGovern, 1990, communication).

In 1985, Byrnes left TE at the end of his five-year contract; Ireland's Minister for Communications had let the contract lapse without signing the seven-year extension on the terms approved by TE's board. In departing, Byrnes minced no words: "the real tragedy, in my view, is that shortsighted, very shortsighted, politicians combined with arrogant power-hungry bureaucrats, have reinstated the same practices which were disastrous for this country prior to 1979" (*Telephony*, 1985, p. 83). As an example, Byrnes cites a 1985 attempt by the government to borrow up to $200 million from private sources through TE's Irish Telecommunications Investments (ITI) subsidiary. ITI was established to help fund TE construction projects, but the Department of Finance used it to relieve Ireland's federal deficit.

Byrnes was succeeded by Fergus McGovern, former head of operations of TE. Some financial help came from the European Community. Ireland was eligible for 64 percent of the budget of the first phase of the EC's $865 million STAR development program. Its dependence on EC funds was likely to nudge Telecom Eireann to comply with Brussels' liberalization policy.

Equipment

The supply of subscriber equipment, including first sets, is largely liberalized. For both equipment and other supplies a private provider must obtain type approval from the government and consent from TE for each connection to the public network. The minister of communications grants equipment approval and TE and the Institute of Industrial Research and Standards administers equipment tests. Each private supplier must also demonstrate technical ability and financial viability.

TE supplies equipment through a wholly owned subsidiary, Telecom Eireann Information System (TEIS), which was established to avoid the cross-subsidization and unfair tax advantages of TE (C. D. Rafferty, 1987, communication). However in 1990, the Telecommunications Association (TA), a group of some twenty Irish equipment suppliers, charged TE and TEIS with unfair competition before the European Commission. TA accused TE of eighty violations, including undercharging TEIS for services, releasing advance information on orders, and operating as a single source despite professed independence (Evagora, 1990a). The TA urged the establishment of an independent watchdog group modeled on the U.K.'s Oftel. TE denied the charges and TA's lawsuits were unable to stimulate EC injunctive action.

In 1979, a decision was made in favor of digital technology. Two switching systems were introduced, Alcatel's E10B and Ericsson's AXE. Both are produced or assembled in Ireland. These modernization plans largely eliminated manual switching, which in 1978 still accounted for 50 percent of exchanges serving 10 percent of subscribers.

For a quarter century, the Swedish L.M. Ericsson supplied exchanges to Ireland from a manufacturing plant in Athlone. For the new digital switching system, a joint venture of the French Alcatel and Telectron was chosen. Active in transmission, Telectron is the main Irish telecommunications firm, with significant exports to the Middle East.

In 1981, AT&T acquired 45 percent of Telectron. This acquisition forced the relationship between Telectron and Alcatel to dissolve. Alcatel then formed Alcatel Ireland, a local affiliate that is 75 percent French and 25 percent Irish.

Services

For a long time, Irish international traffic used to be routed through Britain. In 1984, however, Ireland established an Intelsat earth station near Cork. Since then, it has vied to become an international gateway for European traffic, but this goal clashed with tariff reality. Calls placed from Ireland to a number of other European nations tend to cost considerably more than calls traveling in the opposite direction (*Transnational Data and Communications Report*, 1988). Exceptions are calls to generally high-priced countries (Belgum, Greece, Italy,

Spain, and Portugal). In 1990, however, rates for digital lines were reduced significantly.

Since 1981, international packet switching service has been available, and in 1984, TE introduced the packet-switched network Eirpac. It allows access to bibliographic and full-text databases. Eirpac also connects to national and international videotex services.

A major VAN service is Cognotec, established by the Confederation of Irish Industry in 1984 and restructured in 1987 with strong insurance industry participation. Its Corporate Treasury service provides company controllers with access to financial information. In partnership with Istel (a subsidiary of AT&T), Cognotec launched its Corporate Treasury service in the U.K. market in 1990. Cognotec's other major service is Clientbank, which gives insurance brokers access to host computers of leading insurance companies.

Agriline, an agricultural videotex database, was launched in 1986 following a two-year EC-supported trial. It offers weather, market prices, a calendar of events, and farm business news as well as information on crops and livestock management.

Eircell mobile communication is provided by TE. The system uses the TACS technical standard and had 19,000 subscribers in 1990, the EC's third-highest penetration per working population, at comparatively low rates for Europe (F. McGovern, 1990, communication). Eirpage is a joint venture with Motorola Ireland in which TE has 51 percent. It holds the monopoly on national paging services in Ireland.

Data and Special Services Network (DASSNET), launched in 1990, is a significant improvement of the digital leased-line network, providing 64–kbit-2–Mbit connections. The Government Telecommunications Network, linking government departments in Dublin and five provincial centers, planned to use the advanced DASSNET.

Telecommunications in the Mediterranean Countries and Eastern Europe

21
Italy

No European telecommunications system has been institutionally more complex than Italy's. Through the 1980s, it was best described as a shared monopoly of five organizations. Two of these organizations are government administrations; the other three are nominally private groups. The state directly runs the State Agency for Telephone Services (ASST), which handles long-distance and European telephony, and the Post and Telecommunications Administration (PT), which handles telegraph and telex networks. The three other groups are Società Italiana per l'Esercizio Telefonico (SIP), for local exchanges and some long-distance service; Italcable, for intercontinental service, and Telespazio, for satellite service, all of which are part of the state-dominated Società Finanziaria Telefonica (STET) holding company. In theory, the system separates segments of network control as the AT&T divestiture did in the United States, and it reduces monopoly power. In practice, however, the system in its aggregate is an inflexible bureaucracy, with service problems for small and large users. There are few performance rivalries, but frequent jurisdictional and political disputes. These revolve around financial transfers, particularly over dominance in new fields, such as data transmission and ISDN. Added to these problems are the vertical ties the STET companies maintain with sister firms in manufacturing, notably Italtel, the country's dominant telecommunications equipment maker. The protected market shares make Italy's electronics industry less dynamic than several other segments of its economy. One exception is Olivetti, which is outside this arrangement. On the positive side, the existing complex institutional system would allow for relatively easy modifications. For instance, a privatization of the STET network firms and their separation from equipment suppliers is gradually taking place, although not as part of a planned telecommunications policy. Additionally, equipment liberalization has progressed, partly because users' self-help could not be contained. As the STET firms become more entrepreneurial, the shared service monopoly could break down in the future. But this is counteracted by the government, whose chief initiative in telecommunications seeks to centralize the various institutions into one superprovider.

History

Italy's postal service originated in medieval times when the major cities and trading companies established Europe's first courier services. In Venice, a guildlike messenger organization existed and operated in a monopolistic fashion after 1305. Milan's system dates to 1385, and Naples created a runner course for southern Italy in 1444 (Dallmeyer, 1977). The Tassis family, which became a major presence in the postal system of much of Europe, also established service in Italy. The Italian PTT was established in 1870, during the unification of Italy.

Italian telephony started as a private business. The first large company, Società Generale di Telefonia, was established in 1881 (Holcombe, 1911). Limited telephone service began in Rome in 1878; the American Bell Company opened exchanges in Rome and Milan in 1881. Also in 1881, the first interurban service was provided between Rome and Tivoli on an experimental basis. Rival companies and competitive service emerged in some of the larger cities. Pressure to consolidate soon mounted. Within a short time, only two private telephone companies remained. In 1883, a royal decree established uniform obligations for concessionary firms, and burdensome requirements were imposed to protect the telegraph authority. Concessions were not awarded exclusively, and ran for only three years. The telegraph authority approved all public call offices as well as the private telephone rates. It levied a heavy concession fee on local exchanges and permitted municipalities to purchase the private telephone systems after twelve years. However, only one municipality wound up owning a local telephone ownership. In 1907, there were 141 local networks with 43,000 subscribers. In that year, the Italian parliament voted to purchase eighteen long-distance lines and twenty-seven local exchanges, then operated by the two major private telephone companies (Società Generale Italiana de Telefonia e Applicazione Elettriche and Società Telefonica dell'Alta Italiana, accounting for 75 percent of Italy's telephones). Under the plan, compensation to the owners of these companies was to be paid over eleven years out of future telephone profits.

Between 1907 and 1925, telecommunications were jointly provided by the state and by sixty-three regional private concessionaires. Local telephony was legally franchised to private firms, but long-distance communications remained under state control. Subsequently, under Mussolini, five telephone regions were established and assigned to different concessionaires: STIPEL, TELVE, TIMO, TETI, and SET. The PT organization ASST was established to provide long-distance interconnection between the five regions and international services with European and Mediterranean nations. This interexchange network was completed in 1928.

Forces for further centralization were strong. In October 1933, three of the concessionary firms were absorbed into the government holding company STET, which in turn was part of the government's industrial reconstruction institute, IRI. In 1958, the two remaining regional companies, TETI and SET, became part of STET. In 1965, these five concessionaires were among nine firms merged into the Società Italiana per l'Esercizio Telefonica (SIP), a company that had started as a northern Italian electrical utility. About 70,000 shareholders owned approximately 45 percent of SIP's capital; STET controlled the remainder. In turn, about 50,000 shareholders controlled 42.3 percent of STET, with the remaining 57.7 percent held by IRI.

In the meantime, international communications also consolidated. International telegraph service was initially divided between the radio provider, Italia Radio, and the submarine cable provider, Italcable, and was centralized in 1941 when Italcable acquired its rival. It was further consolidated in 1965, when Italcable became a subsidiary of STET. Telespazio, Italy's satellite communications provider, was established as part of STET in 1963.

Structure

The complexity of the Italian system of telecommunications is largely hidden from the user's view. Virtually all user transactions except telegraph and telex are through SIP, which provides customers with a single telephone bill. The complexity of the system is upstream in the transmission path, where various organizations carved out segments of control. Despite the multiplicity of actors, at no point could users choose a provider, and they faced a monopoly, or more accurately, a shared monopoly. By tradition, politics, or influence, five organizations were able to control geographical or service areas within the monopoly. Virtually all these organizations were in one way or another government controlled, but by different parts of the state bureaucracy. In theory, this system could permit a comparison of performance and diffuse otherwise considerable power. In practice, the organizations were political rivals and not market competitors. Italy's telecommunications structure reflects the more general pervasiveness of politicization. By law, all telecommunications services are the province of the state. The complexity starts because the government operated telecommunications directly, through two of its own administrations, and it also granted operational authority to three outside concessionaires, notably SIP. These concessionaires were controlled by parts of the government other than the PTT ministry. These entities divided domestic and international long-distance service among themselves in no obvious pattern. The lead agency responsible for telecommunications is the Ministry of Post and Telecommunications (MPT). The MPT provides mail service and the vast postal bank transfer system. Two bodies, the Administrative Council and the High Technical Council for Telecommunications, assisted the ministry in its overall control of telecommunications. The Administrative Council included a wide array of governmental interests and is consulted on tariffs, proposed regulations, and concessionaires. The High Technical Council for Telecommunications consisted of experts from government, universities, and the concessionaires. It advised the ministry on technical and economic matters, development plans, and operations.

Subordinate to the MPT through the 1980s were two autonomous administrations: the Post and Telecommunications Administration (PT) and the State Agency for Telephone Services (ASST). The PT conducted postal telegraph, telex, telefax, and radio electric services. ASST, an autonomous public corporation, operated the primary long-distance transmission network that connected the twenty-one telecommunication "compartments" of the country. ASST also operated international telephony within Europe and the Mediterranean basin. Through the PT, the MPT provided a coastal station network (DCR) for communication with ships, minor islands, and Albania. It also provided broadcasting transmission for government operations such as embassies abroad. Two other companies, Sirm and Telemar, operated radio equipment aboard Italian ships, and potentially other services where no private concessioniaries can be secured. The national network's layout consisted of twenty-one regional compartments, subdivided into 231 districts, each with its own area code. These were, in turn, divided into about 1400 sectors and 10,000 local exchanges, of which more than half have less than 500 subscribers.

Perhaps the best way to conceptualize the allocation of services in Italy is to imagine four concentric rings, in which the responsibilities alternated between the government-controlled STET holding company and direct government provision. At the core, STET's subsidiary company SIP operated local distribution. SIP also provided domestic packet-switched service. The next ring around it, corresponding to a greater distance of communication, was domestic long-distance transmission, operated by ASST. (For a long time, SIP also ran long-distance service in many rural districts.) The next ring, international service within Europe and many countries in North Africa, was also in the domain of ASST. The third ring was international transmission outside of Europe and North Africa, which was operated by the STET companies Italcable (for terrestrial and submarine transmission) and Telespazio (for satellites). Both also provided the PT administration with international record traffic.

SIP is by far the largest Italian service operator, with a turnover of 14,900 billion lire and 77,000 employees in 1989; the next largest, ASST, had revenues of 2,400 billion lire and under 13,000 employees.

An interesting side-effect of this system was that the separation of firms by different functions makes internal cross-subsidization more difficult (Benedetti, 1983). The creation of a cross-subsidization fund in 1980, the Cassa Conquaglio per Il Services Telefonico, did not clarify this complex accounting process. SIP's local service was separate from ASST's long-distance service. Thus, where contributions existed, they were by payment to another entity or by contributions to a parent company, and were thus more transparent than internal subsidies would be within a unified PTT system.

In 1985, the PTT ministry (MPT) initiated a study of the feasibility of separating postal and telecommunications activities. The study proposed separate agencies within the ministry to administer each of these activities throughout the country. The recommendations, however, were not instituted. In 1987, a bill was introduced that would change the PTT role from operating services to planning and coordination and that would divide service provision so that Italcable would provide the entire international service and SIP would provide the domestic one. Additionally, the bill proposed that Telespazio operate independently, providing satellite service for SIP, Italcable, and RAI. ASST's operations would be assumed by SIP, Italcable, and the ministry. The bill's opponents focused on job relocation and preserving the state control.

Subsequently, the Christian Democrats offered a plan in 1988 to consolidate the telecommunications agencies into a "Super-STET"—including SIP, ASST, Italcable, and Telespazio—aggregated as "Italia Telecom." It would have relegated the ministry to a watchdog role (Rosenbaum, 1988). But this project was blocked by the PTT minister, trade unions, and southern Italian Christian Democrats, who traditionally were influential in MPT matters and were concerned with loss of telecommunications and postal patronage. An example for the politicization of the decision process: ASST was headed by the leader of the Christian Democratic Italian Union Workers' Confederation. After the proposal failed, an alternate plan to create a "Super-SIP" was introduced by Socialists, but this was also blocked by the Christian Democrats as well as by top management. In 1990, two bills were introduced to break the logjam. One bill proposed a change in the union contract for ASST, to protect those members opposed a move to the private-sector IRI-STET group where they would lose the right to retire after twenty years and receive a smaller pension. The other bill proposed separation of post and telecommunications activities of the PTT.

In 1990, the telecommunications ministry recommended a "Super-STET" under which the government's ASST would be transferred to STET. But the push for structural reform lost some of its steam when a government crisis led to the replacement of Minister Oscar Mammi, a member of the economically liberal Republican Party.

Italy was slow to focus on the role of telecommunications in the development of its economy. Although it was advanced in completing a universal subscriber trunk dialing, the system stagnated in the late 1970s, when, for political reasons, rate increases lagged behind rapid inflation. The major problem in upgrading Italian telecommunications has been reconciling the cost of modernizing the network and of trade union demands for high wages and flexible working conditions with political pressures to keep telephone rates from rising. This dilemma became particularly acute in the late 1970s, when local rates were frozen even with inflation raging at 20 percent. In consequence, no funds remained for investment. The ratio of SIP's self-financing (the contribution of a company's own earnings to capital formation) plummeted to 10 percent in 1980, when the firm reported losses of 538 million lire (Benedetti, 1983). SIP had to resort to indirect ways to increase rates, such as requiring subscribers to increase their deposits. It also had to borrow at the prevailing high interest rates. Subsequently, interest payments at times ate up 30 percent of its total income. The investment slowdown, in turn, adversely affected equipment suppliers and penetration. Italy's telephone density was about half of West Germany's; there were only half as many telex subscribers as in France and one-third as many as in the United Kingdom. Telephone switches were largely electromechanical rather than electronic, and the system was chronically congested. Italy was also late in introducing national data networks, which were implemented eleven years after Germany and seven years behind France's Transpac (Pozzi, 1987).

Tariffs were often set by politics, resulting in a complex split of local, long-distance, and international revenues. A parliamentary committee finally recommended streamlining the cumbersome and restrictive rate-setting process and permitting rates to reflect inflation. The government responded in 1986 by increasing rates, giving SIP more pricing flexibility and fine-tuning the rate structure with time-measured local calls and peak load pricing. It also used a compensation fund, the Cassa Conquaglio, to transfer carrier profits from ASST and Italcable to SIP. It even temporarily reduced SIP's concession fee from 4.5 percent to 0.5 percent of its revenues, invested in its shares, and guaranteed purchase of the remainder. SIP's self-financing ratio increased to almost 50 percent by 1983 as a result of these actions—still low by comparison. France's DGT had a ratio of approximately 65 percent, that of British Telecom was 60 percent, and the Bundespost's was 100 percent (Benedetti, 1983). By 1988, SIP's self-financing had reached 90 percent of its capital expenditures.

In 1982, the PTT ministry also formulated a ten-year plan for the telecommunications sector. The targets for 1990 were a density of thirty-eight subscribers and fifty-seven telephones per 100 population (up from twenty-four and thirty-eight in 1981), and a digitalization, by the year 2000, of 50 percent local and 80 percent long-distance switching. In 1989, digitalization predictions were revised upward for 55 percent of all switches by 1993 and 100 percent by 2000. Trunk lines would be 85 percent digital by 1993 (Benzoni, 1990).

Even after streamlining, the rate-setting process was extremely complex. Users making fewer than fourty calls per month paid 40 lire per billing unit, and others paid 127 lire. Italy's 3.9 million business users paid rates well above the OECD average, and telex service was Europe's most expensive. International rates were also the highest in Europe in 1988, with a three-minute call from Milan to London costing 33 percent more than a call in the other direction (OECD, 1990, p. 30; Schenker, 1990). Perhaps because of its high rates, Italy's international traffic was half that of France's and one-third of Germany's, accounting for less than 1 percent of network usage. Even Switzerland generated more total minutes of international calling. Those three nations accounted for 50 percent of Italy's traffic, with an additional 20 percent going to the United States and the United Kingdom (Staple, 1990; Smau, 1990).

SIP greatly reduced the waiting list for basic service, from 750,000 in 1981 to 118,900 in 1988, though penetration rates were relatively low (34.9 main lines and fifty-one telephones per 100 persons). A great disparity persisted between telephone penetration in the industrial north/central region (fifty-seven per 100 persons) and the rural south (thirty-seven per 100) (ITU, 1990).

In 1989, SIP launched a four-year investment and expansion plan called Piano Europa to invest $8 billion above the already budgeted $18 billion to connect 4 million new basic subscribers by the end of 1992, 43 percent of which reside in southern Italy.

The Equipment Industry

Most equipment procurement is from Italian companies, or Italian operations of foreign companies. Italtel, known originally as SIT-Siemens, is Italy's major telecommunications equipment manufacturer, with 1986 sales of around $1 billion and 17,745 employees. It supplies more than half of SIP's switching equipment needs and 40 percent of its transmission equipment. Under Marisa Bellisario, Italy's only woman CEO of a major firm, Italtel emerged from near bankruptcy in 1981 to financial solvency, mostly by cutting employment from 30,000 in 1981 to 19,000 three years later.

In 1985, SIP bought 75 percent of Italtel's production. Italtel's exports are relatively anemic. In 1985, they totaled about $30 million, or 5 percent of total sales, which consisted primarily of government-subsidized aid to developing countries, including Zambia and Guatemala.

In 1986, STET and Fiat attempted to merge Italtel and Telettra against increasing international competition. The Italtel/Telettra merger would have joined the leading public switch manufacturer with the top transmission and radio communications supplier. Plans for the new company, to be known as Telit, were approved by parliament, but later suspended because of bickering. The fundamental logic behind the Italtel/Telettra merger was not enough to overcome the struggles for managerial control. Fiat's chairman, Giovanni Agnelli, disapproved of allowing Bellesario to run Telit, fearing the influence of bureaucrats at IRT/STET, Italtel's parent firm. Tragically, Bellisario died at a relatively young age in 1988.

Another manufacturer is Ericsson's subsidiary, FATME, which employs 4500 workers in nine factories around the country. FATME had about 20 percent of the market. Alcatel, controlled by the French CGE with minority participation by ITT, employs about 10,000 at its Italian subsidiary, FACE. GTE had a substantial presence in Italy for many years. In 1986, as part of a global agreement with Siemens, it sold its manufacturing facilities and contracts to the German firm. Hewlett-Packard joined forces with Telettra, the telecommunications arm of the Fiat group, for advanced private communications and data-processing systems and equipment.

Conversion to digital switches in Italy was launched in the early 1970s, when SIP began a program for the introduction of PCM systems. Following the example of Alcatel in France, Italtel bypassed the semielectronic stage of switching and installed digital switches, except in some smaller exchanges. In 1980, the first digital exchanges were introduced, Italtel Proteo's TN-16, and AXE of Ericsson's Italian company FATME.

In 1982, the governmental interdepartmental committee for economic planning decided that telecommunications modernization was to be based on electronic switching equipment provided by a competition between two systems, one of which had to be Italian. The primary system, known as the first "pole," was awarded to the Italian joint venture based on the Proteo technology.

SIP planned to procure the majority of its exchanges from the National Pole and the remainder from either FACE, then an ITT subsidiary, or FATME, Ericsson's subsidiary, both of which were domiciled in Italy. However, since the employees of the loser among FACE and FATME would likely have to lay off employees, both companies were chosen as suppliers with the vague expectation that their systems would be modified into a uniform switch. In 1985, the National Pole (Italtel, GTE, Telettra) received two-thirds of the $900 million contract, FACE had 14.2 percent, and FATME had 20.4 percent. This was a continuation of their already existing and quasi-established market shares. Those steady market shares for switching equipment had been Italtel, 52 percent; Telettra, 1 percent; FATME, 18 percent; FACE, 17 percent; GTE (later Siemens), 12 percent (R. Lauro, 1987, communication).

In developing the Proteo system, Italtel first entered into a joint venture cooperation agreement with the American-owned GTE Telecomunicazioni and Telettra, the Fiat subsidiary. It soon required another major partner. This led to a major joint venture between AT&T and Italtel, which won a large portion of the $28 billion that Italy planned to spend on network equipment by 1992 (Colby and Hudson, 1989, p. 27). The Italtel–AT&T deal followed some heavy-handed lobbying for the partnership position, including personal intervention by François Mitterrand for Alcatel and Ronald Reagan for AT&T. Alcatel chairman Pierre Suard played the European card, stating that the "goal of European telecommunications policy must be to maintain and improve the leadership of European industry" (Roussel, 1990). Germany, on behalf of Siemens, threatened to block $4 billion in subsidies for Italy's steel industry. Former Prime Minister Bettino Craxi, a socialist, supported AT&T (Hayes, 1988). Ultimately, AT&T paid the government $130 million, the difference in value of the stock swap of its 20 percent share of Italtel and Italtel's 20 percent stake in AT&T's Network Systems International.

In response to the AT&T–Italtel partnership, Alcatel acquired Telettra in 1990, thereby gaining Teletra's thirty-three percent market share in transmission equipment in Italy and forty-five percent in Spain. But the European Commission first required Spain's Telefonica telephone monopoly to divest itself of its shares in Alcatel (21 percent in the Spanish subsidiary) and Telettra (10 percent), as well as to open its purchasing policy.

The STET Group

Società Finanziaria Telefonica (STET) is the mainstay of Italian telecommunications. With its array of local, domestic long-distance, and international telephone services, as well as manufacturing, it is a formidable presence in Italian communications. In 1990, STET's revenues were 17,200 billion lire, including exports of $1 billion; investments were 5000 billion lire; employment numbered 130,000 people, almost 6000 in R&D (ITU, 1990). STET is controlled in turn by the Institute for Industrial Reconstruction (IRI), the major national holding company for all government-controlled economic enterprises. IRI, a vast company, was created in the 1930s by Mussolini to control the government's operations in telecommunications, transportation, utilities, and several other fields. STET was formed by IRI in the same year as the umbrella organization for its telecommunications activities. In 1986, IRI controlled 84.6 percent of STET, with the rest widely held, and there was a continuing discussion of permitting greater participation by outsiders. In 1985 STET began to sell 30 percent of its subsidiary SIP to the general public as part of a quiet trend toward privatization. Whereas in 1984, private ownership in SIP had been 8.17 percent, two years later, it had grown to 35.69 percent and was expected to reach 46 percent in 1989, almost half of a privatization and not much less than that for British Telecom (*La Repubblica*, 1987). The move was inspired more by IRI's efforts to reduce its substantial losses than by telecommunications policy.

Customer premises equipment (CPE) markets were severely restricted, largely because services were vertically integrated through STET, which favored its equipment subsidiary, Italtel. In 1984, SIP provided 97.6 percent of all additional telephone sets and 45.4 percent of PBXs (R. Lauro, 1987, communication). SIP held an 88 percent market share in key telephone systems and a 60 percent share in facsimile markets. Maintenance of CPE, even that purchased elsewhere, was a SIP or PTT responsibility; this situation changed after 1988, except for first sets. Applicazioni Elettro Telefoniche (AET), an outside plant installer whose core business was cable installation, was acquired by STET in 1989 (G. Pozzi, 1990, communication).

Liberalization began when it became clear that existing regulations were being circumvented and were ultimately counterproductive. Equipment can be purchased from outside vendors, but it has to meet Ministry specifications for type approval, and SIP had to provide the interconnections. The 1987 national ten-year plan liberalized modems and provided for the liberalization of the remaining telephone and telex. Modem liberalization was carried out in 1989 only after the European Commission filed an Article 90 complaint against the Italian government.

SIP is the largest of the STET firms, with about 77,000 employees, 10,000 exchanges, and $4.8 billion in revenues. It had 20 million main lines and 29.2 million telephones at the end of 1988. For a long time, SIP was perceived as an organization barely keeping pace with demand, and not as an innovator in service development.

To improve this situation, SIP initiated a 500 billion-lire ($350 million) program in 1987. As network modernization became a priority, SIP allocated 36,000 billion lire ($26 billion) over four years (1989–1992), 33 percent of which would go to southern Italy (Benzoni, 1990).

Italcable, created in 1921 as an operator of submarine cables, has been part of STET since 1965 and provides transoceanic services outside of Europe. Its 1989 turnover was 659 billion lire, and it employed 3500. From 1968 to 1985, Italcable's telephone traffic grew from 3.7 to 226 million minutes, and telex traffic grew from 3.0 to 71 million minutes. Italcable operates the message and data packet switching network IRICON and provides access services to international databases.

Telespazio is Italy's satellite carrier and its signatory in Intelsat, Inmarsat, and Eutelsat. Like the American Comsat, it is a carriers' carrier. It also provides remote sensing services. Its revenues in 1985 were $43 million, and it employed about 640. One-third of Telespazio is held by the broadcast authority RAI, which uses its services.

The Selenia-Elsag group was another major STET subsidiary. It is extensively involved in manufacturing civilian and military electronic systems and industrial automation and employs 13,000. Elsag won a major contract award from the U.S. Postal Service to automate its system, an export achievement that received much attention because of its size and because of the implicit affirmation of Italy's high-technology capability. In 1989, STET sold its control in Selenia and Elsag.

SGS, until 1989, was a STET company in the microelectronics field and is the major Italian manufacturer of integrated circuits. In 1985, its revenues were $300 million and it employed almost 10,000. In 1987, it entered into a joint venture for component manufacture with the French electronic giant Thomson. But the venture did not flourish and STET sold its share in 1989. Other major STET subsidiaries include Seat, a publishing company for telephone directories and electronic yellow page directory service, and Consultel, a telecommunications consulting firm active in the developing world. STET's research & development organization is CSELT, established in 1984.

Olivetti

Olivetti (formally Ing. C. Olivetti & Co.), headquartered in the northern city of Ivrea, is perhaps Italy's most noted entrepreneurial firm in advanced electronics. For a time it was renowned for its equipment's design rather than its marketplace success. This changed when Carlo De Benedetti assumed its leadership. De Benedetti is to Italy's electronic sector what Silvio Berlusconi is to its broadcasting: an empire builder of the first order. He managed the automobile firm Fiat for a short while, until he had a falling-out with the Agnelli family, which controls it. In 1978, De Benedetti acquired 15 percent of the financially ailing Olivetti.

Within a few years Olivetti became Europe's largest office equipment maker and the world's second largest producer of personal computers. In 1982, AT&T acquired 25 percent of the company for $230 million, with an option to raise its share to 40 percent in 1987. With its AT&T connection in the United States, Olivetti aimed to become the world's number 2 company in professional desktop computers. But in 1988, AT&T, frustrated at its absence of control, declined to increase its financial involvement and cut its computer order by 75 percent (Guyon and Colloy, 1988).

In 1988, the West German firm Volkswagen acquired a 5 percent stake in Olivetti, for which Olivetti received the large German office equipment maker, Adler-Triumph. Olivetti also bought interests in dozens of international high-tech firms, many of them in the United States. In the United Kingdom, Olivetti bought most of the small computer maker Acorn. It also joined with GeDa, a computer services company, to form Olinet, providing database management, data processing, and so forth. Thus, Olivetti had a highly international set of owners, subsidiaries, and markets, all part of De Benedetti's strategy of making it a global electronics company.

In the process, De Benedetti's own shares multiplied in value. He had acquired 15 percent of Olivetti for $17 million. By 1986, this was worth half a billion dollars. He also embarked on building a personal business empire distinct from Olivetti. He acquired for a time Italy's largest food company, Buitoni, and several smaller food companies, an automobile component maker, a tobacco equipment manufacturer, a share in the publishing house Mondadori (where he fought with Silvio Berlusconi for control), and an investment bank. He also established close relations and an ownership share with Pirelli, the large tire manufacturer. In 1987, he embarked on a take-over bid for Belgium's huge but stodgy conglomerate Société Générale de Belgique (SGB). Though established Belgian and French interests succeeded in beating him back, the effort proved profitable for De Benedetti. In the early 1990s, Olivetti experienced serious deficits again, raising questions about its long-term prospects as an independent company.

Services

In data transmission, the structure of the system reflects the complexity of the underlying carriers. The PT administration (not to be confused with the State Administration for Telephone Services, ASST) provides slow-speed data transmission services. Italcable provides intercontinental data transmission lines. SIP supplies slow data transmission over the switched network, and higher rates over leased circuits.

Telex emerged under restrictive regulation. A message could only be sent by its originator; only PTT-supplied devices could be attached to the equipment; and a deposit of $2,000 to $3000 plus annual fees of $2000 made use expensive. Poor service and installation waits that exceeded two years compounded the problems. Users circumvented some of these restrictions by forming associations enabling members to use a community-owned telex.

Since 1983, SIP has operated a circuit-switched data network, Rete Fonia-Dati (RFD), using a technology by Telettra. In 1986, a new digital circuit-switched network, CDN, went on line. Itapac, the packet-switched network operated jointly by SIP and MPT, opened in 1986 for general use. In the first year of full operation, it expected 5000 subscribers but only had 2700. Itapac's main problem was operational, since each of the two partners controls separate parts of the network. In addition, high tariffs and low-speed connections presented problems. Switches were Italtel-modified Siemens equipment. After 1989, Itapac was run by SIP alone.

Dedicated private network facilities are permitted only for services not provided by the public network and exist in a gray zone of tacit agreement among large corporations. Resale is technically prohibited, but appears to exist.

Because of the administrative complexity of the Italian telephone system, moves toward ISDN required more coordination than in most countries. In 1984, the PTT Ministry announced a national plan for telecommunications for the next decade, addressing in particular network digitalization (MPT, 1984). After 1989, only digital equipment was cut over. SIP also introduced the CCITT Common Channel Signalling System 7 into the national network. In Milan, a fiber local loop trial project capable of videotex data, TV, and teleconferencing transmission was started in 1987.

Videotex began experimentally in 1980 under the name Videotel and has operated on a regular basis since 1986. Users can access the system center in Milan from anywhere in Italy with a local call. Videotel is based on the Italtel and CEPT standards, and is concentrated on business subscribers.[1] In 1991, SIP had an installed base of 100,000 terminals and planned to become the second largest videotex system after France.

SIP controlled cellular telephony as the only service provider of its kind in Italy. SIP introduced a 900–MHz system and aimed at a digital system. But increased demand brought pressures to end SIP's monopoly in mobile service. To apply for licenses for digital mobile services, Media czar Berlusconi's Fininvest joined Fiat and the U.K.'s Racal; Olivetti formed the Omnitel consortium with Bell Atlantic and Sweden's Televerket; and Pacific Telesis was part of a third applicant group.

Telecommunications in Malta

Telephone service in Malta, an island nation between Italy and Tunisia, dates back to 1882. Service is operated by the private Malta Telephone Company, which was taken over by the government in 1933. The telephone network was largely destroyed during World War II. In 1957, the manual system was upgraded by STC to a stronger automated system. Later, Siemens exchanges were added. Overseas telephone service to London was established in 1947, and service to Rome began in 1952. A submarine cable to Italy soon became the main connection.

22

Spain

Spain's telecommunications system is unusual. It is dominated by one semiprivate firm, Telefónica de España, which is strongly integrated vertically into equipment manufacturing and horizontally into Latin American telecommunications. Telefónica has been assigned the role of a locomotive in Spain's rapid industrialization, and its powerful and entrepeneurial presence is likely to increase still further, as long as its primary mission of providing basic service does not lag.

History

In 1884, a royal decree established a government monopoly over telephony. Two years later, service concessions were awarded to private firms through an auction of monopoly franchises for each city. Contracts were awarded to applicants who promised to provide the state with the highest percentage of gross receipts of at least 10 percent; bids for some cities far exceeded that percentage. Thirty-five local exchanges were established under the system, but problems soon became apparent; rate reductions could not be instituted, and the private companies were unwilling to extend service to rural and isolated areas. As a result, the government decided in 1890 to drop the monopoly system and to allow any interested parties to establish exchanges, while absolving the existing licensees of their revenue-sharing obligations. Commercial long-distance lines were also left to private firms. No competition emerged, however, since companies were unwilling or unable financially to enter into each others' territories. Thus, de facto unrestricted monopolies remained in existence and were institutionalized in 1903. However, service remained unsatisfactory, and in 1924, the government granted a major concession to operate all of Spanish telephony to the Compañía Telefónica Naçional de España S.A. (CTNE), a firm that had only recently been formed by the American firm International Telephone and Telegraph (ITT) and private Spanish investors. Later that year, ITT acquired all the company's shares. This purchase was the first major step taken by ITT in its efforts to become a major international presence in telecommunications. ITT's founders, the Behn brothers, had little capital and no manufacturing support behind them. Despite its grandiose name, the company was a midget in comparison to AT&T. The Behns now sought a manufacturing base; at the same time, AT&T happened to be looking to unload its European manufacturing operations because of U.S. domestic pressure. ITT bought them, and acquired a major presence in international telecommunications. ITT rapidly became Spain's dominant service and equipment firm. In 1945, however, it was forced to relinquish ownership of its network operation CTNE to the Spanish government, which then directly or indirectly controlled about half of its shares. In 1986, ITT's equipment subsidiaries became part of the French-dominated Alcatel. Also in 1986, CTNE's name was formally shortened into Telefónica de España.

Organization

Overall regulation of the Spanish telecommunications sector lies with the Junta Nacional de Telecomunicaciones (National Telecommunications Board), an interministerial commission answering to the Ministry of Transport, Tourism, and Communications. The board is responsible for assigning radio frequencies, setting investment guidelines, and maintaining relations with foreign administrations.

Within the Ministry of Transport, Tourism, and Communications, two separate agencies have responsibility for telecommunications matters: the Dirección General de Correos y Telecomunicaciones (Directorate General of Post and Telecommunications, or DGCyT), which provides postal service as well as telegraph, telex, facsimile, electronic mail, and message switching; and Dirección General de Electrónica y Informática (Directorate General for Electronics and Informatics, or DGEI), which is in charge of promoting the development of a domestic electronics industry.

An independent communications network is run by the broadcast authority RTVE, which operates its own transmitters and relay stations (Lopez-Escobar, 1985). Most of telephone operations, however, are the domain of Telefónica, which was given monopoly status by government decree in 1970. Television and limited voice and data services have also been offered by Retevision since 1989. Holding about 36 percent of shares in Telefónica, the Spanish government acts as the majority holder of the company and, importantly, appoints its chairman. The remainder of the firm's stock is held by more than 750,000 private shareholders, including a number of foreign interests—mostly American, British, and German institutional investors. American investors held about 17 percent of the company's stock in 1990.

The company's stock was a favorite of small investors; in 1985, CTNE accounted for 17.2 percent of the entire Spanish stock market's capitalization! In comparison, the ten largest stocks on the New York Stock Exchange account for 15 percent (*The Economist*, 1985). Because Telefónica's capital needs are so great relative to the size of the Spanish economy as a whole, it had problems in raising adequate funds to finance its investments, and in 1985 it began to offer its stock on foreign exchanges. As a "strategic sector" firm, the Spanish government refused to raise the ceiling on the amount of Telefónica stock that could be held by foreign interests from 25 percent. A large portion of the state's holdings in Telefónica are administered by the central bank of Spain and the Instituto Nacional de Industria (INI), a public holding authority that was established in 1941 modeled after Mussolini's IRI. By 1982, INI firms had more than 200,000 employees, about 7 percent of the country's labor force. Its losses, however, amounted to $1 billion. Telefónica's semiprivate, semigovern-mental structure has made the privatization versus nationalization debate less pressing than that in most European countries.

Telefónica's presence in the Spanish economy is colossal and is reinforced by its vertical integration. With 71,000 employees, Telefónica is Spain's larg-est company. It holds stock in numerous firms, including Amper-Elasa, SIN-TEL, TEFISA, TIDSA, and Cetesa (de Moragas et al., 1987). It accounts for nearly 4 percent of gross national capital formation in Spain and 2.7 percent of the gross added value in the service industry. Telefónica has one of Europe's highest rates of telecommunications investment as a share of gross fixed capital formation (3.9 percent) (ITU, 1990).

In 1985, the government proposed legislation to reorganize and centralize the telecommunications sector, with the specific objectives of creating an inte-grated network, defining telecommunications services in a consistent manner, and coordinating CTNE, RTVE (broadcast transmissions), and DGTyT (tele-graph, telex). But the proposed expansion of governmental influence was crit-icized by large users as running counter to the trend of reducing the state's role in telecommunications.

In 1986, three narrower bills were substituted for the more comprehensive effort, providing for the reorganization of telecommunications, private tele-vision, and the postal service. The telecommunications bill provided for keep-ing CTNE's monopoly as a telephone carrier intact and for the liberalization of the terminal equipment and VAN markets as well as for the transfer of respon-sibility for equipment approval from the telephone authority to the Ministry of Industry (White, 1986). The liberalization, intended to proceed gradually from 1988 to 1992, began with three corporations requesting Ministry of Industry approval. Under this plan, Telefónica's carrier monopoly was extended for an-other thirty years.

Services

The penetration of telephone service in Spain has lagged behind that in other European countries. In 1990, there were 30.4 telephone lines per 100 people (ITU, 1990). In the same year, however, applications for basic service in-creased 51 percent over the previous year, and the growth of usage of existing lines increased 5 percent. The wait for a new telephone connection was typi-cally still over half a year, although this figure varied, depending on the region. In metropolitan areas service was faster, but in rural areas there were longer waits and greater costs of connection.

Luis Solana, a former banker, took over management of Telefónica in 1982 and led to a major expansion into worldwide markets. Eventually, this led to criticism that the globalization of Telefónica's activities was at the expense of the country. In 1989, there were 1.4 million applications for new lines, 535,000 of which went unfilled. This led business groups like the Madrid Chamber of Commerce and the Catalan Industrialists Association to complain that telephone failures and high costs hurt Spanish business (Purton, 1990). Public dissatisfaction with Telefónica's failure to keep pace with demand for new connections then forced Solona to resign in 1988. He was replaced by Cándido Velazquez-Gaztelu. Telefónica increased network investment by 60 percent from 1988 to 1989, reaching $5.8 billion in 1990, and it allocated another $35 billion through 1994. As a result, Telefónica reduced in 1989 the length of its waiting list for the first time in four years. In 1990 Telefónica lost its monopoly over extension telephone terminals, and by 1992 also over the first set, in accordance with EC rules.

The telegraph administration, DGCyT, originally provided the bulk of data services but in time collided with the telephone carrier. DGCyT operates a telex network and leased telegraph circuits for slow transmission rates. But in 1970, the government granted CTNE the authority to provide data transmission services, electronic mail, facsimile, and videotex. As a result, it began to infringe on its rival's business, for example, through the successful public packet-switched data transmission network Iberpac, which originated as the first European packet-switched network. Data transmissions comprise 9 percent of Telefónica's total income.

Limited ''Ibertex'' videotex operations began during the 1982 World Cup soccer competition. Attempts were made to involve the Spanish-speaking countries of Latin America in the project.

Telefónica is remarkably active internationally. Latin America became the site of Telefónica expansion, particularly in Argentina and Chile. In 1988, the Argentine government announced that, after forty-two years of state ownership, Argentina Empresa Nacional de Telefónica (Entel) would be privatized. In 1990, Telefónica outbid six European and American competitors in 1990 for a controlling interest of Entel's southern operations. The winning package offered $114 million in cash, $2.18 billion in debt, and $540 million in forgiven interest for a 60 percent share of the new company, to be called Telcosur. The Telefónica consortium consisted of an investment company including Citicorp (20 percent), Telefónica (10 percent), and the Argentina's Techint Group (15 percent). Telefónica, the operator, agreed to install 610,000 phone lines and 12,900 public phones by 1996, at a cost of $1 billion The new entity was named Telefónica Argentina, and it planned to invest $400 million a year.

When Chile's telephone system was privatized, Telefónica initially lost to Australian financier Alan Bond in the bidding for a portion of Compañia de Teléfonos de Chile (CTC). But in 1990, Bond's financial difficulties forced him to sell his 43.7 percent stake to Telefónica for $388.5 million. However, soon after the purchase, Chile's antimonopoly commission ruled that Telefónica could not own part of both CTC and ENTEL, Chile's long-distance carrier, in which it also held a 20 percent stake. Telefónica appealed the decision to Chile's Comisión Resolutiva.

Telefónica was also a bidder for a part of Mexico's telephone system; it also purchased a stake in the U.S. firm Infonet (5 percent), along with other European telecommunications organizations, as well as in Geostar (3 percent) and in Mercury's PCN subsidiary (10 percent). It also gained a 40 percent share in 1991 in Venezuela's privatized system, in a consortium led by GTE.

Equipment

Telefónica has a direct stake in determining which firms are allowed access to the equipment market, since it owns a majority of the stock of a dozen equipment firms and holds minority interests in several others. Telefónica controlled 21 percent of Alcatel Standard Eléctrica; 20 percent of Citesa, another Alcatel subsidiary; 10 percent of Telettra, the Spanish subsidiary of the Italian telecommunications manufacturer of the same name, then owned by Fiat; and 7.6 percent of Amper, a Spanish telephone set manufacturer (Telefónica, 1989). Thus, until the 1986 reform giving equipment approval power to the Ministry of Industry, the manufacturer not only had to meet both CCITT and CTNE technical standards, but also often needed to cultivate a good relationship with Telefónica, their own competitor, including the disclosure of information, in order to secure approval for the sale of their products.

In the past, CTNE gave clearance only to its own or to Spanish-made equipment. In 1981, foreign suppliers provided only 13 percent of the company's equipment (MarTech, 1983). However, the 1987 regulatory statute *ley de ordenación de las telecomunicaciones* (LOT) partially opened CPE markets. But it was challenged by the European Commission since it still enabled control over terminal equipment by the vertically integrated Telefónica. Telefónica's practices were also subject to two 1990 investigations, one by the Spanish antimonopolies board over bundling of connection to the network with purchase of more expensive equipment, and one by the Spanish consumer's advocate over a tariff structure that decreased the advantage of off-peak rates.

The Socialist government that came to power in 1982 increased Telefónica's importance in the equipment field by giving it a central role in its ambitious high-technology plans. Telefónica, RTVE, and the Ministry of Defense were each required to establish four-year plans of investment and development. When Standard Electric threatened to eliminate 6000 manufacturing jobs in 1985, the government pressured Telefónica to increase its purchases of that company's equipment.

In 1991, Telettra was acquired by France's Alcatel. This lead the European Commission to require that Telefónica divest itself of its shares in Alcatel and Telettra, as well as to open its purchasing policy.

Luis Solana, Telefónica's president until 1988, actively sought to spur the development of Spanish telecommunications by entering into still more joint ventures with Spanish and foreign companies. Pacific Telesis, the American regional bell holding company, was invited to design a Telefónica telecommunications research center in Madrid. The main partner of Spain's Intelsa, Ericsson, also financed the establishment of a large research center in Madrid, and in 1990 won 43 percent of a major equipment contract through Intelsa. In 1990, half of the digital exchanges in the Spanish public network were Ericsson's AXE exchanges (Martinez, 1990). Telefónica entered a large semiconductor venture with AT&T in 1984. Together, the two firms built a plant in Spain that produces microcomponents, largely for export. Of the project's $65 million direct investment, AT&T put up 80 percent and Telefónica provided the remainder. In addition, the Spanish government provided subsidies totaling $60 million and credits worth another $75 million. The transaction made Spain the major European manufacturing base for AT&T. In 1987, this collaboration was expanded as Telefónica contracted with AT&T/Philips for 20,000 lines of an "intelligent" overlay for the Spanish network (Williamson, 1987). In 1990, Telefónica joined AT&T's Europe-wide equipment efforts by obtaining a 6 percent share in AT&T's network systems (Philips had 15 percent; Italtel, 20 percent; and AT&T, 53 percent), in return for its shares in the joint microelectronics venture with AT&T in Spain.

Telefónica is involved in other joint ventures: In cooperation with Corning Glass, it entered the market for optical fiber; it also engaged in a $200 million computer production venture with Fujitsu. Given its history of close ITT connections, Telefónica also tried, unsuccessfully, to obtain a 10 percent stake in the CGE/ITT Alcatel venture.

In 1990, jointly with Amper, Telefónica won a contract to produce between 500,000 and 1 million telephones in the Soviet Union.

Piher Semiconductor, a firm headquartered in Barcelona, is the primary Spanish component producer, outside of Telefónica's ventures. The firm, part of the state-owned INI group, was fined $1 million in 1985 by an American court, given five years probation, and denied all American export privileges for ten years after it pleaded guilty to illegally diverting more than $2 million worth of semiconductor manufacturing and testing equipment to Cuba and the Soviet Union.

Telecommunications in Gibraltar

In Gibraltar, the British possession at the tip of Spain, telephone service first operated in 1892 for civilian service, with a parallel military system. In 1926, the city council established an automatic Strowger exchange service. In 1969, the operation of the telephone service was taken over by the government of Gibraltar, and in 1973 a crossbar exchange was opened.

International service was opened to Spain in 1927. This service was broken off in 1969 for several years because of the dispute over control of Gibraltar.

In 1989, the Gibraltar government chose NYNEX to enter into a fifty–fifty partnership to run its domestic telecommunications network. NYNEX will invest $10 million over five years to deploy an advanced intelligent network, with a fiber backbone, to serve Gibraltar's needs as a burgeoning financial center.

23

Portugal

The telecommunications sector in Portugal reflects the country's relative poverty and its struggle to catch up with the rest of Europe in industry and advanced services during a period of domestic turmoil. Although it has made much progress, it has not yet reached a level where the policy issues that affect most other Western European countries are part of the Portuguese agenda. Portugal is, however, affected by these issues in its procurement decisions.

Portuguese telecommunications are the charge of three organizations, two of which, Correios e Telecommunicacoes de Portugal (CTT) (renamed Telecom Portugal) and Telefones de Lisboa e Porto (TLP), operate according to the directives of a common General Board; the third, Compania Portuguesa Radio Marconi (CPRM), derives from the Anglo-Portuguese telephone company. Telecom Portugal's service area covers most of the country; it is also responsible for international telephony within Europe and for the Portuguese telex network. TLP operates telephone service and networks within a 30 kilometer radius of Lisbon and a 15 kilometer radius of Porto, the two largest Portuguese cities. The nominally private CPRM provides satellite links and submarine cable service, including connections to the Azores and Madeira. Its franchise covers all public overseas international telecommunications, as well as the concession for maritime mobile service in the whole Portuguese territory.

Telephone and telex service to the European countries are operated by Telecom Portugal in agreement with CPRM, using the latter's transmission facilities. Although it is technically an independent operation with its own budget, 51 percent of CPRM shares are held by IPE, a holding company for state participation in private firms. The chairman of the CPRM board and two of its members are government appointees. For years, relations between the two exchange companies and ITT's Portuguese manufacturing subsidiary Standard Electrica were extraordinarily close.

All three telephone enterprises report to the Ministry of Public Works, Transport and Communications, which also supervises the postal service. Government control over telecommunications is exercised through appointments to the General Board, as well as through legislation on tariffs, the budget, borrowing, and other financial matters. A merger of the three organizations was expected.

The Portuguese telecommunications sector, although relatively underdeveloped by European standards, began to receive increasing attention from the government in the 1980s, as reflected by raises in budgetary allocations. From

1978 to 1987, the investment per line rate was the third lowest among OECD nations. However, 1988 figures show a significant shift in priorities, placing Portugal first in the European Community in terms of telecommunications investment as a percentage of fixed capital formation (ITU, 1990).

In addition, the separation of the telecommunications and postal authorities and the merger of the three telephone service companies became topics of discussion. Telecom Portugal and TLP agreed in principle to a statute that provided for their merger; they share administrative and fiscal counsel, as well as the same chairman as part of the General Board. Legislation passed in 1989 brought Portugal more in line with E.C. directives, (de la Cal, 1990, p. 13). The law also created a Communications Institute of Portugal to coordinate development and liberalization.

To increase capital resources and to prepare for the single European market in 1992, the center-right government which came to power in 1987 announced a process of "partial privatization" to begin after 1990. The government would keep 51 percent of the three companies, with the remaining shares sold to private investors. Foreign holdings were limited to 10 percent, and 20 percent are owned by small investors and employees.

A 1990 law created a holding company for the telecommunications operators, named Telecom Portugal. The state retained control over 51 percent of TLP. The law also created the Instituto das Communicacoes de Portugal to coordinate development and liberalization; regulatory powers remained with the Ministry of Communications.

Services

Telephone density in Portugal stood at eighteen lines per 100 persons in 1988, the lowest in Western Europe. The government's goal is to have 32 connections per 100 population by 1993. In 1988, the average wait for a telephone was 9.4 months, down from almost three years. The waiting list was still 15 percent of the total of main lines (ITU, 1990).

Data transmission service is available on analog leased lines over the public switched telephone network at rates of up to 2.4 kbps. Portugal restricted the creation of private networks based on the use of leased circuits, and customers were consequently not allowed to install their own data multiplexers (*Eurodata Foundation Yearbook*, 1983). This provision was lifted in 1986. Telpac, a packet-switched network featuring Northern Telecom equipment, was opened in 1984 under the control of Transdata, an organization set up by CTT and TLP. The expansion of data usage was curtailed by the limitations of the Portuguese network. A 1990 survey by the European Association of Information Services (EUSIDIC) found that 64 percent of international data test calls made in 1990 from Portugal failed at three times the average rate for the fourteen countries studied, which were themselves low in performance (EUSIDIC, 1990).

Portuguese international rates are high; calls placed from Portugal to other

European nations tend to cost twice as much as calls traveling in the opposite direction (*Transnational Data and Communications Report,* 1988).

Given the priority of developing basic services, Portugal has been slower than other European countries to introduce cellular mobile telephony, teletext, and videotex. In 1984, public telefax service was introduced through the post office. In 1987, Portugal selected Germany's C-Netz standard for cellular radio and contracted Siemens to supply the infrastructure (Purton, 1987). By 1990, cellular phone service was available to 90 percent of Portugal's population in 30 percent of the country, but subscription levels were low.

Equipment

The two local operating organizations held a monopoly over the first telephone sets. Since 1983, it has been legal to obtain second sets from other sources. There is no government monopoly over the PBX or modem market, although they are also supplied by operating companies.

There are two main telecommunications manufacturers in Portugal: Standard Electrica, a subsidiary of ITT and subsequently of Alcatel, which has had a presence in the country since 1932, and Centrel, a wholly Portuguese company (ITT, 1983). Centrel goes back to the British Plessey, at one time the second leading telecommunications equipment supplier in Portugal, which left the country in 1979 and sold its Portuguese factory for £1 to the then unknown local firm, Centrel.

Standard Electrica is the country's largest communications equipment and electronics manufacturer. According to its own estimates, the company has trained about 60 percent of Portugal's telecommunications engineers, a fact that reflects the extremely close relationship that it maintains with the operating companies. Standard Electrica supplies 50 percent of Portugal's telecommunications equipment, producing two crossbar exchange switches (one of which is Portuguese developed) as well as System 12 switches. It also provides PBXs (holding a 90 percent market share), telephone sets, television sets (60 percent of all black-and-white sets sold in the country), and transmission equipment. Its share of Portuguese telex switch sales rose to 35 percent after Siemens's thirty-year hold over supply was ended.

Products by Centrel, the other manufacturer, include systems, repeaters, public switches of the crossbar and Strowger types, handsets, coin box telephones, and transmission equipment. Centrel's public switch division, using Siemens technology, accounted for more than half of the company's total revenue. Although the bulk of the firm's output is purchased within Portugal, it also exports.

The allocation of the larger Portuguese procurement orders for central electronic switches was a multiyear story of intrigue on many levels. Throughout much of the organization's history, the traditional Portuguese supplier to CTT/TLP had been ITT's Standard Electrica. In March of 1985, however, a coalition government opened up the switch contract bidding to seven different companies to demonstrate openness to the European Economic Community. These six additional firms were Ericsson, which had been a supplier to Portugal's former African colonies, AT&T/Phillips, Northern Telecom, Siemens, Plessey, and Alcatel/Thomson. At the time of the awarding of the contract, Centrel had just entered into a joint venture with Siemens for the production of switches developed by the German firm, with some production to be undertaken in Portugal. This gave Siemens an inside track in the competition for the switch contract because it was a European company and could assure Portuguese jobs.

The lobbying for the contract became highly political. Alcatel's interests were personally pushed by French President Mitterrand, who was a friend of Portuguese Prime Minister Mario Soares. German politicians involved themselves in similar lobbying for Siemens, and ITT's interests were advanced by the telephone operating companies CTT/TLP. The government took away the telephone authorities' power to allocate the order, and instead gave it to a more politically oriented interministerial commission. Ericsson, Northern Telecom, AT&T/Phillips, and Plessey were next excluded from bidding; surprisingly, so was ITT. The commission allocated 55 percent of the order to Siemens and 35 percent to Alcatel, despite the latter's lack of Portuguese production facilities, a disadvantage that had been stressed throughout the allocation process. The remaining 10 percent was allocated in a complex fashion among the two victorious companies, which were forced to compete for the last slice by offering technology transfer, guarantees of local production content, and software production (Smith, 1986).

The selection of Alcatel, made just before the election of 1987, raised a major controversy because, in addition to having no Portuguese production facilities at the time, the company had no history of working with the country's telephone organizations. To deal with this problem, as well as with the Standard Electrica employees who felt abandoned because their firm had been left out of the running entirely, the government ordered the ITT subsidiary to turn its physical plant and 20 percent of its equity over to Alcatel so that the French company could use it for the production of switches. This was considered a blatantly political act, and allegations of impropriety followed. After the election, the Socialists were replaced by a more conservative Social Democratic government, which immediately reopened the case. The Siemens/Centrel contract was not controversial and was allowed to stand, but the Alcatel share was opened for bidding, with the operating companies regaining their traditional leverage in the decision process. In the end, Standard Electrica received a 45 percent share. Alcatel was out in the cold, or so it seemed. But within a short time, it pulled a major coup when its parent company, CGE, acquired controlling interests in most of ITT's international telecommunications operations, allowing Alcatel to crack the Portuguese market after all.

24

Israel

Israel is closely related to Western Europe in its telecommunications system. Its dynamics of institutional change are similar, and are therefore included in this study.

For a long time, Israel's telecommunications system was that of the classic postal–industrial complex, with the state PTT nurturing the electronics industry in close collaboration with the trade unions. The government, meanwhile, regarded telecommunications as a source of revenue. This system led to dissatisfaction because the expansion and quality of the network were inadequate for the rapidly modernizing society. In 1982, it was decided to spin off telecommunications from the Ministry of Communications and to establish the independent operating company Bezeq. Bezeq (also often spelled Bezek) is still a state monopoly, albeit a regulated and part-private one, but its service orientation and performance have greatly improved.

The telephone system dates back to the years of the Turkish and British governmental rule over the country. After the founding of Israel in 1948, the telephone network greatly increased in penetration and technical capability and was enhanced by the development of a domestic electronics industry. In 1948, there were only 11,000 lines and usage was 45 million meter pulses; in 1987, there were 1.3 million lines, and usage was almost 9 billion meter pulses. In the same year, 90 percent of households in the major cities had a telephone. This is despite the fact that Israeli telephone service is among the most expensive in the world because of the very high up-front connection charge and the significant government levies on telephone services as part of attempts to raise revenues.

An important change was the transfer, in 1984, of the telecommunications operations from the Ministry of Communications to the separate but state-owned Bezeq Israel Telecommunications Corporation Ltd.

The governmental service had been unable to keep up with the pace of the emerging sophisticated business environment in Israel, and this had led to substantial unhappiness among the public and in the business community. The backlog could have been reduced, of course, by substantial investment programs, but this was constrained by the need to coordinate investments within general governmental priorities. Under governmental control, the telephone system was not able to move as rapidly as the public wished. Greater managerial independence was one reason that the telephone organization wanted to reduce direct governmental operational supervision. Another factor was that many of the telephone administration employees sought to extricate themselves from civil service salaries, particularly when they had technical skills and prestigious engineering degrees. Telecommunications were also subsidizing postal services, a bottomless pit since postal rates were kept low for political reasons.

In the 1960s, the Dinstein Committee was formed to examine the status of public utilities. It recommended splitting these operations from government control, but nothing came of it. In 1970–1972, the Herzog Commission (chaired by the future president of the state, Chaim Herzog) was appointed by the minister of communications (and later Prime Minister) Shimon Peres, to report on the status of telecommunications.

In 1978, under a newly created right-of-center government, an expert consulting body was created that consisted primarily of academics from the fields of business administration, economics, law, and engineering. Their task was to prepare a concrete proposal to transfer the governmental function to a new company. The proposal was completed in 1979, with Yitzhak Modai, the then minister of telecommunications providing strong support. The Bezeq law was prepared and passed by the Knesset in 1982. A prime bone of contention was the status of employees. Without union agreement the plan was politically infeasible. In 1982 and 1983, intensive negotiations took place. The labor unions did not actively oppose the reform, once they received a virtual veto right over certain aspects of the organization and had them written into the law. Within the Labor party, Gad Yaacobi, a future minister of communications, was also supportive. The strongest opposition came from the bureaucracy, particularly the Ministry of Finance, which feared the loss of substantial revenue contributions from the telephone service. This reflected the main problem of the past: the perception of telecommunications as a cash cow rather than as a public service or infrastructure.

Two collective bargaining agreements preserved the various rights and seniorities that telecommunication employees had accumulated. Another agreement with the government settled the transfer of the assets and service obligations. On January 31, 1984, the reorganization became effective, including the transfer of 8000 employees from government service to company service. The government changed from a service provider to a service receiver, and the Communications Ministry was transformed from an operating department to a policymaking, regulatory, and supervisory department.

The reorganization of the telephone system was undertaken under Minister of Telecommunications Mordechai Zippori. After the elections of 1984, Professor Amnon Rubinstein, a prominent reformist member of parliament, became minister and established early agency direction for policy planning, regulation, development, licensing, spectrum management, and equipment approval. The Ministry of Communications regulates Bezeq's tariffs by approving rate increases and general changes in rate structure, in consultation with the finance minister and the economic committee of the Knesset. Rubinstein considered the feasibility of a partial privatization of Bezeq, and advocated full equipment liberalization, including the first telephone set. These proposals, however, were not instituted.

The significance of Bezeq's status outside the government must be viewed in its historical context. In Israel, more than in most European countries, a large number of companies, including those providing infrastructure services in all parts of the economy, are either controlled directly through the government or indirectly through the Histadrut trade union federation and other semipublic bodies. Public ownership of the key means of production in Israel—by government or the trade unions—had been for a long time an article of faith in the ideology of the state, even more than in Western Europe. In its purest reflection, this belief led to the collectivist kibbutz settlement. The partial loosening of governmental control over the telephone system was therefore a major step.

Through the change, the relationship between the company and the public was transformed to some degree. Bezeq attempted to be more responsive to the public, although it is still a monopoly service provider. Bezeq organized itself into six divisions: Finance; Economics and Logistics; Human Resources; Engineering; Marketing and Consumer Services; and Systems and Computers. It divided Israel into twenty-four telecommunications districts within four regions to foster local service (TRC, 1990). The new company's primary goal was to deal with an abominable waiting list for service, as long as 260,000 in a country of less than 1.5 million households. Where in the last year of the old ministry arrangement, $110 million was invested, Bezeq spent $250 million in 1985, $300 million in 1987 (Louisson, 1987), and $412 million in 1989 (Hai, 1990).

In 1986–1987, 22,000 trunk lines were added, compared to about 5000 in 1983–1984. Bezeq established a five-year plan during which time it planned to install 600,000 new lines, thereby increasing the system by 50 percent and doubling the annual installations. Given Israel's population, 550,000 new lines in five years is the equivalent of about 25 million new telephone lines installed in a five-year period in the United States. Bezeq was active in the Arab villages of Israel, where the demand for telephones had increased rapidly. By 1988, almost 1.5 million main lines were installed. The number of new public telephones increased by 65 percent during four years, and the directory information service was fully computerized (Hai, 1990).

By 1988, Bezeq claimed a productivity increase of 100 percent for its 9000 employees; workers per 100 lines were reduced from 7.6 in 1984 to 6.3 in 1988. The backlog of installation requests was reduced to 75,000 in 1989 (TRC, 1990). The annual growth rate of telephone lines was 10 to 12 percent, almost seven times higher than that in the United States. In terms of telephone density, Israel became comparable to Belgium or Italy, with thirty-two main lines per 100 population in 1989 (ITU, 1990).

Private leased lines rose from 1350 in 1981 to 4440 in 1984 and 10,500 in 1988. Bezeq also implemented the ISRANET public packet-switching network, operating at speeds of up to 1.2 kbps, with modems supplied by either Bezeq or the customer and approved by the Ministry of Communications. The network connects to similar networks in other countries, but at a higher usage cost than similar networks. Also, the initial cost of connection is high. The high-speed data network SIFRANET, designed to serve large users, began service in 1988, with the government signing on as the first customer. Demand for data services consistently outpaced supply. One study found that the 16 to 18 percent annual growth rate for leased data circuits would not keep pace with the 45 percent annual growth for VANS (Bainerman, 1989). A government-appointed panel, the Fogel Commission, recommended that rates be reduced. This was done in 1990, as part of a tariff rebalancing.

Bezeq also provides radio paging, alarm systems, and, in a joint venture with Motorola and Tadiran, cellular telephone service, where it holds 35 percent of the market. Competitors in paging services are Iturit, Page-call, and Beeper.

By law, Bezeq is the only company to receive a "general permit" for tele-communications services, although there are no restrictions on the minister's granting special licenses to others for particular services. A wide-ranging license was granted to the Postal Authority in 1990. Other organizations provide telex service, data transmission, and remote data processing. The leading company is Aurec, which supplies electronic mail services as a node of Dialcom in addition to other value-added services in partnership with Bezeq. Other companies provide wireless communications and wireless telex or licenses in the international field (Israel Statutes, 1982). The license fee is 11 percent of revenues.

Rival international telex service is provided by the Postal Authority, Ram Telex, and Cosmic Telex, all of which use Bezeq's telephone and data transmission lines to capture a combined market share of about 25 percent. Bezeq competes with these firms, subject to its own tariffs. The large labor union-controlled industrial group Koor owns a domestic value-added network under the name of Koornet, offering telefax, telex, and data transmission services. Koornet also competes with Aurec and Kav Manche in electronic data interchange (EDI) and VANS. Two popular services are telefax and BITNET, a heavily used standard mode of communications both domestically and internationally. Israel participates in three Mediterranean submarine cables: Tel Aviv–Marseilles, which has operated since 1968; also Tel Aviv–Rome–Marseilles, in operation since 1975; and the Eastern Mediterranean Fiber Optic Cable System, in operation since 1990.

In 1986–1987, Bezeq's contribution to the government was $169 million, out of a total revenue of $738 million for royalties, interest, and taxes. In the same year, Bezeq's rate of return was only 2.5 percent because of a general governmental price freeze in 1985 (S. Hai, 1988, communication). This made even a partial privatization unattractive to potential investors. In 1988, the Ministry of Communications approved a tariff increase of 8 percent. That year Bezeq's revenues grew to $932 million, but it returned only $6.5 million in profits (ITU, 1990). Bezeq was also required to transfer $190 million to the government. In 1990, proposals to privatize Bezeq and sell 20 percent of the company to a foreign owner were made. Fifteen percent of Bezeq's stock was offered to the general public. A ceiling of 25 percent was set, but soon raised, with an anticipated additional nine percent going to foreign shareholders and fourteen percent to strategic investors. A government commission also recommended partial opening to competition.

The major manufacturer of telecommunications equipment in Israel is Telrad, wholly owned by Israel's largest industrial group, Koor Industries, which is in turn owned by the Histadrut labor union federation. Telrad was established in 1951 and became a major developer of the civilian and defense communications network. By 1990, the company had installed more than 165,000 civilian telephone lines per year and had supplied more than 750,000 lines of electronic digital equipment for public systems. Telrad also supplies secure communication systems to the Israel Defense Forces (R. Sitter, 1990, communication).

Telrad's products include electronic switches, key telephones, terminal equipment, modems, transmission equipment multiplexers, and PBXs. Of the telephone handsets in the country, more than 90 percent are manufactured by Telrad. In 1990, the company employed 1200 people and sales totaled $150 million, about a fifth of which were from exports.

Another Israeli telecommunications producer is Tadiran, which has a broad-based product line and is one of the world's leading manufacturers of lithium batteries. Tadiran has 12,000 employees and is owned by the labor unions' Koor. Like Telrad, Tadiran and its subsidiary Tadiran Elisra supply systems and equipment to both defense and commercial markets. Among its products are tactical radios and data terminals, communication devices and radio telephones. Tadiran also manufactures and installs public telephone exchanges (Alcatel's System 12) and PBXs. Among industrial firms, Tadiran has Israel's largest research and development effort.

Elron Electronics, a large electronics concern, owns several subsidiaries, among them Elbit Computers, Elscint (for computer-based diagnostics), and Fibronics (for fiber-optic systems). Other Israeli telecommunications firms are ECI Telecom, Electric Cable, Zion Cables, and Paliadent. Because of the rapid growth of demand for data services, numerous small firms arose to challenge the "Big Three" Telrad, Tadiran, and ECI. These firms—Adacom, Rad Data, Bitcom, Efrat Future Technologies, Keren, Teledata, IAI, Fiobronics, Cvalim, Motorola—have filled niche markets, often teaming up with American firms.

In 1990, Raphael Pinhasi of the ultra-religious Shas party became communications minister, leading to a replacement in Bezeq's leadership. Chairman Yoram Alster was succeeded by Akiva Atoun, a founder of Ofek Computers and Software Research and Development. Atoun's father was a member of the Council of Torah Sages, which oversees the Shas party, and this raised questions over the minister's ability to exercise regulatory functions over Bezeq.

In 1991, the so-called Boaz Committee recommended further liberalization in equipment approval, international telephony, data communications, VANs, and mobile service.

25

Turkey

Telephone service began in Turkey in 1881 with lines connecting various post offices, government buildings, and banking branches. In 1909, a more complete network was created in Istanbul. In 1913, three government exchanges were established, followed by an exchange operated by a foreign company. International telephony was established during World War I, with service to Germany, Turkey's ally. After the war, international service was interrupted until 1931, when service to Sofia, Bulgaria, was reopened.

In 1926, the first automatic exchange was opened by the state in Ankara. In Istanbul, foreign companies played an increasingly important role. In 1935 and 1937, however, the state acquired the private exchanges in Istanbul and Ismir. In the 1940s, new exchanges used equipment made by Ericsson and the LMT Company.

The initial development of telecommunications was part of the modernization of Turkey after World War II. However, the pace of development was markedly slow. In 1954, Ericsson was contracted for switches to serve thirty cities, but it was not until the mid-1960s that telecommunications again became a priority. Fully automatic domestic telephone service was finally established in 1976, followed by similar international service in 1979.

The Turkish PTT holds a monopoly control over telecommunications and is supervised by the Ministry of Transportation and Communications. In the mid-1980s, the government considered a separation of telecommunications from postal services and the privatization of telecommunications services.

In 1982, the average waiting time for a telephone was seven years (OECD, 1982)! More than 70 percent of villages had no telephones. In 1983, the PTT announced its plans to give high priority to an expansion of service to all parts of the country and to an increase in penetration. At the time, telephone line density was only 3.5 per 100 population (Altay, 1987). The goals of the plan included the elimination of the waiting list for telephone service by the end of 1995, modernization, and new services.

From 1985 to 1988, investment quadrupled to more than $365 million annually (ITU, 1990). Financing was accomplished through the PTT's own sources and through domestic and international borrowing. By 1986, the PTT had achieved a number of improvements. The number of subscribers to telephone service increased by 67 percent, and the ratio of the number of demands for telephone service to the number of subscribers had fallen from a huge 1.09 in

1985 to a still considerable 0.27 in 1988. Penetration went from 4.3 phones per 100 population in 1985 to 12.2 in 1989. The waiting list dropped from 2.1 million to 1.3 million in 1988, but it increased again to 1.9 million in 1990 (ITU, 1990; General Directorate of the PTT, 1990). The percentage of villages without telephones decreased in a few years from 72 percent to 28 percent in 1989. Although the wait for service had dropped to two to three days in Istanbul and Ankara by 1990, in more remote areas the wait was still two to three months (Anik, 1990). But there was no longer a waiting list for telex service. In 1990, Turkey had a total of 7 million phones.

After 1984, the PTT also introduced new services. These include digital exchanges, fiber-optic cables, digital radio relay, multiaccess radio relay in rural areas, paging, dial-up modems, telecard payphones, cellular and cordless telephones, teletext, and public telefax. The circuit-switched DATEX-1 data network and the packet-switched data service Turkpak were also introduced.

The government embarked in particular upon an ambitious plan to improve the infrastructure of Istanbul, a city of 6 million inhabitants that experienced especially rapid growth during the 1980s. Istanbul was attempting to position itself as an international business center linking the Middle East and Europe, but it woefully lacked advanced telecommunications. In 1986, booking overseas calls sometimes required several attempts. In 1988, the country's two international gateway switches were replaced with DMS 300 digital exchanges in Istanbul and Ankara. Turkey's first communications satellite was scheduled for launch in 1993.

After 1988, telephone sets, telefax machines, and mobile telephones were available from private sources, as well as from the PTT. Equipment not supplied by the PTT is subject to its approval. For terminal equipment, Turkish-made equipment that meets established standards is generally used. Procurement by the PTT is in principle by public tender, but with the major loophole that tenders need not be undertaken where the equipment is produced by companies in which the PTT holds an interest.

In 1967, the PTT embarked on a course to upgrade Turkish equipment manufacturing: to design and construct transmission equipment, partly under license from the Belgian ITT subsidiary BTM. It established the firm Netas in collaboration with Northern Telecom for the production of crossbar exchanges. It also decided to spin off its Arla research laboratories, which had become quite large, into the new firm Teletas, a joint venture with Alcatel-BTM, and expanded it to serve as a second source for digital switches with its System 12. In 1987, Siemens became Turkey's third digital switch supplier with 100,000 digital EWSD lines, and it has since added 300,000 more. Yugoslavia's Iskra was brought in to provide small rural switches.

Though the PTT privatized Netas and Teletas, it maintains a strong influence through its research labs. Netas also manufactures telephone sets and the locally developed rural switch ELIF, as well as PBX equipment. Teletas also manufactures transmission equipment, teleprinters, and telephone sets, and the firm TTE produces rural switches. According to the PTT, about 85 percent of network equipment is produced in Turkey (Raggett, 1986). Supported by this high level of domestic PTT procurement, Netas and Teletas also sought export markets in northern Africa and the Middle East, and in 1991 Netas won a contract in the Soviet Republic of Azerbaijan.

26

Greece

By European standards, Greek telephone service is backward. This situation is partly due to the poverty of the country relative to Western Europe and the turmoil and polarization of its politics, including military dictatorships, foreign occupation, and divisive elections. It is also attributable to the problems of its telecommunications monopoly, the Hellenic Telecommunications Organization (OTE).

Compounding the problem is the rugged landscape of the interior areas of Greece, the need to reach the many islands, and the politicization of OTE. Given this scenario, it will be difficult for Greece to become the crossroads rather than the weak link of communications between Europe and Asia.

Greek telephony started in 1895 with two local systems. For a long time, the system was rudimentary. In 1930, the private Anonymous Eteria Telepikononion Ellados (AETE) was established to operate and develop local telephone service. In 1931, the AETE installed three automatic telephone exchanges in Athens and later expanded service into the provinces. The system used equipment from Siemens, which dominated Greek telecommunications before World War II. After the war, the system was nationalized and OTE was created. Siemens is still the main supplier, and its close ties to OTE continue. By 1949, there were fifteen automatic local exchanges in Athens and twenty-three in the provinces, with a total capacity of 6500 lines; 364 manual exchanges provided another 4230 lines. Telephone penetration at this time was only one per 100 population. During the same year, the government established OTE to take over telephony. Its sole share is held by the government. OTE operates under the supervision of the PTT, which is part of the Ministry of Transportation and Communications, and has a monopoly over most forms of communications, including broadcast transmission. One exception is local mobile telephone service, which may also be provided by private operators as long as it does not connect to the public network.

Greek telecommunications are lagging. The conservative Karamanlis government assigned a fairly low development priority to telecommunications. It also entered into a barter deal with Romania and East Germany for switches in return for agriculture products, which led to the introduction of low-quality equipment. The socialist Papandreou government that followed emphasized telecommunications and undertook a program of digitalization, but implementation of these plans was slow. From 1978 to 1987, Greece's yearly investment per line was Western Europe's lowest by far, a paltry $21.71, compared with the OECD average of $572.13 (OECD, 1990).

In 1984, telephone density in some districts was only seven to fifteen per 100 (OTE, 1985). The telephone failure frequency per 100 inhabitants was 57.5. About one-half of switches were still of the rotary type, with the rest being crossbar and other varieties. In 1983, the time required to satisfy the last application for main connection was 4.04 years. The mean waiting time to establish an operator-assisted international call was sixteen minutes in the main cities and in Athens (OTE, 1985, p. 30).

In 1985, the waiting list for main connections was over 970,000, about a third of total main lines (3 million, half of which were in the greater Athens region). By 1988, telephone density had grown to approximately thirty-six per 100 and there were about 3.6 million main lines. The wait for a private telephone installation was typically three to five years, and the waiting list had grown to 1.05 million requests (ITU, 1990). Even the highest-priority orders, those for hospital and business users, required at least several months and as much as one year to fill. Digital exchanges began to be introduced in 1986 and 1987, but in 1990, OTE was unable to supply digital lines to private VAN operators (Schenker, 1990, p. C5).

Equipment used by OTE is supplied primarily by Ericsson and the Greek subsidiaries of ITT and subsequently Alcatel, Philips, and Siemens. OTE provides Siemens PBX equipment, but users are free to order from other vendors. Telephone handsets, however, are supplied and maintained by the PTT. OTE's approval policy for private terminal equipment is relatively liberal, but the submission of a detailed technical description in Greek is required, and the procedure usually necessitates a representative in Greece. Modems for leased circuits are privately supplied, although OTE will install them. Telefax equipment is also available from private suppliers, but attachment requires OTE permission. Telex equipment can be obtained from either the OTE or private firms and must have both Latin and Greek characters.

Relatively little data transmission takes place over the public switched network because of its poor quality. Though rates of more than 1200 band are available, error rates are relatively high. As a result, only 5 percent of all Greek modems were connected to the PSTN in 1985. OTE regulations specified that each leased line may be used to transmit only one form of information. For example, despite the backlog in request for lines, a line could not be used for both voice and data. In 1987, the public-packet switched data network Hellaspac began operation, with transmission rates of up to 40 kbps. Its largest customer in 1980 was the on-line documentation center of the Greek Ministry of Industry, Trade, and Research.

In 1984, OTE decided to replace 400,000 telephone sets. It rejected several international supply offers and instead chose an offer from a joint venture of Eommex and the Greek firms Intracom, Elinda, Azinko, and Hourdakis. Eommex is an organization of small and medium-sized businesses headed, in 1984, by Vaso Papandreou, no relation to then Prime Minister Andreas Papandreou, but a close associate of his. Eventually, Intracom handled most of the order.

The primary argument for using the Greek suppliers was the promise of substantial domestic manufacturing. It soon was charged, however, that most parts were imported from abroad and merely assembled in Greece. An outside investigation revealed a 47 percent Greek value added instead of the guaranteed 73 percent.

At that time, OTE was also embroiled in charges of improprieties involving its new headquarters building. Construction of the building proceeded at a very slow pace for ten years, and the building stood empty for a number of years thereafter.

In the early 1980s OTE decided to introduce digital technology into its network and exchanges. A 1988 agreement with Greek assembly chose Ericsson's AXE and Siemens's EWSD switches among four bidders. Northern Telecom supplied crossbar equipment. A special committee headed by a high-ranking official of the Industrial Development Bank was established to negotiate their purchase. The negotiating team included two economists, two university-based technologists, and the deputy managing director of the OTE. This structure, over which OTE did not predominate, led to constant clashes with the managing director of OTE, Theofanis Tombras, who was accused of continuous intervention in the negotiations.

Influential in OTE personnel matters is the PTT union, which plays an unofficial but important role in managerial appointments. It is about one-third conservative, one-third socialist, and one-third communist.

In 1987, the minister of transport and communications expressed pessimism about the future of OTE: "OTE desperately tries to identify capital sources to satisfy over one million pending petitions for new service . . . but the required amount is presently a dream." And he pledged to "bring order to OTE's chaos." Shortly thereafter, the minister was removed. The real power in Greek telecommunications was OTE's director general Tombras, who was appointed by Prime Minister Papandreou in 1981. Tombras had been a military officer who was part of a leftist army group; he was accused of a plot, went into exile, returned, and was close to the prime minister. In that position, he was useful to the government. Tombras bragged to the press about wiretapping opposition leaders by a special department of OTE. He also cut communication links to broadcast stations of the opposition during the election campaign.

Telephone investments were made based on political considerations (where loyal voters were), and it was alleged that to receive priority on the waiting line required political patronage.

As the government's point man, Tombras became well known in Greece, and the opposition announced its intention to bring him to trial if it were to win the election.

The elections were held under a cloud of scandal in government, when a former Crete banker confessed to massive improprieties in the handling of state-owned organizations' funds, which benefited government officials and the ruling Pasok party. After several inconclusive elections, the conservatives came to power in 1990.

Not surprisingly, this climate was not conducive to the development of telecommunications infrastructure. (Tombras found enough time, however, to unsuccessfully intervene with the president of Columbia University, asking him to censure my observations about Greek telecommunications, which I had repeatedly sent to OTE for corrections and comments. The draft did not include the political discussion of the last several paragraphs, since this was not known to me at the time. When I flew to Athens, with an appointment to meet members of Tombras's staff to receive corrections, I was refused the meeting.)

When a conservative government came to power, the hope of many Greeks for better telephone service rested with the possibility of its winning the bid for the 1996 Summer Olympic Games, an event that would have established a firm deadline for improvement of the country's infrastructure. But that bid failed, leaving Greek telecommunications still a weak link in Greece's infrastructure. In 1990, the new government announced an ambitious three-year plan to add 1.2 million digital lines to the OTE network. It also proposed the introduction of cellular service and the liberalization of VANs.

Since Greece was the only EC country left without a cellular telephone system, the government invited in 1991 bids for two competitive cellular telephone systems, which could be foreign owned. Although OTE would own one third of each, thus first opening in the service monopoly, the change augured that Greece, too, was following the broader European trend.

Problems persisted. Procurement contracts were awarded to Greek firms which largely reassembled parts from the Far East. After OTE Director General Kyriakos Kioulafas refused to halt negotiations with Siemens Greece over an underseas cable project (when Denmark's NKT had proposed a similar deal for $5.5 million less), he and others in OTE's top management were dismissed. OTE's digital exchange procurement led to bitter disputes over the suppliers and politicized the decisions process. These procurement scandals encouraged calls for reform which included proposals for the sale of 49 percent of OTE to private investors to raise capital needed for massive modernization programs (Kotsonis, 1990). Due to the less-developed state of the Greek network, the EC proposed in 1991 to apply a special set of telecommunications policies for Greece.

Cyprus

In 1955, the Cyprus Telecommunications Authority (CTA) was formed to replace Cable and Wireless as the telephone provider for the newly independent country. CTA telephone service reaches 35 out of every 100 persons, with one-third of traffic digitally switched. CTA holds a monopoly over telex, facsimile, and data services. Cellular service based on the NMT 450 standard was started in 1988. The equipment market in Cyprus was liberalized in 1988 after CTA could no longer keep pace with demand. CTA did, however, retain type approval powers as well as its complete monopoly on services.

27

Telecommunications in Eastern Europe

Introduction

Telecommunications in pre-reform Eastern Europe resembled that of the West in one important aspect: monopoly control over all aspects, under the aegis of a state PTT. Technical capability, performance quality, and service availability, however, were far behind. Telecommunications had long been neglected. According to a World Bank study, networks in Eastern Europe had growth rates of only 3 percent over the last thirty years, and what little investment was made went to new lines, not maintenance or infrastructure (Nulty, 1990). Penetration figures therefore did not reflect poor service quality and outdated equipment.

Disparities in telephone penetration existed between neighboring countries and between urban and rural areas. Throughout Eastern Europe a typical applicant for new telephone service had to wait a decade or more for service. A post-reform report in Poland noted that a thirty-three year wait for telephone installation was not unheard of. Some of the equipment dated back to World War II or before; international service was often limited to less than 100 inbound and outbound lines, and advanced applications such as cellular mobile phone service were unavailable. Given that the poor quality of transmission prevented facsimile and data services, telex service was heavily used.

This neglect partly reflects the view that telecommunications is a nonproductive consumption sector of the economy, as opposed to agriculture and industry. Telecommunications profits were typically used for other projects. In Czechoslovakia, for example, 87 percent of PTT profits were diverted to the general budget. Another problem was state control: international direct dialing was often prohibited and telephone directories were made classified documents.

Once economic and political reforms were introduced, the upgrading of the telecommunications infrastructure received high priority as central to overall economic development. East European governments sought to almost quadruple growth to 10–11 percent annually. Change was introduced in several areas: improvement of existing networks and customer service, accommodating new technologies such as digital switching and VANs, and institutional and legal reform.

East European governments had to balance competing pressures. The upgrade of public networks requires huge investments, as much as $140 billion in the next decade (Pearce, 1990). There is pressure to target investment for special user groups and to allow private providers of telecommunications services to enter the market.

East European countries traditionally exported telecommunications equipment to the Soviet Union. These industries existed without competitive pressures to develop or modernize and were in fact protected by the West's so-called CoCom restrictions that kept advanced technology from the East. With the easing of restrictions, more efficient Western firms could compete to supply equipment to fill these countries' huge needs. However, all the Eastern Bloc countries shared a similar obstacle: They lacked the hard currency to import Western equipment. Most countries either had to strike barter agreements or had to trade an equity stake as a means of acquiring badly needed technology.[1]

The following sections provide capsule descriptions about change in the various Eastern European countries. Because of the pace of transition, these surveys are brief.

Hungary

Despite its relatively high per capita income, Hungary has one of the least developed telecommunications networks among East European countries (EESTR, 1990a). At the same time, Hungary earned a reputation as a leader: It was the first Eastern Bloc country to invest in Western digital switching technology, first to introduce cellular service, and first to apply for membership in the Conference of European Postal and Telecommunications Administrations (CEPT), the organization of (West) European PTTs.

Hungary's first telephone exchange was installed in 1881. Development slowed during and after World War II, when priorities shifted toward economic centralization and the military. Existing facilities deteriorated for lack of investment funds; annual growth in telephones from 1967 to 1987 was 4.3 percent, the lowest among countries of similar economic development (Datapro, 1990).

Demand for telephone lines grew with the economic reforms of 1968, when economic planners allowed greater horizontal relations between companies. In 1983 the PTT Magyar Posta was turned into an organization separate from the Ministry of Transport, Communications and Construction. In 1989, Magyar Posta was split into three bodies, for telecommunications, broadcasting, and traditional postal service. In anticipation of a privatization, the telecommunications group was renamed the Hungarian Telecommunications Company (HTC). The Telecommunications Act was revised in 1989 to allow limited private investments in Hungarian service providers (EESTR, 1990a). Shares of HTC were offered to Hungarian firms in 1990 and to foreign investors in 1991, with total foreign ownership limited to 25 percent. HTC's investments were still directed by the Ministry for Transport, and rates are approved by the State Price Control Office. Further legislation proposed competition in value-added services and the establishment of private local telephone companies, leaving the PTT with a monopoly over long-distance services.

In 1984 Magyar Posta announced plans for fully automatic switching by

1995. Equipment production was converted from electromechanical to electronic switches in the same year (*Budapress,* 1984). In 1985 Hungary finally expanded direct access for international calls to seventy-three countries from major cities. A $70 million loan from the World Bank in 1987 was used by the PTT to purchase cable and switching equipment from West Germany, Turkey, and France.

The five-year plan for 1986–1990 called for 420,000 new lines to increase telephone penetration to seventeen main lines per 100 people by 1990 and to 40 per 100 by the year 2000. Estimates of telephone penetration for 1990 fall between 7.6 and 9.1 main lines per 100 people. Residential telephone service is inexpensive. The monthly line charge is $1.50 and 3 cents for each local call (Rocks, 1990). The wait for phone service averages ten to twelve years, and 550,000 people are on the waiting list. The PTT's goal is to cut the waiting time to one year by the year 2000.

Two-thirds of calls in 1988 could not be completed in the main cities, with service even worse in the outlying areas. The government estimated that a 1 percent loss in national income could be attributed to poor telephone service. Since over 80 percent of local exchanges are manual, many subscribers cannot obtain service after the post office closes at 4 P.M. Urban areas and the trunk network have crossbar switches, and a few digital switches are in place. Hungary's service problems are worsened by the fact that over half of its 1.4 million lines serve the 20 percent of the population that lives in major cities.

Modernization plans call for replacement of all rotary switches in the local network by the early 1990s and in the toll network by 2000. Investments of $5 billion were projected to satisfy demand and deploy digital switching equipment. HTC expected to generate 50 percent of investment from revenues and 10 percent from government, with the remainder coming from outside sources. To that end, Hungary sought additional loans of $100 to $150 million from the World Bank and the European Investment Bank (Prónay, 1990).

Hungary manufactures telecommunications equipment through its main equipment firms Budavox and Beloyanis Telecommunications Factory (BHG). It exports to the ex-Soviet Union and Eastern Bloc nations as well as to Greece, Italy, and England. Joint ventures with Western firms were crucial in Hungary's post-reform policy. Siemens, which was blocked under CoCom restrictions from exporting its switches to Hungary, in 1984 entered a joint venture with the Hungarian firm Videoton to manufacture equipment in Hungary. Similarly, Alcatel Austria entered a joint venture with HT Hirdastechnika Szovetkezet to manufacture the Alcatel 5200 PBX in Hungary. Northern Telecom formed a joint venture to build digital switches for HTC and private business customers.

A contract for cellular service was awarded in 1990 to a joint venture between HTC and US West for a system that would ultimately interconnect with the pan-European GSM digital mobile system. Critics argued that Hungary should instead invest in the more basic aspects of the existing telephone system. However, rival cellular providers were likely. In 1989, Bond Hungaria Telecom— a joint venture between Coopinvest, Australia's Bond Corporation, and others—announced plans to start a separate 900MHz system. The old government had awarded a cellular license to the American firm Contel, but the new one switched the franchise to US West and HTC.

Poland

The Polish public telecommunications system suffers from forty years of neglect on top of a devastating war. It was not a priority to allow citizens access to a well-developed communications network, and there was consequently little investment or R&D in telecommunications. As a result, the system suffered from inadequate technology and bottlenecks at every level. With political and economic reform, Poland's financial limitations led to an approach toward institutional reform that went further than that of Hungary, embracing full demonopolization of the PTT and allowing foreign interests to compete directly with it.

Communications in Poland dates back to 1558, when King Sigismund Augustus established the Polish mail between Cracow and Venice. The Polish Post Office, Telegraph and Telephones (PPTT) was formed between the two world wars and built a telecommunications network with foreign financial assistance. The system was greatly damaged in World War II. By 1944, the Soviet Union, Britain, Sweden, and the United States were supporting efforts to rebuild it.

The number of telephones more than doubled between 1960 and 1972, reaching a penetration of 3.62 per 100 (*Poland: A Handbook*, 1974). In 1990, there were 3.28 million subscribers, or 8.3 phones per 100 people. The average wait for service was thirteen years, and delays as long as thirty-three years were reported. The 2.2 million people waiting for a phone may be only a portion of those actually interested in telephone service. Poland's network employs local exchanges dating from the 1930s and the 1960s. Fifteen percent of switches are over thirty years old, and the 1990 call completion rate was only 30 percent (*EESTR*, 1990b).

The PPTT was removed from the control of the Ministry of Communications in 1987, after the ministry was merged into the Ministry of Transport and Shipping, which gained control over rates and technical policies. In 1990 a new ministry was created to oversee the PPTT, the Ministry for Posts, Broadcasting and Telecommunications.

The PPTT operates the national network and ran postal and broadcast services (Datapro, 1990). The PPTT is financially self-sufficient but must contribute 40 percent of its income to the government and is obligated to subsidize the post office. In 1991, postal, broadcast, and telecommunications services were separated into individual operating units as a step toward privatization. Telecommunications were provided by Telekomunikacja Polska SA. Long distance services were also separated from local ones, which were to be offered by independent regional companies, potentially private and with minority foreign participation.

The 1991 Telecommunications Act permitted competition with the TPSA in many services, such as local, cellular, and domestic long-distance. Regulation was by the Ministry and its subagencies PIT and PAR. The government's reform plans were ambitious. TPSA was to be privatized in the future, and perhaps divided into a national long-distance organization and several regional companies. Foreign applicants could not own a majority of shares, except for local service companies.

The post-reform Polish government made upgrading the telecommunications system one of its two economic development priorities and targeted Warsaw and the Silesia region. PPTT goals were to quadruple telephone penetration by 2000, setting a goal of 10–12 million subscribers by that time. In addition, the PPTT estimated that as much as 60 percent of the embedded network will also have to be replaced or significantly improved. The PPTT sought to upgrade international capacity and to modernize the network through AT&T. To improve the domestic network the PPTT bought eight transit exchanges from Alcatel-Spain on generous terms arranged for by the Spanish government.

In 1990, the PPTT installed Kommertel, a separate overlay business network in Warsaw. Installation fees and line charges were five times the normal, but interconnection was immediate. Poland had Eastern Europe's highest telex service penetration. Satellite services were offered through Intersputnik. Poland joined Eutelsat in 1990.

Before the reforms of the late 1980s, manufacturing had been handled by United Telekom (UT), a state monopoly with 20,000 employees. In 1989, UT was split into three separate entities that are to compete with one another: ZWUT, Teletra, and the Polish Transmission Works. The three firms were expected to produce 1.8 million lines; of those, the PPTT orders came to 1 million lines per year, and the remainder was aimed for export (Datapro, 1990).

The country was open to joint ventures with Western equipment providers. Domestic manufacture was directed by the Ministry of Industry in partnerships with Western firms. ZWUT produces the EWSD switch with Siemens, and Alcatel produces its E10 and System 12 switches with Telettra and the Polish Transmission Works (PZT). In 1990 Siemens bought a 49 percent stake of ZWUT for DM 50 million. Ericsson was involved with Telecom Telfa. AT&T, Italtel, and Samsung were also active. Customer premises equipment was liberalized subject to type approvals of the PPTT's Institute of Telecommunications.

Twenty-five companies offered bids for cellular overlay networks. Sweden's Televerket, Finland's P&T, and British Telecom formed the Baltic Mobile Telephone System (BMTS) consortium, which bid to expand the NMT 450 cellular system now operating in the Scandinavian countries to the Baltic-rim countries, including Poland. A franchise was won by a consortium of Ameritech and France Télécom.

Czecho-Slovakia

Czecho-Slovakia's telecommunications network is controlled by the Federal Ministry of Posts and Telecommunications (PTT), which was separated from the Ministry of Transport in 1990. All equipment is produced under the supervision of the Federal Ministry of Metallurgy, Engineering and Electrotechnical Industries. In 1989, legislation was passed that required the PTT to earn a profit, but the amount of those profits that would be transferred to the state was left unspecified.

The PTT's structure is federal. The two republic-level operators are SPT Praha and SPT Bratislava. And the struggle over the extent of centralism led to creation of a Slovak PTT Ministry. Despite limited investments and growth rates under 3 percent from 1978 to 1989, the infrastructure is above average for East European nations. Telephone penetration led the Eastern Bloc, with twenty lines per 100 households in 1978 and twenty-seven in 1990, and per capita penetration at fourteen main lines per 100 persons. Nevertheless, the 1990 waiting list was 370,000 names long with a ten-year wait. The figure rises to over 700,000 when those who have dropped off the list are included. The network is mostly analog, with 3 percent of lines served by Alcatel E10 digital exchanges. It also serves the broadcast needs of radio and television (Antono, 1990). Two international exchanges are located in Prague. The SPTs announced ambitious plans for expanded digital switching, packet-switched service, paging, videotex, e-mail, and private networks.

After taking bids from British Telecom, McCaw, and a West German consortium, the PTT awarded a twenty-year license for an analog cellular network to a joint venture of the PTT and US West and Bell Atlantic. Bell Atlantic and US West won a related contract to build a public packet-switched data network (Eurotel).

The Czechoslovak equipment industry was dominated by the state-controlled manufacturer Tesla Karlin, part of the Tesla Electronics Group. After the government decided to privatize industry and allow joint ventures, Tesla Karlin formed a joint venture with Siemens to manufacture switches. Alcatel SEL formed a joint venture with Tesla-Liptovsky. Modems are manufactured by ZVTf Banska Bystrica. There were about 5000 modems connected in 1989 (Datapro, 1990, p. 264). The PTT also sought to improve services by purchasing Ericsson, Alcatel, Philips, and Telettra equipment for switching and data transmission.

In 1992, a new telecommunications law provided for eventual competition, except in basic voice service, regulated nationally.

Yugoslavia—Croatia—Slovenia

The Yugoslav postal and telephone system was highly decentralized, with six republic PTTs under a weak federal administration. Although each of these individual organizations ostensibly determined the prices for its services, the government oversaw rates and manages revenues and expenses within the state budget (Lakicevic, 1970).

The number of telephones and automatic exchanges doubled from 1939 to 1950 (Byrnes, 1957), but growth was slow until the mid-1970s. Since 1979,

Yugoslavia encouraged foreign investment, which led to 9 percent yearly growth and the deployment of a packet-switched network. In 1988, telephone penetration was 13 main lines per 100 population. Digital service began in 1986 with the purchase of twelve ITT System 12 switches. In 1987, satellite communication began under an agreement between Mitsui, NEC, and the PTT to construct a satellite station linking Yugoslavia with Western Europe via Eutelsat (*Business Eastern Europe*, 1987).

Yugoslavia also imported foreign technology and expertise through its equipment manufacturers. A partnership of GTE and Elektronska Industrija of Nis, known as GTE-Pupin, produces PBXs and exchanges. In 1990 it installed its first digital phone exchange near Ljubliana, as part of a joint venture between Siemens of Germany and Iskratel of Yugoslavia (U.S. Department of State, 1990). Iskratel also has technology transfer agreements with ITT and American Microsystems. Other joint ventures included Alcatel with Elektronska Industrija, and Ericsson with Tesla.

Despite these moves to integrate modern technology into its telecommunications infrastructure and a 50 percent increase in investments, Yugoslavia's telephone penetration was only slightly above the Eastern European average. The subsequent secession of Croatia and Slovenia, the ensuing civil war, and the establishment of Bosnia-Herzegovina and Macedonia disrupted and damaged the telecommunications infrastructure and institutions.

Bulgaria

Telecommunications in Bulgaria began with government ownership under the General Directorate of Post, Telegraph and Telephone in 1878. Telegraph lines were completed between Sofia and Plovdiv in 1892. Services continued to expand, and in 1938 there were 8600 km of telegraph lines with 750 stations and 21,086 km of telephone lines with 584 exchanges and over 27,000 phones, processing 54 million calls annually (Dellin, 1957).

When the Communists seized power in 1944, they made no legal changes to the PTT. By 1950, over 57,000 lines were reported to be in service, compared to 27,500 in 1939. Revenues and expenses of this system were included in the state budget. Government reports at the time claimed a fourfold increase in land-based wire line facilities, compared to prewar levels.

According to OECD figures, Bulgaria had the greatest number of main lines, 18.4 per 100 population in Eastern Europe by 1988 (Kelly, 1990). This relative strength came from Bulgaria's investments in telecommunications in the 1980s, which gave it a reputation as Eastern Europe's best developed system (Nulty, 1990).

Bulgaria's plan to upgrade telecommunications, which involved installing electronic and semiautomatic exchanges to enable 155,000 new subscribers to join the system, anticipated a foreign equity participation in a privatized BPT. The main equipment manufacturer, Sofia Telecommunications Plant, exported

16 percent of its output to the Soviet Union, including over 50 percent of handsets. BPT aimed to liberalize the equipment market.

Romania

Romania's telephone network has been operated with some rotary switch equipment since 1933. The equipment in the network's central offices is estimated to be thirty years old on average (U.S. Department of State, 1990). Following the overthrow of President Ceaucescu, however, the new government moved to significantly upgrade all its basic services and to establish some value-added services. It also separated the Ministry of Post and Telecommunications from the Ministry of Transportation. As in most Eastern Bloc nations, telecommunications heavily subsidizes the postal service.

Romania's first automatic telephone exchange, a rotary switch built by ITT, began operation in 1927 in Bucharest. The network continues to rely on such rotary equipment, although in 1968 a licensing agreement was signed with ITT's Belgian BTM that allowed domestic production of more advanced Pentaconta automatic switches for local and trunk traffic (Popescu, 1990). In 1990, Romania contracted Alcatel FACE to provide System 12 switches for Bucharest.

Estimates of Romanian telephone penetration vary from 6.7 to 7.4 main lines per 100 in 1990 (Fidler, 1990). The government's own official estimate is ten lines (including party lines) per 100 persons. Service is unevenly distributed between urban and rural areas. Penetration in Bucharest runs at thirty lines per 100 persons, with other urban areas averaging fifteen per 100. The rural average is 2.5 lines, and 3300 villages have yet to receive service (Popescu, 1990).

The number of subscribers tripled from 1965 to 1975, and an aggressive five-year plan was proposed for 1976–1980 that called for a minimum expansion in facilities of 30–40 percent to accommodate international traffic, with special emphasis on data (Avramescou and Celac, 1980). By 1990, 89 percent of telephone subscribers were served by some form of automatic switch, but data services had not improved. For example, there were only 200 facsimile machines in the country in 1990.

A backlog of 800,000 orders for telephone service in urban areas alone has resulted in a ten-year wait for service. The government forecast an additional 2.5 million lines to meet rural needs and has set a goal of 50 percent penetration in the next fifteen to twenty years. To meet these needs, the aim was 400,000 new lines per year, assisted by a joint venture to manufacture digital equipment at Romania's Electromagnetic Plant.

The government also planned to upgrade the network by completing the existing analog trunk network and adding electronic switches, digital microwave lines, fiber-optic cable, digital multiplexing systems, and a cellular network. In addition, there were plans to develop a high-speed, packet-switched data transmission network to upgrade the previous ROMPAK network.

In 1990, all international traffic was handled by a single crossbar switch with a 340–line capacity that had been in place since 1974. To modernize international access, the PTT purchased a Siemens EWSD digital switch. Siemens also acquired 49 percent of the manufacturer EMCOM. Romania joined Eutelsat and became the first Eastern Bloc country to gain membership in Intelsat in 1990.

For much of this technology, the new Romanian government sought joint ventures with Western companies, and the PTT indicated that it will privatize mobile cellular systems, packet switching equipment, and terminal equipment for value-added services, but not for basic services. Rom Telecom was separated from the PTT and assisted by France.

Albania

The close government control over telecommunications in Albania allowed little information about its network to be disseminated. In 1939, the country had fifty-six hand-operated exchanges serving fewer than 900 lines. Only one automatic switch existed, serving 150 lines in Tirana. Telegraph connections were in place with both Greece and Yugoslavia (Skendi, 1956, p. 251). Albania joined the ITU in 1922 but has not participated in any working groups or assemblies, or reported penetration statistics.

The Italian occupation of Albania from 1939 to 1943 first brought some expansion for the country's system, in establishing international connections with Yugoslavia, Bulgaria, and Italy. The domestic telecommunications infrastructure suffered extensive damage in the war.

Albania's telecommunications systems are owned and operated by the state through the Directorate of Post, Telephone, and Telegraph, within the Ministry of Communications. Network expansion was never a priority. In 1956, only fifty-six telegraph and seventy-five telephone exchanges were in service, the largest of which served 500 lines. Residential telephones were almost unheard of except for officials and doctors. In 1990, direct-dial long distance access started in several cities, though all traffic is routed through a single switch in Tirana.

With a democratic government elected in 1992, major changes were anticipated.

Russia[2] and Commonwealth of Independent States

Telecommunications were long neglected in the former Soviet Union because they were viewed as a consumptive rather than a productive activity. The Soviet telecommunications system was probably not simply a failure in terms of management, but also a fairly accurate reflection of the low priority held by the state for individualized and decentralized civilian communications. The country's centralized economy, compartmentalized bureaucracy, and wariness about citizen access to communications flows were reflected in the rigid hierarchical structure and poor condition of the public network. The result was a communications system that was inadequate for the economy of a superpower. By comparison, the United States had more than seven times the number of telephone lines and nine times the number of residential lines. However, the Soviet Union under Mikhail Gorbachev put telecommunications development more into the forefront. Whereas 1 million new lines were installed annually from 1980 to 1985 (already a major increase over the 1970s), twice as many were added in the second half of the decade, and residential service became a greater priority. At the same time, the process of disintegration into constituent republics led to an increasingly decentralized telecommunications system.

Organizational Structure

In the former Soviet Union, telecommunications facilities, services, and manufacturing were state monopolies, long under the Federal Ministry of Posts and Telecommunications (MPT). The Ministry of Communications, known as Minsviaz, operated national and international networks and services, as well as postal services and TV and radio broadcasting. In addition to national Minsviaz, each of the fifteen republics had its own Minsviaz, which was subordinated to the national ministry as well as to the government of the respective republic. (The Russian Minsviaz was created fairly late, its functions having been undertaken before by the national ministry. Even then, telecommunications in the city of Moscow were still run by the national ministry.)

The national Minsviaz' responsibility was for overall system coordination and operation of overarching activities, such as national long-distance service, communication satellites, and national broadcast services. Minsviaz seemed to have no oversight responsibility over important intraorganizational networks, such as those of the defense establishment, the KGB, and the ministry of Internal Affairs (Campbell, 1988).

Subordinated to Minsviaz were several chief administrations, including those for industrial enterprises (GUPP), science and technology (GNTU), satellite and radio broadcasting (GKRU), postal services (GUPS), long-distance transmission (GUMTS), telegraphy (GTU), and urban and rural services (GUTS). The republic ministries were responsible for services in their territory, provided through regional organizations (PTUS) and production enterprises (RUS). Most of Minsviaz' 7000 such enterprises had some financial independence, but financial subsidies and redistribution were also necessary, especially since more than 1000 lost money. Overall development plans were formulated by Minsviaz and were part of the national five-year plans. But actual investment funds had to be provided by the republics, regional and local governments, and even industrial and agricultural users. Thus, network construction was to some extent at the mercy of the investment priorities and red tape of numerous agencies. With the increasing independence of the republics, telecommunications became increasingly controlled by the various republics' ministries, and their coordinating committees' became critical.

Services

The Soviet telecommunications network was organized to serve official and administrative rather than household needs. Military and industrial communications were especially well developed for utilities departments such as railroads, pipelines, and power, which have separate networks comprising about 6.5 million lines, 40 percent of which are connected to the public network. Frequently, those systems utilize Minsviaz leased lines. The department networks occupied 20 percent of Soviet exchanges (Campbell, 1988). The 1966–1970 Five Year Plan (FYP) mandated a Unified Automated System of Telecommunications (EASS), conceptualized as an integrated network with the capacity to carry voice, video, and data traffic in anticipation of an ISDN-type facility. However, little network integration actually took place and common facilities were used only to a limited extent.

Once telecommunications became more of a priority, penetration increased from 29.1 million phones in 1980 (of which 23.7 million were connected to the public network) to 37.2 million in 1985, with 31.1 million connected to the public network. Of all lines in Russia, 55 percent are residential, compared with 84 percent in the United States.

In 1985, the central government initiated a program for telecommunications growth and converted some military communications manufacturing to civilian production. The twelfth five-year plan, covering 1986 to 1990, sought to add 12.1 million new lines to the system, shift to semielectronic exchanges, and introduce fiber-optic and digital technology. Telecommunications budgets grew from 1.2 billion rubles annually in the eleventh five-year plan to 2 billion in the twelfth. Keeping with the emphasis on residential service, 75 percent of the new installations were to be residential. As part of the ongoing effort to develop the EASS, 2Mbps and 8Mbps digital lines were put in some major cities (Datapro, 1990).

Structurally, the network consisted of a fairly rigid hierarchy of local single or interlinked exchanges; zonal systems (about 175–200) that were assigned area code numbers; and a third-level national trunk network with fifteen interregional transit offices linked through Moscow, using foreign equipment such as the French MT-20. Moscow was also the prime link with the Intersputnik and Intelsat systems.

Domestic long-distance voice communications are mostly terrestrial. But extensive satellite facilities are available, as befitting a space power. The Orbita–Molniia and Raduga satellite systems are used primarily for broadcasting and play only a limited role in telecommunications. The next generation of satellites, named Mayak, aimed to have high elliptical orbits. Also planned was a giant 18-ton, 30-meter diameter communications satellite platform for launch in 1993.

In 1989 there were 40 million telephones or 13 per 100 population inhabitants. But regional disparities in penetration are great; 25 percent of urban households have phones, compared with 10 percent of rural households. Relatively high penetration (from 30–50 lines per 100 households) was reported for Moscow, St. Petersburg, Kiev, Armenia, and the Baltic republics, whereas Siberia and the Central Asian regions have less than one line per 100 homes. Moscow accounts for 11 percent of all telephones; 20 percent of all residential subscribers use party lines.

Tariffs were set favorably for users. Although handsets and installations were costly, subscribers paid only 2.5 rubles per month for unlimited local service (Campbell, 1988), among the least expensive rates in the world. Local measured billing was introduced experimentally in a number of locations but was unreliable. Installation costs rose 500 percent, but they were below the actual cost of 250–500 rubles (Frankl, 1989). Rural service was heavily subsidized; in 1980 its loss was 74 percent of cost. Partly in response, a 1983 price reform moved prices closer to cost. All state and collective farms have been connected to the network. The allocation of telephone service was not by price, but frequently as a privilege for well-connected individuals. The wait in 1989 averaged four years and the waiting list included twelve million households. The availability of pay phones was limited. Nationally, in 1987, there were only 35,000 pay phones that could reach out of the local exchange (in the United States, the number was sixty times as high), and one survey found that half of pay phones were out of service. In 1988, GEC Plessey Telecommunications (GPT) formed a joint venture called Comstar with Minsviaz to provide and operate approximately 100 credit card pay phones, principally for use by foreigners in airports and hotels (Dixon, 1988a). Comstar failed to show significant results after two years.

Two joint ventures with the United States for international data transmission were also planned. Sovam Teleport, which began operations in 1990, connects to public data networks and electronic mail service around the world. Sprint Networks U.S.S.R. was a 1990 joint activity of US Sprint and the Moscow telephone organization.

In 1985, one-third of all long-distance calls still required operators. Where operators are necessary, it can often take a very long time to establish a connection. Even for automatic trunks blockage rates are 3 percent or more on almost one half of the automatic trunks. At the same time, the rigid hierarchy of network architecture leads to underutilization of many circuits. All international calls were routed through one gateway switch in Moscow with 1500 lines and approximately twenty operators to serve the entire country. In 1989, 11 million international calls were made from the Soviet Union.

The goal for the year 2000—to reach 90–100 percent urban penetration and 50 percent in rural areas—will require 60 million lines in the 1990s (i.e., 6 million lines per year as opposed to 2 million in the late 1980s and 1 million earlier in the decade). To meet these targets, the republics, like other East European administrations, must increase spending to more than three times their already accelerated investment rate of the late 1980s (Nulty, 1990). It was not clear where the funds would come from. In one effort to develop innovative financing, Minsviaz formed a commercial bank for deposits from the public and as a financial clearinghouse for its various operations. Another strategy was for Minsviaz to retain more of its earnings for reinvestment. Its profits in 1988 totaled 5.3 billion rubles, but it claimed that 75 percent of this was returned to the central government budget (Campbell, 1990).

The analog network supported data transmission at 9.6 kbps on some dedicated lines (which are very expensive), but the number of users was low because of the lack of transmission devices (i.e., modems) and minicomputers. There was one X.25 packet-switched network, Academnet. There was limited 64 kbps ISDN service in Moscow to leased line business subscribers through a joint venture with IDB (U.S.). Facsimile technology was introduced for newspapers in 1990, but was not available to the public.

. Telex and telegraph services developed as reliable alternatives to telephone service; as a result, they enjoyed high traffic volume. All telex and telegraph traffic passed through a gateway in Moscow. The telex network had 110,000 subscribers in 1990, growing by 5000 subscribers per year. Soviet telegraph volume was greater than that of all other industrialized countries together, with 450 million telegrams sent yearly, and there were no public facsimile, videotex, or e-mail services. A more general state system for data transfer (OGSPD) was proposed in 1972 for speeds above telex's anemic 50 baud. Such a system, PD-200, was online in the late 1970s. It did not evolve further, partly because of lack of terminal equipment, and partly because Minsviaz permitted data access only to organizations, not to individuals (Campbell, 1988). Even authorized users could use the system only for several minutes each hour or had to pay very high rates for access.

Nokia of Finland proposed a cellular network for Moscow. A group of Western telecommunications firms—including Televerket of Sweden, British Telecom, Finnish Telecom International, and NordicTel—joined to provide a cellular network, called the Baltic Mobile Telephone System (BMTS), for the Baltic region (Estonia, Lithuania, and Latvia). The republics of Armenia and Kazakhstan reached agreement with AT&T for international switching, and, in Ukraine, for network operations, with Dutch and German PTOs participation.

Equipment

A key reason for the backwardness of the Soviet telephone system was the country's weakness in the design and production of advanced equipment. And this had structural reasons. Whereas in the telecommunications industry Minsviaz controlled the operations of the network, it had only weak powers when it came to the guidance of the development and production of the equipment that in the aggregate constituted the network. Although Minsviaz had some production plants under its own control, the equipment area was the province of several ministries—Minradioprom (radio equipment), Minelektronprom (electronic components and transmission systems), Minelektrotekhprom (electrical equipment), and especially Minpromsviaz (Communications)—that were part of the defense industry and were controlled by the military industrial commission, VPK. Within the Soviet bureaucracy, Minsviaz was no match for the powerful VPK, which allocated resources to defense and space and away from civilian electronics uses. The telecommunications equipment ministry did not even have a civilian branch. In one year, 30 percent of the telegraph equipment received by Minsviaz from Minpromsviaz was defective. One of the important changes of the twelfth five-year plan in 1985 was to shift some control over the electronics to Minsviaz and to civilian goals. To further the separation of military and civilian institutions, the government in 1989 abolished altogether the Ministry of the Industry of Communications Equipment (Minpromsviaz, or MPSS). Most of MPSS's responsibilities for manufacturing and service provision and 12,000 workers were transferred to Minsviaz. But the former MPSS minister, Erlen Pervyshin, became Minsviaz' new head.

Much of the Soviet telecommunications system relied on outdated equipment, some of which was installed before the 1917 revolution! Soviet authorities acknowledged that copper wire laid by Ericsson in 1907 was still carrying traffic (Gulyaev, 1990). Most of the switches were analog and electromechanical. Forecasts indicate that local industries cannot produce more than a fraction of the equipment needed for the ambitious expansion plans (Frankl, 1989). Since the 1970s, terminal equipment was owned by subscribers. PBXs, although rare, could also be owned by the user. In the past, much of Soviet switching equipment, handsets, and cables had been imported under a deliberate program of support for East European countries. Over 600,000 handsets were imported from Bulgaria in 1986, mostly from the Sofia Telecommunications Plant, and constituted more than half of that country's production. Czechoslovakia had also provided 2 million handsets to the Soviet Union by 1976 and several million more since. East Germany (NEK) was a major supplier of exchanges, and Hungary served the Soviet Union with the some advanced equipment, under Western license. Poland and Yugoslavia were also equipment sources, as were a number of Western countries, most notably Finland. The Finnish firm Nokia supplied exchanges and cables, and France's Thomson CSF also provided switching equipment. With the abolition of Minpromsviaz, Minsviaz wrested control of the main Soviet telecommunications manufacturers from the military industrial commission VPK. Even before, Minsviaz also controlled a number of relatively small and undersupported manufacturing plants.[3] But the more significant development efforts were those of the VPK ministries, which were traditionally shrouded in secrecy. Among these enterprises, of particular importance is VET in Riga, Latvia, a company originating before the Soviet annexation. Other major plants are in Peraa, Kaunas, Vilnius, and other locations (providing a nucleus for electronic industries in the newly independent Baltic States). VEF developed the semi-electronic Kvant PBX. Kvant was plagued by design and production problems. It did not interconnect easily with the Soviet network. It was used only within bureaucratic administrations' private networks and developed outside of Minsviaz' own priorities. It was being adapted as a rural exchange. After eight years the switch could only handle 62 percent of its designed capacity. The first electronic automatic exchange was not introduced until 1986, and domestic manufacturers were still producing step-by-step switches as late as 1988.

Because of the variety of foreign suppliers and the increase in transmission capacity without modern switching equipment, the Soviet network was poorly interconnected. Among the major switches used were Alcatel's MT-20 (imported or built under license), the Finnish Nokia's EATS-200, the Czech ATS-K crossbar, the East German ATS-K, the Yugoslav Metaconta or 10C (licensed from old ITT technology), and Soviet-made Kvarts and Istok switches. The

Istok switch, a joint U.S.S.R.–G.D.R. effort, exemplified the problems of Soviet research and development efforts. The switch took ten years to develop and was stalled by software problems, lack of skilled technicians, and design flaws. One member of the Istok design team claimed the switch would never have been produced without the East German pressure to complete the project. In the end, the Soviet Union entirely depended on East German production by Robotron and Nachrichtentechnik. Kvarts, a semi-electronic switch designed for local or transit exchange, was also a joint design of VEF with the East German's Robotron and the Soviet Union's VEF and TsNIIS.

In 1990, Belgium's BTM Alcatel won a contract to supply almost $1 billion worth of System 12 digital switches, produced both in Belgium and through joint production with local companies. Siemens and GPT will also produce switching systems under joint venture agreements. In 1990, Minsviaz signed a memorandum of understanding with AT&T to explore cooperation on telecommunications services, equipment manufacturing, and R&D.

The Soviet Union helped develop fiber optics in the late 1960s, and it was used primarily for military applications. The network had only one long-distance fiber-optic line, running between Leningrad and Minsk and a few local fiber trunk lines (Gulyaev, 1990). One ambitious part of modernization was a $500 million trans-Siberian fiber optic line to be built by a Minsviaz and foreign consortium of US West, Japan's KDD, DBP Telekom, British Telecom, Italy's Societa Finanziaria Telefonica, Australia's OTC, and others. The goal, to provide domestic service and establish a high-capacity land-based link from Europe to Japan, was stalled by CoCom restrictions against the export of sensitive technology. Behind the American government's opposition was the intelligence community, which did not wish its eavesdropping ability curtailed by a shift of Soviet communications from radio-based transmission to fiber.

There were two major Minsviaz scientific research institutes, NIIR for radio and NsNIIS for network technology. R&D efforts also included design bureaus, research laboratories and higher educational institutes. The overall total of Minsviaz R&D personnel was 10,000. Other research institutions were outside Minsviaz and part of the Academy of Sciences of the Soviet Union (e.g., the institutes for information transfer, microelectronics, cybernetics, and television). Many of the research organizations were linked with each other and to Eastern Europe by the packet-switched network Academnet.

Research and development was the weak spot for Soviet telecommunications. Bureaucracy, aging administrators, an exodus of talented personnel, poor coordination, lack of direction, and low scientific productivity of several institutions have stalled innovation. These points of criticism were made public in 1987 by the deputy head of the Central Committee's department of transport and communications, I. F. Trofimov. The problems with R&D increased reliance on Eastern European suppliers. Given the changes in Eastern Europe, this source of supply will not be accessible in the future without hard-currency transactions.

Reforms

Under proposed legislation, the Russian Ministry of Communications would become more of a regulator and less of an operator, with responsibility over frequency allocations, equipment standards, and licensing service providers. Minsviaz would own the local, trunk, and international network through a holding company and license competitors for local service, maintaining a monopoly over international voice service. Coordination among the republics would be through a committee.

The R&D institutes are being reorganized, put on a self-financing basis, and given greater independence in their projects.

Joint ventures with foreign firms are encouraged. Research institutes may also operate as commercial enterprises and compete in services such as packet-switched networks with Minsviaz. The manufacturing firms formed a cartel named Telekom.

Given the magnitude of the investments and upgrade tasks, and the reorganization of the former Soviet Union into a new substructure of republics, no European telecommunications system has a more formidable challenge ahead in serving the transition to a high-technology economic system.

III

BATTLEFRONTS IN TELECOMMUNICATIONS POLICY

28

The International Organizations of Telecommunications

PTT Institutions

From the inception of early postal systems, communications were a highly international affair. The checkered map of central Europe usually permitted alternative postal routes and thus made intergovernmental agreements desirable. As postal administrations evolved throughout Europe, they prioritized the maintenance of stable international arrangements as a central policy concern. Rooted in this tradition, "integration" and "harmonization" achieved importance in the value system of PTTs beyond purely technical needs. They led to international organizations, one of whose important function was to shore up internationally the domestic arrangements and to anchor national monopolies in an international cartel arrangement. These international organizations worked very successfully to coordinate the old order. Not surprisingly, they were not particularly well-suited to be vehicles for reform. Given their traditional role, as well as their control by traditional PTTs, change was not initiated by the international organizations of telecommunications, but essentially outside and even despite them. Of course, the international organizations served useful functions as fora for discussion and as structures to channel change. But the main reforming countries were quite prepared to ignore the restrictiveness of the traditional international regime if necessary. They also began to activate international organizations associated with interests other than the PTTs, such as the Organization for Economic Cooperation and Development (OECD), the European Community (E.C.), and the General Agreement on Tariffs and Trade (GATT).

The International Telecommunication Union (ITU)

The oldest and most venerable of institutions among international organizations for telecommunications is the International Telecommunication Union (ITU), founded in 1865 by several European telegraph administrations. It is both an organization and a model for international collaboration in telecommunications. Its history traces back to 1850, when several German states created, through the Dresden Convention, the German-Austrian telegraph union as an extension of their earlier postal cooperation, in order to coordinate telegraph operations. A few years later, in 1855, several West European states set up their own telegraph collaboration. In 1865, a Europe-wide conference of these two groupings convened in Paris and established the International Telegraph Union (ITU). European members were joined by Egypt, Persia, British India, and the Netherlands' East Asian possessions.

The ITU was established as a purely intergovernmental organization, and despite its claim to primarily coordinate the technical aspects of telegraphy, it took implicitly political positions by not encouraging the participation of private telegraph firms. Thus, Britain's role was limited until the 1870s, when its telegraphs came under government control; similarly, some American telegraph firms or the private submarine cable firms were outside the ITU. Britain lobbied strongly to be included in the ITU meetings and for a while participated through its Indian colonial administration, which operated a governmental telegraph system. British interests became concerned that intergovernmental agreements that would be decided by the ITU without their participation would threaten Britain's dominant position in submarine cables. This was one argument advanced in favor of the nationalization of the domestic British telegraph system in 1870.

The Paris conference that established the ITU resulted in an international convention and a set of telegraph regulations. The ITU is arguably the first specialized international organization in any field, although that depends on the definition. In 1868 it was agreed to establish a permanent ITU secretariat, the International Bureau. Under the initiative of Heinrich von Stephan, the architect of Germany's Reichspost, the ITU adopted principles of international rates, first developed in the 1850 Dresden Convention and modeled after even earlier postal agreements.

The major European powers controlled the ITU. Not only were these countries at the forefront of telegraph technology and usage, but they had provided themselves voting membership through the colonial telegraph administrations of their overseas colonies. In 1925, France, Great Britain, Italy, and Portugal each had seven votes in the ITU.

Technical coordination was only one aspect of the ITU activities, and it turned out, in the early phase, not to be a particularly difficult one (Codding and Rutkowski, 1982). It was only later that technical standards issues became increasingly complex, leading to nonbinding standards known as "recommendations." Issues of international rate making (i.e., economic collaboration) were important from the beginning, and many ITU meetings were spent establishing rates, arguing over uniform pricing, and agreeing upon the charges for coded messages. An American observer to the 1875 International Telegraph Conference in St. Petersburg wrote critically, "The interest of the public who use the telegraph seemed to be entirely subordinated to the interest of the states and to the administrations: that is, to a fear lest any improvement (in the rate structure) might produce less revenue than is got at present, and lest it might throw more work on the telegraph bureau" (Codding and Rutkowski, 1982, p. 8).

The Telegraph Union gave little attention to the coordination of the emerging telephony. Until 1925, it was not even obligatory for the various telephone administrations to interconnect with other countries. Eventually, national telephone administrations led by the French PTT created a new body, the International Consultative Committee for Long Distance Telephony, initially outside of the ITU, to address telephone coordination issues.

Radio communications were also organizationally separate from the ITU; coordination began in 1903 at a conference convened by Germany. Here too technical issues coexisted with economic and political ones. Various countries tried to counter the market power in wireless communication by the Marconi Wireless Telegraph Company, which had instructed its radio operators to communicate only with those using Marconi equipment and to refuse all others. This was an economic and strategic threat to other countries' emerging wireless operations, manufacturing, and shipping. Germany had embarked on an ambitious naval build-up in rivalry with Britain, and, given the importance of radio communications for fleet operations, sought to break Marconi's power. Great Britain and Italy, both of which had Marconi's interests at heart, consequently boycotted the 1903 conference. The meeting established a protocol that provided rules of noninterference and interconnection. Another international convention was passed in 1906, again in Berlin, establishing the framework (still in existence today) of allocating radio bands to particular services to avoid intermixing. Frequencies could be used on a first-come basis, but notification had to be given. In 1912, the Marconi Company agreed to stop refusing communications with rival equipment. World War I put an end to collaborative arrangements. After the war, a 1920 conference drafted many of the principles upon which today's ITU operates. The most difficult issues, not surprisingly, dealt with a mechanism for frequency allocation and allotment; no agreement was reached. Parallel to these efforts, the emergence of private radio broadcasting led to a meeting in 1925, convened by the BBC, that created an international radio conference to deal with problems of interference. Eventually, at a joint meeting in Madrid in 1932, the International Telegraph Union and the loose International Radio Telegraph Conference were merged in 1934 and renamed the International Telecommunication Union.

Initially, the Swiss government staffed, financed, and managed the ITU's office in Berne. But as the ITU became a specialized diplomatic agency to the League of Nations (and later part of the United Nations), its secretariat was moved to Geneva and both its staff and financial support were internationalized. To induce the United States to join, the new ITU convention was kept general and flexible. A major meeting was held in Washington in 1927. The U.S.S.R. was precluded from attendance, because of opposition to its government. Thus, the alleged "nonpolitical" history of the ITU and U.S. adherence to such principles should not be exaggerated.

Until World War II, the United States maintained an attitude of benign neglect toward the ITU and its policies. It did not send government delegates or observers to the ITU (leaving this to private firms) and did not participate in the international consultative committees when they were formed in the 1920s.

It opposed the creation of the unified telecommunication ITU since this extended the potential for an international cartel (Rutkowski, 1982, p. 33). The United States participated more actively, but still reluctantly, in the international radio telegraph conferences, though it made clear its suspicions that they served to retard the development of radio. The exceptions in the U.S. attitude were the periods following the world wars, when it was more closely interested in creating stable international arrangements. For the United States to sign the telegraph regulations took until 1949, eighty-four years after the first set had been approved and only after major changes.

The postwar interest of the United States led to Atlantic City conferences in 1947 that reshaped international communications into structures that have endured until today. At the end of the meeting, the ITU framework was in place. In 1952, an International Frequency Registration Board (IFRB) was created as a body for the record-keeping of international frequency use and for dispute resolution. In subsequent years, membership increased dramatically with decolonization.

The ITU's system is complex. It includes four secretariats, a multinational Administrative Council, Plenipotentiary Conferences, World Administrative Radio Conferences, World Administrative Telegraph and Telephone Conferences, the IFRB, Regional Administrative Radio Conferences, Consultative Committees on Radio (CCIR) and on Telephone and Telegraph (CCITT), and droves of subcommittees and study groups. The ITU currently performs clearing house activities, coordinates standards and spectrum allocations, and provides technical assistance to developing countries. Despite the elaborate structure, or perhaps because of it, the pace of discussions, particularly in comparison with the rapid advance of technology, has been torpid for a long time, though there have been exceptions.

Private sector experts, particularly in the equipment industry, can participate in the Consultative Committees of the ITU. In the American case, a majority of committees were attended only by private-sector representatives.

The ITU was run in the 1980s by Richard Butler of Australia. Butler ably managed an unprecedented expansion of membership and scope of responsibilities and initiated reforms to move the organization from a federal to a more centralized structure. He was succeeded as secretary general by Pekka Tarjanne, a former physics professor, leader of Finland's Liberal party, and director general of the Finnish PTT. A merger of CCITT and CCIR was proposed but postponed. An independent Bureau for Telecommunications Development (BDT) was created with status equal to CCITT and CCIR, subsuming the existing Center for Telecommunications Development, strengthening recommendations made in 1982 in the so-called Maitland Report, "The Missing Link" (Butler, 1989). Since assuming his post, Tarjanne has advocated greater regional cooperation and a lessening of state control over telecommunications for economic and administrative reasons.

A majority of ITU members in the 1980s were against any form of liberalization. In this matter, the European PTTs until recently saw eye to eye with virtually all developing countries and with the Soviet bloc. Hence, for the liberalization-minded countries, the ITU was a basically uncongenial body in which they are automatically a tiny minority. Nevertheless, the victories of the traditionalist majority are hollow if the minority, consisting of important high-technology countries such as the United States, the United Kingdom, Japan, and increasingly continental Europe, go their own way and are joined by some developing countries. Partly in consequence, the ITU began to slowly change its organization in the 1980s (Drake, 1989). For example, it strengthened the participation of private telecommunications providers, and scheduled reform-oriented conferences.

The ITU and its sister PTT organization, the Universal Postal Union (UPU), conduct most of their affairs in closed meetings, in contrast with most international organizations, including the United Nations and the Security Council (Codding, 1984). Between 1947 and 1965 the ITU was unenthusiastically open to the press. At the 1958 meeting in Geneva, for example, the media were excluded with the argument that the press, as a customer of telecommunications, should not witness decisions that affect their business. This argument was maintained in the 1980s. Its weakness is evident if one considers that in most CCITT and CCIR committee meetings, private manufacturers, who often have an enormous stake in the recommendations, participate officially and actively.

The CCITT

Of particular importance in the telecommunications field is the Consultative Committee on International Telegraph and Telephone. The CCITT's predecessor was established at the initiative of Britain and France subsequent to a Paris meeting in 1923. In its first years it mainly concerned itself with the establishment of desirable characteristics for long-distance international telephone lines. In 1924, the organization was given the name of International Consultative Committee on Long-Distance Telephone Communications, and it established a permanent secretariat in Paris. Later it was renamed CCIT (International Consultative Committee on Telephone), which became in 1956 the CCITT. It was largely separate from the ITU for almost a quarter century. The organizations, with the International Consultative Committee on Radio (CCIR), were brought under the umbrella of the ITU in 1949 subsequent to its 1947 Atlantic City meeting. The technical committees of the CCIR and the International Broadcasting Union were united at that time.

The CCITT operates through administrations, operating agencies, non-common carrier enterprises, and international organizations (A. Rutkowski, 1990, communication). Working groups include representatives of governments and private operating firms. After 1927 it also operated a laboratory under the name of the Telephonometric Laboratory. The CCITT issues only recommendations and has no enforcement power. It does not function as a treaty organization with binding resolutions. Though developing countries and new electronics firms have become more active, developed countries and established manufacturers still dominate the discussion. Government representatives as well as representatives of fifty-five recognized private companies, several regional telecommunications organizations, and other institutions also participate in the study groups. Private companies with committee representation must contribute financially to the cost of the meetings; members of scientific institutions also often participate (Scherer, 1985).

The role of the CCITT is to develop operational and technical standards and to harmonize international telecommunications tariff issues. Its expert groups draft recommendations that are submitted for adoption by the CCITT Plenary Assemblies held every four years. At the Assembly held in Spain in 1984, almost 650 recommendations or amendments were submitted for approval. With growing numbers of equipment firms, applications, and standards committees, the CCITT's Book of Recommendations grew from 5,000 to 21,000 pages in the past decade. This forced organizational change in 1988: an accelerated approval procedure, consolidated study groups, and new internal organization. This allowed CCITT to deal more expeditiously with standards issues where its role was being reduced by a regionalization, taking place through Bellcore and American standards bodies, ETSI in Europe, the Technical Telecommunications Committee (TTC) in Japan, and other standards bodies, including the International Organization for Standardization (ISO).

A major conference (WATTC-88) was held in Melbourne, Australia, to deal with new telecommunications services such as enhanced or value-added services, with the notion of protecting them from excessive regulation. It reached an agreement on integrating telephone and telegraph service under the International Telecommunication Regulations (Drake, 1988; Codacovi, 1989). However, difficult problems of accounting rates and tariffs were left unresolved.

The CCITT's policy recommendations can clash not only with liberalization policies of individual countries, but also with other standards bodies, and with other international bodies and agreements. The European Community's Treaty of Rome provides for the elimination of restrictions in trade of goods and services among European countries. In the 1970s, so-called telex bureaus emerged in Britain that would route telex messages from continental Europe to North America through London at a considerably cheaper rate than that charged for direct service by the European countries' PTTs. CCITT recommendations, however, prohibit such third-country traffic, and the PTTs attempted to eliminate such telex bureaus by invoking the rules. But as the chapter on U.K. telecommunications described, the telex bureaus fought back and sued under the EEC's Treaty of Rome, and eventually won a resounding victory before the European Commission and the European High Court (*Official Journal,* 1982).

In 1992, CCITT's head Theodor Irmer proposed to transform it into a private non-governmental organization.

Intelsat

Intelsat is the international organization providing international civilian satellite communications. By the terms of the Intelsat Agreement entered into by member states, it has exclusivity over these services, though this is under dispute.

Intelsat was formed in 1964 largely at the initiative of the United States, and is headquartered in Washington, D.C. At the time, the United States was still firmly in the camp of monopoly; Intelsat is a reflection of the U.S. desire to embed its own technical lead in satellites and launchers in an international regime of coordinated monopoly, subject to a weighted voting that benefits industrialized countries. Intelsat operates through an Assembly of Parties (representatives of government members to the agreement), which usually meets every two years to discuss long-term issues. There are also Signatories' Meetings in which the designated telecommunications entities are represented. A board of governors, whose members are representatives of the larger users and regional groups, deals with budget matters, procurement, and policy issues. Intelsat business itself is conducted by its executive organ, which is headed by a director general and employs about 600 people.

Intelsat satellites have evolved seven full and two half generations. The first Intelsat satellite was Early Bird in 1965, with Hughes as the private contractor. Its capacity could accommodate up to 240 telephone circuits or one TV channel. Design life was a brief eighteen months, though it operated satisfactorily twice as long. In 1967 and 1968 the Intelsat II and III generations were launched, produced by Hughes and TRW. Intelsat III had a capacity of 1500 circuits or four TV channels. Multipoint communications were possible, and design lifetime was now five years. In 1971, the Intelsat IV generation was put aloft, produced again by Hughes, and providing 4000 circuits. The satellite antenna system was much more advanced and permitted spot beams and other features. In 1975, the Intelsat IV-A satellite generation expanded capacity to 6000 two-way circuits. Five years later, the first Intelsat V was launched with Ford Aerospace as the prime contractor. Capacity doubled to 12,000 two-way telephone circuits and two TV channels. The system was further improved in 1985 with Intelsat V-A/B to 15,000 circuits and a variety of antennas. Hughes' Intelsat VI was launched in 1986, with a capacity of 30,000 circuits and three TV channels, using a variety of polarizations that make multiple usage possible. The next generation, Intelsat VII, is ready for the 90s. Most of these satellites are physically quite large. Intelsat VI measures 6.4 meters high and 3.6 meters wide. These are very heavy pieces of equipment, densely packed with high-performance electronics, and they are correspondingly expensive.

Critics contend that Intelsat created an overcapacity in order to reduce incentives for others to enter. It also operates on very-low-power systems, which require an expensive earth station segment that makes usage by smaller parties other than the national PTT's less desirable. This also makes it expensive for smaller countries with low traffic density to participate (Cowhey and Aronson, 1985).

Intelsat's director general in the beginning of the 1980s was Richard Colino, an American lawyer. In 1986, it was discovered that Colino and a close associate had arranged a real estate transaction in which they personally benefitted. Colino was dismissed from his position and later convicted by an American criminal court and sentenced to six years in prison. He was succeeded by Dean Burch, former chairman of the American FCC and an insider in Republican politics since 1964, when he was the campaign manager for Barry Goldwater's conservative candidacy. Burch died in 1991. In 1990, Intelsat was criticized by competing operators, who claimed it had set monopoly prices and refused to use the most cost-effective technology. PanAmSat filed a $1.5 billion lawsuit against Comsat, charging anticompetitive behavior.

Faced with added capacity and dropping prices, Intelsat's revenues stagnated in 1989 and dropped almost by 20 percent in 1990. Jolted, this organization of (largely) government organizations began to consider selling 49 percent of its shares to the public, and its new head Irving Goldstein sought renegotiation on launch contracts.

Policy issues involving Intelsat are discussed in greater detail in the chapter on international communications and new entrants, both satellites and fiber cables.

CEPT

On the European level, the Conference of European Postal and Telecommunications Administrations (CEPT) provides PTT coordination. CEPT was established in 1959 as the organization representing the interests of European PTTs and included the telecommunications administrations from the twenty-five West European countries, Hungary, and Yugoslavia. Other Eastern European countries were to join after 1990. It operates by annual plenary meetings and committees that are responsible for specific issues, such as transatlantic telecommunication, harmonization of telecommunications, commercial action, data transmission, and satellites (Quander, 1982). Since it synthesized the views of the powerful European PTTs that subsequently dominate worldwide CCITT proceedings, CEPT wielded substantial power. CEPT was characterized by an insider *modus operandi* that reinforced its image as a very conservative organization, concerned with enforcing a European telecommunications cartel. In theory, CEPT made only recommendations. In practice, however, these proposals, which are often quite detailed in the areas of technology, were mostly followed (Le Boucher, 1984).

CEPT meetings too were closed to the press, and its working papers unavailable to the public. It argued that public meetings would politicize expert bodies, reduce the free exchange of opinions, and lead to distorted reporting (Scherer, 1985). Even industry participation in CEPT deliberations was exclusive. For example, the Bundespost coordinated its position on issues pending in CEPT within a German committee, whose meetings until 1983 included only the classic telecommunications equipment industry. It took repeated attempts for the Office and Information Technology group of the German Industry Association to be included in the body also.

In 1984, CEPT adopted some measures to set technical norms and to open the national European markets. These standards, established by a commission, would gradually become obligatory. But the U.S. complained that PTT control of CEPT foreclosed industry involvement, especially by foreign firms, in the standards-setting process (Dougan, 1987).

In 1990, under pressure from the European Commission and telecommunications users, CEPT's Telecommunication Commission accepted the need to separate network regulation from network operation. A new CEPT regulatory committee sets policies relating to all activities apart from the network agreements among its member PTOs. CEPT also agreed to shed some of its secrecy. CEPT was also challenged in its economic coordination role. When it recommended a tariff structure for leased lines for large users that opt for digital technology that would reaquire a 30 percent access charge for connection to the public network or carriage of third-party traffic, the European Commission attacked the arrangement.

In 1989, the E.C.'s directorate for competition policy (DG IV) began an inquiry into the legality of CEPT tariff recommendations. It found the CEPT tariff plans to be cartel actions under Article 85 of the Treaty of Rome. Consequently, CEPT withdrew its recommendations in 1990.

Following the tariff debate and the E.C.'s creation of the European standards body ETSI that was outside CEPT, CEPT instituted a set of reforms, transferred most of its standards activity to ETSI, created a Commercial Action Committee to deal with user demands, and reorganized its spectrum management division. Most CEPT member organizations formed the European Telecommunication Network Operators group (ETNO) as a carrier association to represent their interests. They also formed the European Institute for Research and Strategy Studies in Communication (Eurescon). This institute, located in Heidelberg, Germany, has similar functions as Bellcore in the United States.

Eutelsat

Eutelsat was created in 1977 with an objective of creating and operating a European system of satellite telecommunications. The organization is headquartered in Paris. It includes an Assembly of Signatories, which sets general policy and objectives for the organization and addresses questions related to external organizations and the division of markets. Another agency, the European Space Agency, deals mainly with the coordination of satellite development. It places satellites in orbit for Eutelsat.

Although established for telecommunications, Eutelsat's main business became the transmission of television programs to cable networks and national broadcasters. In 1990, telephony and business telecommunications accounted for a quarter of revenues, and television broadcasting for the rest.

The newer satellite generation, Eutelsat II, in operation after 1990, has 60 percent more communications capacity than the Eutelsat I series. It has sixteen television transponders at 50 watts of power. Eutelsat II is built by a consortium of Aerospatiale and Alcatel Espace, of France; Aeritalia, of Italy; CASA, of Spain; Germany's MBB; and Sweden's Ericsson. Eutelsat was shaken in 1991 by the E.C. Commission's intention to seek an "open skies" policy that would free users to interconnect into other satellite systems and deal with Eutelsat directly rather than through a PTT.

International Institutions Outside the PTTs

The emergence of telecommunications policy discussion in other international organizations such as the European Community and the OECD is a reaction to the often narrow perspective of the PTTs in their own international bodies, ITU, CCITT, CEPT, Intelsat, and Eutelsat. It is an extension to the international level of domestic conflicts that exist in many advanced countries between the PTTs, on the one hand, and the ministries of economics or industry and of antimonopoly agencies, on the other. Generally speaking, the ministries of economics or industry see telecommunications issues in the broader context of high-technology development and national competitiveness of the information sector.

The Organization for Economic Cooperation and Development (OECD) has displayed particular initiative on matters of information policy, where it took a role in identifying and discussing the issue of transborder data flows, privacy, and national sovereignty. It has also issued several influential reports discussing the problems of national compartmentalization of telecommunications, and comparing services, rates, and performance in various countries. The OECD's important role is referred to in other parts of this book.

Another international body into which telecommunications issues have spilled is the General Agreement on Tariffs and Trade (GATT). GATT goes back to 1947 attempts to re-energize world trade after World War II and avoid protectionism and bilateralism. The new framework of fairly open trade was remarkably successful. However, it applied only to commodities, and not to services. In 1986 GATT had only two full-time professionals dealing with services. Starting in the 1970s, several major U.S. companies such as insurance and tourism firms began to advocate inclusion, and to ally themselves with the weakening free-trade coalition that included, among others, retailers and farmers. Telecommunications and information firms joined, too, but construction and shipping companies were opposed to foreign competition. Other countries resisted, but did not wish to provoke retaliatory restrictions of their nonservice exports into the large American market. In 1980, the U.S. demanded GATT treatment for services. This was rebuffed in 1982, primarily due to Third World opposition. In time, Great Britain, Japan, Canada, and Sweden supported a services trade negotiation but continental European countries were mostly opposed. France eventually began to support the negotiations, and GATT decided in its 1986 Punta del Este meeting to proceed. When telecommunications were introduced into the topics under negotiations in the "Uruguay round," traditional international organizations such as the CCITT were unenthusiastic, viewing it as either a trespass by free-marketeers and American business interests, or at least, the application of trade policy to what should be sovereign regulatory policy. Issues for negotiation were reciprocal market access; national treatment; most favored nation treatment; right of establishment; access to local distribution; competition and transaction with government monopolies; free flows of information; and nondiscriminatory technical standards and pricing policies (Aronson and Cowhey, 1988). Perhaps the most important issue was the interconnection of networks across frontiers (*Transnational Data and Communications Report,* May 1988, pp. 18–22; Drake, 1988).

Four years of negotiations followed. A broad but vague consensus was reached on VAN services, which were to be granted access to the public network, though with considerable national discretion, in a cost-based, transparent, fair, and unrestricted fashion. But no similar consensus was reached for basic services and facilities. Here, the original U.S. position had been pro-liberalization. However, U.S. international carriers, large user organizations, and even the federation of consumer organizations began to oppose that position and the policy of giving countries the ability to exempt certain services. The groups lobbied instead for bilateral agreements, fearing asymmetric access opportunities due to the more deregulated U.S. market, as well as concessions in telecommunications in favor of other industries. AT&T in particular concluded that "national treatment" in a restrictive country would not give it any opportunities, in contrast to foreign countries which would be able to operate freely in the United States.

This view complicated the American bargaining position, which had always been hampered by vague linkages to financial and human services that had not been carefully thought through. The U.S. position, in effect, switched to a priority of regulatory policy in telecommunications (i.e., national liberalizations) in preference to trade policy and bilateral trade agreements.

As tortured as the progress in the telecommunications services basket was, it was actually the most developed among the GATT service trade negotiations. Agreements on tourism, professional services, construction, finance, and banking and transportation were far behind telecommunications.

Telecommunications was part of a much larger international trade package, which included textiles, patents and copyrights, and agriculture, among others. The package collapsed in 1990, largely due to disputes over European agricultural subsidies.

Other Standards Setting Bodies

The International Organization for Standardization (ISO), whose Committee 79 sets standards for data-processing systems, computers, and office automation, is a particularly important organization. Another international standards body is the International Electrotechnical Commission (IEC), joined with the ISO, which also deals with information technology equipment. European standards coordination also takes place in the Comité Européen de Normalisation (CEN) and the European Committee for Electronic Technology Norms (CENELEC). CEN/CENELEC is mostly geared toward development of OSI protocols. Two other OSI standards groups are SPAG (Standards Promotion and Applications Group), a consortium of major European electronics firms, and EWOS, the

European Workshop for Open Systems. Another standards group, the European Computer Manufacturers Association (ECMA), was founded in 1961 with the participation of US and European firms. ECMA, which specializes in private networks, works more quickly than its bureaucratic cousins and frequently submits its reports to CCITT and ISO for adoption (Gibbons, 1989a).

29

Brussels Takes On the Traditional System

Until recently, telecommunications matters were outside the jurisdiction of the European Community and its commission. The Commission's first attempt in the 1960s to play a role in the field was unsuccessful. In 1978, Commissioner Count Davignon introduced a telematics initiative at the EC summit meeting in Dublin. There was little activity on this issue until 1983, when the commission accepted recommendations that it play a major role in the high-technology and information industries. It concluded that the nationally protected environment that fragmented European telecommunications was an important factor in Europe's weak competitive position relative to the United States and Japan. This led to decisions that initiated the ESPRIT high-tech technology development program. Although ESPRIT excluded hard-core telecommunications, it laid the foundations for the RACE program that the commission established in 1985 specifically for telecommunications. The EUREKA program, another Europe-wide support program, also grew from these beginnings. Davignon wanted to go considerably further and advocated a European telecommunications agency to enhance equipment production and service supply.

The European Commission's growing role in telecommunications followed two paths that can easily be at tension with each other: antimonopoly policy and industrial policy. The antimonopoly actions, in addition to the repeatedly mentioned British telex case, which involved the abuse of BT's dominant position by imposing restrictions on telex message-forwarding agencies, also soon included challenges to the following: the Bundespost's intent to extend its monopoly to cordless telephones; the extension of the Luxembourg broadcasters to telemarketing into neighboring markets; the Bundespost's exclusive marketing and ownership of computer modems; the extension of the Belgian RTT monopoly to include medium-sized PBXs; excessively long-term leasing contracts for telephone equipment; and IBM's extension of its Systems Network Architecture for interconnecting computers and other equipment (requiring it to publish formats and protocols) (CEC, 1986), the PTTs' joint Managed Data Network Services project, and the price cartel in international telephone rates and in leased line tariff principles.

An example of the E.C.'s successful action involved the pricing of international lines leased to SWIFT, the international interbank electronic transfer network. CEPT had repeatedly changed the rules applied to SWIFT with the aim of recouping revenue lost to telex service. SWIFT, not a meek organization itself, lodged a complaint with the commission charging a price cartel and abuse of individual and collective dominance. Negotiations then took place that ultimately resulted in the lowering of its rates.

Another case was a 1986 complaint by the French DGT against the German Bundespost. The DGT charged the Bundespost with restraint of marketing when it did not accept the French Minitel videotex terminal, preferring to keep the distribution of more integrated models for itself (Schulte-Braucks, 1986).

In 1984, the member states of the European Community agreed on the details of a European telecommunications technology policy. The E.C. proposals included the following: definition of medium- and long-term European policy objectives; a new forum for European telecommunications issues; collaborative European technological projects; common equipment interconnection standards; a common European front towards outsiders; opening of national European markets to unbiased procurement from other European countries; and collaboration in the development of new transnational services, such as ISDN, broadband networks, and satellites.

France was initially active in pushing for a joint European telecommunications policy. Given its own high standard of telecommunications technology within Europe, it saw itself as a potential beneficiary. The French PTT minister Louis Mexandeau argued for a reciprocal and open European Community market, which could also include the non-European Community members of CEPT. His plan specified a delay in the reciprocal opening of the market with the United States, Canada, and Japan.

In 1987, eleven out of the twelve E.C. countries (with the exception of Greece) were separately and actively reassessing their telecommunications policies. Assuming a responsibility for preventing diverging paths and seeking to accelerate the process, the commission issued a Green Paper aimed at "achieving maximum synergy between current developments and debates within the Member States" and "to launch a debate" (CEC, 1987, p. 2). The paper's recommendations included a phased opening of competition in the terminal equipment market. This was, in part, merely an acknowledgment of gray-market liberalization. Accordingly, the paper sought mutual recognition of type approvals for terminal equipment and mutual opening of procurement contracts. Most importantly, the paper asserted unequivocally that the (liberal) competition rules of the Treaty of Rome apply to telecommunications, in particular where PTTs engage in commercial practices rather than basic 'reserved' services. It called for the creation of a European telecommunications standard body to set common standards.

The paper's second recommendation aimed at the unrestricted provision of competitive (in particular nonvoice) services both within and among member states, including an obligation for PTTs to provide access to transfrontier value-added networks. This "open network provision" would permit such a network, once licensed in one country, to operate throughout Europe. Such liberalization would require agreement on definitions, termination points, tariff principles, and so on.

The paper further recommended a clear separation of the regulatory and operational functions of telecommunications administrations, which "cannot continue to be both regulator and market participant (i.e., referee and player)" (CEC, 1987, p. 17). It also warned of cross-subsidization of competitive activities and cautioned against excessive restrictiveness toward the use of private lines. Regulatory "methods must be limited to a legitimate level of protection of financial viability and must not represent the abuse of a dominant position." It observed that charges for leased lines among member countries "show in some cases wide and unexplained divergences."

The PTTs' dominance over network infrastructure and over basic services was accepted in the commission's Green Paper. However, the document conveyed the message that the PTTs' efforts at protecting their turf were counterproductive to European high-technology capability and economic competitiveness and that change ought to be encouraged. Instead of letting inter-European harmonization be used defensively as in the past, the commission now wanted to initiate the reverse and let supranational coordination create a force for change. Thus, the Green Paper was an important step, despite the modest scope of its proposals. It marked a signal that the days in which PTTs defined the public interest in telecommunications were drawing to a close.

As the European Community approached 1992, the date for widespread harmonization, the role of the commission in setting telecommunications policy grew increasingly contentious. The commission repeatedly used Article 90 of the Treaty of Rome, which permits the bypassing of national governments (i.e., of PTT authority). In 1988, Italy, Germany, and Belgium joined France in unsuccessfully filing suit against the commission in the European Court of Justice over the use of this article in telecommunications. But an unrepentant commission kept using Article 90 to extend its guidelines for open competition in terminal equipment markets to telecommunications service provision (CEC, 1988). It also presented plans for open network provision, including harmonization of tariffs, network interconnection, technical standards, quality targets, common numbering, and a common ISDN policy. It was increasingly evolving into a European regulatory agency.

In 1988, the commission, in the 'bloodless coup' of its Equipment Directive, took standards setting authority from CEPT's notoriously slow Technical Recommendations Applications Committee (TRAC). ETSI, the European Telecommunications Standards Institute, was established in Sophia Antipolis, near Cannes in France. PTTs' users and manufacturers are included in ETSI's General and Technical Assemblies. Over 135 organizations had joined ETSI by 1990 (Besen, 1990).

The commission also protested the activities of non-E.C. organizations. It won the elimination of two CEPT tariff plans that allowed a 30 percent access charge on international leased lines, on the grounds that it amounted to price-fixing. That, on top of the creation of ETSI, significantly reduced the regulatory and cartel powers of CEPT.

The commission's approach to liberalization of terminal equipment by litigation was supplemented by gradual Directives for equipment and services. In 1988 it required first telephone sets to be liberalized by June 30, 1990. But when that date arrived, monopoly control over modems and telex terminals still existed in Spain and Belgium, which also joined Ireland, Greece, and Italy in retaining PTT monopoly rights to first sets. Denmark's PBX market was closed, and France was accused of delaying type approvals for foreign companies (Schenker, 1990). The commission challenged Belgium's and Spain's equipment rules. It also challenged cartel-like coordination of PTTs for private network services.

In 1989, the European Community reached agreement over data services, after France along with other southern E.C. countries had sought to block data service competition by requiring national licensing. National licensing conditions were retained, but they became subject to approval by the commission. To assist VAN access, the commission passed open network provision (ONP) guidelines but retained the power to set mandatory standards (ITU, 1990).[1]

In 1992, the commission even edged toward establishing general tariff principles, including price caps, acceptance of discounts to large users and the needy, and a common stance on international settlements reform. And it proposed a European licensing and regulatory agency—the Community Telecommunications Committee—based on national authorities.

Development Programs: ESPRIT, RACE, EUREKA

The second type of policy pursued by the European Community was to encourage technology development. Several joint projects were initiated. In addressing domestic protections, the commission argued that the Common Market represents 30 percent of the world market for information technologies but that it produces only 15 percent of such products. The European Strategic Program of Research and Development in Information Technology (ESPRIT) whose goal was to triple the E.C.'s share in the world market by 1990, was initiated to alleviate this imbalance.

ESPRIT was established in 1984, seeking to promote cooperation between European enterprises, research institutes, and universities. The total budget for the first four years was $1.2 billion. A report of the French Senate delegation for the European Communities noted, somewhat breathlessly, that, ''The program is a chance—perhaps the last—for the countries of Europe to rejoin the pack at the head of the industrial nations in new technologies, and to therefore maintain technological autonomy . . .'' (*TDR*, 1985, p. 49). Major European manufacturing companies, including Bull, CGE, Thomson, ICL, Plessey, GEC, Siemens, Nixdorf, AEG, Philips, and Olivetti supported ESPRIT, hoping for its largesse.

In its first year, ESPRIT selected 90 projects out of 441 proposals, matching industry financing with equal subsidies for projects joining firms from at least two E.C. countries. Although small companies and universities gained, the prime beneficiaries were the established large electronics firms.

ESPRIT has five main research themes: microelectronics, software, advanced information processing, office electronics, and integrated computerized design and production. Biotechnology, nuclear energy, and processing of radioactive wastes were added later. Because of various turf-battles, telecommunications policy was conspicuously missing, except indirectly through components and applications.

To deal with this absence, the European Commission established the Research and Development in Advanced Communications Technologies for Europe (RACE) program to target telecommunications issues. The program's research priorities are very-high-speed integrated circuits; high-complexity integrated circuits; broadband switching; fiber-optic components; components for long-distance, high-power links; specialized communications software; and large format, flat-screen display technology (Télédiffusion de France, 1985).

A major goal for RACE is to develop a European integrated broadband communications network (IBN) by 1995. Given its planned and periodically uncertain budget, only a relatively minor amount could be spent at first on development. In its initial phase, RACE defined a European model of IBN and provided the necessary equipment and cooperation methods among different firms and countries. The main phase, from 1986 onward, includes field trials (systems), technology development (technology), and standardization (integration) undertaken in integrated broadband technology to provide a "framework for subsequent competitive product development" (CEC, 1987). The commission contributed $500 million.

In 1990, the European Commission considered a plan to accelerate RACE and achieve pan-European broadband communications as early as 1993. Under the three-phase plan, broadband "islands" would be linked by existing 140 Mbps fiber optic lines. By 1994, the system would connect about 100 companies. Starting in 1996, fiber-optic cable would bring residential subscribers into the broadband network.

EUREKA, the European Research Coordination Agency, is a third joint European development program and is based on an initiative proposed by French President Mitterrand. EUREKA concentrates on six broad scientific areas: optronics, high-speed microelectronics, large computers, artificial intelligence, high-power laser and particle beams, and new materials.

For each of these areas, a management committee is made up of members from governments, industry, and research institutes. Financing is shared by the national governments and the firms. EUREKA's goal was defined as the development and potential manufacture of marketable products, with an eye toward the perceived major European weakness—not research, but its translation into successful products. EUREKA is not specifically a project of the European Community. Non-E.C. nations also participate in the program.

EUREKA was stressed as the European and civilian alternative to the American militarized research effort. Skeptics like *The Economist* described EU-REKA as ''[promising] to take more money from taxpayers to bribe rich European companies to do the sort of R&D they should be doing anyway if they want to stay in business.''

Another program, the Special Telecommunications Action for Regional Development (STAR), began in 1988 to assist development of telecommunications services in less-developed E.C. nations, primarily Portugal, Greece, Ireland, Spain, and southern Italy (Lalor, 1987). The JESSI program (Joint European Submicron Silicon Initiative) was developed to provide $4 billion in financing for chip makers.

Data Base Development

The distinctions between organizations that coordinate policies and those establishing joint operations is a fluid one. Euronet and DIANE are in the latter category. Euronet, a packet-switched data transmission network, was run primarily for E.C. countries by the European PTTs. Its main purpose is to provide international on-line database access, specifically to DIANE (Direct Access Information Network for Europe).

Euronet was decided upon in 1971, and it was set up by 1979. To remove locational advantages, the Euronet tariff structure was distance-independent. Total cost to the European Community was approximately $25 million, about two-thirds of the required budget. The PTT administrations contributed a smaller amount (CEC, 1982). Once the system was operational, the European Community terminated its financial involvement in the project.

The Euronet-DIANE system's role was multifold. First, the projects aimed to establish a European Community-based public data network specifically for on-line information retrieval. Not only would this make intra-European flows of information easier, but it would encourage the use of information by European scientists and business firms and government institutions. Second, it sought to establish standards that would permit the interaction of users and multiple databases within Europe by creating similar database standards, switching principles, and a unified command language. In this respect, the network was a success. Third, Euronet aimed to establish and promote the concept of databases, to create a Europe-wide market for them, and to encourage the setting up of host computers for their use.

The European Community's statistical office also established the CRONOS data bank, which includes economic data from various countries. Another inter-European information project is INSIS (Inter-Institutional Integrated Services Information Systems), which aimed to provide information links between institutions of the European community and its member states (Van Rosenthal, 1983). The E.C. also ventured into the electronic publishing field, subsidizing a number of experiments by a consortium of thirty-five publishers, software manufacturers, and data processing firms. And a $130 million program to develop information services was launched, as well as a program to fund personal computer acquisitions in less developed regions of Europe.

Space Development

In 1975, eleven European countries created the European Space Agency (ESA). Its origins began with European efforts to catch up with the American and Soviet space programs. In 1960, the European Preparatory Commission for Space (COPERS) was established, and in 1964, the conventions for the European Space Vehicle Launcher Development Organization (ELDO) and the European Space Research Organization (ESRO) were signed. These organizations were forerunners of ESA (ESA, 1984).[2] ELDO developed a European booster using British, French, and German rockets as stages and launched them from Woomera, Australia. Three European scientific satellites were developed and launched—by American rockets—in 1968.

ESA began operations in 1975, when eleven European countries signed its convention. It moved into the development of weather forecasting and telecommunications satellites, and in 1985 launched a mission to explore Halley's comet. Meteorological satellites were first launched in 1981 and operated by the European Meteorological Satellite Organization (EUMETSAT), established in 1983. In 1983, the American space shuttle launched Spacelab, the European space laboratory, which carried the first ESA astronaut into space.

The Ariane space launcher program was started in 1973. In 1979, the first successful test flight was completed, followed by consecutively more powerful Ariane generations. Ariane IV can lift 4 tons into a stationary orbit. Technical responsibility for the development of the launcher lies with CNEE, the Centre National d'Etudes Espace. The firm Aerospatiale coordinates its systems integration. Arianspace operates commercial launches, and competes with NASA for customers in the launching of telecommunications satellites. NASA's space shuttle requires launch to a low orbit in a manned vehicle, from where a second launch is undertaken to reach the geostationary orbit. In that second boost, a number of problems occurred. Both organizations charge each other with unfair competition by subsidized launches, and it is difficult to determine what the "economic" cost is, particularly in a multipurpose mission such as a manned space shuttle flight.

In 1983, the Ariane rocket launched the first European Communications Satellite (ECS). The ECS system, in turn, is operated by Eutelsat, the satellite organization of the European PTTs. A new generation of European satellites was approved in 1984 under the name of Apollo.

Within Europe, some of the larger countries felt reluctant to share their technology and its application with other countries. For example, France and Germany did not develop broadcast-strength satellites through ESA, but instead collaborated and produced them (joined later by Sweden).

30
Telecommunications Policy as Industrial Policy

Convergence?

It is possible to view international telecommunications as merely a hodgepodge of national systems, each reflecting its society's history and economics, and each happily self-contained except for collaboration on technical issues. It is equally possible to see national developments as variations on a single technology theme, inexorably driven by an underlying technological determinism, such as the convergence of telecommunications and computers. Or one can argue, as this book does, that common and often non-technical dynamics are changing the institutions of telecommunications: On the demand side, the sharing coalition of network users is breaking down, whereas on the supply side, the coalition in support of the monopoly system is eroding. For a long time the traditional arrangement was remarkably stable, successful, and undisputed. For a number of years, however, it has been subject to forces of disintegration. Although it was at first possible to dismiss change as the policy initiatives of an economically conservative America, later events in Britain, Japan, the Netherlands, and developing countries such as Pakistan and Malaysia, and even a mainstay of the traditional system such as Germany, suggest a broader trend.

The question of convergence in economic systems has been extensively discussed in reference to the development paths of Western and socialist countries. One argument for predicting convergence was that similarities in basic economic processes, in particular the prerequisites of large scale manufacturing, must lead to fundamentally similar structures: large production organizations, centralized planning, and large social programs (Wiles, 1960). The culture, ideology, and technology of industrialized societies may differ in early stages of their development. But industrialization, it is asserted, is a standardizing force that creates common institutional arrangements.

This view goes back to Marx and Engels, who interpreted society and technology as different aspects of the same process of social production, or with certain social and institutional inevitabilities. In the United States, Thorsten Veblen saw as one of the central tensions in modern economic society the interaction of the market system with dominant engineering and science. Similarly, many dominant European intellectuals believe that "technique has become autonomous; it has fashioned an omnivorous world which obeys its own laws and which has renounced all tradition" (Ellul, 1964, p. 14).

Western Europe and the United States are of course diverse in their economic institutions, as are European countries among themselves. But if one looks at the first derivative—the change—rather than at the absolute, the United States and Europe exhibited roughly similar trends for more than half a century. After a relatively free-wheeling 1920s, the interventionist role of the state increased considerably in the 1930s on both sides of the Atlantic under the effect of the Great Depression. World War II led to a still increased governmental role. In the 1950s, Europeans and Americans pursued an essentially conservative pro-business policy in economic development, coupled with adherence to the welfare state programs of the 1930s and late 1940s. Central to the economic system of the postwar years was reliance on the large business corporation. In the 1960s, more liberal or social democratic trends emerged on both sides of the Atlantic, followed by a tumultuous period of internal unrest.

In the mid-1970s, however, the economic theories of the Chicago School—a noninterventionist philosophy—became influential among economists and provided the economic legitimization of a policy that called for a reduced governmental role. During that period and not unrelated, American economic development shifted from the traditional centers of production, primarily in the northeast, to the west and south. The new firms responsible for the shift were smaller or medium-sized, frequently run by entrepreneurs rather than by corporate bureaucracies, and hostile to unionization. Meanwhile, the American government had been substantially discredited by the disasters of Vietnam, Watergate, inflation, and social problems despite the reform programs of the 1960s. These interacting forces contributed to America's move toward an increasing withdrawal of the state from economic control.

In Europe, the state had not squandered public trust to the same extent. European intellectuals were not moving generally to the right as in America, though there were increasingly exceptions. European societies were comfortable with large bureaucratized firms; a pro-competitive policy had genuine support only from small liberal parties of the center. A further stabilizing force was environmentalism. "Green" parties called for strict governmental regulation and specifically advocated control over technology-driven change.

In continental Europe, corporatism as an ideology is palatable both to the political right and left. Accordingly, in Europe the state has frequently acted to encourage consolidation in order to make national industry viable in world competition. In the United States however, antitrust policy, rooted in anti-bigness populism, was important for a century, even though its enforcement had its ups and downs.

Thus, the 1980s witnessed a marked divergence of the paths of European and American high technology development: In Europe, large firms were more important than ever; in the United States, the giants were attacked by small competitors and challenged by various take-over financiers, corporate empire-builders, and government. The telecommunications and information sector provides a good illustration for this divergence. In the same decade that AT&T's power declined, Silicon Valley was in ascendancy.

In Europe, economic growth became a major concern to governments and began to affect telecommunications policy. In the decade from 1963 to 1973, E.C. economies grew at a healthy average annual rate of 4.6 percent. In the next ten years, annual growth slowed to 2 percent, and in the early 1980s it practically ceased, as did the previously steady increase in individual income and social services. For the first time in a generation, unemployment rose and living standards stagnated and sometimes even fell. The slowdown of economic expansion meant a move toward what Lester Thurow called the "zero sum society," in which social tensions are sharpened by one group's gain being another group's loss.

Though growth rates rose again, the concern of the early 1980s led to industrial development policy receiving priority in most European countries. In markets for simple, mass-produced goods, heavy manufacturing products, and other industrial mainstays, the European and North American economies were slipping behind low-cost, high-volume producers, particularly those of the Far East. There was no reason to assume that this was a temporary situation to be rectified as soon as these countries' wage levels increased. Other low labor-cost countries were waiting in the wings, eager to assume a role similar to that played by Hong Kong, South Korea, Taiwan, and Singapore.

The main competitive advantage held by European and North American countries is superior knowledge and experience in technical matters, which allows them to develop products whose manufacture requires a substantial degree of manufacturing know-how and sophistication. Rather than "brawny" goods, such as steel, "brainy" or science-based production is better suited to maintaining competitiveness. Also, such production better serves the domestic preferences of countries that have developed more middle-class and more environmentally conscious societies. Electronics and information are therefore an ideal sector, since it is sophisticated in terms of design, production, and application and can provide employment for the large number of university graduates generated by the industrial countries. Over time, success in this field has become an indicator of international standing. Although it is acceptable to buy steel, grain, or watches from abroad, the importation of electronic brains seems to touch a sensitive nerve, especially since success or failure are not based on locational or geological coincidences.

The path of technological development is littered with lofty but failed national prestige projects. One example is the World Center for Computer Science and Human Resources (Centre Mondial de l'Informatique et Resource Humaine), which opened in Paris in 1982. President François Mitterrand personally supported the venture, proclaiming as its goal an understanding of the computerization of society and the development of computer applications for social and economic growth, particularly in the Third World. A noted journalist and politician, Jean-Jacques Servan-Schreiber, was the primary French organizer, and several eminent American computer scientists from the Massachussetts

Institute of Technology (MIT) were chosen to direct research. The project would fuse American technical know-how with European social concern and humanism in the service of society and the Third World. It was generously financed by the French government and was lavishly presented to the public (Etheridge, 1983).

Yet within one year the center was paralyzed and the Americans had left. What had gone wrong? Among other reasons, the American scientists and the French politicians had different conceptions of the center. The French wanted to demonstrate France's national commitment to technological leadership. The MIT technocrats took the humanist mission of the center more seriously and favored a democratic style of management, which clashed with the style of the French government officials who controlled it. Instead of becoming a world forum with an international outlook, the center became a backwater catering to domestic manufacturing interests.

This episode illuminates the dilemma facing European leaders. They are aware of the importance of this sector, they want to attain rapid results, and are willing to commit money and prestige. In the end, however, their efforts are hampered by fundamental constraints: the self-interests of bureaucracies, the narrow perspective of domestic manufacturers, and technological nationalism, even in the European context.

The History of the Electronics Gap

Despite Europe's proud scientific and technological traditions, well-functioning R&D infrastructures, sophisticated users, and large financial markets, European views of a role in electronics were often colored by a surprisingly Spenglerian pessimism.

This had not always been the case. Even after World War II, the United States and Europe were at similar levels of technological development, with Japan trailing. The war had accelerated major electronics R&D projects in countries such as Britain and Germany, and although many German production facilities were destroyed or dismantled, the technical know-how was there. European firms were as advanced in tube technology as their American counterparts, and they were performing research in solid-state technology, including research that led to the development of semiconductor diodes.

In late 1947, the transistor was invented at Bell Labs, and its superiority over traditional receiving equipment was soon apparent. On both sides of the Atlantic, large established tube manufacturers quickly expanded into transistor manufacturing. And although Americans had a head start and a larger and richer market, European companies managed to keep pace with the new developments. Philips, with its various European subsidiaries; Siemens; AEG-Telefunken; Plessey; Ferranti; GEC; and Lucas were all doing quite well technologically, and many had close development links with American manufacturers or with each other. By the late 1950s, Philips and Siemens were particularly strong, innovative, and internationally competitive (Malerba, 1985).

Much more significant than war and devastation in creating a disparity in high technology was the different evolution of market structures on the two sides of the Atlantic. In the United States, the needs of military, space, and the emerging computer sectors were met not so much by the traditional tube manufacturers as by new firms. Furthermore, computer manufacturers themselves moved into component production. In Europe, meanwhile, much of the development of the integrated circuit technology was undertaken by the traditional large tube manufacturers, which were slower to innovate than their American and later Japanese rivals. American producers gained an advantage that translated into larger market shares in Europe. European manufacturers were left with the development of less innovative discrete devices and linear integrated circuits for consumer and industrial markets. Among the tube manufacturers, competition between new and existing technologies was frequently determined by in-house bureaucratic rivalries instead of by competing companies.

The key development in the acceleration of high technology electronics in the United States was the switch from the earlier discrete devices to the newer integrated circuits that had been introduced by Texas Instruments in 1959 and Fairchild in 1960. Instead of being based on germanium and the alloy-and-mesa process, the new technology was based on silicon and on planar fabrication. These innovations made mass production easier and facilitated substantial component integration within one chip. Young companies that were wedded neither intellectually nor financially to the older ways moved into the new technology. These firms left the traditional, vertically integrated European and American tube manufacturers far behind. For the most part, European firms also made incorrect choices of American partners for technology transfers by choosing their traditionalist counterparts across the Atlantic, such as RCA and General Electric, both of which soon dropped out of integrated circuit production.

The integrated circuit period lasted a decade, until the introduction of large-scale integration (LSI) in 1971 with the development of the microprocessor. The LSI period in turn lasted a decade and was followed by the very large-scale integration (VLSI) stage, beginning in the early 1980s. At the beginning of the LSI period, American firms were dominant in high technology and increased their lead over their European competitors, while the Japanese also made serious advances. American firms also took a lead in several VLSI products. Meanwhile, European public policy began to focus on microelectronics. Finished goods producers such as telecommunications and consumer electronics firms started to integrate vertically into component manufacture, and government projects provided investment funds. On the whole, however, none of these efforts were successful in significantly challenging the overall American and Japanese strength, though achievements were made in niche markets. For example, French firms were strong in developing digital exchanges, and the "Smart Card" had a great number of future possibilities. The Prestel videotex system in Britain established a novel information medium. Several Italian companies were creative in software applications and in assembling robots. Siemens was a leader in many products.

Still, European semiconductor sales declined from the 30 percent share in the early 1970s to 18 percent in 1980, less than half the volume of the United States alone. By 1984, the share of European firms in the world market had decreased further to 8.5 percent. During that same period, Europe's share of total global chip consumption dropped from 27 percent to 18 percent (Wiegner, 1985). By 1990, European chipmakers' market share was slightly up (7.5 percent worldwide, 36.5 percent in Europe). Philips alone among European firms ranked among the top ten suppliers of semiconductors in 1990, but much of its worldwide semiconductor sales were attributable to its Silicon Valley subsidiary Signetics. Japan and the United States were far ahead in semiconductor production: 50 percent and 40 percent respectively in 1991.

In the 1980s, there were twice as many data processing terminals in the United States as in all of Western Europe, and the ratio of European to American data processing terminals fell from 62 percent to 54 percent from 1978 to 1988.

American computer companies dominated the European market, holding for a long time a collective share of more than 80 percent. IBM was the leader, particularly in mainframes, and was strong in the medium-sized market, along with DEC and Hewlett-Packard. Apple and Tandy were large suppliers of microcomputers.

European efforts to strengthen their industries were substantial.[1] Even so, the European computer industry had only two of the world's top ten manufacturers in 1989. Olivetti was eighth, with $7.26 billion in revenues, and Bull was ninth, with $6.47 billion. IBM had revenues greater than the combined earnings of its top six rivals in 1989 (de Jonquieres, 1990). In contrast, European firms in telecommunications constituted three of the top six firms. In that sector, which is technically similar to that of computers, government procurements rather than markets govern.

It is often claimed that there is not enough R&D in Europe, an assumption accompanying calls for more public subsidies. But the countries of the European Community spent only slightly less than the United States on high technology R&D, and they spent nearly *ten times* as much as Japan.[2] A related misconception is that European firms are not large enough to carry out R&D. This belief frequently leads to recommendations that firms be consolidated to establish larger units. Such observations confuse cause and effect. Size is not a precondition to success, but its result (Ergas, 1985).

Eventually, European governments began to encourage the formation of new firms. France granted six months of unemployment benefits in a lump sum if the benefits were used for investment in a new business. In Britain, unemployment benefits were paid in some instances while a person's new business took hold. The main purpose of these programs, however, was to help potentially unemployed people, not high-technology entrepreneurs.

Perhaps the greatest impedance to new firms was the low availability of venture capital in Western Europe. Banks tended to be conservative in their lending policies. They viewed themselves as lenders rather than underwriters, even though most European countries do not separate commercial and investment banking by regulation as in the United States.[3] In France, the use of venture capital to finance business was not widespread. In 1983, an attempt was made to change this through the reform of the French over-the-counter stock market.[4]

The failing of the private sector financing set the stage for the significance of governmental institutions in high-technology ventures with much greater success.

Development Projects and Joint Ventures

Every European country has some government-sponsored development program in semiconductor and computer technology. In Germany, three successive data processing programs were funded in the 1960s and 1970s. In France, two Plan Calculs were instituted amid much publicity in 1966 and 1971.[5]

In 1978, the French government launched the *Plan Circuits Intègres,* providing subsidies and preferential access to the French market in which the government is the dominant purchaser, and buying 40 percent of all chips sold.[6] The costly French efforts in the computer and consumer electronics fields are detailed in the chapter on that country's telecommunications.

In Britain, development by the main computer firm ICL was subsidized by the government. Other support programs were also set up, but until 1978 this assistance was relatively limited.[7]

Despite its missionary stress on private initiative, the Thatcher government strongly supported government-backed development of the information industry. In 1982, the Alvey Report recommended substantial government investments in VLSI software engineering and artificial intelligence research and development, with the goal of developing a fifth generation computer. A £120 million government semiconductor development program called Inmos was then implemented. Inmos was later privatized and sold to Thorn EMI.

In Italy, an electronics industry development plan similar to the British one was part of a large industrialization program formulated in 1978, most of which remained largely a blueprint.

The strengthening of the electronics industry in Europe became a subject of particular interest for the European Community. As discussed, a number of supranational subsidy programs exist with the aim of helping multinationals' efforts, such as EUREKA, RACE, and ESPRIT.

A large number of private European joint ventures were also established (Aronson and Cowhey, 1987). Olivetti owns a major part of the British firm Acorn Computers. Philips, in addition to its link with Siemens and AT&T, entered into joint ventures with Ericsson in Sweden, and with Bull, Alcatel, and Thomson in France. In 1983, Philips took control of the German consumer electronics firm Grundig when that company had financial problems. Similarly, Thomson acquired the consumer electronics division of AEG-Telefunken in Germany when it was near bankruptcy, as well as the German television producers Nordmende and Saba, and the stereo equipment maker Dual. CGE collaborates with the Belgian holding company ACEC. The Belgian SGB, part owned by Olivetti's De Benedetti, is also a part owner of Alcatel. Alcatel, Siemens, Plessey, and Italtel have a joint research effort for telecommunications switches and transmission. Siemens and GEC own Plessey.[8]

Interfirm collaboration is not without limits. Multinational joint ventures can be hampered by some countries' promotion of high technology companies as "national champions," making it difficult to have these firms as junior partners in a collaborative effort.

Those wishing to establish intra-European joint ventures must also consider the European antitrust laws of the Treaty of Rome. Additionally, they must take into account the various national antitrust legislation, particularly the British and German laws. The German Cartel Office, for example, vetoed a joint project for fiber-optic cables that would have brought together Siemens, Philips, and other smaller companies.[9]

Industrial Policy: PTTs to the Rescue

As the 1990s began, Europe's and America's microelectronics industries had serious problems. Philips, Groupe Bull, SGS, and Thomson incurred huge losses and were forced to lay off thousands of employees. No European firm held more than 4 percent of the world market, and the Japanese dominance in advanced components was increasingly worrisome.

The difficulties in establishing a strong, self-sustaining, and self-financing electronics industry outside the telecommunications sector and of breakthrough government projects strengthened the role of the PTTs. They are best able to supply resources, field trials, standardization, and procurement markets. They accomplish their activities while maintaining a stress on civilian rather than on military projects, which have fallen increasingly into political disfavor.

PTTs were able to provide nontariff protection and export advantages to the companies with which they work. They accomplished this through their buy-domestic and preferential standards-setting policies, which generally favored the purchase of domestic-manufactured equipment. This is particularly important because tariff barriers within the European Community largely disappeared and made industry more vulnerable to competition from European imports, while the international free trade rules of GATT reduced the scope of protectionism for non-European manufactured goods.

An assured domestic base was important as development costs were rising. One compilation of R&D costs of digital exchanges for the major manufacturers is listed in Table 30.1. The cost ranges from half a billion to three times as much.

(These large numbers, however, must be used with caution. It is always more expensive to develop an entirely new technological generation than to upgrade it.)

The PTTs served as large-scale purchasers of almost every kind of electronic equipment. For many manufacturers, PTT orders meant the difference between survival and bankruptcy. The PTTs underwrote part of the development and

Table 30.1   R&D Expenditure on Development of Digital Exchanges, 1987

Types of Switches	Cost (billions)
AXE (Ericsson)	$0.5
EWS-D (Siemens)	0.7
DMS (Northern Telecom)	0.7
ESS-5 (AT&T)	0.75
E1O (Alcatel)	1.0
System 12 (ITT)	1.0
System X (GEC-Plessey)	1.4

Source: Palmer and Tunstall, 1990, p. 22.

trial costs of a new product by tending to be its first major user and assuming some of the costs of the early shake-outs and of the early production runs. PTTs therefore subsidized the development of products that were then offered in the world market, often at costs below the domestic ones. Domestic telephone users, in effect, subsidize the export activities of industrial firms.

For example, deviations from competitive world market prices of up to 120 percent existed for PTT central office equipment procurement in 1985. In Belgium, this 120 percent markup allegedly supported company R&D. Germany and Italy paid prices 100 percent above cost. France's payments for equipment were only 50 percent above world prices, but the DGT funded R&D directly, not through equipment purchases (Müller, 1987, p. 12). The attempts to use the telecommunications network as a motor for more general industrial policy is not uniquely European. Japan, Korea, Singapore and Taiwan, for example, have pursued similar policies. In the United States, too, there have been many voices recommending such a direction in light of the decline of U.S. strength in electronics. Their weight is partly dependent on the success of the European efforts and its demonstration effects.

Toward Vertical Integration?

The weakness of some equipment firms once the protective bond of the postal-industrial alliance is loosened means that, at least in the short term, the traditional network operator may gain rather than lose strength in a liberalized environment. It would be naive to expect that reorganizing a PTT as an independent corporation—whatever its ownership status—would lead it automatically to strive for improved efficiency. If the exhortations to act like a business are taken seriously by a PTT and are acted upon, they result in an expanded set of activities. In Europe, the network operators, now often permitted to do so, have integrated horizontally and vertically and extended their reach. It is likely that we are merely at the beginning of a process in which effective telecommunications carriers move into adjacent lines of business.

In the United Kingdom, British Telecom began to pursue several avenues of vertical integration. In the equipment field, it bought the Canadian PBX manufacturer Mitel. The regulatory body, Oftel, and almost the entire British equipment industry then argued that the acquisition would not be in the public interest because it would strengthen BT's power in terminal equipment and threaten British PBX manufacturers. Although it acknowledged the problem, the Monopolies and Mergers Commission accepted the merger, with some conditions attached. But even those conditions were waived by the government, which approved the acquisition. In the end, the acquisition was not successful economically, but that does not mean that future vertical integration is precluded.

BT is not unique in seeking to expand its market power vertically. In Spain, the semi-private telecommunications monopoly, Telefónica, has a strong involvement in manufacturing. It held a large interest in the Spanish ITT-Alcatel subsdiary Standard Eléctrica, which was by far the largest electronics manufacturer in Spain, and it had major stock interests in a dozen other equipment firms and minority interests in seven more. The aggregate output of these firms accounted for about a third of total Spanish telecommunications production.

Vertical integration also existed for a long time in Italy. The predominant telephone carrier, SIP, is part of the holding company Societa Finanziaria Telefonico, which in turn is partly private, and mostly controlled by the government holding organization Institut per la Reconstruzione Industriale (IRI). STET also owns several major manufacturing firms, including Italtel, the country's largest telecommunications equipment firm, and several leading components and high technology firms.

Similarly, the Swedish national telephone administration, Televerket, has substantial manufacturing operations in its TELI and other subsidiaries. Japan's NTT formed within one year of privatization almost seventy subsidiaries or new ventures that were active in new products, services, and marketing.

These instances of vertical integration by the network operators indicate that liberalization transforms the relationship between PTTs and equipment firms from one of partnership into one of potential rivalry. And while this has competitive advantages, at least in the lengthy transition phase, the potential for vertical integration increases rather than decreases the role of the network operator.

The conclusion is that in their role as the state-sanctioned engine of domestic technological developments, and through their ability to extend their market power vertically, the PTTs, now transformed into semi-independent PTOs with greater flexibility, will be even more important and powerful than in the past. It is also conceivable that a similar role might be assigned in the U.S. to telephone companies, as alarm grows over the Japanese lead in high technology. Several congressional bills point in that direction. Thus, convergence may be resurrected, after all.

31

Transatlantic Trade Friction

European Interpretation of U.S. Telecommunications Policy

Developments in the United States challenged the traditional status quo in the European telecommunications field, threatening its traditional postal–industrial coalition. For a long time, European interpretation of U.S. developments was colored by the prevailing views of telecommunications experts, most of whom were closely affiliated with the traditional system. The AT&T divestiture itself was generally described as advantageous to AT&T: It was dropping the costly baggage of the regulated operating companies and could now take on IBM.

European PTTs had a great amount of respect and sympathy for the old AT&T. Although the American telephone operating company was privately owned, its dominance was similar to that of European administrations. International cooperation in such areas as transatlantic communications resulted in close links as partners rather than competitors. The dismantling of AT&T bewildered the PTTs. The decision seemed arbitrary, inefficient, and political. It should be noted that the belief that the competent and successful AT&T had been needlessly dismembered by the government is at odds with the view that the divestiture was a great success for AT&T.

The notion that the United States, with its advanced technology and successful telecommunications monopoly, would choose voluntarily to dismember such a system was unsettling. Whereas in the past, the development and adoption of new technologies provided security to the PTTs, it now seemed to undermine them. This perception resulted in strong defensive reactions. The American circumstances were generally portrayed as inherently different from those in European countries and hence not applicable to their situation, and little effort was made to isolate those elements that could be seen as part of a generalizable network evolution.

In some ways, the PTTs' views closely resembled the instant nostalgia that occurred in the United States after the announcement of the AT&T divestiture agreement. AT&T, which had been a favorite object of criticism, was suddenly seen as an efficient and benevolent organization torn apart by economic zealots. This ignored decades of major complaints about AT&T and its vast power in the American economy. The lawsuit against AT&T by the Antitrust Division of the Justice Department was the result of long-standing problems and was pursued by both Democratic and Republican administrations.

Generally the negative distributional impact of U.S. developments was stressed by PTTs. It is true that the AT&T divestiture threatened the system of cross-subsidies from business customers to residential customers, from long-distance service to local service, and from urban and suburban users to rural users. But these cross-subsidies did not disappear. Congressional reaction and state regulatory actions have shown that the protection of affordable universal service is a high political priority. In New York State, for example, the Public Service Commission, in a 1987 plan designed by the author, set rates for poor people at a low $1 per month for a basic subscription, plus two discount packages for usage, and a reduced installation charge for new subscribers of $2 per month over a year. In many areas of the United States, similar basic "lifeline" telephone service was instituted. In rural areas, low-priced telephone service is maintained, among other means, through direct subsidies to providers of such services, for example, through low interest loans from the Rural Electrification Administration. Telephone rates for rural America are also often lower than for urban users, because charges vary by exchange size. Small exchanges offer services at markedly lower rates.

In the United States, the decision process for telecommunications is not controlled by any political party. There is a multitude of decision points—the FCC; the Departments of Justice, Commerce, and State; U.S. District Court Judge Harold Greene; Congress; and the state regulatory commissions.[1] This system of decision making, resembling a war with a hundred local battles, is different from the process in Europe. But for all its untidiness, this decentralized process can accommodate change. Changes in European telecommunications policy may seem more orderly, better planned, and less disruptive. But much of the orderliness of the policy debate derives from the fact that for a long time there was no real public debate on telephone issues in most countries. European telecommunications policy discussions were carried on by government insiders. When regulation and operation coexist within the same institution, little information flows to the public. Although there is often heated criticism of the quality of service, as took place in France in the early 1970s, this rarely touches on the nature of the system itself, only on the level of investment or the competence of its managers.

Of course, policymakers within European governments try to accommodate the interests of a variety of groups that have a stake in telecommunications, but this is done by emphasizing the participation of insiders rather than by launching disruptive challenges to the status quo. These participants are typically technologists and government officials. For a long time, the PTTs transformed domestic policy questions into issues of electrical engineering or international diplomacy that must be dealt with at a governmental level.

The Containment of American Equipment Manufacturers in Europe

Although the traditional postal–industrial coalitions in European countries were sharply critical of U.S. liberalization, they were not above benefiting from it in terms of trade. This created problems of trade reciprocity that spilled into the political arena.

The AT&T divestiture led to the emergence of AT&T as a competitor in international markets, a sharp break with the past. This development received much attention and led to fears of an American telecommunications equipment offensive into Europe. But the opposite happened in the 1980s. American telecommunications equipment makers were repulsed and almost expelled from the European market, with ITT, GTE, and Honeywell largely departing. AT&T and the Bell regional holding companies were only partly successful after large scale efforts.

For more than fifty years, AT&T had stayed out of international equipment activities, despite its position as the largest such manufacturer in the world. But this had not always been the case. In the early years of the telephone, the Bell System had licensed several European equipment manufacturers, acquired others, built its own facilities in Europe, and had a substantial manufacturing and distribution presence in several major countries. But in the 1920s, the company was under much U.S. pressure to sell its international operations, as American critics of AT&T charged that American ratepayers were subsidizing AT&T's international operations. For that and other reasons, the company in 1925 decided to sell its European operations to the then relatively insignificant firm ITT, run by the Virgin Islands entrepreneur Sosthenes Behn and his brother.

This event marked ITT's entry into the big league of telecommunications. ITT's major European operations included Standard Telephone Company (STC) in the United Kingdom; Standard Lorenz Elektrik (SEL) in Germany; FACE in Italy, Bell Telephone Manufacturing Company (BTM) in Belgium, Standard Electrica in Spain, and LMT and CGCT in France. Other subsidiaries existed in Norway, Denmark, Portugal, Austria, Ireland, and so on. Given the nationalistic nature of the telecommunications equipment market, it was to ITT's advantage to have a physical presence in each country, because this allowed it to present itself as a domestic rather than an American company; local ITT companies often downplayed their U.S. connections.

The ITT companies included, among others, Standard Radio and Telefone AB, Sweden; the Bell Telephone Manufacturing Company, Belgium; FACE, Italy; ITT, Austria; ITT, Netherlands; Standard Electric Kirk A/S, Denmark; Standard Electrica, Spain; Standard Electrica, Portugal; Standard Elektrik Lorenz (SEL), Germany; Standard Telephone and Radio, Switzerland; Standard Telefone og Kabelfabrik A/S, Norway; Standard Telephone and Cable (30 percent ITT owned), Britain; and an Australian subsidiary. ITT's sales were not normally broken down by country, though one study reported the following 1976 sales figures (Northern Telecom, 1980):

West Germany	$516 million
France	$456 million
Spain	$439 million

United Kingdom	$330 million
Italy	$259 million
Belgium	$255 million
Brazil	$130 million
Australia	$ 96 million
Norway	$ 88 million
Switzerland	$ 71 million
Netherlands	$ 65 million
Austria	$ 44 million

ITT was a huge conglomerate, employing over 350,000 in 1980. At some point, it owned telephone companies—later nationalized—in Peru, Chile, Puerto Rico, and Spain. Its original holding in the Virgin Islands Telephone Company was still intact, and it owned an international record carrier (ITT Worldcom) and a U.S. domestic long-distance carrier (USTT). In equipment, where about three-quarters of its sales were in Europe, ITT had an impressive array of footholds with aggregated economies of scale, as in the case of its advanced System 12 digital exchange, while at the same time assuming a certain national stance by downplaying its American connections.

But the company, which had become a far-flung conglomerate in the 1960s and 1970s, was unable to sustain the costs of extending its System 12 digital switch to the U.S. market or financing development of the next generation of technology. In 1986, control in ITT was acquired by France's CGE, then a state company. For details, see the country chapter on France.

GTE was another American telecommunications company with a presence in the European equipment market. It had substantial manufacturing involvements in Italy and Belgium. But it could not make headway with its products, and in 1986 it sold 80 percent of its equipment interests to Siemens.

Following divestiture, the international market became interesting to AT&T. Since the domestic equipment market had been opened to all comers, its U.S. market share had nowhere to go but down. Hence, the rest of the world was its field of growth. AT&T's strategy was to align itself with domestic interests, thus overcoming the barriers an American company would face. The first such toehold alliance was a joint venture agreement with the Dutch electronics giant Philips, with the latter contributing access to the politicized European procurement field. Philips eventually decreased its investment.

Another significant alliance was with Olivetti, the Italian office equipment and small computer manufacturer. AT&T purchased 25 percent ownership of Olivetti for $260 million, with the option to acquire another 15 percent after four years.

Olivetti's ambition was to become a major European player in the world computer markets. But the collaboration did not work out well. In 1988, AT&T chose not to increase its financial and managerial involvement in the joint venture and cut its computer orders by 75 percent.

Perhaps the greatest AT&T breakthrough was with Italy's Italtel, a sister company of the main operating company SIP. Italy had slated its lagging telecommunications network for a major upgrade and expansion. But Italtel, the main domestic supplier, was in need of a foreign technology source. A struggle between Siemens, Alcatel, and AT&T for the huge contract ensued and led to lobbying efforts by Presidents Mitterrand and Reagan. In 1989, AT&T was selected. Italtel, in return, received a share of AT&T's European operations. AT&T also entered into other international involvements in Korea, Spain, Ireland, and Taiwan, all primarily off-shore manufacturing efforts that provided some local presence. In 1990, Spain's Telefónica upgraded its involvement with AT&T. Telefónica became a participant in AT&T Network Systems International, with 6 percent of the equity. AT&T had 59 percent, Italtel 20 percent, and Philips 15 percent, until the latter ran into financial difficulties and sold out to AT&T. These partnerships opened the prospect for AT&T's entry into Spain's expanding equipment market. Next, it established itself in Ukraine's network operations, and in Armenia and Kazakhstan. Thus, AT&T seemed to have finally established a European presence.

Another major move by AT&T was to try, unsuccessfully, for an agreement with the dominant French firm of CGE, which unleashed a round of diplomatic and economic intrigue. In particular, the German government began to lobby on behalf of Siemens, pressuring the French government at the highest levels to substitute Siemens for AT&T-Philips in the spirit of European solidarity, as well as in reciprocity for the newly acquired German Alcatel subsidiary SEL. The tug of war grew acrimonious. FCC Chairman Mark Fowler sent pointed inquiries to major American telephone companies regarding their use of equipment from countries where U.S. firms were being discriminated against. Within the French government, the PTT preferred APT, but other ministries did not wish to antagonize Germany. In the end, the French government chose the Swedish Ericsson as a neutral compromise, together with the French defense firm Matra, which thus gained a foothold in its country's telecommunications market. Further details on AT&T and ITT in France are provided in the chapter on that country.

Overall, the European equipment market was $18 billion in 1987 and had grown to $28 billion by 1990, with huge modernization and digitalization programs in Spain, France, Italy, and other countries; the European Commission predicted a 9 percent yearly growth rate for equipment and services. Within the European market, Alcatel, Siemens, and Ericsson were the dominant suppliers. In 1987, Alcatel was the largest supplier of public switching equipment (with 40 percent of the market), private switches (20 percent), terminal equipment (19 percent), and transmission systems. Siemens was second in public switches (20 percent), terminal equipment (16 percent), and transmission equipment (15 percent), followed by Ericsson in each category. Northern Telecom was the only non-European company to break into the top three, with an 18 percent share of private switching equipment. But with the saturation of the domestic market for basic service expansion, exports became more important to equipment manufacturers.

European Exports to America

The U.S. market is not only the largest domestic market in the world for tele-communications products, but it is also relatively free, and it has a large number of potential customers in the 1200 local exchange companies, the various new carriers and telephone companies. There are more networks as potential customers in the United States than in the rest of the world put together. (Most of the companies are, of course, quite small.)

The U.S. market for local exchange and transmission equipment was characterized before the AT&T divestiture by competition only in the procurement of equipment by non-AT&T telephone companies. Even GTE's local exchange companies were tied to their parent company's manufacturing units. AT&T was largely precluded from the independent market by the terms of legal agreements with the Justice Department, but—perhaps as a result—many other companies were active in it, including foreign suppliers such as Ericsson and Northern Telecom. On the other hand, the vast Bell system and all of its customers—comprising 80 percent of the local market—were largely inaccessible to other suppliers because of AT&T's ties to its manufacturing subsidiary Western Electric.

The U.S. liberalization provided non-U.S. manufacturers with opportunities. The Bell operating companies, which prior to divestiture of AT&T had relied mostly on Western Electric, were now free to buy equipment from other suppliers, and have indeed actively done so.

Interconnection of customer premises equipment was also significantly liberalized in the United States. Whereas it once was more restrictive than in many European countries, it became much freer in the wake of regulatory and court decisions. The relaxed rules ("Part 68") followed the 1968 *Carterfone* case. Now equipment sellers need only to register their products with the FCC as complying with standards before marketing them. Registration requires the disclosure of a unit's technical specifications, so that the FCC's staff can, if it wishes, identify possible system degradation prior to installation of the equipment. But there is no approval process. (There is a national security exception to the registration requirement. If a federal agency certifies that compliance with registration procedures would jeopardize security interests, equipment may be connected to the network without publication of technical data.)

Although most analysts expected the BOCs to cling to AT&T as their equipment supplier, they in fact rapidly embraced a wide variety of non-AT&T equipment. In one instance involving equipment allegedly affecting defense communications, the Defense Department reportedly used pressure to influence a carrier not to buy Japanese equipment. But this was a widely noted exception. Generally, the opening of the U.S. market to non-AT&T and foreign equipment was rapid.

Network standards are coordinated for the BOCs by their joint organization, Bell Communication Research (Bellcore). Although Bellcore's information requests to vendors of central office switches are formidable, there is no economic reason for it to use its role to favor AT&T or other U.S.-owned manufacturers. The rapid growth and large market share of the Canadian-owned Northern Telecom would tend to indicate that neither the FCC nor the state commissions have shown a desire to set standards.

Procurement of network equipment by local telephone companies is governed by their obligation to state regulators to pay the lowest possible prices for qualifying equipment. The loss of subsidies from long-distance service created pressures in keeping local rates low. The ability to compare costs for the twenty-two companies also forces them to seek low-cost equipment. The "gold plating" (overcapitalization) of the past is unlikely to persist in the new environment. Because of the divestiture, the BOCs no longer have any incentive to increase Western Electric's profits, because none of those profits benefit the BOCs or their managers. Furthermore, the partial substitution of price cap regulation, or negotiated rates, for rate-of-return regulation provides an incentive for cost cutting. Thus, the potential for new entry by suppliers existed.

Aiming at the U.S. market, George Pebereau, then president of the French CGE, declared:

> It is obvious that no European company, French or not, can remain a world company if it does not have a significant position in the American market, which represents 40 percent of the world market and, in addition, is from the point of view of technology the best testing grounds one can imagine. Happily, we have a historic opportunity to develop ourselves in the U.S., with the deregulation of AT&T. . . . If, sadly, CGE's presence in the U.S. failed, we would need more than a decade to regain the confidence of our American customers [*L'Expansion,* 1985].

But Alcatel, which bought ITT's switching systems division worldwide (including the United States), was not successful at introducing ITT's switch into America. It closed its U.S. switching division and cut back its efforts to sell cable and transmission equipment. Northern Telecom, however, performed very well in the U.S. market, securing a leadership position as a second source. Three contenders for the number three slot were Siemens, Ericsson, and Fujitsu. None of them emerged as a clear leader. Siemens, with the strongest presence, had over 1 million installed lines as of 1990. Ericsson's success has been mostly in rural applications of its AXE switch, and Fujitsu had various trials in place throughout the United States.

The major problem, from the U.S. perspective, is that the opening of the U.S. telecommunications equipment market to foreign suppliers was not matched by a reciprocal opening of their markets to U.S. producers.

In 1981, the United States had a $6.04 billion trade surplus in electronics-based products, which included telecommunications and computer goods. By 1986, the U.S. deficit in this area was $16.06 billion (NTIA, as cited by Robinson, 1987).

In the subcategory of telecommunications products, the United States had a $817 million trade surplus in 1981, and a $2.5 billion deficit in 1987. In the same period, exports of telecommunications products increased by 41 percent, whereas imports increased by 320 percent (Robinson, 1987). By 1989, the deficit had dropped to $1.9 billion (Department of Commerce, 1990, p. 227).

On the other hand, the E.C. imported 21 percent of its equipment from Japan and 11 percent from the United States, whereas exports to the United States amounted to only 4.3 percent of E.C. exports. The United States had a positive trade balance with E.C. nations of $417 million in 1988 and $800 million in 1989 (Department of Commerce, 1990, p. 229).[2] Nevertheless, U.S. companies felt increasingly higher walls around a "Fortress Europe." It was much easier for Siemens, Alcatel, or Ericsson to do business in the U.S. than it was for AT&T to have a presence in Germany, France, or Sweden.

It was highly unlikely that the U.S. government would stand by as foreign firms sold freely in America while U.S. manufacturers were shut out. The FCC initiated a *Notice of Inquiry* in 1987 in which it invited comments on whether there should be restrictions on the approval of equipment exported from countries that discriminated against American equipment. In 1988, the FCC ordered large U.S. firms to report purchases of switching equipment from foreign sources. This action came in retaliation to French and German resistance to AT&T operations in Europe (Davis, 1988).

Another response to these developments was the introduction of proposed federal legislation to require reciprocity. The United States also exerted pressure on Japan and Europe to lower its nontariff barriers in equipment procurement. For example, the U.S. International Trade Commission ruled that a number of Japanese manufacturers had "dumped" (i.e., sold below cost) cellular car telephones in the United States. The decision allowed the U.S. Customs Service to increase duties on these manufacturers' products.

Thus, the opportunity to enter the U.S. market is a double-edged sword, threatening to bring about a reduction of European and Japanese firms' own protected positions. This tends to split the telecommunications industries of other countries: strong and advanced manufacturers who can compete successfully in the world market based on the merits of their products can accept imports to their home base, but weak firms in need of protection have little to gain and much to lose from lowering the barriers.

A round of accusations began in 1989 with a U.S. Trade Representative (USTR) report finding that the European Community had "needlessly burdensome" type approvals and discriminated against U.S. suppliers in procurement and services. Two days later, the E.C.'s Directorate General for External Affairs issued its own counterreport, entitled "U.S. Barriers to Trade," which claimed that the cost of adapting equipment to the U.S. market and lengthy Bellcore approvals effectively cut E.C. firms out of U.S. contracts (*TDR*, 1989).

This followed a 1986 report by the Commission of the European Communities criticizing the slowness and complexity in the American approval of equipment and the oligopolistic features of the market. But this applies to central office equipment; for terminal equipment, the charge is largely incorrect. It is true, however, that the costs for foreign switch manufacturers to enter the United States can be substantial. Not only must they pay $5 to $10 million to Bellcore for testing the system (the so-called Phase E review), but it also costs $100 million or more to modify the system to North American standards and software practices. There are technical differences that create barriers to entry by European suppliers. But there is no evidence that these technical standards, which evolved over decades some time ago, were set or are applied with a protectionist purpose.[3]

In 1990, the European Commission issued a directive on public procurement that included a "buy Europe" clause, stipulating that E.C. bids must be accepted if they are less than 3 percent higher than non-E.C. offers (for orders over 600,000 ECU). Only bids from firms with more than 50 percent E.C. ownership would be given this preference. The law was scheduled to take effect in 1992, except in Spain, Portugal, and Greece. Shortly after the directive was passed, the French Ministry of European Affairs called for resistance to the "invasion" by U.S. and Japanese firms. It claimed that Japan had a 95 percent share of the facsimile machine market, that Motorola had 25 percent of cellular equipment, and that AT&T had increased from a 2.5 percent market share in switching in 1985 to 13 percent in 1990 (Roussel, 1990).

The following are unconfirmed (and quite likely non-comparable) numbers for digital switches that were provided by several market participants about competitors' and suppliers' bids and contracts. The figures should be treated with great caution, because each deal may include different packages of hardware, software, and support. But the numbers, nevertheless, serve to illustrate the order of magnitude of the high premiums charged domestically over the lowest bid made by the same firm internationally in the early 1990s. The figures show a very significant domestic premium, indicating that much of R&D and other initial costs are paid for by PTTs and borne by domestic rate payers in those countries where foreign entry is disfavored over domestic "industrial champions." The U.S. seems to have competitive pricing, with a small premium only. Japan, despite the four major vendors of the "NTT family," has prices above world market prices. And European premiums are substantial.

Company	Market Share in Home Market	Home Price ($/Line)	Int'l Lowest Bid($/Line)	% Home Market
Alcatel (France)	84	335	110	204
AT&T (U.S.)	42	110	100	10
Ericsson (Sweden)	100	325	130	150
Fujitsu (Japan)	24	290	110	164
NEC (Japan)	25	290	140	107
Northern Telecom (Canada & U.S.)	80*	250	100	150
Siemens (Germany)	83	450	100	350

Sources: figures provided by various market participants (unverified).

*Canada

32

International Telecommunications Services

The clash between the different policy approaches taken on the two sides of the Atlantic was particularly acute in international communications, partly because of its great profitability. Historically, U.S. policy on international telecommunications had carved up the market into distinct segments, assigning each segment to different kinds of carriers. In the 1970s and 1980s, however, the United States radically restructured its own rules of the game and forced the European countries to respond to a new situation. This led to frequent disputes. American changes destabilized the traditional European system, as analyzed later with the theoretical model of Chapter 40.

The volume of international telecommunications traffic increased much faster than international trade in general. From 1970 to 1981, for example, international calls originating in the United States increased by a factor of 11.3, whereas American international trade grew, in real terms, by a factor of 3 (Antonelli, 1984).

One part of the impetus behind this rise in international traffic was the dramatic decrease in investment cost for a transatlantic circuit, from $1.4 billion per voice circuit on TAT-1 in 1956 down to $44,356 per circuit for the fiber-optic TAT-8 cable in 1988 (Stanley, 1988). An FCC study found that the cost per minute on transatlantic cable dropped from $2.53 in 1956 to $0.04 in 1988 and was expected to fall to $0.02 in 1992. In the same period, the number of available voice circuits grew from 89 to 37,800. Satellite circuit costs similarly fell from $32,000 each on the Early Bird satellite in 1968 to $4,680 for the Intelsat-VI satellite generation in 1982.

However, this drop in costs was not matched by an equal drop in prices; consequently, the profit margin on international service remains very high. According to one study, British Telecom charged $750,000 for a direct-broadcast-grade connection between London and New York in 1981, whose cost to BT was only $53,000, which in turn contained an Intelsat charge that already was well above actual economic cost (Stapley, 1981).

Closely related to these high prices is their asymmetry. An FCC study showed that the weighted average for foreign tariffs was almost 95 percent higher than the American tariff (Kwerel, 1984).

Lower rates in the United States are partly the result of a long struggle among various market segments and participants. In 1964, clear boundaries existed, and the FCC prohibited AT&T from entering the international record market (i.e., telegraph and data transmission) to protect the so-called International Record Carriers (IRCs). Authorization of the transatlantic TAT-4 cable was contingent upon AT&T's exclusion from such services (GAO, 1983).

Among record services, the FCC made a further distinction between domestic services, from which Western Union was restricted, and international services, which were provided by the IRCs, including Western Union International, which had been divested from Western Union to become a wholly independent and unaffiliated entity. IRCs could only operate in the United States from certain limited and approved "gateways." A telegram from Cleveland to Paris, for example, would be routed by Western Union to an IRC gateway, transmitted by an IRC to Europe, and then passed on to the French PTT. Price competition among the IRCs was restrained.

The market segmentation led to a lack of competition, as well as to substantial earnings margins. Partly because of the high profitability, the situation became unstable and cracks began to appear. The artificial nature of the market segmentation then became evident and led to a policy response within a relatively short time.

The FCC set maximum rates for international telecommunications services in theory on the basis of rate-of-return regulation. In practice, however, these rates were not closely monitored because AT&T's international department was not examined separately from its overall operations. Figures for 1979, the first year that AT&T was required to provide separate reporting, show that the net return of overseas voice service represented a very high 36.5 percent on its total investment.

Similarly, the FCC did not investigate the rate of return for any IRC between 1958 and 1976. A 1979 audit report found that telex service was subsidizing telegraph and private services. The IRCs' rate of return for telex services ranged from 34.4 to 58.3 percent for the most profitable carrier and from 18.6 to 25.4 percent for the least profitable carrier, with the variation in the percentages depending on methodology (GAO, 1983).

High profits and differential pricing encouraged the emergence of arbitrage. In 1981, a telex message from Germany directly to the United States cost $2.58 per minute, but it cost only $1.76 if routed via the United Kingdom. This led to substantial transatlantic traffic through London telex bureaus. The European PTTs tried to stamp out this arbitrage, citing CCITT rules they themselves had authored, but they were rebuffed by the European Commission and the European High Court of Justice, as detailed in the chapter on U.K. telecommunications.

Not surprisingly, as the FCC's liberal domestic policies took shape, its restrictive entry and service policies for international telecommunications appeared to make less and less sense, at least from the U.S. perspective. In 1976, the FCC allowed competitive entry into international telecommunications, and thereafter routinely approved applications by MCI, US Sprint, and others to provide international service.

In a series of rulings in 1979 and 1980, the FCC also largely removed the dichotomy of voice and record carriage, eliminated the rules prohibiting AT&T and the IRCs from entering each other's markets, and expanded the number of gateway cities from which international traffic could be sent.[1]

The FCC also eliminated rate-of-return regulation and tariffing. Only dominant carriers (i.e., AT&T and GTE's Hawaiian Telephone Company) needed to file international tariffs. Other carriers had merely to report their activities.

The PTTs observed all this with some misgivings, for these rulings challenged long-established partnership arrangements and rate structures. But once their initial distaste for the increased complexity in the international telecommunications regime subsided, they recognized the potential advantages. As the only address within their countries for AT&T, MCI, Sprint, and others, the PTTs were in a position to profit by forcing rival American carriers to compete against each other for operating agreements.

To prevent the IRCs from being thus "whipsawed," the FCC in 1977 enforced a Uniform Settlements Policy requiring all U.S. carriers to have uniform settlement rates with all other carriers for the same routes. When the Benelux PTTs and Nordtel (the Inter-Scandinavian telecommunications body) invited all potential suppliers of data communication services to submit bids that included the division of accounting (i.e., an element of price bids), the American reaction was swift. Despite normally championing liberalization, the FCC ironically requested that U.S. carriers collectively defer negotiations with Nordtel. Nordtel backed off and notified the carriers that it did not plan to use its monopoly power for exclusive bids.

When different entities provide international telecommunications service at each end of a circuit, they agree upon a division of the revenues between them. The entities create an "accounting rate" or "settlement rate" to be paid to one carrier by the other carrier collecting from a customer. The accounting rate may bear little or no relationship to the actual customer charge or "collection" rate. As a hypothetical example, the accounting rate for the first three minutes of a telephone call between New York and Paris might be $3.00; the charge for the call in the United States, $4.50; and the charge in France, $6.00. When U.S. customers call, they pay $4.50 to AT&T, which credits $3.00 to the French PTT. When French customers call, they pay $6.00 to the French PTT, which credits $3.00 to AT&T. The Uniform Settlements Policy does not regulate U.S. carriers' rates on the U.S. end, but attempts to protect U.S. companies from whipsawing by foreign PTTs by requiring that all U.S. carriers pay them a uniform rate.

But given the profit margins it must be difficult to prevent non-price concessions. In 1985, an example of whipsawing occurred when RCA filed a complaint with the FCC, charging TRT and FTCC, two other international record carriers, with using so-called special drawing rights instead of the established gold franc settlements in their international telex accounts with the PTTs of Finland, France, Norway, and Spain. RCA charged that this arrangement reduced the accounting rate they would receive from $1.38 to $1.14. FTCC defended itself, arguing that it would actually receive $1.21 under the special drawing right settlement, but it admitted that the figure was still lower than the gold franc rate.

In 1984, the European PTTs affirmed their policy on the limitation of entry by American competitors. The PTT organization CEPT recommended that its members not open their markets to any new American carriers unless they would provide better technical service at a lower cost (to PTTs) than at present. New carriers were permitted for new types of communications services such as videotex, teletext, facsimile, and packet switching, but the CEPT guidelines restricted each to providing only one type of new service.

In an attempt to reduce the barriers to entry created by the PTTs' negotiation requirements, MCI bought an existing IRC, Western Union International (renamed MCI International) from Xerox. MCI International created a convenient international outlet for MCI's American involvement in electronic mail and also provided MCI with an already established relationship with the PTTs. The company concluded agreements with several countries and established London and Hong Kong as international hubs for its traffic to other countries. It also complied with a host of burdensome requirements and procedures that made service to some countries unprofitable.

A related question was the way in which European PTTs pick American long-distance carriers for communication originating in Europe. For European customers calling American cities, the PTT chooses which U.S. long-distance carrier will transmit the call within the U.S. and realize the subsequent revenue.

Of course, it would be possible to permit the European users to indicate which American long-distance carrier they prefer. This could be accomplished through the use of not one but several country codes for the United States (or North America), with a different numeric access code assigned to each U.S. international carrier.[2] But such a choice of services, together with the possibility of advertising campaigns by various carriers directed at European customers, would have visibly demonstrated that network competition was feasible, and this type of consumer choice was not granted to most European users. Instead, negotiations centered on the ways in which the PTTs might allocate their U.S.-bound traffic between AT&T and its competitors. One possibility was to negotiate market shares in advance; another was to use a fixed share allocation formula. The easiest was to allocate America-bound traffic to American carriers in the same proportion that those carriers supply traffic to Europe.

In addition to extending its pro-competitive and deregulatory policies to international services, the FCC sought to increase competition between types of transmission media and service providers.[3]

An important distinction is made in international communications between transmission by submarine cable and transmission by satellite. The several submarine cables linking North America and Europe are owned and operated by consortia of European and North American telecommunications administrations and firms. In contrast to their part-ownership in the submarine cable operations, AT&T and the other American international carriers as well as domestic satellite operators were specifically excluded from international satellite transmission, which was reserved for Comsat, the American designated carrier of the international satellite organization Intelsat. Created in 1964 at the instigation of the United States, Intelsat is a cartel-like organization with a considerable monopoly over satellite transmission of international public telecommunications. Each member country designates a carrier to manage outgoing and incoming Intelsat communications traffic. For most countries, this carrier is the governmental PTT authority. Following intense domestic debate in the United States, however, Congress denied AT&T this role in an attempt to limit its power. The role was instead given to Comsat, which was created through the Communications Satellite Act of 1962 as a publicly chartered, privately owned company. Under the 1962 legislation, Comsat was solely a "carrier's carrier"; neither AT&T nor the IRCs were permitted direct access to Intelsat, and Comsat could not connect directly with users. In 1965, Comsat had a 61 percent share in Intelsat, reflecting its share of traffic. Its share later declined to approximately 25 percent.[4]

The FCC subsequently permitted Comsat to go beyond its role as a carrier's carrier and to provide services to customers directly. The FCC made this conditional upon a major restructuring of Comsat separating its unregulated competitive activities from its regulated activities. Comsat sold its earth stations and divested its manufacturing subsidiaries in 1988 and 1989.[5]

New International Carriers

Because some PTTs made almost one-quarter of their profits in international services, it was not surprising that new entrants arrived, first by sky and then by sea. In 1983, the FCC extended its domestic "Open Skies" satellite policy and accepted an application for a license from a tiny entrepreneurial venture, Orion Telecommunications, to build a private satellite system for North Atlantic service. Orion planned to aim at customized business services and private lines that were not well served by Intelsat. Just as MCI had done for domestic services, Orion denied that it was trying to enter the market of the dominant firm and instead argued that it would create a new market. Orion's application was followed by similar filings from International Satellite, Inc. (backed by TRT), Cygnus (backed by the earth station manufacturer MA/COM), RCA Americom (for modification of an American domestic satellite), and Pan-AmSat.

The applications caused a debate within the American government concerning whether the United States should endorse or permit international systems to "bypass" Intelsat. This kept the applications pending at the FCC and culminated in 1985 with the issuance of a policy paper intended to provide guidance to the FCC. It cautiously approved the concept of separate private systems, as long as they did not interconnect with public switched networks. The FCC eventually agreed. Not surprisingly, Comsat opposed the private satellite systems vehemently, and sought legislation that would preclude such systems or restrict their operations.

According to a provision of the Intelsat agreement (Article 14D), no satellite competition is permitted that would cause economic harm to Intelsat operations and profits. Intelsat uses vague criteria in making such assessments, however. It did not find that the PTTs' Eutelsat system was causing "significant harm" because the European PTTs asserted, with logic more political than economic, that they would use no satellite system other than one that they would operate.

Several regional and intercontinental satellite systems were established outside of the Intelsat organization. They included Arabsat, Eutelsat, a project run by a Scandinavian consortium, and the French system (which is "domestic" but which stretches that term to encompass communications with French possessions in the Western Hemisphere). These projects arose partly because several countries believed that they could more easily reach their telecommunications goals if they had greater control over satellite communications, and partly because they pursued various industrial policy goals in electronics. The aggregate result was to weaken the argument that for reasons of economic and technical efficiency, international satellite telecommunications must be controlled by a single organization.

As both users and shareholders of the Intelsat consortium, Intelsat's constituent organizations did not want to see their profits whittled down by competition. To that end, they enlisted the traditional cross-subsidy argument. In international terms, the argument stated that the profits from the high-density transatlantic and North Pacific routes were needed to provide a subsidy for low-density traffic to and among Third World countries. But the monopoly profits are far larger than those subsidies, and PTTs could assist less developed countries also by more direct contributions in the form of equipment, expertise, financial subsidies, lower communications tariffs for calls to those countries, or more advantageous settlement rates.

The conflict is not simply between Intelsat and its potential rivals, but just as much between the PTTs and the new carriers. Consequently, various defensive strategies were pursued against potential rival satellite carriers. An "up-link" strategy was aimed at preventing the FCC from granting licenses to both American and foreign applicants. This was supported by the argument that the member states of the Intelsat agreement gave Intelsat the monopoly over commercial international satellite telecommunications. The American applicants contended that the agreement covered only public switched communications and not private line leasing, and that the terms of the Intelsat agreement prohibited only those rival systems that would cause "significant economic harm" to Intelsat.

A preemptive strategy by Intelsat sought to deter potential entry by offering new satellite service options at reduced rates. Similarly, submarine cable capacity was increased by the traditional service providers. In 1991, two additional trans-atlantic fiber cables were agreed upon by European and North American carriers.

A "down-link" strategy tried to prevent new satellite carriers from connecting into national networks. But this required a unified front of all PTT countries in a region against the establishment of a beachhead or, if such were established, against its use as a transfer point to other countries. As with other cartel-like agreements, this was only as strong as its weakest link. Given its general evolution toward liberalization of telecommunications and its privatization of British Telecom, the United Kingdom did not remain agreeable to the plan. Similarly, as in the case of tax havens, one could expect other European countries to find it advantageous to become international transmissions hubs by permitting down-links from non-Intelsat carriers. Moreover, limitations against retransmission might not be supported by the European antitrust laws, as the case of the British telex bureaus demonstrates.

Still, the delaying tactics took their toll. After a while, PanAmSat was the only project that could afford to pursue its goals actively. In 1988, the Pan-AmSat, with twenty-four C-Band transponders, was launched. Its combative chairman, Rene Anselmo, promised to crack the monopoly of Intelsat with service to Central and South America, the continental United States, the Caribbean, and, significantly, Western Europe. In 1990, PanAmSat filed a $1.5 million lawsuit against Intelsat and won an easing of restrictions. In 1991, Intelsat, having in 1985 been forced to agree to coordinate with separate systems, agreed for PanAmSat to be interconnected with public switched networks in the Caribbean and Eastern Europe, with up to 100 circuits. Orion restructured itself into a limited partnership including British Aerospace, General Dynamics, and Matra, with a 1994 launch date.

Although a single global system may be desirable because of its economies of scale, a distance- and border-insensitive technology such as satellite transmission cannot be successfully restricted for long. Sooner or later, companies larger than Orion and PanAmSat will establish themselves in the market. Domestic or regional PTT satellites with spare capacity will play a similar role. Intersputnik, the Soviet-dominated Eastern European system was another possibility, and it began to offer its services to Western countries as its East European customer base declined. Partly to preempt competitive entry, several European operators began VSAT (very small aperture terminals) service, aimed at the private networks of large users, particularly those with pan-European communications needs such as automobile makers. Both British Telecom and Mercury made plans for VSAT service. In 1990, only in Germany and potentially in Britain could such service be offered outside the traditional carriers. In 1991, the European Commission drafted a directive to create a competitive European satellite market. Soon, various PTOs began to coordinate their VSAT plans, partly out of concern that VSAT service could be used to bypass national networks.

Intelsat's revenues stagnated in 1989 and dropped by almost 20 percent in 1990. Jolted, it considered privatizing itself by selling 49 percent of its shares to the public.

Even in the absence of competing satellites, Intelsat arrangements are threatened by rivalry from already emerging competitors in private submarine cable facilities. Two companies, Tel-Optik and Submarine Lightwave Cable Company (SLCC), applied for licenses to operate an international submarine cable (PTAT) in the United States. The submarine cable applications did not raise issues under the Intelsat agreements. Moreover, AT&T, the major American owner of submarine cable systems, did not file any substantial objections. The FCC thus moved expeditiously to grant the Tel-Optik application in 1985. Cable & Wireless and E. F. Hutton participated in that venture. Soon one Bell regional holding company, NYNEX, acquired an option, thereby raising the question of the permissibility of Bell companies' international involvement in this form, which was eventually denied. The plan was for two cables to be operated in conjunction with Cable & Wireless in the United Kingdom, with the first cable completed in 1989 and the second in 1992. Similar applications were made and approved for Pacific routes.

Liberalization of entry led to the emergence of international carriers in Britain, Japan, and Sweden. Cable & Wireless (C&W) was the prototype for the new generation of international carriers. As discussed in the chapter on U.K. telecommunications, C&W's goal was to become the first global telephone carrier, and its strategy targeted the world's financial centers: London, New York, Tokyo, Hong Kong, and Bahrain. It was already a dominant presence in Hong Kong, where it owns the local telephone company. In Britain, C&W became the sole owner of Mercury, which provided it with domestic long-distance capability within Britain and access to several European countries. C&W was a major partner in the PTAT transatlantic fiber-optic cable to New York and held transcontinental rights in the United States through its ownership of TDX, an American long-distance carrier.

In Japan, the liberalization of long-distance communications also reached international service. Two consortia applied for a license to provide such service in competition with the previous monopolist KDD. The first was International Telecom Japan (ITJ), owned by fifty-three large users, including Mitsubishi, Somitomo, Mitsui, Matsushita, and the Bank of Tokyo. The second consortium was International Digital Communications (IDC), in which C. Itoh & Co. and Cable & Wireless were the largest partners from among thirty-five companies, including Toyota. The Ministry of Posts and Telecommunications tried to convince the two ventures to merge. Part of the agreement would have been to reduce C&W's share to 3 percent for reasons of "national security" and to exclude it from a role in management. The British and American governments opposed these restrictions as nontariff barriers. Both services were launched in 1989. By 1990, they had captured 35 percent of all international traffic between Japan and the U.S.

Challenges to the Traditional Rate System

In time the distortions of the traditional system reached the attention of the public. Hugo Dixon of *The Financial Times,* in particular, argued that users were overcharged by $10 billion because of cartel-like tariff arrangements. Costs for international calls were estimated at $0.25 to $0.50, but rates averaged $1 per minute. It was estimated that $30 billion in revenues would generate $20 billion in profits in 1990 (Dixon, 1990a). BT reported 60 percent profit rates internationally (Malik, 1990, p. 5). In 1990, the European Commission began an investigation into artificially high international rates, and CCITT admitted that its tariff recommendations needed to be revised. In defense, it was argued that these profits subsidized residential local rates.

A related issue was the asymmetry in incoming and outgoing traffic to the United States, which paradoxically created a major American deficit because of its lower rates. A study by the International Institute of Communications found that the United States originated 5.3 billion minutes of calls and received only 3.1 billion minutes of traffic (Staple, 1990).

International telephone service in the United States grew more rapidly than that of other countries, causing a rise in the deficit from $1.4 billion in 1987, to $2.2 billion in 1989 (Stanley, 1988), and almost $3 billion in 1990. In 1990, the FCC instituted a proceeding on this matter. The FCC required U.S. international carriers to negotiate a reduction in accounting rates in order to alleviate the U.S. telecommunications deficit. And it announced that it could take unilateral steps if necessary. Proposals were also made to reform the entire system of settlements (Ergas and Patterson, 1989). In 1991, the OECD proposed replacing the traditional accounting rate system with access charges. The new system would be cost-based and non-discriminatory against low-cost carriers. But it would require international regulatory action.

Comparison of International Performance

We will now turn briefly to some comparisons of carriers. As was stated in the introduction to this book, this is not a comparative study in the sense of measuring the performance of various countries' PTTs and issuing report cards. The study is concerned more with vertical changes over time than with horizontal cross-country analysis. However, some comparative data will be provided in the following section, largely from OECD figures. But first, it is necessary to discuss the difficulties of cross-country analysis.

The difficulties inherent in any comparison task can be shown with the example of Sweden's Televerket reporting of its own performance.

One Televerket study shows the number of working hours required for an average industrial laborer to pay for annual fixed telecommunication service basket (Roos and Loenqvist, 1984). In Sweden, the basket required thirty hours of work. For Great Britain, in contrast, it was eighty hours; for France, sixty-five; for Germany, fifty-five; and for the United States, fifty. But nowhere in the report is the telecommunications "basket" defined, and attempts to obtain that information from Televerket were unsuccessful. Mitchell (1983) comes to very different conclusions in that forty-two hours of work purchased one year of residential service in the United States. In Sweden, the same service requires fifty-five hours; in the United Kingdom, ninety-eight; in Italy, 111; in Germany, 126; and in France, 165. Clearly, every country has different prices and usage patterns for different components, permitting arbitrary comparisons. In the United States, there are very different rates among customer types and geographic regions; there are alternative competing carriers and substantial off-peak discounts. For example, while Televerket assumes that U.S. terminal equipment is rented by users, most Americans buy it, since that is much cheaper. The same study uses the average industrial wage as a measuring rod, which creates a bias toward richer countries, and within these countries toward those with strongly unionized economies, where industrial wages are relatively high. Televerket uses for local rates New York City as a typical representative. Unfortunately, for a variety of reasons, New York is at the high-cost end.

It is also difficult to define services. In the United States, operator assistance and itemized bills are included. Swedish network quality, as measured by the percentage of unsuccessful calls due to overload or technical faults, was at 2.4 percent of trunk calls in 1985 (Televerket, 1986, p. 9). In the United States, the percentage of unsuccessful trunk calls was 1 percent for only twenty peak hours per year, with the other times being lower.

It appears that in some comparisons virtually every judgment call ends up with unfavorable assumptions, or noninclusion of favorable factors. Although some simplifications are unavoidable, an analysis should not consistently err to one side if it is to shed light.

In the decade between 1972 and 1982 alone, at least fourteen international comparative studies of residential telephone rates were undertaken (see Mitchell, 1983). Subsequent comparisons include Siemens (1988); Logica (1989); McDowall (1987); and Horton and Donovan (1987). The results vary widely but are consistent insofar as they usually favor the sponsoring administration. Normally, the definition of the basket (local versus long-distance) can strongly affect results, depending on the extent of subsidization of local calls. Given the large number of variables to be considered and judgments to be made, one could conduct defensible statistical studies that would show probably several countries as the cheapest telephone country.

Perhaps the most thorough comparative study of rates and quality is a lengthy OECD report issued in 1990. But it too makes numerous assumptions that are problematic for the U.S. system, which has a structure considerably different from European ones.

The OECD methodology uses an average ratio between fixed and usage-sensitive charges (2:3 for residential subscribers 1:4 for business users). In applying these ratios to the U.S. situation, the OECD study apparently does not take into account the fact that most U.S. monthly residential fixed service charges include provisions for unlimited local calling. It is hard to understand how the study could find residential fixed charges of $175.10, higher than those of business charges, which were calculated at $174.67 (OECD 1990, p. 46). This misconception skews the subsequent analysis. Other assumptions are similarly unfavorable, such as the use of New York City as the comparison city; the absence of quality factors; the lack of credit for operator availability and itemized billing; the assumption of AT&T as long-distance carrier; and the use of only partial off-peak discounts.

The study itself concedes that: "on balance, the model works best for the countries of Western Europe which tend to have similar tariff structures and similar geographies'' (p. 57). In consequence, it is best to use the following figures as a comparison of traditional or semi-traditional systems, and to be wary of applying them to the U.S., Canada, and perhaps Japan.

OECD calculations show that the lowest rates in Western Europe for a basket of *business* telephone charges, including fixed and usage costs, are found in Iceland ($365) and the Netherlands ($430). Swedish rates are $600 while the highest charges are found in Austria ($1,409), Ireland ($1,320) and Germany ($1,326). The OECD average is $930 (OECD, 1990, p. 52). When purchasing power parities are held constant (Figure 32.1), Iceland, Denmark, the Netherlands and Sweden are least expensive for telephone charges (Figure 32.1a); Portugal, Italy, and Ireland are the most costly. Germany is also above average (OECD, 1990, p. 52).

The OECD's comparison of a basket of *residential* services shows similarly that consumers in Iceland, Sweden, Denmark, and the Netherlands enjoy the lowest rates, whereas rates in Portugal and Ireland are highest (Figure 32.2a). Iceland's rates are only $191, representing 34 percent of the OECD average of $354. Austrian consumers, on the other hand, pay $529—64 percent above the OECD average (OECD, 1990, p. 53).

Europe's lowest *international* charges are found in Scandinavia, with Denmark ($76) being the cheapest of all OECD countries for business service. On the other end of the scale, Spain, Greece, and Portugal have the least favorable business rates. Turkey and Portugal, at $165 and $131, have the highest rates in Europe. They are followed by Greece ($124) and Spain ($123).

The residential basket of international charges (Figure 32.3) shows that among the five least expensive countries in the OECD survey, Sweden (at $78) is the cheapest European country. Turkey, Greece, Portugal, and Spain have the highest charges in Europe.

The highest European charges for mobile services are found in Luxembourg, France, and Germany. Germany, the highest at $2944, reflects a ratio of usage-to-fixed charges of almost 3:1. France, which follows with $2630, has higher fixed charges than Germany; Luxembourg ($2573) has the highest fixed costs of the three.

The OECD's basket of mobile telephone charges calculated in purchasing power parities (Figure 32.4) shows Iceland as the least expensive nation, with the second cheapest, Denmark, over three and a half times more expensive ($189 versus $687). At the other end of the scale, Luxembourg had the highest charges for mobile service ($2405) followed closely by Germany ($2358) and France ($2316). The OECD average for mobile service is $1681 ($1116 for usage and $565 for fixed charges).

The OECD comparison of charges for leased data lines with 1.5–2.0 Mbps of capacity (Figure 32.5) shows a relatively even distribution for all OECD countries except Germany. Here charges were about three times higher than the OECD average. Another study by Logica showed that leased line rates varied widely. It found for 64 kilobits per second, 100-kilometer leased lines, a range from $545 (Mercury) to $4,904 (DBP Telekom). France ($3,403), Belgium ($3,457), and Spain ($4,332) were also on the high end. Comparable service

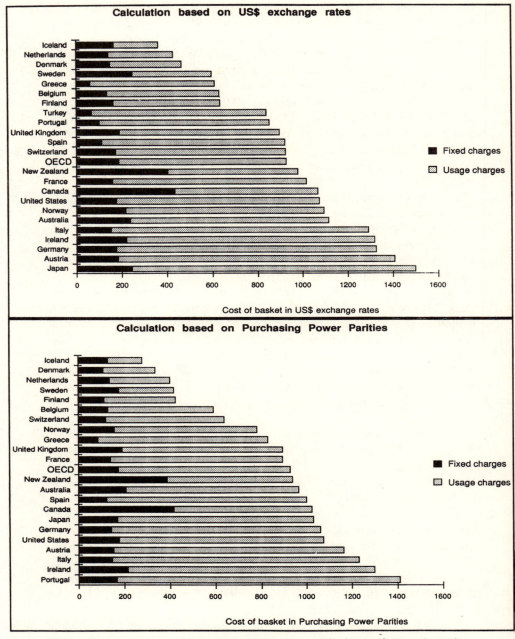

Figure 32.1 and 32.1a.   OECD Basket of Business Telephone Charges, in US$
Exchange Rates and PPPs, November 1989. (*Source:* OECD, 1990, p. 52.)

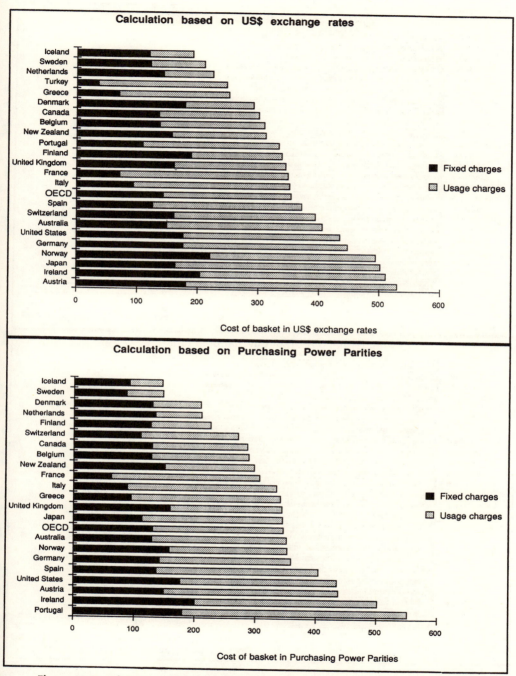

Figure 32.2 and 32.2a. OECD Basket of Residential Telephone Charges, in US$ Exchange Rates and PPPs, November 1989. (*Source:* OECD, 1990, p. 53.)

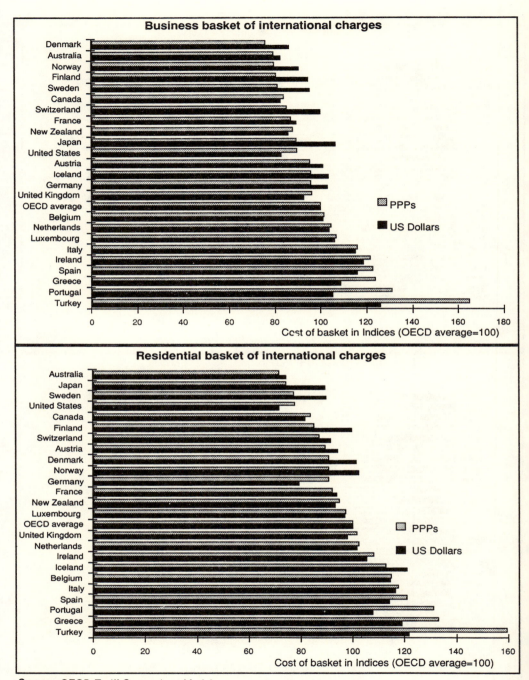

Source: OECD Tariff Comparison Model.

Figure 32.3 and 32.3a. OECD Basket of International Telephone Charges, Ranked by Country, November 1989. (*Source:* OECD, 1990, p. 61.)

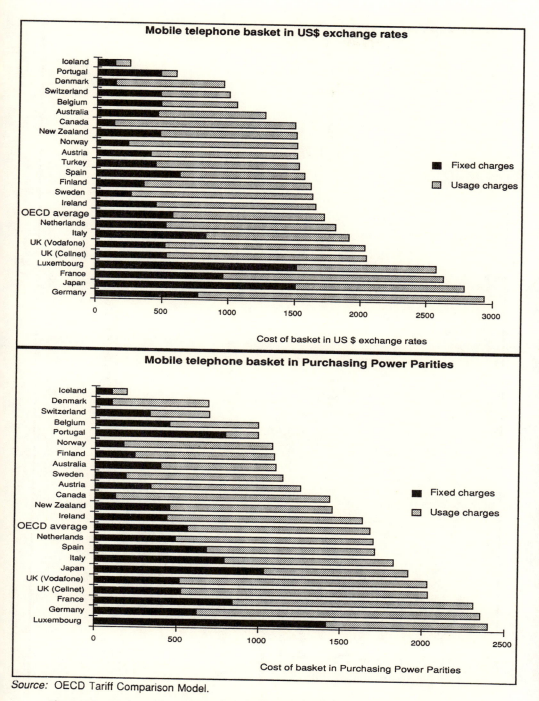

Source: OECD Tariff Comparison Model.

Figure 32.4 and 32.4a. OECD Basket of Mobile Telephone Charges, Ranked by Country, November 1989. (*Source:* OECD, 1990, p. 64.)

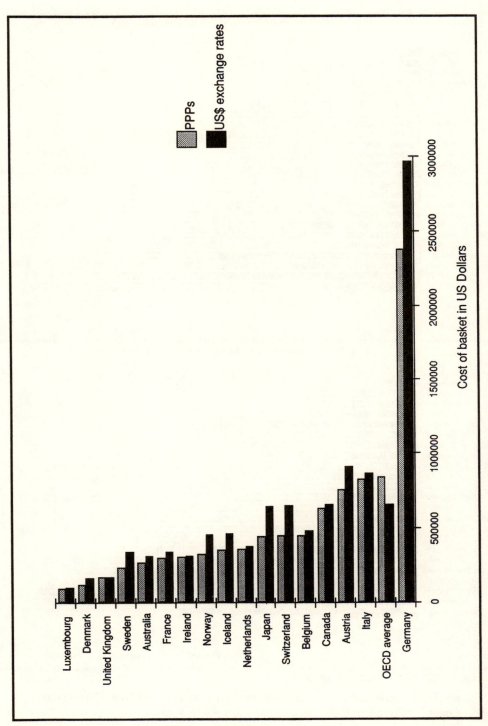

Figure 32.5. Basket of Charges for 1.5/2.0 Mbit/s Leased Lines. (*Source: OECD, 1990, p. 70.*)

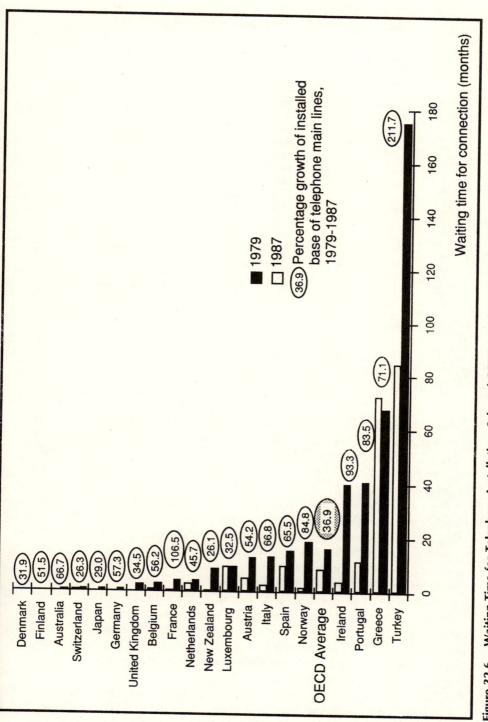

Figure 32.6. Waiting Time for Telephone Installation, Selected OECD Member Countries, 1979–1987. (*Source:* OECD, 1990, p. 126.)

Table 32.1 Fault Reporting Rates in Selected OECD
Countries

Country	Year	Faults per 100 main lines	Comments
Belgium	1985	41.3	
Denmark	1988	31.7	Jutland Telephone
Finland	1987	23.0	
France	1986	21.7	
Greece	1987	62.5	
Ireland	1988/89	52.0	
Japan	1988	2.2	
Norway	1988	30.9	
Portugal	1985	59.0	
Spain	1986	46.3/31.0	Complaints/Faults
Sweden	1986	16.0	
Turkey	1989	19.4	Jan.-Oct. only
United Kingdom	1988	22.0	
United States	1990		July-Dec.
			Consumer trouble,
New York Telephone		4.7	all types
SW Bell		2.4	
			Unweighted aver-
US West		1.8	age

Sources: FCC, Industry Analysis Division (J. Kraushaar, 1991, communication);
New York State Public Service Commission, 1991, communication; OECD, 1990,
p. 131.

costs in the U.S. $267 using MCI. For 2 megabits per second capacity, prices
in Europe ranged from $3,415 (Mercury) to $49,044 (DBP Telekom). Other
major European countries charged more than $10,000. In the United States,
this service is offered by U.S. Sprint for $3,100 (upwardly prorated T-1 line)
(Heywood, 1991).

Price is not the only performance dimension of significance. OECD figures
adapted from the ITU statistics reveal great variation in the amount of time it
took to obtain telephone service (Figure 32.6). The OECD average shows a
significant drop in the amount of waiting time between 1979 and 1987 to around
ten months, and the installed base of main lines grew 37 percent. Potential
subscribers in Greece and Turkey had to wait six and seven years, respectively,
for installation. This stood in stark contrast to the situation in Denmark and
Finland, where waiting time was negligible. Greece was the only country among
those shown where the wait actually increased between 1979 and 1987, while
at the same time its installed base of main lines increased 71.1 percent. Portugal and Ireland both cut waiting periods significantly between 1979 and 1987,
but still ranked weak on this dimension.

The growth rates of installed lines in OECD countries for the same eight-
year period were remarkable (see also Figure 32.6), with Turkey (211 percent),
France (106 percent), and Ireland (93 percent) leading the way. Growth was

Table 32.2 Public Payphones in OECD Countries

Country	No. of Payphones	Payphones per 1,000 Population
Australia[1]	34,135	2.19
Austria	28,018	3.71
Belgium	11,373	1.15
Canada[1]	143,682	5.86
Denmark	5,792	1.13
Finland	17,739	3.61
France	213,126	3.86
Germany	162,458	2.66
Greece	21,815	2.20
Japan	910,000	7.54
Luxembourg	640	1.75
Netherlands	8,020	0.55
Norway	13,353	3.22
Portugal	18,126	1.77
Spain[1]	40,720[2]	1.06[2]
Sweden	18,700[3]	2.10
Switzerland	57,526	8.90
Turkey	35,500	1.55
United Kingdom	76,500	1.35
USA	1,714,055	7.18

Notes: 1. 1985 data.
2. Call box telephones—i.e. excluding public call offices.
3. 1988 data including privately operated payphones.
Source: OECD, 1990, p. 129.

less dramatic in percentage terms in more mature telephone systems (e.g., 26 percent in Switzerland).

OECD statistics reveal the range of faults, apart from network congestion, reported per 100 main lines. Only fourteen countries compiled such statistics nationally (Table 32.1). Japan's rate—in 1988, 2.2 faults per 100 lines—is far below that of any European country participating in the survey. Greece (62) has the highest rate, followed by Portugal (59) and Ireland (52). Some of Europe's most reliable networks include Sweden at 16 and France at 22 (both for 1986). In the United States, corresponding figures for two Bell regional companies for which figures are available are 2.4 for Southwestern Bell and approximately 1.8 for US West (Table 32.1). The OECD estimates a 40 percent likelihood of line faults occurring in OECD countries (OECD, 1990, p. 131).

OECD figures also show that the availability of pay phones per 1000 population in European countries (1985) ranged from a low in the Netherlands of 0.55 to a high in Switzerland of 8.9 (Table 32.2). Between these extremes lay the United Kingdom (1.35), Germany (2.66), and France (3.86). In the United States, the number was 7.18. But this did not include the many privately operated pay phones. The bulk of the world's payphones are in Japan and the United States.

33

The Economics of ISDN Integration

The past chapters have discussed the evolution taking place in various countries. The next sections will deal with more general issues of European communications. The first of them is ISDN.

The Setting

The integrated Services Digital Network (ISDN) is a major development priority of many European PTTs and equipment manufacturers. It is also one of those subjects at once complex, obscure, and important. Deterred by the dense technological jargon that surrounds ISDN, only a few social scientists, let alone commentators or politicians, have ventured near the subject (Schiller, 1984). Similarly, there has been no public discussion. Instead, decisions on this major infrastructure investment were made almost entirely outside the public view by engineering bureaucracies in government and established equipment manufacturing firms. This is not to say that the basic concept of ISDN is flawed as a matter of technology or policy. (The author, while serving as a member of the New York State Public Service Commission, was supportive of the concept and initiated an ISDN trial that linked five different carriers and multiple users.) But it is remarkable how the process of decision making had been transformed into expert discussions of technical specifications. A book by a participant in the international ISDN negotiations in the Consultative Committee on International Telephone and Telegraph (CCITT) and its Study Group XVII provides detailed accounting of the discussion that lasted several years (Rutkowski, 1985). Remarkable in these negotiations is the near total absence of references to considerations of the cost or economic issues involved.

The Concept of ISDN

The term *ISDN* encompasses several subconcepts; thus, some confusion exists about its primary rationale. It is, first, a movement toward end-to-end *digitalization*. As such, it continues a development of several decades, accelerated by advances in computers, from analog to digital electronics. Digitalization has been moving from data processing to telecommunication transmission and switching, similar to its spread to consumer electronics, and is moving to broadcasting and motion picture technology. The evolution of the network toward digitalization precedes ISDN, and the development of ISDN lies squarely within that trend.

The second element of ISDN is that of upgrading user access to the telecommunication network to a *higher data transmission* rate. In past decades, the increased merging of computers and communications, together with the greater information needs of users, have led to a vast increase in data communications traffic. Data communications rose during the period from 1970 to 1985 almost fortyfold, and communications and data processing increased about fivefold (NTIA, 1983). This raised the importance for data communications links of a high capacity, greater than could be provided on analog networks. Digital transmission is also a more efficient means for the transmission of voice traffic at points in the network where it is highly concentrated.

Whereas good-quality, regular analog voice-grade switched communications links support a transmission rate of about 9.6 kbps, international ISDN recommendations provide a much higher total transmission of 144 kbps for two switched channels of 64 kbps (B channels) chosen for voice quality, and one "signalling" channel for housekeeping functions of 16 kbps (the D channel). It is this CCITT-recommended narrowband system that will be referred to in the following as "ISDN." Although analog technology does not stand still (newer modems can upgrade the data capacity of analog lines to over 20 kbps), the data transmission superiority of ISDN over the existing public network is clear.

The third element of ISDN is *integration* and is much weaker in its rationale. ISDN claims to put together separate communications networks into one unified superpipe. From the technologist's perspective, this is a more elegant solution than duplication and multiplication.

Almost all ISDN discussions start out invoking the wasteful existence of several parallel telecommunications networks—if they bother to articulate a rationale at all. Some historic perspective is necessary: Parallel networks existed from the moment that the telephone emerged more than a century ago as a voice network separated from the already existing telegraph—the data network of its time. Eventually, telex networks replaced much of the telegraph; still later, the advent of computer communications led to specialized data transmission, and in particular to packet-switched networks, which move certain types of digital data better than the standard telephone networks.

Digitalization often led to the establishment of integrated digital networks (IDN) for various data services. But it did not yet reach the subscriber loop and subscriber equipment itself (though it came in many instances to within a few hundred feet of them). Thus, subscribers in need of digital data communications of more than slow speeds had to operate over special lines outside the public switched analog network. ISDN represents the completion of network digitalization by going the last mile and reaching subscribers and their equipment. It thus provides the capability to dispense with parallel lines for analog voice and for digital services and instead puts them together in one integrated bit stream of digitalized voice and data.

As long as ISDN simply implies no more, it is hard to find fault with this development, which is part of a broad technological trend. ISDN, however, is more than such upgrading, in Europe and elsewhere; it is also part of a business and political strategy of telephone administrations. "Integration" is thus not simply an issue of technology.

Economies of Scope

The classical arguments in favor of integration are the benefits of "economies of scale" and the joint production benefits of "economies of scope." The latter occurs since the duplication of equipment and personnel is eliminated; similarly, less spare capacity is necessary to handle peak demand loads in integrated production than is required to provide for them separately. If one denotes C as cost, and assumes two services, voice service (V) and data service (D), economies of scope exist if the joint cost is less than the two separate costs; that is, if the following inequality holds:

$$C(V + D) < C(V) + C(D) \tag{1}$$

That this relation exists is generally asserted by ISDN proponents as a matter of a priori reasoning. The same logic—that substitute and complementary products are cheaper if jointly provided—applies similarly to such product pairs as orange juice and beer, beer and aluminum cans, aluminum and aircraft, and aircraft and communications equipment. In the extreme, if one truly wants to eliminate all duplication, the entire economy should consist of one giant integrated enterprise. Thus, the significance of economies of scope is not necessarily as clear-cut a matter as it may appear at first.

Furthermore, the question is not how best to structure a *new* network, but how best to upgrade an already *existing* network. In the short term, virtually all capital in the networks V and D is sunk, whereas a modification for the integrated network ($V + D$) may require new investments I, as well as the premature retirement R of some equipment used for the separate networks. Hence, the test for integration should be expanded to require

$$C(V + D) + C(I) + C(R) < C(A) + C(B) \tag{2}$$

The adjustment costs $C(I)$ and $C(R)$ can offset the pure economies of scope. In the longer term, their significance diminishes as equipment gets replaced naturally. But there are costs to a very gradual integration too, because it requires parallel technologies of different generations to coexist for a long time.

Another problem with the argument of economies of scope is its implicit assumption of static cost functions. That is, costs are defined by the relations $C(V)$, $C(D)$, and $C(V + D)$ without a provision for change. However, separate networks are partial substitutes. Hence, a rivalry between separate specialized networks can provide a competitive environment that can lead to cost reductions and technical innovation. In other words, the cost curves in a separate environment can be dynamic. What starts out as the cost relation $C(V)$ and $C(D)$ can become, under rivalry, $C'(V)$ and $C'(D)$, with the assumption that

$$C'(V) < C(V) \text{ and } C'(D) < C(D) \tag{3}$$

The integrated network should then be more accurately required to meet the condition

$$C(V + D) < C'(V) + C'(D) \tag{4}$$

which is much less obvious than relation (1).

It is, of course, true that institutionally almost no country's telecommunications systems permit competitive networks under separate control. But this is not to say that no rivalry exists at all. Most studies of organizational behavior within government bureaucracies would lead one to predict that different network services will have their own advocates, and constituencies, both inside and outside of the organizations. Hence, at least a bit of rivalry between different networks could exist even in a monopolistic situation.

Another problem with economies of scope is their lack of generality when the number of services is large, as demonstrated with the earlier orange juice example. For example, suppose that instead of two networks V and D there exist n different types of data networks—for example, for different transmission rates, different error rates, and so on, denoted by $D_1 \ldots D_n$. Similarly, let there be a third type of telecommunications network, used for transmission of television programs and denoted by TV. Then we have the separate cost functions

$$C(V), C(D)_1, \ldots, C(D)_n, C(TV) \tag{5}$$

It is far from clear where the economies of scope exist. Even if we assume that each service has economies of scope with its immediate neighbors, this does not prove that a total integration across the entire spectrum of networks would produce economies of scope over stand-alone provision. To prove total integration, one would have to show economies of scope between every pair of services (e.g., between voice and television). Furthermore, each service may have its own and different economies of scale, and a bundling may lead to suboptimal pairing.

Thus, the question of integration then becomes one of choosing clusters of services to integrate, such as $[V, D_1, D_3]$, or $[V, D_2, TV]$. It is far from obvious which groupings of service networks are optimal. Should high-speed data be integrated into broadband cable systems, as is the case in some American cable systems (Noam, 1986)? Or should it be part of an intermediate integration of data networks? Should it be integrated with voice service, even at a high cost? Should it stand on its own? Or should it simply not be provided? None of these questions is answered by the simple reasoning that avoidance of duplication is cost efficient. As the various telecommunications services are bundled into packages of various integration, invariably some services will be dropped. Integration is a standardization process, which is always a trade-off between the cost reduction of compatibility and the benefits of diversity. A process of integration is hence usually a process of reduction of options.

Furthermore, even where total integration may be cheaper than stand-alone services, the integration may not be stable—"sustainable"—if some of the services could drop out of the integrated package. To understand this, it is necessary to distinguish between three cost concepts: first, the stand-alone cost of service of type i, denoted by C_i. Second, the cost of operating i as part of a service package, which is $C(I_i)$. Third, the incremental total cost IC_i of adding it to the service package.

$$IC(_i) = C(1 \ldots n) - C[a \ldots (i-1), (i+1) \ldots , n] \qquad (6)$$

IC may be lower than the cost of integration, positive externalities of i on the services, if it acts, for example, as a backup. Suppose, for example, that the cost of providing i is 10 as a stand-alone service and 20 as an integrated service because of technical problems of integration. This would suggest that integration is uneconomical. However, total incremental cost of the integrated service may be only 5, because of the positive externalities on the other services. Thus, integration would be economically efficient, but it would not be a stable solution. If each network could act independently, it would drop out of an integrated network, since this would reduce its cost from 20 to 10. Its positive network externalities to the overall service would then be lost to the remaining network. Thus, the integrated system, if it is voluntary, is unstable, or "unsustainable."

The sustainability argument for integration, presented here in very simple terms, is one not made specifically by the telecommunications administrations. It is based on a more complete general theory of industrial organization (Baumol et al., 1983), with which PTTs are gradually becoming familiar (Weizsäcker, 1987). In any event, the sustainability argument is a theoretical one and depends on the underlying cost characteristics, which may or may not exist for telecommunications networks.

Economies of Scale

We now widen the discussion to economies of scale, the intellectual ancestor of economies of scope. This concept, probably the single favorite idea in the intellectual armory of telecommunications administrations, states that the cost of providing additional users continuously decreases, and that is thus cheaper to service all users by one large entity. The concept, closely related to the vague notion of "natural monopoly," has been questioned on empirical grounds as to its actual existence beyond a certain size. (For a review of the empirical literature, see Meyer, 1980.) It can also be challenged along the lines used above, namely, that the inefficiency of monopoly more than offsets its economies of scale. In the American context, for example, the system of rate-of-return regulation created built-in incentives toward an overcapitalization, known as the Averch-Johnson effect. As discussed earlier, competition can move cost curves downward, which may result in greater efficiencies than through relying on a movement *along* a downward-sloping static cost function.

In the context of integrated service, economies of scale are used to argue that the integration of services creates cost efficiencies by bringing various new communications services to the population at large. Whereas it would be uneconomic for a residential or small business user to have digital data links, this would become affordable in an integrated universal network. By making such services prevalent, their cost per user drops, benefitting also the earlier large users.

If strong economies of scale exist in ISDN, one policy implication could be to subsidize the early stages of its growth. Even if its cost cannot be recovered for a while, eventually costs come down and benefits rise. Early users deserve a subsidy, because their participation lowers the cost for previous and subsequent users; otherwise, they may well never sign up and start the chain of economies of scale down the cost curve. (For a discussion of network externalities, see Katz and Shapiro, 1985.) This argument is a plausible one for a subsidy, though it does not prove a case for integration or for governmental control. But it is true for almost all start-up operations, in any line of business, whether public or private. To judge the justification for subsidies in the ISDN context one needs to have information about the size of the economies of scale.

The need for a start-up subsidy can be used to justify a variety of restrictive policies:

1. Prohibition against alternative network options—certainly private, but also public—in order to gain the economies of scale and avoid a loss in revenue, which is termed *cream skimming*.
2. A tariff structure that reduces the required subsidy as much as possible by increasing revenues through a rate system that charges according to the *value* of the service to different users (i.e., their elasticity of demand), rather than on the basis of cost. *Value to user*—which is not a pricing criterion for economic efficiency—means discrimination between different users on the basis of the service's value to them. Charges are made on the basis of actual usage rather than on the basis of cost. To be effective over time, price discrimination requires market power, although such power need not be governmental. Introducing such usage-sensitive pricing was part of PTT policy; the German Bundespost introduced it to the displeasure of large users of data communications and of equipment firms such as IBM. (A volume-based pricing system was employed by IBM itself years ago when it required the use of IBM-produced punched cards to go with rented IBM computers, thus creating a usage metering and pricing system, and by Xerox Corp., which rented its equipment and charged according to the metered number of copies.) One optimal discriminatory policy is known as Ramsey pricing (i.e., charging according to the inverse of the demand elasticities of different customers).

Table 33.1   Cost of Providing Voice and Data Service to
Firms and Residents (Schematic)

	V	D	(V+D)
F	8	9	16
R	11	12	21
(F+R)	16	20	35

The two policies are interrelated. The establishment of price discrimination that is not based on cost leads to incentives for arbitrage and for competitive alternatives. Hence, it becomes more important than ever to stem these threats of cream skimming by prohibitions against competitive networks of reselling.

In other words, the start-up subsidy necessary for the service becomes an argument for protection against competition and for maintenance of monopoly. Indeed, a highly perverse incentive is built in, because the greater the required subsidy, the greater the political support will be for a monopoly status that reduces its cost to the taxpayers. An expensive project helps raise not only the economic but also the political barriers to entry. This encourages the introduction of successive large projects that remain in deficit long enough to justify barriers against cream skimming.

Scale and Scope

Economies of scale are used as an argument for the expansion of network integration to all classes of participants in the public network. As with most of the pro-integration arguments, this is true only under certain conditions. The theoretical problem with the argument can be demonstrated with the following table. Assume again two types of networks, voice (V) and digital data (D), and two types of users, firms F and residents R. Service can be provided separately or jointly across services ($V + D$), across user classes ($F + R$), or across both services and user classes. Table 33.1 demonstrates schematically a situation in which economies of scale and scope exist yet the integration is uneconomical. Each number corresponds to the cost of providing a service of type i to user class of type j.

In Table 33.1, economies of scale exist in the vertical columns, where integration across customers lowers costs for voice service from $8 + 11 = 19$ to 16 and for data service D from $9 + 12 = 21$ to 20.

Similarly, economies of scope exist horizontally in the rows of Table 33.1. For firms they reduce cost from $8 + 9 = 17$ to 16, and for residents from $11 + 12 = 23$ to 21. Furthermore, full integration—both across services and customers—combines economies of scale and scope and lowers total costs to 35, where they would be 40 in total separation and 36 and 37 in partial integrations. This would argue for total integration. The economies of integration (scale and scope) are greater than each of the subeconomies. Both horizontal or vertical integration are cost-reducing.

Table 33.2 Benefits of Voice and Data Service to Firms and Residents (Schematic)

	V	D	(V+D)
F	9	10	19
R	11	6	17
(F+R)	20	16	36

This analysis, however, is based purely on cost considerations and is devoid of any discussion of revenues, benefits, and demand. If the price for each of the four subcategories is arrived at by simply dividing total cost equally, the price for each subservice would be 35/4 = 8.75. This means that firms are now charged for the integrated voice service 2 × 8.75 = 17.5, rather than the 16 of partial integration or the 17 of full separation. Thus, they pay more than before.

Of course, it would be possible to structure a pricing scheme that would distribute the cost savings to all types of usages. This would mean price discrimination according to usage type or user category, or both. Yet such price discrimination would establish incentives for arbitrage. Under certain circumstances no price vector could exist that would not make it preferable for some service to be provided separately (nonsustainability).

A second problem exists if one considers, realistically, that the different service types are of varying benefit to their users. For example, the benefit of data services users may actually be quite small to residential users. Let us assume for illustration that the benefits of the four categories are given by Table 33.2. These benefits also establish the maximum willingness to pay.

In this situation it will increase welfare—defined as benefits minus costs—to integrate voice and data on the firm level, since benefits are 19, against costs, which are 16 (from Table 33.1). But it would not cover cost to integrate the residential service, the cost of which is 21, whereas maximum revenue would be only 11 + 6 = 17. Similarly, it would make sense to integrate voice services for firms and residents, but not for data. Any inclusion of residential data service would have a deficit of 16 − 21 = −5. This could be done through an outside subsidy, as by using the total cost gains of integration (8 + 9 + 11 + 12 − 35 = 5) to offset the deficit, or by charging some or all users and services above cost, up to the limit of their willingness to pay.

Of course, this means that three of the service types do not pay less, because of integration; to the contrary, they are likely to be called upon to pay more than before, since earlier they paid less than their benefit (i.e., had a consumer surplus). On the other hand, the fourth service benefits. An otherwise lost benefit of 5 is gained, though at a cost of a subsidy of 5.

Another pricing policy would be to eschew a subsidy from one *user* type to another and to limit it to a subsidy within a category. This could be done by requiring the residential user to obtain a package of the two services, or none at all. Maximum total payment would be 21, from Table 33.1. This would not be sufficient, and hence an additional subsidy of 4 would be necessary, either from outside governmental services or, more likely, from the other user category. This then creates the incentive to go beyond partial to full integration, to find more services or user surplus for purposes of subsidy.

But in terms of welfare, is this the optimizing policy? Suppose that instead of integrating all four services, one integrates only three and forgets about data service for residents. This would generate costs of 28 (for the three separate services) and benefits of 30, for a total net welfare of 2 ($30 - 28$), whereas in the fully integrated system net benefits are only $36 - 35 = 1$. In other words, aggregate societal benefit may not be improved by a cross-subsidy to a user whose benefits from the service are small, even where one can show economies of both scale and scope. Thus, technical efficiencies by themselves do not prove societal benefits of integration in the absence of consideration of user benefits (i.e., of demand conditions). And it is not enough to show that there are *some* benefits to residential users from data service, which is what ISDN boosters do with anecdotal evidence. Instead, it is necessary to illustrate the magnitude of these benefits relative to their costs.

This discussion can be extended beyond a 2 × 2 matrix to additional types of telecommunications services and additional user categories. What is intended here is only a schematic sketch of economic arguments that could be made more rigorously. Economic reasoning suggests that a trade-off exists between variety and specialization and that an optimal product diversity exists (Lancaster, 1975; Salop, 1979; Hemenway, 1975; Spence, 1975). There can easily be too much standardization or inefficient standardization (Farrell and Saloner, 1985, 1986a; Besen and Johnson, 1986). [1]

An important cost of systems standardization, such as that sought for ISDN, is that it tends to lock equipment manufacturing, systems development, and user applications into a pattern revolving around the one standard that may soon be obsolete technologically. However, for any one agent to move to another standard may prove prohibitively expensive. Hence, standards include an element of discontinuity and retardation of innovation. For example, the keyboard of typewriters and other input terminals has remained with the traditional "QWERTY" key system, even though studies have shown that a different configuration (Dvorak) of keys increases typing speed and reduces errors (David, 1984).

Such discontinuities exist in particular when, as in a network, positive externalities are generated by each participant. To leave a standardized integrated system is costly, because those departing lose the benefits conveyed by the other members. Only large agents could then be expected to move on their own toward a new technical specification. However, because their departure imposes a cost (lost positive externalities) on the remaining adherents to the network, the decision to move to another standard may be blocked by administrative fiat as imposing a social cost.

Similarly, the early announcements of new standards, such as those for ISDN, is not necessarily the efficient information-enhancing act claimed by its proponents. Instead, it can be the act of a monopolist or of oligopolists aimed at preventing users from moving toward superior technology that they would otherwise choose, by signalling to them that they will lose the benefits of leaving the coalition around the major standard that the monopolist controls (Farrell and Saloner, 1986b).

The investment in a major upgrading of the network has the effect of raising barriers to entry in the following ways: First, it increases the required initial investment that a potential rival needs to match the upgraded technical capabilities of the existing network. Second and similarly, where there is a trade-off between fixed costs and marginal costs, as there often is, the latter are lowered by the investment, making it more difficult for a rival to enter and match marginal cost pricing. Third, by raising the initial investment, one can stretch the range of economies of scale (declining average cost) and thus of "natural monopoly." The trough of a U-shaped cost curve is shifted to a higher level of production by an increase in fixed costs.

The theoretical analysis of the past sections demonstrated that the economic case for ISDN, on purely analytical grounds, has not been made persuasively. Empirical figures have not been presented in support of ISDN which would prove the advantages of integration in light of the issues discussed earlier. This is not to say that such a case cannot be made. However, the battles over ISDN have never been fought on the grounds of economics. To understand why, one has to go back to the history of ISDN. This will be done in the next chapter.

34

The Political Economy of ISDN

Computer Industry versus Telecommunications Providers

Debates over narrowband ISDN mirror the key conflicts in the information sector. In the 1960s and early 1970s, the PTTs had failed to appreciate the potential of data communications, and much of equipment, packet switching, and so on, was developed outside the telephone industry and its traditional suppliers. For the PTTs, the threat was that the computer industry would reach standards that would be incompatible with the existing public or specialized networks and would instead accelerate the creation of private networks. Computer standards were the purview of the International Standards Organization, ISO, whereas telecommunications standards were those of the ITU's CCITT, the Consultative Committee on International Telephony and Telegraphy. Though significant coordination between ISO and CCITT exists through Joint Technical Committee 1 (JTC1), there is also a built-in rivalry between administrations and private network operators. This is partly due to "forum shopping" by interested parties, with the computer community preferring ISO. Joint development of standards was undertaken through the JTC1. Given the complexity and contiguity of technology, the dividing line between standards set by network authorities and those of computer manufacturers is a meandering one. Standards control varies, depending on the type of service (e.g., telephones, telex, teletext, electronic mail) and depending on the layer in the OSI reference model.

After years of preliminary research, the CCITT decided to study ISDN in 1980 and to issue recommendations. It established Study Group XVIII headed by Theodor Irmer of the German Bundespost, which proceeded very actively to issue recommendations (Irmer later became head of CCITT, having won respect for his ISDN work). While these efforts were significantly escalated in 1980, the origin of CCITT-defined ISDN (narrowband with two 64 kbps channels and a signaling channel of 16 kbps) goes back to a 1970s view of technology, markets, and strategic vision (A. Rutkowski, communication, 1990). For a detailed chronology of these proceedings, see Rutkowski (1985). ISDN was left in the domain of the technical study groups (H. Marks, 1987, communication).

The ISDN concept was, in part, a defensive response by the telephone administrations to assert control over the network. Technologists and inside experts may see ISDN merely as a technical issue, but massive investment programs are rarely free of other considerations. ISDN is no exception, unless one entirely ignores the historic struggles over exclusivity in which most major PTTs are engaged.

A similar implicit assertiveness to expand the range of the PTTs' activities also lies in the potential of future integrated broadband networks (B-ISDN, or IBN). This is likely to become a major issue. The cost of glass fiber terminal equipment will soon permit the use of fiber to a point near the home or even into it. The development of broadband switching has also progressed enormously. Given these favorable technological and economic trends, telephone carriers will be able in the foreseeable future to provide video program services (even switched ones), and become rivals of traditional cable television carriers and over-the-air transmitters. Conversely, cable carriers could engage in alternative local telecommunications transmission, challenging the PTT exclusivity over the local loop (Noam, 1986). The British government's duopoly review of 1990 recognized and encouraged such evolution.[1]

The conflict of telecommunications providers with the computer industry centered on IBM. For a long time, many Europeans endowed IBM with near-mythical abilities, which justified drastic government actions. The preoccupation with IBM led to recommendations to use telecommunications, which governments control, as a lever over the computer industry, now that the two sectors are overlapping. This strategy was spelled out in the influential 1978 Nora–Minc report to the French president, which was discussed earlier, and which, with its combination of brilliance, gloom, and nationalism, deeply influenced French and European policymakers and intellectuals.

> Controlling the network system is thus an essential objective. This requires that its framework be designed to serve the public. But it is also necessary for the state to define access standards; otherwise the manufacturers will, utilizing the available routes but subjecting them to their own protocols. The level of standardization will thus shift the boundary between the manufacturers and the telecommunications organizations; it will be a bitter struggle, since it will develop out of a reciprocal play for influence. But the objective of public control indicates the strategy to follow: increase the pressure in favor of standardization [Nora and Minc, 1980, pp. 74–75].

ISDN and its standardization thus promised to be a tool of the kind advocated by Nora and Minc at the time when ISDN planning moved into its serious stage.

United States versus the PTTs

Given this perception, it is not surprising that there were conflicts between the United States and the major PTT countries. The concept of ISDN, by itself, does not require exclusivity and power. Strictly speaking, all it means is that the same communication link is able to provide a range of digital telecommunications services. It could be provided by multiple and competing ISDNs or by private customized ISDNs. However, the usage has, at least within the PTTs, implied a de facto exclusivity. The abolition of duplicative networks is stressed as a main goal of integration. Economies of scale and scope are the arguments. With such justification, the idea of permitting rival networks seems self-defeating, and deeply at odds with the motivations for ISDN. In the United States, on the other hand, an ISDN cannot be one of exclusivity, neither geographically nor functionally, but must involve the interconnectivity of multiple networks, several of which could be ISDN types.

For United States policymakers, the ISDN creates several problems. Much of the early ISDN discussion was technical, and not necessarily in tune with the broader concerns of U.S. telecommunications policy (Marks, 1984). It was advanced by the still undivested AT&T system, for reasons similar to those motivating the PTTs.

Because ISDN calls for standardization, integration, and international coordination, centralized telecommunications systems such as those in Europe had an easier time formulating their ISDN goals than in the United States, where such central decision making does not exist in telecommunications. Particularly after the AT&T divestiture, American industry was fragmented, and coordination was difficult to achieve. The Bell operating companies formed a central technical organization, Bellcore, to provide some of the services that the old AT&T had provided; but by the nature of decentralization, it could move only slowly. Furthermore, independent telephone companies, including ones as large as GTE, are outside of Bellcore, as are the computer and component industries and telephone uses. It was a matter of concern in America that international standards could be agreed upon by entities whose operative philosophy was very different from the American one.

As the chief of the FCC's Technical Analysis Division wrote:

> [S]ince only two other countries out of 159 members of the International Telecommunication Union (ITU) have any aspect of competition in their carrier industry, technical decisions made in this forum have a tendency to be biased toward monopoly. This is not to imply that other countries seek to impose their industry structure on the United States intentionally; rather they are focusing on their own situations and honestly do not understand the implications of the US industry structure [Marcus, 1985, p. 33].

The FCC declared that customer provision of the network termination device (NT1) should be a national option.[2] It described as fundamental that CCITT recommendations must be flexible enough for national options and that the American distinction between basic and enhanced services must be maintained.

It turned out to be complicated to work out the proper interface point between the domain of the network and that of the users. Essentially, three demarcation points are possible, known, respectively, as the S, T, and U points in CCITT terminology. The S point is closest to the end user, and hence carries the network-controlled portion furthest upstream.[3] The PTTs wanted point S as the interface between user and network because they could control equipment standards up to that point. Users and independent equipment manufacturers, on the other hand, did not want to see PTT control reach that far.[4] The FCC supported U as the demarcation point in order to encourage the development of more advanced and versatile terminal equipment.

Hegemonic ISDN

ISDN has always meant different things to different people, from a simple and partial upgrading of digitalization to more ambitious undertakings encompassing everything up to video transmission. However, recent international standardization efforts have narrowed the term for the present. But these different definitions revolve around technology. A different classification of ISDN is based on its *purpose:* it distinguishes "hegemonic" from "upgrade" ISDN. The latter is a step in the technical evolution of telecommunications. The former, on the other hand, is part of a general attempt at maintaining control over networks.

The key element of the coalition between bureaucracy and established equipment manufacturers is strongly evident in the discussions on ISDN, and for good reason. In most European countries, the decades following World War II were periods of very active expansion in telecommunications. The combination of war-damage repair and the expansion of telephone penetration from the business and upper classes to universal use has kept telephone authorities busy and manufacturers profitable. But this expansion reached its natural plateau when most households were served. Whereas in 1960, only some 20 percent of the German households had telephones, by 1982, over 80 percent did. In France, after a major development push, penetration by 1984 was over 80 percent. The implications for equipment manufacturers were clear; the domestic market was close to saturation in terms of standard equipment and would decline; this would leave them only with the export market, of which, according to an OECD study, only 15 percent was free from protectionism. Furthermore, the absence of a strong domestic market is also likely to make exports more costly, since they would not benefit from economies of scale in production. One way to activate the sagging domestic market was therefore to launch an ambitious program of upgrading, and ISDN was just such a project. Figure 34.1 illustrates, for Germany, the role of ISDN digital upgrade for both transmission and switching (Schön, 1985).

The PTTs, seeking support for their domestic position, courted their traditional allies by dangling ISDN before them. Germany's Bundespost, for example, argued that ISDN was important for the export success of domestic industry and that it required the ability of the Bundespost to play a role in the equipment supply field, a role that was under attack by Germany's Monopoly Commission and the Ministry of Economics.

> The PTT that takes on the leading role internationally when a new service is standardized gives the communications industry in their country a big head start in this

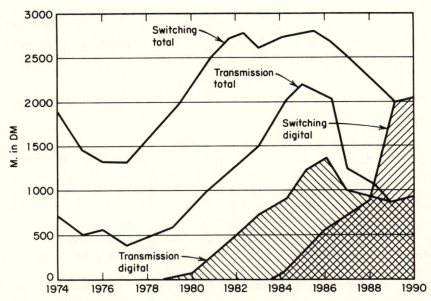

Figure 34.1.   Annual Investments in Transmission and Switching Technology in Germany. (*Source:* Schön, 1985.)

service. . . . The Deutsche Bundespost has so far played a prominent part in this context. . . . *Anyone who blocks this influence in his own country damages the innovative force of a future technology and ultimately the entire economy* [Schön, 1984, p. 22; emphasis in original].[5]

Network Segmentation and the Open Network Architecture Concept

In America, the idea of all telecommunications under one organization was never palatable. Even in AT&T's heyday, it shared the field geographically with almost 2000 other independent telephone companies (covering more than half the country and 20 percent of subscribers) and functionally with the domestic and international record carriers. Deregulation and divestiture accelerated the segmentation of networks. These developments led to yet another and still more radical approach that that begun to emerge, known as *open network architecture* (ONA). This approach is *not* incompatible with ISDN in terms of technology; and in the United States they are likely to coexist. But in terms of underlying philosophy, ONA derived from a diametrically different concept of the future environment of the telecommunications networks, and of the different role of the major carriers in it than those held by ISDN's major international supporters.

Open network architecture expanded the concepts of service alternatives and network fragmentation into the very core of the networks, and lowered barriers to entry for rival and varied communications services. ISDN, in contrast, raised entry barriers by providing a highly integrated network. ONA unbundles, whereas ISDN consolidates.

The concept of open network architecture must be distinguished from the similarly named *open systems interconnection* (OSI) of the International Organization for Standardization which provides a definitional framework of seven broad layers of the entire network process. ONA takes this further by not only going into more detailed subfunctions of several of these layers, but also proposing their functional separation, together with a business and regulatory policy concept. It must also be distinguished from the E.C.'s Open Network Provision, a concept that established access for value-added services, especially across European frontiers, and which is much less far-reaching in its unbundling.

A preliminary variant of ONA is also known as *comparably efficient interconnection,* or CEI.[6] The FCC required the major carriers to submit ONA plans in 1988 as a step in its evolution. The states (most notably New York and California) also began to evolve ONA regulatory concepts (Noam, 1988a).

ONA is a framework of network components that disaggregate in such a way as to permit open access; it operates on the concept that all central office functions consist of fundamental components or Basic Service Elements (BSEs) and that these components can and should be unbundled. Different communications services use different BSEs, or different configurations of them, sequenced in various ways. The open network architecture permits the use by outside parties (users or third-party service providers) of the building blocks of their choice. Where any of the blocks could be provided cheaper or better from another supplier, it could be substituted and combined with BSEs or equipment of the local exchange company. In other words, competition would exist for the various functions of the central exchange switch by unbundling its multiple functions. To make such a system work, service providers conceivably could in some instances collocate their own nodes on the physical premises of the local exchange company. The third-party service providers are partly a form of value-added networks, competing physical networks on the local level, and simple resellers. In all of these functions they would compete head on with the local exchange companies, who act both as retailers and as wholesalers of these services (Noam, 1989).

Through ONA, local exchange carriers in effect permit the resale of separate parts of their services, down to separate functions of the local exchange. This is a radical reversal of past practice, where the monopolistic telephone companies tried to prevent resale. Now they have begun to recognize that their network is their prime asset and that they should sell its capabilities as much as possible, to the point of encouraging use by outsiders. In this fashion, the network can be utilized more and a telephone company can still profit.

Once the building blocks are separated from each other, a pricing mechanism need be put into place that can establish transparent and nondiscriminatory pricing. For those building blocks where competition exists, deregulation can be instituted. Elsewhere, tariffed rates would be set. Clearly, a wide array of complex regulatory questions needs to be resolved in the process of introducing

ONA (Marks, 1986; Noam, 1988b, c). For example, the FCC announced the possibility of extending ONA in the future into basic service access arrangements (BSAs) of the local carriers. This step was taken by the New York State Public Service Commission, which established ONA rights for basic transport and created a type of access (collocation) in which alternative transport providers can physically locate their equipment in the central offices of the traditional carriers, and vice versa (or do so in a functionally equivalent, i.e., "virtual" form). Collocation also permits alternative carriers to provide network monitoring and control of their own.

In *technical* terms, the ONA approach is not contradictory to ISDN, since an ISDN operator could similarly provide for the subdivision of its functions, selling them separately and permitting various reconfigurations and resale to third parties. This is likely to happen in the United States in the future. But *attitudinally,* the ISDN concept, as presently held by its champions abroad, is widely different. Whereas the open network architecture is another step in the segmentation of American networks, the PTTs' purpose for ISDN is another step in its centralization.

ONA is not the only move toward segmentation in central office switching. Already mentioned were shared tenant services, by which multiple users share a common (nonpartitional) PBX. This concept has already begun to move into the clustering of office buildings and provides a nucleus of alternative central switches (Noam, 1986). Another manifestation is the emergence of interorganizational networks (IONs) or enterprise networks.

Europe's ONP seeks to harmonize conditions of access, usage, interoperability, and data protection among the networks of E.C. member states by eliminating the need for special adaptation of services between countries; it thus provides a framework for a pan-European liberalized market for value-added services. In 1988, the E.C. commission outlined its goals for ONP, including the gradual establishment of technical standards, rules of interconnection, and equal access to value-added services (Ungerer, 1989). Decisions concerning technical standards were referred to the European Telecommunications Standards Institute (ETSI). Parameters were developed concerning service quality, shared use, and resale of network capacity. Also, the commission intends to implement a mutual recognition process of authorization for services, whereby one member state can certify a supplier to serve the entire European Community.

ONP has none of the unbundling elements of ONA and its establishment of central office subfunctions, nor its related collocation and transport competition. (Avoiding the latter two is also the position of the American local exchange telephone companies.) Yet ONP, while a modest step, nevertheless created a European rift.

Several PTTs (those of France, Italy, Belgium, Greece, and Portugal) were reluctant to accept the liberal ONP guidelines. A compromise was reached. The French proposed the licensing of data service providers, but the E.C. retained approval of licensing procedures. Less-developed European countries were given extensions to 1996 to implement ONP, and harmonization of technical standards was made voluntary.

In 1990, an E.C. directive was issued adopting technical interface and service feature standards. Although compliance is voluntary, the directive gives the European Community the option to make it mandatory in the interest of interoperability. The directive's ONP framework provides the following: policies for leased lines and voice telephony to follow; standards for ISDN and packet-switched services by 1991; recommendations for ISDN and packet-switched services by 1992; and an examination by the European Community and further recommendations after 1992 (European Commission, 1990, pp. 294–95).

Technical Capability: Toward the Integrated Broadband Network

The two main narrowband ISDN channels operate on a speed of 64 kbps, but user needs vary widely. Some services need only a very slow bit rate (e.g., telemetry, such as meter reading and alarm services). Inquiry response applications, such as airline flight reservations, electronic banking, or electronic shopping, require rates of less than 4.8 kbps. A 64 kbps rate supports transmission of high-quality facsimile as well as simple fixed graphic images and slow video scan. Voice transmission in the United States is principally encoded at 56 kbps, but 32 kbps seems to be emerging as the conventional rate. By various methods of compression, voice transmission of sufficient quality has been accomplished with as little as 9.6 kbps. Thus, one need not expect the 64 kbps requirement for digitalized voice to endure. It is a fairly high standard for digital voice encoding, and it had been chosen because of the need for voice quality in the context of an analog network with frequent demodulation.

On the other hand, the transfer of bulk data, such as large data files or communications among mainframe computers, uses much higher rates. In the United States, they are often in the T1 rate range of 1.544 Mbps (i.e., more than twenty times faster than rates for the ISDN); and in Europe, they are at the 2.048 Mbps rate.

Full-motion broadcast-quality video requires, depending on the protocols, an analog signal of about 4.5 MHz, or about 100 Mbps as a digital signal. Using signal-compression techniques, or a smaller number of lines, the signal can be compressed down to 1.5 Mbps (i.e., the T1 rate).

Its name notwithstanding, ISDN, as defined by the CCITT, does not fully integrate all communications services. The transmission of broadband services—most important, of video programs—cannot be accommodated, except through bundling of several lines. The bandwidth of the ISDN network is too narrow for it; four-wire transmission of one video signal can be accomplished with some technical effort. In comparison, a standard coaxial cable television link can easily carry seventy or more simultaneous video channels. At present, digital switches are not yet well suited for large-scale switching of broadband services. ISDN, as defined by the CCITT, thus results in a compromise rate: faster than necessary for most small and medium-sized data users but too slow for video.

The next technological step after integration and digitalization is integrated broadband service (IBN). Such a broadband service could be more fully integrated, carrying also video programming and mass media entertainment as well as high-speed data streams.

The underlying technological development is optical fiber with its large transmission capability. Experimentally, transmission rates of dozens of gigabits/sec over a single fiber strand have been achieved. At present, fiber is largely used for high-capacity trunk transmission. Its cost (supporting equipment, installation, etc.) is still too high for regular subscriber loops, though some large end users have already been reached (Egan, 1990; Elton, 1991). But it is likely that fiber will be used in the future for small users too. At the same time, development work is taking place for broadband electronic and optical switches. The latter can process an optical flow without requiring its transformation into electrons for the switching functions. It will take some time for these developments to be completed, but their eventual arrival is clear. Therefore, one may ask whether it makes sense to move to the narrowband, electronic, copper-based (for subscriber loops) ISDN if it is merely a transitional technology. Should one postpone the next generation of communications technology to wait for the one after it? This depends on the speed of innovation and the cost of replacement, questions that call for analysis along technical and economical lines. For some theoretical considerations, see Wilson (1984) and Rohlfs (1974).

It does not appear that fiber will rapidly replace already embedded copper loops. And where separate coaxial cable television lines exist, the most demanded broadband services are already provided to subscribers. Thus, the time-frame for the deployment of basic narrowband digitalization has a duration longer than its stay in the technical labs, giving it a role in a transition to broadband-ISDN.

Outlook

The past two chapters have asserted that the issue of integration stands for much more fundamental questions of control over the telecommunications network.

In a wider sense, it is part of a contest over where the intelligence in the network resides (i.e., at the center or the periphery), who controls it (users or network operators), who builds it (the telecommunications or the computer industry), and who runs the network (public providers or private ones).

Whether ''segmentation'' or ''integration'' are optimal solutions for networks is a matter that cannot be determined a priori. It is a trade-off of four economic principles in two combinations: the efficiency of specialized production and of a competitive environment versus the productivity contributions of economies of scale and scope and the reduction of uncertainty. One cannot generalize on which might work best.

35

Value-Added Networks and Services

Value-added networks receive greater attention in European policy discussions than in the United States, and it is important to understand from the outset why this is so. The key policy issue with respect to value-added networks is their potential to resell basic transmission to third parties. Arbitrage by a service reseller leads to loss of control by the basic network provider and to revenue reduction, at least in the short run. In the United States, such resale is possible and widely practiced; lessees of circuits can do almost anything they want. Regulatory constraints exist only to prevent basic carriers from using internal subsidies to extend their market power into the applications stages. In contrast, European PTTs generally prohibit resale, though it exists unofficially in some instances. But in time, European countries realized that the use of leased lines can give rise to sophisticated applications and that such services should be encouraged. They have consequently moved toward permitting the provision of services that "add value" to basic transmission, and the sale of such VAN services to third parties. This technical addition legally transforms what would otherwise be an illegal resale into a legal sale. Another alternative to containing resale is to establish usage-sensitive pricing for leased circuits. But this creates problems of efficient pricing.

However, as with any kind of attempt at price discrimination that is not cost based, one can never underestimate the ingenuity of arbitrageurs. Those who still wish to resell basic transmission but can only sell "value-added" service may try to add a trivial amount of value or an entirely unnecessary amount, solely to cross the line into legality. To prevent this it becomes necessary for PTTs or governments to require formal licensing of these value-added networks, which would involve scrutinizing the nature of their "value added" and of their pricing. A formal approval process, or at least some form of ongoing monitoring, is necessary to protect the system of price discrimination.

In the United States, as mentioned, such procedures do not exist. As a result, VANs are merely a functional description and not a regulatory category. Being not officially defined, they have different meanings for different people, and often simply refer to packet-switching networks. It is true that in the United States there is a regulatory distinction between "basic" and "enhanced" services affecting VANs. But this distinction serves an entirely different purpose. Whereas PTTs seek regulation of VANs to prevent the resale of leased capacity (i.e., to protect the PTT service monopoly), the U.S. regulations serve to prevent the cross-subsidization by a dominant carrier of its value-added services through revenue gained in those dominant activities. In other words, the American "basic/enhanced" dichotomy is established to protect the newcomers from the established carriers, and the PTTs' licensing of VANs aims at protecting themselves.

A Conceptual Framework for the VANs

The VAN system is dynamic, but also organizationally complex and interrelated, to the despair of tidy minds. Terminology on VANs is vague, and some attempt at clarification is in order. Conceptually, it is useful to think of VANs as a system of multiple levels of sale and transformation. The first level consists of the basic transport carriers such as the PTTs, AT&T, or the local Bell companies. These carriers all provide lines to basic value-added networks (in the United States, private firms such as Telenet, Tymnet, or AT&T Accunet; in Europe, PTT entities and sometimes subsidiaries such as Transpac), which constitute the second level. These essentially provide basic packet-switched transmission service and some basic protocol conversions as common or private carriers.

The third layer consists of "generic service providers." Such firms, also called VANs, provide the additional software and organizational features that make for added value beyond transmission. The third-level providers can be identical to the second-level providers, and the operations can be functionally integrated. Conceptually, however, the distinction is necessary. In the case of AT&T and the BOCs, in fact, any third-level service must be provided by an entity that keeps strict accounting separations from the rest of the firm (i.e., from its levels 1 and 2). AT&T offered level 3 service under the name of Net 1000, for which it leased time from its level 2 Accunet Packet Service, which in turn used AT&T network dedicated lines (level 1).

However, things are never neat in this field. Level 2 VANs can also provide capacity directly to end users, who can then provide their own level 3 enhancements in private networks for their own operations. In effect, these users create intrafirm "private" VANs. They can also make these private VANs available to their customers, suppliers, or business partners, and thus create a private "closed-user group" VAN. Level 2 VANs can also provide their transmission capacity to other level 2 VANs, where legally possible, when these have not established access of their own to a particular region. (This adds another layer to the resale hierarchy.)

The level 3 VANs, in turn, sell their services. Buyers can be end users of the generic applications, but they can also be providers of specific applications who add value to the generic services as level 4 VANs. For example, a level 4 VAN can be a network of electronic store-and-retrieval service (a generic offering) that is made to fit the specific needs of the insurance industry, together with other generics, such as a bulletin board, or a level 4 insurance network. A combination of several generic services may be involved in such an application. Another example is that of networks that connect automatic teller machines. Providers of these network services often retail them to a number of banks, which thus need not establish their own systems. The banks, in turn, give their customers access to their fourth-level VAN. Through open or hidden service charges, they in effect resell electronic banking services to the public. Thus, when a customer uses a bank teller machine to withdraw money, the communications may easily involve four layers of communications services and several firms, all contributing to the end service in a distinct way.

Because of the peculiarities of the American divestiture of AT&T, one can often add to the U.S. scenario a long-distance carrier (which may in turn lease its capacity from another), and two local exchange companies at each end that have several sets of VAN relationships. The communications process could thus involve almost a dozen firms.

The system is incestuous because competitors can be at the same time each others' suppliers and customers of software, hardware, and transmission capacity. In the United States, they can compete on level 1, collaborate on level 2, and compete again on level 3. These relationships are unavoidably complicated, as are the production and distribution of almost any sophisticated product. Rarely are all stages of production of a complex product vertically integrated within one company.

Level 2 VANS: Basic Packet Transmission

Packet transmission originated with a Pentagon effort, whose Defense Advanced Research Projects Agency (DARPA) had the firm of Bolt, Beranek and Newman (BBN) develop in the early 1970s the "Arpanet" nationwide network to link researchers. Arpanet was a major success and induced BBN to start the commercial network Telenet, which has been in operation since 1975 as the precursor to packet-switched (so-called X.25 protocol) networks around the world.

Basic packet-switching transmission has two main advantages. The first, technical in nature, is error detection and correction, which is enormously useful for data transmission. The second advantage, economic/regulatory in nature, is the ability to slice transmission time into minute quantities, which can be resold to provide a profit where there is a differential between retail and wholesale prices. Data transmission rates, however, are not high enough for high-traffic users of data. That, together with the tendency of packet networks to charge by volume, means that leasing private lines may make more sense for large users than using a "public" VAN. (However, packet switches are getting faster—from 1500 packets/sec to 5000 packets/sec, and even to 60,000, anticipated through parallel processing).

Telenet was not profitable and it was eventually sold to GTE. In the period 1978–1983 Telenet grew at rates of up to 40 percent annually. After this period, growth slowed to a still high 30 percent. But it reached critical mass and broke even only after 1983, with revenues of about $100 million. At that time it connected about 2000 host computers, and in 1984, it averaged 200,000 sessions a day (Link Resources, 1984). In 1986, GTE Telenet was combined into GTE's joint venture with United Telecommunications, soon dominated by the latter, which in turn contributed its own Uninet (levels 2 and 3) and a substantially fiber-optic physical network (level 1).

Tymnet was originally an internal operation of Tymshare, but its initial advantage of having a customer base of time-sharing computer users turned out to be a problem later on, as time-sharing went into a steep decline with the advent of inexpensive mini- and microcomputers. Users typically accessed the packet-switched networks' nodes either through leased lines (digital or analog) or through a regular public dial-up line. Tymnet and its parent Tymshare were acquired by the aircraft manufacturer McDonnell Douglas, which resold it in 1989 to British Telecom.[1]

Other U.S. entrants were Graphic Scanning (Graphnet), PCI, CompuServe Network, Autonet, MarkNet, Cylix, IBM Information Network, and MCI Data Transport and EDS.[2]

In 1986, the FCC's Computer III ruling established the important policy concept of open network architecture (ONA), discussed in the previous chapter of this book. Under ONA, VANs can obtain special unbundled service elements from the telephone carriers, add network building blocks of their own choice, and add their own blocks to them.

The PTTs and Value-Added Networks in Europe

All European countries have some forms of upper-level value-added services; but in the past, such services were at the discretion of the PTTs, which would set service conditions and technical specifications that were often influenced by the desire to protect their own services and equipment offerings. For independent VANs to become vigorous required strengthening their rights and independence vis-à-vis the PTTs.

Liberalization took place first in Britain. The Telecommunications Act of 1981 provided for the secretary of state for industry to grant licenses for value-added networks. To operate a VAN, a general license was required. Because of the complexity of enforcing these separations, VAN licensing rules have been constantly modified.

The Dutch PTT reform of 1987 opened that country's network to competition in VAN services. Germany's 1988 legislation restructuring the Bundespost permitted considerably liberalized VAN services, including pure resale of data (not voice) services. In all instances, however, the PTTs secured their own right to participate in VAN offerings, and did so vigorously. This led to the E.C.'s policy on open network provision, discussed in Chapter 34.

The market for European VANs reached about $4.7 billion in 1991. The U.K. market was the largest ($918 million), followed by those of France ($665 million), Germany ($428 million), and Italy ($230 million) (Whitehouse, 1990; Boult, 1990; Blau, 1990).

The top VANs firms in Europe were Telenet ($500 million), IBM ($500 million), and GE Information Services ($450 million). Tymnet (BT after 1989) and Istel (owned by AT&T after 1990) were the fourth and sixth largest providers, with revenues of $430 million and $170 million in 1989.

In some instances, technical problems slowed the spread of VANs. In 1988, a survey by an end-user association found a failure rate of 25 percent in 5700 attempted data calls (Lill, 1988). Similar large-scale surveys found a 24 percent failure rate in 1989 and 25 percent in 1990 (18.7 percent failing for telecommunications reasons) (Roussel, 1989; Schenker, 1990a).[3]

Another barrier to VAN services was the high cost of leased lines. A 1989 report noted that the average cost in Europe of 9.6 kbps leased-lines was, on average, $1,500 for national circuits and $2,400 for international circuits. But for national service, Spain charged eleven times that amount ($16,000) and Germany's tariffs were six times costs. On international circuits, Italy charged a 1700 percent markup, to $42,500, followed by Spain ($31,000) and Sweden ($30,000) (Woollacott, 1989a). Another study claimed that most European PTTs priced their public data networks too low and lost money on them, while leased lines were priced very high (Purton, 1989).

In 1987, after many large European users expressed dissatisfaction with the CCITT X.25 public packet-switched network structure, the European PTTs, through CEPT, promoted a joint Managed Data Network Services project. But the European Commission, concerned about cartel behavior, limited MDNS to offering three pan-European services and restricted it from advanced gateways and network management. The project was abandoned after a year, and the PTTs focused on their own projects, such as Eucom, Tymnet, Infonet, and Syncordia.

Infonet was the fifth largest European VAN. In 1989, it was acquired by a powerful cast of owners: France Télécom, DBP Telekom, Telefónica, Belgacom, PTT Netherlands, and the Swiss PTT. MCI held the largest share, 25 percent. The European Commission investigated France Télécom, the Bundespost, and others for conflicts of interest in their investments in Infonet.

In 1988, the DBP and France Télécom also formed Eunetcom, a joint venture for industry-specific VANs. In 1991, several major carriers—British Telecom, DBP Telekom, and NTT—announced their intention to set up a global facilities management service named Syncordia, possibly with France Télécom.

Level 3 VANS: Generic Services

The following sections describe the more important upper-level VAN services.

Voice Mail

Voice messaging (also known as VSR, or voice storage and retrieval, not to be confused with electronic mail) is a service that permits a computer to store digitalized voice messages, like an answering machine. Different configurations are possible: voice mail can be part of PBXs; it can be resold by service bureaus; and it can be embedded in the central telephone switch. Typical level 4 users' applications of voice mail (level 3) are purchase-order-taking systems, ticket reservations, scheduling of work crews, hospital paging, and hotel reservations and guest messaging.

Voice Retrieval (Audiotex)

Voice retrieval (audiotex) is related to voice mail, but with the emphasis on *retrieval* rather than on input and storage. A computer typically stores a large variety of information in digital voice form that can then be recalled from afar by calling in. One application is detailed weather forecasts, which pilots can access and select according to region. Similarly, a theater reservation system can have the ticket availability of each play stored separately, along with a brief description of the play and the cast. Other applications are train schedules, ordering of merchandise, airline ticket reservations, and mass announcements such as dial-a-joke or music juke-box. These services can be lodged in customer equipment or in the network itself. These applications will be considerably boosted as synthetic voice technology develops.

Electronic Mail

In Europe, CEPT has set standards for "e-mail" service known as teletext (not to be confused with broadcast videotex known in many countries as teletext too). Particularly active in the development was the German Bundespost and the firm of Siemens. In the United States, electronic mail, much more heterogeneous, was offered by a number of firms. ITT's ailing Dialcom was acquired by British Telecom in 1986.

Data Retrieval and Search

The large number of personal computers and office desk-top terminals, many with built-in modems, greatly increased the number of parties with the ability and interest to access data banks. This led to the emergence of an electronic publishing industry and on-line databases. There are specialized services as well as more general "information utilities" that include a portfolio of data services. In some ways these are similar to videotex, though usually without the graphic capability, but with more data, faster response rates, and "smart" computer terminals that can process the called-in information rather than TV screens or dumb terminals. European PTTs have chosen the videotex approach, which is discussed in a separate chapter. Videotex has not been a success in the United States, partly because on-line data services have preempted much of its role in the commercial field.

Telephone (Audio) Conferencing

In addition to the standard teleconference bridges, more advanced systems permit dial-up (operator-free) conferencing, for both voice and data/text, and without subscription. A "meet me" option permits conference participants to call in to join the conference, without having to wait to be contacted.

Video Conferencing

Video conferencing is an active but commercially not particularly successful area. Many large firms have video-conferencing facilities but do not use them to capacity. Several U.S. hotel chains have nationwide interconnected video-conferencing facilities.

Part of video conferencing's slow acceptance derives from the need for expensive dedicated studio-like conference rooms and wide-band transmission. Both of these problems are being reduced through equipment capable of slow-scan transmission and data compression and enhancement, which permit video use in regular offices and require only one regular telephone line.

Telemetry

Alarm systems can be offered based on a new "derived channel transport" that overlays the regular voice channel with a second narrow channel, creating an independent transmission path for low-rate data. In addition to alarms, it can be used for utility meter reading and for pay-per-view cable television control. Alarm service can also be carried by cable television networks.

Computer Bulletin Board Systems

Computer bulletin board systems (BBSs) have proliferated in recent years with the increase in personal computers. In the United States, there were an estimated 25,000 in 1988. They are run by a "sysop" (systems operator), mostly amateur enthusiasts, and often include a wide menu of subgroups and services, including personal mailboxes. Specialized BBSs include professional conferences and matchmaking services.

Call Forwarding

For some years, telephone service providers have offered enhanced services such as call waiting, automatic call forwarding to other numbers, speed dialing, and three-way calling.

Call Identification

New common channel signaling systems permit an identification of the incoming call and make possible several features: call screening (blocking of undesired callers), a selective call forwarding, identification of incoming call numbers, call-back of last number(s) that had called in but were not connected, and special rings for preselected incoming calls, to permit, for example, separation of incoming personal and business calls. These services are important in a broader sense, since they give some measure of choice over the telecommunications process to the party being called, who in the past has had to guess at the nature of the incoming call. They also permit verified billing arrangements. They also raise important privacy issues.

Electronic Data Interchange (EDI)

Generic form transmission can replace traditional practices of purchase orders, invoices, bills of lading, and so on, that require separately processed documents. Instead, the documentation of an entire transaction is electronic, integrated, and nearly instantaneous. An important level 4 application for EDI is for "just-in-time" production, such as for automobiles. Some automobile manufacturers established an EDI system with their suppliers. Purchase orders are entered entirely automatically, according to programmed instructions, and sent to suppliers, who confirm, process, ship, bill, advise, get paid, and so on, all within the same set of documentation. The system provides some of the advantages of vertical integration and single sourcing without the cost. EDI systems can be provided by the private network of a firm, an industry group, or a public VAN. The EDI market is potentially quite large.

Level 4 VANS: Specific Applications

Telekurs and the Society for Worldwide Interbank Financial Telecommunications (SWIFT) are two examples of level 4 application VANs. Telekurs AG was an early entrant in the VAN market. An independent Swiss firm, jointly held by 350 Swiss banks and the Swiss stock exchanges, it began operations in 1930 as Ticker AG by transmitting stock market information via telegraph lines. Its business evolved to include financial information services, interbank clearing, and management of Eurocard, a travel and entertainment card issued by Swiss banks. Telekurs AG's most important financial information service, Investdata, provides strong competition to Reuters, offering direct access to eighty stock exchanges worldwide. Its interbank clearing service produces 30 percent of Telekurs' income. The Eurocard network serves over 850,000 card holders, who can conduct their transactions at any of about 500 Bancomat machines throughout Switzerland. In 1985, Telekurs employed 850 people and had sales totaling SFr 150 million (von Weizsäcker, 1987).

SWIFT is a particularly important participant in the financial VAN market. A consortium of European and American banks created SWIFT in 1973, and it went on line in 1977. All SWIFT participants are also shareholders. In 1977, 240 banks in fifteen countries were members, and SWIFT processed 27,000 transactions daily. In 1985, the ranks had grown to include 1275 banks in forty-six countries, generating 192 million transactions. By 1989, the system was handling up to 1.3 million transactions a day. SWIFT's main communications activities are customer transfers, accounting for 30 percent of total volume; bank transfers, another 30 percent; and statements and conformations, with 25 percent. Participating banks derive benefits from the service because of reduced transactions and better control of costs. A SWIFT message costs BFr 18 ($0.48) independent of distance.

To start operating, SWIFT had to establish standards for international transactions; these have since been instituted worldwide. The nature of its business requires strict security measures. SWIFT accepts liability for all losses due to errors or cheating, underscoring its confidence in the system. It has never had to fulfill this guarantee. SWIFT achieves this level of security with a hierarchical network structure. Individual banks connect to national nodes (regional processors or RPs) via leased or dialed lines. The RPs encrypt, store, and pass the messages on to the System Control Centers (SCCs) in Washington, D.C. or Leyden, Holland.[4] In 1989, European, African, and Middle Eastern banks generated 68 percent of SWIFT's transactions. About 13 percent of messages came from the Pacific Rim nations, and North America accounted for 18 percent (Hayes, 1989).

To obtain its leased lines, SWIFT had to negotiate special arrangements with each country. It pays a set amount per message plus a volume-based tariff; the volume-based pricing often causes SWIFT to pay more than four times the ordinary leased-line tariffs. The PTTs thus extract a premium from SWIFT for leased lines, but this was also an advantage, since SWIFT obtained special licenses when there was no similar offering. It is therefore more difficult for new entrants to emerge.

In time, SWIFT encountered competition from IBM, which set up a global banking network of its own, and from Reuters. Furthermore, some of SWIFT's bigger members set up their own networks to counter what they see as SWIFT's subsidization of smaller banks. Thus, the exit mechanism discussed in Chapter 4 applies also to subnetworks.

The SWIFT network grew from 27,000 messages daily in 1977 to 1 million in 1989, and rapidly neared its capacity.[5] A more advanced network, SWIFT II, was authorized, and SWIFT chose Northern Telecom for network equipment. It will be a distributed network, unlike the more centralized SWIFT I, with more value-added services, including messaging and EDI. Fast-packet switching was introduced in 1991.

The following services are part of the variety of specific applications of level 4 VAN-type services that have emerged. Several other applications have already been mentioned.

1. *Accelerated international trade payments.* This service, its providers claim, accelerates international payments often by two weeks.
2. *International trade shipment data service.* Helps trade shipment transactions, documentation, billings, insurance, and so on.
3. Company dealer networks. Used for orders, product information, service problems, billing, and customer information. Also referred to as *Electronic Order Exchange* (EOE).
4. *Health care providers and insurance networks.* Permits transactions between hospitals and insurers.

5. *Credit card verification and processing.* Merchants have terminals that can read credit card magnetic stripes and transmit the information to a central location for approval and processing. Some transactions are handled by local banks or bank associations, such as VISA for its members. Others are offered by public level 4 VANs. Credit authorization is being integrated into electronic record keeping and transaction accounting.

6. *Point-of-sale services.* These retail services permit merchants to transfer payments, send bills, verify credit, and reorder inventory. Because of the high cost involved to set up such a system, several point-of-sale switching networks exist. Some are affiliated with automated teller machine networks and often are owned by several banks or by more general service providers.

7. *Manufacturing design.* Computer-aided design and manufacturing (CAD/CAM) has led to private VAN applications. GM's blueprints are electronically accessible by its suppliers (which are thus forced into the electronic mode of design themselves). The high cost of a CAD/CAM terminal (plus computer, software, and know-how) has been a problem for small suppliers. In response, reselling has emerged in this segment.

8. *Factory production.* Automation produces and requires constant data flows. One development priority for the near future is to permit equipment to interconnect better with each other and with support services. Electronic data interchange (EDI) systems offered by several VANs provide some such integration and permit a ''just-in-time'' production process, with interconnection with suppliers and programmed purchase orders. GM adopted a manufacturing automation protocol (MAP). It acquired the major data-processing firm EDS, which set up sophisticated networks with dealers and suppliers.

9. *Spare-parts service.* Industrial database/transaction systems provide information on and transactions for millions of products, parts, and supplies.

10. *Service dispatch.* A combination radio beeper/access terminal permits input and communications with service personnel in the field.

11. *Electronic banking and brokering.* A number of financial institutions enable customers to use their computers to reach their account information, obtain investment data and place stock orders.

12. *Electronic Fund Transfers (EFT).* This is one of the earliest network transaction uses. Various clearinghouse arrangements exist domestically and internationally, and were discussed earlier with the examples of Telekurs and SWIFT.

13. *Automated teller machine (ATM) networks.* The popularity and low cost of the automated bank presence of ATMs spread enormously. In the United States, a 1986 Supreme Court decision permitted ATM placement out of state, and thus enabled banks to move across state lines, which they could do before only to a limited extent.

    Large banks can offer these services on private networks. Smaller and medium-sized banks depend on VAN intermediaries. Several ATM switching networks exist, often owned by a consortium of banks. Large data processors also provide such services. Increasingly, the ATM of one bank accepts transactions for others.

14. *Commodity trading.* Trading in commodities and precious metals, where time is of the essence, has been enhanced by networks with brokers in some instances simultaneously using regular voice call, viewing market data, transacting trades, retrieving customer information, and entering notes about the call.

15. *Insurance industry networking.* Because many independent insurance agents deal with many underwriter firms, it was important to provide them with a network for communications. Such a network had to fit many firms' modus operandi and business forms and had to be compatible with thousands of different equipment systems in agents' offices.

16. *Medical communications.* An information and transaction network exists to connect doctors and drug companies as well as reference services and advanced medical education databases.

17. *Moving CAT-SCAN images.* Medical CAT-scanning procedures are expensive and very data intensive. One VAN transmits image data from smaller hospitals to larger data facilities for processing and storage.

18. *Consumer information.* VANs provide a variety of consumer information and transaction services.

19. *Job searches.* There are data banks for employment, particularly for data-processing professionals.

20. *On-line databases.* These are discussed in Chapter 37 of this book.

21. *Teleshopping.* Several varieties of teleshopping exist: on computer on-line services, on cable television, and by automated phone-in orders. One supermarket chain permits call-in orders with automated reception from a 4000-item catalog, with the teleshopper picking up the order soon thereafter.

22. *Agricultural networks.* Information and transaction systems exist for commodity trading, weather, help, and advice.

23. *Hotel in-room services.* Services permit guests to access information and electronic mail from their rooms and to receive information about city or hotel activities, airlines, and so on.

24. *Grocery networking.* VANs can provide an electronic data interchange (EDI) for a grocery industry group, which permits them to pool their purchases and realize bulk discounts.

25. *Up- and downloading with personal computers.* PCs can be used as data input and output terminals for a mainframe. Data can be exchanged, software can be shared, and so on.

26. *Yellow Page service.* On-line service permits nationwide and international compilations and searches of businesses.

27. *Automobile collision estimation.* This service permits garages and insurance companies to estimate repair costs.

28. *Animal breeder services*. Permits matching of livestock.
29. *Library shared cataloguing*. Permits interlibrary searches, exchanges, acquisitions, and automation in cataloging.
30. *Credit history*. Several commercial systems permit lenders to check on the credit history of borrowers. This application, more than any other, has been controversial and has led to laws protecting privacy and accuracy.
31. *Telemarketing*. Automatic dialing machines call potential customers randomly or from prescreened lists. The sales message is taped; responses are given either to a person who comes on the line or to a voice mailbox.

Outlook

The list of VAN services and applications is not indicative of their commercial or technical success. There is no reason to assume that today's mix of offerings is more than temporary. It would not be surprising if half of today's offerings and services would be gone in a few years and replaced by other services and offerors. Given the rapid developments in hardware, software, and user organizations, the main attribute of a VAN system is not predictability of success but flexibility of process. It is hard to see how restrictive rules on VANs could be effective in the long run. If VAN services are successful—and it is important to a competitive economy that they are—they will dance electronic circles around the restrictions.

When it comes to policy liberalization, VANs ride on the coattails of equipment. A liberalization of equipment has meaning primarily when the equipment can be used in varied ways. Conversely, one cannot expect dynamic VAN development if users are limited in their choices of equipment to a few slowly approved models. VANs can be important to manufacturers because much of the pure equipment can become a merchant market, with East Asian countries serving as the low-cost producers. Hence, a link of equipment to services, of hardware to software, and of hardware elements to each other by networks can be critical to competitiveness.

This raises a final question. Are VANs another instance of "supply-side telecommunications," with appeal to computer enthusiasts, equipment manufacturers, and telecommunications carriers, but not to regular users? There is no question that many VAN services have been excessively hyped, and the reality invariably fails in comparison. In the aggregate, the VAN service industry is not yet particularly large in dollar terms. In the United States, level 2 VANs (packet switching) were in 1988 estimated at $850 million; for the higher-level application levels 3 and 4 they were about $1.5 billion. In comparison with basic voice telephony, these amounts are trivial. However, the market is very innovative and is developing expertise in fashioning configurations of users, equipment, and services. A market cannot move much faster than the users, which had to absorb entirely new systems, work procedures, and organizational patterns. These things take time. But users are steadily becoming more applications-conscious; several industries have already reached the stage of dependence on them. Thus, the VAN services sector is riding a favorable trend.

Today VANs are "discretionary" services. Over time, however, some of them may become first essential, and then basic services, as happened to voice telephony.

36

Videotex

The New Technology

Videotex emerged in 1970, when the British Post Office started work on its viewdata system Prestel, with the aim of integrating the telephones, computers, and the television sets. France followed suit in 1972 with Antiope. In Germany, the Bundespost bought and built upon British rights in the development of its Btx system. In 1979, Canada developed Telidon, which, unlike the others, is based on a geometric rather than an alpha-mosaic display.

All systems contended before the CCITT for recognition as the single international standard. The American position held that it was too early to implement standardization because of the rapid development of technologies. Europeans suspected that this view was based on the Americans' absence from the forefront of videotex development. In 1980, the CCITT recognized three systems—Antiope, Prestel, and Telidon—and agreement on a common protocol seemed impossible. In 1981, AT&T established its Presentation Level Protocol (PLP), closely related to the Canadian standard. In 1982, the American National Standards Institute (ANSI) agreed upon a more mature version of PLP, the North American Presentation Level Protocol Standard (NAPLPS), and submitted it to the CCITT. The European PTTs agreed on a common overarching CEPT standard in an attempt to harmonize their systems and make them compatible. They also induced other European countries, including Italy and Spain, to join them in those CEPT standards, and launched an export offensive.

In the meantime, a variety of nonvideotex computer information host systems emerged in the United States. These host systems are accessed over telephone lines by a microcomputer as a terminal and a modem, usually via a packet-switched network such as Telenet or Tymnet. Other database providers are accessed directly, without an intermediary host. The on-line service provision has become known as electronic publishing, and traditional and new publishers have entered the field. Compared to videotex, these on-line services require more intelligent terminals, but they can also perform more tasks. With the rapid decline in the cost of microcomputers and monitors, there has been a great increase in the number of households with microcomputers. For these users, access to databases such as computer and mail-box service becomes relatively simple. These data services do not package the information in multicolored graphics, as videotex often does. In 1990, there were about twenty-seven million microcomputers in U.S. businesses and homes—a much larger number than Minitel terminals in France, and with greater intelligence of equipment.

Videotex offers primarily five basic types of services: information (such as news, weather, financial data, and regional movie listings), commercial transactions (such as airline ticket orders), closed user-group interactions, electronic mail and mailboxes, and information processing. For the latter, an interconnected computer system (such as the one implemented by the German Bundespost) facilitates customer use. In effect, a PTT's videotex system can operate as a computer utility. With interconnection, it can also interact with computers of other service vendors.

By 1990, videotex had not become a success in any European country, with the exception of France, where over 5 million Minitel terminals had been distributed. Germany had 200,000 subscribers; Great Britain, 95,000; Italy, 100,000; and the Netherlands, 28,000. All other countries had less than 5000. There were only 5000 subscribers in Japan, and 10,000 in Canada, mostly for farm reports.

The differing philosophies on telecommunications policy are reflected in four countries' approach to videotex. Britain's service developed only slowly, caught between the government's prevalent indecision between deregulatory telecommunications policy and pro-active technology policy. In Germany, the Bundespost set up a huge centralized system and promoted it heavily, but demand was low. In France, in contrast, the government was massively engaged in direct subsidization, buying millions of terminals from domestic manufacturers and literally giving them away. It financially supported the usage, information production, and equipment, in the hope that in time the subsidized egg would hatch a chicken. Usage has been brisk, but the costs of keeping the system going have been high. In the United States, videotex was left to the market, and the local Bell telephone companies were restricted to protect competition. There is little videotex in America, though much usage of its on-line cousins.

Videotex in the United Kingdom

Using the Prestel protocol, interactive videotex is offered by British Telecom (BT) under the name of Viewtel. Prestel was the world's first public interactive videotex system, developed in the early 1970s at the Post Office Research Center by researcher Sam Fedeida from work involving a "viewphone." The system was demonstrated in 1975, and a pilot project was initiated the following year with the participation of the main manufacturers—GEC, ITT, Philips, Pye, Rank, and Thorn-EMI. About 400 organizations provided information, including the *Financial Times,* the London Stock Exchange, and several government enterprises. Testing with a sample of domestic and business users began in 1976, and regular service was initiated in 1979 (Tydeman, 1982). In 1990, about 95,000 terminals were attached to the Prestel network and more than

2000 main providers offered information. As a premium service at an extra charge, information pages could be stored for closed user groups.

The success of the service was important to the British government as a highly visible indicator of British scientific and engineering knowhow. Referring to videotex and broadcast teletext, the former minister for information technology, Kenneth Baker, exclaimed:

> First, we see them as two technological developments in that Britain now leads the world and which must be promoted, because of the commercial and industrial benefits which can accrue to the nation. Second, we see teletext and viewdata as swing doors through which the country can gain an entry into what some people are calling the "second microelectronics revolution." I mean, of course, information technology. Third, it provides employment for set manufacturers, component manufacturers, and software companies. The government is convinced that information technology is going to be the key growth sector in this country's economy [*British Business*, 1981, p. 1480].

Prestel service was enthusiastically welcomed not only by the government and BT, but also by electronic firms and television set manufacturers, who saw a potentially large consumer market for new types of equipment. Furthermore, mail-order houses, travel agencies, and banks were interested in using Prestel as a new marketing tool. Because of the belief that videotex could fulfill many of the functions currently handled by newspapers, the service was viewed warily by newspaper publishers, who feared the potential loss of advertising revenue and newsstand sales. Other publishers, however, recognized that their long-range role was not merely to publish news on paper but to collect, edit, and distribute information in various forms; they moved to become videotex information providers. Although Prestel was originally conceived as a residential customer service, businesses were the most eager customers during the first few years that the service was offered. Of the 7605 subscriptions in January 1981, 87 percent were for businesses, and only 13 percent were from residential locations (*British Business*, 1981). Both figures fell far below BT's original forecast of 50,000. By 1988, the proportion of residential users had increased to 39 percent of Prestel's 80,000 subscribers (British Telecom, 1988, communication).

In 1986, Prestel began to provide more specialized services, such as home banking, teleshopping, and educational offerings. British Telecom entered the information provider market itself by purchasing a majority in Farmlink, a specialized service aimed at the rural population. BT also acquired a substantial share of Telemap, the operator of Micronet 800 service, which provides computer news, advice, and games for computer users.

The Prestel protocol was adopted by other countries, including Italy, Belgium, the Netherlands, Switzerland, Hong Kong, and Australia. Although Prestel is an impressive display of advanced British engineering, development of other systems did not stand still. Partly as a consequence, BT developed Photovideotex, a substantially upgraded standard that can transmit picture-quality reproductions for use in picture databases.

Videotex in Germany

Initially, the German telecommunications equipment industry was not particularly interested in videotex. The Bundespost bought British rights and expertise and built upon Prestel in the development of its Bildschirmtext, known as Btx. Following recommendations by the blue-ribbon commission KtK and an affirmative government decision, Btx pilot projects were initiated in 1980 in Düsseldorf and Berlin. Interconnected financial institutions and mail-order firms were soon active. One travel organizer made forty to fifty bookings per week. The government institutions decided to advance the development of the new technology, and in 1981, the Bundespost awarded the major contract to IBM Germany.

The advantage of Btx is its uniform technical standards, which allow a wide range of applications in an integrated and commonly used system. Thus, even rarely used services share the benefits of a mass service. The concept is based on uniformity and centralization and is concerned with economies of scale. The entire national Btx system was centralized in one giant IBM computer located in Ulm and known as the "Mother." This central location, which allegedly can be infinitely expanded, stores participant data, all personally addressed information, and all supplied information for the entire Federal Republic. Users are linked through regular telephone lines with regional Btx offices, which are in turn linked to the central computer by a packet-switched network. The regional offices consist of two data bank computers and up to six communications computers for storage of regionally relevant information. Btx's design innovation over Prestel is its use of private computers connected to the central PTT computer.

Most of the Btx's information is provided by travel agencies, insurance companies, banks, publishers, and mail order houses. However, most retailers have discounted Btx's efficacy for transactional purchases unless the user also has a catalogue. Home banking requires a special alphanumeric keyboard. One bank reported that the turnover on their Btx accounts was higher than that for their general accounts (Tonnemacher, 1982).

One problem has been the high cost of decoders. Although new television sets of high quality have built-in decoders, most other television sets must be supported by a separate box. In a 1985 analysis by the Bundespost of its videotex strategy, it was found that the terminal equipment supply by the equipment sector was problematic in that the necessary diversity at acceptable prices did not exist. The system was also not fulfilling the desired expectations of information seekers. One early survey indicated that only 27 percent of information providers had expected Btx to move as slowly as it had (*Neue Medien*, 1985). Only 18 percent of service information providers considered their Btx investment to have paid off. When information providers were asked for their opinions about the causes of the slow demand for Btx, virtually everyone criticized the Bundespost: 46 percent for the flawed advertising concept, 19 percent for the incorrect forecasts that had led to false expectations, 12 percent for overly complicated or expensive standards, 10 percent for high DBP telephone rates, and 2 percent for the system of search trees. The Bundespost was receptive to the criticism. It took the long view, expecting slow going until take-off. In 1990, the DBP had 200,000 subscribers and 3,000 providers.

Videotex in France

During the 1970s, the French telecommunications administration DGT (later France Télécom) and its research labs CNET investigated the use of television sets for novel telecommunications data and text services. In 1977, the Nora-Minc report galvanized the public with concern about the "informatization" of society. Prodded by the British videotex advances, the DGT adopted a new initiative in the area of videotex in 1977. In 1978, it gave videotex the green light, with the economic rationale that human directory assistance service and paper telephone directories would be replaced by the cheaper electronic service. This concept neatly side-stepped opposition to the new and competitive medium by the newspaper publishers. In 1979, field trials took place in Brittany, and the DGT then decided to distribute, for free, 30 million terminals over fifteen years (Vedel, 1987).

The DGT's technocratic moves aroused opposition by the press, civil libertarians, and some economists, and led to the establishment of a permanent monitoring commission in 1981 and to stronger attempts by the DGT to place its technological goals within a broader social policy rhetoric. Following the change in government in 1981, these principles were incorporated into a large trial in Velizy, near Paris. The DGT began to subsidize press applications in order to encourage development of their Teletel videotex service and set rates in an advantageous "Kiosk" system. By 1983, mass distribution of Minitel terminals was begun, and by the end of 1984, half a million terminals had been given away. Usage was encouraged by a generous charging system, no subscription cost, free terminals, and incentives to service providers.

The electronic directory service was officially launched in the Ile-et-Vilaine department around Rennes in February 1983. After some experience, the policy on electronic directories shifted from forced to voluntary usage. This shift undermined some of the economic logic of substituting electronic for paper directories.

Initially, each household used the electronic directories only about twice a week. After a while, surveys showed that residents used Teletel about one-half hour per week, calling four or five services in a single fifteen-minute access session. The surveys also showed that teenagers between twelve and fourteen years of age were the most frequent and most proficient users of the service, and people over sixty years old largely ignored it (Sichel, 1983).

In 1991, there were nearly 12,000 private information providers and three levels of private information service: Teletel 1, which is mainly for commercial usage, costs $0.08 per 20 minutes. The user must subscribe to each service individually and pay local telephone rates, while the provider pays the rest of the telecommunication fees. Teletel 2, which is for both private and commercial usage and for which the user pays all communication costs, costs $0.08 per two minutes. And Teletel 3, or "Kiosk," which is also for private and commercial usage, requires the user to pay the communication costs of $0.10 per minute plus a time-sensitive service fee. On the Kiosk system, there are five levels of service fees, with the private providers and the telecommunications authority receiving varying proportions.

Penetration has been large because the terminals have been distributed at no charge. Government support was also given to information providers to encourage them to use the medium.

France Télécom's own 1987 figures for total hours of usage divided by the number of households results in an average monthly usage of sixty-two minutes per household (*Telematique News,* 1987). Disregarding the revenue loss because of lower long-distance calling, and making the generous assumptions that two-thirds of the network usage is newly generated traffic rather than replacement of calls to airlines, for example, and that two-thirds of new revenue is pure France Télécom profit, the added revenue should come to an average of FFr 90 million (about $15 million) per month. At that rate, a terminal, which costs about FFr 2000, is paid for in about five years.

For the total actual and planned Minitel investment of FFr 17 billion from 1984 to 1995, 54 percent goes toward the development of Minitel, 18 percent to the packet-switched network Transpac, 15 percent for additional lines, and 13 percent for the DGT network. Annual investment costs are FFr 1.5 billion ($240 million). At the present utilization and revenue rate given earlier, annual system investments per subscriber are FFr 750 ($150), while revenues are only FFr 550 ($90) (T. Vedel, 1988, communication).

The financial performance of the project is not readily apparent, since several public subsidies are involved. In 1984, Teletel expenses were FFr 2 billion ($320 million) and brought in FFr 407 million ($68 million). According to French critic Jacques Darmon, there will be a permanent deficit (Darmon, 1985, p. 108). France Télécom disputes this, claiming that Teletel increases usage of the network.

On the revenue side of France Télécom performance, there are a number of empirical and conceptual problems to overcome. France Télécom discloses revenue and minutes of usage on Teletel, but it does not provide net figures. A Teletel call for travel information provides revenues, but at the same time it may replace a regular telephone call. Indeed, the distance-insensitive (local) Teletel call may replace toll calls, thus causing a net revenue loss. Similarly, an electronic directory assistance call replaces the revenues of a similar call to a human operator.

In addition, not all revenues of new types of calls, such as those of the chat-lines, should be allocated to Teletel per se. Such conversations could have occurred on privately provided bulletin boards or computer conference systems. In the Unites States, there are about 25,000 such systems, many of which are arranged by teenagers and computer hackers. The resources of the centralized state are not required to accomplish communications among the people. Thus, even without videotex, new and revenue-producing calls would be generated by communicating terminals.

Extensive marketing campaigns were used to increase Teletel usage. As a result, the number of calls to information services rose from 104 million in 1985 to 513 million in 1987, and the hours of connection time rose from 11.7 to 52.4 million over the same period (Booker, 1989). Growth in the average number of yearly connection hours per terminal leveled off in 1987, dropping from twenty hours to eighteen in 1988 and seventeen in 1989 (*France Télécom News*, 1990).

Despite the marketing push, the state accounting agency for state-owned companies, the Cour des Comptes, reported that the Teletel system lost $742 million in 1988, and projected 1995 losses at $574 million. To bolster revenues, a monthly charge was suggested. However, the analysis did not include Transpac revenues.

France Télécom denounced the results of the Cour des Comptes report. It commissioned an analysis by Coopers & Lybrand showing a breakeven starting in 1991, and a rate-of-return of 11.3 percent. The 5 millionth Minitel was delivered in 1990. But this growth was primarily in business use (plus 26 percent), whereas there was an 8 percent decrease in residential use (*France Télécom News*, 1990, p. 3; Roussel, 1989b, p. 52). The average household made twelve calls and used less than one hour of service per month (*The Economist*, 1989, p. 55).

Among the Teletel services, the *messagerie* service has proven popular among users and lucrative for the telecommunications administration. The messaging service was allegedly invented by a newspaper in Strasbourg that encouraged users to talk to each other. The service provides an on-line dialogue capability between users, similar to the electronic mailboxes and bulletin boards of computer hackers. It also offers various bulletin board services, such as classified and personal ads and electronic messages. Cost is about FFr 260 per hour (about $10 per hour) of connection time. Users often adopt pseudonyms or "handles." In 1989, a best-selling book by Denis Perier chronicled the story of a Paris call girl whose brutal murder was arranged over the Minitel. The case led to a round of protests from French family and church organizations about the very character of messaging services (Kramer, 1990).

A majority of the users of the service are young men, and many of the dialogues are flirtatious in nature. When the service was first offered, peak usage occurred at the end of the lunchtime break, indicating usage by employees at the workplace, and employers began to block Teletel usage. Because of the newspaper involvement and the human interest angle, the Kiosk offerings received lavish media attention in France and abroad.

Partly because of their classified ads, the Kiosk offerings could be offered until late 1985 only by newspapers. The major presence was *Le Parisien Libéré*, with about 1 million monthly connections in 1985. The newspaper *Libération* had 300,000 calls per month.

Teletel reaped its highest yield from "messaging," which accounts for 8 percent of calls and 22 percent of revenues. The electronic directory, on the other hand, was a loss-leader, providing 18 percent of revenue from 33 percent of the calls (Thomas, 1988).

As applications and familiarities grow, per capita usage of Teletel could well increase. On the other hand, as the novelty of the chatlines, the main revenue source, wears down, their per capita usage may decline. Furthermore, usage among the present users may not indicate future usage patterns in the general populace. Although Minitels were distributed around the country, they were given first to the heavy telephone users within each district. Light users may be less comfortable with Teletel or have less of a need for its services.

Minitel terminals under the Antiope system are provided by a number of suppliers, including Alcatel, Matra, and TRT. In addition to the simple terminals, French manufacturers have developed several more expensive models with added features. The Minitel 12, for example, is geared toward professional users. For other foreign markets, particularly in Arab countries, these firms developed videotex terminals with more than one character set, but have received relatively few export orders. An upgraded M10B terminal has a separate screen and memory telephone; an intelligent Minitel costs between FFr 10,000 and FFr 15,000. CNET developed a Minitel model with the capability of running various peripheral functions as a microcomputer. However, according to the associate director of industrial and international affairs at the DGT, there are several obstacles to upgrading the Minitel:

> Changing a screw on a Minitel takes a year! Then there is the price. Our ambition is to see the price of the Minitel reduced. To give it the advantage of added functions would condemn us to pay more, and just imagine the PTT having to manage a market of several million microcomputers which would very quickly become obsolete. That would be untenable. And who would rapidly develop software for these micros? Not the PTT! We are not a service company [Clavaud, 1984, p. 37].

At France Télécom, there are two contrasting strategies for the future development of the Minitel. One strategy advocates the rapid development of an intelligent second-generation Minitel in order to forestall the flood of cheap microcomputers. The other stresses the expansion of the market for the first-generation Minitel by freely distributing the terminals and allowing the private market to supply more advanced attachments.

France has exported Teletel development worldwide. In the United States, the Minitel Services Company has made French services available over Bell-South, US West, and Southwestern Bell gateways. In 1987, Intelmatique established Minitelnet, an international interconnection service with Transpac. Agreements with Germany, Belgium, and Luxembourg to permit access to its services were reached in 1988, and in 1989 Intelmatique made services available to Japan's Mitsui Knowledge Industry Co., complete with a Japanese language interface. Switzerland and Spain also allowed interconnection with the Minitel network, as did Italy in 1990. Also, in 1989 Mercury considered adopting the French standard for its service instead of the Prestel system. However, despite the number of countries reached, only 30,000 hours of connection time out of 85 million hours of total traffic came from outside France in 1989, or

0.05 percent of total traffic (*France Télécom News, 1990;* Roussel and Rockwell, 1989).

For all its birth-pains that were described above, French engineering in the videotex field is indisputably outstanding. As an example of forward looking government strategy, Teletel may well provide a triumph in the future. This high visibility project can succeed in technical, social, and economic terms, and prove the viability of videotex—and more generally of PTT support—in establishing a critical mass for a new information service.

Videotex in Other Countries

Many other European nations have experimented with videotex and similar electronic information services. None have matched the penetration of the French system.

In Finland, databases and data processing industries have developed at a fast pace, and the country's dynamic publishing industry has been a leader in developing electronic information services. The remote access data processing industry is fairly open to outside suppliers. Finland was the second country to offer videotex, known as Teleset; it was started experimentally in 1978 by the Helsinki Telephone Company, together with Nokia Electronics (equipment) and the Sanoma Corporation (information), using a Prestel-like system. Teleset standards conform to European standards. American DEC computers are used; decoders are supplied by the two Finnish TV set manufacturers. The information provided is primarily business and consumer information, news, statistical data, and local municipal announcements. No P&T license is necessary for videotex, but initially the P&T unsuccessfully argued that videotex, as a text transmission, was part of its monopoly on "telegraphy." The P&T also operates its own videotex operation, Telset, which had some paying subscribers in its Helsinki system (Howkins, 1982). Other local telephone companies in Turku and Tampere also followed the model, entering cooperative ventures with newspaper publishers.

In Italy, videotex services are provided by a number of STET subsidiaries—SARIN, SIP, and SEAT. In 1980, these services began experimental operation under the name Videotel, and the telephone company, SIP, has operated videotex on a regular basis since 1986. Users can access the host computer, located in Milan, from throughout the country with a local call. Videotel is base on Italtel and CEPT standards, and concentrates on business subscribers. SARIN handles the engineering and market research aspects of telematics. It develops the mainframe and system software to support Italy's Mediatel terminals and provides the X.25 and Italpac packet-switched services. On the marketing side, SARIN offers telemarketing, advertising services and user profiles, all geared toward encouraging on-line usage.[1]

In the United States there have been several unsuccessful pilot videotex projects in the period from 1981 to 1985, including such companies as the New York Times and AT&T, in Coral Gables, Florida; Time, Inc., and AT&T, in

Ridgefield, New Jersey; Times Mirror, in Los Angeles; and Knight-Ridder, in Lake Forest, Ill. Though these experiments were targeted to wealthy suburbs, only few subscribers were willing to pay connection fees of up to $20 a month along with one-time charges for terminals of $400 or more. A second wave of videotex ventures in the late 1980s involved Prodigy, a joint venture of Sears and IBM, which has a user-friendly system and aims at the personal computer user. Its billing is simple too, with a usage insensitive flat monthly charge of $12.95 for most services. Prodigy offered transactional and travel services, news, sports, and an on-line encyclopedia. Its membership in 1991 was about 1 million, although many were inactive. Sears' and IBM's investment was estimated to be between one half and one billion dollars, but it was losing money and was reliant on continued financial support.

Another joint venture of Citicorp, NYNEX, and RCA, CNR Partners, folded in 1988 after two years. Likewise, the Covidea project, involving Chemical Bank and CBS, folded in 1987. The government and telephone companies have so far played only minimal roles, although Judge Greene's 1987 relaxation of restrictions has encouraged the Bell companies to enter this field. They established the concept of "gateways" to provide easy connections to any database or enhanced service provider by offering user-friendly menu services. These data and information providers can usually also be accessed directly rather than through the gateway, although in that case other billing arrangements are necessary. Information service gateways were begun by several regional Bell companies in 1988 and 1989, but most failed soon after their introduction. In 1991, the Bell companies succeeded in court and won the right to offer information services. This made it likely that they would enter videotex markets more actively than by providing gateways.

The absence of success of U.S. videotex stands in contrast to more decentralized services of on-line databases and information hosts. By 1990, the leading on-line service was Compuserve, with 620,000 subscribers, followed by Dow Jones News Service, with 400,000; and GENIE, with 150,000. An estimated 25,000 bulletin board services were operating in the United States, and 6.5 million out of 27 million microcomputers were equipped with modems.

37

Transborder Data Flows

Impediments to the free flow of information predate the advent of electronic communications by centuries. From the earliest years of book printing, some published materials were prohibited from importation to other countries or jurisdictions for reasons of politics, religion, or economics. Written correspondence was often censored, although this practice had some limits because of its expense. The advent of wire-line communications gave individuals new means to communicate across borders, but it also provided states with a smaller number of entry channels that needed to be controlled. In the case of the telegraph, state employees handled each word of the messages, and often kept copies. Broadcasting proved harder to contain, since over-the-air messages could cross political boundaries with impunity. Some states deterred individuals from listening to unwelcome news from outside sources by making the activity a crime and by interfering with foreign broadcasting frequencies through electronic jamming. On the whole, however, a strong tradition of unimpeded information flow during peacetime emerged in Western democracies, including the freedom to speak, compose, and distribute messages nationally and internationally. Even as European governments continued to control the transmission channels for electronic communications between individuals, they did not control or tamper with the *content* of the communications—at least in the democratic countries—and limited themselves to indirect restrictions governing tariffs, technical standards, and attached equipment.

Given this strong tradition, the advent of new technologies that generate, process, and transmit information might be expected to reduce or even eliminate restrictions. Yet the proliferation of electronic transmission in Europe created new types of issues that raised the free-flow question again.

Data Protection and Transborder Flows

Computers and information storage led to fears about the use and abuse of electronic data.[1] The tremendous ability of computers to store vast amounts of information, to centralize individual data from a large number of sources, and to recall and disseminate it rapidly makes this new technology an effective tool for government surveillance and business power. For example, government investigations can rapidly correlate an individual's medical history, financial transactions, consumption patterns, travel, reading habits, and so on. Many fears expressed in the 1970s were based on the notion of computers as vast centralized mainframes, which roughly corresponded to the nature of technology of the 1960s. Since then, technology has moved toward decentralized systems, with millions of interconnected computers. This has reduced the need for centralized storage and has shifted the problem of protecting individual privacy from one of data storage to one of data flow.

Protective legislation on electronic data collection and storage began in the early 1970s with a law in the German state of Hesse (1970) and a national law in Sweden (1973). From there, the movement spread to most of Western Europe. Most European countries used similar approaches to data privacy. They include a uniform national law (in contrast to the piecemeal American approach), an independent specialized agency for enforcement and regulation, registration or licensing of data files that include personal information, access and correction rights for individuals, use and disclosure limitations, and a structure for the internal management of databases (Pipe, 1984b; Turn, 1979).

Though the origin of concern over privacy was the potential abuse of data by government agencies, the focus of remedial action shifted to control of the data collection activities by private organizations. Rules against the government's collection of data were also set, but with less severity. At the same time that Germany promulgated the first data protection laws against private data abuse, its federal and state governments took a quantum leap in the use of data-processing technology for the surveillance of its citizenry. During the 1970s, political violence by the so-called Baader-Meinhof gang prompted the German police to institute a chillingly efficient system of border checks, citizen registration, and domestic road blocks, all of which were interconnected by data banks and communications links. Although the terrorism was mostly stopped, many control mechanisms were not.

In the meantime, it was recognized that privacy laws had a loophole: international data transfers permitted the evasion of data protection laws. Under the Swedish Data Protection Law of 1973, for example, a data file on any Swedish employee is subject to certain protections from disclosure to third persons. However, if a Swede works for a foreign firm, it is possible that the data would be routinely transmitted to the headquarters of the firm, where it would be less protected. Conceivably, given this loophole, some countries could set themselves up as "data havens" in order to attract businesses determined to circumvent privacy laws. Although these threats were more theoretical than real, they led to a movement to harmonize data protection practices or to restrict the flow of sensitive data in the absence of such harmonization.

The Organization of Economic Cooperation and Development (OECD), through the initiative of Hans-Peter Gassmann, was instrumental in formulating the principles. It created a Committee on Information, Computer and Information Policy (ICCP). In 1979, the OECD drafted a first set of guidelines for its member states: Data collection should be limited to necessary information obtained lawfully, and, where appropriate, with consent; data should be accurate, complete, up-to-date, and relevant to the needs of the collector; use of the data ought to be specified at the time of collection, and its disclosure should be in conformity with the purpose of collection; assurances must be made against unauthorized access, use, and disclosure; and data should be open to inspection and correction by the individual to whom it refers (OECD, 1979).

The Council of Europe had considered privacy issues since 1969. In 1980, it incorporated the OECD guidelines in a convention on the Protection of Individuals with Regard to Automatic Processing of Personal Data. The proposal achieved binding status after ratification in 1985 by a majority of Council of Europe members. The convention affected all transborder data flow among European countries and with other countries, such as the United States. Multinational firms became nervous about all this, since the convention provided that any country could restrict the transmission of data to another country that did not have data protection legislation comparable to its own or that had not ratified the convention. This provided a means of affecting transnational operations. Theoretically, any country could restrict the flow of data to other countries by the simple device of raising the level of its own privacy protection. Since firms conducting international transactions generally prefer to have uniform procedures for transactions in various countries, procedures were likely to conform to the strictest of the national rules.

In 1985, the OECD's ICCP adopted a Data Declaration on transborder data flows as a more specific framework for data flow policy, or "rules of the road on TDF" (Robinson, 1990). TDF issues were also examined by the U.N.'s Intergovernmental Bureau for Informatics (IBI) a Rome-based Third World-oriented communications body that eventually folded for financial reasons. UNESCO also showed involvement (Roche, 1984). The United Nations' Center on Transnational Corporations similarly initiated a TDF project to increase developed and developing countries' sensitivity on the issue (Sauvant, 1986). Even the Vatican took a position: "There is important work to be done to harmonize [national regulations] at the international level and finalize them by using suggestions coming from different social contexts and by employing continuing technological developments" (in Pipe, 1984a).

Europe-wide efforts at ensuring privacy continued with a 1989 Council of Europe recommendation on protection of personal data used for employment purposes (*TDR*, 1989). In 1991, the E.C. passed a directive covering also manual files, and forcing legislation by member states. Yet, at the same time, European police data collaboration was substantially upgraded (Masden, 1992).

Data Protection in a National Context

France

In 1974, a Commission on Information Policy and Civil Liberties was established within the Ministry of Justice to regulate databases and protect individual privacy. Subsequently, in 1978, a law on Information Processing, Files, and Civil Liberties was passed that became effective two years later and affected domestic databases and cross-border data flows. The law attempts to regulate biased and unfair methods of data collection and prohibits the recording of information on race, politics, religion, union membership, and so on. The law also acknowledges the individual's right of access to the information, imposes the obligation to correct false or incomplete information, and sets rules for its distribution.

All data systems must be registered with a special agency, the National Commission on Informatics and Liberties (Commission National d'Informatique et Liberté, or CNIL). The CNIL is an independent administrative authority, similar in some ways to the independent American regulatory commissions, and as such is a rare body in French administration. A majority of its seventeen members are chosen by the judicial and parliamentary bodies. The commission can issue advisory opinions about data protection and data processing, which are then subject to judicial review by a higher administrative court, the Conseil d'Etat.

A database must be registered with CNIL, so that the commission will be able to analyze it. A declaration must state the purpose of the database, the nature of the personal data collected, and its sources as well as destinations. In 1985 and 1986, the commission received almost 10,000 filings of data banks (*TDR,* 1986). In 1987, the number rose to some 45,000. Simplified procedures are available for routine personal data such as payroll, banking accounts, utility billings, and mailing lists.

The first case in which the CNIL recommended criminal prosecution involved the Swedish ball bearing company SKF and its French subsidiary. During a labor dispute, the company was occupied by trade unionists, who discovered a notebook with 600 entries on employment applicants for the years 1971–1982. Although the data collections had been discontinued and were not electronic, the CNIL recommended prosecution. Another case that nearly led to criminal prosecution involved an infraction by the Communist trade union CGT, which had used the automated payroll list of the electric and gas company for mailing election materials on the eve of workers' council elections (Kuitenbrouwer, 1985).

In 1986, the CNIL brought a criminal case against a director of an information bureau in Nantes. The director had not registered his data bank and refused to cooperate with the CNIL. Found guilty of illegally collecting personal data and obstructing a CNIL investigation, he received a FFr 20,000 fine and a suspended prison sentence of two months.

In 1986, the CNIL required that caller identification services in the Biarritz fiber-optic trial offer a blocking function to all subscribers. Call-by-call blocking was also included in the French ISDN service Numeris in 1988, and protections were instituted in the Mestel and Minicom electronic messaging services (Gebhardt, 1990). Another case limited collection of genealogical records by Mormons.

Germany

As mentioned, the state of Hesse enacted the first data protection law in 1970; in 1977, a national law was passed. The discussion of data privacy in Germany in the 1970s was colored by a fierce debate over how to contain a small group of political extremists who engaged in terrorism. Data issues were described as a choice between *Datenschutz* versus *Tatenschutz* (protection of data versus protection of criminal deeds). Social Democrats were concerned with protection of employees' privacy. Law-and-order conservatives, on the other hand, pushed for elaborate police matching of various databases in order to identify potential criminal suspects. They also supported a national machine-readable personal identification card that would permit the tracking of individual movement; this led to an anti-data-collection backlash. The 1983 national census was opposed by many groups, and in an important decision, the Federal Constitutional Court invalidated the holding of the census on the grounds of "informational self-determination." In the meantime, several social democratic states pushed ahead with their own legislation. In the state of Hessen, for example, the automated processing of medical and psychological data is prohibited where information is judgmental rather than factual. The use of data laws was not confined to matters of privacy. It also provided a lever in other disputes. A 1984 decision of the German High Court for Industrial Relations required the express consent of a workers' council for the introduction of a computer system that would be used to collect information on the performance of data technicians. The decision gave unions some influence over computerization where it affects employment security.

In 1988, telecommunications regulations were instituted that provided some protection in calling identification and collection of subscriber data through ISDN. Data compiled on Btx videotex and Temex may be used only for billing and must be erased six months after collection (Gebhardt, 1990). Unification extended privacy laws into the Eastern *Länder*.

United Kingdom

In the United Kingdom, the Advisory Council on Applied Research and Development (ACARD), a consultative body to the prime minister and the cabinet, recommended that one government agency coordinate all policies concerning information technology and its applications, development, and operations. In November 1982, the government adopted ACARD's recommendation by appointing a minister of state for industry and information technology to serve under the secretary of state for industry. It was the first such appointment anywhere.

In response to another ACARD recommendation and spurred by the Council of Europe's Convention on Data Protection, which the United Kingdom signed in 1981, the government introduced a bill that eventually became the Data Protection Act 1984. The Act requires the registration of data banks containing personal information and sets other limitations on data collection and access (Niblett, 1984). The home secretary designated as the first data protection registrar a computer expert, Eric Howe. Initially critical of the legislation, the data-processing industry was partly mollified by Howe's appointment. The duties of the registrar include the establishment of public files of data users and data-processing bureaus. He is also an ombudsman for complaints of data abuse and inaccessibility of records. Data subjects have the right to a copy of the data held about them, and if such information is not provided, they may complain to the registrar or to a court, both of which are empowered to order access. There is also a right to compensation for damages resulting from inadequate data security precautions. By 1990, approximately 153,000 companies and organizations with computerized lists of information on individuals had registered with the Home Office representing 130,000 data users (*Sixth Report of the Data Distribution Registrar*, 1990, p. 22).[2]

In 1987, the United Kingdom adopted a Model Code of Practice for telecommunications service operators that forbids unauthorized dissemination of data on users (Gebhardt, 1990).

Other European Countries

In Sweden, government involvement in a large number of areas has led to the evolution of many data banks in different government agencies. It was estimated that the average Swede is registered in about 150 governmental computer databases. This situation led to a special government commission and subsequent legislation in 1973, the first nationwide comprehensive privacy law anywhere. The law set up a Data Inspection Board for administration and policy development that has the right to grant permits for the maintenance of personal data files. A Data Policy Commission (subsequently the Information Policy Commission) was created to include representatives of federal agencies, political parties, the private sector, unions, employers, and local authorities.

Denmark passed two of the most complex and specific TDF laws in Europe, based in part on Swedish and British privacy law (Feldman and Garcia, 1982). A Data Surveillance Authority must provide a license for any database to be collected or transmitted abroad. The authority also reviews proposals for international communication links to assure that data flows will not lower Denmark's standard of protection, and registers sensitive files.

In Austria, privacy policy illustrates how data protection laws can potentially operate as a nontariff barrier. To transmit personal data abroad, a license must be obtained from the Austrian Data Protection Commission. For countries where similar data protection standards exist, no license is required (Wigand, 1985).

Switzerland provided privacy protection in its 1987 draft law on telecommunications. Article 16 of the law prevented data on telephone users from appearing in statements and extended protections to videotex (Gebhardt, 1990).

In 1988, privacy legislation was passed in Ireland and the Netherlands. In the Netherlands, the legislation followed twenty years of parliamentary debate. The Dutch law permits any subject of a database file to inspect and correct collected information for a small fee (de Pous, 1989; Gassman, 1989; Fauret, 1989). Italy, Spain, Portugal, and Belgium were slow to pass privacy laws.

A Comparison of European and American Approaches to Data Privacy

Legal and historical traditions, as well as economic motivations, explain the disparity between European and American conceptions of TDF, particularly in the realm of privacy protection.

In the United States, a generally more pragmatic approach to legislation has led to the tackling of specific data abuses rather than to comprehensive laws. Numerous laws exist, some of which are quite far-reaching (Noam, 1990)[3]. The so-called Buckley Amendment, for example, permits students access to files that are kept on them by public or private schools and universities, even including letters of evaluation. Similarly, the Freedom of Information Act gives the public access to government documents, excluding only information that is deemed vital to national security, that is needed for the protection of confidential sources or the conduct of an ongoing criminal investigation, or that contains trade secrets of other firms.

Nevertheless, U.S. privacy legislation remains considerably less strict than European law in the regulation of *private* databases, and the coverage of American governmental organizations by privacy law is not comprehensive. Although the Privacy Act of 1974 restricts collection and disclosure by the federal government, only a few states and local governments have passed similar fair information practices laws. The Privacy Act requires each federal government agency to issue a public notice on its record-keeping activities. The Office of Management and Budget (OMB) coordinates the government's efforts in this area, and the protections cover all data files, electronic and conventional. The Privacy Act explicitly protects only U.S. citizens and permanent residents, thus excluding foreign nationals, whose personal data is exported from their national place of employment to U.S. headquarters. Furthermore, the U.S. has no government agency specifically charged with data protection similar to the centralized data protection commissions or authorities established in European countries, though proposals have been advanced in Congress.

U.S. federal data protection requirements cover only consumer credit and reporting agencies, and educational and financial institutions. Several of the states have similar provisions. Under the Fair Credit Reporting Act of 1970, individuals have the right to access their credit-rating file, to have corrections included in the file, and to know the sources of information in credit files (Noam, 1990).[4]

Whereas the European approach is to protect data by making its collection and security requirements explicit, in the United States the abuse of information rather than its collection is the target, and harm must be shown for laws to apply (Feldman and Garcia, 1982). In many European countries, electronic record-keeping systems must be registered with or licensed by a national data protection board and may be subjected to inspection for compliance with the law. Where private recordkeeping involves a large number of individuals, it is permissible only if the individuals have a clear relationship with the record-keeping organization (OTA, 1983).

Privacy and Free Speech

Privacy is not an absolute value. As the traditional clash between the privacy rights of the individual and the free speech rights of the press illustrates, different societal objectives must be balanced against each other. It is by no means clear that a maximum of privacy is desirable. If files that included personal information could not be maintained, it would be difficult for the press to develop an investigative story or for banks to extend credit.

Free speech is perhaps the main consideration that must be balanced against the data privacy principle. Western democracies guarantee freedom of speech in their constitutions. Labeling some types of speech "information flows" and subjecting them to restrictive rules of a tradelike nature does not remove the constitutional protection. Thus, the U.S. government may not enter into agreements restricting the free speech of its citizens without subjecting itself to court challenges.

Privacy protection can conflict with other societal interests. Law enforcement is a consideration, as is technological advancement. Other countervailing factors to consider are protection of consumers (who may be preyed upon by third parties whose identity is being protected), operational ease for networks, and conflicting privacy interests. Although these factors do not obviate the need for privacy protection, they suggest that a balancing of interests needs to take place.

Privacy, broadly defined, consists of two distinguishable but related aspects:

1. The protection against intrusion by unwanted information. This is sometimes termed "the right to be left alone" (Warren and Brandeis, 1890), analogous to the constitutional protection to be secure in one's home against intrusion by government.
2. The ability to control information about oneself and one's activities; this is related in some ways to proprietary protection accorded to other forms of information through copyright laws.[5] A related aspect is the protection of information about oneself from being tampered with by others.

The common aspect of both these elements is that they establish a barrier to information flows between the individual and society at large. In the first case, it is a barrier against informational outflows.

The concept of privacy is not without its detractors. There are three major criticisms:

1. "Only the guilty need privacy." To the contrary, privacy is one of the touchstones of a civilized and free society.[6] Authoritarian or backward societies do not value a private sphere, since they rarely respect individuality and subordinate it to the demands of rulers or social groups.[7]
2. "Privacy is a drag on the economy." Privacy protections raise the cost of information search. Potential employers and buyers, for example, would have to spend more effort and money to find out who they are dealing with if access to personal information is restricted. Deception becomes easier, and transaction costs rise (Posner, 1981).

But there are also good economic arguments for privacy. It ensures the ability of companies and organizations to hold on to their trade secrets and details of their operations and to protect themselves from leaks of insider information and against governmental intrusion. Information often has actual value, and since much of it has no protection through property rights, it must be protected through confidentiality or secrecy.[8] To permit its easy breach[9] would lead to a lesser production of such information. It has been shown in a theorem by Noam and Greenawalt (1979) that under normal conditions "information of value, once released to one person (or very few persons at most) will spread—in the absence of collusion—to all participants." Hence, the absence of privacy protection to stem outflow of information will lead to suboptimal production of such information.

Similarly, anonymity may increase economic risk taking (though increase risk for the partners to a transaction); certain investments may be curtailed if the identity of their investors were disclosed. In that sense, privacy protection acts as a spur to investment, as does the protection of limited liability offered to corporations. (Of course, illegal activities are also made easier.)

The loss of privacy also leads to inefficiency in information flows, just as excessive privacy protection may. In the absence of privacy, people use all kinds of hints or codes to reduce the outflow of information. Or they may meet face to face instead of using the telephone.

Partly in response to economic and social needs, many transactions have been specifically accorded special informational protection, known as privileges (e.g., between attorney and client, penitent and clergy, patient and doctor, citizen and census taker). The idea in each case is that the protection of information leads to a socially superior result even if it is inconvenient in an individual instance to others.

3. "Privacy is of interest to a small elite only." To the contrary, attention to privacy is widely shared. For example, according to information from the New York Telephone Co., 34 percent of all residential households in Manhattan and 24 percent of all its residential households in the state have unpublished telephone numbers at subscribers' request. Most policemen, doctors, or judges, to name but a few professionals, have unlisted numbers. Elsewhere, it appears that the spread of unlisting is still further advanced, reaching 55 percent in California.[10]

Pacific Bell planned in 1986 to sell subscriber information such as new phone orders; more than 75,000 complaints came in, and the company backed off.[11]

Will competition take care of privacy problems? Not necessarily. A competitive environment may resolve some privacy issues, especially if it is possible for a user to select a service provider that offers the desired level of privacy protection. Carriers would lose business if customers felt unsure about privacy of usage. But in many other instances, the greater openness of a competitive system and the greater complexities of its multiple networks may also mean a greater openness of information. It is probably easier to restrict the dissemination of information in a monopoly setting. By its nature, a network is a sharing arrangement. In the past, this sharing encompassed mostly physical assets such as trunks and switches. But as the "intelligence" of networks increases, and as enhanced service networks and physical networks that particpate in communications services evolve, the sharing also reaches data and other informational resources.

In telecommunications, privacy can be protected by either hardware or software options. It makes sense to provide a guaranteed level of privacy protection as a basic right and at no extra charge, and to offer enhanced privacy measures on a for-pay basis for those that need them. It makes sense to define property rights and transaction-generated information as belonging to both sides of the transaction; to require the disclosure of privacy jeopardies; and to limit monitoring of employee calls. These principles, and others, were based on the proceeding initiated by the author (NYPSC, 1991).

Data protection laws can have unintended and paradoxical results for political action. The case of the French section of the human rights organization Amnesty International presents an extreme example. The organization maintains personal records on "prisoners of conscience" and victims of capital punishment and torture. French data protection law prohibits personal files from including information on prison sentences or convictions. Such information, however, is fundamental to AI's activities. The law also prohibits the recording of information about the racial, political, philosophical, religious, or union affiliation of individuals. Again, such information is essential to Amnesty International's activities. Under the French law, personal information collected can be transmitted only to the few countries that have similar data protection laws. But the essence of AI's work is to disseminate information widely about prisoners of conscience, and this would be impossible under a literal reading of the law. In proposing a solution to these problems, a study group of international data protection commissioners recommended the creation of a committee to deal with "bona-fide international organizations pursuing humanitarian goals or defending human rights on an international basis, such as Amnesty International or the International Red Cross" (TDR, 1983). Yet the selection and certification of such organizations enables government authorities to certify some organizations as worthy and humanitarian and others as not.

Privacy protection has become especially important in the telecommunications field, as new technology such as automatic number identification began to be offered.

In 1990, the European Commission issued a draft directive establishing basic telecommunications privacy rights across the twelve member states. The directive includes restrictions on unsolicited calls, calling number indentification, and use and storage of data collected by telephone carriers for electronic profiles.

Sovereignty

The fact that foreign institutions and governments have access to domestic data can be troublesome to many countries. A 1979 Canadian study found that nearly 50 percent of U.S.-based information bureaus storing data on Canadian transactions would have provided data access to U.S. organizations such as credit bureaus, law enforcement agencies, employers insurance firms, and government agencies (CCITCS, 1979).

Similarly, Sweden became alarmed when the fire department of the city of Malmö accessed data on chemical storage and truck routing on a computer of the American firm TRW, located in Cleveland, Ohio. Swedes feared that the U.S. government could interfere with Malmö's fire-fighting efforts. In consequence, the fire department began using a data file located, apparently more safely, in Holland (Feketekuty and Aronson, 1983).

The French government was concerned with the use of American-based econometrics models in the projection of French economic trends. It feared that the U.S. government could access those models and gain insight into the French economy.

To be fair, the United States has given Europeans some cause for concern. In one often retold episode, it tried unsuccessfully to pressure European countries to cancel a major gas pipeline deal with the Soviet Union. When that failed, the American government ordered the producer of the essential compressors for the project, Dresser Industries, to lock out French engineers from the design database (Botein and Noam, 1986). Another example involved Lockheed's Dialog on-line database. Dialog contracted with the International Institute for Advanced Systems Analysis (IIASA) in Vienna to provide access to its publicly available database. Since the Soviets had access to the IIASA data gateway, the U.S. government became concerned that they could establish easy access to U.S. data systems, and it restricted Dialog access through IIASA (Pipe, 1984b).

The United States is not consistent in its advocacy of a free flow of information (Cass and Noam, 1990). In fairness, however, these departures are exceptions. Furthermore, to argue legitimately for the principles of free flow of information, one need not be virtuous beyond reproach.

Industrial Policy and Data Flows

The United States enjoyed a headstart in on-line databases from which it still benefits. In 1983, worldwide revenue from on-line services was about $2 billion, of which the United States accounted for more than three-quarters (Anderla, 1983). In 1983 figures, an OECD report found sales of on-line data services in Western Europe to be less than 10 percent of sales in the United States.

As with most information produced initially for a domestic market, the marginal cost for the export of these databases is low. With a head start and a substantial domestic customer base, U.S. databases provide tough competition for European systems. Although the availability of low-cost and well-tested foreign databases would be in some cases welcome, since domestic replication is made unnecessary, in most cases, other countries fear informational dependency.

Given this database and data-processing discrepancy, some American firms believe that what TDF is really about is economic protectionism in favor of local data processing firms. A Canadian study found that, in 1985, the value for imported computing services was about $1.5 billion, which could fund an estimated 23,000 jobs in the Canadian data-processing industry. With greater frankness than is normally offered, the study conceded that issues of privacy and protectionism are closely intertwined. The report found that the major problem inherent in flows of Canadian data to the United States is "not one of privacy of Canadian data subjects being invaded by data about them being stored in the United States. It is rather that data processing in the communications business may be lost to Canadians as a result of this foreign flow" (Turn, 1979, p. 6). To combat this trend, the Canadian Banking Act of 1980 required that customer data be processed and stored in Canada, thereby forcing U.S. banks to duplicate their hardware and software instead of relying on existing data-processing facilities across the border.

Among Third World countries, Brazil has been particularly active in data and telematics issues, and its policies have received wide publicity. Instituted during the military dictatorship, the thrust of Brazil's policy is evident in the statement of its top information officer, in both senses of that title:

> [T]he administration [i.e., restriction] of TDF appears to be an effective government instrument for the creation of an environment that makes the emergence of an internationally viable national data-service industry possible. By itself, such an industry would have had great difficulties in overcoming the obstacles of a completely "laissez-faire" environment. The country's TDF policy altered that situation [Pipe, 1984b].

In Brazil, a license must be obtained from the special Secretariat for Informatics before establishing international data links. Applications for foreign processing, software import, and database access are rejected if domestic capability exists. The rules are an attempt to strengthen and develop the domestic industry. The policy was strongly embraced by the Brazilian military dictatorship and its business and industrial allies, and it was admired by many observers who otherwise feel no kindness toward right-wing juntas.

Beyond the issues of privacy, sovereignty, and protectionism, data flows also affect the future of PTT monopolies. The 1980s witnessed an acceleration in the creation of private data networks, and technology offered many possibilities for data flows bypassing PTTs. Privacy protection provides an argument for service monopoly, given that private systems, especially if they are shared by several users, cannot be trusted to enforce data protection provisions. Thus, in Germany, the media policy spokesman and secretary general of the Social

Democratic party, Peter Glotz, argued that the network monopoly of the German Bundespost was necessary for data protection.

Another German official, Spiro Simitis, the pioneering data protection commissioner for the state of Hesse, argued that it was necessary to enact special hardware standards:

> [T]he rudiments of a possible set of regulations are emerging. Until now legislation has been chiefly concerned with storage; the conditions governing processing having been abstract and controlled general procedures. Now we must turn our attention directly to hardware, in order to find out whether and how far technical devices conforming to data protection laws can be built into all the equipment in question. A decisive number of statutory requirements could then be met through construction standards [Simitis, 1985].

At present, the possible effect of TDF restrictions on trade has been largely theoretical. But since the United States will probably not adopt data protection legislation to match West European strictness, data flows across the Atlantic could be impeded. This would affect trade, because the amount of electronic data flow that accompanies business transactions has increased dramatically.

Can one truly expect a leak-proof system of data protection? Not surprisingly, "data havens" soon began to emerge, including Monaco and Liechtenstein, and Andorra.

In the friction that ensued on TDF issues and in the traditional manner of international compromise, which acknowledges that there is merit to the claims of both sides, the formula of "regulated free flow" emerged. But no elegant formula could easily cover the differing attitudes toward transborder data flow on the two sides of the Atlantic.

IV
THE FUTURE OF TELECOMMUNICATIONS

38

Networks in the Future

The scenario of the future of telecommunications that is held by traditionalists is well-known: increased integration, broader bandwidth, wider mobility, greater ubiquity. All these tendencies are anticipated correctly, yet they represent only one side of the coin. The discussion of earlier sections of this book aimed at demonstrating the dynamics of disaggregation in networks. If one gives individuals the freedom of association and if the economics are right, in time they will form new types of interlinkages that we call networks. What are some of the long-term implications for networks?

1. Networks will become transnational. As the cost of transmission continues to drop, networks will not be territorially organized. Territoriality was based on the need for a network architecture that primarily minimized cost by minimizing transmission distance. It led to the creation of the "German network," the "French network," and so on. This technological and economic territoriality suited governments everywhere, because they too were based on territoriality of jurisdiction and could thus conveniently exercise control and even ownership over "their" network. But that is changing. Networks are increasingly becoming pluralistic group affairs. Groups break off parts of their communications needs from the public network and aggregate them in their own associations, usually on the facilities of a public carrier, but under different rules and prices.

Territoriality becomes secondary. Many of these communities of interest transcend national frontiers. Their interests are continental and global, and so are their networks. When the computers of brokers and investment banks in New York are interconnected by a continuous network and interact with those in Tokyo and London to trade and clear transactions, one can no longer say that there is a New York or Tokyo market. There is no longer a physical locus for transactions; *the network itself becomes the market.*

2. New electronic neighborhoods will emerge. A few years ago, it became fashionable to speak of telecommunications creating the "global village." There was something inspiring in this image, communal and peaceful. But there is nothing villagelike in the unfolding reality. Instead, groups with shared economic interests are extending national group pluralism into the international sphere through the opportunity to create global interconnections with each other. Indeed, communications make international pluralism easier because it is easier to reach a critical mass for subnetworks if one aggregates users across several countries. *The new group networks do not create a global village; they create the world as a series of electronic neighborhoods.*

In the past, neighborhoods had economic and social functions. In New York, for example, there are Chinatown, Little Italy, the Garment District, Wall Street, Madison Avenue, and the Theater District. All have defined social and economic functions. There are regions with specialized production—Solingen and Sheffield for cutlery; Lyon for silk; Hollywood for films; Silicon Valley for microelectronics (Piore and Sabel, 1984). Production clusters create economies of aggregation that substitute for the economies of scale and scope of the giant multiproduct firm. Physical proximity was a key. But now group networks can serve many of the functions of physical proximity. They interconnect specialized producers, suppliers, buyers, experts, and markets. They create new ways of clustering, spread around the world.

Some of these electronic neighborhoods will be nicer than others. They will perform better, faster, and often even cheaper. In developing countries, the networks of those transacting with the world are already becoming better than those of local people. In places like China or Egypt, a two-tier communications system has emerged.

Networks might also be stratified along socio-demographic dimensions. Already, some long-distance resellers in the United States offer bonuses to churches if they sign up their members. Such marketing efforts can lead over time to identification of some network with particular ethnic, religious, or political groups. Similarly, some networks may be shunned by labor union members if they have a history of labor problems.

3. Personal networks will emerge. But why stop at networks for *groups?* If the trend is from national public networks covering the entire population to a pluralist system, why not expect still further disaggregation? This additional step means individualized networks. Before dismissing the notion of personal networks (PNs) as extravagant, let us remember that twenty years ago nobody expected computers on everybody's lap either.

What does a personal network mean? It means an individually tailored network arrangement. It does not mean a separate physical system, except for inside wiring and maybe the last mile of circuits, plus some radio-mobile links and terminal equipment. The rest could consist of virtual networks, provided by a whole range of service providers and carriers, and packaged together to provide easy access to an individual's primary communications needs: friends and family; work colleagues; frequent business contacts, both domestic and foreign; data sources; transaction programs; frequently accessed video publishers; telemetry services, such as alarm companies; bulletin boards, and so on. Contact to and from these destinations would move with the individuals, whether they are at home, at the office, or moving about.

4. Networks will assume political power as quasi-jurisdictions. Historically, the nation-state was at tension with cross-border allegiances—whether proletarian international solidarity, rebellious youth culture, international financial capital, or ethnic minorities. The new network environment weakens national cohesion. It strengthens particularism and internationalizes it. It is difficult for a state to extend its powers beyond traditional frontiers, but it is easy for the new networks to do so.

Furthermore, these network associations possess and acquire powers of their own. They already may link powerful entities and can bring their combined powers to bear. For example, the combined weight of the members of the SWIFT banking network got the powerful national PTT monopolies to cave in on a number of crucial issues. And there is no reason to expect the power of network combinations to be directed only at communications issues. Once groups are in constant touch, they may as well get organized on other issues too. *The communications network becomes the political network.*

They will coordinate in the economic sphere. When it comes to the role of information, the line between competition and cartel coordination has always been a fine one. In the 1920s, various American industries established so-called fair-price bureaus that gave each member of the industry a convenient look at what its competitors were charging. This practice was outlawed in a series of antitrust cases. Imagine if one leaves instead information exchange to a series of artificial intelligence programs communicating internationally. One has a real problem of conceptualizing, detecting, and preventing international cartels. One person's collusion is another person's programmed trading. *The network becomes the cartel.*

The network associations are also likely to become quasi-jurisdictions themselves. They have to mediate the conflicting interests of their members. They have to establish cost shares, sometimes creating their own de facto taxing mechanism as well as redistribution. They have to determine major investments, to set standards, to decide whom to admit and whom to expel. As a network becomes more important and complex, control over its management is fought over. Elections may take place. Constitutions, bylaws, and regulations are passed. Arbitration mechanisms are set up. Members are assessed financially. *Networks become political entities.*

Thus, we may be witnessing the creation of new and often extraterritorial forms of new quasi-jurisdictions that are not clearly subordinated to others. In response, governments might create forms of domestic and international regulatory mechanisms for specified sets of problems, possibly based on global networks themselves that continuously collect and exchange information, track activities, and coordinate enforcement.[1]

5. Networks will exercise power toward their members. A major question is whether a network group can dominate its own members or be restrictive in allowing others to join. The power of the network becomes most obvious when it is operated by a dominant entity. For example:

- The network of a university such as Columbia can legally exercise restrictions toward its members. It can and does limit terminal equipment and options and charge monopolistic prices, and it could legally refuse to serve political groups that are disfavored.

- The major U.S. videotex service, Prodigy, prevents its users from discussing politics or Prodigy itself on the system. When Prodigy, which provides an extensive messaging service, announced that it would raise the rates for such messages, a group of subscribers posted notices in a "public area" of the system encouraging other subscribers to protest. When Prodigy removed these messages, the protesters turned to the private message feature, and sought help from advertisers. Thereupon, Prodigy canceled the subscriptions of the protesters.[2] It later permitted the discussion of politics, only to become the subject of protests when such discussions became nasty.

- On the public networks, too, content control emerges. American telephone companies recently sought to establish their right to the restrict otherwise lawful "adult" communications if they were harmful to telco's image. The three major U.S. long-distance carriers (AT&T, MCI, and US Sprint) all instituted restrictions on their audiotex ("900") services.

- Employers frequently block the ability of their employees to reach certain numbers. While this is based on protections against running up telephone bills generated by dial-it services, the principle could be extended to exclude messages of a type undesirable to employers, such as those of labor unions. A growing number of businesses maintain electronic mail systems for internal communications, and some have asserted their right to monitor employees' messages. In one instance, a mayor read the private messages that city council members had sent over the municipal system.

- In so-called intelligent buildings, landlords provide communications to occupants. These "shared-tenant services" are largely under the control of the building owners, whose interconnection decisions determine which networks tenants can reach.

Petty monopolies can thus emerge, largely unencumbered by the protections built into the public network, at least in the past, by law, custom, and regulation. The option is to exit, which may mean giving up a job or an apartment—usually not a realistic option.

Are there freedom-of-speech rights for users (in network terminology "common carriage obligations") in group networks? The scope of these rights is undefined. Constitutional rights are unclear in the case of a private group network. Regulatory impositions of such obligations are possible but are limited by the rights of groups to substantially define their membership and the rules under which they operate, especially where a major purpose of the groups is communication, and thus the exercise of a fundamental right itself (i.e., free speech). In such circumstances group activities have strong protection from restrictive regulation.

Even where network groups are organized democratically, they may well be restrictive. A major function of liberties, after all, is to protect minorities from unsympathetic majorities. In the public sphere, guarantees of free speech against governments are part of constitutions. In the network environment, the granting of access and nondiscriminatory content-neutrality is required of the general "public" networks by law or by common carriage regulation. But common carriage does not necessarily apply to group networks. Groups may institute restrictions on the exercise of speech over their network and assert that their status is akin to publishers, with no rights for users. They can exclude certain subjects from being discussed or certain speakers from having access to the network. This could become particularly an issue when telecommunications networks gain the ability to transmit video programs. It is true that individuals could form alternative networks if they are being restricted. Thus, market forces could help, but not if some of the networks control some segments of a chain of communications, or where the ability of any link in such a chain to institute content-based tests would impose transaction costs on the entire system.

In this context, the exercise of freedom of association may lead to group formations that restrict speech. Hence, the evolving pluralistic structure of telecommunications may bear the seeds for a new type of bottleneck to the free flow of information that did not exist on the traditional public network and its common carriage.

These conclusions point to bottlenecks, instability, conflict, and new forms of restrictions, all within an environment rich with communications. What are the long-term implications for policy? In the past decade, policy discussion was correctly focused on creating *openness* by reducing barriers and permitting entry. In Europe, this process is only in its early stages. But as the diversification of the network environment is proceeding, the next set of issues is to create points and rules for *integration* that permit the continued *interoperability* of a "network of networks." These issues are more difficult to deal with than the policy questions of the past. They require the conceptualization of a post-liberalization environment.

39

Toward a Modular Network

In the future it will become increasingly difficult to define what "the network" is. The distinctions between private and public, basic and enhanced, terminal and network equipment, national and international, will fade. It is best to think of the network as a federation that must interact. The traditional arrangement was based on the notion of *sharing* of resources in terms of technology, economics, and politics. But the evolution of networks moves away from this sharing arrangement, because of new entry by suppliers, and, perhaps even more important, of *exit* of major users from the old sharing coalition. It may be more efficient on some level to share, but by the same logic one should not buy books but use the library, or one should not buy a car but hire a taxi. In other words, the efficiency of capacity utilization is not the only economic force driving an economic system. What is important for policy is not to ban the private car, figuratively speaking, but to make sure that there are basic rules of the road for interaction, based on the principles of compatibility, interconnection, nondiscrimination, and reciprocity, that make it possible for the emerging quarrelsome network family to live and work together. It is true that in the short term, revenues may be lost to the public network operator and that additional costs may be incurred. But one must take the long view: Cost tends to come down with competition; network revenues will go up as utilization goes up, and new applications should increase utilization. Where there are still revenue losses, regulators should help make them up elsewhere, such as through access charges, rather than stop the evolution of the network. Contributions to traditional social services could also be made by the newer members of the network family.

The trends toward technical integration and toward institutional and business diversity are, to some extent, substitutes for each other. To advance technologically, one can upgrade a telecommunications system by more powerful integration, such as through integrated narrowband and broadband networks (ISDN and IBN), and benefit from their economies of scale and scope and from their greater technical standardization and compatibility. Or one can choose a more competitive diversity and benefit from its dynamism and cost consciousness. Figure 39.1 maps the strategies of several countries over the past few years.

Generally speaking, the European PTTs stressed ISDN-style integration, whereas the United States mostly followed the path of diversity, the comparative advantage of its society. Japan's approach has been fairly balanced in com-

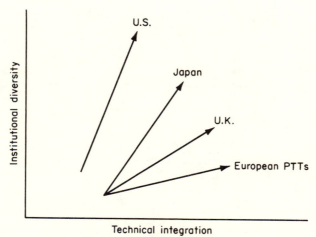

Figure 39.1. National Strategies for Network Evolution.

bining a major push for both in terms of diversity and integration. Diversity can lead to innovation, but it can also retard innovation where there are many independent parts of a system that must interact. Then change can become much harder.

The implication is not that one should go to the other extreme and protect a monopoly system, but rather that it is necessary to provide the system with some tools of integration where they are not self-generating.

Mapping the Network

Analyzing the network environment requires a more systematic look. Obviously it is possible to provide access and interconnection of networks to each other in ways that are technically and economically inefficient.

It is helpful to think of a network as consisting of hardware and software functions.[1] In software the tendency is toward modularity.[2] An example for modular software hierarchy is the Open Systems Interconnection (OSI) model, which was adopted in 1986 by the International Standards Organization (ISO). OSI is based on a hierarchy of seven layers, each of which has defined functional responsibilities. An upper level layer is reliant on the lower layers. But they are, in principle, independent modules, and in theory one can rewrite the software protocol for any layer, and replace it without having to change any of the other layers. In actuality, some layers are integrated, but this need not affect a conceptual map.[3]

The other dimension is hardware. Here it is helpful to think of a network architecture as a sequence of physical segments. For example, the subscriber terminal itself. Or the inside wiring from the terminal to the network termination point. Or the trunk between the local office and the tandem office higher

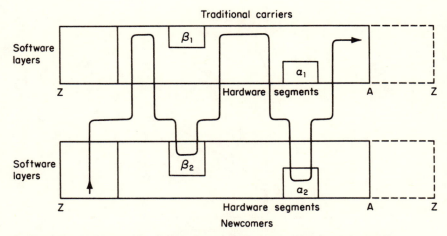

Figure 39.2. Mapping the Network and Interconnecting the Competitive Islands.

up in the switching hierarchy. In the context of defining ISDN standards, the international standards body CCITT defined the segments close to the user very carefully and separated them with demarcation points known as the *R, S, T, U,* and so on. One can use the same technique to define segments throughout the network.

One can put together the software and the hardware presentations into a system of coordinates. On the horizontal axis of Figure 39.2, we have the physical segments, from the periphery of the end user (say a point Z) up through the network hierarchy to point *A,* and back to another end user, *Z.* On the vertical side, one has a software hierarchy.

The boxes of Figure 39.2 thus graph the networks schematically. Each part of the network is defined by a set of coordinates for its software and hardware location, and each service element can be graphed into this map. Element α, for example, could be an interoffice transmission trunk. It is located between two points, which we assume hypothetically to be the physical coordinates for interoffice transmission, and it occupies the first three layers of the OSI hierarchy. Element ß, similarly, is an applications module, located in the top layer and physically in the central office port that lies between some horizontal points. Element β is terminal equipment, such as a fax machine.

Almost all this territory used to be occupied by telecommunications monopolies such as AT&T or the PTTs. But one of the developments of the last two decades has been that other suppliers are available too. The alternatives are schematically graphed in Figure 39.2. In this case, there are α_2 and β_2 elements that are offered by alternative vendors, in competition with the α_1 and β_1 of the traditional monopoly carrier. But, and this is important, the alternative service blocks that are offered usually lack the connecting physical and software elements that are necessary for an end-to-end connection with users, which the traditional carriers possess. This is why, if alternative service elements are to exist and survive, one must provide a framework of interconnection with the other elements of the network, in a way shown schematically by the winding path in the graph, so that one could use the alternative α_2 and β_2 and still not be left cut off from the rest of network functionalities. And this is the major rationale for ONA and similar access and interconnection arrangements. Eventually, the islands will grow larger and fill the entire map. In the meantime, however, one can establish islands of competition only if one assures the ferry service to them.

A Network Grid

As these islands grow, they must operate together in a sensible manner in terms of technical standards, protocols, and boundaries. This is why it is necessary to establish a network blueprint. It would be, conceptually, a grid of defined vertical and horizontal coordinates, and the technical standards of interconnection and interface between them. In this fashion it would set out a system of *modularity* that would make possible an interconnecting modular network system. Within the modules, providers could do more or less whatever they wanted. And they could connect modules together. But one could replace one module with another, and it could interact with the rest of the network.[4]

The transfer from one module to the next will not be free. The charges can be structured to support traditional concerns, such as universal service, and assure the viability of the core network.

Modularity enhances competition and will therefore be viewed negatively by the traditional carriers. On the other hand, it would make them much less dependent on any particular equipment manufacturers, since there is likely to be more competition to supply any specialized module than to provide an entire central office switch, which is a billion-dollar development effort. Thus, the modularity of software will free carriers from switches with multimillion-line programs.[5]

Today most computer hardware is designed to accommodate an operating system such as DOS or UNIX with applications programs such as spreadsheets and word processing. Telephone digital switches, though similar to computers, in effect mix the operating system with the applications, so that it is difficult for telephone companies or independent software companies (as opposed to switch manufacturers) to write the new applications software either because its millions of lines are impenetrable or because they cannot touch it legally. Modularity would also deal with the inevitably increasing competitive overlap between telecommunications and computer industries and would assure that intelligence does not migrate into the terminal equipment periphery of the network for purely regulatory reasons.

Market niches for small hardware suppliers would open. The carriers could encourage the development of software applications by outside suppliers, just as IBM did by opening software applications for its personal computers. This would enhance the telephone carriers' flexibility. Right now, changing network capability and services is a ponderous process.

It would be similarly possible for the VAN service providers to provide new applications by placing them among the central office software functions themselves. In other words, software by outsiders would be put into the central exchange. This could be called software collocation. PTTs will shudder today at the notion. But it may be attractive commercially to them, as long as it conforms with standards and protocols, does not displace their own functions because of limited capacity, is limited to higher-layer applications rather than network control functions, and of course yields revenues. This could open up a scenario of exciting applications.

40

Telecommunications Liberalization: An Expansionary Process?

A Model of Interaction in Telecommunications Policy

A look across countries and across different economic sectors shows a spreading in the liberalization of previously strictly controlled economic activities. In the United States, deregulation expanded *functionally* from one line of business to adjoining ones (e.g., in transportation, from airlines to railroads and then to trucks; in telecommunications, from equipment to long-distance service, local transmission, and central office functions). Liberalization has also spread *geographically*. In telecommunications it has moved from the United States to the United Kingdom, Japan, and to some extent continental Europe. In air transportation, too, it proceeded from the United States to Britain and Europe. One should note that in other historical periods the opposite trends have occurred, and regulation has expanded. In the United States, for example, state railroad regulation led to federal railroad regulation in the 1880s, which in turn spread in the 1920s and 1930s to trucking, buses, and airlines. In financial services, regulation of savings and loan banks expanded to commercial and investment banks and brokerage services. In telecommunications, national telegraph regulation of European countries was extended, in the 1850s, to international arrangements, and later, to telephone service.

This leads to the question of why these long-term international trends are taking place. Is it a change in *ideology,* in which the Chicago School of Economics follows, for example, the Fabian Society? Or is it the political *dominance* of one country, which is then reflected in international trends of policy? Or is it a dialectic cycle, in which the inevitable shortcomings of any policy lead in time to the adoption of another? Chapters 5 and 6 discussed this question, largely in domestic terms. We shall now add the element of international interaction.

Interaction creates instability. The more interrelated countries and economic activities are, the less likely are stable solutions to separate policies. And where instabilities exist, they ripple throughout the entire system. It becomes increasingly difficult to control all the elements in a complex matrix of interrelations. Ultimately, overarching control over many countries and many economic activities would be necessary to restore stability. And since this power does not exist, or is usually not deemed desirable, regulatory strictness may unravel.

The following pages provide a simple analysis of regulation in its intersectoral and international dimensions. We start off by narrowly defining regulation as the setting, by a regulatory agency, of a price vector R for a set of economic activities. A total prohibition is an infinite price set by the state; a totally laissez-faire regime means a market price. Most regulation, however, is somewhere in between and can be viewed as a way of making an economic activity costlier (as in pollution control) or cheaper (as in residential telephone usage). Various interest groups are affected by the setting of these prices, and they seek favorable P's by exercising pressure through the political process.

Where will R be set? This depends on the optimizing function of the regulator. For purposes of the argument, it is not necessary to specify this function in detail, but to assume an interest group model of politics. Regulatory behavior is affected by the groups according to their power and stake in the outcome. Let us assume two interest groups, A and B, each with a "political weight" of W_A and W_B. Each group is affected by the regulation R, with the effect E described by $E_i = g_i(R)$. We assume for simplicity that the two groups are impacted differently by regulation, in that one gains from a higher R, whereas the other loses from it.

$$E'_A > 0 \qquad E'_B < 0 \tag{1}$$

Each group asserts pressure P_i according to the strength of impact E_i, weighted by the group's political weight W_i.

$$P_i = E_i W_i = g_i(R)W_i \tag{2}$$

The various pressures are in equilibrium when

$$P_A + P_B = g_A(R)W_A + g_B(R)\text{w}_B = 0 \tag{3}$$

which is where the ratio of the benefit functions is equal to the inverse of the political weights of the respective groups. Since the W_i and g_i are given, we can determine the expected regulation R in such a system as

$$R = h\left[\frac{g_A}{g_B}, \frac{W_A}{W_B}\right]^{-1} \tag{4}$$

We now introduce a second and related economic activity and denote it by 2. This activity affects both A and B in their activity 1. For example, activity 2 could be telephony, which affects telegraphy (activity 1) and two interests affected by it, carriers and users. Similarly, activity 2 could be functionally the same as 1 but exercised in a different political jurisdiction. The demand and supply for one activity tend to be related to the other, either as substitutes or as complements. Hence, in an interrelated world, the politically optimal regulations may be different from those for a single activity in an isolated jurisdiction.

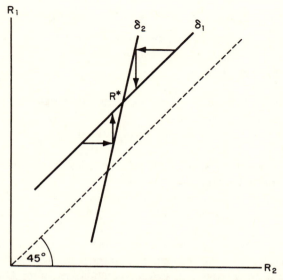

Figure 40.1. Reaction Functions of Regulatory Policy by Two Jurisdictions.

$$R_1 = f\left[\frac{g_A}{g_B}, \frac{W_A}{W_B}, R_2\right] \tag{5}$$

In most instances, we will encounter a cross-elasticity C that is positive:

$$\frac{dR_1}{dR_2}\frac{R_2}{R_1} = c_1 > 0 \tag{6}$$

But in some instances, cross-elasticity of regulation C would be negative. For example, if banking laws are tightened in Italy, they may be lowered in Switzerland, since its banking industry, which benefits from inflows from Italy, would be worse off than before without counter-relaxation. Similarly, if Switzerland lowers the strictness of its banking regulations, Italy may have to tighten up its own to reduce outflow. This can lead to instability. As Italy successively tightens up, Switzerland keeps liberalizing.

An example in telecommunications is transborder data flow protection laws. The less protected data is in one country, the tighter the other country may become in response.

Now for activity 2 the same holds true. Here too are two interest groups, denoted by C and D, and an effect of R_1 with a cross-elasticity of C_2. Therefore, we can think of two "reaction functions" f_1 and f_2, that track the response of one regulation to the other's given level.

A point such as R' would denote the two independently set regulatory policies (Figure 40.1).

But once we postulate reactions to each other, there would be a shift to R^*.

$$R^*_1 = (R^1_1, R_2) \, C_1 \, exp(1/1 - C_1 C_2) \tag{7}$$

Under moderately sized and positive cross-elasticities, there will be an equilibrium point such that regulation will be lower for desirable activities and higher for undesirable ones.

Examples are

(a) lower telephone rates, if one wants to attract business from the other jurisdiction; and

(b) stricter local zoning laws, to prevent undesirable activities from spilling in.

There is no need for *coordination* between 1 and 2; an equilibrium can be reached by unilateral actions and reactions.

However, an equilibrium requires that the reaction functions 1 and 2 are such that 2 is steeper than the inverse of 1 at the point of intersection (i.e., that 2 cuts 1 from below).

If the reverse is true, then there is no equilibrium, and the regulatory strictness either moves successively higher or lower to corner solutions. Examples are the "race to the bottom" in state corporation law in the United States, or tax havens internationally. The reverse is the increasing exclusion by strict regulation of chemical waste dump sites. These are instances of corner solutions. For other configurations of the reaction functions, cyclical change is possible.

Instability raises questions of how to prevent it, and therefore leads to the issue of *policy coordination*. But even in stable situations, R^* may not be the optimal result for either 1 or 2, or both, and policies may be sought to affect moving R^* back to R'.

There are several possibilities for such policy coordination and they are touched upon in the following:

Supraregulation

Supraregulation is encompassing regulation, either across jurisdictions (e.g., a supranational policy) or across functions (i.e., "supra-modal"). This expands regulation to a *higher* level of institutions (e.g., to the European Commission) or to a *wider* institution, such as the Interstate Commerce Commission in the United States which regulates all modes of surface transportation.

How is supraregulation set? By analogy to the single-jurisdiction case, the two sets of interest groups are assumed to affect the joint jurisdiction in an aggregated fashion, if the suprajurisdiction is answerable to the body politic.

$$R_s = f_3 \, [(P_{1A} + P_{2A}), (P_{1B} + P_{2B})] \tag{8}$$

This can be higher or lower than uncoordinated outcomes. Supraregulation is not invariably stricter than particularist regulation, for the reasons discussed. In telecommunications, for example, the regulatory principles of the European Commission are less strict than those of most of the member states. In the United States, the same holds true for the FCC vis-à-vis the state Public Utility

Commissions. But the reverse is also often the case (e.g., in the regulation of securities).

One question is "Why would interest groups (or a whole country) consent to supraregulation?" Would this not dilute the power of dominant groups? This is indeed true. Therefore, a dominant group will normally consent to a shift to supraregulation only where its favored policy would be enhanced (e.g., if the balance of power of interest groups in the other sector is even more favorable to its concerns). However, for symmetrical reasons, the dominant group in the other sector would then oppose supraregulation lest it dilute its own influence. Log rolling aside, this then leaves two primary scenarios (the second of which is the more important) in which mutual joining of supraregulation will occur:

1. When the balance of power is essentially equal in the two sectors, so that supraregulation does not make much difference. This is why policy co-ordination is easier among Western European countries than, for example, East Asian ones.
2. When supraregulation establishes a *policy cartel* to avoid separate regu-lation to affect each other and to lead to results that are considered sub-optimal by the dominant groups. This is more likely to be important where the cross-elasticity of regulation is high, which is likely to be the case with sectors or countries that interact strongly with each other.

In other words, the advantage of the elimination of uncontrolled interaction must be greater than the value attributed to control and independence. Of course, de facto independence already had been lost through the mechanism of inter-action, and supraregulation reflects this.

A related issue is that of uniformity in regulation. Here the issue is not the strictness per se, but the importance of being identical. There are situations where efficiencies exist in uniformity or connectivity. (The width of railroad gauge or protocols in telecommunications are examples.)

Technologists tend to favor standardization. Economists have more mixed views, because uniformity has its costs. To have cars with identical pollution controls in both Norway and Belgium may not necessarily be optimal for either or for both jointly.

In terms of the model, uniformity is given by the 45° line, which is likely to be off the equilibrium point R^*. Uniformity is the dominant policy throughout if at least one reaction function is sloped at 45° (i.e., where at least one juris-diction reacts to the other's change by an identical change so as to preserve uniformity). But that is an exceptional situation.

There may be great incentives for one state to be nonuniform. Examples are large countries for whom international interaction may be small in relative terms (e.g., the United States, which for example affords a nonmetric system of mea-surements). At the same time, many other examples are small jurisdictions: Switzerland in banking; Delaware in corporation law; Hong Kong in tariff du-ties; Liechtenstein in taxes; Monaco in gambling; and Luxembourg in broad-casting. These examples suggest that small countries have incentives to be non-conforming, probably since the loss in revenue, control, and so on, from their own relatively small domestic economies is more than offset by the inflow from the larger countries resulting from nonconformity. To prevent such nonuniformity, the other states may have to impose substantial pressure on the maverick jurisdictions or pay significant compensation.

Regulatory Treaties

Another possibility of coordination is to establish interjurisdictional or intersectoral treaties. Here there is no supraregulation by a suprabody, only an agreement, and each side must be better off than before to enter into it. Agreement will stop at the point where marginal benefits of marginal regulation will begin to be negative for at least one jurisdiction. Thus, such a system is a convoy traveling at the speed of its slowest ship. It can be extended further where compensation to some participants is possible, which is one of the ways the European Community operates in the agricultural field.

Regulatory Colonialism

An extreme example for regulatory coordination could be called regulatory colonialism, when one jurisdiction can set regulations for another jurisdiction solely to benefit itself. Britain's imposition of regulations on cotton spinning in India or on opium trade in China are examples. Other illustrations are the use of the Interstate Commerce Commission by American railroads to impose regulations on trucking, or the successful pressure put on the FCC by American broadcasters to restrict cable television for a number of years.

Instability

The problem of any coordinated regulatory structure is its instability. First, no equilibrium may be possible, because the reaction functions do not meet the stability criterion described earlier. Second, one jurisdiction's adherence to an agreement provides the other with an opportunity of gain by seeking a noncooperative policy. In each jurisdiction there are pressures to seek one's own ideal regulatory level, which is likely to be different from the agreed upon level or from the interactive equilibrium. Going it alone can be due to shortsightedness or lack of understanding of the interaction involved. But it can be based on the rational desire to gain advantages over others by breaking joint policy, at least in the short run.

In telecommunications, for example, communications "havens" are possible and likely to emerge. The example of telex service is instructive. As discussed repeatedly in this book, in the 1980s, London-based telex bureaus started to retransmit traffic between North America and continental Europe in defiance of CCITT cartel "recommendations" against such retransmission. It was profitable for U.K. firms to break these rules, since this generated more traffic and made the United Kingdom more attractive as a business location. In time, the cartel rules were held to be illegal.

It is important to recognize that domestic intersectoral instability is linked to international instability in regulation. A matrix describes the set of intersectoral (vertical) and international (horizontal) regulatory cross-elasticities.

$$c_{11}, c_{12}, \ldots, c_{1n}$$
$$c_{21}, c_{22}, \ldots, c_{2n}$$
$$\cdot$$
$$\cdot$$
$$\cdot$$
$$c_{m1}, c_{m2}, \ldots, c_{mn}$$

Generally, a stable solution is less likely as:

1. The sectors increasingly overlap (higher vertical cross-elasticities), for example, due to "merging" technology. (Example: telecommunications, mass media, computers.)
2. Jurisdictions increasingly interrelate (higher horizontal cross-elasticities), for example, because of lower transportation costs.
3. The relative weight of interest groups in different jurisdictions varies, as their economies develop on different trajectories. This can be a self-feeding mechanism, as some countries become specialized in certain sectors.
4. The regulatory price set diverges from cost, generating incentives for breaching the set.

These changes lead to unstable situations that affect the entire system. A single inconsistency has multiple secondary effects, which in turn lead to further inconsistencies. At the same time, collaborative regulatory adjustments become more difficult, because they cannot be confined to subsectors.

Outlook

Is there anything to stop the process? At some point, the cost of instability and diversity becomes high enough for a coordinated regime to be reestablished. But this is not likely to be stable over time, especially since no real international enforcement or compensation mechanisms exist, and their absence has domestic reverberations. For example, if international airline cartels break down, domestic ones are threatened. One can fly from Toronto to Vancouver through the United States, if Canadian prices are too high.

Applied to telecommunications, one should therefore expect an overall trend toward liberalization, though accompanied by efforts to stabilize its collaborative aspects. As the matrix of interrelations becomes steadily more cross-elastic, one could have some oscillations. But the overall tendency should lead to reduced regulatory strictness internationally. In that sense, liberalization is an expansionary process. It may not be just an ideological choice but a response to an internal inability to structure a stable equilibrium that serves multiple domestic interests and goals. One has to predict that similar inconsistencies will spread throughout the system, even where they are not based on the same domestic pressure to change that led to the original instability in the other jurisdiction.

Traditional telecommunications operated through national monopolies protected internationally by a cartel arrangement. Now, a challenge to domestic monopolies threatens the international cartel, and the breakdown in international arrangements threatens the domestic stability of others. It is difficult to see how the simplicity of the traditional system can be maintained or restored. Most likely we are merely at the beginning of a lengthy, dynamic, and untidy process, of which the presently asymmetric liberalization across the two sides of the Atlantic is a manifestation.

41

Regulatory Tasks for the Future: Interconnectivity in the Pluralist Network

Two basic forces shape change in today's telecommunications networks in Europe and elsewhere: the integrative forces of technology that push towards ISDN and integrated broadband networks, raising barriers to entry; and the social and economic forces of pluralism, which move the network toward a decentralized and segmented federation of subnetworks. The tension between these forces is most pronounced on the front where they intersect: the rules of interconnection of the multiple hardware and software subnetworks and their access into the integrated whole. Such interconnection and access extend traditional common carrier principles from users to networks. In coming years, policymakers must structure ways in which network interconnection is granted, defined, policed, priced, and harmonized. Many questions must be resolved involving technical standards, national uniformity, and international collaboration.

Regulatory structure in telecommunications has paralleled the stages of the industry itself. The monopoly stage of industry structure was accompanied by state ownership and price and profit regulation. The breach of monopoly was tracked and sometimes facilitated by regulation focusing on industry structure. In the next stage, the network is being rearranged from a centralized starlike structure into a matrix of interconnected but decentralized networks. This moves the focus of regulation to encompass not only traditional consumer protection, but also network protection where necessary, mediating the interaction of carriers, network operators, value-added service providers, end users, and equipment manufacturers.

Where does a pluralist network leave future policy? It would be naive to expect fewer regulatory tasks. Many disputes become less intraorganizational within the single network and more public in nature. The main regulatory tasks that the pluralistic network system raises for the future would deal especially with interconnectivity issues—technical, legal, content, financial, social, international, and otherwise. They are characterized by *inter* words: interoperability, interconnection, integration, intermedia, international. These issues include the following:

1. *Technical interconnectivity: protection of a balance between standardiza-*

tion and diversity. The advantages of uniformity derive from greater industry and service stability, and increased compatibility and portability between different hardware and software. Its primary disadvantages involve reduced freedom to innovate and experiment, and the loss of flexibility to adopt to changing conditions. What is needed is a process to weigh and balance the various needs, and a hierarchy of uniformity.

Experience and the theoretical economic literature on standards setting and game theory show that standards do not necessarily evolve optimally, smoothly, or speedily in a purely voluntary setting. This would suggest a governmental role in interoperability, as long as one can prevent their use for protectionist purposes. Europe's ETSI is an institutional response to that need.

2. *Legal interconnectivity: protection of interconnection and access.* The tension between the integrative and pluralistic forces is most pronounced on the front where they intersect: the rules of interconnection of the multiple hardware and software subnetworks and their access into the integrated whole. Policy must structure ways in which network interconnection is granted, defined, priced, and harmonized. To control access arrangements is to control the network. This is detailed in Chapter 42, where an open network system is discussed (NYPSC, 1989; NYPSC, 1990c).[1] The liberalization of terminal equipment interconnection and open network provision in Europe are steps in that direction. But they are only the first steps in a long journey.

3. *Content interconnectivity: regulatory treatment of telephone carriers in their capacity as mass media.* The upgrading of the telephone network toward broadband capability and its use for video, data, and text transmission brings telephone transmission ever closer to mass media. Audio mass announcement services are already widely offered, and video broadband is a likely future scenario for telecommunications carriers.

In the United States, there have been claims by network operators to possess the status of "broadcasters" or "publishers" of information, or at least the arbiter of what fits their organization's image, with the right to select the information carried over their network. In Europe, these issues are beginning to arise, and the television field itself is in the turmoil of change, as discussed in the companion volume to this book (Noam, 1991c).

In the common law tradition, carriers and other businesses "affected with the public interest" had an obligation to provide service to all indiscriminately. They provided transport or transmission function, with no influence over or liability for the content of transmissions, as *common carriers.* Common carriage is among the most important long-term issues in telecommunications policy. Common carriage is a form of content interconnection in an intermedia environment. As such, it is a cousin of the other forms of interconnection.

What does common carriage mean? That is a surprisingly difficult question for such a well-worn term.[2] It is often used imprecisely as a synonym with other terms. For example, it does not mean universal service, that is, the requirement to serve anyone equally, regardless of geography. Nor is it a synonym for *monopoly, public utility,* or *regulated firm.* It is best defined for our purposes as a "carrier of electronic information offering service on demand to the general public, for hire." Its attributes are neutrality among similar users and usages, content neutrality, and no liability for content and user actions. This is nothing new. For centuries under English common law, transportation carriers had special obligations when dealing with the public, primarily the responsibility to treat customers equally.

Early forms of common carriage date back at least to the Roman Empire, which developed law on the duties of shipowners, innkeepers, and stable keepers. Early English common law established rules on businesses that were considered "public callings." These included bakers, brewers, cab drivers, ferrymen, innkeepers, millers, smiths, surgeons, tailors, and wharfingers (Phillips, 1988, p. 83). *Common,* in this sense, meant "open to public service." [3] By force of common law enforced by the courts, common carriers were required to serve, upon reasonable demand, any and all who sought their services (Aust, 1990).

The concept of common carriage crossed the Atlantic and became part of the American legal system. Common carriage was applied to railroads and later to other distribution mediums. In 1901, the U.S. Supreme Court affirmed that under common law a telegraph company is a common carrier and owes a duty of nondiscrimination. [4]

In today's legal terms, common carrier obligations translate into nondiscrimination and noninterference with content. What are the benefits of such a system? In economic terms, common carriage is one of those arrangements whose purpose is to reduce transaction costs, like limited liability, legal tender, or negotiable instruments.

As with other efforts to balance private and public interests, common carriage is at times burdensome to the carrier. Yet it is probably fair to say that the common carrier system has served telecommunications participants well: It has permitted society to entrust its vital highways of information to governmental administrations or for-profit companies, without the specter of discrimination and censorship by government or private monopolies; it helped establish a free flow of information; it reduced administrative costs and the burden of liability because the network operator did not need to concern itself with content; and it protected the carriers from pressure groups who wanted to exclude telephone service to some other groups or activities they opposed. This system has probably resulted in a broader, more useful, lower cost, and more profitable network system than would have developed without it.

Although common carrier principles go back a long time, their applications are in a constantly shifting terrain and require continuous updating, particularly in an extraordinarily dynamic period in telecommunications.

Perhaps the most important change has been the emergence of the telephone network as a carrier of mass media messages, provided mostly by other information suppliers. Examples include videotex, dial-it, mass announcement services, interactive services, and future telephone broadband services, including video. This raises the question of the regulatory status of such a new mass medium. Here it is helpful to understand what the options are. Mass media are basically treated in one of three ways. The print media is virtually unregulated;

in the United States and Europe, free speech governs. The main restrictions are the prohibition of libel, the protection of privacy, and some protection from obscenity. Other countries have similar, though usually somewhat more restrictive, free-speech protection. Private broadcasters and cable operators are treated somewhat differently. They require licenses and franchises to operate and are subject to certain obligations, such as, in the United States, the fairness doctrine, the must-carry rule, and so on. They still enjoy significant free-speech rights; in particular, they are able, to a large extent, to determine what will be shown on their medium. The third type of treatment is common carriage. This is the traditional way for telephone carriers to operate. That is, any user, and any form of content, as long as it is lawful and as long as it pays the regular price, will be carried over the telephone network.

The question now arises, how should the telephone carriers' increasing mass media role be handled: Should it become something akin to a second cable television system (i.e., with the powers of selecting and programming many of its channels and excluding others)? This would give an unprecedented gatekeeper role over mass media to private or governmental organizations with considerable market power. Instead, telephone organizations' role as mass media carriers should be governed by the conduit and nondiscrimination principles of common carriage, which is the traditional way that telephone carriers have provided services in the past.[5]

It is important to distinguish *conduit*, or transmission, functions from *content* functions involving information provision or modification. This is the most basic way to distinguish common carriage from publishing.

Whether or not telephone carriers offer program services does not affect the validity of common carriage principles. Common carriage applies only to a communication carrier's provision of conduit services. If a conduit provider is also permitted to offer content, the basic principles of common carriage are not reduced; On the contrary, they are even more important, because otherwise the carrier could keep its content competitors out, or discriminate against them.

There is a simple way to summarize common carriage. *All electrons and photons are created equal.* (In 1990, the New York State Public Service Commission established the first U.S. rules to this effect, drafted by the author, denying telephone carriers censorship rights for lawful messages, or the ability to institute discriminatory access arrangements for information providers or listeners.) In the United Kingdom, on the other hand, under traditionalist pressure, the regulatory agency Oftel established a censorship board and other forms of control. Most countries also permit or require various forms of content discrimination.

4. *Financial Interconnectivity: Protecting the Viability of the Core Network.*
Clearly, an expanded, upgraded, and enhanced network utilizing the best technology requires significant capital investment. A competitive network system may drive prices not only to costs but to marginal costs, making it impossible to cover fixed costs, let alone to have monopoly profits to support upgrades. Furthermore, as discussed, there may be a problem of investing in a critical mass (i.e., in generating externalities) when the risk is borne by the initiating

network but the rewards are shared by others through the mechanism of interconnection. Finally, a technologically dynamic environment means shorter economic lives for equipment, requiring faster amortization. It is therefore a challenge for future policy to structure arrangements such that adequate investments in the network are available in a decentralized environment.

5. *Social interconnectivity: establishing new mechanisms of redistribution.* The pluralistic network will make it increasingly difficult to maintain the traditional system of *internal* transfers from one class of users to another. But this does not spell the end of transfers as such. There is still ample possibility and opportunity to subsidize some categories of service for reasons of social policy or regional development, or for the positive benefits that new subscribers provide to existing users. One type of support mechanism is a "lifeline" program to insure access by the poor.[6]

A new mechanism to finance desired subsidies and end the primary reliance on the PTTs and their customers would be to establish a "universal service fund" with contributions by all network providers, instead of the present system of internal transfers. Such funds could be raised through various access charge mechanisms, or, more neutrally and efficiently, through a value-added tax on communication services.

6. *Informational interconnectivity: privacy protection.* The new telecommunications environment raises privacy problems. Privacy issues, in effect, are the flow of information beyond the intended recipient. Privacy protection in telecommunications is not a new issue. In the past, manual operators and party lines all created their own problems. The first patent for a voice scrambling device was issued in 1881, only five years after the invention of the telephone.[7] Relatively strong expectations of privacy developed in time. Today a new generation of privacy problems has emerged. The reasons include:

a. More and more transactions are conducted electronically.[8]
b. It has become easier and cheaper to collect, store, match, and redistribute information about transactions and individuals.[9]
c. The number of carriers and service providers has grown enormously, leading to an increasingly open network system in which information about use and user is exchanged across companies.
d. Transmission conduits increasingly include unsecured portions—for example, because of mobile communications.

Concern with electronic privacy has led to different policy approaches. In Western Europe, attention to privacy issues has led to data protection laws and the establishment of institutionalized boards and commissions that have often imposed fairly rigorous restrictions on data collection and data flows. This is discussed in Chapter 37 on transborder data flows. In the United States, the approach has instead been based on a variety of ad hoc federal and state legislation.

The policy challenge is to structure a more flexible approach: a framework in which the user would have several hardware and software "privacy options" of service.

A competitive environment may resolve some privacy issues, especially if it is possible for a user to select a service provider that offers the desired level of privacy protection. But as mentioned before, the greater openness of a competitive system and the greater complexities of its multiple and networks may also mean a greater openness of information (NYPSC, 1990a, Noam 1991a). In the absence of protection it is likely that advocates of the traditional system will argue that a monopoly is required for privacy protection.

7. *Service quality interconnectivity: monitoring and maintaining service quality.* Quality issues are becoming important with price regulation. There are more incentives to cut corners as a hidden way of increasing prices. As society becomes ever more dependent on communications streams, it may reach a point of great vulnerability because of a technical failure or intentional harm.

Furthermore, the network system is increasingly nontransparent to end users. In a chain of several carriers that are strung together for a transmission path, which one causes faulty transmission? This difficulty in identifying the culprit could encourage "free riding" by some companies (Noam, 1991b). Also, there may be selective deterioration (red-lining). As PTTs become entities that are more driven by profit motives than in the past, these issues will become important.

8. *Infrastructure interconnectivity: the role of telecommunications policy as economic development policy.* The competitiveness of an economy is affected by the state of its communications. Many European countries are active in using telecommunications as a strategic tool for technological development.

Planning horizons in telecommunications are very long and suggest the need to facilitate coordination among carriers, where governments assume infrastructure responsibility. Depending on the success of such policies, the U.S. may embark on a similar course, as its recent science network, NREN, demonstrates.

9. *Competitive interconnectivity: the prevention of oligopolistic behavior and of cyclical instability.* A decentralized and pluralistic network system is less efficient in terms of minimizing resources, and there is likely to be excess capacity. There is nothing unusual about this. Almost every industry has excess productive capacity, and the competitive effect is usually beneficial for customers. In the telecommunications field, with its low marginal costs, we must expect that the competition will cause periodic price instability. One of the functions of future regulation will therefore be to moderate the worst effects of price volatility and at the same time prevent industry efforts at collusion. In the future, volatility may be most pronounced in international communications.

10. *Interconnectivity of planning information.* A decentralized network system will have much less of a comprehensive planning role than in the past. To planners and engineers this may seem heresy, but most markets for products and services have no long-range, industry-wide plan. However, since telecommunications are characterized by interconnectivity issues and large-scale investments, it is useful to establish clearinghouses of information about network deployments. That is, there may be a need for some form of disclosure.

11. *International interconnectivity: establishment of global arrangements to*

match the global scope of networks. The openness of the evolving network system will not stop at the national frontiers. In the long run, telecommunications will move beyond the territorial concept, and the notion of each country having full territorial control over electronic communications will become anachronistic. Communications are becoming distance insensitive. Rerouting, arbitrage, and the establishment of communications "havens" become easily possible. This undermines attempts to set rules administratively for prices and service conditions. No country can be a telecommunications island anymore. The more interrelated countries and economic activities are, the less likely it is that there are stable solutions to separate policies. Moreover, instabilities in one country affect the entire system. It becomes increasingly difficult to control all the elements in such a complex matrix of interrelations (See Chapter 40). This means conceding a greater role to international bodies, while recognizing their limitations, and similarly conceding a greater role to the coordination powers of markets.

Conclusion

These issues will, no doubt, lead to significant regulatory controversies and will occupy policy discussions in the United States, Europe, and elsewhere for a long time. None of the tasks is beyond the grasp of policy makers in terms of complexity or political feasibility. But it requires an end to the nostalgia for the simplicity of the golden age, a vision of a very different network environment, and the willingness to engage in an analysis that goes beyond that of competition versus monopoly, because most future issues cannot be analyzed in such simple terms.

42

The Pluralist Network

The New Network Coalitions

In the first part of this book, we analyzed the incentives and forces for centrifugalism in the previously all-encompassing network. We then turned to the various countries and issues to observe these centrifugal tendencies. Now, we close the circle and return to the nature of change. The incentives to group formation, discussed in the model of Chapter 3, can lead, where they are permitted to do so legally, to new "network associations." It is a process that we called earlier the "tragedy of the common network," because it is not its failing but rather its very success which undermined the public network. As we observed, the success of a communal network creates overexpansion, cost shifting, and the forces for particularism. For example, the largest of users increase their electronic communications to huge volumes, and their technical requirements are increasingly differentiated from those of average users. Because the combined volume of large users has risen so much, they can account for much of the cost savings of sharing just between themselves. They can form alternative network associations for large parts of their communications needs, first in-house, then with their closest suppliers, customers, or market partners.

Examples are large private intraorganization networks, shared tenant services, local area networks, wide area networks, and other specialized services.

These groupings of users need not be territorial. The notion of telecommunications as consisting of interconnected national systems is likely to be transcended in many instances, and specialized transnational networks will emerge. This becomes possible with the drop in cost of international circuits.

For satellite transmission, in particular, the marginal cost with respect to distance is close to zero. Fiber-optic links also have lower distance-sensitive costs. The implications are that communication flows can be routed in indirect ways to exit previous shared arrangements or to join new and more congenial ones. Arbitrage becomes easily possible. This undermines attempts to set rules administratively for prices and service conditions.

In the future it is likely that specialized global networks will emerge for a variety of groups that communicate with each other intensely. Their relation to each other is functional rather than territorial, and they can create global clustering of economically interrelated activities in much the way that, in the past, related activities clustered physically near each other.

This has begun with the private networks of large users. These private networks, some of whose operation and administration require hundreds of skilled technicians and managers, even where they usually rely on the infrastructure of the regular carriers, have emerged in developed countries. These activities are spearheaded by private firms, but are pursued also by nonprofit and public organizations. Similarly, users with common interests and activities have begun to interlink through private value-added networks such as SWIFT.

Examples for actual or potential group networks are those of (1) advertising agencies linked to media firms and printers; (2) chemical manufacturers and environmental protection agencies; (3) insurance firms, hospitals, record rooms, police departments, and so on; or (4) of automobile manufacturers, dealers, suppliers, and shippers.

In some instances these networks will have special performance features that distinguish them from the general "public" network. In the first example just cited, network bandwidth must be high to permit transfer of high-resolution graphics. In the second example, the usefulness of the network may be in supporting software and databases. In many instances, such as the third example, it is probably the price of intercommunications that drives the arrangement. In the fourth example, the standardization of transactions may be the primary advantage.

Most users are likely to participate in several networks. Furthermore, such a pluralist network arrangement does not mean separate transmission links for each subnetwork at every point. It will often make sense to transport the traffic of several low-volume users part of the way on the general network until the point where there is enough aggregate traffic to branch off. The economics of sharing are not abolished. But they must prove to be superior as a matter of choice, not imposed by a legal requirement. Hybrid arrangements like virtual networks are therefore likely to be popular.

The earlier observations suggest that no specific event undermines a European PTT's role; instead, the aggregate of challenges will lead to the "tipping of the monopoly." Restrictions in one area are interconnected with others; conversely, liberalization in one field is hard to contain. Thus, equipment liberalization leads to the demand for new services, such as value-added networks, which in turn creates pressures for resale opportunities. It is unlikely, given the nature of PTT organizations, rapid technological developments, and resultant market pressures, that they will be able to put out every fire, man every rampart, and seal every dike successfully. At the same time, a partial liberalization also provides opportunities for the traditional telecommunications authorities, and they may seize them for the temporary advantage, though change will undermine their exclusivity in the long term.

The conclusion is that European telecommunications will, in the short run, experience a push by PTTs to extend and defend their monopoly position and to expand in the direction of new services and equipment operations. However, long-term forces are at work that are likely to lead in time to an unraveling of the monopoly system. These factors, in combination, make it unlikely that the PTTs will maintain the present extent of their monopoly control.

Liberalization will first be granted for value-added networks and customer terminal equipment because these are the least controversial. Once the genie is out of its bottle and different service options are available, all kinds of new incentives for entry will be created. In those areas where monopoly service is not necessary or preferable—that is, where neither social policy reasons nor the strong economies of scale of a natural monopoly exist—some form of competition will emerge. This will leave for a while a natural monopoly core under the control of the PTT and its affiliated system. Such a system may be termed *creeping liberalization.*

Thus, the days of the PTTs—in their present manifestation as PTOs, public telecommunications operators—are in no way numbered. Just as AT&T, even after its massive divestiture, is still a major supplier of long-distance communications services and equipment, so will the PTTs maintain a formidable presence. Indeed, they will be able, for a time, to leverage their formidable resources and market power in core markets. They will become more independent, more powerful, less controllable, and less socially oriented. But in time they will lose their exclusivity and a more pluralist network system will emerge. This will require the development of alternative forms for the PTTs' cross-subsidies to support local exchange traffic, residential users, and the rural population. But the system will no doubt be able to adapt. In the end, large PTT organizations will still be linked with powerful groups in society, but without the status of a monopoly. European countries will gradually discover that a monopoly in telecommunications, controlled by PTTs, is not a prerequisite to a technically efficient and socially equitable communications system.

The new system will considerably lower terminal and central office equipment prices and reduce the profitability of the postal-industrial coalition. The equipment market will become much more open to foreign manufacturers and to members of the "second" electronics industry. Traditional telecommunications firms will accelerate their rate of innovation. Equipment itself will become unbundled, modular, and specialized, so that multiple suppliers can seek their niches. The conventional wisdom that there is room for only a handful of switch manufacturers worldwide will prove as nearsighted as the "mainframe thinking" in the computer industry of the 1960s. Over time, developments will push telecommunications rates toward cost, particularly in the highly profitable international services. These prices will be unstable, since the excess capacity will lead to periodic price wars, and they will be differentiated among routes of different traffic density and competitiveness.

As this process of normalization takes place, those identified with the traditional system, who are rightly proud of its technical and social accomplishment, will defend it as best as they can. The transition will, therefore, be a difficult one, but it is unavoidable.

We are merely at the beginning of a lengthy process of change in the network: The centrifugal forces discussed earlier are encouraging the evolution of a new network model of telecommunications characterized by a great deal of openness, transforming its structure from a centralized star into an interconnecting matrix as noted above. The new structure has various forms of openness: of entry (be it a carrier, specialized service provider, or equipment vendor), of interconnection into other networks, of access to other networks, and of standards. What are the main characteristics of this open network system?

Network of Networks

The network system of the future is one of great institutional, technical, and legal complexity. The network environment will consist of an untidy patchwork of many subnetworks, serving different geographical regions, customer types, user groups, categories, and service, with no neat classification or compartmentalization possible. It includes a hodgepodge of participants, governmental and private, national and regional, general and specialized, narrow and wideband, terrestrial and satellite, tiny and vast, domestic and multinational. The American experience demonstrates the long-range instability of structural regulation, such as compartmentalization of the telecommunications sector along different functional and geographic dimensions and the assignment of market segments to different carriers. This is due to the overlapping and ever-changing nature of services, the inability to define clear boundary lines, and the incentives for participants to breach restrictions. Hence, the future telecommunications network environment will have carriers engaged in multiple functions, though there will be no shortage of official attempts to establish order.

Substantial Reduction of Central Control

The primary characteristic of the open network model is a substantial reduction of central control, though with a significant PTT role and some military planning functions. The network becomes a composite of numerous separate planning decisions. This notion is alien to the engineering world-view of traditionalists in telecommunications. To leave an integrated system to the vagaries of hundreds of uncoordinated and selfish actors seems to invite disaster. Can it work? Perhaps this is not the right way to frame the question. Can there be a stable alternative in economies that otherwise favor a market mechanism and that want to stay on the leading edge of technology and applications?

Nonsustainability of Most Regulation

Telecommunications is in the process of moving from one of the most regulated industries to one of the least regulated. One reason is that the growing complexity of the system makes it increasingly difficult to fashion consistent rules, whether behavioral or structural. The American experience with the FCC's Computer Inquiry decisions gives an early taste of this difficulty.

In addition, rules are not likely to be enforceable. The subject of the regulation—streams of electrons and photons, and patterns of signals that constitute information—is so elusive in physical or even conceptual terms, and at the same time so fast and distance insensitive that a regulatory mechanism, to be effective, must be draconian, and for that the traditional system has neither the will nor the political support. Yet there is need for regulatory oversight of the rules under which networks and users interrelate in the future, as detailed next. To bridge this tension will be one of the central challenges for future policy.

The Public System as Core

The telecommunications system will evolve into a mixed public–private arrangement. The public network will not cease to exist. It is likely to remain for a long time the core of the system and its prime standard setter, with public support for the same reasons that have existed before, but without the exclusivity that characterized it for over a century. This is comparable to the situation prevailing in transportation. A state railroad system exists in most industrialized countries, often subsidized directly and indirectly, but it is supplemented by a mixture of trucking firms, airlines, barges, passenger automobiles, and small railroads. No one advocates a transportation system that bans all private trucks just because they reduce the scope and revenues of public railroads.

Gradualism

As the earlier discussion of interconnection of old and new networks demonstrates, it is not necessary to cut one's links to other participants. Multiple networks need not lead to multiple telephone sets on the desk. This is not more necessary than having multiple currencies if there are several banks in a country. In the situation of multiple networks, the functioning of the network federation depends on rules of interconnection. Such rules are being structured in regulatory approaches of open network architecture (ONA) in the United States and of open network provision (ONP) in Europe. Such arrangements provide additional impetus for new networks in that they permit the gradual establishment of a new network. They also permit a wide range of options between a full and separate physical network, and the use of an existing network in different and innovative ways, somewhat apart from the general "public" usership.

The concept of gradualism inherent in open network architecture is important. Many advocates of the traditional shared network system believe that the demands of pluralism could be met by a flexibility for software network options, without altering the exclusivity of the physical network of the traditional monopolist. This is wishful thinking. Granted, to permit software networks on a transmission monopoly is a correct first response to the emerging pressures. However, it is unlikely to be adequate in the long run. Soon users will want to supplement transmission offerings with additions to satisfy their preferences in terms of technology, control, and economics. The exclusive network cannot be the superior solution in each instance, particularly if it has to follow political mandates, or if it cannot bargain individually on prices.

Expansion of the Public System

The traditional public system may be losing its exclusivity, but it is gaining the flexibility of moving into new activities. The experience of British Telecom, Sweden's Televerket, the semi-independent public system of the STET group in Italy, and of the Telefónica group in Spain indicates strong tendencies of dominant carriers to expand vertically into equipment and manufacturing, even internationally. These tendencies are similar to the developments in the United States, where the scope of activity of the AT&T successor companies is steadily increasing. Such new horizons are an attraction to the PTTs as they consent to the loss of monopoly; for policymakers, they raise regulatory issues on how to deal with the substantial economic power of independent PTTs now renamed PTOs, but with market power intact.

Universal Service: Narrower but Deeper

The traditional public network system operated with the obligation of universal service, that is, virtually any interested customer had to be served, regardless of location. In a pluralist network system, the question is whether universal service obligations apply to all participants. The answer is likely to be differentiated. For some of the more specialized services, the obligation will not exist. But for "basic" service, it will continue, and the definition of basic is likely to expand. The boundary line is likely to be an ongoing issue of policy discussion.

Internal Subsidies

In a pluralist network system it is unlikely that the traditional system of internal transfers from one class of users to others can be maintained. But this does not spell their end. There is still ample reason and opportunity to subsidize some categories of service and of user classes, just as in the case of railroads. Services for that subsidy can be raised and distributed in the normal way of taxation and budget allocation in which income redistribution takes place in society. It is incorrect to consider a monopoly as a necessary condition for redistribution. Justification of the subsidy exists for reasons of general social policy or regional development, and because of the positive externalities that new subscribers provide to previous subscribers. Nevertheless, the extent of the subsidies could be smaller once their scope is open to scrutiny. As a result, they are likely to become more targeted toward the truly needy (i.e., the poor), and away from the middle class. The remainder of residential users will be forced to pay more than before and will also increase their usage of the telephone as its functions grow, making telecommunications a larger budget item than in the past.

Quality and Price Differentiation

There will be more choice but less equity. Whereas in the past all subscribers had a fairly similar quality of telephone service and equipment, an open network system will have much variation, depending on the preferences of customers and their willingness and ability to pay. There will also be a much greater differentiation in the cost of communications. Just as two adjoining passengers in an airplane may have paid widely different prices for their ticket, so will telecommunications users pay different rates for similar service. Those with small usage and few alternatives will pay more per volume than large users, and more than alert consumers. This reverses the traditional price relationship of business users subsidizing residential and rural service, yet it does not necessarily point to the end of universal telephone penetration. Given the low elasticity of demand, the increasing importance of telecommunications, and new ways to raise and distribute subsidies, the drop-off of subscribers is not likely to be large, despite some negative redistributory effects.

Transnationalism

The traditional centralized system was directly mirrored internationally. It held together well because of a similarity in views—the values of engineering and bureaucracy—and because of a common interest in protecting the domestic arrangements. For a long time, national PTT administrations almost joyfully participated in the international sphere, because they could return home with an international agreement that would buttress their domestic position. But in the age of satellites, internationalism became a threat, because it was initiated by users and new carriers. International communications are the most vunerable part of the domestic service monopoly. In the long run, telecommunications will go beyond the territorial concept. Communications are becoming too varied, complex, and significant for one organization to do it all well. Similarly, the notion that, in the age of information, all communications flows in societies operating largely on the market principle would pass through one streamlined super pipe controlled by a single organization is hard to entertain on technical, economic, or political grounds, except by reference to the present balance of power.

Once the notions of the centralized network are breached in some respects, the process is hard to contain. This development is inevitable not because it leads necessarily to a superior result, but because the traditional network is an anomaly once it moves beyond its cost-sharing and redistributory stages—though it is an anomaly too familiar to notice. As long as the economic system of Western industrialized democracies is based on markets and private firms, the exclusion of major economic parties from a major field is an unstable affair. It is hard to maintain a dichotomy between telecommunications and the rest of the economy. To differentiate it as an infrastructure service is too vague to be useful. The traditional public network was an appealing idea. It incorporated a notion of sharing which reached every member of society. Yet these are also the concepts of authoritarianism. The historical origin of the system, rooted as it is in seventeenth-century absolutism, does not support those who view its defense as a progressive act. The telecommunications field will more closely resemble the rest of the economic system. It may be much more complex, and in some aspects less resource-efficient than the old system, but it will be a truer reflection of the underlying pluralist society.

Notes

Preface

1. There are, of course, semiofficial volumes in which various countries' PTTs report about themselves, but these reports are neither analytical nor probing.

2. The Establishment of the PTT System

1. From *Hansard's Parliamentary Debates*, March, 1895, p. 214, in Meyer, 1907, p. 117.

3. Network Tipping: The Rise and Fall of the Public Network Monopoly

1. Galbraith—Interview with Francis Cairncross, *The Observer*, November 22, 1970.

2. One attempt was a U.S. Department of Justice report on the postdivestiture network (Huber, 1987). Another approach is that of Koichiro Hayashi of NTT (1988). An earlier version of the present model was Eli Noam, *The Next Stage in Telecommunications Evolution: The Pluralistic Network*, paper presented at the ITS Conference, June 1988.

3. Exceptions were CoCom restrictions to East bloc countries that were fading, together with the latter.

4. It should be noted that this model can be easily adopted for "standards coalitions" rather than for "network coalitions." For the literature on standards, see David (1987).

5. I will follow the network analysis as developed in Noam (1988). Also see Heal (1989).

6. The case of n assumes that users are homogeneous. Of course, some network participants are much larger than others, but that poses no problem if we define a large organization to consist of multiple members of type n (e.g., telephone lines or terminals). Later, we will drop this assumption.

7. Strictly speaking, income is allocated to telephone and to other consumption

$$y = cp + C(n)/n.$$

A subscriber's utility is then given by

$$u \{(y/p - [C(n)/n]p; n\}$$

8. For convexity, assume $u(c, P, 1) > u(c, P, 0)$ (i.e., the first user has positive benefits even if no one else is on the network).

9. For simplicity, utility is expressed in monetary units. Then $u(P,n) = P(n) + u(n)$

10. Heal defines it, similarly, as

$$u (y/p—[F + f(n)]/np; n) = u(y/p; 0)$$

See also Allen (1988).

11. This analysis should not suggest that a voting mechanism is governing in reality (although it exists for telephone cooperatives in Finland and the United States); rather, it helps us to understand the pressures and dynamics that are transmitted to the governmental institutions that embody the different user interests.

12. For simplicity, we use in the following $n/2$ rather than $(n/2) - 1$.

13. A very similar analysis can be undertaken for a political system in which network outsiders have a vote, as in a governmentally directed system.

14. I owe the terminology of "tipping" to Schelling (1978).

15. This corresponds to reality; new networks such as those of MCI and Sprint have lost money for a number of years until turning profitable with growth.

16. The results discussed would not hold if the marginal costs of new network participants drop continuously more than their marginal benefit to an existing network user. The latter is unlikely, since marginal cost, beyond a certain range, is either flat or very slowly decreasing, or in fact increasing.

4. Forces of Centrifugalism

1. The author served as a member of the Advisory Board for the selection.

2. NYNEX data, see Noam (forthcoming).

3. New York PSC data, see Noam (forthcoming).

4. Encompasses all U.S. carriers; translated for new telephones from data on access line using 1975 ratio. Sources: *Telecom Factbook*, 1986; FCC, *Statistics of Communications Common Carriers*, 1945, 1955, 1965, 1975, 1985.

5. This classification extends those of Ergas (1989).

5. Defense of the Telecommunications Monopoly

1. Residential penetration is not the entire story. In public (i.e., coin) telephones of several European countries, Switzerland had the highest density (8.90 per 1000 population). Densities are substantially lower in the rest of Europe. In the United States, the corresponding density is 7.18, to which figure one must add the many private coin telephone networks that have mushroomed since liberalization of this sector. In New York State in 1988, privately owned coin telephones amounted to an additional 20 percent of those operated by the telephone companies, suggesting a density of 8.6 per 1000 population. The OECD countries apart from Switzerland and Japan have substantially lower densities. See Table 32.2.

7. Germany

1. In a letter to a colleague in both the party and the Reichspost, Ohnesorge rhapsodized in 1931 about Hitler, then still in the opposition:

Dear God, what luck that the country has been blessed with a man of such stature! . . . He is the only, the last great German! And everything is right as he approaches it and as he wishes it. . . . Haase, dear Haase, when finally the marching steps of the battalions will sound again through the streets of Berlin! Both of us are still young! Then we will march, too, unyielding, unrelenting to wherever Adolf Hitler wants [Nagel, 1937, p. 24].

Such sentiments, expressed also publicly, had not slowed Ohnesorge's career in the Reichspost during the Weimar Republic; he was promoted to considerable responsibility, including being in charge of the Reichspost's priority project of transition to automatic exchanges.

2. In 1972, Germany's high-technology exports had been a respectable 26.3 percent of the six major countries. However, by 1983, this share had fallen to 17 percent. The French share in the same period declined from 11.1 percent to 8 percent, Britain's share from 13.8 percent to 10 percent, and Switzerland's share from 3.5 percent to 3 percent. In contrast, the non-European countries improved their situation significantly. Japan's market share almost doubled from 13 percent to 25 percent, and that of the United States rose from 32.2 percent to 37 percent, amounting to more than one-third of the total. Furthermore, the market as a whole increased sixfold, from $8.4 billion in 1972 to $54 billion in 1983. In telecommunications, Germany's share fell from 22.8 percent to 14.5 percent: in electronic tubes and transistors, from 17.4 percent to 11 percent (Bundesbank, Annual Report, 1983).

3. It also invested extensively in America and acquired 20 percent of the American company Advanced Micro Devices (AMD), a company that second-sourced Intel and Zilog microprocessors. It also bought 100 percent of Microwave Semiconductor, 80 percent of Litronix, and 60 percent of Advanced Microcromputer (AMC). Through Corning Glass it established the successful optical fiber venture Siecor and acquired the floppy disk operations of Perkins-Elmer. Siemens also formed joint ventures with Intel and Westinghouse, in 1988.

4. Today the Bundespost's record of service in the rural population is often used to support the argument for its monopoly. According to the Bundespost, the Bell System in the United States concentrated on the lucrative urban areas to the disadvantage of less profitable and more sparsely populated areas: "A telephone connection in structurally weak areas is either not offered at all, or even today is offered more expensively and maintained or provided technically less accomplished than in urban regions" (DBP, 1981, para. 96a). In fact, rural telephony in the United States is often cheaper than an urban one. In typical farm states such as Iowa and Kansas, the percentage of households having telephones in 1987 was even higher (95.1 percent and 95.2 percent, respectively) than the national average of 92.4 percent (Federal-State Joint-Board, 1988), and a high 96 percent of all American farms had telephone service in the same year (Rural Electrification Administration, 1988). This was despite the significantly lower density of population, particularly in the American West, as compared to that in Europe. Population density in the state of Wyoming is 12.4 inhabitants per km^2. In comparison, density in Germany is 246 inhabitants per km^2; in the United Kingdom it is 233 per km^2; and in France, 100 per km^2. In some instances, the technical quality of independent rural telephony has not been as high as that in urban areas, but it is often better, too. In 1985, the average residential flat rate for unlimited local-call service was $13.80 per month in urban U.S. areas and $10.15 per month in rural areas.

5. The Bundespost planned for a natural evolution from ISDN to broadband ISDN,

with a structure suitable for higher-speed applications like television or video telephony (Ohmann and Armbruster, 1986; Armbruster, 1986).

6. A study undertaken by the Deutsches Institut für Wirtschaftsforschung (DIW) in 1980 found that for each *additional* billion DM in investment in telecommunications beyond the existing 10 billion, 21,000 to 22,000 jobs would be generated if such investment continued (Schnöring, 1982). However, another study, commissioned by the Ministry of Economics in 1983 and carried out by the IFO Institute and looking at the period 1983–1990, found that an additional billion DM a year in telecommunications investment would result in only 4000 additional jobs per year. This is not an impressive figure; it means that for each new job, a new and ongoing investment level of DM 250,000 ($134,000) per year would have to be maintained.

7. To ascertain the efficacy of this system, the FCC also asked that AT&T and eleven public utility commissions determine whether network damage has occurred. They concluded that there had been no negative effects on the network or physical impact on personnel.

8. The interest of private households and business customers in various new features of telephone service and equipment grew dramatically. There was a demand, approaching two-thirds of all businesses and residences, for detailed specification of billings. Such billings are not normally provided (Schulte, 1982, p. 322, Table 12B).

Another common U.S. service, call-forwarding, began to be introduced in Germany under the name of GEDAN only in the 1980s. But the basic rate for this service was between DM 133 and DM 160 ($71 and $85) per month. Cost for call forwarding in New York is, for businesses, $6 per month after an initial installation fee of $54; for residences it is $4 per month after an initial fee of $15.50. (Frequently, the initial installation rate is cut or dropped to attract usage.)

9. It should be noted, however, that although Wagner advocated public ownership of the railroads as essential, another eminent German institutionalist economist, E. Sax, argued that a form of private enterprise could fulfill public tasks just as well (Sax, 1887). Wagner's views, however, won in the political sphere.

8. The United Kingdom

1. Carsberg was knighted in 1989 for his service, and promoted in 1992 to head the Fair Trade Office (FTO).

2. In the first year after being granted its license, BT applied for price changes. The inflation rate for the period had been 7 percent, making the average permissible price increase 4 percent. BT increased the price of local calls by 6.4 percent after allowing for changes in the categories of a calling unit. Coupled with increases for five types of long distance calls and reductions for four, the weighted average price increase was 3.7 percent, slightly below the allowable rate. Among residential customers, rates increased by 7.1 percent for low-volume users, 6.3 percent for moderate users, and 5.7 percent for high-volume users. For business users on average, however, rate increases were lower. To minimize rate increases for the lightest business users, BT instituted a low-user rebate in 1983. For moderately high business users, rates went up by about 2 percent (Oftel, 1985a).

3. In 1988, Oftel granted six satellite licenses to Robert Maxwell; British Satellite Broadcasting (BSB); EDS U.K.; British Aerospace; Satellite Information Services; and Uplink Ltd. The firms were allowed to offer point-to-multipoint services, but were barred from two-way communication (Hayes, 1988).

9. France

1. Although the DGT installs and maintains customer equipment, authorized independent installers and their subcontractors can also provide such services. There are about 500 primary installer authorizations in the country, employing about 15,000 people (Voge, 1986).

2. The digitalization of central office switches permitted the introduction in 1983 of itemized billing (at a separate charge), conference calls, call forwarding, free-phone (800 service), and call waiting (Bruce et al., 1985).

3. When the agreement expired in 1990, Thomson won a France Télécom contract for broadband switches and CGE's Alcatel made defense electronics one focus of a new division (Boult, 1990, p. 10).

4. The reorganization was also believed to help French telecommunications exports by avoiding head-on competition between two suppliers for international contracts. For example, in the case of major Egyptian telecommunications contract, CIT–Alcatel bid against Thomson and Siemens. The merger eliminated the potential for such intra-French competition.

5. In the United States, Alcatel's sales efforts began in 1984 and resulted in orders for several dozen of a U.S. switch version, the E-10–5, primarily for small independent telephone companies, such as the Clay County Rural Telephone Cooperative in Indiana, rather than to the Bell Operating Companies (*Telephony*, 1985, pp. 32–33). For equipment other than local exchanges, Alcatel's customers in the United States were MCI and AT&T for multiplexing systems. Having adapted ITT's System 12 switch, Alcatel reentered an American central exchange market that ITT had abandoned in 1986 when adapting the System 12 proved too expensive and time-consuming.

In 1990 Alcatel pulled many of its operations out of the United States except for cable television and SONET transmission equipment development (Roussel, 1990d).

10. The Netherlands

1. Until 1987, when the zones were redrawn, the small call areas—with an average of 31 square kilometers versus 2673 square kilometers in the United Kingdom (Dabbs et al., 1982)—allowed for untimed local calls. After 1987, only two charging zones remained. Areas for local and long-distance calls were extended and local calls became timed.

2. The PTT is required to meet performance standards in "reserved" services and has lowered rates for several services since the reform.

3. To enhance its position as the dominant supplier in the newly liberalized value-added services market, PTT Telecom acquired 45 percent of a Dutch networking firm, Impact Automation, and began negotiations with France Télécom and the DBP Telekom about an international consortium (Schenker, 1989, p. 8).

11. Belgium

1. Although it opposed the loosening of its own monopoly, the RTT was not above benefiting from the opportunities presented by the liberalization of others. After an agreement between the U.S. carrier MCI and the Belgian Post Office, the PTT became the major entry point to Europe for the American alternative long-distance carrier.

2. In Turkey, BTMC has a particularly large contract, which includes the transfer of technology and manufacturing expertise to the Turkish equipment producer Teletas in a turnkey arrangement.

3. Also, under its guidelines for the licensing of VANs providers, RTT granted approval to five service providers: GEIS, Sabena, SITA, SWIFT, and Infonet. However, the licensing process was criticized because the requirements for VANs providers were unclear and because the RTT's 95 percent ownership of Infonet's Belgian operations could result in preferential treatment (Tutt, 1990, p. 15).

13. Switzerland

1. Part of the telecommunications profits are used to subsidize the postal services within the PTT. Swiss mail service is excellent, but partly at the expense of telecommunications users and network quality. Transfers in 1983 were more than SFr 600 million; in addition, about SFr 90 million, or 3 percent of value added, were transferred to the general federal treasury (Knieps, 1985b, p. 19).

14. Austria

1. Unlike many PTTs, the Austrian PTV does not operate broadcast transmission services, though it distributes broadcast programs to transmitters and cable networks.

2. In 1984, a reduced-cost phone service (Service 660) was introduced in which recipients pay part of the tariffs for received calls. Starting in 1985, the PTV in conjunction with Radio Austria initiated a text mail and data service "Telebox," which attracted about 2100 subscribers by 1988.

3. ITT Austria was a successor to Czeija & Nissel, Austria's first telephone equipment firm, which was at one time partly owned by AT&T and which exclusively supplied large manual exchanges from 1896 to 1913.

4. There are claims that Austria was the first place in Europe with a transistorized computer, the "Mailüpferl" (Smith, 1984, p. 14).

15. Sweden

1. In West Germany, in contrast, the Bundespost had a monopoly on low-speed modems, although private supply of high-speed modems was permitted; in Sweden, the opposite was the case. In each market, extensive arguments were made about why it was in the public interest to maintain its role in a particular market segment, but the glaring contradictions of the different approaches illustrates the weakness of the arguments. These restrictions were subsequently dropped in both countries.

2. When total purchases, including such items as vehicles, are considered, 20–25 percent of equipment is imported (OECD, 1987).

3. Teletext electronic mail was started in 1983. "Telebox," an electronic mailbox, has been offered since 1986. In 1987, "020" free-phone service was introduced.

16. Finland

1. In 1989, Motorola filed a patent suit against Nokia related to cellular handsets. Nokia held 16 percent of the U.S. cellular equipment market (O'Dwyer, 1989b, p. 8).

The suit was resolved out-of-court, with Nokia and Korea's Tandy Corporation signing a license agreement favorable to Motorola (O'Dwyer, 1989a).

20. Ireland

1. Its first operator was a boy who was dismissed for playing marbles while the switchboard was idle.

21. Italy

1. Since 1984, broadcast teletext has been offered under the name of Televideo. The PT administration also provides public bureaufax service with facsimile equipment installed at post offices; paging (Teledrin); electronic mail teletex (since 1985), and a slow scan video system useful for traffic control and surveillance.

27. Telecommunications in Eastern Europe

1. Some of the joint East–West ventures would not have been possible had not the Coordinating Committee for Multi-Lateral Export Control (CoCom) moved in June 1990 to relax certain trade barriers against exporting telecommunications technology to Eastern Europe, especially those that have demonstrated that they have ended "intelligence cooperation" with the Soviet Union (Datapro, 1990). As a result, high-speed fiber optics as well as data equipment (up to 9600 bps), analog mobile interface equipment, and small digital PABXs could be sold to Hungary, Poland, and Czechoslovakia, though not to Romania, Bulgaria, and Soviet Union, which were identified as more problematic from a strategic perspective (Woollacott, 1990).

2. This section owes much of its information to Campbell (1988).

3. In Minsk, Kiev, Barabinskii, Erevan, Akhtyrskii, Perm, Sverdlovsk, Taldom, Tashkent, Ufa, Kaunas, and Navlinskii and in Estonia (under that republic's control) (Campbell, 1988, pp. 83–84).

29. Brussels Takes On the Traditional System

1. The E.C. also faced disagreements among member states on satellite policy and spectrum management. Tensions over service development especially in the area of VSATs led to the postponement of the E.C.'s Blue Paper on satellite policy in 1990 (Roussel, 1990). Frequency coordination problems beyond the scope of CEPT's Radio-communications Committee led the E.C. to call for a European Frequency Research Institute to allocate spectrum for mobile services.

2. In order to satisfy the various national demands for participation, they were extraordinarily complex in structure and acronyms. ESRO was headquartered in Paris, while its two main technical centers were located in the Netherlands (ESTEC) and in Germany (ESDAC, later ESOC). Other centers were ESLAB in the Netherlands, ESRIN in Italy, and ESRANGE and ESTRACK in Sweden.

30. Telecommunications Policy as Industrial Policy

1. For example, Siemens produced computers during the 1960s under licenses obtained from RCA, but was left in the lurch when RCA abandoned its computer business. Siemens then joined Philips and CIT to form Unidata, a joint computer venture that faltered in the mid-1970s. After the failure, Siemens entered into an arrangement with Fujitsu for the manufacture of IBM plug-compatible machines, but the Japanese backed out in 1985. In 1974, Siemens acquired an unsuccessful joint computer venture of AEG-Telefunken, which also produced specialized mainframe computers under license from RCA.

In Britain, the major computer manufacturer has been ICL, which has had some success in mainframes, but less in the market for smaller units. Its overall market share declined throughout the 1970s.

2. With the onset of integrated circuit technology, the role of the American government as a purchaser of electronic components, until then a major factor, began to decline. In 1960, public procurement of semiconductors was $258 million, 48 percent of the total. By 1973, it had fallen to $201 million, 6 percent of the total U.S. sales (Levin, 1982). In 1987, because of the military buildup, government procurement (military and civilian) had risen again to about $1.2 billion, or 12 percent of domestic sales (Semiconductor Industry Association, 1988, communication).

3. Capital markets in America, and to a lesser extent in Japan, were vastly more active than their European counterparts, with the exception of London after the liberalization of its trading practices. For the first ten months of 1985, for example, the turnover on U.S. security exchanges was $755.9 billion. In Japan, it was $267.1 billion. In Britain, capital market turnover was only $48.8 billion, in Germany $29.7 billion, in France $10.2 billion, and in Italy $3.8 billion (*The Economist*, 1985, p. 77). By 1990, total turnover was greatest in Japan ($2,313 billion), followed by the U.S. ($1,542 billion), Germany ($661 billion), the U.K. ($379 billion), France ($65 billion) and Italy ($36 billion) (NYSE, 1990, communication).

4. In Germany, capital investment in private entrepreneurial operations also developed only slowly. An OECD report found that "Germany has long stood out by the virtual absence of venture capitalism, in contrast to the dynamism that its small and medium-sized firms display" (OECD, 1985, p. 31).

5. In absolute terms, support levels for the French plans were small: for the first five-year plan, funding was $140 million; and for the second five-year period, $263 million.

6. A hierarchy of procurement preferences was established: top priority was given to French companies, and lowest to imports to France. This system tended to exclude some of the firms that produced the most advanced designs of chips, and thus restricted French computer manufacturers at times from the use of the newest technology.

7. The Micro-Electronics Support Scheme, for example, provided only £12 million of research and development money to British microelectronic manufacturers, mostly to established firms such as GEC, Ferranti, and Plessey. Similarly, the Advanced Computer Technology Project provided a tiny £.8 million per year to British semiconductor manufacturers between 1976 and 1979. During that same period, the Component Industry Scheme distributed about £20 million (Malerba, 1985). Subsequently, the government increased its support by contributing a quarter to a third of R&D expenditures and a quarter of total necessary investments. The Micro-Electronics Industry Support Program (MISP), the Micro-Electronics Application Project (MAP), and the Electronic Component Industry Scheme (ECIS) were all launched in 1978. Also, the memory com-

ponent firm Inmos was created through the National Enterprise Board. Britain even provided support to foreign companies that were domiciled in the United Kingdom.

8. International joint ventures often present difficult problems in practice. In addition to the obstacle of incompatible products, problems include selection of the physical location, the operational language, the composition of management, and labor sensitivities. The collaborative effort of Siemens, ICL, and Bull to develop fifth-generation supercomputer technology was launched with a French director, English as the language, and a shared R&D lab located in Germany. For the same reasons that firms like to see duplication of efforts reduced by joint ventures, trade unions are suspicious of such efforts. They are fearful of employment reduction and of the ability to deflect the effects of strikes in one country.

9. One of the consequences of joint venturing is that it leads toward greater stress on standardization. In March 1984, the twelve leading European computer and communication firms agreed to draft common standards for the interconnection of their products. In 1985, six European computer manufacturers—STC, Nixdorf, Siemens, Olivetti, Philips, and Bull—jointly determined to base their future computer systems on AT&T's Unix operating system and to develop software for such uses. In 1986, they further agreed to collaborate on OSI interconnection standards. Membership was open to other European firms, but non-European companies (i.e., American and Japanese) were excluded.

31. Transatlantic Trade Friction

1. The indirect influence of technology must be sharply distinguished from a direct role of technologists. American engineers, despite the widespread respect for technology in the abstract, do not have much of a direct political role in society. In 1984, Congress had only five engineers as members but 261 lawyers (Frey, 1984).

2. Even with the deficit to the United States, the E.C. had a positive trade balance with the rest of the world of $730 million in 1987, with $2.7 billion in imports and $3.43 billion in exports (Whitehouse, 1990).

3. Some modification is unavoidable, because European equipment does not match North American standards. In digital multiplex systems, pulse code modulation (PCM) is different. Different coding systems translate the amplitude of the analog voice signal into digital code. Whereas Europe uses the so called "A" law, North America, Japan, and some others use the "μ" law. The number of voice channels and the signalling and synchronization are also different. The standard high-volume rate in North America provides for twenty-four voice channels at 1.544 megabits per second. In Europe, the equivalent is thirty channels with a total bit rate of 2.048 megabits per second.

In microwave radio equipment, North American equipment interleaves the "go" and the "return" path frequencies at 20 MHz intervals. On the other hand, the CCIR frequency plan, to which Europeans and Japanese usually adhere, allocates the "go" frequencies at one end of the band, and the "return" frequencies at the other, spaced at 29 MHz each. Furthermore, the frequency transmission band itself is slightly different. There are also differences in the number of radio and voice channels on each radio frequency. In North America, twelve are carried on each radio frequency channel, as opposed to the CCIR standard of six. In contrast, there are 1200 voice channels per radio channel, whereas for the CCIR, the number is 1800. Other differences exist for signal level and pilot frequencies and in noise performance specifications. For cables, the attenuation, wire diameters, cable construction, and color coding are different.

32. International Telecommunications Services

1. This meant that the majority of the large business centers could now be served directly by an international record carrier, rendering Western Union unnecessary for the domestic leg of international transmissions. At the same time, the IRCs were required to unbundle their rates into separate charges for terminal equipment, transmission, and local access and to interconnect so that customers could use one telex machine to access all IRCs.

To permit Western Union to offer international communications services, the FCC had to overcome the opposition of the IRCs, which feared that Western Union would provide far stronger international competition than domestic competition because of public recognition of its name and the large number of telex machines already operating in the United States. Although the U.S. Court of Appeals, 2nd Circuit, overturned this decision in 1980, the International Record Carrier Competition Act subsequently amended the Communications Act of 1934 to permit Western Union IRC service. At the same time, the legislation permitted the IRCs to provide domestic record service.

2. Although there are a number of technical objections to this proposal, none of them is particularly convincing, considering the sophistication of telecommunications technology. Another objection is that multiple codes would impose an extra cost on the PTTs. This extra cost, however, could be compensated by payments from the carriers, which would benefit from access.

3. Prior to the advent of communications satellites, the FCC focused on authorization for and ownership of submarine cable facilities. It scrutinized applications for these facilities to decide whether their need justified an increase in a carrier's rate base. The commission's close review of the applications resulted partly from the fact that investments in international submarine cables were quite large in comparison to investments in most domestic facility applications.

AT&T, the IRCs, and other carriers used these cables and were at least theoretically subject to rate base regulations and thus sought to obtain ownership interests in these facilities, in the form of "indefeasible rights of use" (IRU). The FCC concluded that it was impossible to audit the IRCs and that no benefits would flow from rate regulation of the industry. The carriers sought ownership interests in order to expand their rate bases and to realize certain benefits under the U.S. tax code. The IRUs still exist, and the ownership interests in addition to the PTTs' interests have added new parties to the negotiating process.

4. Following enactment of the Comsat Act, the FCC developed various policies to establish and protect Comsat's role as the U.S. signatory and monopoly U.S. provider of international satellite service. A key component of this role was the construction and operation of these stations. Comsat and the U.S. international service carriers, AT&T and the IRCs, would own and operate stations jointly through a cooperative Earth Station Ownership Committee (ESOC). This approach gave Comsat the major role in earth station management as well as in investment decisions and allowed Comsat to bundle earth station costs with space segment costs in setting rates.

Following pressure from various carriers and users, the FCC proposed a more liberal international earth stations policy in 1982. Carriers and users wanted Comsat to separate out charges for its space segment (satellite) and earth segment (earth station), and they also wanted the option of building their own lower-cost earth stations at sites with efficient access to Intelsat. In 1984, the FCC authorized international earth stations (Frieden, 1983).

Not surprisingly, the competitive pressures that led to modifications of policies regarding earth station ownership and authorization of users necessitated an examination of whether Comsat should continue to be the sole source of access to Intelsat.

5. The FCC also gradually decreased its role in the planning aspects of international facilities in favor of reliance on the market. In the past, the FCC had been jointly involved in the international facilities planning process with carriers and foreign authorities. The planning process had begun as simple negotiations between the FCC and the PTTs for landing rights and terminal points. As technology became more varied, the planning process also became increasingly complex. With the advent of satellite communications, the FCC began to regulate the ratio of satellite to cable circuits for transatlantic telecommunications services. For the TAT-5 cable, the FCC required AT&T to use one cable circuit for every five satellite circuits activated. After considerable pressure from PTTs and American carriers, this ratio was reduced to 1:1 in the 1972 approval of the TAT-6 cable, subsequently applied only to AT&T. The carriers traditionally preferred submarine cables because of their proven technology and the carriers' ownership of the IRUs. Moreover, carriers used satellites under leases, which could not be included in a carrier's rate base. Following the PTTs initiative for comprehensive planning, the FCC agreed in 1976 to substitute a long-range planning process for the disruptive and time-consuming review process previously used. In 1988, the FCC terminated AT&T's traffic balance restrictions, thus allowing Comsat and AT&T to reach their own agreement on facilities usage.

Using the planning process, the FCC consulted with interested parties and in 1977 rejected the TAT-7 cable as being economically unjustified. The rejection caused strong protests from many of the European PTTs, other governmental agencies, AT&T, and the IRCs. In 1979, the FCC reversed its decision, claiming that the new cable would result in increased service reliability. Although the FCC still believed that TAT-7 was unnecessary to satisfy demand through 1985, the strong European pressure led the commission to balance the economic efficiency arguments, which were supported by the revenue requirements of the new facilities of about $68 million, with its desire to maintain good international relations.

33. The Economics of ISDN Integration

1. Other contributions to the standardization literature include Arthur, 1983; Kindleberger, 1983; Wilson, 1984; Besen and Johnson, 1986; and Katz and Shapiro, 1985.

34. The Political Economy of ISDN

1. A large research project on broadband-ISDN was conducted at Columbia University, funded by the Markle Foundation and led by Professor Martin Elton. It marshals technological, economic, and policy issues of broadband fiber (Elton, 1991).

2. To deal with the ISDN issues, the FCC issued a Notice of Inquiry in 1983. Its goals were both to generate comments on the FCC's role in ISDN and to stimulate interest in the policy discussion on ISDN itself. The first report, issued in 1984, restated the FCC's intention to take a limited role. It set, however, several policy principles for ISDN design: a flexible numbering plan that permits user choice of carriers, domestically and internationally (this was possible for international telex, but not for international telephony under the existing numbering plan); and no limitations of satellite hops in international connections. On the numbering issue, the 1984 Brasilia meeting of the

CCITT adopted a numbering plan that permits a multivendor system in the United States, and also accommodates in PTT countries alternative providers of databases and local area networks (Schiller, 1984).

3. Between the transmission line and the user, two sets of network termination equipment exist, known as NT1 and NT2. NT1 provides the subscriber functions such as test loops, power feedings, timing, multiplexing, and synchronization. The network termination point T is located between NT1 and NT2. NT2 equipment is more sophisticated and provides functions of switching, multiplexing, and protocol handling by equipment such as PBXs, local area networks, and terminal controllers.

4. The original American telephone companies' position had been to go with T as the demarcation point; this point had to be defined by the CCITT Study Group, which had thought in terms of an integrated rather than separated NT1 and NT2. PTTs can integrate them if they wish to do so; and the German Bundespost's elaborate graphic representation of ISDN architecture omits even an acknowledgement of point T's existence.

5. Going one step further, the German telecommunications equipment industry commissioned a report on ISDN by another former head of the governmental telecommunications department, Franz Arnold. That study was, if anything, critical of the Bundespost's ISDN and cable television plans as too timid. Arnold called for a "national effort," which would include private and public funds, in which ISDN was a first step in the right direction. This would provide German export industry with future potential, which the present traditional copper-wire-oriented technology does not offer. For such support, public funds must be available to reduce private risk (Müller-Sachs, 1984, pp. 6–7). In pursuit of goals, the Bundespost took an administrative leadership role in the CCITT Study Group XVIII, which was chaired by one of its officials, Theodore Irmer, who subsequently became the head of the CCITT itself. The DBP was also the first PTT administration to announce a tariff structure for ISDN.

6. An operational framework for a CEI was reached in March 1986 by three major firms with diverse interests: Pacific Bell (carrier), IBM (equipment supplier), and Tymnet (value-added provider).

35. Value-Added Networks and Services

1. AT&T's involvement in packet switching service was tumultuous and has so far been unsuccessful. Regulation caused some of its problems, but others were a result of its own operations, and indicate that economies of scale should not be overvalued in this field.

Following the divestiture decree in 1982, it was unclear whether the Bell Operating Companies could provide VAN service and whether the Computer II rules regarding separation of enhanced from basic services applied. This was clarified by the FCC when it declared basic packet switching (X.25-to-X.25) to be a "basic" service that BOCs therefore could provide, subject to regulation.

2. In 1985, the FCC removed barriers from the BOCs and permitted a bundled provision of basic packet transmission with the "enhanced" protocol conversion asynchronous X.25-to-X.25 and X.25-to-X.75. However, they were also required to provide such services to their competitors at nondiscriminatory terms; they had to file an accounting plan of separation, and they could not unfairly cross-subsidize their service. Specific rules were established for cost allocation and pricing.

3. EUSIDIC later revised its 1990 findings to a 19 percent failure rate after discount-

ing a one-day Transpac failure. However, CEPT challenged the survey, claiming that 96 percent of calls were completed successfully in 1989. The CEPT figures measured only X.25 and not dial-up access (Schenker, 1990b).

4. The SCC also stores the message and relays it to the addressee. The RPs and SCCs interconnect with leased lines since both the sender and receiver are encrypted so that it is impossible to control which banks communicate with each other. The RPs cannot communicate directly with each other, but must go through the SCCs. The lines between the RPs and SCCs are doubled as insurance against lines failure, and the SCCs also have back-up installations.

5. SWIFT supplies users with the necessary hardware and software through its subsidiary STS SWIFT terminal services, with equipment by IBM, DEC, NCR, Burroughs, and others. About 70 percent of the member banks opt to purchase SWIFT equipment over equipment supplied directly by computer products vendors.

36. Videotex

1. SEAT is the official "publisher" of on-line information with its main product being the Pagine Gialle Elettroniche (Electronic Yellow Pages). SEAT has data from 1 million Italian firms classified into 1400 categories. The system allows companies to include technical and commercial data on their products, yet had only 25,836 users in 1987. Of the user sessions, 39 percent were to access PGE, 11 percent made use of teletourism services, and 42 percent were on Amadeus, a real-time credit rating and financial facts service aimed at business users. The PGE system developed by SEAT runs on two simple commands, cerca (find) and mostra (show). Other services offered by SEAT include Mastermail (electronic mail), Banca dati Tributaria (home banking), teletourism, and an Official Airlines Guide. These services are generally not used much beyond corporate applications. In 1990, there were 100,000 terminals in use, and SIP had invested only 100 billion lire ($1 million).

37. Transborder Data Flows

1. Technological advances in general facilitate invasions of privacy. Electronic data banks can be abused to obtain vast amounts of personal data, as discussed in this chapter. However, other privacy abuses exist as well. For example, cellular, mobile, and satellite telephony increase the chance that conversations may be intercepted and monitored. Beepers and intraorganizational networks can be used by corporations to track employee activities. Call forwarding and facsimile machines make it easier to intrude on an individual. Almost every new telecommunications service has raised new types of privacy issues and concerns.

2. In 1990, over 100,000 registration entries were received by the Home Office for renewal, and 37,000 amendments to register entries and over 19,000 new applications were filed.

3. For a summary of these laws as they deal with telecommunications, see Noam (1990 and forthcoming).

4. One initiative was taken by the author in 1990 when he served as a commissioner in New York State. A draft set of privacy principles for telecommunications service was adopted by the New York Public Service Commission (Noam, 1990; NYPSC, 1991).

5. The common law copyright protection provided primarily that if one had not pub-

lished information in one's possession, no one else could take it and publish it. This was similar to a trespass and conversion action.

6. Justice Louis Brandeis, in a famous dissent, wrote of "the right to be left alone— the most comprehensive of rights and the right most valued by civilized men" (*Olmstead* v. *U.S.,* 1927).

7. On the history of privacy, see Posner (1981); Simmel (1906); Westin (1967); Seipp (1978). In the United States, privacy is a nonpartisan issue. The Privacy Act of 1974 was cosponsored by Senators Edward Kennedy and Barry Goldwater.

8. In the extreme, private information is so valuable to an individual as to make him a target for blackmail. See also Brown and Gordon (1980) for an economic perspective from the FCC.

9. In an information-based society and economy, the incentives to acquire information are continuously increasing. See Posner (1981, pp. 231–347) for the most comprehensive discussion of the economics of privacy.

10. Another indication is provided by a survey conducted by American Express among its card holders, which showed that 90 percent felt that mailing list practices were inadequately disclosed, 80 percent felt that information should not be given to a third party without permission, and more than 30 percent believed federal legislation was needed to restrict the use of lists ["Privacy Study Reveals Lack of Consumer Confidence," *Direct Marketing,* December 1988, p. 8, in McManus (1989)]. It should be noted that American Express makes extensive use of the data it has accumulated on its cardholders. According to *Fortune,* the company computers "maintain and update weekly a profile of 450 attributes—such as age, sex, and purchasing patterns—on every cardholder" (Newpert, 1989, p. 82).

A 1988 survey by the Massachusetts Executive Office of Consumer Affairs of the main consumer complaints found them topped by telemarketing and promotional mailings (Marchocki, 1989, p. 47; McManus, 1989, p. 82).

11. "Pac Bell backs off selling lists," *Alameda Times Star,* April 16, 1986, p. 16, as cited in McManus (1989).

38. Networks in the Future

1. The optimal size of jurisdictions was always dependent on communications. French departments were based on the distance that a horseback rider could cover in a day. Transportation and communications technology changes the optimal size. It is hard to imagine a voluntary European integration without telecommunications.

2. Professor Henry Niman, per Marc Rotenberg; communication.

39. Toward a Modular Network

1. These can partly substitute for each other.

2. First for data and in an ISDN network also for voice service.

3. One can similarly use software hierarchies other than OSI.

4. It is easiest to set the horizontal physical coordinate where segments are defined in purely spatial terms, such as "inside wiring." But for central office functions the dividing lines are more complicated and controversial. Central exchanges combine several physical as well as software segments. (The switch generics of SPC central offices combine functions of access, features, functions, and transport.) One may need some

underlying operating protocol across modular lines. (Such a system, if it is proprietary, could give its owner-manufacturer an advantage. But this could be resolved by nonproprietary standards.)

This does not mean modules and interface points everywhere, since this would be technologically burdensome. Nor would there have to be more unbundling than before. Nor does it mean that one would have to set all points at once. Setting the specifics of interfaces is complex and need not be ahead of demand (Some embedded technology today may straddle several modules and separation may be impractical). That is a regulatory policy decision that will have to take into account cost and performance implications. But it would require a more systematic approach to however much disaggregation is decided upon.

5. At present, one cannot, for example, upgrade an analog SPC switch by a digital adjunct or overlay; instead, one must replace the entire switch.

41. Regulatory Tasks for the Future: Interconnectivity in the Pluralist Network

1. The New York State Public Service Commission established, as the first state, principles of ONA (Noam, 1990); it was also the first to establish collocation (NYPSC, 1989; NYPSC, 1990c).

2. In the United States, the fundamental 1934 Communications Act, for example, defines it in a totally circular fashion. Section 153(h) states that "a common carrier means any person engaged as a common carrier for hire. . . ."

3. The origins of common callings arose from the medieval custom of carrying on business at stated periods in fairs within defined market areas. Fraudulent commercial practices were prohibited and disputes were settled by the steward of the fair with the assistance of the other merchants.

4. *Western Union Telegraph Co.* v. *Call Publishing Co.*, 181 U.S. 92, 98 (1901).

5. These are part of the questions that the New York Public Service Commission addressed. After public comment, the commission adopted common carriage principles of content–neutrality–nondiscrimination and separation of content and conduit functions. Issues include line-drawing problems. For example, are supplementary or subsidiary functions such as the signaling channel and network management functions part of common carriage? Or is the central office affected, which is an issue in collocation? Or billing and collection services, which are important to VANs?

Another kind of a question is whether common carriage and private carriage can coexist in the same entity, or in the same service. For example, can a carrier be a common carrier to users at one end of a communications link, but a private carrier to the user at the other end?

Similarly, there is the question of how market power or monopoly should enter into common carrier issues. Or the questions of what would qualify as legitimate distinctions between classes of users, or what forms of prior subscription may be used for "adult" programming.

6. New York State has a $1 per month lifeline plan, with installation spread over a year to be $2 per month (NYPSC, 1987).

7. There is evidence for telephone wiretaps by private parties and individuals ten years after Bell's patent (Westin, 1967). The New York Police Department tapped telephones since at least 1895. In 1916, this led to a scandal about listening in on private conversations of Catholic priests and to those of a law firm involved in competition to J.P. Morgan & Co. for World War I munitions contracts (Seipp, 1978).

8. For example, in 1962, the U.S. federal government had 1030 computer central processing units; in 1972, 6731; in 1982, 18,747; and in 1985, over 100,000 (Linowes, 1989).

9. In the past twenty years the cost of access to a name on a computer-based mailing list has come down to about one thousandth of its earlier cost.

References

1. Public Telecommunications: A Concept in Transition

Dallmeyer, Martin. 1977. *Quellen zur Geschichte Des Europäischen Postwesens 1501–1806.* Bern: Verlag Michael Lassleben, Kallmünz, vol. 1.

Ministry of Communications. 1990. *Political Agreement on the Telecommunications Structure.* Copenhagen. June 22, p. 2.

Schulte, Josef. 1982. Endgerätekonzeption im Fernsprechdienst der Deutschen Bundespost. In *Telekommunikation in der Bundesrepublik Deutschland,* ed. Dietrich Elias. Heidelberg: R. V. Decker's Verlag, G. Schenck, pp. 319–48.

Stephan, Heinrich. 1859. *Geschichte der Preussischen Post von ihrem Ursprunge bis auf die Gegenwart.* Berlin: Verlag der Königlichen Geheimen Ober-Hofbuchdruckerei, (R. Decker).

Wolf, Thomas. 1983. Akzeptanz und Kosten des Schnurlosen Telephons. *Neue Züricher Zeitung.* October 26.

2. The Establishment of the PTT System

Brock, Gerald W. 1981. *The Telecommunications Industry: The Dynamics of Market Structure.* Cambridge, MA: Harvard University Press.

Clear, C. R. 1940. The Birth of the Postal Service. In *Penny Postage Centenary,* ed. Samuel Graveson. London: The Postal History Society, pp. 21–33.

Collis, Maurice. 1960. *Marco Polo.* New York: New Directions.

Dallmeyer, Martin. 1977. *Quellen zur Geschichte des Europäischen Postwesenes 1501–1806.* Bern: Verlag Michael Lassleben Kallmünz, vol. 1.

Edwards, Eliezer. 1879. *Sir Rowland Hill.* London: Frederick Warne & Co.

Grosse, Oskar. 1931. *Stephan: Von Postschreiber zum Minister.* Berlin: Mittler und Sohn.

Hemmeon, J. C. 1912. *The History of the British Post Office.* Cambridge, MA: Harvard University Press.

Hill, Sir Rowland, and George Birbeck Hill. 1880. *The Life of Sir Rowland Hill.* London: Thomas de la Rune & Co.

Kramer, Richard. 1991. *A Faith That Divides: Competition Policy in European Telecommunications.* Master's Thesis. Philadelphia, PA: Annenberg School for Communication.

Meyer, Hugo Richard. 1907. *Public Ownership and the Telephone in Great Britain.* New York: Macmillan.

Organization for Economic Co-Operation and Development (OECD). 1983. *Telecommunications: Pressures and Policies for Change*. Paris: OECD.

———. 1990. Committee for Information, Computer and Communications Policy. *Performance Indicators for Public Telecommunications Operators*. DSTI/ICCP/TISP/ 89.10. February. Paris: OECD.

Perry, Charles R. 1977. The British Experience 1876 to 1912: The Impact of the Telephone During the Years of Delay. In *The Social Impact of the Telephone*, ed. Ithiel de Sola Pool. Cambridge, MA: MIT Press, pp. 64–96.

Smyth, Eleanor C. 1907. *Sir Rowland Hill: The Story of a Great Reform*. London: T. Fisher Unwin.

Stephan, Heinrich. 1859. *Geschichte der Preussischen Post von ihrem Ursprunge bis auf die Gegenwart*. Berlin: Verlag der Königlichen Geheimen Ober-Hofbuchdruckerei (R. Decker).

von Beust, Christopher. 1748. *Versuch einer auführlichen Erklärung des Post-Regals*. Berlin: Jena, vol. II, sec V.

3. Network Tipping: The Rise and Fall of the Public Network Monopoly

Allen, David. 1988. New Telecommunications Services: Network Externalities and Critical Mass. *Telecommunications Policy* 12(3): 257–71.

Aronson, Jonathan, and Peter F. Cowhey. 1988. *When Countries Talk*. Cambridge, MA: Ballinger.

Barnes, J. A. 1954. Class and Committees in a Norwegian Island Parish. *Human Relations*, 7.

Baumol, William J., John C. Panzar, and Robert D. Willig. 1982. *Contestable Markets and the Theory of Industry Structure*. New York: Harcourt Brace Jovanovich.

Boissevain, J. 1979. Network Analysis: A Reappraisal. *Current Anthropology*, 20.

Bott, E., 1971. *Family and Social Network*, New York: Free Press.

Buchanan, James M. 1965. An Economic Theory of Clubs. *Economica* 32(125): 1–14.

David, Paul A. 1987. Some New Standards for the Economists of Standardization in the Information Age. In *Economic Policy and Technological Performance*, ed. P. Dasgupta and P. L. Stoneman. Cambridge: Cambridge University Press.

Dumey, Richard. 1983. Telecommunications and the BT Case Competition Rules. Unpublished Speech at Antitrust Luncheon. Commission of The European Communities, Directorate General for Competition, Brussels.

Economides, Nicholas. 1989. Desirability of Compatibility in the Absence of Network Externalities. *American Economic Review* 79(5): 1165–81.

Elmaghraby, Salah E. 1970. *Some Network Models in Management Science*. New York: Springer.

Hardin, Garrett. 1968. The Tragedy of the Commons. *Science* 162 (December 13).

Hayashi, Koichiro. 1988. *The Economies of Networking—Implications for Telecommunications Liberalization*, paper presented at the IIC Conference, Washington, D.C., September.

Heal, Geoffrey. 1989. *The Economics of Networks*. New York: Columbia Institute for Tele-Information. Working Paper Series.

Huber, Peter. 1987. *The Geodesic Network*. Washington, D.C.: U.S. Government Printing Office.

Karni, Shlomo. 1986. *An Analysis of Electrical Networks*. New York: Wiley, pp. 1–4.

Klingman, David J., and J. Mulvey eds. 1981. *Network Models and Associated Applications*. New York: Elsevier.

Knox, Robert. 1830. *Elements of General Anatomy,* Translated from Inst. edition of *Beclard's Anatomy* by D. A. Beclard. Edinburgh: Maclachlan & Stewart, p. 214.

McGuire, Martin. 1972. Private Good Clubs and Public Good Clubs: Economic Models of Group Formation. *Swedish Journal of Economics* 74(1):84–99.

Mueller, Milton. 1988. *Interconnection Policy and Network Economics.* Paper presented at Telecommunications Policy Research Conference, Airlie, Virginia, October 31.

Noam, Eli M. 1986. The "New" Local Communications: Office Networks and Private Cable. *Computer Law Journal* 6(2).

———. 1988. The Next Stage in Telecommunications Evolution: The Pluralistic Network. Paper presented to the International Telecommunications Society, New York: Columbia Institute for Tele-Information Working Paper Series.

Richardson, Jeremy John, Gunnel, Gustafson, and Art Jordan. 1985. In R. A. W. Rhodes, *Power Dependence, Policy Communities and Intergovernmental Networks.* Colchester, Essex: Department of Government, University of Essex, Wivenhoe Park, pp. 6–8.

Rothenberg, Jerome. 1976. Inadvertent Distributional Impacts in the Provision of Public Services to Individuals. In *Public and Urban Economics,* Ronald Grieson, ed. Lexington, MA: Lexington Books.

Schelling, Thomas. 1978. *Micromotives and Macrobehavior.* New York: W. W. Norton.

———. 1969. *Models of Segregation.* Santa Monica, CA: RAND Corporation.

Shepherd, William. 1983. Concepts of Competition and Efficient Policy in the Telecommunications Sector. In *Telecommunications Today and Tomorrow.* ed. Eli M. Noam. New York: Harcourt Brace Jovanovich.

Tiebout, Charles. 1956. A Pure Theory of Local Expenditures. *Journal of Political Economy* 64(5): 414–24.

Tullock, Gordon. 1971. Public Decisions as Public Goods. *Journal of Political Economy* 179(4): 913–18.

Woroch, Glenn A. 1990. On The Stability of Efficient Networks. Waltham MA: GTE Labs. Mimeo.

Zacharisen, W. M. 1932. The Atomic Arrangement in Glass. *Journal of the American Chemical Society* 54(10): 38–42.

4. Forces of Centrifugalism

AT&T Communications. 1983. *The World's Telephones.* Morris Plains, NJ.

Beniger, James. 1986. *The Control Revolution.* Cambridge, MA: Harvard University Press.

Cole, Barry, ed. 1990. *After the Break-up: Assessing the New Post-AT&T Divestiture Era.* New York: Columbia University Press.

Crandall, Robert W. 1988. *Fragmentation of the Telephone Network: Implications for the Policymaker.* Washington, DC: Brookings Institution.

Egan, Bruce. 1990. *Information Superhighways: The Future of Broadband Communications.* Dedham, MA: Artech House.

Elton, Martin, ed. 1991. *Integrated Broadband Networks: The Public Policy Issues,* Amsterdam: Elsevier.

Ergas, Henry. 1989. International Telecommunications Accounting Arrangements: An Unsustainable Inheritance? Paper presented at Colloque Villefranche-sur-Mer. June 1–3.

FCC. 1945. *Statistics of Common Carriers.* Washington, D.C.: U.S. Government Printing Office.

———. 1955. *Statistics of Common Carriers.* Washington, D.C.: U.S. Government Printing Office.

———. 1965. *Statistics of Common Carriers.* Washington, D.C.: U.S. Government Printing Office.

———. 1975. *Statistics of Common Carriers.* Washington, D.C.: U.S. Government Printing Office.

———. 1985. *Statistics of Common Carriers.* Washington, D.C.: U.S. Government Printing Office.

Guérard, A., G. Lafarge, and C. Pautrat. 1979. Les Régions dans la Course au Téléphone. *Economie et Statistique* 117 (December):37–49.

Ito, Yoichi. Historical Review of Japanese Telecommunications Policies. In *Pacific Basin Telecommunications,* ed. Eli Noam and Seisuke Komatsuzaki, forthcoming.

Komatsuzaki, Seisuke. 1986. The Economic Impact of Informatization. In *KEIO Communication Review* 7(March): 13–24. Tokyo: Institute for Communications Research.

Nagai, Susuma. On the Deregulation Process in Japanese Telecommunications. In *Pacific Basin Telecommunications,* eds. Eli Noam, and Seisuke Komatsuzaki, and Douglas Conn, forthcoming.

Nambu, Tsuruhiko. A Comparison of Telecommunications Policies for Deregulation. In *Pacific Basin Telecommunications,* eds. Eli Noam, Seisuke Komatsuzaki, and Douglas Conn, forthcoming.

Noam, Eli M. 1986. The "New" Local Communications: Office Networks and Private Cable. *Computer Law Journal* 6(2): 247–82.

———. Divestiture Plus V and the Coming Regulatory Agenda. In *New Regulatory Concepts, Issues, and Controversies,* ed. Harry Trebing, forthcoming.

Nora, Simon, and Alain Minc. 1980. *The Computerization of Society: Report to the President of the French Republic.* Cambridge, MA: MIT Press.

Pfeiffer, Günter, and Bernhard Wieland. 1990. *Telecommunications in Germany: An Economic Perspective.* New York: Springer-Verlag.

Piore, Michael J. and Charles F. Sabel. 1984. *The Second Industrial Divide: Possibilities for Prosperity.* New York: Basic Books.

Pool, Ithiel de Sola. 1990. *Technologies Without Boundaries: On Telecommunications in a Global Age,* ed. Eli Noam. Cambridge, MA: Harvard University Press.

Porat, Marc U. 1978. Communication Policy in an Information Society. In *Communications for Tommorrow, Policy Perspectives for the 1980s,* ed. Glen O. Robinson. New York: Praeger.

Schiller, Dan. 1982. Business Users and the Telecommunications Network. *Journal of Communication* 32(4): 84–97.

Schulte, Josef. 1982. Endgerätekonzeption im Fernsprechdienst der Deutschen Bundespost. In *Telekommunikation in der Bundesrepublik Deutschland,* ed. Dietrich Elias. Heidelberg: R. V. Decker's Verlag, G. Schenck, p. 321.

Steckel, Marie-Monique, and Marc Fossier. 1990. *France Télécom: An Insider's Guide.* Chicago: Intertec.

Strassman, Paul. 1985. *The Information Payoff: The Transformation of Work in the Electronic Age.* New York: Free Press.

Telecom Factbook. 1986. New York: Television Digest.

5. Defense of the Telecommunications Monopoly

AT&T. 1976. An Econometric Study of Returns to Scale in the Bell System. Bell Exhibit 60, FCC Docket 20003 (Fifth Supplemental Response), August 20.

Baumol, William J., John C. Panzar, and Robert D. Willig. 1982. *Contestable Markets and the Theory of Industry Structure.* New York: Harcourt Brace Jovanovich.

Brock, Gerald W. 1981. *The Telecommunications Industry: The Dynamics of Market Structure.* Cambridge, MA: Harvard University Press.

Chrust, Steven. 1985. MCI Communications Corporation. New York: Bernstein Research.

Dobell, Rodney A., et al. 1972. Telephone Communications in Canada: Demand, Production, and Investment Decisions. *Bell Journal of Economics and Management Science* 3(1): 175–219.

Federal-State Joint Board. 1988. *Monitoring Report of the Federal-State Joint Board.* CC Docket No. 80–286, 87–339.

Fuss, Melvyn, and Leonard Waverman. 1977. Multi-product Multi-input Cost Functions for a Regulated Utility: The Case of Telecommunications in Canada. NBER Conference on Public Regulation. Washington, D.C., February 15–17.

Mantell, L. 1974. *An Econometric Study of Returns to Scale in the Bell System.* Staff Research Paper. Office of Telecommunications Policy, Executive Office of the President. Washington, D.C., February.

Meyer, John R., Robert W. Wilson, M. Alan Baughcum, Ellen Burton, and Louise Caoulette. 1980. *The Economics of Competition in the Telecommunications Industry.* Cambridge, MA: Oelgeschlager, Gunn & Hain.

Nadiri, Ishaq and Mark Schankerman. 1981. Production, Technological Change and Productivity in the Bell System. In *Productivity Measurement in Regulated Industries,* ed. Thomas Cowing and Rodney Stevenson. New York: Academic Press, pp. 219–48.

OECD. 1990. Committee for Information, Computer and Communications Policy. *Performance Indicators for Public Telecommunications Operators.* DSTI/ICCP/TISP/ 89.10. February. Paris: OECD.

Schulte, Josef. 1982. Endgerätekonzeption im Fernsprechdienst der Deutschen Bundespost. In *Telekommunikation in der Bundesrepublik Deutschland,* ed. Dietrich Elias. Heidelberg: R. V. Decker's Verlag, G. Schenck, pp. 319–48.

Shepherd, William. 1983. Concepts of Competition and Efficient Policy in the Telecommunications Sector. In *Telecommunications Regulation Today and Tomorrow,* ed. Eli Noam. New York: Harcourt Brace Jovanovich, pp. 79–120.

6. Policy Directions

Le Boucher, Eric, and Jean-Michel Quatrepoint. 1984. La Guerre Mondiale de la Communication (four parts). *Le Monde* (January 11): 1, 44.

Le Monde. 1984. La Guerre Mondiale de la Communication. January 11–14.

Nora, Simon, and Alain Minc. 1980. *The Computerization of Society: Report to the President of the French Republic.* Cambridge, MA: MIT Press.

7. Germany

Alcatel Annual Report. 1989.

Allentier. 1973. *Die Telegraphenstation Köln-Flittard, Eine Kleine Geschichte der Nachrichtentechnik.* Rheinisch-Westfaelisches Wirtschaftsarchiv, Köln.

Äppel, Timothy. 1990. Siemens Unveils East German Investment Plan. *Communications Week International,* March 26, p. 6.

Armbruster, Heinrich. 1986. Breitband-ISDN erfüllt die wachsenden Telekommunikationswünsche. *Telecom Report* 9 (3): 168–75.

Bauer, H. 1982. Future Outlook for Communications in the Light of New Technologies. *Telecommunications Journal* 49(9): 579.

Blau, John. 1989. Telecoms Show Biggest Profit. *Communications Week International,* September 4, p. 17.

———. 1990. Siemens May Shed Parts of Nixdorf. *Communications Week International,* January 29, p. 12.

Blau, John, and Karen Lynch. 1990. Germany Opens Satcoms. *Communications Week International,* July 2, p. 3.

Bruce, Peter. 1986. Bundespost Reaches Deregulation Milestone. *Financial Times,* July 31.

Communications Week International. 1989. German Cellular Race Is On. May 15.

Deutsche Bundepost (DPB). 1981. "Stellungnahme der DBP zum Sondergutachten der Monpolkommission 'Die Rolle der DBP in Fermeldewesen." Referat 603. May.

———. 1982a. *Deutsche Bundespost Annual Report.* Bad Windsheim: Georg Heidecker.

———. 1982b. *Harmonization of the Tariffs for Fixed Connections with Those for Switched Connections in the Public Telecommunications Network.* Bad Windesheim: Verlag für Wissenschaft und Leben—George Heidecker.

———. 1985. From the Analogue Telephone Network to the Integrated Broadband Telecom Network. DBP.

———. 1987. *Statistisches Jahrbuch 1986.* London/Pfalz: Pfälzische Verlagsanstalt.

Dodsworth, Terry. 1987. Manufacturing with Passion. *Financial Times,* June 29, p. 15.

Dörrenbächer, Christoph. 1988. Telecommunications in West Germany. *Telecommunications Policy,* 12(4): 344–52.

The Economist. 1985. March in the EEC Competition. April 6.

Elias, Dietrich (ed.). *Telekommunikation in der Bundesrepublik Deutschland 1982.* Hamburg: R. V. Decker.

———, Roland Klett, and Eberhard Witte. 1980. *Neue Kommunikationsdienste der Bundespost in der Wirtschaftsordnung und Gemeinwirtschaft.* Heft 19. Baden-Baden: Nomos.

Engals, W., A. Gutowski, W. Hamm, et al. 1988. *More Competition in Telecommunications.* Frankfurt: Frankfurt Institute.

Federal Ministry of Posts and Telecommunications (PTT). 1990. Documents Concerning the Licensing of Private Satellite Network in the FRG. Bonn. June 19.

Federal-State Joint Board. 1988. Monitoring Report in CC Docket No. 80–286, CC Docket No. 87–339. March.

Fuhrman, Peter. 1990. Papa Siemens. *Forbes,* May 28, p. 100.

Gilhooly, Dennis, and Jennifer Schenker. 1989. Germans Rethink ISDN. *Communications Week International,* March 13, p. 1.

Gärtner, Bernhard, and Georg Habenicht, eds. 1990. *Doing Business with DBP Telekom in the Center of Europe.* Bonn: Deutsche Bundespost Telekom.

Glotz, Peter. 1983. Unpublished manuscript of speech.

Goetzler, Herbert. 1976. 100 Jahre Fernsprechtechnik. *Sonderdruck aus der Nachrichtentechnischen Zeitschrift* 29(2): 105–8.

Goodhart, David. 1990. Combining Resolution and Tradition. *Financial Times,* June 21, p. 20.

Hafner, Katie. 1990 German Phone System is Taxed By Unification. *The New York Times,* December 10, p. D8.

Hayes, Dawn, and Candee Wilde, 1988. NYNEX Teams in German Bid. *Communications Week International,* December 19.

Henneman, Gerhard. 1984. Ein Gigant rekelt sich. *Neue Medien* 1(June): 70–77.

Heuss, Theodor. 1946. *Robert Bosch: Leben und Liestung.* Stuttgart: Rainer Wunderlich Verlag.

Hoffmann-Riem, Wolfgang. 1984. Policy Research on Telecommunications in West Germany. In *Policy Research in Telecommunications,* ed. Vincent Mosco. Norwood, NJ: Ablex.

Holcombe, A. N. 1911. *Public Ownership of Telephones on the Continent of Europe.* Boston: Houghton Mifflin.

Inquiry Commission. 1984. Bericht der Enquete Kommission. "Neue Information und Kommunikationstechniken." Deutscher Bundestag: D. Bopnn.

ITU. 1990. *Annual Telephone Statistics.* Geneva: International Telecommunications Union.

ITU. 1985. *Telecommunications Journal:* 191.

Kelly, Tim. 1990. *Telecommunications and Eastern European Economies.* Paris: OECD.

Knieps, Günther, Jürgen Müller, and Carl Christian von Weizsäcker. 1981. *Die Rolle des Wettbewerbs im Fernmeldebereich.* Baden-Baden: Nomos.

Körner, E. 1937. Die Deutsche Reichspost—Eine Hoheitsverwaltung. In *Die Reichspost im Staate Adolf Hitler,* ed. Jakob Nagel. Berlin: Verlag Georg König.

Lange, Bernd-Peter. 1984. Dokument Einer Einseitigen Politik. *Medium,* May.

Malerba, Franco. 1985. *The Semi-Conductor Business.* Madison, WI: University of Wisconsin Press.

Markoff, John. 1988. I.B.M. to Sell Rolm to Siemens. *New York Times,* December 14, p. D1.

Mestmäcker, Ernst-Joachim. 1980. Fernmeldenmonopol und Nachfragemacht—Wirtschaftsrechtliche und ordnungspolitische Probleme der hoheitlichen und unternehmerischen Funktion der DBP. In *Kommunikation ohne Monopole,* ed. Ernst-Joachim Mestmäcker. Baden-Baden: Nomos, pp. 185, 196.

Mestmäcker, Ernst-Joachim, ed. 1980. *Kommunikation Ohne Monopole.* Baden-Baden: Nomos.

Möschel, Wernhard. 1988. (No) Restructuring of Telecommunications in Germany? Unpublished paper.

Monopolkommission. 1981. *Die Rolle der Deutschen Bundespost im Fernmeldewesen.* Sondergutachten 9. Baden-Baden: Nomos.

Nagel, Jakob, ed. 1937. *Die Reichspost im Staat Adolf Hitler.* Berlin: Verlag Georg König.

Neumann, Karl-Heinz. 1986. Economic Policy Toward Telecommunications, Information and the Media in West Germany. In *Marketplace for Telecommunications:*

Regulation and Deregulation in Industrialized Democracies, ed. Marcellus Snow. White Plains, NY: Longman, pp. 131–52.

———. 1990. The Unification of Telecommunications in Germany. Paper prepared for the Brussels Meeting of the International Institute of Communications Telecommunications Forum, July 16–17.

Ohmann, Friederich, and Heinrich Armbruster. 1986. Beiträge zur Fernmeldepolitischen Diskussion in der Bundesrepublik Deutschland. April.

Pfeiffer, Günter, and Bernhard Wieland. 1990. *Telecommunications in West Germany.* Berlin: Springer-Verlag.

Purton, Peter. 1990. Siemens to Go East. *Communications International,* February, pp. 7–28.

Roth, Terrence. 1990. West German Firm to Supply Phones for East Germany. *Wall Street Journal,* March 12, p. A7.

Rural Electrification Administration. 1988. *A Brief History of the Rural Electric and Telephone Programs.* Washington, D.C.: U.S. Government Printing Office.

Sax, E. 1887. *Die Verkehrsmittel in Volks-und Staatswirtschaft.* Vienna: Grundlegung der theoretischen Staatswirtschaft.

Schares, Gail. 1989. Siemens: A Plodding Giant Starts to Pick Up Speed. *Business Week,* February 20, p. 136–37.

Schenker, Jennifer. 1990. German Angst. *Communications Week International,* January 29, p. 1.

Scherer, Joachim. 1985. *Telekommunikationsrecht und Telekommunikationspolitik.* Baden-Baden: Nomos.

Schnöring, M. 1982. Direkte und indirekte Investitionsaufwendungen der Deutschen Bundespost fur Fernmeldeanlagen auf die Produktion und die Beschäftigung in der Bundesrepublik Deutschland. Berlin: DIW.

Schulte, Josef. 1982. Endgerätekonzeption in Fernsprechdienst der Deutschen Bundespost. In *Telekommunikation in der Bundesrepublik Deutschland 1982,* ed. Dietrich Elias. Heidelberg: R. V. Decker's Verlag, G. Schenck.

Schwarz-Schilling, Christian. 1990. Germany. *Telephony,* January 22, p. 58.

Scott, John Dick. 1958. *Siemens' Brothers, 1858–1958: An Essay in the History of the Industry.* London: Weidenfeld and Nicholson.

Siemens, Georg. 1949. *Geschichte des Hauses Siemens.* 3 vols. Munich: Verlag Karl Alber.

———. 1957. *History of the House of Siemens, English Translation.* Munich: Verlag Karl Alber.

Siemens, 1989. Keeping You Posted. Siemens Press Release. January 5.

Snow, Marcellus S. 1983. Comparative Policy Research and Policy Making in Telecommunications: The Case of West Germany. Paper prepared for the Eleventh Annual Telecommunications Policy Research Conference. Annapolis, MD.

Stuebing, Heinz Volkmar. 1982. *Der Deutsche Kraftwagenpostpersonenverkehr in seinem rechtlichen Aufbau.* Weimar. Ph.D. dissertation.

Tagliabue, John. 1984. Nixdorf takes on the Americans. *New York Times,* September 16, p. F4.

Telekom. 1990. Telecommunications "Made in Germany" *Annual Report.* Deutsche Bundespost Telekom.

Thiemeyer, Theo. 1983. Deregulation in the Perspective of the German Gemeinwirtschaftslehre. *Journal of Institutional and Theoretical Economics* 139:405–18.

U.S. Department of State. 1990. *Eastern Europe: Please Stand By.* Washington, D.C.: U.S. Department of State.

von Weizsäcker, Carl Christian. 1980. Wirtschaftspolitische Begründung und Abgrenzung des Fernmeldemonopols. In *Kommunikation ohne Monopole,* ed. Ernst-Joachim Mestmäcker. Baden-Baden: Nomos.

Wagner, Adolf. 1887. Finanzwissenschaft und Staatssozialismus. *Zeitschrift für die Gesamte Staatswissenschaft,* 43: 37–122, 675–746.

Witte, Eberhard. 1987. *Neuordung der Telekommunikation.* Heidelberg: R. V. Decker's Verlag, G. Schenck.

Wittiber. 1934. *Die Entwicklung und Neuregelung des Fernsprechnebenstellenwesens in Deutschland, Deutsche Verkehrszeitung 1934.* Nv. 19. As quoted in Mestmäcker, 1980, p. 184.

Wolf, Roswitha. 1982. Telefonladen und Telefonmobil—Teile des Marketing-Konzepts der Deutschen Bundespost. In *Telekommunikation in der Bundesrepublik Deutschland,* ed. Dietrich Elias. Heidelberg: R.V. Decker's Verlag, G. Schenck, p. 26.

ZVEI. 1983. *Telecommunications in the Federal Republic of Germany.* Frankfurt: Fachverband Fermeldetechnik.

8. The United Kingdom

Abel, Glen. 1989. BT is Planting Global Seeds. *Communications Week International,* May 29.

Arlandis, Jacques, and Laurent Gille. 1989. Performance Under Different Regulatory Regimes: A Comparison of British Telecom and France Télécom. Montpellier: IDATE.

Beesley, Michael E. 1981. *Liberalization of the Use of the British Telecommunications Network.* Report to the Secretary of State. London: Her Majesty's Stationery Office.

Beesley, Michael, and Bruce Laidlaw. 1990. *The Future of Telecommunications.* London: Institute of International Affairs.

Bird June, and John Huxley. 1984. Tomorrow the World? *The New York Times,* October 7.

British Telecom. 1981. *Further Considerations Relating to the British Telecommunications Network and Proposal to Permit Competition.* London: British Telecom.

Bruce, Robert R., Jeffrey P. Cunard, and Mark D. Director. 1986. *From Telecommunications to Electronic Services: A Global Spectrum of Definitions, Boundary Lines, and Structures.* London: Butterworths.

Cable and Wireless. 1990. *Report and Accounts,* p. 8

Connections. 1985. British Telecom License Out of Reach? May 24, p. 32.

Court of Justice of the European Communities. 1985. Judgement of the Court of 20 March, 1985 in Case 41/83: Italian Republic of Commission of the European Communities. Reference No. 85/c96/06, April 17.

Department of Industry. 1982. The Future of Telecommunications in Britain. *White Paper.* London: Department of Industry.

Department of Trade and Industry. 1985. Government Proposals for the Future Licensing of Value Added and Data Services. Unpublished document of the Department of Trade and Industry.

———. 1987. Registrations Under the VANs General License OSAT. Unpublished document. February.

Dixon, Hugo. 1990a. Freeing the Phone Networks. *Financial Times,* February 5, p. 20.

————. 1990b. U.K. Watchdog Launches Plan to Cut International Telephone Charges. *Financial Times,* October 2, p. 24.

————, and Alan Cane. 1990. STC to Use Fujitsu's £743m for Expansion in Telecoms. *Financial Times,* July 31, pp. 1, 22.

Dumey, R. 1983. Telecommunications and the BT Case Competition Rules. Unpublished speech given at an Antitrust Luncheon. Commission of the European Communities, Directorate General for Competition. Brussels.

The Economist. 1985. A Hull of a Difference. November 16, p. 90.

————. 1989. Telephones That Get Up and Go. September 16, p. 71–72.

————. 1990a. Gnatwork. March 31, p. 56.

————. 1990b. Duopoly Rhymes with Monopoly. July 7, p. 72.

Evagora, Andreas. 1990. Cable TV–Telecoms Showdown. *Communications Week International,* May 21, p. 16.

Financial Times. 1990. British Telecom Pushes Up Prices. July 19, p. 6.

Foreman-Peck, James. 1985. Competition and Performance in the UK Telecommunication Industry. *Telecommunications Policy,* 9(3): 215–28.

Fortune. 1990. August 28, p. 15.

Fuller, Claire, and Pam Mitchell. 1986. A "Jolly Good" Start for Cellular. *Telelocator,* March, pp. 42–46.

Garnham, Nicholas. 1985. Telecommunications Policy in the United Kingdom. *Media, Culture and Society.* London: Sage, vol. 7, pp. 7–29.

Garrett, John. 1984. Tacs: The UK Standard for Cellular Radio. *Telephony,* July 23, pp. 58, 62.

Gebhardt, H. P. 1989. *Analysis of the Present Situation and Future Trends in Telecommunications Regulation in the Member States in the Light of EC Policy.* Brussels: EC.

Gist, Peter. 1990. The Role of Oftel. *Telecommunications Policy,* February, pp. 26–51.

Green, Jeremy. 1989. BT Looks Westward. *Communications International,* September, p. 8.

————. 1990a. At Last, UK ISDN. *Communications International,* January, p. 10.

————. 1990b. PCN: A Role for ETSI? *Communications International,* January, p. 14.

Hayes, Dawn. 1988. Carrington's Mobile Vision. *Communications Week International,* September 12.

————. 1989a. U.K. Spurs New Competition. *Communications Week International,* July 26, p. 3.

————. 1989b. BT to Raise Leased Line Prices. *Communications Week International,* October 30, p. 3.

————. 1989c. BT to Run Video Trial Over Fiber. *Communications Week International,* November 27.

————. 1990a. BT Reorganizes to Meet Competition. *Communications Week International,* April 9, p. 2.

————. 1990b. PCN Market Faces Sobering Reality. *Communications Week International,* July 16, pp. 10–11.

Heuermann, A. and K. H. Neumann. 1983. Die Neue Fernmeldepolitik Grossbritanniens—Eine ökonomische Darstellung. Bad Honnef: Wissenschaftliches Institut Für Kommunikationsdienste der Deutschen Bundespost.

Hudson, Richard L. 1987. British Telecom's Modernization Falters. *Wall Street Journal,* August 27.

ITU. 1990. *Annual Telephone Statistics.* Geneva: ITU.

Jason, Chris. 1985. Mercury Dials the Right Number. *Financial Times*, October 2, p. 4.

Jones, Phil. 1989. UK Frees Leased Line Resale. *Communications International*, July, p. 5.

Journal of Commerce. 1983.

Laws, Malcolm. 1989. U.K. Vendors Target New Network Niche. *Communications Week International*, July 26, p. 1.

Littlechild, Stephen. 1983a. Deregulation of UK Telecommunications: Some Economic Aspects. *Economic Review* 1(2): 29.

———. 1983b. *Regulations of British Telecommunications Profitability*. London: Department of Industry.

Locksley, Gareth. 1982. *The EEC Telecommunications Industry: Competition, Concentration and Competitiveness*. Brussels: Commission of the European Communities.

———. 1983. Europe and the Electronics Industry: Conflicting Strategies in Positive Restructuring. *West European Politics* 6(2): 128–38.

Lynch, Karen, and Dawn Hayes. 1990. Telepoint Operators Refocusing. *Communications Week International*, July 16, p. 11.

Manning, D. 1988. Telecommunications in the United Kingdom. In *European Telecommunications Organizations*, ed. James Foreman-Peck and Jürgen Müller. Baden-Baden: Nomos.

Maremont, Mark. 1989. British Telecom Is Getting Less British All the Time. *Business Week*, August 14.

Monopolies and Mergers Commission, The General Electric Company, PLC, and The Plessey Company. 1986. *PLC: A Report on the Proposed Merger*. London: Her Majesty's Stationery Office.

Morgan, Kevin. 1987. Breaching the Monopoly: Telecommunications and the State in Britain. Working Paper Series on Government-Industry Relations. No. 7. University of Sussex.

Noam, Eli M. 1982. Towards an Integrated Telecommunications Market: Overcoming the Local Monopoly of Cable Television. *Federal Communications Bar Journal*, 34(2): 209–57.

———. 1985. *Video Media Competition*. New York: Columbia University Press.

———. 1986. The "New" Local Communications: Office Networks and Private Cable. *Computer Law Journal* 6: 901–42. New York: Columbia University Press.

Official Journal L360. 1982. Congressional Record, U.K. December 21, p. 36

Oftel. 1985a. British Telcom's Price Changes. Oftel press notice. December 16.

———. 1985b. Professor Carsberg Congratulates BT for Achieving Call Box Target. Press release. April 20.

———. 1988. Chatlines and Other Message Services. Statement from Professor Bryan Carsberg. July 19.

———. 1990a. Director General of Telecommunications Publishes Sixth Annual Report. June 27.

———. 1990b. PCN Licenses. *Oftel News*, March.

Purton, Peter. 1989. Slow Progress of VANS. *Communications International*, July, pp. 27–32.

———. 1990. Old Player Returns to UK Telecom. *Telephony*, March 26, p. 14

Raggett, R. J. 1986. Racal Vodaphone Fights for Its Share. *Telephony*, April 28.

Redux, Huber. 1989. BT Ventures Proliferate as International Markets Complicate. *Telecommunications*, September, pp. 57–58.

Reiter, Alan. 1989. Focus on Technology. *Telocator*, July, pp. 36–42.

Sims, Calvin. 1989. Licenses Awarded by Britain for 3 New Phone Networks. *The New York Times*, December 12.

Staple, Greg. 1990. *The Global Telecommunications Traffic Boom*. London: International Institute of Communications.

Stapley, Barry. 1981. Managing Communications—The Value of Choice. *Telecommunications Policy* 5(2): 149–51.

Telecommunications Reports International. 1990. Seven UK Paging Operators Sign MOU on ERMES Message System. February 16, p. 7.

Thomas, David. 1987. Mercury Communications: Making Good Headway. *Financial Times*, October 19.

Williamson, John. 1986. Cellnet Intends to Keep Its Lead. *Telephony*, April 28, pp. 37–40.

———. 1987. ISDN in the UK: Enthusiasm Overshadows Skepticism as Private Applications Emerge. *Telephony*, April 27.

Woollacott, Emma. 1990a. BT Slims and Prices ISDN. *Communications International*, May, p. 7.

———. 1990b. Small Screen Services. *Communications International*, February, pp. 41–43.

Young, Peter. 1983. *Power of Speech: History of Standard Telephones and Cable 1883 to 1983*. Winchester, MA: Allen and Unwin.

9. France

Alletier. 1973. *Die Telegraphenstation Koeln-Flittard, Eine Kleine Geschichte der Nachrichtentechnik*. Rheinisch-Westfaelisches: Wirtschaftsarchive zu Koeln.

Arlandis, Jacques and Laurent Gille. 1989. Performance Under Different Regulatory Regimes: A Comparision of British Telecom and France Télécom. Montpellier: IDATE.

Attali, Jacques, and Yves Stourdze. 1977. The Birth of the Telephone and Economic Crisis: The Slow Death of Monologue in French Society. In *The Social Impact of the Telephone*, ed. Ithiel de Sola Pool. Cambridge, MA: MIT Press, pp. 97–111.

Aurelle, Bruno. 1986. *Les Télécommunications*. Paris: Editions de la Couverte.

Benedetti, Marino. 1983. Télécommunications Services: Policy in Europe. Paper presented at the European Institute of Public Administration, Maestricht/Valkerburt.

Bertho, Catherine. 1987. Origins of the Organization of Telecommunications in France. New York: Columbia Institute for Tele-Information. Working Paper Series.

———, et al., ed. 1984. *Histoire des Télécommunications en France*. Toulouse: Editions Erés.

———, and Michelle Nouvion. 1986. In *Les Télécommunications*, Bruno Aurelle. Paris: Editions de la Couverte.

Bienaim, Jean-Pierre, and Michel Picaud. 1984. Télécommunications et le IXème (ninth) Plan. *Revue Française des Télécommunications*, January 19, pp. 35–41.

Bonan, M., Dominique Roux, and Jean Michel Delbarade. 1985. *L'importance de Télécommunications sur la Croissance Économique*. Paris: Université de Paris-Dauphine.

Boult, Raymond. 1989. Users Back PTT Split. *Communications International*, October, pp. 13–14.

————. 1990. Alcatel Takes Military Turn. *Communications International*, March, pp. 10–12.

Bransten, Thomas R., and Stanley H. Brown. 1964. Machines Bull's Computer Crisis. *Fortune*, July, pp. 154–55, 242–44.

Bright, Julian. 1990. The Smart Card: An Application in Search of a Technology. *Telecommunications* 24(March) 3.

Brock, Gerald W. 1981. *The Telecommunications Industry: The Dynamics of Market Structure*. Cambridge, MA: Harvard University Press.

Bruce, Robert R., Jeffrey P. Cunard, and Mark D. Director. 1985. Country Report: France. In *Study of Telecommunications Structures*. Washington, D.C.: Debevoise & Plimpton, p. 34.

Business Week. 1982. Thomson: First Test of a Socialist Theory. May 5, p. 53.

Chamoux, Jean-Pierre. 1988. The Current-French Telecommunication Policy. Mission à la Réglementation.

Connaughton, Bernadette. 1982. The French Telecommunications Industry. Unpublished paper. University of Pennsylvania, Wharton School of Finance.

Crane, Rhonda J. 1979. *The Politics of International Standards: France and the Color TV War*. Norwood, NJ: Ablex.

Curien, N., and J. de la Brunetière. 1984. Les Transferts de Revenus Induits par la Tarification Téléphonique entre Catégories d'Abonnés et entre Types de Prestations. *Télécommunications*, vol. 39. pp. 11–12.

Darmon, Jacques. 1985. *Le Grand Dérangement: La Guerre du Téléphone*. Paris: Editions Jean Claude Lattes.

Dawkins, William. 1990a. France Makes a Point of Catching Up in the Mobile Phone Race. *Financial Times*, March 1.

————. 1990b. Shackles to Be Removed. *Financial Times*, June 26, p. 11.

Delamaide, Darrell. 1982. Will the Socialist Experiment Work? *Institutional Investor*. March, pp. 161–75.

The Economist. 1967. Knocking Microheads Together. December 23, p. 1245.

————. 1989. Silicon Ballet. February 18.

Gleckman, Howard. 1990. CGE Gains a Chunk of Alcatel. *Business Week*, June 25, p. 34.

Guérard, Agnes, Guy Lafarge, and Charles Pautrat. 1979. Les Régions dans la Course au Téléphone. *Economie et Statistique*, 177(December): 37–49.

Holcombe, A. N. 1911. *Public Ownership of Telephones on the Continent of Europe*. Boston: Houghton Mifflin.

Hudson, Richard. 1990. Groupe Bull's Loss Widened Sharply During First Half. *Wall Street Journal*, July 31.

Locksley, Gareth. 1983. Europe and the Electronics Industry, Conflicting Strategies in Positive Restructuring. *West European Politics* 64(2): 128–38.

Logica. 1979. Structure and Performance Comparison, vol. IV (France). Oct. 12:5.

Malerba, Franco. 1985. *The Semi-Conductor Business*. Madison, WI: University of Wisconsin Press.

McInnes, Neil. 1964. The Story of Machines Bull. *Barron's*, February 24, pp. 9–21.

Monsen, R. Joseph. 1984. French Socialists March to the Right. *Challenge*, September/October, pp. 37–42.

Morley, Meg. 1986. French Telecoms Place Call. *Connections*, 59(June): 1.

Nouvion, Mireille. 1984. L'Automatisation du Réseau Téléphonique Français. *Revue Française de Télécommunications*, January, pp. 76–85.

Parry, John. 1989. Cashless Europe. *International Management* 44(September): 8.

Pautrat, Charles. 1984. La Nouvelle Structure Tarifaire. *Revue Française des Télécommunications,* January, pp. 127–34.

Petersen, Thane. 1989. A New CEO Is Taking Bull by the Horns. *Business Week,* July 17, p. 80.

Pierrand, Jean. 1984. Thomson Voit Grand pour ses "Micro." *Le Monde,* April 23.

Quatrepoint, Jean-Michel. 1984. CIT-Alcatel n'a Fait qu'une Perce Limite sur les Marchés Européens. *Le Monde,* May 15, pp. 20–21.

Rice, Valerie. 1989. It's Now or Never for Europe's Biggest Chip Makers. *Electronic Business* 15(August 7): 16.

Roussel, Anne-Marie. 1989a. French Clarify VAN Regulation. *Communications Week International,* May 15, p. 13.

———. 1989b. French Revision. *Communications Week International,* May 29, p. 22.

———. 1989c. The Top 25. *Communications Week International,* October 24, p. C10.

———. 1989d. Quilés Offers Reform Plan. *Communications Week International,* November 13, p. 13.

———. 1990a. French Reform Still Hotly Debated. *Communications Week International,* April 9, p. 3.

———. 1990b. Reforms Gaining Ground. *Communications Week International,* May 21, p. 3.

———. 1990c. French Senators Want More Reform. *Communications Week International,* June 18, p. 13.

———. 1990d. Report Warns of Foreign "Invasion." *Communications Week International,* August 13.

Schenker, Jennifer. 1989a. Bull Reorganizes in Aftermath of Merger. *Communications Week International,* February 6, p. 13.

———. 1989b. New Minister on the Spot in France. *Communications Week International,* July, p. 24.

———. 1989c. Users Combat French Initiative. *Communications Week International,* November 27, p. 2.

———. 1990. Transpac Ready to Branch Out. *Communications Week International,* January 29, p. 2.

Scientific American. 1983. Special Issue on French Telecommunications. October.

Simon, Jean-Paul. 1990. Aftermath: Deregulation in France in the Eighties. Paper presented at the 18th Annual TPRC, Airlie VA. September.

Steckel, Marie-Monique, and Marc Fossier. 1990. *France Télécom: An Insider's Guide.* Chicago: Telephony.

Stephan, Heinrich. 1859. *Geschichte der Preussischen Post von ihrem Ursprunge bis auf die Gegenwart.* Berlin: Verlag der Königlichen Geheimen Ober-Hofbuchdruckerei (R. V. Decker).

Telecom France. 1990. *Revue Française des Télécommunications.* International Edition. April.

Telecommuncations Reports. 1990. National Assembly Approves Government Plan to Separate France Télécom, Postal Service. May 28.

Telephony. 1985. A Partnership in Progress. February 11, pp. 32–33.

Tully, Shawn. 1989. Europe Goes on a Telephone Binge. *Fortune,* August 28.

U.S. Department of Commerce, Bureau of the Census. 1939. Cited in *Telephone and Telegraph Statistics of the World, January, 1938,* American Telephone and Telegraph Co. Comptroller's Department, Chief Statistician's Division. Washington, DC: Government Printing Office.

U.S. Department of Commerce, Domestic and International Business Administration. 1975. Communications Equipment and Systems-France. September.

Vasseur, Frederic. 1984. Bull: C'est Reparti pour un Tour. *L'Expansion*, April 20/May 10, pp. 39–40.

Voge, Jean. 1986. Survey of French Regulatory Policy. In *The Marketplace for Telecommunications: Regulation and Deregulation in Industrial Democracies*, ed. Marcellus Snow. White Plains, NY: Longman.

Western Electric. 1978. Study: Telecommunication Services in France.

10. The Netherlands

Dabbs, P., J. J. E. Swaffield, C. M. Aust, and I. Sarwar. 1982. Going Dutch! *British Telecom Journal.* Spring.

de Pous, Victor. 1988. Dutch Privacy Bill Again Delayed. *Transnational Data and Communications Report.* December, pp. 6–7.

———. 1989. Dutch Data Protection Act in Force. *Transnational Data & Communications Report.* December, pp. 21–22.

Forden, Sara Gay. 1990. AT&T-Italian Joint Venture Targets and U.K., Greece, Portugal, Spain Markets. *The Wall Street Journal*, July 28, pp. A3E, 3.

Hayes, Dawn. 1989. Suppliers Split Over GSM. *Communications International*, September 18, p. 1.

Hins, Wouter, and Bernt Hugenholtz. 1986. *The Law and Economics of Transborder Telecommunications: Report on the Netherlands.* Hamburg: Max-Planck Institut.

Holcombe, A. N. 1911. *Public Ownership of Telephones on the Continent of Europe.* Boston: Houghton Mifflin.

ITU. 1990. *Annual Telephone Statistics.* Geneva: ITU.

Kingdom of the Netherlands. 1981. *Facts and Figures: Transport and Communications.* Amsterdam: Ministry of Foreign Affairs.

Lablans, Peter. 1989. Privatization of the Dutch PTT: New Telecommunications Opportunities. *Telecommunications Business* 1(3): 61–66.

Malerba, Franco. 1985. *The Semiconductor Business.* Madison: University of Wisconsin Press.

Montgomery, Page, Lee Selwyn, and Paul Keller. 1990. The Telecommunications Infrastructure in Perspective. Economics & Technology, Inc. March.

Netherlands PTT. 1985. *PTT in Motion.* Amsterdam: Netherlands PTT.

Philips, Frederik. 1978. *Forty-Five Years With Philips.* Dorset, UK: Blandford Press.

Prokesch, Steven. 1990. Philips Sees $1 Billion Loss in Reorganizing 2 Divisions. *New York Times.* July 3, pp. D1–D2.

PTT Telecommunicatie. 1983. *The Dutch Telecommunications Service in Brief.* Amsterdam: PTT Telecommunicatie.

Schenker, Jennifer. 1989. Dutch PTT Enters Datacoms Market. *Communications Week International.* October 16, p. 87.

———. 1990. Judging the PTTs. *Communications Week International.* July 16, pp. C11–12.

Staple, Gregory. 1990. *The Global Telecommunications Traffic Boom.* London: IIC.

Tagliabue, Paul. 1987. *New York Times.* January 15, p. F8.

Transnational Data and Communications Report. (TDR). 1989. Equipment Approval Row Mars Start of Dutch PTT. February, p. 3.

Tutt, Nigel. 1990. Belgium Belies Status as Netherlands Reforms. *Communications International*. July, pp. 15–19.

Van de Krol, Ronald. 1990. Philips Reorganises After Rationalisation Costs. *Financial Times*. July 3, p. 1.

The Wall Street Journal. 1989. April 4, pp. A19, 6.

———. 1989. March 9, pp. A13, 4.

Wieland, Bernhard. 1986. *Die Neuordnung des Fernmeldewesens in den Niederlanden*. Bad Honnef: Deutsche Bundespost, Wissenschaftliches Institut fuer Kommunikationsdienste.

———. 1988. Telecommunications in the Netherlands. In *European Telecommunications Organizations*, ed. James Foreman-Peck and Jürgen Müller. Baden-Baden: Nomos, pp. 203–19.

Wilde, Candee. 1990. Philips Pulls Out of AT&T Venture. *Communication Week International*. October 1.

11. Belgium

Belgian National Committee for the World Year of Communications. 1983. *Belgian Communications Technology*, November.

Cheeseright, Paul. 1985. Key Decisions Still Awaited. *Financial Times*, January 14, p. 8.

Euro-Telecom News. 1987. Belgium. 1(10).

ITU. 1990a. *Annual Telephone Statistics*. Geneva: ITU.

———. 1990b. European Digital Mobile Telephone Network: Belgium Chooses System Suppliers. *Telecommunications Journal* 57(3): 191.

Kellaway, Lucy. 1990. Don't Ring Us. . . . *Financial Times*, June 18, p. 4.

Müller, Jürgen. 1988. Telecommunications in Belgium. In *European Telecommunications Organizations*, ed. James Foreman-Peck and Jürgen Müller. Baden-Baden: Nomos, pp. 87–102.

Pichault, François. 1985. La Télématique dans le Cadre Réglementaire et Institutionnel de la Belgique. *Courier Hebdomadaire, CRISP*, December 6.

Poullet, Yves. 1989. *The Belgian Telecommunications Case*. Presented at FNRS International Conference on Telecommunications. Brussels. January 20.

RTT. 1985. Current Situation and Development of Telecommunications in Belgium. *Telecommunication Journal*, pp. 52, 191.

———. 1987. *Belgium Telecommunications*. Brussels: RTT.

Schenker, Jennifer. 1990. Judging the PTTs. *Communications Week International*, July 16, p. C13.

Tutt, Nigel. 1989. A Question of Balance. *Communications International*, August, pp. 21–26.

———. 1990. Belgium Belies Status as Netherlands Reforms. *Communications International*, July, pp. 15–19.

U.S. Department of Justice. 1987. The Geodesic Network: 1987 *Report on Competition in the Telephone Industry* (The Huber Report). Washington, D.C.: Government Printing Office. January.

12. Luxembourg

Bode, Leon. 1985. *Les Origines et l'Extension du Téléphone au Grand-Duché de Luxembourg (1884–1920)*. Luxembourg: Administration des Posts et Télécommunications.

ITU. 1990. *Annual Telephone Statistics*. Geneva: ITU.

Schenker, Jennifer. 1990. Judging the PTTs. *Communications Week International*, July 16, pp. C12–C13.

13. Switzerland

Association Suisse d'Usager de Télécommunications (ASUT). 1983. *Asut Bulletin*, No. 28, October, pp. 108–9, 114.

Blankart, Charles D., and Friedrich Schneider. 1984. Schweizer Fernmeldetarife in Internationalen Vergleich. *ASUT Bulletin*, No. 32, December.

Blankart, Charles B., and Günter Knieps. 1985. Die Herausforderungen des Technischen Fortschrittes an das Fernmelderecht. *Neue Zürcher Zeitung*, November 1, p. 37.

Bütikofer, Jean-Fredy. 1987. The Swiss Response to a Changing Telecommunications Environment. Speech given at the Annenberg Washington Forum. Berne, October 29.

Ducommun, Maurice. 1987. SWISSNET-the Swiss ISDN. *Bulletin Technique PTT* Berne: General Directorate of the Swiss PTT.

———, and François Keller. 1980. Telecommunications Today and in the Near Future. *Bulletin Technique PTT*, October.

Hofmann, Max. 1980. The Telephone and Its Significance to Switzerland's First Subscriber, *Bulletin Technique PTT*, No. 10, pp. 390–92.

ITU. 1989. More and More Main Stations in the World Telephone Network. *Telecommunications Journal* 56(7): 764.

Knieps, Günter. 1985a. *Entstaatlichung im Telekommunikationsbereich*. Tübingen: Mohr, pp. 167–81.

———. 1985b. Die Notwendigkeit einer Reform des Telegrafen-und Telefonverkehrsgesetzes. *Neue Zürcher Zeitung*, April 9.

Kobelt, Christian. 1980. 100 years of Telephone Service in Switzerland. *Bulletin Technique PTT*, No. 10, pp. F344–63.

Northern Business Information. 1990. *European Telecom Market*. New York: McGraw Hill.

Piquet, Jacques. 1980. Cooperation of Switzerland's Telecommunications Industry with the PTT. *Bulletin Technique PTT*. October.

Purton, Peter. 1990. More than a Crossroads. *Communications International*, June, pp. 13–18.

Staple, Gregory. 1990. *The Global Telecommunications Traffic Boom*. London: International Institute of Communications.

Swiss PTT. 1983. *Telecommunications in Switzerland*. Swiss Posts, Telephones, and Telegraphs.

Trachsel, Rudolf. 1987. Pending Changes in Telecommunications Policy: The United States, Europe, and Japan. Keynote Speech, Annenberg Washington Forum. Berne. October 29.

Union Bank of Switzerland. 1986. *Telecommunications Industry in Switzerland.* Industry Studies.

Wührmann, Karl. 1989. Swiss PTT's Approach to the European Market Unification. *Bulletin Technique PTT.* Berne: General Directorate of the Swiss PTT.

————. 1990. Switzerland. *Telephony,* January 22, p. 56.

14. Austria

Bauer, Johannes M. 1986. Telekommunikation in Österreich: Innovationspolitik in einem dynamischen Infrastrukturbereich. In *Stahl und Eisen Bericht: Industrie und staatliche Politik in Östereich,* ed. M. Scherb and I. Morawetz. Vienna: Verlag für Gesellschaftskritik.

————, and Michael Latzer. 1987. Ökonomische Analyse des Österreichischen Telekommunikationsektors. In *Technikbewertung neuer Telekommunikationsdienste.* Vienna: Österreichische Akademie de Wissenschaften.

————, and Michael Latzer. 1988. Telecommunications in Austria: Past Developments and Prospects for Change. In *European Telecommunications Organizations,* ed. James Foreman-Peck and Jürgen Müller. 1988. Baden-Baden: Nomos, pp. 53–82.

Bruckner, Georg. 1982. *Background Report: Austria.* Committee for Information, Computer Communications Policy, Special Session on International Implications of Changing Market Structures in Telecommunications Services. Paris: OECD.

Communications Week International (CWI). 1990. Austria Modernizing Telecoms. May 21, p. 4.

Eward, Ronald. 1984. *The Competition for Markets in International Telecommunications.* Dedham, MA: Artech.

Holcombe, A. N. 1911. *Public Ownership of Telephone on the Continent of Europe.* Boston: Houghton Mifflin.

ITU. 1990. *Annual Telephone Statistics.* Geneva: ITU.

Montgomery, Page, Lee Selwyn, and Paul Keller. 1990. The Telecommunications Infrastructure in Perspective. Boston: Economics & Technology, Inc., March.

PTV. 1984. *Geschäftsbericht 1984.* Vienna: PTV.

Purton, Peter. 1990. More Than a Crossroads. *Communications International,* June, pp. 13–19.

Sindelka, Josef. 1988. Austria. *Telephony,* February 22, p. 46.

————. 1990. Austria. *Telephony,* January 22, p. 50.

Smith, Gordon. 1984. Can Austria Meet the Challenge of the Electronics Industry? *Focus on Europe,* June 25, pp. 12, 14.

Transnational Data and Communications Report (TDR). 1988. European Consumers Voice Telephone Goals. October, p. 9.

15. Sweden

Boan, Kelley. 1990. The Future of Co-Location in Sweden: An "Unoffical" View. Presented at Central Office Interconnection Conference, Washington DC.

Brown, David. 1985. Televerket's Monopoly Remains Impregnable. *Financial Times,* 14 (January).

Connections. 1984. Corporate Report. Ericsson. December 3.

Dabbs, P., J. J. E. Swaffield, C. M. Aust, and I. Sarwar. 1982. Going Dutch! *British Telecom Journal*, Spring.

Evagora, Andreas. 1990. Privatization Proposed. *Communications Week International*, October 1, p. 10.

Gilhooly, Denis. 1990. Swedes Opening Resale Market. *Communications Week International*, June 4, p. 1.

Gleiss, Norman. 1983. Connection of Privately Owned Equipment. *Tele*, XXXVI(21). English edition.

Gustafsson, Karl Erik. 1987. Televisioner—en studie i branschutveckling. Kristianstad: Raben & Sjogren.

Heimburger, Hans. 1931. *The State Telephone System 1881–1902*. Gothenburg.

Holcombe, A. N. 1911. *Public Ownership of Telephones on the Continent of Europe*. Boston: Houghton Mifflin.

ITU. 1990a. *Annual Telephone Statistics*. Geneva: International Telecommunications Union.

———. 1990b. Swedish Telecom Introduces Information and Entertainment Service. *Telecommunications Journal* 57(4): 258.

Krzywicki, John. 1990. Japan and Sweden: Comparative Regulatory Frameworks. Cambridge Strategic Management Group. Presented at the Telecommunications Reports Price Caps Pre-Conference Seminar. July 13.

Ministry of Transport and Communications. 1987. Telecom in Change. Stockholm. June.

Mitchell, Bridger M. 1983. The Cost of Telephone Service: An International Comparison of Rates in Major Countries. *Telecommunications Policy*. March.

OECD. 1985. Report to the Committee for Information, Computer and Communications Policy. Special Session on Telecommunications Policy. Paris.

———. 1987. *The Swedish Telecom Market*. Report No. 1437. Unpublished paper. Paris. May.

———. 1989. *Telecommunication Network-Based Services: Policy Implications*. Paris.

———. 1990. Committee for Information, Computer and Communications Policy. *Performance Indicators for Public Telecommunications Operators*. DSTI/ICCP/TISP/89.10. February. Paris: OECD.

O'Dwyer, Gerauerd. 1990a. Nordic Free Market Looms. *Communications International*, April, pp. 5–6.

———. 1990b. Televerket to Face Appeal. *Communications International*, June, pp. 6–7.

Qvortrup, Lars. 1989. The Nordic Telecottages. *Telecommunications Policy*, March, pp. 59–68.

Satellite Communications. 1988. Comvik Receives Permission to Transmit to North America. December, p. 8.

Siemens. 1985. *Study on National Tariffs Worldwide*.

Swedish Telecommunications Authority. 1987. *Facts About Televerket: 1987*. Farsta: Televerket Information Unit.

Telephony. 1984. A Commitment to Quality. October 7, p. 7.

———. 1987. Ericsson Divests Office Equipment Firm. October 26, p. 26.

Televerket. 1983. *Organization and Operation of the Swedish Telecommunications Administration*. Stockholm: Televerket.

———. 1984. *Annual Report*. Stockholm.

———. 1989. Who Represents Europe? Paper presented at Assessment 1989. Luxembourg. May 11.

Thorngren, Bertil. 1990. The Swedish Road to Liberalization. *Telecommunications Policy*, April, pp. 94–98.

Whitehouse, Bob. 1989. The Swedes Try Out Liberalization. *Communication International*, November (supplement): pp. 2–7.

16. Finland

Association of Telephone Companies in Finland. 1986. *Facts About Telephony in Finland, 1986*. Helsinki: ATCF.

AT&T. 1975. *Calling the World*. New York: AT&T Long Lines.

Bruce, Robert R., Jeffrey P. Cunard, and Mark D. Director. 1986. From Telecommunications to Electronic Services. *Telecommunications Policy* 10(1).

Communications Systems Worldwide. 1987. Firms Decide Soon on Open Networks. September.

The Economist. 1985. Privatization: Everybody's Doing It Differently, December 21, pp. 71–86.

Evagora, Andreas. 1990. Finland Serving FDDI. *Communications Week International*, July 16, p. 4.

Finland PTT. 1983. *Postal Service Today*. Helsinki: PTT.

———. 1985. *Telecommunications*. Helsinki: PTT.

ITU. 1990. *Annual Telephone Statistics*. Geneva: ITU.

Karvonen, Mati. 1984. Ah, Wilderness . . . Telephones! *Telephony*, May 28, pp. 52–63.

Myllo, Heikki. 1984. Telecom Reform Legislation Nears Completion. *Telephony*, June 25, pp. 58–63.

Nokia. 1989. *Nokia Annual Report*. pp. 3–19.

Northern Business Information. 1990. New York, McGraw-Hill, p. 79.

O'Dwyer, Gerard. 1989a. PTT Rival. *Communications International*, December, pp. 8–11.

———. 1989b. Finnish Ministers Back Nokia. *Communications International*, November, p. 8.

OECD. 1982. Committee for Information, Computer and Communications Policy. *Special Session on the International Implications of Changing Market Structures in Telecommunications Services*. Paris: OECD. December 13–15.

———. 1990. Committee for Information, Computer and Communications Policy. *Performance Indicators for Public Telecommunications Operators*. DSTI/ICCP/TISP/89.10. February. Paris: OECD.

Qvortrup, Lars. 1989. The Nordic Telecottages. *Telecommunications Policy*, March, pp. 59–68.

Tanhuanpää, Arno. 1990. Finland. *Telephony*, January 22, p. 50.

Telephony. 1990. News Bytes. July 30, p. 25.

Whitehouse, Bob. 1989a. "IT in the ITU" Says Doctor Tarjanne. *Communications International*, October, pp. 20–23.

———. 1989b. Finland Pushes Forward. *Communications International*, November, pp. 21–22.

———. 1989c. PTT Rival. *Communications International*, November, p. 21.

Williamson, John. 1986. The Finnish Telecom Industry: As Unusual as the County Itself. *Telephony*, January 27, pp. 50–54.

17. Norway

Foreman-Peck, James, and Dorothy Manning. 1988. Telecommunications in Norway. In *European Telecommunications Organisations,* ed. James Foreman-Peck and Jürgen Müller. Baden-Baden: Nomos.

Green, Jeremy. 1989. Norway's Middle Path. *Communications International,* November (supplement), pp. 9–18.

Holcombe, A. N. 1911. *Public Ownership of Telephone on the Continent of Europe.* Boston: Houghton Mifflin.

ITU. 1990. *Annual Telephone Statistics.* Geneva: ITU.

Norwegian Telecommunications Administration (NTA). 1988. *Annual Report 1987.* Oslo.

Nyheim, Jan Henrik. 1984. Norwegian Broadcasting and Telecommunications. *The Norseman* 5(November): 39–41.

———. 1987. Norway: Regulation—Who Needs It? *Intermedia* 15(4–5): 61–62.

18. Denmark

Barnes, Hillary. 1987. Low-Cost Calls. *Financial Times,* October 19, p. 29.

Feldman, Mark B., and David R. Garcia. 1982. National Regulation of Transborder Data Flows. *North Carolina Journal of International Law and Commercial Regulation* 7(1): 1–25.

Green, Jeremy. 1989. The Unconventional Ways of Danish Comms. *Communications International,* November supplement, pp. 29–32.

NKT. 1987. *NKT at Telecom 87,* October.

OECD. 1982. Committee for Information, Computer and Communications Policy. Background Report: Denmark. Unpublished report for Special Session on the International Implications on Changing Market Structures in Telecommunications. Paris.

Olsen, O. Jess. 1988. Deregulation and Reorganization—the Case of Danish Telecommunications. Memo 4. Copenhagen: Institute of Economics, University of Copenhagen.

Pedersen, Mogens Kuhn. 1987. The State and Telecoms Policy: Convenient or Contrived? Unpublished paper.

———. 1988. The Danish Telecommunications Equipment Industry. Paper presented at European Association for Research in Industrial Economics, Rotterdam. August.

P&T Directorate General. 1988. Liberalization of the Rules Governing Text and Data Transmissions on the Danish Telecommunications Network. June 21.

Qvotrup, Lars. 1984. Cable Television: Public Infrastructure or Private Business, Cable Politics in Denmark. *Le Bulletin de l'Idate: Le Prix des Nouveaux Medias* 17(October): 173–79.

TeleDenmark. 1987. Strongest Growth Is in International Telecom Traffic.

Transnational Data and Communications Report. (TDR) 1989. Europe Achieving Telecom Reforms. October, pp. 6–8.

Williamson, John. 1990. Danes Buy Back Local Telcos. *Telephony,* April 2, p. 16.

19. Iceland

Eurodata Foundation Yearbook. 1987. London: Eurodata Foundation.
ITU. 1990. *Annual Telephone Statistics*. Geneva: ITU.
OECD. Committee for Information, Computer and Communications Policy. 1990. *Performance Indicators for Public Telecommunications Operators*. February, DSTI/ICCP/TISP/89.10. Paris: OECD.
Post and Telecommunications Administration. 1986. *Telecommunications in Iceland*.
Tomasson, Olafur. 1990. Iceland. *Telephony*, January 22, p. 54.

20. Ireland

Central Statistics Office. 1979. *Statistical Abstract of Ireland*. Vol. 43.
Department of Industry and Commerce of Ireland. 1944. *Irish Trade Journal and Statistical Bulletin*. Vol. 19
————. 1969. *Irish Trade Journal and Statistical Bulletin*. Vol. 44.
Dillon, Liam. 1987. Ireland Boosts Its Operational Efficiency. *Telephony*, December 22.
Ergas, Henry, and Jun Okavana. 1984. *Changing Market Structures in Telecommunication*. Paris: OECD.
Evagora, Andreas. 1990a. Irish Suppliers Charge Favoritism. *Communications Week International*, May 21, p. 12.
————. 1990b. Terminal Equipment: Opening the Door. *CWI*, September 3.
Garnett, Nick. 1987. Substantial Progress. *Financial Times*, October 19.
ITU. 1990. *Annual Telephone Statistics*. Geneva: ITU.
Keenan, Brennan. 1985. Growing-up Pains for State Infant. *Financial Times*, January 14, p. 7.
Litton, A. J. 1961. *The Growth and Development of the Irish Telephone System*. Dublin: Institute of Electrical Engineers.
NTIA. 1985. *Telecommunications Policies in Ten Countries: Prospects for Future Competitive Access*. Washington, D.C.: U.S. Government Printing Office. March.
Raggett, R. J. 1984. The Fall and Rise of Irish Telecommunications. *Telephony*, February, p. 31.
Schenker, Jennifer. 1990. Judging the PTT's. *Communications Week International*, July 16, pp. C1–16.
Statistical Abstract of Ireland. 1979. Central Statistics Office. Vol. 43.
Telecom Eireann. 1987. *Step by Step to the Digital Exchange*.
Telephony. 1985. Irish Telecom Chief Quits. June 24, pp. 13, 83.
————. 1987. Northern Ireland May Get FO Ring. February 23, p. 26.
Transnational Data and Communications Report. *(TDR)* 1988. European Consumers Voice Telephone Goals. October.
————. 1989. Europe Achieving Telecom Reforms. October, pp. 6–8.

21. Italy

Antonelli, Cristiano. 1988. The Emergence of the Network Firm. In *New Information Technology and Industrial Change: The Italian Case*, ed. Cristiano Antonelli. Dordrecht: Kluwer.

Benedetti, Marino. 1983. Telecommunications Services: Policy in Europe. Paper presented at the European Institute of Public Administration. Maastricht/Valkerburt.

Benzoni, Paolo. 1990. Italy. *Telephony*, January 22, p. 56.

Bonafield, Christine. 1988. AT&T May Redefine Partnership with Olivetti. *Communications Week*, May 30, p. 6.

Colby, Laura, and Richard Hudson. 1989. AT&T Learns Right Choices for Europe. *The Wall Street Journal*, February 2, p. 27.

Communications Week International (CWI). 1990. Italians Consort. June 4, p. 3.

Dallmeyer, Martin. 1977. *Quellen zur Geschichte des Europäischen Postwesens 1501–1806*. Kallmünz: Verlag Michael Lassleben.

Del Terra, Laura. 1989. SIP's Four Year Plan. *Communications International*, September, p. 53.

The Economist. 1989. Meeeow. July 22, pp. 62–63.

Friedman, Alan. 1987. The War of Words that Surrounds Telit. *Financial Times*, October 19.

Graziosi, Guiliano. 1988. Telecommunications in Italy. *Telecommunications Policy*, December, pp. 303–10.

Green, Jeremy. 1989. Italy in the Fast Lane. *Communications International*, December, pp. 15–17.

Greenhouse, Steven. 1989. AT&T Deal with Italtel Advances. *The New York Times*, February 10, p. D1.

Guyon, Janet, and Laura Colloy. 1988. Firm Declines to Boost Stake in Olivetti. *The Wall Street Journal*, April 12, p. 4.

Hayes, Dawn. 1988. Italian Leaders at Odds Over AT&T-Italtel Deal. *Communications Week International*, August 22, p. 21.

Holcombe, A. N. 1911. *Public Ownership of Telephones on the Continent of Europe*. Boston: Houghton Mifflin.

Italtel. 1989. *Guatemala Telecommunications Development Project, Zambia Rural Radiotelephony Project, Zimbabwe 140 Mbit/s Fiber Optic Link*. Milano: Italtel Societá Italiana Telecomunicazioni.

ITU. 1989. Supply of Modems: Liberalization in Italy. *Telecommunications Journal* 56(8): 533.

———. 1990. *Annual Telephone Statistics*. Geneva: ITU.

La Repubblica, Il Grande Salto della SIP. 1987. February 10.

Lynch, Karen. 1990. Italy Struggles with 1992. *Communications Week International*, May 21, p. 6.

Ministero delle Poste e delle Telecomunicazioni (MPT). 1984. Piano Nazionale delle Telecomunicazioni 1985–1994. Rome: Ministero delle Poste e delle Telecomunicazioni.

OECD. 1990. Committee for Information, Computer and Communications Policy. *Performance Indicators for Public Telecommunications Operators*. February, DSTI/ICCP/TISP/89.10. Paris: OECD.

Pozzi, Giovanni. 1987. The Evolution of the Italian Telecommunications System. Milan: Reseau.

Rosenbaum, Andrew. 1988. Country by Country, The Old Rules Change. *Communications Week International*, September 12, p. C4.

Rossant, John. 1988. Does AT&T Have a Real Shot at This Juicy Contract? *Business Week*, November 21, p. 59.

Roussel, Anne-Marie. 1988. Italy Weighs Telecom Restructuring. *Communications Week International*, November 22, p. 15.

————. 1990. Italians, French Pushing Videotex. *Communications Week International*, March 12, p. 17.

Sabel, Charles F. 1982. *Work and Politics: The Division of Labor in Industry.* New York: Cambridge University Press.

Schenker, Jennifer. 1990. Judging the PTTs. *Communications Week International*, July 16, pp. C1–16.

Smau. 1990. *Information Technology.* Milan: L'osservatorio Smau, pp. 74–111.

Staple, Gregory. 1990. *The Global Telecommunications Traffic Boom.* London: IIC.

STET. 1985. *Annual Report.*

Symonds, Williams. 1987. A Failed Merger Blows Italy's Shot at the Big Time. *Business Week*, November 23, p. 52.

Telephony. 1983. After Ten Years of Neglect, Italian Telecommunications Comes of Age. September 25–26, pp. 32–37.

Wilson, Carol. 1987. BellSouth lands Italian net contract. *Telephony*, December 7.

22. Spain

Bradsher, Keith. 1990. Allure of Spain's Phone Company. *The New York Times*, March, p. D12.

Burns, Tom. 1985. ITT's Redundancy Plans Unacceptable, Says Spain. *Financial Times*, October 1, p. 2.

de Moragas, Miguel, Rosario de Mateo, and Emilio Prado. 1987. Spain. *Electronic Mass Media and Politics in Western Europe*, ed. Hans J. Kleinsteuber, Denis McQuail, and Karen Siune. Frankfurt: Campus Verlag, pp. 251–72.

The Economist. 1985. Hello World, Madrid Calling. May 25.

————. 1990. Please Try Again. May 12, pp. 71–72.

Eurodata Foundation Yearbook. 1986. London: Eurodata Foundation.

Financial Times. 1989. Nynex Sees Gibraltar As Its Telecoms Showcase. October 5.

ITU. 1990. *Annual Telephone Statistics.* Geneva: ITU.

Lopez-Escobar, Esteban. 1985. Spain Telecom's Monopoly. *Intermedia*, July/September, pp. 3–4.

Manning, Dorothy, Diego Bader von Jagow, James Foreman-Peck, and Jürgen Müller. 1988. In *European Telecommunications Organisations*, ed. James Foreman-Peck and Jürgen Müller. Baden-Baden: Nomos.

MarTech Strategies, Inc. 1983. *Telecommunication Policies in Ten Countries: Prospects for Future Competitive Access.* Washington, D.C.: Government Printing Office.

Martinez, Miguel. 1990. A Digital Missing Link. *Communications International*, February, pp. 18–20.

Morgan, Jeremy, and Charles Mason. 1990. Argentina's Entel Deal Postponed as Banks Struggle to Meet Terms. *Telephony*, August 20, p. 8.

Purton, Peter. 1989. What the EC Is Trying to Achieve. *Communications International*, July, pp. 28–29.

————. 1990. Nineties May Be Fiesta for Spanish Telecoms. *Communications International*, February, pp. 15–17.

Ryser, Jefferey. 1988. Getting South America's #!*% Phones to Work. *Business Week*, April 18.

Taylor, Robert. 1990. Ericsson Offshoot Wins Spanish Telecoms Order. *Financial Times*, July 6.

Telefónica. 1990. *1989 Annual Report* Madrid: Telefónica.

Warden, Becky. 1990. Playing Safe. *Communications International*, May, p. 8.

White, David. 1986. Clarification of Game Plan After EEC Entry. *Financial Times*, January 6.

Whitehouse, Bob. 1990. Telefónica's Waiting List. *Communications International*, March, pp. 13–16.

Williamson, John. 1987. AT&T/Philips Inks Spanish Contract. *Telephony*, October.

Woolacott, Emma. 1990. Telefónica in Cartel Debate. *Communications International*, June.

23. Portugal

Baptista, Jose Viana. 1988. Portugal. *Telephony*, February 22.

de la Cal, Martha. 1990. Portugal: A Radical Transformation of the Telecommunications Sector. *1992 Single Market Communications Review* 1(4): 12–17.

Eurodata Foundation Yearbook. 1983. London: Eurodata Foundation.

EUSIDIC. 1990. *1990 PDN Study*.

ITT. 1983. ITT in Portugal: The First 50 Years. February, No. 2.

ITU. 1990. *Annual Telephone Statistics*. Geneva: ITU.

Purton, Peter. 1987. Last European Country Chooses Cellular Standard. *Telephony*, December.

Roussel, Anne-Marie. 1990. Portugal to Privatize. *Communications Week International*, November 12.

Smith, Diana. 1986. Portugal Ends Battle Over Telephones. *Financial Times*, August 19.

Transnational Data and Communications Report (TDR). 1988. European Consumers Voice Telephone Goals. pp. 6–8. October.

———. 1989. Europe Achieving Telecom Reforms. October, pp. 6–8.

Warden, Becky. 1990a. Portugal Sets Out Reforms. *Communications International*, March, p. 7.

———. 1990b. Fresh Face for Privatisation. *Communications International*, July, p. 10.

24. Israel

Bainerman, Joel. 1988. Israeli Upstarts Target Niches. *Communications Week International*, November 7, p. 24.

———. 1989. The Pragmatic Approach. *Communications Systems Worldwide*, September, p. 50.

Eres, Beth. 1989. *Status and Trends in the use of Computers and Telecommunications in Israel*. Interdisciplinary Center for Technological Analysis and Forecasting, TelAviv University.

Hai, Shaul. 1988. Israel. *Telephony*, January 22, p. 62.

Israel Statutes. 1982. *1060: The Telecommunication Law*. Jerusalem. August 22.

ITU. 1990. *Annual Telephone Statistics*. Geneva: ITU.

Louisson, Simon. 1987. After Three Years Success Still on Hold for Bezeq. *Jerusalem Post*.

TRC. 1990. Market Report. Bezeq-Israel. *World Telecom Daily*. February 26, pp. 15–19.

25. Turkey

Altay, Sefik. 1987. *The Development of Telecommunications in Turkey.* October 30.
Anik, Gengiz. 1990. General Directorate of PTT, personal communication. August 29.
AT&T. 1975. *Calling the World.* New York: AT&T Long Lines.
General Directorate of the PTT. 1990. *Brief Report on Telecommunications in Turkey.* August.
ITU. 1990. *Annual Telephone Statistics.* Geneva: ITU.
OECD. 1982. Committee for Information, Computer and Communications Policy. *Special Session on the International Implications of Changing Market Structures in Telecommunications Services.* Paris: OECD. December 13–15.
Raggett, R. J. 1986. Emir Outlines an Ambitious Program for the Turkish PTT. *Telephony,* July 28, p. 42.
TRC. 1990. Market Report: Turkey. *World Telecom Daily,* April 30, pp. 6–7.
Williamson, John. 1988. Turkey Heads for the Next Decade with a 21st Century Telecom System. *Telephony,* December 26, pp. 21, 24–25.

26. Greece

Efstathiou, James. 1990. Greece Going Digital. *Communications Week International,* September 17.
Eurodata Foundation Yearbook. 1984. London: Eurodata Foundation.
ITU. 1990. *Annual Telephone Statistics.* Geneva: ITV.
Kotsonis, Stefan. 1990. "Greek Telecoms Shake-up" *Communications International* December, pp. 14, 16.
OECD. 1990. Committee for Information, Computer and Communications Policy. *Performance Indicators for Public Telecommunications Operators.* DSTI/ICCP/TISP/89.10. February. Paris: OECD.
OTE. 1985. *Annual Report 1984.* Athens.
———. 1985. *Telecommunications Statistics in Greece '84.* Athens.
Schenker, Jennifer. 1990. Judging the PTTs. *Communications Week International,* June 12, pp. C1–16.

27. Telecommunications in Eastern Europe

Antono, Miroslav, and B. Kubin. 1990. *Czechoslovakia.* Bucharest: Federal Ministry of Posts and Telecommunications.
Avramesou, Aristita, and Sergiu Celac, eds. 1980. *Romania: An Encyclopaedic Survey.* Bucharest: Editura Sciintifica si Enciclopedica, pp. 158–60.
Budapress. 1984. Telephone Network Expansion. XXIII(14). Budapest: Hungarian News Agency. April 4, p. 8.
———. 1988. 420,000 New Telephones. XXVII(32). Budapest: Hungarian News Agency. August 12, pp. 5–6.
Business Eastern Europe. 1986. December 8, p. 392.
———. 1987. October 26, p. 344.
Byrnes, Robert F., ed. 1957. *East Central Europe Under the Communists: Yugoslavia.* New York: Frederick A. Praeger, pp. 386–87.
Campbell, Robert W. 1988. *The Soviet Telecommunications System.* Indianapolis: Hudson Institute.

———. 1990. The Soviet Telecom Challenge. *Eastern Europe and Soviet Telecom Report* 1(6).

Communications International. 1989. December, p. 12.

Datapro. 1990. *Datapro Reports on International Telecommunications.* New York: McGraw-Hill.

Dellin, L. A. D., ed. 1957. *East Central Europe Under the Communists: Bulgaria.* New York: Fredrick A. Praeger, pp. 369, 383–84.

Dixon, Hugo. 1988a. UK Group in Soviet Pay Phone Venture. *Financial Times,* July 5, p. 3.

———. 1988b. UK Digital Telecoms Switch for Moscow. *Financial Times,* October 18, p. 6.

———. 1990. The Paranoia Eases. *Financial Times,* April 19.

Eastern European and Soviet Telecom Report (EESTR). 1990a. Hungarian Telecom: Catching Up With Europe, 1(3).

———. 1990b. Polish Telecom: New Directions, 1(4).

The Economist. 1990. Sorry, Reformer, the Line Is Dead. July 21, p. 2.

Fidler, Stephen. 1990. Western Companies Hold Lifeline for Eastern Europe. *Financial Times,* April 17, p. 4.

Financial Times. 1987. October 19, p. XXIV.

Frankl, Judy. 1989. The Telecoms Glasnost. *Communications International,* July, pp. 39–41.

Gilhooly, Denis. 1989. Hungary Heralds Telecoms Reform. *Communications Week International,* October 30, p. 1.

Goodhart, David. 1989. Siemens to Modernize Soviet Telephones. *Financial Times,* August 3, p. 3.

Gulyaev, Yuri V. 1990. Directions in Telecommunications Policy in the USSR. Paper presented to the International Telecommunications Society. Venice, Italy, March.

Hayes, Dawn. 1990. Cellular Network Proposed for Baltic. *Communications Week International,* June 18, p. 18.

Kelly, Tim. 1990. *Telecommunications and Eastern European Economies.* Paris: OECD.

Lakicevic, Ognjen, ed. 1970. *A Handbook of Yugoslavia.* Belgrade: Beogradski Graficki Zavod.

Lewis, Patrick. 1976. Communications Output in the USSR: A Study of The Soviet Telephone Systems. *Soviet Studies,* July, pp. 406–17.

Major, Iva. 1980. *The Progress of the Hungarian Telephone.* Hungarian Academy of Sciences: Institute of Economics Series, 17.

Nulty, Timothy. 1990. *Considerations in Telecom Investment in Eastern Europe.* Washington, D.C.: World Bank.

Pearce, Alan. 1990. A Capital Question. *Network World,* April 30.

Poland: A Handbook. 1974. Warsaw: Interpress, pp. 276–77.

Popescu, Virgil. 1990. *Romania.* Bucharest: Ministry of Communications.

Pronay, G. 1990. Freedom of Speech. *IEEE Review,* July/August.

Purton, Peter. 1990. Western Firms Plan Baltic Service. *Telephony,* June 11, pp. 16, 20.

Rocks, David. 1990. Hungary Grants Second Cellular Net. *Communications Week International,* June 4, p. 7.

Satellite Communications. 1990. July, p. 9.

Schenker, Jennifer. 1990. Upgrade in Czechoslovakia. *Communications Week International,* July 2.

Selin, Ivan. 1986. Communications and Computers in the Soviet Union. *Signal*, December, pp. 91–95.

Skendi, Stavro. ed. 1956. *East Central Europe Under the Communists: Albania*. New York: Frederick A. Praeger.

U.S. Department of State, Advisory Committee on International Communications and Information Policy. 1990. *Eastern Europe: Please Stand By*. Washington, D.C.: U.S. Department of State.

Woollacott, Emma. 1990. Relaxation on a Sliding Scale. *Communications International*, July, pp. 32–33.

28. The International Organizations of Telecommunications

Aronson, Jonathan, and Peter Cowhey. 1988. *When Countries Talk*. Cambridge, MA: Ballinger.

Butler, Richard. 1989. ITU Plenipotentiary Conference: Closing Address. June 30.

Codacovi, Lawrence. 1989. WATTC: Impact on Services. *Transnational Data and Communications Report*, June–July, pp. 18–20.

Codding, George A., Jr. 1984. Public Access to International Organizations: the ITU. *Intermedia* 12(6).

———. 1990. The Nice ITU Plenipotentiary Conference. *Telecom Policy*, April, pp. 139–50.

———, and Anthony M. Rutkowski. 1982. *The International Telecommunication Union in a Changing World*. Dedham, MA: Artech

Cowhey, Peter S., and Jonathan B. Aronson. 1985. The Great Satellite Shoot-Out. *Regulation*, May–June, pp. 27–35.

Dougan, Diana Lady. 1987. *The High Stakes Game of International Standards Setting*. Washington D.C.: U.S. Department of State.

Drake, William. 1988. WATTC-88: Restructuring the International Telecommunication Regulations. *Telecommunications Policy*, September, pp. 217–23.

———. 1989. The CCITT: Time for Reform? in *Reforming the Global Network*. London: International Institute of Communications. pp. 28–43.

Gibbons, Roger. 1989a. Surveying Europe's Standardization Scene. *Communications International*, November, pp. 25–31.

———. 1989b. European Standards. *Communications International*, December, pp. 19–22.

Gilhooly, Denis. 1989. Finland's Tarjanne Elected ITU Head. *Communications Week International*, June 26, p. 41.

———. 1990. CEPT Faces Up to Its Changing Role. *Communications Week International*, March 12, p. 13.

Le Boucher, Eric. 1984. Europe des Télécommunications S'Organise. *Le Monde*, January 21.

Lynch, Karen. 1990. U.S. Turnaround. *Communications Week International*, October 29, p. 4.

Northern Telecom. 1980. *Nature of the Telecommunications Industry Throughout the World*. Submission to the Canadian Restrictive Trade Practices Commission. May.

Official Journal L360. 1982. Congressional Record, December 21, p. 36.

Quander, Peter. 1982. Internationale Zusammenarbeit? In *Telekommunikation in der Bundesrepublik Deutschland*, ed. Dietrich Elias. Heidelberg: R.V. Decker's Verlag, G. Schenck, pp. 375–90.

Rutkowski, Anthony M. 1982. The U.S.A. and the ITU: Many Attitudes, Few Policies. *Intermedia* 10(4–5).

Satelllite News. 1990. Execs Spar at Philips Satellite IX Conference. March 19.

Schenker, Jennifer. 1989. CEPT Revamping Rates. *Communications Week International,* February 6, p. 1.

Scherer, Joachim. 1985. *Telekommunikationsrecht und Telekommunikationspolitik.* Baden-Baden: Nomos.

Schnurr, L. E. 1988. The Single European Act: Towards an Open Market in 1992. Essex: Essex Institute of Higher Education.

Warden, Becky. 1990. The Curtain Rises on a New Satellite Generation. *Communications International,* July, p. 5.

Whitehouse, Bob. 1989. "IT in the ITU" Says Dr. Tarjanne. *Communications International,* October, pp. 20–23.

———. 1990. CEPT Accedes Under Siege. *Communications International,* April, p. 6.

29. Brussels Takes On the Traditional System

Besen, Stanley M. 1990. The European Telecommunications Standards Institute. *Telecommunications Policy.* December.

Commission of the European Communities (CEC). 1982. *Euronet-DIANE: Towards a Common Information Market.*

———. 1986. *EC Competition in Telecommunications.* Unpublished document IV/B/1. March 4.

———. 1987. *Green Paper on the Development of the Common Market for Telecommunication Services and Equipment.* COM (87) 290 Final. Brussels. June 30.

———. 1988. Directive 88/301. *Official Journal of the European Communities.* L.131.

European Space Agency. 1984. *European Space Agency, 20 Years of European Cooperation in Space.* Paris: ESA.

Gilhooly, Denis, and Malcolm Laws. 1990. New Course Set for RACE. *Communications Week International,* July 2, p. 1.

Green, Jeremy. 1989. Who Rules on Radio. *Communications International,* November, p. 10.

ITU. 1990. A European Market for Telecommunications. *ITU Telecommunications Journal,* 57(6): 294.

Lalor, Eamon. 1987. Action for Telecommunications Development. *Telecommunications Policy,* June, pp. 115–20.

Roussel, Anne-Marie. 1990. Satcoms Policy Up in the Air. *Communications Week International,* June 4.

Schenker, Jennifer. 1989. Services Clash Could Derail Deregulation. *Communications Week International,* May 1, p. 6.

———. 1990. Putting off 1992. *Communications Week International,* July 2, p.1.

Schulte-Braucks, Reinhard. 1986. European Telecommunications Law in the Light of the British Telecom Judgment. *Common Market Law Review.* vol. 23.

Télédiffusion de France. 1985. Europe: Vers une Europe de la (Haute) Technologie. *Actualité des Techniques de Communication dans le Monde.* June.

Transnational Data and Communications Report (TDR). 1988. Europe Adopts New Standards Approach. August-September, p. 6.

———. 1989. Euro-Parliament Favors Network Monopoly. February, p. 8.

van Rosenthal, C. Jansen. 1983. *The Implications of Telecommunications for a European Community Information Market Policy*. Commission of the European Communities, Directorate General for Telecommunications and Information Industries and Innovation. Luxembourg.

von Martin, Klaus and Walter S. Kirchen. 1981. Euronet: Growth of A Direct-Access Information Network. *ESTA Bulletin*. January.

Woollacott, Emma. 1990. Leased Cost Solution. *Communications International*, April, p. 5.

30. Telecommunications Policy as Industrial Policy

Aronson, Jonathan David, and Peter F. Cowhey. 1987. *When Countries Talk*. Cambridge, MA: Ballinger.

Cane, Alan. 1985. Producers Pin Hopes on New Alliances. *Financial Times*, June 24, p. 3.

Dang-Nguyen, Godefroy. 1986. A European Telecommunications Policy—Which Instruments for Which Prospects? ENST-Bretagne. August.

The Economist. 1985. Privatization: Everybody's Doing It Differently. December 21.

Ellul, Jacques. 1964. *The Technological Society*. New York: Knopf.

Ergas, Henry. 1985. Exploding the Myths About What's Wrong. *Financial Times*, June 26.

Etheridge, James, 1983. Center of Controversy. *Datamation* 240(June): 31–34.

de Jonquieres, Guy. 1990. Shadows Over the Sunrise Sector. *Financial Times*, July 25, p. 12.

Knieps, Günter, Jürgen Müller, and Carl Christian von Weizsäcker. 1981. *Die Rolle des Wettbewerbs im Fernmeldebereich*. Baden-Baden: Nomos, 1984.

Levin, R. C. 1982. The Semi-conductor Industry. In *Government and Technical Progress: A Cross Industry Analysis*, ed. R. R. Nelson. New York: Paramount Press.

Malerba, Franco. 1985. *The Semi-conductor Business*. Madison: University of Wisconsin Press.

Müller, Jürgen. The Benefits of Completing the Internal Market for Telecommunications Equipment in the Community. Research on the Cost of Non-Europe. Fontainbleau: INSEAD. vol. 1.

OECD. 1985. Committee for Information, Computer and Communications Policy. *Venture Capital in Information Technology*. Paris: OECD.

Palmer, Michael, and Jeremy Tunstall. 1990. *Liberating Communications: Policymaking in France and Britian*, Oxford: Basil Blackwell.

Wiegner, Kathleen. 1985. Europe Fights Back. *Forbes*, August 12, p. 82.

Wiles, Peter. 1960. Will Capitalism and Communism Spontaneously Converge? *Foreign Affairs*, February.

31. Transatlantic Trade Friction

Colby, Laura, and Richard Hudson. 1989. AT&T Learns Right Choices for Europe. *Wall Street Journal*, February 2. p. 27.

Davis, Bob. 1988. FCC Orders Phone Companies to Report Yearly Purchases of Foreign Equipment. *Wall Street Journal*, February 26.

Department of Commerce. 1990. *U.S. Telecommunications in a Global Economy.* Washington, D.C.: Government Printing Office.

Frey, Carl. 1984. What is Due the Engineer? *IEEE Spectrum,* June.

Greenhouse, Steven. 1989. AT&T Deal with Italtel Advances. *The New York Times,* February 10, p. D1.

Guyon, Janet and Laura Colloy. 1988. Firm Declines to Boost Stakes in Olivetti. *The Wall Street Journal,* April 12.

Hoffman-Riem, Wolfgang. 1984. Policy Research on Telecommunications in West Germany. *In Policy Research in Telecommunications,* ed. Vincent Mosco. Norwood, NJ: Ablex.

L'Expansion. 1985. Pebereau joue quitte ou double. June 7–20, pp. 67–81.

Northern Telecom. 1980. *Nature of the Telecommunications Industry Throughout the World.* Revised May 1980, Submission to the Canadian Restrictive Trade Practices Commission, p. 74.

Robinson, Kenneth. 1987. The International Competitiveness of Judge Greene's Recent Order. Paper presented at the 1987 USTA Convention, Orlando, Florida. October 13.

Roussel, Anne-Marie. 1990. Report Warns of Foreign Invasion. *Communications Week International,* August 13, p. 7.

Transnational Data and Communications Report (TDR). 1989. Telecom Trade Barriers Alleged by EC and US. May, p. 12.

Tully, Shawn. 1989. Europe Goes on a Telephone Binge. *Fortune,* August 28, p. 102–08.

Whitehouse, Bob. 1990. Euroboom. *Communications International,* January, pp. 47–48.

Woollacott, Emma. 1990. Transatlantic Battle Lines. *Communications International,* p. 22.

32. International Telecommunications Services

Antonelli, Cristiano. 1984. Multinational Firms, International Trade and International Telecommunications. *Information, Economics, and Policy,* 1: 333–43.

Chase, Scott. 1990. An Interview with Comsat's Bruce Crockett. *Satellite News.* May 7, p. 4.

Cowhey, Peter S., and Jonathan B. Aronson. 1985. The Great Satellite Shoot-Out. *Regulation,* May–June, pp. 27–35.

Dickinson, Tim, and Charles Leadbeater. 1990. Brussels to Probe World Telephone Cartel Allegations. *Financial Times,* April.

Dixon, Hugo. 1990a. Phone Companies Overcharge Callers $10 Billion a Year. *Financial Times,* April 3, p. 1.

———. 1990b. Phone Club Days Are Numbered. *Financial Times* (international edition), May 15, p. 7.

Ergas, Henry, and Paul Paterson. 1989. International Telecommunications Accounting Arrangements: An Unsustainable Inheritance. Presented at Colloque Villefranche-Sur-Mer, June 1–3.

Frieden, Robert. 1983. Getting Closer to the Source: New Policies for International Satellite Access. 37 *Fed. Comm. L.J.* 293.

General Accounting Office (GAO). 1983. FCC Needs to Monitor a Changing International Telecommunications Market. March 14, GAO/RCED-865–892.

Horton, R. and J. Donovan. 1987. International Comparisons of Telecommunications Charges. *Telecommunications Policy*. 11(3): 269–90.

International Telecommunications Deregulation Act of 1982. Hearings Before the Sub-committee on Communications of the Committee on Science, Commerce, and Transportation, U.S. Senate, 97th Congress, 2nd session on S.2469. June 14, 15, 17, 1982. Serial No. 96–126. Washington, D.C.: U.S. Government Printing Office.

Kwerel, Evan. 1984. Promoting Piecemeal Competition in International Telecommunications. OPP Working Paper Series. Washington, D.C.: Federal Communications Commission.

Logica Consultancy Ltd. 1989. *The TARIFICA Annual Review*. London: Logica.

Malik, Rex. 1990. A Press Commentator's Guide to the Complexities and Economics of Telephone Call Charging. *Intermedia* 18(3): 4–7.

McDowall, M. E. 1987. International Comparisons of Telephone Charges. OFTEL Working Paper No. 2. London.

Mitchell, B. M. 1983. The Cost of Telephone Service: An International Comparison of Rates in Major Countries. *Telecommunications Policy*. March, pp. 53–63.

OECD. 1990. Committee for Information, Computer and Communications Policy. *Performance Indicators for Public Telecommunications Operators*. February, DSTI/ICCP/TISP/89.10. Paris: OECD.

Roos, Ingevar, and Ivar Loenqvist. 1984. Telephone Rates in Various Countries. *Tele* (English edition), XXXVII(2): 1–37.

Siemens. 1988. Study on National Telephone Tariffs Worldwide: A Detailed Comparison. Munich: Siemens

Stanley, Kenneth. 1988. The Balance of Payments Deficit in International Telecommunications Services. Washington DC: Industry Analysis Division, Federal Communications Commission.

Staple, Gregory. 1990. *The Global Telecommunications Traffic Boom*. London: International Institute of Communications.

Stapley, Barry. 1981. Managing Communications: The Value of Choice. *Telecommunications Policy*, June.

Televerket. 1986. Facts about Televerket. Stockholm. p. 9.

Walter Hinchman Associates, Inc. 1984. The Economics of International Satellite Communications. Unpublished report. May 18.

33. The Economics of ISDN Integration

Baumol, W. J., J. C. Panzar, and R. D. Willig. 1983. *Contestable Markets and the Theory of Industry Structure*. New York: Harcourt Brace Jovanovich.

Besen, S., and L. Johnson. 1986. *Compatibility Standards: Innovation and Competition in the Broadcast Industry*. Santa Monica, CA: RAND Corporation.

David, P. A. 1984. Understanding the Economics of QWERTY, or Is History Necessary? Mimeo. Stanford University.

Digital NCTE Decision. *FCC Docket* No. 81–216.

Farrell, Joseph, and Garth Saloner. 1985. Standardization, Compatibility, and Innovation. *Rand Journal of Economics* 16(1): 70–83.

———. 1986a. Standardization and Variety. *Economics Letters*, January.

———. 1986b. Installed Base and Compatibility: Innovation, Product Preannouncements and Predation. *MIT Working Papers*, No. 411, February.

Hemenway, D. 1975. *Industrywide Voluntary Product Standards.* Cambridge, MA: Ballinger.

Katz, Michael, and Carl Shapiro. 1985. Network Externalities, Competition, and Compatibility. *American Economic Review* 75(3): 424–40.

Lancaster, K. 1975. Socially Optimal Product Differentiation. *American Economic Review* 64: 567–85.

Meyer, J. R., Wilson, R. W., Baughcum, M. A., Burton, E., and Caouette, L. 1980. *The Economics of Competition in the Telecommunications Industry.* Cambridge, MA: Oelgeschlager, Quinn & Hain.

National Telecommunications and Information Administration (NTIA). 1983. Primer on Integrated Services Digital Network (ISDN): Implications for Future Global Communications. NTIA Report No. 1983–138. Washington, DC: U.S. Department of Commerce.

Noam, Eli. 1986. The "New" Local Communications: Office Networks and Private Cable. *Computer Law Journal* 6(2): 247–82.

Rutkowski, Anthony. 1985. *Integrated Services Digital Networks.* Dedham, MA: Artech.

Salop, S. C. 1979. Monopolistic Competition and Outside Goods. *Bell Journal of Economics and Management Science* 10(1): 141–56.

Schiller, Dan. 1984. The Emerging Global Grid: Planning for What? Paper presented to the Final Plenary Session of the 14th IAMCR Conference and General Assembly. Prague, Czechoslovakia. August 27–September 1.

Spence, A. M. 1975. Monopoly, Quality, and Regulation. *Bell Journal of Economics and Management Science,* Autumn.

von Weizsäcker, Carl Christian. 1987. The Economics of Value Added Network Services. Unpublished study. Cologne.

34. The Political Economy of ISDN

Egan, Bruce L. 1990. *Information Superhighways: The Economics of Advanced Public Communications Networks.* Dedham, MA: Artech.

Elton, Martin, ed. 1991. *Integrated Broadband Networks: The Public Policy Issues.* Amsterdam: Elsevier.

European Commission. 1990. A European Market for Telecommunications. *ITU Telecommunications Journal* 57: 294–95.

Frey, Carl. 1984. What is Due the Engineer? *IEEE Spectrum.* June.

Gilhooly, Denis. 1988a. EC Report: ISDN Rollout Is 2 Years Behind. *Communications Week International,* November 21.

———. 1988b. Dismal Report on European ISDN. *Communications Week International,* August.

Green, Jeremy. 1989a. A Deadline for ONP. *Communications International,* December.

———. 1989b. High Noon for ONP. *Communications International,* December.

Marcus, Michael J. 1985. The Regulatory Point of View: ISDN in the United States. *Telephony,* March.

Marks, Herbert E. 1984. ISDN in the United States. Paper delivered at the Twelfth Annual Telecommunications Policy Research Conference. Airlie, Virginia. April.

———. 1986. Comparably Efficient Interconnection: Equal Access Is Better. Unpublished paper presented at EIA Roundtable.

Mueller-Sachse, Karl H. 1984. Noch fehlt di nationale Anstrengung. *Medium*. February.

Noam, Eli. 1986. The "New" Local Communications: Office Networks and Private Cable. *Computer Law Journal* 6(2): 247–82.

———. 1988a. Filing and Review of Open Network Architecture Plans. CC Docket No. 88–2, Phase I. Federal Communications Commission, Washington, D.C.

———. 1988b. Implementing ONA: Federal-State Partnership Needed to Connect Network of Networks. *Communications Week*, May 2.

———. 1989a. Beyond ONA: Designing Modular Network as a Strategy for National Competitiveness. New York: Columbia Institute for Tele-Information Working Paper Series. May.

———. 1989b. Network Pluralism and Regulatory Pluralism. Paula R. Newberg. ed. *New Directions in Telecommunications Policy*. vol. 1. North Carolina: Duke University Press, pp. 66–91.

———. 1989c. ONA: The Need for Partnership. *Hearing before the Subcommittee on Commerce Science and Transportation*. Senate Hearing 100–510. Part 2.

Nora, S. and A. Minc. 1980. *The Computerization of Society. Report to the President of the French Republic*. Cambridge, MA: MIT Press.

Purton, Peter. 1989. What the EC Is Trying to Achieve. *Communications International*, July, pp. 28–29.

Rohlfs, J. 1974. A Theory of Interdependent Demand for a Communications Service. *Bell Journal of Economics and Management Science*, vol. 5.

Rutkowski, Anthony. 1985. *Integrated Services Digital Networks*. Dedham, MA: Artech.

Sapronov, Walt. 1985. Technical and Regulatory Issues Are Challenging ISDN's Progress. *Data Communication*, November.

Schenker, Jennifer. 1990. Europe Sets ONP Timeframe. *Communications Week International*, February 2, p. 3.

Scherer, Joachim. 1985. *Telekommunikationsrecht und Telekommunikationspolitik*. Baden-Baden: Nomos.

Schön, Helmut. 1984. The Deutsche Bundespost on Its Way Towards the ISDN. *Zeitschrift für das Post- und Fernmeldwesen*, 6(27). Joseph Keller Gimbolt & Co. (English language version).

———. 1985. Das ISDN im Investitions-, Industrie- und Fernmeldepolitischen Kontext. In *Intergrierte Telekommunikation*, ed. W. Kaiser Münchner Kreis (No. 11). Berlin: Springer-Verlag.

Ungerer, Herbert. 1989. EC Position and Green Paper Implementation. Paper presented at Conference on Telecommunications, Brussels. January.

U.S. Department of Commerce, NTIS. 1983. *Primer on Integrated Service Digital Network (ISDN): Implications for Future Global Communications*.

Weiss, Ernest O. 1984. ISDN-User and Social Aspects. Paper presented to the World Telecommunications Forum. Geneva, Switzerland.

Wilson, C. 1984. Games of Timing with Incomplete Information. Mimeo. New York University.

35. Value-Added Networks and Services

Beesley, Michael. 1981. *Liberalization of the Use of the British Telecommunications Network*. Report to the Secretary of State. London: Her Majesty's Stationery Office. January.

Blau, John. 1990. Germany Lags in VANs. *Communications Week International*, June 4, p. 10.

Boult, Raymond. 1990. French Review of Services. *Communications International*. April, p. 6.

Gilhooly, Denis, 1990. CEPT Revamps X-25. *Communications Week International*, July 2, p. 1.

Hayes, Dawn. 1989. Swift Upgrades—But Slowly. *Communications Week International*, October 2, p. 3.

Lill, A. 1988. European Public Data Network Service Marginally Improved. Stamford, CT: Gartner Group.

Link Resources. 1984. *Competition in Value Added Networks*. New York: Link.

Purton, Peter. 1989. European Public Data Networks Losing Money. *Telephony*, June 5.

Roussel, Anne-Marie. 1989. Public Data Nets Still Failing Users. *Communications Week International*, September 4.

Schenker, Jennifer. 1990a. Data Networks Disappoint. *Communications Week International*, July 16, p. 1.

———. 1990b. CEPT Rebuts EUSIDIC Study. *Communications Week International*, August 13, p. 16.

Sherrat, William. 1988. Important New Initiatives for European Packet Data Networks. *Telematics International*.

Tully, Shawn, 1989. Europe Goes on a Telephone Binge. *Fortune*, August 28, pp. 102–08.

von Weizsäcker, Carl-Christian. 1987. The Economics of Value Added Network Services. Mimeo. Cologne.

Whitehouse, Bob. 1990. Adding Value. *Communications International*, July, p. 39.

Woollacott, Emma. 1989. Hiding the Real Cost. *Communications International*, July, p. 43.

Yankee Group. 1986. *VANs: Vertical Market Implementations*. Boston. January.

36. Videotex

Booker, Ellis. 1989. Vive le Minitel. *Telephony*, August 8, pp. 23–25.

British Business. 1981. CCITT. 1980. Study Group VII. Recommendation S.100. London: Crown Publishing. January.

Clavaud, Richard. 1984. Le Destin Incertain de Minitel. *L'Expansion*, April, p. 37.

Darmon, Jacques. 1985. *Le Grand Dérangement: La Guerre du Téléphone*. Paris: Editions Jean Claude Latles.

The Economist. 1989. Highwired Society. August 9, p. 55.

France Telecom. 1990. Teletel Meets with Worldwide Success. *Revue Française des Télécommunications*, No. 12 (April).

France Telecom News. 1990. Minitel Penetrates French Business. Winter.

Howkins, John. 1985. Communications in Finland. *Intermedia*, 10(4–5): 48–49.

Kramer, Richard. 1991. Misapplying the Model: The French Minitel and U.S. Video-
    tex. New York: Columbia Institute for Tele-Information Working Paper Senes.
Neue Medien. August 1985.
Roussel, Anne-Marie. 1989a. Italians, French, Purchasing Videotex. *Communications
    Week International,* March 12, p. 6.
————. 1989b. Minitel Gets New Terminal. *Communications Week International,* April
    17, p. 52.
————. 1989c. France's Minitel Shows Major Losses. *Communications Week Interna-
    tional,* July 10, p. 14.
————. 1989d. France Telecom Rebuts Teletel Drain. *Communications Week Interna-
    tional,* August 14, p. 8.
————, and Mark Rockwell. 1989. Minitel Spreads Beyond France. *Communications
    Week International,* June 12.
Sichel, Bertha. 1983. How the French Are Using Videotex. *ITP Report,* No. 1 (Spring–
    Summer): 23.
Telematique News. 1987. 1987 Minitel Statistics: January to June. Fall.
Thomas, Hilary. 1988. Mintel USA. Mimeo. November.
Tonnemacher, Jan. 1982. The New Media in West Germany. *Intermedia* 10(2).
Tydeman, John, et al. 1982. *Teletext and Videotex in the United States.* New York:
    McGraw Hill.
Vedel, Thierry. 1987. New Media Politics and Policies in France from 1981 to 1986:
    What Is Left? New York: Columbia Institute for Tele-Information Working Pa-
    per Series.
Woollacott, Emma. 1990. Small Screen Services. *Communications International,* Feb-
    ruary, pp. 41–43.

37. Transborder Data Flows

Anderla, G. 1983. *The International Data Market Revisited.* Report to the Second Sym-
    posium on TBDF. Paris: OECD. October.
Botein, Michael, and Eli M. Noam. 1986. U.S. Restrictions on International Data
    Transmission by Telecommunications Networks. New York: Columbia Institute
    for Tele-Information Working Paper Series.
Cass, Ron, and Eli Noam. 1990. Services Trade and Services Regulation in the United
    States. *Rules for Free International Trade in Services,* eds. D. Friedman and
    E. J. Mestmäcker. Baden-Baden: Nomos.
Commission of the European Communities (CEC). 1990. Concerning the Protection of
    Personal Data and Privacy in the Context of Public Digital Telecommunications
    Networks. June 5.
Consultative Committee on the Implications of Telecommunications for Canadian Sov-
    ereignty (CCITCS). 1979. *Telecommunications in Canada.* Ottawa: Information
    Canada.
de Pous, Victor. 1989. Dutch Data Protection Act in Force. *Transnational Data and
    Communications Report,* December, pp. 21–22.
Fauret, Jacques. 1989. Privacy in the New Europe. *Transnational Data and Commu-
    nications Report.* November, pp. 17–18.
Feketekuty, Geza, and Jonathan David Aronson. 1983. The World Information Econ-
    omy. Background Paper of the George Washington and McGill Universities'

Conference on Policy Issues in the Canadian-American Information Sector. November 17–18.

Feldman, Mark B., and David R. Garcia. 1982. National Regulation of Transborder Data Flows. *North Carolina Journal of International Law and Commercial Regulation* 7(1): 1–25.

Gassman, Hans-Peter. 1989. Privacy Protection and Computer Networks. *Transnational Data and Communications Report,* November, pp. 19–20.

Gebhardt, H. P. 1990. The Legal Basis of Data Protection and Data Protection in the Field of Telecommunications in Seven Countries. *ITU Telecommunications Journal* 57(1): 40.

Gesellschaft für Information und Dokumentation (GID). 1983. *Analyse des Informationsmarkets.* AIM Projekt. March.

Gilhooly, Denis. 1990. EC Tackles Privacy. *Communications Week International,* July 16. p. 1.

Kuitenbrouwer, Frank. 1985. CNIL Warns Against Breach of Privacy Act. *Transnational Data Report* 8(5): 226–27.

Madsen, Wayne. 1992. *Handbook of Personal Data Communications.* New York: Stockton Press.

McManus, Thomas E. 1989. Telephone Transaction-Generated Information: Rights and Restrictions. Harvard Program on Information Resources Policy. August. Permission to cite gratefully acknowledged.

Newpert, John Paul, Jr. 1989. American Express: Service That Sells. *Fortune* 120(12) :82.

New York Public Service Commission (NYPSC). Case 90-C-0075, *Proceeding on Motion of the Commission to Review Issues Concerning Privacy in Telecommunications: Statement of Policy.* March 22, New York: NYPSC.

Niblett, Bryan. 1984. *Data Protection Act 1984.* London: Oyez Longman.

Noam, Eli. 1990. Telecom Privacy Policy Elements. *Transnational Data and Communications Report,* March, p. 9.

———. Privacy in Telecommunication Services. In *Critical Yearbook on Telecommunications.* vol. 1. Karlsrühe: C.S. Mueller, forthcoming.

———, and Kent Greenawalt. 1979. Confidentiality Claims of Business Organizations. In *Business Disclosure: Government's Need to Know,* ed. Harvey J. Goldschmidt. New York: McGraw-Hill, 1979, pp. 378–412.

OECD. 1979. *Draft Guidelines Governing the Protection of Privacy and Transborder Flows of Personal Data.* Paris. June 22.

———. 1983. Second Symposium on Transborder Data Flows. London. November 30–December 2.

Office of Technology Assessment, Communications and Information Technologies Program (OTA). 1983. Institutional Options for Addressing Information Policy Issues: A Preliminary Framework for Analyzing the Choices. Staff Memorandum. Washington, D.C. November 29.

Olmstead v. *U.S.,* 277 U.S. 438, at 478 (1927).

Pipe, G. Russel. 1984a. Getting on the TDF Track. *Datamation* 30(1): 211–13.

———. 1984b. International Information Policy: Evolution of Transborder Data Flow Issues. *Telematics and Informatics* 1(4): 409–18.

Posner, Richard. 1981. *The Economics of Justice.* Cambridge, MA: Harvard University Press.

Robinson, Peter. 1990. TDF Issues: Hard Issues for Governments. *Telecommunications Policy* 14(1): 64–70.

Roche, Edward M. 1984. New Agency on Technology Takes Flight. *The Independent* 10(4).

Sauvant, Karl P. 1986. *Trade and Foreign Direct Investment in Data Services*. Westview Special Studies in International Economics and Business. Boulder, CO: Praeger, Westview Press.

Seipp, David John. 1978. *The Right to Privacy in American History*. Cambridge, MA: Harvard Program on Information Resources Policy, pp. 78–83.

Simmel, Georg. 1906. The Sociology of Secrecy and of Secret Societies, *American Journal of Sociology* 11: 441, 446, 450.

Simitis, Spiros. 1985. Data Protection: New Developments, New Challenges. *Transnational Data and Communications Report* 8(2): 95–96

Sixth Report of the Data Distribution Registrar, 1990. London: Her Majesty's Stationery Office, June.

Transnational Data and Communications Report (TDR). 1983. European Data Base Searches Chapter Than Using US. 6(8): 423.

———. 1986. OECD Weighs Future Telcom Policy Role. 9(1).

———. 1989. Protection of Personal Data Used for Employment Purposes. March, pp. 26–29.

Turn, Rein, ed. 1979. *Transborder Data Flows: Concern in Privacy Protection and Free Flow of Information*. Washington, DC: American Federation of Information Processing Societies, vol. 1.

Warren, Samuel D., and Louis D. Brandeis. 1890. The Right to Privacy. *Harvard Law Review* 4: 193,196.

Westin, Alan. 1967. *Privacy and Freedom*. New York: Atheneum.

Wigand, Rolf T. 1985. Transborder Data Flow and Its Impact on Business and Government. *Information Management Review* 1(2).

38. Networks in the Future

Piore, Michael, and Charles Sabel. 1984. *The Second Industrial Divide: Possibilities for Prosperity*. New York: Basic Books.

41. Regulatory Tasks for the Future: Interconnectivity in the Pluralist Network

Adler, E.. 1914. Business Jurisprudence. *Harvard Law Review* 28(135).

Aust, Thomas. 1990. *Principles in the New Telecommunications Environment*. Attachment to Case 89-C-009–Opinion No. 90–9. Opinion and Order Adopting Regulation Concerning Common Carriage, Appendix A. February 20, New York: NYPSC.

Linowes, David E. 1989. *Privacy in America: Is Your Private Life in the Public Eye*. Chicago: University of Illinois Press.

New York Public Service Commision (NYPSC). 1987. Case 28961, *New York Telephone Company—Rate Moratorium*. August 21, New York: NYPSC.

———. 1989. Case 29469, *Proceeding on Motion of the Commission to Review Regulatory Policies for Segments of the Telecommunications Industry Subject to Competition*, Opinion No. 89–12. Issues and Effective May 16, New York: NYPSC.

———. 1990a. Case 90-C-0075, *Proceeding on Motion of the Commission to Review*

Issues Concerning Privacy in Telecommunications. January 31, New York: NYPSC.

―――. 1990b. *Report on the ISDN Trial in New York State.* March 14, New York: NYPSC.

―――. 1990c. Case 88-C-004, *Order Accepting in Part and Rejecting in Part Comparably Efficient Interconnection (CEI) Task Force Recommendations.* June 7, New York: NYPSC.

Noam, E. 1990. *Beyond ONA: Beginning a Modular Network.* New York: NYPSC.

―――. 1991a. Privacy in Telecommunication Services. In *Critical Yearbook on Telecommunications,* vol. 1. Karlsrühe: C.S. Mueller, forthcoming.

―――. 1991b. The Quality of Regulation in Regulating Quality: A Proposal for an Integrated Incentive Approach to Telephone Service. *Price Caps and Incentive Regulation in Telecommunications.* Michael Einhorn, ed. Norwell, MA: Kluwer Academic Publications.

―――. 1991c. *Television In Europe.* New York: Oxford University Press.

Phillips, Jr., C. 1988. *The Regulation of Public Utilities,* 2nd ed. Arlington, VA.

Seipp, David John. 1978. *The Right to Privacy in American History.* Cambridge, MA: Harvard Program on Information Resources Policy, Harvard University.

Westin, Alan F. 1967. *Privacy and Freedom.* New York: Atheneum.

Index